THE LAW OF CORPORATIONS
IN A NUTSHELL

Fifth Edition

By

ROBERT W. HAMILTON

Minerva House Drysdale Regents Chair in Law

The University of Texas at Austin

WEST
GROUP

ST. PAUL, MINN.
2000

COPYRIGHT © 1980, 1987, 1991, 1996 WEST PUBLISHING CO.
COPYRIGHT © 2000 By WEST GROUP

> 610 Opperman Drive
> P.O. Box 64526
> St. Paul, MN 55164–0526
> 1–800–328–9352

All rights reserved
Printed in the United States of America

ISBN 0–314–24132–9

TEXT IS PRINTED ON 10% POST
CONSUMER RECYCLED PAPER

2nd Reprint — 2003

OUTLINE

		Page
Table of Cases		xxv

Chapter One. Modern Business Forms and the Corporation — 1

Sec.

1.1	Historical Dominance of the Corporation in the United States	1
1.2	Publicly Held and Closely Held Corporations	2
1.3	Adjustment of Law School Curricula to Current Trends	4
1.4	Traditional Business Forms: Introduction	5
1.5	Proprietorships	6
1.6	General Partnerships: Introduction	7
1.7	General Partnerships: Financial Provisions	8
1.8	General Partnerships: Participation in Management	10
1.9	General Partnerships: A Separate Entity?	11
1.10	General Partnerships: Artificial Entities as Partners	12
1.11	General Partnerships: Dissolution, Winding Up and Termination	12
1.12	General Partnerships: Revisions Made by the 1994 Act	14
1.13	Limited Partnerships: In General	16
1.14	Limited Partnerships with a Corporate General Partner	18
1.15	A New Business Form: The Limited Liability Partnership	19

Sec.

1.16 Another New Business Form: The Limited Liability Company 23

1.17 A Menu of Modern Business Forms Based on the Number of Owners 26

1.18 Factors Influencing the Selection of Business Forms 27

1.19 Federal Tax Regimes 28

1.20 Impact of Tax Rates on Tax Minimization Strategies 30

1.21 Tax Classification of Unincorporated Limited Liability Entities: The Kintner Rules and "Check the Box" 32

1.22 A Comparison of Taxation under Subchapter K and Subchapter S 36

1.23 Non–Tax Differences Between an LLC and a Corporation 40

1.24 Differences Between the LLC and Various Partnership Forms 42

1.25 Selection of Business Form for a Start-up Business 43

1.26 What Does the Future Hold? 45

Chapter Two. The Corporation in Theory 46

2.1 The Corporation as an "Artificial Entity" 46

2.2 Limitations of the "Artificial Entity" Theory 48

2.3 The Corporation as a Privilege or Contract 50

2.4 The "Nexus of Contracts" Model 52

Chapter Three. Development of American Corporation Law 62

3.1 The Early History of Corporation Law in the United States 62

3.2 The "Race for the Bottom" 63

3.3 What Explains Delaware's Success in Attracting Corporations? 66

Sec.

3.4 The Debate Over Social Responsibility Within The Publicly Held Corporation 69
3.5 Modern Corporation Statutes 72
3.6 The Model Business Corporation Act (1984) 74
3.7 Federal Regulation.. 76

Chapter Four. Formation of Corporations 77
4.1 In General 77
4.2 Selection of the State of Incorporation 77
4.3 Mechanics of Creating a Corporation 78
4.4 Incorporators 81
4.5 Articles of Incorporation: In General 82
4.6 Articles of Incorporation: The Corporate Name.. 84
4.7 Articles of Incorporation: Period of Duration 87
4.8 Articles of Incorporation: Capitalization............ 88
4.9 Articles of Incorporation: Registered Office and Registered Agent 89
4.10 Articles of Incorporation: Initial Board of Directors 90
4.11 Articles of Incorporation: Limitation of Directoral Liability... 91
4.12 Articles of Incorporation: Purposes and Powers 92
4.13 The Common Law Doctrine of Ultra Vires.......... 95
4.14 The Modern Role of Ultra Vires 97
4.15 Ultra Vires Problems in Connection With Corporate Powers 99
4.16 Completion of the Organization of the Corporation: In General.. 104
4.17 Nature and Purpose of Bylaws............................. 105
4.18 The Corporate Seal 106
4.19 Organizational Meetings 107

Chapter Five. Preincorporation Transactions 110
5.1 Introduction... 110
5.2 Subscriptions for Shares 110

Sec.

5.3 Agreements to Form Corporation 114
5.4 Promoters in General 115
5.5 Promoters' Contracts 117
5.6 Liability of Corporations for Promoters' Con-
      tracts 122
5.7 Promoter's Fiduciary Duties 124
5.8 Organizational Expenses Incurred by Promoters 125
5.9 Premature Commencement of Business and the
      De Facto Doctrine 127
5.10 Corporations by Estoppel 131
5.11 A Unified Conception of "Defective Incorpo-
      ration" 133

**Chapter Six. "Piercing the Corporate Veil" and
      Related Problems** 134
6.1 "Piercing the Corporate Veil" In Context 134
6.2 Shareholder Responsibility for Corporate In-
      debtedness: Introduction 135
6.3 The Rhetoric of "Piercing the Corporate Veil" ... 136
6.4 Piercing the Corporate Veil in Contract and
      Tort Cases 138
6.5 Inadequate Capitalization 142
6.6 Failure to Follow Corporate Formalities 145
6.7 Parent–Subsidiary Cases 147
6.8 The Concept of "Enterprise Entity" 151
6.9 Choice of Law and "Piercing the Corporate
      Veil" 152
6.10 The Federal Law of "Piercing the Corporate
      Veil" 154
6.11 Reverse Piercing 156
6.12 "Piercing the Corporate Veil" to Further Public
      Policy 157
6.13 "Piercing the Corporate Veil" in Taxation and
      Bankruptcy 159

Sec.
6.14   Other Generalizations About "Piercing the Corporate Veil" ------------------------------------ 161

Chapter Seven. Financing the Corporation -------- 163
7.1   Introduction------------------------------------- 163
7.2   Common Stock: The Basic Definition--------------- 164
7.3   Common Stock: Authorized and Issued Shares--- 165
7.4   Common Stock: The Price at Which Shares Are Issued -- 166
7.5   Common Shares: Par Value and "Watered" Stock --- 168
7.6   Common Shares: Par Value and the Capital Accounts of the Corporation ----------------------- 171
7.7   Common Stock: No Par Shares in a Par Value Regime-- 176
7.8   Common Stock: Shares Issued for Property or Services--- 178
7.9   Common Stock: Liability for Watered Shares----- 182
7.10   Common Shares: Options, Warrants and Rights 187
7.11   Common Stock: Non–Voting Shares ---------------- 188
7.12   Common Stock: Classes of Common Shares in Closely Held Businesses----------------------------- 189
7.13   Common Stock: Classes of Common Shares in Publicly Held Businesses ---------------------------- 190
7.14   Common Stock: Tracking Shares -------------------- 192
7.15   Common Stock: Treasury Shares -------------------- 192
7.16   Common Stock: Circular Ownership of Shares --- 194
7.17   Common Stock: Current Trends Regarding Par Value --- 195
7.18   Common Stock: Preemptive Rights ----------------- 196
7.19   Oppressive Issuance of Shares ----------------------- 201
7.20   A Cautionary Postscript: The Risk of Violating Securities Acts While Raising Capital ----------- 203
7.21   Preferred Shares -------------------------------- 204
7.22   The Distinction Between "Equity" and "Debt"-- 210

Page

Sec.

7.23   Equalizing Capital and Services When Forming a Corporation 212

7.24   The Advantages of Debt Financing 215

7.25   Tax Consequences of Excessive Debt Capitalization in C Corporations 219

7.26   Debt as a Second Class of Stock in S Corporations 221

7.27   The Deep Rock Doctrine Revisited 221

7.28   Publicly Traded Debt Securities 223

Chapter Eight.   The Distribution of Powers Within a Corporation: Special Problems 228

8.1   The "Statutory Scheme" in General 228

8.2   The Power to Vary the Statutory Scheme 229

8.3   The Statutory Scheme: Shareholders 231

8.4   The Statutory Scheme: Directors 232

8.5   The Statutory Scheme: The Power to Remove Directors 235

8.6   Elimination of the Board of Directors 238

8.7   The Statutory Scheme: Officers 239

8.8   Shared Responsibility With Respect to Corporate Operations 240

8.9   Shared Responsibility: Approval of Fundamental Corporate Changes.. 241

8.10   Shared Responsibility: Bylaw Amendments 243

8.11   Restrictions on Directors in Close Corporations 244

8.12   Ameliorating Trends 251

8.13   Delegation of Management Powers and the Statutory Scheme 252

Chapter Nine.   Shares and Shareholders 254

9.1   Annual and Special Meetings of Shareholders 254

9.2   Shareholder Action by Consent 257

9.3   Record and Beneficial Ownership of Shares 258

9.4   Record Dates... 260

Page

Sec.
9.5   Preparation of Voting List ------------------------------- 262
9.6   Election of Directors: Cumulative or Straight
          Voting--- 263
9.7   "Classified" Boards of Directors --------------------- 270
9.8   Other Devices to Minimize Cumulative Voting--- 272
9.9   Voting by Proxy--- 273
9.10   Irrevocable Proxy Appointments --------------------- 275
9.11   Vote Buying-- 277
9.12   Shareholder Voting Agreements---------------------- 278
9.13   Voting Trusts: Purpose, Operation, and Legisla-
          tive Policy--- 281
9.14   Voting Trusts: Use in Public Corporations ------- 284
9.15   Voting Trusts: Powers and Duties of Trustee----- 284
9.16   Creation of Floating Voting Power Through Dif-
          ferent Classes of Shares---------------------------- 286
9.17   Share Transfer Restrictions: Purposes, Opera-
          tion, and Effect--- 288
9.18   Share Transfer Restrictions: Scope and Validity 291
9.19   Share Transfer Restrictions: Duration of Re-
          straints -- 293
9.20   Share Transfer Restrictions: Procedural Re-
          quirements -- 294
9.21   Option or Buy/Sell Agreements: Who Should
          Have the Right or Privilege to Buy? ------------- 295
9.22   Option or Buy/Sell Agreements: Establishment
          of Purchase or Option Price ----------------------- 297
9.23   Option or Buy/Sell Agreements: Life Insurance-- 301
9.24   Selection of the Purchaser in Deadlock Buyouts 302
9.25   Deferred Payment of the Purchase Price---------- 303

Chapter Ten.   Directors ------------------------------------ 304
10.1   Number and Qualifications of Directors ----------- 304
10.2   Directors' Meetings: Notice, Quorum, and Simi-
          lar Matters -- 306
10.3   Compensation of Directors -------------------------- 310

Page

Sec.

10.4	Filling Vacancies	311
10.5	Hold–Over Directors	313
10.6	Necessity for Meeting and Personal Attendance	313
10.7	Telephonic Meetings	315
10.8	Action Without a Meeting	316
10.9	Directors' Objections to Actions	316
10.10	Committees of the Board of Directors	318

Chapter Eleven. Officers ... 322

11.1	Statutory Designations of Officers	322
11.2	An Introduction to Principles of Agency Law	324
11.3	Sources of Authority of Corporate Officers	325
11.4	Bylaw Provisions Describing Roles of Corporate Officers	326
11.5	Express Authority Created by the Board of Directors	328
11.6	Inherent Power of the Corporate President	330
11.7	Implied Authority, Ratification, Estoppel, and Unjust Enrichment	331
11.8	Fiduciary Duties of Officers, Employees and Agents	334
11.9	Liability of Officers and Agents to Third Parties	335
11.10	Imputation of Knowledge to Corporation	337
11.11	Tenure of Officers and Agents	338
11.12	Long–Term Employment Contracts	339

Chapter Twelve. The Closely Held Corporation ... 343

12.1	The Meaning of "Closely Held" and "Publicly Held"	343
12.2	The Economic Importance of Closely Held Corporations	344
12.3	The Reality of Management, Control and Participation in a Closely Held Corporation	346
12.4	Advance Planning in Closely Held Corporations	348

Sec.

12.5   Limitations on the Power to Contract Within
        Closely Held Corporations 352
12.6   Classes of Shares 353
12.7   Increased Quorum and Voting Requirements 356
12.8   Special Close Corporation Statutes 357
12.9   Section 7.32 of MBCA (1984) 360
12.10   Deadlocks 362
12.11   Resolution of Disputes by Arbitration 363
12.12   "Oppression," "Freeze–Outs" and "Squeeze–
        Outs" 365
12.13   Share Transfer Restrictions and the "Market"
        for Shares in a Closely Held Corporation 366
12.14   Receivership and Involuntary Dissolution: The
        Traditional Solutions to Oppression and
        Deadlock In Closely Held Corporations 369
12.15   Court–Ordered Buy–Outs 371
12.16   Section 14.34 of MBCA (1984) 372
12.17   Fiduciary Duties of Controlling Shareholders 373

Chapter Thirteen.   The Publicly Held Corporation 376
13.1   The Publicly Held Corporation in Perspective 376
13.2   The "High Tech" or "Dot.com" Company 377
13.3   The Impact of Technology on Public Trading of
        Securities 380
13.4   Description of The Very Large Publicly Held
        Company 382
13.5   The Internal Structure of Very Large Corpora-
        tions 384
13.6   Profit Centers 386
13.7   The Home Office 388
13.8   The Chief Executive Officer 391
13.9   Compensation of Senior Executives 392
13.10   Shareholders as "Investors" or "Owners" 394
13.11   Institutional Investors 397

Page

Sec.

13.12	Street Name Registration of Securities; Book Entry	399
13.13	The Board of Directors of Large Publicly Held Companies: Theory and Reality	402
13.14	The Election of Directors	404
13.15	"Inside" and "Independent" Directors	405
13.16	Historic Dominance of the Board by the CEO	406
13.17	The Modern Board of Directors	408
13.18	The "Chicago School" of Law and Economics	412
13.19	Share Prices and The Changing Body of Shareholders	416
13.20	The Takeover Movement of the 1980s	417
13.21	Proxy Regulation in Publicly Held Corporations	418
13.22	Disclosure Requirements in Connection With Proxy Solicitations	420
13.23	Shareholder Proposals	424
13.24	Private Actions for Violations of Federal Proxy Rules	427
13.25	Proxy Contests	429
13.26	Cash Tender Offers During the 1970s and 1980s	433
13.27	Combination Strategies Involving Proxy Fights and Cash Tender Offers	436
13.28	Defensive Tactics	437
13.29	State Intervention in the Takeover Movement	440
13.30	The Takeover Movement in the 1990s	442
Chapter Fourteen. Duties of Directors		444
14.1	Directors, Controlling Shareholders and Senior Officers as "Fiduciaries"	444
14.2	Duties of Shareholders and Junior Officers	445
14.3	Sources of Law Relating to Duties of Directors— Common Law, State and Federal Statutes	446
14.4	Duty of Care	447
14.5	The "Business Judgment Rule"	453
14.6	The Famous Case of Smith v. Van Gorkom	455

Page

Sec.
14.7	Section 102(b)(7) of the Delaware GCL	459
14.8	The Business Judgment Rule in Takeover Contests	460
14.9	The Business Judgment Rule in Derivative Litigation	463
14.10	The Duty of Loyalty	467
14.11	Self Dealing	467
14.12	Interlocking Directors	473
14.13	Executive Compensation	474
14.14	Corporate Opportunities In General	478
14.15	What is a Corporate Opportunity?	479
14.16	When May a Director Take Advantage of A Corporate Opportunity?	481
14.17	Must a Director First Offer the Opportunity to the Corporation?	482
14.18	Competition with the Corporation	483
14.19	Fairness to Minority Shareholders	484
14.20	"Fairness" and the Merger of a Subsidiary into Its Parent	486
14.21	The Effect of Shareholder Ratification	489
14.22	Provisions That Exonerate Directors	490
14.23	Statutory Duties and Statutory Defenses	490
14.24	Purchase or Sale of Shares or Claims Under State Law	493
14.25	Duties of Directors of Financially Distressed Corporations	497
14.26	Disclosure Obligations Under State Law	498
14.27	Rule 10b–5	499
14.28	Rule 10b–5 as an Anti-fraud Provision	502
14.29	Insider Trading: The Beginnings	503
14.30	Insider Trading: The Defining Case Law	504
14.31	Insider Trading: Statutory Recognition and SEC Enforcement Policies	509
14.32	Insider Trading: The Possession/Use Debate	510

Page

Sec.

14.33	Insider Trading: The Policy Justifications	511
14.34	Rule 10b–5 as a Protector of the Issuer	512
14.35	Rule 10b–5 as a General Prohibition Against Wrongful Conduct	513
14.36	Section 16(b) of the Securities Exchange Act of 1934	514
14.37	Transfers of Control	517

Chapter 15. Indemnification and Insurance 524

15.1	Definitions of Terms	524
15.2	The Need for Protection of Directors and Officers	525
15.3	Public Policy Limitations on Indemnification	526
15.4	Statutory Treatment of Indemnification	527
15.5	Advances for Expenses	530
15.6	D & O Insurance	532

Chapter Sixteen. Derivative Litigation 535

16.1	Direct and Derivative Suits in General	535
16.2	Derivative and Direct Claims Distinguished	536
16.3	Alignment of Parties in a Derivative Suit	538
16.4	Role of the Plaintiff's Attorney	539
16.5	Derivative Litigation as Strike Suits	542
16.6	Contemporary Ownership	543
16.7	Demand on Directors and Shareholders	544
16.8	Security–For–Expenses Statutes	546
16.9	Verification of the Complaint	548
16.10	Resolution of Derivative Litigation by Board Committees	548
16.11	Defenses in a Derivative Suit	552
16.12	Private Settlement of Derivative Suits	554
16.13	Res Judicata Effect of Derivative Suits	555

Page

Chapter Seventeen. Class Actions Under Federal Securities Acts ------------------------------------- 556

Sec.

17.1   Securities Class Actions in General ----------------- 556

17.2   SEC Disclosure Requirements and the "Safe Harbor" -- 557

17.3   The Growth of Class Action Securities Litigation--- 559

17.4   Original Judicial Response to "New Era" Class Actions--- 561

17.5   The Private Securities Litigation Reform Act of 1995 --- 562

17.6   PSLRA Class Action Provisions --------------------- 562

17.7   New Safe Harbor Provisions for Forward Looking Statements ----------------------------------- 563

17.8   PSLRA Discovery Provisions --------------------------- 565

17.9   PSLRA Proportionate Liability Provisions-------- 566

17.10   PSLRA Settlement Provisions ----------------------- 567

17.11   PSLRA Fee Shifting Provisions---------------------- 567

17.12   PSLRA Pleading Provisions--------------------------- 568

17.13   PSLRA Damage Provisions --------------------------- 570

17.14   PSLRA Aiding and Abetting Provisions----------- 570

17.15   PSLRA Auditor Disclosure Provisions-------------- 570

17.16   The Securities Litigation Uniform Standards Act of 1998 (SLUSA) --------------------------------- 572

Chapter Eighteen. Dividends, Distributions, and Redemptions --- 575

18.1   Cash or Property Dividends and Distributions --- 575

18.2   Share Dividends and Share Splits-------------------- 577

18.3   Distributions of Rights or Warrants ---------------- 580

18.4   Share Reacquisitions as Distributions; Treasury Shares-- 581

18.5   Shareholders' Rights to a Dividend------------------ 583

18.6   Statutory Restrictions on the Declaration of Dividends --- 585

18.7   Contractual Provisions Relating to Declarations of Dividends--- 590

Sec.

18.8   Liability of Directors and Shareholders for Illegal Dividends 592

18.9   Shareholders' Right to Compel a Dividend 592

18.10 Corporate Repurchase of Its Own Shares: Installment Sale 594

18.11 Redeemable and Convertible Securities 597

Chapter Nineteen. Inspection of Books and Records 599

19.1   Inspection by Directors and Shareholders Compared 599

19.2   Common Law and Statutory Rights of Inspection by Shareholders 600

19.3   Corporate Records: What May Be Examined? 602

19.4   What Is a "Proper Purpose"? 604

19.5   Who Is Entitled to Inspect? 605

19.6   Inspection of Shareholders Lists 606

19.7   Financial Reports for Shareholders 608

Chapter Twenty. Organic Changes: Amendments, Mergers, and Dissolution 609

20.1   Introduction and Caveat 609

20.2   Amendments to Articles of Incorporation in General 610

20.3   Vested Rights 611

20.4   Voting by Classes 613

20.5   Mergers and Consolidations 615

20.6   Triangular Mergers, Cash Mergers, Short Form Mergers, and Related Developments 619

20.7   Cash-out Mergers 621

20.8   "Upstream" and "Downstream" Mergers 622

20.9   Short Form Mergers 623

20.10 Fiduciary Duties in Mergers 624

20.11 Sales of All or Substantially All the Assets of a Corporation 625

OUTLINE

Page

Sec.
20.12 The Right of Dissent and Appraisal 627
20.13 Voluntary Dissolution 631
20.14 Changes Made by the 1999 MBCA Amendments 633

Glossary 637
INDEX 675

RESEARCH REFERENCES

Am Jur 2d, Corporations §§ 1 et seq.; Judgments §§ 693, 696; Negligence § 1764; Process §§ 263-284; Products Liability §§ 757, 768, 1679-1681; Quo Warranto §§ 73-78; State and Local Taxation §§ 254-306

Corpus Juris Secundum, Constitutional Law §§ 348-362; Corporations §§ 1 et seq.; Evidence §§ 445, 448, 1099, 1100; Executions §§ 39, 40; Internal Revenue §§ 329-372

ALR Index: Corporate Officers, Directors, and Agents; Corporate Opportunity; Corporate Responsibility Doctrine; Corporate Stock and Stockholders; Corporations; Piercing Corporate Veil

ALR Digest: Constitutional Law §§ 204-236; Contracts § 4; Corporations §§ 1 et seq.; Courts §§ 186-193; Evidence §§ 249-254; Mandamus §§ 66-80; Pleading §§ 105, 244, 444, 501; Taxes §§ 101-113; Writ and Process §§ 30-43

Am Jur Legal Forms 2d, Corporations §§ 74:1 et seq.; Estoppel and Waiver § 102:17; Sale of Businesses §§ 226:241-226:340; Stock and Commodity Exchanges §§ 240:84-240:86

Am Jur Pleading and Practice (Rev), Captions, Prayers, and Formal Parts §§ 99-106; Commercial Code §§ 8:70, 8:71; Corporations §§ 1 et seq.; Federal Practice and Procedure §§ 1381-1403; Process §§ 149-166

68 Am Jur Trials 503, Hidden and Multiple Defendant Tort Litigation; 45 Am Jur Trials 113, Third-Party Accountant Liability-Prospective Financial Statements Used in Securities Offerings; 42 Am Jur Trials 419, Lender Liability Litigation: Undue Control; 2 Am Jur Trials 409, Locating Public Records

46 POF3d 431, Liability of Nonprofit Corporation for Engaging in For-Profit Business Activities; 29 POF3d 133, Liability of a Director to a Corporation for Mismanagement; 17 POF3d 685, Tortious Interference by Parent Corporation with Subsidiary's Contract with Third Party; 16 POF3d 583, Corporate Director's Breach of Fiduciary Duty to Creditors

46 POF2d 313, Products Liability: Continuation of Business Enterprise or Product Line by Successor Corporation; 30 POF2d 291, Corporate Opportunity Doctrine-Fairness of Corporate Official's Acquisition of Business Opportunity; 24 POF2d 71, Proper Purpose for Shareholder's Inspection of Corporate Books and Records; 15 POF2d 417, Improper Issuance of Corporate Stock to Directors or Officers; 9 POF2d 57, Corporate Officer or Director as Alter Ego of Corporation; 8 POF2d 315, Corporate Opportunity Doctrine-Business Opportunities in "Line Of Business" of Corporation; 5

POF2d 645, Oppressive Conduct by Majority Shareholders, Directors, or Those in Control of Corporation

Use Westlaw® to Research Corporations Law

Access Westlaw, the computer-assisted legal research service of West Group, to search a broad array of legal resources, including case law, statutes, practice guides, current developments and various other types of information. Consult the online Westlaw Directory to determine databases specific to your needs.

Searching on Westlaw

With Westlaw, you can use the Natural Language search method, which allows you to simply describe your corporations law issue in plain English. For example, to retrieve documents discussing the amendment of by-laws, access the Delaware Business Organizations Cases (Delaware and Federal) database (DEBUS) and type the following Natural Language description: amendment of by-laws

You can also use the Terms and Connectors search method, which allows you to enter a query consisting of key terms from your issue and connectors specifying the relationship between those terms. For example, to search for the terms amend, amended or amending, in the same sentence as the term by-law, type the following Terms and Connectors query: amend! /s by-law

Use KeyCite® to Check Your Research

KeyCite is the citation research service available exclusively on Westlaw. Use KeyCite to see if your cases or statutes are good law and to retrieve cases, legislation or articles that cite your cases and statutes.

For more information regarding searching on Westlaw, call the West Group Reference Attorneys at 1-800-REF-ATTY (1-800-733-2889).

*

TABLE OF CASES

References are to Pages

Abercrombie v. Davies, 36 Del.Ch. 371, 130 A.2d 338 (Del.Supr.1957), *279, 283*
Application of (see name of party)
Aronson v. Lewis, 473 A.2d 805 (Del.Supr.1984), *465*
Auer v. Dressel, 306 N.Y. 427, 118 N.E.2d 590 (N.Y.1954), *241*
Austin v. Michigan Chamber of Commerce, 494 U.S. 652, 110 S.Ct. 1391, 108 L.Ed.2d 652 (1990), *100*

Baker v. Commercial Body Builders, Inc., 264 Or. 614, 507 P.2d 387 (Or. 1973), *370*
Barnes v. Andrews, 298 F. 614 (S.D.N.Y.1924), *452*
Bartle v. Home Owners Co-op., 309 N.Y. 103, 127 N.E.2d 832 (N.Y.1955), *137*
Basic Inc. v. Levinson, 485 U.S. 224, 108 S.Ct. 978, 99 L.Ed.2d 194 (1988), *559*
Bateman Eichler, Hill Richards, Inc. v. Berner, 472 U.S. 299, 105 S.Ct. 2622, 86 L.Ed.2d 215 (1985), *508*
Benintendi v. Kenton Hotel, 294 N.Y. 112, 60 N.E.2d 829 (N.Y.1945), *357*
Berkey v. Third Ave. Ry. Co., 244 N.Y. 84, 155 N.E. 58 (N.Y.1926), *138*
Bestfoods, United States v., 524 U.S. 51, 118 S.Ct. 1876, 141 L.Ed.2d 43 (1998), *155*
Birnbaum v. Newport Steel Corp., 193 F.2d 461 (2nd Cir.1952), *522*
Blau v. Lehman, 368 U.S. 403, 82 S.Ct. 451, 7 L.Ed.2d 403 (1962), *517*
Bradshaw v. Jones, 152 S.W. 695 (Tex.Civ.App.-Texarkana 1912), *121*
Browning v. C & C Plywood Corp., 248 Or. 574, 434 P.2d 339 (Or.1967), *202*
Broz v. Cellular Information Systems, Inc., 673 A.2d 148 (Del.Supr.1996), *483*
Burkin, Application of, 154 N.Y.S.2d 898, 136 N.E.2d 862 (N.Y.1956), *364*
Burnett v. Word, Inc., 412 S.W.2d 792 (Tex.Civ.App.-Waco 1967), *245, 246*
Business Roundtable v. S.E.C., 905 F.2d 406, 284 U.S.App.D.C. 301 (D.C.Cir. 1990), *191*

Cady Roberts & Co., Matter of, 40 SEC 907 (1961), *503, 511*
Caplan, Petition of, 20 A.D.2d 301, 246 N.Y.S.2d 913 (N.Y.A.D. 1 Dept.1964), *522*

Caremark Intern. Inc. Derivative Litigation, In re, 698 A.2d 959 (Del.Ch. 1996), *448, 455*

Cargill, Inc. v. Hedge, 375 N.W.2d 477 (Minn.1985), *156*

Carpenter v. United States, 484 U.S. 19, 108 S.Ct. 316, 98 L.Ed.2d 275 (1987), *506*

Central Bank of Denver, N.A. v. First Interstate Bank of Denver, N.A., 511 U.S. 164, 114 S.Ct. 1439, 128 L.Ed.2d 119 (1994), *501, 571*

Cheff v. Mathes, 41 Del.Ch. 494, 199 A.2d 548 (Del.Supr.1964), *496*

Chiarella v. United States, 445 U.S. 222, 100 S.Ct. 1108, 63 L.Ed.2d 348 (1980), *505, 506, 512*

Cinerama, Inc. v. Technicolor, Inc., 663 A.2d 1156 (Del.Supr.1995), *488*

Clark v. Dodge, 269 N.Y. 410, 199 N.E. 641 (N.Y.1936), *247, 248, 249*

Clearfield Trust Co. v. United States, 318 U.S. 363, 318 U.S. 744, 63 S.Ct. 573, 87 L.Ed. 838 (1943), *154*

Cohen v. Beneficial Indus. Loan Corp., 337 U.S. 541, 69 S.Ct. 1221, 93 L.Ed. 1528 (1949), *548*

Cooke v. Oolie, 1997 WL 367034 (Del.Ch.1997), *473*

Credit Lyonnais Bank Nederland, N.V. v. Pathe Communications Corp., 1991 WL 277613 (Del.Ch.1991), *498*

CTS Corp. v. Dynamics Corp. of America, 481 U.S. 69, 107 S.Ct. 1637, 95 L.Ed.2d 67 (1987), *441, 442*

Dartmouth College v. Woodward, 17 U.S. 518, 4 L.Ed. 629 (1819), *51*

Demoulas v. Demoulas Super Markets, Inc., 424 Mass. 501, 677 N.E.2d 159 (Mass.1997), *483*

Diamond v. Oreamuno, 301 N.Y.S.2d 78, 248 N.E.2d 910 (N.Y.1969), *494*

Dirks v. S.E.C., 463 U.S. 646, 103 S.Ct. 3255, 77 L.Ed.2d 911 (1983), *506*

Dodge v. Ford Motor Co., 204 Mich. 459, 170 N.W. 668 (Mich.1919), *593*

Donahue v. Rodd Electrotype Co. of New England, Inc., 367 Mass. 578, 328 N.E.2d 505 (Mass.1975), *373, 374, 375, 594*

Edgar v. MITE Corp., 457 U.S. 624, 102 S.Ct. 2629, 73 L.Ed.2d 269 (1982), *440*

Farris v. Glen Alden Corp., 393 Pa. 427, 143 A.2d 25 (Pa.1958), *618, 619*

Fidelity Federal Sav. and Loan Ass'n v. Felicetti, 830 F.Supp. 262 (E.D.Pa. 1993), *532*

First Nat. Bank of Boston v. Bellotti, 435 U.S. 765, 98 S.Ct. 1407, 55 L.Ed.2d 707 (1978), *100*

Fletcher v. Atex, Inc., 68 F.3d 1451 (2nd Cir.1995), *151*

Fliegler v. Lawrence, 361 A.2d 218 (Del.Supr.1976), *472*

Foremost–McKesson, Inc. v. Provident Securities Co., 423 U.S. 232, 96 S.Ct. 508, 46 L.Ed.2d 464 (1976), *517*

Francis v. United Jersey Bank, 87 N.J. 15, 432 A.2d 814 (N.J.1981), *451*

Gall v. Exxon Corp., 418 F.Supp. 508 (S.D.N.Y.1976), *549*

Galler v. Galler, 32 Ill.2d 16, 203 N.E.2d 577 (Ill.1964), *251, 252, 358, 373*

Gearing v. Kelly, 227 N.Y.S.2d 897, 182 N.E.2d 391 (N.Y.1962), *357*

Geyer v. Ingersoll Publications Co., 621 A.2d 784 (Del.Ch.1992), *497*

Goodnow v. American Writing Paper Co., 69 A. 1014 (N.J.Err. & App.1908), *587*

Graham v. Allis–Chalmers Mfg. Co., 41 Del.Ch. 78, 188 A.2d 125 (Del. Supr.1963), *449*

Gustafson v. Alloyd Co., Inc., 513 U.S. 561, 115 S.Ct. 1061, 131 L.Ed.2d 1 (1995), *501*

Hall v. Staha, 303 Ark. 673, 800 S.W.2d 396 (Ark.1990), *283*

Heckmann v. Ahmanson, 168 Cal.App.3d 119, 214 Cal.Rptr. 177 (Cal.App. 2 Dist.1985), *496*

Heller v. Boylan, 29 N.Y.S.2d 653 (N.Y.Sup.1941), *477*

Honigman v. Green Giant Co., 309 F.2d 667 (8th Cir.1962), *520*

Hospes v. Northwestern Mfg. & Car Co., 48 Minn. 174, 50 N.W. 1117 (Minn.1892), *183*

Hunt v. Rousmanier's Adm'rs, 21 U.S. 174, 5 L.Ed. 589 (1823), *275*

Hyman v. Velsicol Corp., 342 Ill.App. 489, 97 N.E.2d 122 (Ill.App. 1 Dist. 1951), *202*

In re (see name of party)

J. I. Case Co. v. Borak, 377 U.S. 426, 84 S.Ct. 1555, 12 L.Ed.2d 423 (1964), *427, 428*

John Kelley Co. v. Commissioner, 326 U.S. 521, 326 U.S. 698, 66 S.Ct. 299, 90 L.Ed. 278 (1946), *220*

Jones v. H. F. Ahmanson & Co., 81 Cal.Rptr. 592, 460 P.2d 464 (Cal.1969), *521*

Kahn v. Lynch Communication Systems, Inc., 638 A.2d 1110 (Del.Supr.1994), *473*

Klang v. Smith's Food & Drug Centers, Inc., 702 A.2d 150 (Del.Supr.1997), *491*

Klinicki v. Lundgren, 298 Or. 662, 695 P.2d 906 (Or.1985), *482*

Lehrman v. Cohen, 43 Del.Ch. 222, 222 A.2d 800 (Del.Supr.1966), *190, 286, 355*

Long Park v. Trenton–New Brunswick Theatres Co., 297 N.Y. 174, 77 N.E.2d 633 (N.Y.1948), *249*

Louis K. Liggett Co. v. Lee, 288 U.S. 517, 53 S.Ct. 481, 77 L.Ed. 929 (1933), *64*

Malone v. Brincat, 722 A.2d 5 (Del.Supr.1998), *498*

Marciano v. Nakash, 535 A.2d 400 (Del.Supr.1987), *472*

Matter of (see name of party)

McQuade v. Stoneham, 263 N.Y. 323, 189 N.E. 234 (N.Y.1934), *246, 247, 248, 249, 250, 251*

Meinhard v. Salmon, 249 N.Y. 458, 164 N.E. 545 (N.Y.1928), *10, 11*

Mills v. Electric Auto–Lite Co., 396 U.S. 375, 90 S.Ct. 616, 24 L.Ed.2d 593 (1970), *428, 429*

Minton v. Cavaney, 56 Cal.2d 576, 15 Cal.Rptr. 641, 364 P.2d 473 (Cal.1961), *142*

Moran v. Household Intern., Inc., 500 A.2d 1346 (Del.Supr.1985), *439, 461*

Munford v. Valuation Research Corp., 97 F.3d 456 (11th Cir.1996), *592*

Nixon v. Blackwell, 626 A.2d 1366 (Del.Supr.1993), *250, 375*

Northeast Harbor Golf Club, Inc. v. Harris, 661 A.2d 1146 (Me.1995), *481*

Obre v. Alban Tractor Co., 228 Md. 291, 179 A.2d 861 (Md.1962), *214*

O'Hagan, United States v., 521 U.S. 642, 117 S.Ct. 2199, 138 L.Ed.2d 724 (1997), *505, 507*

Old Dominion Copper Mining & Smelting Co. v. Bigelow, 203 Mass. 159, 89 N.E. 193 (Mass.1909), *124*

Old Dominion Copper Mining & Smelting Co. v. Lewisohn, 210 U.S. 206, 28 S.Ct. 634, 52 L.Ed. 1025 (1908), *125*

Ostrowski v. Avery, 243 Conn. 355, 703 A.2d 117 (Conn.1997), *483*

Panter v. Marshall Field & Co., 646 F.2d 271 (7th Cir.1981), *460*

Paramount Communications Inc. v. QVC Network Inc., 637 A.2d 34 (Del. Supr.1994), *439*

Paramount Communications, Inc. v. Time Inc., 571 A.2d 1140 (Del. Supr.1989), *439*

Perlman v. Feldmann, 219 F.2d 173 (2nd Cir.1955), *518, 522, 554*

Petition of (see name of party)

Pinson v. Hartsfield Intern. Commerce Center, Ltd., 191 Ga.App. 459, 382 S.E.2d 136 (Ga.App.1989), *135*

Piper v. Chris–Craft Industries, Inc., 430 U.S. 1, 97 S.Ct. 926, 51 L.Ed.2d 124 (1977), *435*

Quaker Hill, Inc. v. Parr, 148 Colo. 45, 364 P.2d 1056 (Colo.1961), *122*

Quickturn Design Systems, Inc. v. Shapiro, 721 A.2d 1281 (Del.Supr.1998), *439*

Radaszewski by Radaszewski v. Telecom Corp., 981 F.2d 305 (8th Cir.1992), *143*

Radom & Neidorff, Inc., In re, 307 N.Y. 1, 119 N.E.2d 563 (N.Y.1954), *371*

Randall v. Bailey, 23 N.Y.S.2d 173 (N.Y.Sup.1940), *586*

Revlon, Inc. v. MacAndrews & Forbes Holdings, Inc., 506 A.2d 173 (Del. Supr.1985), *439, 462*

Ridder v. CityFed Financial Corp., 47 F.3d 85 (3rd Cir.1995), *532*

Ringling Bros.–Barnum & Bailey Combined Shows v. Ringling, 29 Del.Ch. 610, 53 A.2d 441 (Del.Supr.1947), *280*

Rogers v. Hill, 289 U.S. 582, 53 S.Ct. 731, 77 L.Ed. 1385 (1933), *477, 478*

Rooney v. Paul D. Osborne Desk Co., Inc., 38 Mass.App.Ct. 82, 645 N.E.2d 50 (Mass.App.Ct.1995), *179*

Ross v. Bernhard, 396 U.S. 531, 90 S.Ct. 733, 24 L.Ed.2d 729 (1970), *536*

Santa Fe Industries, Inc. v. Green, 430 U.S. 462, 97 S.Ct. 1292, 51 L.Ed.2d 480 (1977), *625*

Schreiber v. Carney, 447 A.2d 17 (Del.Ch.1982), *277*

S.E.C. v. Adler, 137 F.3d 1325 (11th Cir.1998), *510*

Securities and Exchange Commission v. May, 229 F.2d 123 (2nd Cir.1956), *431*

Securities and Exchange Commission v. Texas Gulf Sulphur Co., 401 F.2d 833 (2nd Cir.1968), *503, 511*

Selheimer v. Manganese Corp. of America, 423 Pa. 563, 224 A.2d 634 (Pa.1966), *448*

Sims v. Western Waste Industries, 918 S.W.2d 682 (Tex.App.-Beaumont 1996), *156*

Sinclair Oil Corp. v. Levien, 280 A.2d 717 (Del.Supr.1971), *486*

Singer v. Magnavox Co., 380 A.2d 969 (Del.Supr.1977), *624, 625*

Smith v. Van Gorkom, 488 A.2d 858 (Del.Supr.1985), *91, 455, 458, 459, 460, 462*

Speed v. Transamerica Corp., 235 F.2d 369 (3rd Cir.1956), *485*

Strong v. Repide, 213 U.S. 419, 29 S.Ct. 521, 53 L.Ed. 853 (1909), *493*

Studebaker Corp. v. Gittlin, 360 F.2d 692 (2nd Cir.1966), *608*

Superintendent of Ins. of State of N. Y. v. Bankers Life & Cas. Co., 404 U.S. 6, 92 S.Ct. 165, 30 L.Ed.2d 128 (1971), *513*

Surowitz v. Hilton Hotels Corp., 383 U.S. 363, 86 S.Ct. 845, 15 L.Ed.2d 807 (1966), *548*

Taylor v. Standard Gas & Elec. Co., 306 U.S. 307, 306 U.S. 618, 59 S.Ct. 543, 83 L.Ed. 669 (1939), *160*

Teicher, United States v., 987 F.2d 112 (2nd Cir.1993), *511*

Theodora Holding Corp. v. Henderson, 257 A.2d 398 (Del.Ch.1969), *99*

Timberline Equipment Co., Inc. v. Davenport, 267 Or. 64, 514 P.2d 1109 (Or.1973), *130*

Tomlinson v. Loew's Inc., 37 Del.Ch. 8, 135 A.2d 136 (Del.Supr.1957), *310*

Tomlinson v. 1661 Corp., 377 F.2d 291 (5th Cir.1967), *220*

TSC Industries, Inc. v. Northway, Inc., 426 U.S. 438, 96 S.Ct. 2126, 48 L.Ed.2d 757 (1976), *428*

United States v. _____ (see opposing party)

Unitrin, Inc. v. American General Corp., 651 A.2d 1361 (Del.Supr.1995), *440*

Unocal Corp. v. Mesa Petroleum Co., 493 A.2d 946 (Del.Supr.1985), *439, 461, 496*

USACafes, L.P. Litigation, In re, 600 A.2d 43 (Del.Ch.1991), *101*

Van Schaack Holdings, Ltd. v. Van Schaack, 867 P.2d 892 (Colo.1994), *494*

Virginia Bankshares, Inc. v. Sandberg, 501 U.S. 1083, 111 S.Ct. 2749, 115 L.Ed.2d 929 (1991), *428, 429*

Vogel v. Lewis, 25 A.D.2d 212, 268 N.Y.S.2d 237 (N.Y.A.D. 1 Dept.1966), *364*

Wages v. Weiner, 381 F.2d 667 (5th Cir.1967), *222*

Walkovszky v. Carlton, 276 N.Y.S.2d 585, 223 N.E.2d 6 (N.Y.1966), *144, 145*

Weinberger v. UOP, Inc., 457 A.2d 701 (Del.Supr.1983), *487, 488, 625, 629*

Wheelabrator Technologies, Inc. Shareholders Litigation, In re, 663 A.2d 1194 (Del.Ch.1995), *489*

Wilkes v. Springside Nursing Home, Inc., 370 Mass. 842, 353 N.E.2d 657 (Mass.1976), *374*

Williams v. Geier, 671 A.2d 1368 (Del.Supr.1996), *191*

Zahn v. Transamerica Corp., 162 F.2d 36 (3rd Cir.1947), *485*

Zapata Corp. v. Maldonado, 430 A.2d 779 (Del.Supr.1981), *465*

Zion v. Kurtz, 428 N.Y.S.2d 199, 405 N.E.2d 681 (N.Y.1980), *246, 249, 250*

THE LAW OF CORPORATIONS

IN A NUTSHELL

Fifth Edition

*

CHAPTER ONE

MODERN BUSINESS FORMS AND THE CORPORATION

§ 1.1 Historical Dominance of the Corporation in the United States

The corporation has been the dominant business form in the United States since the early days of independence. The industrialization of the United States during the Nineteenth and Twentieth Centuries occurred through corporations which were incorporated in a single state (often Delaware or New Jersey) but conducted business on a national and international scale. The Twentieth Century has been a period of growth, of modernization, and of adjustment by the corporation to new challenges, including the enactment of the Internal Revenue Code and the Federal securities acts of the 1930s, statutes that have had great impact on modern corporation law in the United States. Section 3.1 of this Nutshell gives a brief description of this history.

In the last twenty years there has been a revolution of sorts in business forms for businesses with a few owners. As of about 1980, the corporation was the business form of choice for most profitable enterprises, small and large. Indeed, with the modernization and simplification of corporation law that occurred during the Twentieth Century, the corporation's role as the principal form of business for both publicly held and closely held enterprises seemed impregnable. Today, just twenty years later, a variety of different business forms have been created for closely held businesses that possess the limited liability characteristics of a corporation but are more attractive for reasons of income taxation and flexibility and efficiency of internal operations. The result is that the corporation, while still dominant in economic terms for businesses with many owners, is no longer the business form of choice for many newly formed enterprises.

§ 1.2 Publicly Held and Closely Held Corporations

Corporations may usefully be classified as "publicly held" or "closely held." Publicly held corporations are corporations whose shares are widely owned and publicly traded on the national securities exchanges, over the counter, and, increasingly, on the internet. Publicly held corporations are typically managed by professional managers who collectively own a relatively small fraction of the outstanding shares. "Closely held" corporations are corporations with relatively few shareholders. There is no public market for their shares. They are typically managed by the shareholders themselves or by persons closely associated with the shareholders. The typical "closely held" corporation has less than ten shareholders. Many may be solely owned by one person, a business form that is called an "incorporated proprietorship." Similarly, a corporation owned by several persons may be referred to as an "incorporated partnership." These phrases are potentially misleading, since the entities involved are corporations, not proprietorships or partnerships. In many closely held corporations, the shareholders will have entered into agreements restricting the transferability of shares to ensure that outsiders cannot become shareholders without the consent of the existing shareholders; these agreements also may provide a device by which existing shareholders may have their shares purchased when they die or decide to leave the corporation. See sections 9.18 through 9.23.

Most publicly held corporations are large and most closely held corporations are small, but size is not the criterion. There exist a few closely held corporations that rival the largest publicly held corporations in size, and there are some publicly traded corporations that consist of little more than a name and hopeful prospects.

This classification is useful even though there is a continuum of corporations in terms of diversification of ownership and professional management. There are many "in between" corporations that have some characteristics of public corporations but whose shares are infrequently or "thinly" traded. A corporation with 300 shareholders, for example, may be quite substantial in terms of size and assets, have professional management, and yet there may be only a sporadic or "thin" market for shares. The existence of such corporations does not destroy the basic validity of the distinction between publicly held and closely held, but recognizes the continuum that exists.

In terms of economic activity, publicly held corporations dominate the American (and world) economy. There are roughly 10,000 corporations with securities that are publicly traded on the securities markets in the United States; these corporations account for the great bulk of economic production and activity in the United States. Most of this Nutshell deals with these large economic entities, their ownership, their management, and their effect on American society.

The corporate model on which state corporation statutes and the Model Business Corporation Act (1984) are based is an idealized model that is not tailored specifically either for the close corporation or for the publicly held corporation. It is a model that is sufficiently broad and generalized that large portions of it are appropriate for both closely held and publicly held corporations. Many states have supplemented their gen-

eral corporation statutes with special statutes providing relaxed rules for closely held corporations that elect to take
advantage of their provisions. See section 12.8 of this Nutshell. Sections 7.32 and 14.34 of MBCA (1984), in particular,
provide an alternative set of provisions designed specifically
for closely held corporations.

As discussed in the latter part of this chapter, current tax
rules favor the use of unincorporated business forms that
provide limited liability for their members rather than a
closely held corporation. It is therefore probable that greater
attention will be paid to these unincorporated forms in the
future. However, closely held corporations will remain an
important part of corporate law. Profitable closely held businesses that were initially formed as corporations are very
likely to continue to retain the corporate form indefinitely.
The income tax rules make conversions from corporate to non-
corporate forms generally unattractive. The corporation may
also be selected by many new business entities as the initial
business form if the owners hope to "go public" in the future.
Some persons also may favor the certainty and familiarity of
the corporate form over newer, less familiar business forms.
However, the central role of the closely held corporation has
declined since 1990, and is likely to decline further in coming
years.

§ 1.3 Adjustment of Law School Curricula to Current Trends

Law school curricula are gradually changing to reflect the
new world of closely held businesses. Ten years ago, the
business law curriculum might have a separate course entitled
"Agency and Partnership," but the principal entity-level business law course was the "Corporations" course, to be followed
by advanced courses in "Corporation Finance," "Securities

Regulation," "Mergers and Acquisitions," "Corporate Income Taxation," and possibly other courses as well. Today most law schools offer an entry level survey course in "Business Associations" or "Business Organizations" that is designed to cover both closely held business forms and publicly traded corporations. Other schools offer separate courses in "closely held" and "publicly held" businesses; the former considers the new business forms as well as closely held corporations, while the latter covers the publicly held corporation. Still other schools offer separate courses in unincorporated business forms and corporations.

The first edition of this Nutshell was published in 1980 when the corporation was the dominant business form for both closely held and publicly held enterprises. Hence the name, "Nutshell on Corporations." For reasons of continuity, later editions retain the same name even though coverage has been broadened to discuss modern alternatives to the closely held corporation.

§ 1.4   Traditional Business Forms: Introduction

As of 1980, there were four principal business forms available for enterprises: the sole proprietorship, the general partnership, the limited partnership, and the corporation. Only the corporation combined the benefits of limited liability for all participants, centralized management, free transferability of interest, perpetual existence, and a tax structure that tended to minimize taxes for profitable business entities. As a result most businesses elected the corporation as its business form.

There were some exceptions, of course. The most important area involved professionals: Lawyers, doctors, architects, and several other occupations were prohibited by law from conducting business in corporate form; they traditionally formed general partnerships, but professional corporations and professional associations permitted some degree of limited liability in many states. A second area involved start-up enterprises anticipating losses in the early years; for federal income tax reasons they might initially be conducted in the form of proprietorships or general partnerships, planning to incorporate at a later date when the business became profitable. Commercial real estate ventures often used partnerships or real estate investment trusts rather than corporations, again for tax reasons. But these exceptions only emphasized the central role of the corporation in most areas of economic activity.

The following sections discuss briefly each of these traditional alternative forms.

§ 1.5 Proprietorships

A proprietorship is a business owned by a single person who has the sole right to manage, is solely entitled to the profits, and is unlimitedly responsible for the debts of the business. A proprietorship is often viewed not as a separate business entity but as an extension of the proprietor himself. For example, a proprietorship is not a separate entity for federal income tax purposes. Rather, when preparing his federal income tax return, a proprietor prepares a "Schedule C" reflecting the business transactions of the proprietorship, and the net profit or loss shown on Schedule C is transferred directly to his personal income tax return, the Form 1040.

Historically, a proprietor who desired a degree of immunity from personal responsibility for the debts of the proprietorship could "incorporate his business" by creating a corporation and having all business transactions be executed in the name of the corporation. There was never serious doubt that the shares of a corporation could be entirely owned by a single person. An "incorporated proprietorship" of this nature was more expensive to operate than a simple proprietorship. However, the "shield of limited liability" provided by the corporate form was a substantial advantage even though it did not protect the proprietor from liability for his personal tortious acts (or possibly a failure to exercise oversight responsibility over the acts of employees). In addition, the incorporated proprietorship created some flexibility in planning tax strategies to minimize income taxation that helped to offset the costs of operating a corporation.

§ 1.6　General Partnerships: Introduction

A general partnership is the simplest form of business organization involving more than one person. In many ways it is a logical generalization of a proprietorship with more than one member. It is widely used today by a variety of different types of businesses.

Originally, the partnership was a common law form of business, but was largely codified by the Uniform Partnership Act (1914), a statute developed by the National Conference of Commissioners on Uniform State Laws ("NCCUSL") and enacted in virtually all states. A revised Uniform Partnership Act was approved in 1994, and has been adopted by somewhat more than half of the states. The description in the following sections is generally based on the 1914 Act with separate discussion of the principal modifications made by the 1994 Act.

§ 1.7   General Partnerships: Financial Provisions

A general partnership is formed simply by an oral or written agreement of the partners, who share the right to manage and the right to participate in the profits. They also share in partnership losses and are personally responsible for all partnership obligations.

The partnership agreement is usually referred to as the "law" for that partnership since it is binding on all the partners. However, it is not binding on persons who are not partners: They may recover on partnership obligations from any partner without regard to the loss-sharing or other arrangements set forth in the partnership agreement.

Profit participations may be allocated by agreement; in the absence of agreement each partner shares equally in profits. If a partnership suffers losses, they are shared by the partners as they agree, or in the event of a failure to agree, in proportion to their profit sharing ratios.

Each partner is also personally liable on partnership obligations; a partner compelled to satisfy a partnership liability is entitled to *indemnification* from the partnership. In effect, the partnership must reimburse each partner who personally satisfies a partnership liability.

Each partner may be required to make a *contribution* to the partnership on dissolution to cover his or her share of any losses, including capital losses of other partners. "Indemnification" and "contribution" are related but different concepts: "Indemnification" relates to the reimbursement of partners who are compelled to pay partnership liabilities in an on-going partnership, while "contribution" relates to payments needed to settle accounts on the termination of the partnership.

It is customary in partnerships to maintain a "capital account" for each partner. The capital account consists of the original contribution of the partner to the partnership, increased by earnings and profits credited to the account, and reduced by losses and distributions to the partner. When a partner withdraws from the partnership he is typically entitled to receive the amount in his capital account. If the account has a negative balance, he may be required to make a contribution to eliminate the negative amount. If the entire partnership is being wound up and terminated, all capital accounts are reduced to zero by distribution or by contribution, as the case may be. Unrealized gains in the values of partnership assets are normally not credited to the capital account until they are realized or upon the final termination of the partnership.

A partner may assign his financial interest in the partnership. The assignee of such an interest does not become a partner but is entitled to whatever distributions the assigning partner was entitled to. He does not automatically become a partner because the partnership relation is a personal one. The legal phrase that describes this concept is *delectus personae.* An assignee, of course, may also be admitted to the partnership, in which case he assumes all the rights and duties of a partner. An assignee who is not a partner is not personally liable on partnership obligations and is not required to make a contribution to the partnership on dissolution. The assigning partner remains liable on those obligations.

A personal creditor of a partner may surcharge the partner's interest in the partnership through a device known as a "charging order." By a charging order, partnership distributions to the debtor partner are diverted to the creditor. The creditor may also be able to foreclose on the interest of the partner and become an assignee of the partner's financial interest.

Partnership creditors, of course may proceed directly against partnership assets. Partnership creditors may also enforce their claim against the partners, who are jointly or jointly and severally liable for partnership obligations. Under the 1914 Act, individual partners are jointly and severally liable for wrongful acts and breaches of trust, and jointly liable for contractual and other obligations. Joint liability may require naming all the partners as defendants. Under the 1994 Act, all liability is joint and several, but a partnership creditor may obtain satisfaction from individual partners only if a judgment is obtained against both the partnership and the specific partners and a writ of execution on the judgment against the partnership has been returned unsatisfied. These rules apply in the absence of a specific guarantee of payment by the partner.

§ 1.8 General Partnerships: Participation in Management

In a general partnership each partner is also an agent of the partnership for purposes of its business and has a right to participate in management. In the absence of a specific agreement, all partners share equally in management decisions. However, the partners may agree among themselves as to how the partnership business is to be managed; management, for example, may be delegated to a committee or to a single partner. Delegation of management authority to a committee is customary in large law and accounting partnerships.

An important aspect of partnership law under the 1914 Act is the broad fiduciary duty that exists among the partners. The leading case describing this duty is *Meinhard v. Salmon* (N.Y.1928), in which Chief Justice Cardozo stated:

Joint adventurers, like copartners, owe to one another, while the enterprise continues, the duty of the finest loyalty.

Many forms of conduct permissible in a workaday world for those acting at arm's length, are forbidden to those bound by fiduciary ties. A trustee is held to something stricter than the morals of the market place. Not honesty alone, but the punctillio of an honor the most sensitive, is then the standard of behavior.

This fiduciary duty has its base in the personal liability of each partner for partnership obligations and the mutual sharing of control inherent in each partnership.

The broad fiduciary duty described in *Meinhard* may be appropriate for a small partnership with relatively few members. However, it creates problems in partnerships with large numbers of members, where relationships are less personal than in small partnerships. The 1994 Uniform Partnership Act contains provisions narrowing the scope of this duty and permitting the partnership agreement, within specified limits, to limit this duty further.

A partner may be expelled by the remaining partners. Under the 1914 Act, a power to expel existed only when that power was specifically provided in the partnership agreement. The 1994 Act retains this provision and in addition recognizes an inherent power to expel a partner by the unanimous vote of the remaining partners in limited circumstances.

§ 1.9   General Partnerships: A Separate Entity?

The 1914 Act defines a partnership as an "association of two or more persons to carry on as co-owners a business for profit." UPA § 6(1). It was not clear under this statute whether this "association" was an entity in its own right independent of the partners. Early case law tended to treat a partnership as an informal association of individuals and not as a separate entity, but this view gradually changed as many partnerships grew in size and clearly possessed many entity characteristics. The 1994 Act states explicitly in section 201 that "a partnership is an entity distinct from its partners." Today each partnership has its own federal tax ID number and files its own information tax return; it owns real and personal property in its own name; it can sue and be sued in its own name; and so forth.

The notion that a partnership is an entity in its own right leads naturally to distinctions being drawn between "partnership assets" and "personal assets" of each partner and between "partnership liabilities" and "personal liabilities" of each partner. Despite these distinctions, of course, each partner remained personally responsible for all partnership liabilities to the extent described in section 1.7 of this Nutshell.

§ 1.10 General Partnerships: Artificial Entities as Partners

The 1914 Act defines "person" as including "partnerships, corporations, and other associations" as well as natural individuals. The 1994 Act adds "joint venture, government, governmental subdivision, agency or instrumentality" to this definition as well, and for good measure also adds "any other legal or commercial entity." Thus, two or more corporations may form a partnership, two or more partnerships may themselves form another partnership, or one or more individuals or corporations may form a partnership with one or more corporations, partnerships, governmental agencies, or other types of limited liability entities. All of these clearly are partnerships.

§ 1.11 General Partnerships: Dissolution, Winding Up and Termination

Under the 1914 Act, a general partnership is apparently a fragile form of business: It is "dissolved" automatically when a partner dies or leaves the partnership or when a partner expressly states that he no longer wishes to be a partner. However, the 1914 Act uses the word "dissolution" in a narrow and limited sense. Section 29 of the 1914 Act defines a "dissolution" as "the change in the relation of the partners caused by any partner ceasing to be associated in the carrying on as distinguished from the winding up of the business." In other words, "dissolution" is the mere change in relationship that occurs when a partner dies or leaves the partnership. Despite the "dissolution," the partnership continues to exist for a period of "winding up," i.e. the process of collecting claims, satisfying liabilities, and reducing assets to cash in order to permit a final distribution and settlement of the partnership accounts. Upon the final settlement and the distribution of remaining assets to the partners, the partnership "terminates" and ceases to exist.

Under the 1914 Act, a partner withdrawing from an at-will partnership was able to compel a winding up and termination. However, as a practical matter, the withdrawing partner was usually paid the value of his interest by the partnership and the partnership business continued in the form of a new partnership consisting of the remaining partners and possibly the addition of new partners as well. Under UPA (1914) a partnership was dissolved and reformed every time there was a change in the members of the partnership but the business was continued.

The 1994 Act uses the word "dissociation" rather than "dissolution" to refer to the change in relationship that occurs when a partner leaves the partnership. The Act also distinguishes between "events of withdrawal" (which permit a partner to leave the partnership and receive the value of his partnership interest but do not cause winding up and termination), and "events causing dissolution and winding up of the partnership business." This alternative, rather confusingly, is described in the 1994 Act as the "*dissolution* and winding up" of the partnership business. Early drafts of the 1994 Act did not use the word "dissolution" at all, but the word was reintroduced in later drafts to refer to the last step of the winding up process.

A partnership dissolution may also be a breach of contract. A partnership may be created by an enforceable contract that states that the partnership is to continue to exist for some stated period; a premature dissolution of that partnership is a breach of that contract. A basic distinction must therefore be made between a "partnership at will" and a "partnership for a term." In a partnership at will, dissolution is usually liability-free; in a partnership for a term, a premature dissolution is a breach of contract and the withdrawing partner may be liable for significant damages.

§ 1.12 General Partnerships: Revisions Made by the 1994 Act

The 1914 Uniform Partnership Act adequately served the needs of business for many years. However, as the size of many partnerships increased, dissatisfaction increased with respect to the dissolution provisions of that Act, the unlimited personal liability provisions involving joint and joint and several liability, and the broad fiduciary duties contemplated by that Act and uncertainty as to whether those duties could be modified by agreement or waived. This dissatisfaction surfaced in the form of enactment of non-uniform amendments in several states. These amendments, of course, destroyed the uniformity of statutory partnership law that had existed for more than sixty years, and led ultimately to the development of a revised Uniform Partnership Act. This new statute was first known as "RUPA" and later renamed the Uniform Partnership Act (1994).

The major changes made by the 1994 Act include:

• A provision expressly defining a partnership to be an entity in its own right independent of its partners.

• Provisions making clear that a partnership agreement may modify most of the partnership statutory provisions (and adding a list of specific provisions that cannot be modified or can only be modified in limited ways).

• A provision defining, and to some extent limiting, the scope of the fiduciary duty within a partnership.

• A provision making it more difficult for partnership creditors to seek recovery from partners individually. Liability may be imposed on a partner only if (1) he or she is named as a defendant along with the partnership and (2) the creditor first seeks exhaustion of partnership assets before seeking a recovery from a partner's personal assets.

• A provision modifying the dissolution provisions to distinguish between "events of withdrawal" and "events causing dissolution and winding up of the partnership business," and making clear that the dissociation of a partner did not cause a dissolution of the partnership.

• A provision authorizing partnerships to merge and to convert from a general partnership to a limited partnership, or vice versa.

• A provision authorizing partnerships to make public filings (typically with the Secretary of State) to establish the authority of specific partners to enter into partnership transactions. These filings may be useful, for example, to establish the authority of a partner to convey real property owned by the partnership.

• Provisions authorizing a partner who has dissociated from a partnership to file a public statement announcing that he is no longer associated with the partnership.

• Provisions authorizing the partnership to file a public statement announcing that it is in the process of winding up and dissolution.

The 1994 Act has been adopted by approximately 27 states as this is written. Several states have adopted new partnership statutes that incorporate many provisions of the 1994 Act but depart significantly from the Act in other respects. Modern partnership law today is therefore an amalgam of the 1914 Act, the 1994 Act, and in many states, some non-uniform provisions. It appears unlikely that partnership law will ever return to the extensive degree of uniformity that existed for many years.

§ 1.13   Limited Partnerships: In General

A limited partnership is a partnership in which there are one or more general partners and one or more limited partners. The general partners are essentially viewed as having the rights and duties of partners in a partnership without limited partners. They are unlimitedly liable for the debts of the business and have general powers of management. Limited partners, on the other hand, have no personal liability for the debts of the business (except to the extent of their capital contributions) and have only very limited rights to participate in management. If they exceed these limited rights, they become general partners and personally liable for partnership liabilities.

A limited partnership is a creature of statute. A Uniform Limited Partnership Act was promulgated by NCCUSL in 1916 and was widely adopted. A revised Act was approved in

1976 and significant amendments were made in 1983 and 1985. Today, all states have limited partnership statutes but there is a considerable degree of diversity among them.

A limited partnership is formed by filing a document or certificate with the Secretary of State or with a specified county or city official. A failure to file (or filing in the wrong office) results in the creation of a general partnership rather than a limited partnership.

In most respects, a limited partnership is governed by the same rules that are applicable to general partnerships. What is unique is the presence of limited partners who are passive investors with very limited power to participate in the management of the firm. Limited partners who do participate in the control of the business or who permit their names to appear in the partnership name may thereby lose their shield of limited liability. A major issue in limited partnership law is the extent to which limited partners may participate in management without loss of the shield of limited liability. ULPA (1916) simply provided that limited partners who "participated in the control of the business" thereby lost the shield of limited liability. The 1976 Act added a "safe harbor" consisting of a list of management-related actions that a limited partner might engage in without incurring additional liability. In 1983, the statute was further amended by adding a provision that states that a creditor may hold a limited partner liable as a general partner only if the creditor dealt with the limited partner "reasonably believing that he was a general partner."

The limited partnership has an interesting history. It developed in Europe during the Middle Ages as a device that permitted nobility and churches to participate anonymously in ordinary commerce. It was introduced in the United States at an early time but has never been widely used. During a brief period in the 1960s and 1970s, limited partnerships with publicly traded limited partnership interests were widely used as tax shelters. (See the discussion of taxation in § 1.19). The curtain came down on these "master limited partnerships" in 1986 with an amendment to the Internal Revenue Code that provided that all businesses that had publicly traded ownership interests must be taxed as a corporation.

Today, traditional limited partnerships are widely used in real estate syndications, particularly for large commercial shopping center and office projects.

One significant feature of limited partnership statutes is that they are not free-standing but rely on the general partnership statutes for matters not specifically dealt with in the limited partnership statute. Section 1105 of the current Uniform Limited Partnership Act, for example, provides, "In any case not provided for in this Act the provisions of the Uniform Partnership Act govern." This "linkage" between the two statutes has created anomalies and practical problems, and as this is written a free-standing revision of RULPA ("ReRULPA") is under consideration by NCCUSL.

§ 1.14 Limited Partnerships with a Corporate General Partner

For many years, a limited partnership was viewed as a device by which passive individual investors could invest in small businesses operated by other individuals. The limited partnership became a distinctly modern business form in the 1970s with the recognition that (1) a corporation (or other limited liability entity) could be the sole general partner in a limited partnership, and (2) limited partners could also be shareholders, directors, or officers of the general partner without losing the shield of limited liability. Limited partnership statutes were amended to make clear that participation by a limited partner in the management of the general partner did not make the limited partner personally liable for partnership obligations. This combination of business forms largely eliminated liability concerns in the limited partnership, so long as the general partner was reasonably financed considering the nature of the business. In a sense the limited partnership with a corporate general partner is a new business form. Typically, the general partner is completely controlled by the limited partners and has a nominal or relatively small equity interest in the enterprise: One per cent for the general partner and 99 percent for the limited partners is a common ratio.

Today, it is unusual to find a limited partnership in which individuals are named as general partners. Basically, there is never any reason to expose any individual to the personal liability that is inherent in the role of general partner.

The major advantage of conducting business in the form of a limited partnership with a corporate general partner today is that it combines limited liability for all with favorable federal income tax treatment, discussed below. It also permits transactions in ownership interests in the general partner to occur without causing a change in the identity of the general partner itself.

§ 1.15 A New Business Form: The Limited Liability Partnership

Historically, certain classes of professionals were prohibited from conducting their practices in corporate form. These professionals were viewed as providing individualized services and it was against public policy for them to limit their personal liability for malpractice or negligence by incorporating. While states varied in determining which services should be viewed as "professional" and subject to this public policy, all states agreed that lawyers, accountants, and medical professionals fell within this category.

Professional partnerships are probably the principal form of general partnership today; many of them have scores or hundreds (or thousands, in the case of accounting firms) of partners. Many readers of this Nutshell will doubtless be, first, employees of, and, later, partners in, large law firms that have hundreds of partners and offices scattered around major cities in the United States and the world.

Of course, there also exist many thousands of small businesses that also are general partnerships.

In light of the modern litigious society in which we live today, the major drawback of the general partnership form of business is of course the potential personal liability of partners for partnership obligations. These problems became evident in Texas during the 1980s during the crisis involving the failure of savings and loan associations, and led to the development of a new partnership business form, the limited liability partnership or "LLP." The principal classes of persons affected were lawyers and accountants. The background that led to this new business form is described in the following excerpt:

The LLP is a direct outgrowth of the collapse of real estate and energy prices in the late 1980s, and the concomitant disaster that befell Texas's banks and savings and loan associations. Texas led the nation in bank and savings and loan failures during the 1980s. More than one-third of all the bank failures in the United States occurred in Texas.

Ever since the collapse of these financial institutions across the state, the Federal Deposit Insurance Corporation ("FDIC") and the Resolution Trust Corporation ("RTC") (and its predecessor, the Federal Savings and Loan Insurance Corporation ("FSLIC")) have devoted a significant part of their total resources to the recovery of funds lost in the collapse of Texas institutions. Suit was brought against hundreds of shareholders, directors and officers of failed financial institutions. However, the amounts recovered from the principal wrongdoers were only a tiny fraction of total losses and attention quickly turned to the roles of the lawyers and accountants who had represented the failed financial institutions before their collapse. "Where were the lawyers?" and "Where were the public accountants?" were cries figuratively heard across the state. Claims against lawyers and accountants for malpractice and breach of duty were attractive because the individual professionals sometimes had been deeply involved in the affairs of their clients. Also, these lawyers and accountants were usually associated with partnerships that had substantial malpractice insurance and numerous wealthy partners. As a result, several highly reputable law firms in Texas found themselves in deep trouble because of their bank and thrift work during the "salad days" of the 1980s.

(Robert W. Hamilton, Registered Limited Liability Partnerships: Present at the Birth (Nearly), 66 Colo.L.Rev. 1065, 1069 (1995)).

In these cases, individual partners, no matter how innocent or unaware of the transactions in question, were threatened with claims running into the hundreds of millions of dollars. Even the largest malpractice insurance policy covered only a fraction of the claim, and each professional in the partnership was faced with the loss of his personal assets and wealth as well as his interest in the firm. Texas responded to this "crisis" by the enactment of amendments to its partnership statute that authorized general partnerships to limit the liability of innocent partners to their investment in the firm. In effect, these amendments created another new business form, the "limited liability partnership" or "LLP." The concept was immediately popular not only in Texas but also around the country, and all states quickly adopted statutes authorizing this new business form. The LLP election also appears in the Uniform Partnership Act (1994).

A general partnership elects to become an LLP simply by filing a statement with the Secretary of State electing LLP status. It must also change its name so that it contains the phrase "Limited Liability Partnership," "LLP," "Registered Limited Liability Partnership," "RLLP," or acceptable variations of those phrases or abbreviations.

As initially enacted in Texas, the shield of limited liability provided by the LLP election was limited. It provided protection only against malpractice and negligence claims; it did not provide protection against contract claims that exceeded the available assets of the partnership. Other states adopting LLP statutes, however, quickly extended the shield of limited liability to claims of all types. Statutes also were broadened to make it clear that the limited liability shield provided protection against claims arising from the obligations of indemnification and contribution that exist in all general partnerships. These broader statutes are called "full shield" statutes while the Texas approach is referred to as a "partial shield" statute. In 1997, Texas broadened its statute to cover contract as well as tort claims.

The shield of limited liability provided by the LLP statute is not available to partners who themselves commit acts of malpractice or negligence. In many states the protection is also not available to partners who have oversight obligations over those partners, and to partners who are aware of the malpractice or negligence and fail to take steps to prevent it. The statutes of several states, including Texas, also require that LLPs maintain certain minimum levels of assets or insurance.

A full broad shield LLP provides limited liability for partners similar to the limited liability available to shareholders in a corporation or to limited partners in a partnership that do not participate in management.

The LLP election is available to all businesses that are general partnerships and is not limited to professional partnerships. However, it is predominantly used by professional partnerships, particularly large law and accounting firms.

Following the development of the LLP, many states authorized a similar election for general partners in limited partnerships. Thus yet another new partnership form was created, the limited liability limited partnership ("LLLP"). An LLLP is a limited partnership in which general partners have the liability protection provided by the LLP election. One of the peculiarities created by the "linkage" problem between the general and limited partnership statutes is that the general partners in an LLLP may have broader protection against liability than the limited partners. This is a result of historical accident and not specific design. In practice, the LLLP is apparently not widely used today; the more common practice in limited partnerships is to have only a single general partner that is itself a corporation that is usually minimally capitalized and has a nominal equity interest in the limited partnership.

§ 1.16 Another New Business Form: The Limited Liability Company

In the 1970s a new business form, the "limited liability company" (an "LLC") was authorized by statute initially in Wyoming, and subsequently in Florida. Once its federal income tax status was established in approximately 1980, all states quickly adopted LLC statutes. In its relatively brief history, the LLC has clearly become the most popular and widely used unincorporated business form that provides limited liability for its members.

An LLC is created by filing a document with the Secretary of State or other state officer. This document, usually called "articles of organization" is a short, summary document similar to modern articles of incorporation. Detailed rules of operation are set forth in an "operating agreement" or (in some states) "regulations." Operating agreements may be patterned either after a partnership agreement or corporate bylaws. Depending on the complexity of the business and the number of participants, operating agreements may be very short or may be 30 pages or more in length.

The LLC combines the corporate benefit of limited liability for all participants with complete flexibility in internal structure and management. However, it does not involve incorporation in the traditional sense but rather traces its heritage back to the continental tradition of statutory limited liability entities that has taken root in Central and South America.

From a liability standpoint, an LLC may be roughly analogized to a limited partnership composed only of limited partners. However, all of the members may freely participate in management of the business without becoming liable for the business's obligations. This protection is provided simply by a provision in the LLC statute that states that members are not personally liable for the organization's debts.

LLC statutes permit the internal management structure to be modeled either after a corporation or after a general partnership. LLC statutes generally provide that each LLC should elect to be either "member managed" or "manager managed." A member managed LLC is governed by a set of rules similar to a partnership while a manager managed LLC is governed by a set of rules more analogous to a corporation. However, the operating agreement may modify these rules as the members desire.

Originally, the statutes of many states modeled the LLC after a partnership and required at least two members; today the statutes of virtually all states provide that an LLC may have only a single member. A one-member LLC is analogous to an incorporated proprietorship but with none of the required corporate formalities. At the other extreme, membership interests may also be made readily transferable like shares of stock and may be reflected by certificates, the transfer of which may or may not be restricted by provision in the governing documents. Duration may be perpetual, for a term, or at will. The LLC is, in short, a genuinely novel business form of great flexibility.

Today, a sole proprietor may obtain a significant limited liability shield simply by forming a one-person LLC to operate the business. A proprietor who formed a corporation to operate an "incorporated proprietorship" twenty years ago would in all likelihood today use an LLC rather than a corporation. A one-person LLC has more desirable federal income tax treatment than a corporation while the shield of limited liability is the same. As a result, the LLC has largely supplanted the one-person corporation for new businesses.

In 1995 NCCUSL approved the Uniform Limited Liability Company Act ("ULLCA"). By this time, however, most states had developed their own statutes. As a result, ULLCA has not played a central role in developing statutes. Indeed, the ULL-CA draws many provisions from the partnership statutes, while many state statutes adopt a more "corporate" approach. A handful of smaller states have adopted ULLCA.

In summary, the attractiveness of the LLC as a form of business is that it combines (1) limited liability for all members, (2) flexibility of management structure, and (3) most importantly, as described in § 1.19, a desirable income tax treatment.

§ 1.17 A Menu of Modern Business Forms Based on the Number of Owners

A new venture obviously must adopt a business form in which it is to operate. Today, with the proliferation of business forms described above, the principal choices (based on the number of owners) are as follows:

(a) If the business has only a single owner, (i) a proprietorship, (ii) a one-person limited liability company, or (iii) a corporation.

(b) If the business has more than one owner but ownership interests are not themselves publicly traded: (i) a general partnership, (ii) a limited partnership, (iii) a limited liability company, (iv) a limited liability partnership, (v) a limited liability limited partnership, or (vi) a corporation.

(c) If ownership interests are (or are likely to be) publicly traded: a corporation. However, there are a few examples of publicly traded limited liability companies or limited partnerships, but they appear to have no advantage over the corporation form, and their very newness and lack of familiarity by the trading public are disadvantages. Publicly traded LLCs and LPs are subject to corporate income taxation and are virtually indistinguishable from corporations.

If a new business venture is simply launched without a conscious selection of business form being made, a partnership or proprietorship has been created, for better or for worse.

§ 1.18 Factors Influencing the Selection of Business Forms

It is not possible to appreciate the issues surrounding the selection of modern business forms without some knowledge of the basic principles of modern federal income taxation. Unfortunately, for many students, the role of federal income taxation in the selection of the business form is a mystery or an enigma. They are not familiar with the broad structure of the Internal Revenue Code which, of course, is a daunting and complex statute that is the subject of separate law school courses. Indeed, in many business association courses, the role of federal income taxes is ignored simply because it is so complex. The following sections describe in broad terms how the income tax interrelates with the selection of business forms.

For many users of this book, this discussion may not be necessary. It may be enough to know that the current federal income tax regime favors the use of unincorporated business forms for closely held businesses. The corporation is thus the least attractive closely held business form from a purely tax standpoint.

All of the unincorporated business forms described above either provide for limited liability of owners or permit limited liability to be obtained by a simple filing procedure. The differences among them that may influence the selection of a specific business form include federal and state taxation (both franchise and income), the ease of internal operations, the probability that the business in the future might "go public," the sophistication of the various participants, their estimate whether their relationship with the business is permanent or temporary, and doubtless other factors as well.

§ 1.19 Federal Tax Regimes

There are three basic tax regimes for businesses. They are usually referred to by the subchapter of the Internal Revenue Code dealing with that regime. Subchapter C describes the traditional corporate income tax; Subchapter K describes the tax regime applicable to partnerships and associations taxable as partnerships; and Subchapter S is an alternative tax regime applicable to electing closely held corporations that meet specific eligibility requirements. Each of these regimes may be briefly described in simplified fashion:

(1) *Subchapter C Taxation.* The starting point for corporate taxation is that a corporation is a separate taxable entity independent of its shareholders. I.R.C. § 11(a) imposes a separate tax on the income of corporations while § 301 in effect imposes a tax on shareholders who receive distributions of cash or property from corporations, to the extent the corporation has earnings or profits. Thus, the earnings of a C corporation that pays dividends to its shareholders are subject to federal income taxation at two different levels: at the corporate level on the corporation's taxable income and a second time at the shareholders' level on the actual dividends or distributions. This method of taxation is applicable not only to corporations but also to a variety of other associations that are "taxable as a corporation." C corporation taxation is the form of taxation applicable to all publicly held corporations.

As indicated previously, there was a brief period in the 1960s and 1970s when "master limited partnerships" were widely sold as a tax-oriented investment. The favorable tax treatment was based on the assumption that the limited partnership would be taxed under subchapter K rather than Subchapter C. The Revenue Act of 1987 effectively ended the tax advantage of publicly-traded entities by defining all such entities as corporations for tax purposes. In short, any business entity that has ownership interests that are publicly traded must be taxed as a C corporation. (The Revenue Act of 1987 did "grandfather" a few existing master limited partnerships, and some of these companies may still be in existence.)

(2) *Subchapter S Taxation.* For many years closely held corporations complained that the double taxation inherent in Subchapter C taxation treated them unfairly and encouraged questionable tax avoidance tactics. In 1957, Congress created a special tax election for qualified closely held corporations. This election permits many closely held corporations to elect to be taxed in a manner that generally avoids the double taxation of distributions. It permits corporate income to be passed through the corporation and be taxed directly to shareholders, whether or not it is actually distributed to them. While Subchapter S tax treatment is similar to the conduit tax treatment applicable to partnerships and unincorporated entities described below, there are numerous significant technical differences. The S corporation election is also sometimes loosely referred to as a corporation "electing to be taxed as a partnership" or "electing partnership taxation;" those statements are only partially accurate.

To be eligible for subchapter S, a corporation must meet the following conditions on the date of election:

(a) It must be a domestic corporation;

(b) It must have no more than 75 shareholders;

(c) Each shareholder must be an individual, a decedent's estate, or certain types of trusts;

(d) No shareholder may be a nonresident alien; and

(e) It may have only one class of stock outstanding (except that classes of common stock differing only in voting rights do not result in the loss of the election).

An S corporation is a true corporation with all attributes of a corporation other than the peculiar tax treatment. Thus, an S corporation has the normal corporate characteristics of limited liability, centralization of management, perpetual existence, and free transferability of interest.

(3) *Subchapter K taxation.* In general terms, partnerships and "associations taxable as partnerships" are not separate taxable units. Rather, the various tax consequences of their activities are passed through to the owners of the enterprise. The partnership files an information return calculating its business income or loss and then allocates the pro rata share of gains, losses, income, deductions, and so forth, to each individual partner who must include those items in his or her individual income tax return. Under subchapter K, allocations need not be strictly in proportion to economic interests. This method of taxation is generically described as "conduit," "pass through," or "partnership-type" taxation. Today it is often referred to as "subchapter K" taxation, or simply as "K" taxation. The rules under subchapter K are much more complex and sophisticated than the rules applicable to C or S corporations.

§ 1.20 Impact of Tax Rates on Tax Minimization Strategies

It should be emphasized that as an abstract matter none of the systems of taxation described in the previous section is inherently superior to the others. It all depends on relative tax rates and the detailed rules as to whether income is taxable at the corporate level and, if so, what deductions and credits are available to shareholders at the shareholder level.

Tax minimization strategies change with changes in rates and tax rules. For example, for many years after World War II individual marginal tax rates for wealthy individuals were as high as 80 percent while the maximum corporate tax rate was capped at 52 percent. Furthermore, the tax rate on long term capital gains was capped at 25 percent. This structure of rates strongly encouraged successful businesses (1) to incorporate and take advantage of the C corporation maximum tax rate, (2) to defer paying substantial dividends, (3) to obtain the benefit of assets accumulated in the corporation through transactions that qualified for capital gain treatment, and (4) to provide benefits to shareholder/officers that were tax deductible by the corporation. During this period, Subchapter K taxation for a profitable business with high-income taxpayers was to be avoided at all costs, since it subjected all the business' income to the very high individual tax rates. Shareholders were much better off if a corporation made no taxable distributions at all. However, reasonable salaries paid to shareholders were deductible by the corporation as an ordinary and necessary business expense. In addition to salaries, corporations also provided tax deductible benefits to shareholders, including company vehicles or country club memberships used for business development purposes. Thus some indirect distributions regularly were made to at least some of the shareholders. Shareholders could ultimately sell their shares to third persons to capture the increases in value at the corporate level resulting from limited distributions. The gain from a sale of stock was taxed at a maximum 25 percent rate. The strategy of allowing earnings to accumulate in the corporation and then selling the shares was so common that it became known as the "accumulate and bail-out strategy." An even better tax result was obtained if a shareholder died owning shares of stock, since a special tax rule permits the appreciation in value of the stock to escape taxation entirely.

It might be added that shareholders who were not employed by the corporation usually had no method of obtaining distributions from the corporation except at a very substantial tax cost.

Tax rates generally trended downward following World War II, reaching their lowest level in 1986. In 1986, individual tax rates were reduced sharply to a maximum rate of 28 percent while corporate tax rates were reduced to a maximum rate of 34 percent. As a result, the rules of the tax avoidance game changed abruptly, as partnership-type taxation became attractive, and C corporation taxation was to be avoided if possible. Current tax rates are higher than they were in 1986; in 1999 the maximum marginal tax rate for individuals is 39.6 percent while the maximum corporate tax rate is 35 percent. Under these tax rates, the most favorable tax regime today for a profitable business is usually subchapter K, followed by subchapter S, followed by Subchapter C. However, if the participants in the business lack the sophistication to take full advantage of the complexities of subchapter K, S corporation taxation should normally be elected (assuming the entity qualifies).

§ 1.21 Tax Classification of Unincorporated Limited Liability Entities: The Kintner Rules and "Check the Box"

The creation of unincorporated business forms that possessed limited liability for all of its owners created serious classification problems for the Internal Revenue Service. For many years it had been accepted wisdom that partnership tax treatment was available only in business forms that imposed unlimited personal liability on the owners for business obligations. The theory apparently was that since the economic benefits and burdens of the partnership business passed directly through to the partners, it was reasonable to impose income taxation on the same basis.

The Internal Revenue Service first considered making unlimited personal liability the touchstone of Subchapter K taxation, but this approach was rejected by the courts as not being justified under the language of the Internal Revenue Code. The Service then created a set of regulations, known as the "Kintner regulations," to identify which unincorporated limited liability entities could qualify for partnership tax treatment under subchapter K. These regulations identified six characteristics that are "found in a pure corporation that distinguish it from other organizations." These six characteristics were (i) associates, (ii) an objective to carry on a business and divide the gains therefrom, (iii) continuity of life, (iv) centralized management, (v) liability for corporate debts limited to corporate property, and (vi) free transferability of interest. The critical test of the Kintner regulations was based on the premise that an entity should be classified as an association taxable as a corporation if it had more corporate than non-corporate attributes. Otherwise it should be taxed under subchapter K. According to these regulations, corporations and unincorporated limited liability entities all have the common characteristics of associates and an objective to carry on a business for profit and divide the gains therefrom. Therefore, an unincorporated entity would be subject to corporate tax treatment only if it had three or more of the remaining four characteristics, or phrased in the opposite way, an entity would be classified as a partnership if it lacked any two of these four characteristics. All the new unincorporated business forms had the characteristic of limited liability. Hence the critical issues were whether the unincorporated entities possessed two of the three remaining "corporate characteristics:" centralized management, continuity of life, and free transferability of interest. This rather mechanical approach toward classification quickly created a cottage industry of lawyers seeking the outer limits of "centralized management," "continuity of life" and "free transferability of interest." The result was an increasing number of rulings and increasingly fine distinctions about the precise contours of these critical characteristics. A fair evaluation of this jurisprudence is that it created a system in which skilled lawyering and careful drafting of documents made it possible for business entities almost always to elect whichever tax regime was most favorable to it.

In 1996 the Internal Revenue Service concluded that the Kintner regulations had failed of their essential purpose because the selection of tax regimes under those regulations had become essentially optional. It announced new regulations, popularly known as "check the box," that explicitly made the election of tax regimes voluntary for unincorporated business forms, while limiting corporations (and a large number of corporate-type entities) to the traditional S Corporation/C Corporation rules. These new regulations became effective on January 1, 1997. They materially simplified the arcane and complex Kintner rules and made new strategies available to lawyers seeking the most favorable income tax treatment for clients.

The stated purpose of the "check the box" regulations was to replace the Kintner rules "with a much simpler approach that generally is elective." The basic rules of "check the box" can be simply stated:

(1) An entity is classified as a corporation for tax purposes if it is created under a statute that "describes or refers to the entity as incorporated as a corporation, body corporate, or body politic" or as a "joint-stock company or joint stock association." Such an entity must be taxed as a C or S corporation. The regulations also list a large number of

foreign entities that are viewed by the Internal Revenue Service as equivalent of corporations for domestic income tax purposes.

(2) An entity that is not classified as a corporation and has at least two members can elect to be classified for tax purposes either as a corporation (Subchapters C or S) or as a partnership (Subchapter K) by making an election at the time it files its first tax return. If the entity does not formally elect to be taxed as a corporation, it will be taxed as a partnership. Existing entities with two or more members retain the tax status they had immediately before the new regulations went into effect.

(3) An entity that has only one member may elect to be taxed as a corporation or it will be taxed as a "nothing," i.e. as though it had no existence separate from its owner.

(4) An entity that is not a corporation has one free opportunity to change its classification after its formation. It may not change its classification thereafter within five years without permission of the Commissioner.

(5) The conversion of an entity that is currently taxable as a corporation to a form of entity that is taxed as a partnership is itself treated as a taxable event, i.e. as though the corporation dissolved and reconstituted itself as a partnership or limited liability company. Dissolution of a corporation results in a tax being imposed on the amount by which the fair market value of the property distributed exceeds the basis (cost) of the property. This tax often makes a conversion from a corporation to a partnership or LLC economically impractical.

(6) A conversion in the opposite direction, i.e. from a partnership or LLC to a corporation is usually (though not always) tax free.

The "check the box" regulations do not apply to business organizations that have publicly traded ownership interests; they continue be taxed exclusively under Subchapter C.

In summary, under "check the box" partnerships and limited liability companies may elect to be taxed under any of the three principal forms of taxation. A corporation, on the other hand is taxed either under Subchapter C or, if it is eligible, Subchapter S. The following section discusses the technical differences between Subchapter S taxation and Subchapter K taxation. Section 1.23 considers additional factors involved in deciding whether a new business desiring limited liability should choose to utilize a corporation or an LLC.

§ 1.22   A Comparison of Taxation under Subchapter K and Subchapter S

Subchapter K dealing with traditional partnership taxation contains exceptionally complex provisions authorizing a variety of elections and allocations. Subchapter S, in contrast, while providing a similar type of "pass through" taxation is much simpler and easier to apply since income is simply allocated in accordance with relative ownership interests. Thus, while the tax treatment of business entities under subchapter S and subchapter K is similar in a basic sense, there are numerous technical differences. These differences may permit significant tax savings by election of Subchapter K. On the other hand, unless a business entity has sophisticated tax advice available to it, there is a risk under Subchapter K either that tax-minimization opportunities available to it may be ignored or that it will claim tax benefits to which it is not entitled. In the absence of considerable tax sophistication, many practitioners therefore recommend that new entities elect S corporation tax treatment even though some tax-minimization benefits may be lost.

Subchapter S and subchapter K differ in a number of technical respects, virtually all of which favor partnership tax treatment as a theoretical matter. For readers unfamiliar with basic tax principles, it may not be necessary to finish reading this section. For others, this is a list of the principal differences:

(1) A shareholder of an S corporation must include in her taxable income the amount of the income of the S corporation allocated to her, based on her proportional interest in the corporation. The tax rules applicable to partnerships, on the other hand, give the business entity some discretion as to how income or loss are to be allocated among the participants, allocations that may produce significant net tax savings. Subchapter K permits the use of curative or remedial allocations in some circumstances that permit the transfer of property in a tax-deferred transaction while enabling the new owner to obtain the economic benefit of a step-up in basis of the property.

(2) Subchapter S and Subchapter K tax treatment differ in the manner in which gain is recognized when a participant in a business contributes appreciated property to the business, and the property is thereafter sold to capture this appreciation in value. This type of gain is called "built-in gain." In a partnership, built-in gain from any sale of property within two years must be allocated back to the contributing partner. In an S corporation, the gain must be allocated strictly in accordance with ownership interests. For example, assume that A contributes $10,000 in cash and B contributes a piece of real estate having a tax basis (roughly, the investment made to acquire the property) of $4,000 and a fair market value of $10,000. There is built-in gain of $6,000 in B's contribution. Assume further that A and B each have a 50% interest in the business. Shortly

thereafter, suppose that the business sells the real estate for $10,000. If the business is subject to partnership tax treatment, the $6,000 gain must be allocated entirely to B, who must pay tax on this gain (presumably as a capital gain). B's basis in the partnership is thereby increased to $10,000. If the business is subject to S corporation tax treatment, on the other hand, $3,000 of the gain must be allocated to A and $3,000 to B. A, in effect, is taxed on a portion of the gain attributable to B's contribution of property, and the tax bases of A's and B's interests in the corporation will not be equal, even though each originally contributed property of equal value.

(3) Another difference in tax treatment arises if the business owns property that has appreciated in value while owned by the business, and distributes that property to its owners. If the business is taxed under Subchapter K, no gain is recognized on the transfer, and the basis of each partner in the property is carried over from the partnership's basis. Under Subchapter S, the distribution of appreciated property results in recognition of gain and its allocation to the owners in proportion to their percentage of ownership. Thus, a tax on the gain is due even if the appreciated property is still owned by the business and has not been sold to third parties.

(4) Another difference between Subchapter S and Subchapter K tax treatment relates to adjustments to basis for liabilities incurred by the business itself. If the business is subject to Subchapter S and money is borrowed by an owner and contributed to the corporation, his basis is increased by the amount of the loan. However, if the indebtedness is incurred directly by the business, there is no adjustment in the owners' tax bases, and a valuable tax attribute is lost entirely (since it is always advantageous to increase the tax

basis in the business). Under Subchapter K the tax basis of all partners is increased by indebtedness incurred directly by the partnership.

(5) Under Subchapter S losses are deductible by the owners of the business only to the extent of the tax basis of their interests in the firm. Under Subchapter K, losses are deductible by partners without limit.

(6) Finally, Subchapter K permits a step-up of basis in assets to reflect the owners' bases in the partnership whenever a single participant's interest is redeemed or liquidated. This privilege is not available under Subchapter S, again with the result that valuable tax benefits may be lost under that tax regime.

While these differences between Subchapter K and Subchapter K are technical, they involve real dollars in the real world. Since the rules favor Subchapter K over Subchapter S, practitioners have naturally gravitated toward that method of taxation. Under check the box, an LLC or limited partnership may elect among C, K or S while a corporation may only elect between Subchapters C and S. Undoubtedly this difference in tax treatment has encouraged many sophisticated lawyers since 1997 to routinely recommend the use of limited partnerships or limited liability companies rather than corporations.

On the other hand, Subchapter S has the advantage of simplicity. Its application in practice is relatively simple and straight-forward since allocations are based on stock ownership. In many instances, Subchapter K may provide only minor benefits over Subchapter S so that the simpler system may be elected despite the possible loss of small additional tax benefits.

§ 1.23 Non–Tax Differences Between an LLC and a Corporation

An LLC differs from a corporation in several respects. From a theoretical standpoint, an LLC, unlike a corporation, does not obtain a "charter" or "franchise" from the state. It may be objected that this is a distinction without a difference, since a filing is required for an LLC, and the two forms of business may be superficially quite similar. However, this difference has implications in several areas.

For example, under many state franchise tax statutes, a corporation is subject to the franchise tax but an LLC is not. In some states, including Texas and Tennessee, an LLC is taxed as a corporation for franchise tax purposes, and this difference disappears. However, that is not true in most states.

The internal management structure of a traditional corporation is three-tiered: shareholders, directors, and officers. Each tier has its own rights and duties established by statute (and by tradition), and the power to vary this structure may be limited. See, however, Sections 12.8–12.9 for a discussion of statutes in some states that permit corporations to vary their internal structure by unanimous consent.

The traditional corporation also has procedural requirements for meetings and for decision-making. Many corporation statutes have fixed rules for such matters as notice of meetings of shareholders and directors, establishment of record dates, quorums, decisions based on formal votes on motions, maintenance of minutes of meetings in minute books, stock registers and stock transfer books, and the like, which are appropriate for publicly held corporations but not for small, closely held businesses. In the small closely held corporation it is very likely that these formal requirements will be ignored and decisions will be made quite informally. Failure to follow corporate formalities in many states is explicitly a factor considered by courts when deciding whether to pierce the corporate veil and impose on shareholders personal responsibility for corporate obligations. See Section 6.6 of this Nutshell.

Ignoring procedural requirements may also raise questions about whether specific corporate actions were validly taken. Many lawyers have had the experience of requesting to see the minute book of a closely held corporation, only to find it contains nothing but the articles of incorporation and bylaws created by the lawyer that formed the corporation. In effect, there is no record of corporate actions and as a result it may be difficult to determine the economic or legal status of the corporation.

The LLC has none of these formal requirements. The internal structure of an LLC may be quite informal, with members acting as though they were partners rather than as shareholders or directors or officers. Decisions in an LLC may be made quite informally, and the question whether a specific prior action was properly taken is simply a matter of evidence, of proof, of testimony, and not of reliance on formal corporate records. The LLC structure is thus not only simpler but more natural for most business persons. The steady growth in the use of LLCs rather than corporations for small businesses should therefore not be surprising.

Many states continue to record the formation of more new corporations than new LLCs. There are several possible explanations. The simplest is that old habits die hard. A second is that documentation for an LLC may be more complex than that of a corporation because of its increased flexibility. Many corporation service companies continue to use corporate forms for this reason. Since almost all entities with publicly traded ownership interests are corporations, a start-up business that contemplates or hopes for an initial public offering ("IPO") may elect to become a corporation from the outset. Venture capital firms also may prefer to deal with a corporation rather than an LLC because of control considerations that revolve around the creation of special classes of preferred shares.

§ 1.24 Differences Between the LLC and Various Partnership Forms

Limited partnerships and limited liability partnerships now provide a significant degree of limited liability for the owners, a degree of limited liability that is comparable to that provided by a limited liability company. There are some differences, however. The LLC provides limited liability for all members (presumably subject to some public policy limitations such as principles analogous to the corporate doctrine of piercing the corporate veil).

In contrast, some state LLP statutes contain specific minimum capital requirements that may, if inadvertently violated, result in the loss of the limited liability shield. Some LLP statutes also limit the shield of limited liability in the case of partners with oversight responsibilities or who have personal knowledge of misconduct that they do not attempt to correct. LLCs do not explicitly recognize this liability, which possibly might be imposed under common law principles.

Similarly, limited partnership statutes in many states continue to provide that the shield of limited liability does not protect limited partners who take part in the control of the business beyond certain safe harbor provisions. While precautions may limit this exposure, there is always a risk that a limited partner will not be aware of the rules and inadvertently incur personal liability.

Another difference is that an LLC may have a single member while partnerships (including LLPs) and limited partnerships, by definition, involve two or more persons. While it is possible for a sole proprietor to create a corporation or limited liability company and then enter into a partnership with that entity, the advantage of doing so seems problematic at best. Where a sole proprietorship is involved, limited liability can be achieved most simply and directly by creating an LLC.

Some aspects of partnership law may not be as well suited to a specific enterprise as the rules applicable to a limited liability company. For example, an individual partner may be able to compel the winding up and termination of a partnership under the 1914 Act. LLC statutes provide for continuity of life equivalent to that provided by a corporation. The broad fiduciary duty that exists in partnerships also may not be desirable in a closely held business if it is contemplated that individual participants may be able to act in their own self interest in specific areas.

Centralized management may be more firmly created in a manager-managed LLC than in a partnership managed by a committee. If the corporate model of centralized management is desired, it may be provided most simply by an LLC. A limited partnership may also provide centralized management analogous to that provided by an LLC.

These differences tend to favor the flexibility of the LLC over the partnership model for most small closely held businesses.

§ 1.25   Selection of Business Form for a Start-up Business

Historically, the selection of a business form revolved around the core issues of limitation of liability and federal income taxation. Many older treatises may still emphasize these factors. Today, however, these factors are not central. Limited liability is routinely available for all businesses that desire it and "check the box" has made the selection of tax regime largely, though not entirely, elective. Attention should therefore be given to additional areas. These areas include:

1. Considerations of internal efficiency, operational cost, and organizational convenience given the nature of the business, the number of owners, and their relationships with each other.

2. The husbanding of scarce capital and resources during the period before the business becomes well established.

3. Considerations relating to the ease of raising capital in the future.

4. The possibility of going public some time in the future.

A sensible rule for newly formed businesses is to keep matters simple at the outset. Small, marginal businesses with limited capital usually benefit by limiting organizational expenses and devoting capital to operations and inventory rather than to lawyers. Simplicity also permits owners to concentrate on business matters and not be saddled with unessential organizational details. It may not be sensible to invest limited capital resources in creating a detailed corporate or limited liability company structure when the money might be better used by being directly invested in the business.

Modern tax rules encourage the use of non-corporate business forms for small start-up businesses. Since a non-corporate business form may elect to convert to a corporation without significant tax costs, it may not be necessary to use a corporation for a newly formed business. See, however, the discussion of IPOs and venture capital in Section 1.23.

§ 1.26   What Does the Future Hold?

The current menu of business forms for closely held businesses is unquestionably confusing and untidy. The business forms that are widely used in the United States today overlap in various ways; each has its own particularized history that leads to unique rules and limitations. Many of these differences are explained only by history and not by logic. However, there has been a strong trend in recent years to increasing the areas in which basic characteristics of business forms overlap.

Suggestions have been made to unify the various business forms into a single model that would permit the owners to select the characteristics most suitable for their specific business without regard to the traditional differences in the various business forms. Rather than having corporations, partnerships, limited liability companies and the like we would have only "business entities" or "businesses." Each "business entity" could then select the business and tax characteristics it desires from a standard list. Such a development would render obsolete the traditional differences among business forms discussed in this initial chapter. It is unlikely that such unification will occur in the near future, if it ever occurs at all. The traditional concepts of corporations, of partnerships, and more recently, of limited liability companies appear to be very strongly ingrained in American legal thought.

CHAPTER TWO

THE CORPORATION IN THEORY

§ 2.1 The Corporation as an "Artificial Entity"

A corporation is formed simply by one or more persons, acting as "incorporators," filing an appropriate document with a state official, usually the secretary of state, and paying the required fee. Acceptance of this filing is traditionally evidenced either by a notation on the filed document itself or by the issuance of a separate document by the state official certifying that the original filing has been accepted. Statutes provide that "the corporate existence shall begin" either with the acceptance of the filing by the state official or with the issuance of the separate document. Assuming that all necessary steps have been taken and the "corporate existence" has begun, what has been created?

The traditional view is that a corporation is an *artificial person* or *artificial entity* independent of the incorporators, owners or investors. This artificial person may conduct a business or businesses in its own name in the same way that a "real" person can. Business is done, assets acquired, contracts entered into, and liabilities incurred, all in the name of the corporation rather than in the name of any individual. This artificial person has most of the legal rights of a "real" person: it may sue or be sued as though it were a "real" person, it must pay taxes, it may apply for business licenses in its own name, it may have its own bank account, it may hire employees, and so forth.

One consequence of this traditional view is that since the corporation is an entity in its own right it is liable for its own debts and obligations and the individual shareholders or incorporators are not liable. Indeed, the separate entity concept is so deeply ingrained in Anglo–American thinking about corporation law that many corporation statutes (unlike partnership or limited liability company statutes) never expressly state that shareholders are not liable for corporate obligations. The shareholders enjoy *limited liability* because the corporation is an entity in its own right, and it is not necessary for statutes to restate the obvious.

Of course, modern partnerships or limited liability companies also are defined to be "entities" in their own right and partners or members may enjoy a significant degree of limited liability. The difference is that corporations have been viewed as artificial entities for centuries while unincorporated business forms have not.

While talking about conceptualizations, it is helpful to describe other traditional characteristics that flow from the concept of artificial entity:

(a) The existence of the corporation is not dependent on who the owners or investors are at any one time. If shareholders die, or decide to sell out, or what have you, the corporation continues to exist as a separate entity. In legal language, a corporation has *continuity of life*.

(b) The corporation does not have a limited life span. Rather it has *perpetual existence*. One should not be misled, however, about what "perpetual existence" means: It does not really mean that all corporations continue until the end of time but rather that a corporation continues indefinitely until the owners decide to dissolve it or merge it into another business.

(c) The management of the corporation is vested in an independent body, the board of directors (which is elected by the shareholders), but not in the shareholders themselves. There is *centralized management* in a corporation. Indeed, shareholders as such have no right at all to interfere with the operations of the corporation (except for very specific rights such as a limited right to inspect the books and records of the corporation).

(d) The ownership interests of the shareholders may be sold or transferred to third persons without the approval or consent of the corporation or other shareholders. There is *free transferability of interest* in a corporation.

These various characteristics of a corporation constitute the default form of corporation. A corporation that is formed without any specialized planning automatically has each of these basic characteristics. However, in real life today there is usually a great deal of contract-type planning that goes on within a specific corporate structure, and these basic characteristics may be eliminated or modified significantly by agreement among the interested parties. Virtually all of this increased flexibility is a result of innovative provisions in corporation statutes developed since World War II.

The artificial entity theory is most likely to be accepted unconsciously when talking about a large publicly held corporation that has billions of dollars in assets and thousands of shareholders. A similar theory may also be unconsciously applied to other institutions in modern society, such as churches, colleges and universities.

§ 2.2 Limitations of the "Artificial Entity" Theory

The artificial entity theory has been criticized as being unrealistic and formalistic. It is true that it is a reification, the personalization of an abstract concept. Reifications sometimes are a substitute for analysis, and so it is with the corporation. The starting point for a realistic examination of a corporation is a fundamental truth: flesh-and-blood people underlie every corporation, and are essential to everything a corporation does. Some individual must decide what the corporation is to do; some individual must actually do the required act on behalf of the corporation, because manifestly an artificial entity has no will of its own and no arms, legs, mouth, or eyes that permit it to take action. Some individual ultimately reaps the profits earned by the corporation, and some person must ultimately bear any loss. In realistic terms, a corporation is simply a device by which individuals join to conduct a business and the same or different individuals share in any profit or loss. Professor Hohfeld summarized this view of the corporation in 1923 when he wrote, "Strangely enough, it has not always been perceived with perfect clearness that transacting business under the forms, methods, and procedure pertaining to so-called corporations is simply another mode by which individuals or natural persons can enjoy their property and engage in business. Just as several individuals may transact business collectively as partners, so they may as members of a corporation—the corporation being nothing more than an association of such individuals * * *." He added, when "we speak of the corporation * * * contracting in the corporate name, * * * we are merely employing a short and convenient mode of describing the complex and peculiar process by which the benefits and burdens of the corporate members are worked out * * *." Hohfeld, Fundamental Legal Conceptions 197 (1923).

Hohfeld's analysis illustrates the fallacy of accepting uncritically the "artificial entity" theory. A corporation may be treated as an entity for many purposes but it need not be treated as an entity for all purposes. At some point the reality which Hohfeld describes may control over formalistic arguments. For this reason, arguments grounded solely on the artificial entity theory and not supported by considerations of fairness, justice, or policy have sometimes not prevailed.

The artificial entity concept in a sense gets things backwards. While useful as a "short and convenient mode" of describing most of the powers of a corporation and the legal relationships surrounding it, a corporation possesses these attributes not because it is an artificial entity but because of statutory provisions, supplemented by history and tradition. And, it should be added, it does not follow that merely because a corporation possesses many entity attributes, it necessarily possesses additional entity attributes as well.

Finally, the artificial entity concept gives no indication of the goals or objectives of a corporation. It does not address the role of corporations in modern society or the complex interrelationships of persons who participate in, profit from, or are affected by, the corporation.

§ 2.3   The Corporation as a Privilege or Contract

In traditional thinking about corporations, the artificial entity theory is supplemented by other theories. These formulations often arise in situations involving the power of states to regulate corporations or the rights or duties of shareholders in a corporation among themselves. They include:

(a) The corporation is a "privilege," "concession," "franchise," or "grant" from the state that permits the owners and investors to conduct business as a corporation. Conceptually, when the secretary of state formally recognizes the creation of a corporation, that action can be viewed as a grant by the state of a franchise to conduct business in corporate form. This conception had greater importance in an earlier day when significant limitations or conditions were imposed on the privilege of incorporating in many states. However, this theory is still sometimes referred to in the literature in connection with the social policy debate about the appropriate role of large corporations in modern society (see § 3.4 of this Nutshell). Further, the notion that a corporation receives a "franchise" from the state of incorporation is the theory on which states selectively apply their franchise taxes to corporations but not to other business forms.

(b) The corporate charter may also be viewed as a "compact" or "contract." Depending on the circumstances, the parties to this contract may be:

(i) The shareholders themselves; or

(ii) The shareholders and the corporation; or

(iii) The corporation and the state of incorporation.

For example, the contract theory often appears in situations where disputes have arisen between classes of shareholders. In a dispute between preferred and common shareholders, for example, it is not uncommon for a court to refer to the provisions of the articles of incorporation that describes the rights of preferred shareholders as "the preferred shareholders' contract." Many cases state that this "contract" constitutes the full and exclusive description of the rights of that class of shareholders as against the common shareholders.

In the famous decision in Dartmouth College v. Woodward [(U.S.1819)], the Court considered the charter of Dartmouth College to be a contract between the corporation and the state that was protected against unilateral impairment by the state under the contracts clause of the United States Constitution. This case is of historic interest today since all states subsequently adopted constitutional provisions or statutes that specifically require every certificate of incorporation granted by that state to be subject to later amendment by the state. An example of such a statute is section 1.02 of the Model Business Corporation Act.

The theories of corporateness discussed in this and the prior section—the "artificial entity" theory, the "realistic" theory, the "concession" theory, the "franchise" theory, and the "contract" theory—are the traditional explanations of what a corporation "really" is. All help to explain the modern concept of a corporation. None is totally correct, none is totally wrong, and each has its place in defining the concept of corporateness.

§ 2.4 The "Nexus of Contracts" Model

The "nexus of contracts" model is a development of economics-trained scholars. This theory broadly applies to "firms," a term that may include business forms other than corporations. This theory is likely to be discussed early in every modern corporation law course and, depending on the background of the instructor, may be a central focus of the discussion of corporation law.

The nexus of contracts has its roots in pioneering economics analysis by Ronald Coase in the 1930s. Among Professor Coase's insights, was the observation that the essence of a firm is a long term relational contract by which each factor of production is affiliated with the other factors contributing to the enterprise. From this insight the nexus of contracts model has developed. Professor Stephen M. Bainbridge describes this model as follows:

The nexus of contracts or contractarian model conceptualizes the firm not as an entity but as an aggregate of various inputs acting together to produce goods or services. Employees provide labor. Creditors provide debt capital. Shareholders or partners, as the case may be, initially provide equity capital and subsequently bear the risk of losses * * *. The firm is simply a legal fiction representing the complex set of contractual relationships between these inputs. * * * In other words, the firm is not a thing, but rather a nexus or web of explicit or implicit contracts establishing rights and obligations among the various inputs making up the firm.

Many commentators have criticized the contractarian model on the ground, *inter alia*, that it is an incomplete theory of how people relate to one another within a firm. If contractarianism claimed to be a valid description of economic reality, this argument might have some traction. In my view, however, contractarianism claims only to offer a richer metaphor than do traditional entity-based theories and as such, a more useful heuristic for understanding corporations. Put another way, I tell my classes that the nexus of contracts model is properly viewed as a metaphor rather than as a positive account of economic reality. I analogize contractarianism to Newtonian physics, which no longer credibly claims to be true, but still provides a simple model that adequately explains a large and important set of physical phenomena.

Even as a mere heuristic, of course, contractarianism makes both positive and normative claims about corporate law. The positive claim is that the (statutory) law of business associations is comprised mostly of default rules, which the parties are free to vary by agreement, not mandatory rules. * * * [This] claim has been disputed insofar as corporate law is concerned. * * * Contractarianism's normative claim is that default rules are generally preferable to mandatory rules. * * *

In the nexus of contracts model, * * * [corporate] statutes and decisions can be thought of as a standard form contract voluntarily adopted—perhaps with modifications—by the [shareholders]. The point of a standard form contract, of course is to reduce bargaining costs. Parties for whom the default rules are a good fit can take the default rules off the rack, without having to bargain over them. Parties for whom the default rules are inappropriate, in contrast, are free to bargain out of the default rules. * * * If transactions costs are zero, the default rules—whether contained in a statute or a private standard form contract—do not matter very much. In the face of positive transaction costs, however, the default rule begins to matter very much. Indeed, if transaction costs are very high, bargaining around the rule becomes wholly impractical, forcing the parties to live with an inefficient rule. In such settings, we cannot depend on private contracting to achieve efficient outcomes. Instead, statutes must function as a substitute for private bargaining. Identifying the party for whom getting its way has the highest value thus becomes the critical question. In effect, we must perform a thought experiment: "If the parties could costlessly bargain over the question, which rule would they adopt?" By providing the rule to which the parties would agree if they could bargain (the so-called "majoritarian default"), society facilitates private ordering.

Bainbridge, Contractarianism in the Business Associations Classroom: The Puzzling Case of Kovacik v. Reed and the Allocation of Capital Losses in Service Partnerships, [34 Ga. L.Rev. (2000)]. As this title indicates, Professor Bainbridge used a partnership case as an example of his thesis about mandatory and default rules, but the analysis is equally applicable to corporation law.

Law and economics, as this new approach to corporation law is generally called, models a corporation essentially as a bundle of contracts entered into by the managers of the enterprise with providers of labor, services, raw materials, capital, and contractual commitments of various types. In this model, the managers are viewed as the essential glue that fits together all the various contributors to the firm in the most efficient way. Managers have broad discretion to structure and run the enterprise. The result is a hierarchical structure of control over employees and agents, perhaps softened by principles of participatory management or team production. The principal problem is control over "agency costs," which are usually defined "as the sum of the monitoring and bonding costs, plus any residual loss, incurred to prevent shirking by agents." Monitoring costs are the costs of oversight while bonding costs are devices to assure the fidelity of employees and agents where oversight is impractical or too costly. Shirking is conduct of an individual that diverges from the interests of the enterprise as a whole, including cheating, negligence, incompetence, and culpable mistakes.

The shareholders are simply contractual suppliers of residual capital, the group whose "contract" entitles them to the residual profits of the business and requires them to assume the primary risk of loss since all other providers to the corporation have priority in payment over them. Shareholders are not viewed as "owners" of the corporation. Rather, they are only one of several contractual suppliers of vital resources to the corporation. At the same time, however, the goal of the corporation is viewed as the maximization of shareholder wealth in the enterprise. A corporation is thus viewed as a set of consensual relationships established by the managers of that corporation with the goal of maximizing the wealth of contractual suppliers of residual capital.

One preliminary problem with the nexus of contracts model is that some relationships within a corporation do not appear to be contractual at all, at least not contractual in the normal legal sense of that term. This is particularly true of corporations whose shares are publicly traded on the securities markets. For example, it is difficult to say that a person who buys 100 shares of General Motors Corporation through a broker on the New York Stock Exchange has entered into a "contract" with General Motors. It is true, of course, that a purchaser of GM shares obtains certain rights. If GM declares a dividend, the shareholder is entitled to receive a payment. But the shareholder has not paid General Motors anything or agreed to do anything with or for General Motors. One might equally well argue that a farmer has entered into a contract with his land when he plants a crop.

The person who buys shares on the open market and becomes a GM shareholder is certainly bound to accept the judgment of a majority of the shareholders even if he is in the minority. Did the shareholder enter into a "contract" agreeing to this? As a positive description of what the world "really" is, the nexus of contracts model stretches the word "contract" way beyond its normal meaning. If the artificial entity or franchise theories described in the previous section are criticized as codifying a fiction, the nexus of contracts approach may equally be criticized for defining economic relationships as "contractual" in many situations where in fact no contract exists.

Some defenders of the nexus of contracts theory have argued that in situations such as the purchase of GM shares, an "implicit" contract nevertheless exists between GM and the new shareholder. To a lawyer, such a statement does not make much sense, since the phrase "implicit contract" suggests (to the extent the phrase means anything at all) a quasi-contract or implied-in-fact contract that the law constructs in the absence of actual agreement between the parties in order to do basic justice in the particular situation. Those concepts seem to have nothing to do with the investor who enters into an economic relationship with General Motors by buying one hundred shares of its common stock.

Law and economics scholars also suggest that the words "contracts" or "implicit contracts" are used by economists in a much broader sense than when the same words are used by lawyers. To a lawyer, the word "contract" means a real agreement that the legal system will enforce if one party tries to welsh. However, "to an economist, an implied contract is one that is enforced through marketplace mechanisms such as reputation effects rather than in a court, a means of enforcement that may not bring relief to the aggrieved party but will over time penalize parties who welsh." Gordon, The Mandatory Structure of Corporate Law, 89 Colum. L.Rev. 1549, 1550 (1989). In other words, to an economist, a "contract" may mean something quite different than what it means to a lawyer.

An alternative explanation that also builds on differences as to what the word "contract" means is the suggestion that the economist views voluntary arrangements as contracts even though they do not involve actual consensual exchanges:

Voluntary arrangements are contracts. Some may be negotiated over a bargaining table. Some may be a set of terms that are dictated by managers or investors and accepted or not; only the price is negotiated. Some may be fixed and must be accepted at the "going price" (as when people buy investment instruments traded in the market). Some may be implied by courts or legislatures trying to supply the terms that would have been negotiated had people addressed the problem explicitly. Even terms that are invariant—such as the requirement that the board of directors act only by a majority of a quorum—are contractual to the extent that they produce offsetting voluntary arrangements.

The result of all of these voluntary arrangements will be contractual.

Easterbrook and Fischel, The Corporate Contract, 89 Colum. L.Rev. 1416, 1428 (1989). It is probably difficult for most lawyers to accept the propositions that an arrangement created by a court "trying to supply the terms that would have been negotiated had people addressed the problem explicitly" is a "contract." Similarly a lawyer might not view an arrangement in which parties "produce offsetting voluntary arrangements" as involving a "contract" that includes the rule that is being offset. One suspects that if the economists' understanding of what "contract" means is accepted the "nexus of contracts" theory virtually becomes a tautology.

However, the serious question is what use is to be made of this theory. Models, it has been suggested, are of two basic types. A "normative" model is one that does not necessarily describe what reality is but what it ought to be. A "descriptive" model is one that describes what reality is. With the use of a descriptive model one can discover internal relationships that may not be visible in the real world. Professor McChesney has neatly encapsulated this distinction when he distinguishes "positive economics"—attempts to understand the world the way it is—from "normative economics"—a study of the way the world ought to be. McChesney, Positive Economics and All That—A Review of the Economic Structure of Corporate Law by Frank H. Easterbrook and Daniel R. Fischel, 61 Geo. Wash. L.Rev. 272 (1992).

It is not clear whether the nexus of contracts model should be viewed as essentially normative, or as descriptive, or as both. Its proponents have used it in both contexts.

At the outset, it seems clear that the nexus of contracts is not truly a descriptive model of today's real world, even though many corporate relationships are undoubtedly based on contractual concepts. It is simply not true that modern corporation statutes today provide "off the rack" default provisions that participants in the corporation are completely free to amend or modify as they wish. While modern corporation statutes give corporations considerable freedom to establish internal rules, they also contain a large number of mandatory requirements that corporations have no power to waive or modify. An even larger number of mandatory rules appear in the federal and state securities statutes that affect capital-raising by corporations.

The more difficult question is whether the nexus of contracts should be viewed as a normative model, a model of what the rules ought to be. It is this issue that has made the "nexus of contracts" theory so controversial. If the nexus of contracts is a normative model, corporation statutes should be changed to grant corporations the freedom to adopt whatever contractual relationships they see fit. That would include the right to "opt out" of currently mandatory legal requirements whenever their "nexus of contracts" suggests that that is efficient to do so. Normative arguments are more difficult to address than descriptive arguments.

The principal argument that the author finds persuasive against using the nexus of contracts model as the general normative model for statutory revisions is that it is based on certain fundamental assumptions about conduct and knowledge of individuals. Law and economics scholars assume, for example, that persons act rationally to maximize their personal satisfaction and wealth, and that they are fundamentally honest in that they follow certain rules of civilized conduct. Many persons, of course, fit this mold. Unfortunately, in the real world, some do not.

Major purposes of mandatory rules in the corporate/securities area are to compel the disclosure of important information and to prohibit certain kinds of undesirable conduct. The federal securities laws mandate disclosure and prohibit certain kinds of conduct that is deemed improper, misleading, or fraudulent. The securities markets in the United States are the envy of other nations because of the wide availability of information and their basic reliability. If the nexus of contracts model is a normative model, all of these principles would become voluntary and waivable. Indeed, some law and economics scholars have argued that there should be at least experiments that would permit publicly held corporations to "opt out" of the mandatory disclosure rules of the securities acts.

Unfortunately, some persons in fact are unsophisticated and easy "marks" for knowledgeable and unscrupulous individuals. Elimination of all mandatory rules would certainly create the likelihood of much greater fraud than occurs today. Economic scholars may respond, (1) that corporations would not actually opt out of the modern disclosure system (if it really is in their best interests to remain in it), or (2) that the reputational affects of fraudulent conduct in the long run may cause a greater loss of wealth than is gained from fraudulent conduct. Unfortunately, the markets in which scoundrels operate do not appear to be self-correcting. There appears to be a never-ending supply of potential victims. The old adage that "there is a sucker born every minute," seems true in the sense that as one person in a totally unregulated market learns a bitter lesson, another unsophisticated person is entering it. The fundamental problem with the nexus of contracts as a normative model is that the assumptions about human behavior on which economic analysis rests are, at best, only partially valid.

The rejection of the nexus of contracts as a normative model should not detract from its value when used in the limited sense that Professor Bainbridge suggests. It provides valuable insight into the role corporations play in modern society. Also, it may be that there are too many mandatory rules in modern corporation law today, and that efficiency would be improved if some of them were made waivable.

In evaluating the "nexus of contracts" theory, it should be noted that most teachers of corporation law today accept it as a useful approach in evaluating legal principles, and some certainly accept it as an appropriate normative model for corporation law.

[For unfamiliar terms see the Glossary]

CHAPTER THREE

DEVELOPMENT OF AMERICAN CORPORATION LAW

§ 3.1 The Early History of Corporation Law in the United States

In the pre-revolutionary period, the original colonies created colonial legislatures that granted a few corporate charters under the presumed authority of the British Crown. Following independence and the adoption of the Federal Constitution, state legislatures continued to grant corporate charters, many of them for banks. After the War of 1812, the number of corporate charters increased rapidly; in addition to banks, corporations were formed to construct canals and turnpikes. Many of these early charters granted special privileges in the form of monopolies or franchises.

The Federal Government incorporated the Bank of the United States by statute in 1791. However, doubt continued to exist as to the general power of the Federal Government to create corporations for general economic purposes, and as a result states continued to form corporations. Even today, with the power of the Federal Government to create corporations firmly established, that power is rarely exercised, and then only for predominantly public purposes.

Intensive industrial development began in about 1825. The corporation proved to be an ideal instrument for this development since it could raise large amounts of capital from numerous investors and yet provide centralized direction of large industrial concerns.

Originally, state legislatures approved each individual corporate charter. Approval of a charter was a political act, involving lobbying, political influence, campaign contributions, and sometimes worse. The first general incorporation statutes permitting businesses to incorporate by action of an administrative agency without specific legislative approval were adopted in Pennsylvania in 1836 and in Connecticut in 1840. This innovation quickly became popular so that by 1859 twenty-five out of the then existing thirty-eight states and territories had enacted general incorporation statutes. By 1890, all states had adopted general incorporation statutes.

The populist movement that developed primarily in the agricultural states in the midwest viewed both railroads and corporations with suspicion and mistrust. In many of these states, legislatures imposed restrictions on corporations in terms of size, period of duration, capital invested, and permissible purposes or powers. These artificial restrictions on corporations were largely ineffective as corporations could be formed in states without restrictions and then do business in other states. These restrictions have been largely removed in all states, though traces of them may still remain in a few states.

§ 3.2   The "Race for the Bottom"

Beginning in the late nineteenth century, several states systematically began to seek to attract businesses to incorporate or reincorporate in their states even though the corporation planned to do business elsewhere. Statutes were amended to simplify procedures, relax restrictions and limitations, reduce fees, and make the applicable rules more attractive, particularly for large corporations doing business in New York and other major commercial states. Competition for this incorporation business rapidly developed in New Jersey, Delaware,

Maine, Arizona, and other states. The uncrowned winner of this "race" in the early years of this century was initially New Jersey. However, that state lost its position to its sister state of Delaware when New Jersey decided to adopt a stronger regulatory stance toward corporations under Governor Woodrow Wilson. Today, at the end of the twentieth century, it is clear that the winner is Delaware. Nearly one-half of all the corporations listed on the New York Stock Exchange are incorporated in that single state even though most of these corporations have both their home office and principal business operations elsewhere.

This competition among states for incorporation business was initially viewed as being unseemly, if not totally inappropriate. It was vividly described in Mr. Justice Brandeis's dissent in Liggett Co. v. Lee (S.Ct.1933) as being a race "not of diligence but of laxity." Forty years later it was described by Professor Cary as a "race for the bottom." Cary, Federalism and Corporate Law: Reflections Upon Delaware, 83 Yale L.J. 663, 670 (1974). This "race" was viewed as leading to the systematic elimination of all regulatory controls on the corporation, the adoption of a "pro-management" stance whenever conflicts arose between managers and shareholders, and the elimination of preemptive rights and cumulative voting, which were widely viewed as providing protection to shareholders generally. Delaware, according to Professor Cary, was successful in attracting corporations to form in that state because it permitted management excessive freedom to use and manipulate corporate assets as they wished, presumably to the detriment of innocent and defenseless shareholders. He proposed the enactment of minimum uniform Federal standards for corporation law, a proposal that went nowhere.

The "race to the bottom" thesis, it is important to emphasize, applied specifically and particularly to large, publicly held corporations.

Modern economic analysis tends to view this issue in a very different light. Agency cost theory does recognize that there is a potential conflict of interest between managers and shareholders. Managers who have an insignificant interest in the ownership of the corporation can make decisions that benefit their own personal interests and ensure their continued role in management rather than acting in the best interests of the shareholders as a whole. The "race for the bottom" advocates assumed that corporate managers can freely make these decisions and that the disorganized shareholders can do nothing about them.

Judge Winter in a well-known book [R. Winter, Government and the Corporation (1978)] questioned this assumption. He pointed out that this analysis is flawed because it overlooks the existence of an efficient and broad market for corporate securities. If Delaware in fact permits management to profit at the expense of shareholders (and other states do not, or do not as much), then earnings of Delaware corporations that are allocable to shareholders will be less than earnings of comparable corporations that are subject to more rigorous control elsewhere. The result must be that shares of Delaware corporations will trade at lower prices than shares of equivalent corporations incorporated in other states. Thus, if the "race to the bottom" theory is correct, corporations formed in Delaware will be at an economic disadvantage, and ultimately this disadvantage should cause shareholders to invest in non-Delaware corporations. Eventually Delaware corporations would migrate to other states, or Delaware would have to change its rules if it wished to remain competitive.

There are a couple of ways in which these inconsistent hypotheses may be tested. One is simply to examine the Delaware General Corporation Law and Delaware judicial decisions and compare them to other state statutes and judicial decisions in an effort to determine whether the differences are material and whether they tend to favor management over shareholders. Admittedly, this is impressionistic rather than scientific since there are numerous variations from state to state and it is often unclear which provisions help management and which do not. However, an attempt to actually make such a comparison yields the conclusion that one cannot find a significant number of principles of Delaware law that are more favorable to management than the principles applied in other states. Indeed, if anything, the opposite appears to be true.

A second method is by using sophisticated statistical techniques to determine whether the reincorporation of corporations in Delaware from another state results in a decline in the share price of those corporations. If so, this would support the "race for the bottom" thesis. Several statistical studies have been made to test the hypothesis; they tend to show that reincorporation in Delaware more often leads to an *increase* in share prices than to a decrease; thus, they generally support Judge Winter's thesis and tend to disprove the "race for the bottom" thesis. Unfortunately, share prices may be affected by numerous factors interacting at the time of a reincorporation decision, and it is not possible to say with certainty that Delaware law is the sole, or even the principal, cause of the favorable price movement. However, the fact that no one has found significant price decreases in any of these studies is itself an indication that the "race for the bottom" thesis is probably not correct.

§ 3.3 What Explains Delaware's Success in Attracting Corporations?

If the "race to the bottom" thesis is not accepted, some explanation must be put forth to explain why Delaware has been, and continues to be, so successful in the incorporation business, particularly for large, publicly held corporations. This also has been the subject of considerable discussion and commentary.

It is useful to first consider the reasons corporation attorneys give as to why they use Delaware as their preferred state of incorporation even though the corporation will have only a minimal contact with that state. Their responses fall into the following general categories: (1) We use Delaware because it has been a leading state of incorporation for many years, and there are answers to most questions of corporation law in the Delaware statute and case law. If there are answers to questions we can work around them; what we cannot deal with is uncertainty, and the law in other states, including heavily populated states such as California, New York, and Texas, has many areas of uncertainty. (2) We use Delaware because the corporation lawyers in our firm are familiar with Delaware law, and it is cheaper and more efficient for our clients if we create Delaware corporations rather than corporations in a number of different states. As evidence of this, we customarily give opinions with respect to Delaware corporation law even though our offices are located in New York City (or Chicago, Los Angeles, Denver, or wherever). (3) We use Delaware law because if a problem arises we will be dealing with state officials who are sophisticated in corporation law, and we will get useful advice and assistance from them. (4) We use Delaware law because if we have to litigate, we will be before sophisticated judges well versed in corporation law and we will have the assistance of sophisticated Delaware corporation lawyers. (5) We use Delaware law because we know that that state will respond promptly if unexpected problems arise by amending its corporation law. Delaware is usually the leader in this regard while other states follow. (6) We use Delaware law because it is stable. It is unlikely that major policy changes will be made in Delaware without the most careful consideration by corporate specialists.

These statements have a convincing air about them, and probably do in fact explain why Delaware is where it is today. It is not because it is more permissive than other states. Rather, it is because Delaware is reaping the benefits of its many years of experience with corporation law, the familiarity of corporation lawyers around the country with its statute, and the stability and responsiveness this small state has shown in addressing corporation law issues.

A final important factor is that the Delaware Court of Chancery is predominantly a "business law" court and its judges have wide experience with corporate disputes. It has achieved a favorable reputation that is the envy of other states. Indeed, several other states have created similar specialized courts, but none have the reputation of the Delaware Chancery Court.

From the standpoint of Delaware's selfish interests, there is no secret as to why it wishes to retain this incorporation business. More than 15 percent of the state's total budget comes from franchise taxes paid by corporations. Mandatory local filings by corporations provide the backbone of support for the three county courthouses in the state. Insurance firms, corporation service companies, and major law firms with principal officers in other states maintain offices in Wilmington that would doubtless be a small fraction of their present size if Delaware's foreign corporation business moved to some other state. Indeed, from a financial standpoint, the Delaware corporation business is the envy of all other states, large and small.

§ 3.4 The Debate Over Social Responsibility Within The Publicly Held Corporation

In some respects, the long debate over the social responsibility of large publicly held corporations resembles the debate over the "race for the bottom." In both instances, influential voices have argued that publicly held corporations should be subject to greater social control while more conservative voices have maintained that the corporation as a business form is doing fine, and since it is not broken, it certainly doesn't need fixing.

The debate over the social responsibility of large publicly held corporations in modern society begins with the fact that such corporations unquestionably wield immense economic power when they make decisions. Corporate decisions where to locate a plant, what environmental equipment to install, what products to manufacture, what safety devices to build into them, and so forth, are all decisions that may fairly be described as "social" as well as "economic." Such decisions may have dramatic consequences for individuals, communities, and entire states. These decisions, furthermore, may be made by corporate management on the basis of internally generated economic studies with limited or no public review or comment. While there has been an increasing amount of governmental review of environmental and related issues in recent years, the effectiveness of this review is sometimes suspect.

The concentration of power in publicly held corporations has been decried by some commentators and defended by others. This debate goes back to before the New Deal era.

The social responsibility debate has several different levels. At the most basic level the issue is the extent to which corporations should take social considerations into account when they make important decisions. The view of conservative scholars is that decisions should be made on the basis of the

"bottom line" of what produces the highest profit for the
corporation and shareholders. The extent non-economic factors should be considered, these scholars add, is the responsibility of government, not the board of directors.

The traditional classroom example of a social responsibility
issue is whether a corporation should continue to operate a
50–year-old, obsolete plant in a small one-plant town in a
northern state. The alternative is to close the plant down and
move the entire operation to a southern state where labor
costs are lower, land is cheaper, and a modern, efficient plant
could be built. Profitability would unquestionably be improved
by closing the plant down and moving to the South. In making
this decision, should the corporation take into account the
adverse effects on the persons currently employed in the
Northern plant, their families, the local stores currently in the
town, the community itself, and the state? These interests are
often described as "other constituencies" of the corporation. If
the response is that the company should consider the effect on
these other constituencies, should not the corporation also
take into account the fact that remaining in the northern
town may result in reduced dividends to shareholders and
higher prices for its products? Should it not also consider
potential injury to residents of the southern city which loses
the plant? Questions like this can go on and on: There are
secondary and tertiary effects of each such decision.

Starkly posed, the question is whether the corporation
should consider only its profitability and the wealth of its
shareholders, or whether it should take into account the
interests of other constituencies. At first glance, these two
alternatives may seem polar opposites, but in fact they are
not. One can always argue that the aim of corporate governance should be to maximize long run rather than short run
profits, and the economic effects of these social factors may

quite legitimately be considered in the long-term profit calculation. For example, a decision to raise prices to monopoly levels (assuming that that is feasible), may maximize short run profits but may have devastating effects on profits in the long run. Adverse publicity, the entry of new competitors in the industry, and governmental intervention under the Federal antitrust laws all may have strongly negative effects on long term profitability. Rational profit maximizers, it is argued, should take these long run consequences into account.

However, there are major difficulties with the long term profit maximization approach. The major problem is that social variables are difficult or impossible to quantify in terms of dollars. Long term effects, in particular, may be highly subjective and the weight to be given to them uncertain. The long term profit maximization thesis could easily be used to justify either alternative, and thus it appears to be more of a shield to paper over differences than a tool for resolving them.

Another branch of the social responsibility debate considers whether membership on the board of directors should be expanded to include representatives of other constituencies. Suggestions typically include adding one or more representatives of government, labor, suppliers, consumers, creditors, etc. to the board. While there has been limited experimentation with this idea, it has never really caught on in the United States, and, where it has been tried, it is difficult to find tangible evidence that the representational directors have made any difference one way or the other. Involvement of other constituencies in management, particularly labor, however, is quite common in several European countries.

In the 1970s the debate over social responsibility received new impetus from the disclosure by hundreds of publicly held corporations that they had engaged in illegal conduct. They had made illegal campaign contributions in the United States or had paid bribes or illegal payments overseas to obtain business. These disclosures were made in connection with the scandals that ultimately led to President Nixon's resignation. They led not only to new calls for greater social responsibility of corporations but also focused on the role of the board of directors and the need for better control mechanisms to insure that corporate management conform with legal and moral principles of conduct. Many public corporations made important changes in their methods of internal governance as a result of these disclosures and other factors. See Chapter 13.

As this is written at the end of the Twentieth Century, it seems that the social responsibility debate has ended. Laissez faire and the goal of profit maximization appear to have carried the day.

§ 3.5 Modern Corporation Statutes

Each state, the District of Columbia, and Puerto Rico has its own corporation statute. There is a considerable degree of commonality among these statutes as well as a considerable degree of divergence on specific provisions. It is not practicable, or indeed desirable, to attempt to describe each state's statute in a Nutshell. Rather, the following general comments may be useful:

1) Corporation law in the United States is still predominantly state law. Federal statutes, particularly the federal securities acts, have important effects on and application to publicly held corporations. However, the basic structure of corporation law is still grounded on state law.

2) In terms of potential applicability and greatest economic impact, the Delaware General Corporation Law is undoubtedly the single most influential statute. The Delaware statute, however, has not been widely copied in other

states; it has been used as a model for corporation statutes in only a few smaller states.

3) The statute that has been mostly widely used as a model by smaller states is the Model Business Corporation Act (1984) ["MBCA (1984)"], as amended. It has served as the model for corporation statutes in roughly half of the states, and specific provisions have been adopted in virtually all states. The author of this Nutshell served as the Reporter for the original MBCA (1984).

In the balance of this Nutshell, the MBCA (1984) is the principal statute used as a model.

4) Several state statutes continue to be based on the provisions of the Model Business Corporation Act (1969), the predecessor of MBCA (1984).

5) Larger states tend to develop their own unique statutes that may be drawn in part from Delaware, in part from the MBCA (1984), and in part from internal sources. States that fall within this category include New York, California, Texas, and Illinois. In each of these states there are active bar committees that follow developments in the corporate area and quite regularly create statutory provisions on their own to address new developments.

6) In general terms, the trend in corporation statutes during the Twentieth Century has been toward simplification and the elimination of formalities or requirements that have little or no substantive effect. Of particular importance has been the elimination of strict rules relating to internal governance that serve little or no purpose in corporations with relatively few shareholders. Also of importance has been the elimination or simplification in many states of technical rules relating to the issuance of shares that tend to be traps for the unwary or unsophisticated incorporator.

§ 3.6   The Model Business Corporation Act (1984)

A brief description of the background of uniform or model corporate statutes may be helpful. The National Conference of Commissioners on Uniform State Laws ("NCCUSL") promulgated a "Uniform Business Corporation Act" in 1928. This statute followed the promulgation of the Uniform Partnership Act (1914) and the Uniform Limited Partnership Act (1917), both of which were adopted by all states. However, the Uniform Business Corporation Act was not a success: It was adopted in whole or in part by only four states. In 1943, NCCUSL renamed this statute the "Model Business Corporation Act" on the theory that corporation law was not a subject upon which uniformity among states was necessary or desirable. In 1958, this statute was withdrawn by NCCUSL, it having had little influence.

In the meantime the Committee on Corporate Laws, a committee created by the American Bar Association, approved a competing "Model Business Corporation Act" ("MBCA") in 1946. (An earlier draft was widely circulated in 1943.) This statute was largely based on the Illinois statute. More widely distributed versions were published in 1950 and 1969. The 1950 and 1969 versions of the MBCA were influential in the development of corporation statutes in more than thirty states.

MBCA (1984) involved a complete revision of the 1969 statute. A new numeration system was developed which permits expansion of the Act. Official comments were prepared for each section. Since its approval, this statute has been the basis for revision of corporation statutes in more than twenty-five states, and portions of it have been adopted in additional states. While MBCA (1984) builds on the provisions of older versions of the MBCA, it adopts innovative provisions in a number of areas and effects a considerable simplification of language in many provisions.

MBCA (1984) is in the tradition of most modern corporation statutes: It is primarily an enabling statute rather than a regulatory statute. Whether or not it (or the Delaware statute, for that matter) is too flexible or too permissive depends to a large extent on the social views of the observer.

The Committee on Corporate Laws of the American Bar Association is charged with the development and review of this statute. This Committee is unique within the ABA in that its decisions are not subject to review by the Section of Business Law or by the ABA itself. Proposed revisions of the MBCA are published for comment in the *Business Lawyer*, an influential publication of the Section of Business Law of the ABA, and then incorporated in the statute. The announcement of the approval of the final revision also appears in the *Business Lawyer*.

The Committee on Corporate Laws is composed of leading corporate attorneys and academics from across the country. It is a very active committee that has continuously monitored the acceptance of the MBCA in individual states. It also has made significant (and often innovative) revisions to the statute on its own motion. These revisions have been approved only after careful and searching examination. For example, significant revisions were made in 1998 and 1999 dealing with rules for approval of fundamental corporate changes, appraisal rights, and the duty of care of directors. These issues are highly controversial and are discussed in this Nutshell even though, as this is written, they have not yet been enacted by any state.

§ 3.7 Federal Regulation

Finally, mention should be made of developments at the federal level. In the early 1930s, Congress enacted two statutes relating to corporate matters. The Securities Act of 1933 largely relates to the process by which corporations raise funds from the general public. The Securities Exchange Act of 1934 is a broader statute relating to a variety of matters, including the regulation of securities exchanges, securities brokers and dealers, corporate disclosure policies, takeover bids and tender offers, securities fraud, and class action securities litigation. These two statutes have formed the springboard for extensive federal regulation of the internal affairs of publicly held corporations. While federal regulation under these statutes is of great importance in corporation law, state statutes still govern many aspects of publicly held corporations.

The Securities Act of 1933 is supplemented by state statutes, called "blue sky laws," that regulate capital raising by corporations within each state. These blue sky laws antedate the Securities Act of 1933. In the National Securities Markets Improvement Act of 1996 Congress preempted a significant portion of traditional state blue sky regulation of public distributions of corporate securities. Blue Sky laws, however, continue to be applicable to private and intrastate offerings.

The Private Securities Litigation Reform Act of 1995 and the Securities Litigation Uniform Standards Act of 1998 are important federal statutes relating to class action securities fraud litigation. These two statutes largely preempt state courts from resolving securities fraud issues and impose significant limitations and rules for such litigation in the federal courts. See sections 17.5–17.18 of this Nutshell.

CHAPTER FOUR

FORMATION OF CORPORATIONS

§ 4.1 In General

The process of corporate formation is essentially a very simple one, and much (though not all) of it may be performed by a competent legal secretary. Indeed, one of the great modern innovations in corporate formation is the computer, which permits the mass production of corporate documents with only special name and other minor changes. Many readers have doubtless also seen advertisements in legal and other journals for "kits" for the creation of corporations; they are also based on mass produced, standard-form incorporation documents. There are two significant pitfalls in the routine use of such forms. The first is the danger that no one with a broad perspective on the law of corporations will bring that perspective to bear on potentially unique problems of the particular venture. The second is the universal danger in the use of "boiler-plate" forms: they may contain some provision that was suitable for the last corporation but is egregiously inappropriate for the next one. This is perhaps most likely in the case of advertised kits, which may be sold on a national basis without regard to specific state requirements. Overall, however, the process by which a corporation is formed is simple and routine and not in any way mysterious.

§ 4.2 Selection of the State of Incorporation

A large, publicly held corporation that transacts business in every state may theoretically choose its state of incorporation from among any of the fifty states. As a practical matter, however, most such corporations have selected Delaware as their state of incorporation. The small corporation doing business in only a single state or locality has the same theoretical freedom as the publicly held corporation in this regard, since it is possible to incorporate in any state and qualify to transact business as a foreign corporation in any other state. However, practical considerations usually dictate that the small corporation be formed in the jurisdiction in which it is solely or principally doing business. There are real costs if any foreign state is selected: The corporation will have to qualify as a foreign corporation in its "home state;" it will be subject to two taxing authorities; and it may be subject to suit in a distant state. If there is some reason not to incorporate in the local jurisdiction despite these costs, the alternative usually is Delaware, with its popular statute. As other states have modernized their corporation statutes, the advantages of Delaware as a state of incorporation for small businesses active in other jurisdictions have lessened, and most local businesses today are probably incorporated in the state in which they primarily conduct business.

§ 4.3   Mechanics of Creating a Corporation

The mechanics of creating a corporation vary from state to state, and the specific statute must be consulted for details.

Every state requires the filing of a document with a state official, usually the secretary of state, together with the payment of a filing fee. Depending on the state, the document may be called the "articles of incorporation," the "certificate of incorporation," the "charter" or some other name. In this Nutshell, this document is called the "articles of incorporation."

Corporate records maintained by the Office of Secretary of State usually are in the form of paper documents. However, computerization of records in this Office offers obvious advantages and many offices now maintain corporate records in electronic form. Some offices maintain both electronic and paper records.

The traditional manner of filing articles of incorporation is to mail them in, deliver them by overnight mail service, or deliver them by messenger or courier to the office of the secretary of state. Many state filing offices now also permit electronic filing, often by telefax. This development usually required special legislation since the traditional language of corporation statutes requires submission of an "executed" original as well as a conformed copy, and telefaxed communications do not comply with these requirements. With further improvements in technology, an electronic filing directly into the computer system maintained by the secretary of state is now practical, and a few states may permit this method of filing.

Each filing is reviewed by the office of the secretary of state, which commonly means by a professional staff member within that office. If the document meets the statutory requirements, the corporate existence is usually deemed to relate back to the date and time the document was originally received, any post-filing delays being ignored. In the case of a traditional document, this is the date evidenced by a time stamp placed on the document when it was received or on its envelope. The secretary of state reflects its approval of the filing by an action, traditionally the issuance of a formal "charter" or "certificate of incorporation" which is attached to a duplicate original or copy of the original filing. Increasingly the approval of the filing is evidenced merely by a notation that the document has been accepted for filing and the issuance of a receipt for the filing fee.

Some 13 states today have additional filing requirements. Delaware, for example, requires local filing in the county in which the corporation's registered office is located (as well as filing in a state office). Twelve states including Arizona, require that evidence be submitted that the statutory agent has accepted his appointment. In Arizona, the articles of incorporation must be published in a newspaper of general circulation in the county in which the corporation's known place of business is located three consecutive times within 60 days after the articles are filed [Ariz. Rev.Stat.Ann. § 10–055]. Georgia and Pennsylvania also require publication of a notice in a local newspaper. Some states may still require recording in every county in which the corporation transacts business. It is generally believed that these publication requirements serve little or no practical benefit; they are retained usually because of the political power of county clerks or newspaper publishers who have come to rely on the fees or charges generated by those requirements.

Local filing or advertising requirements create legal problems if some, but not all of them, are complied with before the corporation begins business. Some states have statutes that deal specifically with this question. Delaware, for example, provides that corporate existence begins with the acceptance of the filing by the secretary of state, and the failure to file locally within the specified period increases the filing fee but does not affect the existence of the corporation [Del. Code Ann. Tit. 8, § 103(d)]. Some states, however, condition the existence of the corporation on the completion of all filing and advertising requirements.

Some six states have a minimum capital requirement, usually $1,000, which must be paid in before the corporation may begin business. See section 4.8 of this Nutshell.

§ 4.4 Incorporators

The person or persons who execute the articles of incorporation are called "incorporators." Traditionally, three incorporators were required; today all states (except Puerto Rico) require only a single incorporator; a few states still have residency or age requirements for incorporators, but most states now permit an individual to act as incorporator if he or she is of legal age without regard to residency or later participation in the corporation. Most states also permit artificial entities such as corporations or trusts to serve as incorporators.

The relaxation of the requirements relating to incorporators reflects the minor role they play in the formation of a modern corporation. Depending on the state, incorporators may serve one or more of the following roles:

(1) They execute and deliver the articles of incorporation to the secretary of state;

(2) They, or their representatives, receive the charter, certificate of incorporation, notice of acceptance, or fee receipt back from the secretary of state;

(3) They either (i) meet to complete the organization of the corporation or (ii) call the first meeting of the initial board of directors (named in the articles of incorporation) at which the organization of the corporation is completed;

(4) They may voluntarily dissolve the corporation if the corporation has not commenced business and has not issued shares; and

(5) They may amend the articles of incorporation by unanimous consent if the corporation has not commenced business and has not issued any shares.

It is generally believed that there is no risk of liability for actions taken while acting as incorporator of a corporation. Indeed, many attorneys or their secretaries or other law office employees routinely serve as incorporators. The same is not always true of acting as an initial director, however, and many attorneys decline to serve as a director of small corporations they form, or do so only reluctantly.

A "subscriber" is a person who agrees to buy shares in the corporation; in other words, a subscriber is an investor and participant in the venture. At one time many states required that an incorporator also be a subscriber of shares; however, that requirement appears to have disappeared in all states.

§ 4.5   Articles of Incorporation: In General

The document filed with the secretary of state must contain certain mandatory information. While the requirements vary from state to state, the following modest list (drawn from § 54 of the 1969 MBCA) is typical:

(a) The name of the corporation;

(b) The period of duration which may be perpetual;

(c) The purpose or purposes of the corporation, which may be generally described as "engaging in any lawful business;"

(d) The number of shares authorized to be issued, including information about the rights and preferences of such shares;

(e) The address of its registered office and the name of its registered agent at that office;

(f) The number of directors and, when required, the names and addresses of the members of the initial board of directors; and

(g) The names and addresses of each incorporator.

Since virtually all modern corporations elect perpetual duration and a purpose of engaging in any lawful business, the
MBCA (1984) simply provides that every corporation has these
attributes unless a shorter duration or narrower purpose is set
forth in the articles of incorporation. Also, if the corporation
has only a single class of shares and elects to be created and
organized by a single incorporator the resulting articles of
incorporation fits conveniently on a post card!

In addition, state statutes provide that a corporation may
elect to be governed by certain statutory provisions, the election of which must be reflected by an appropriate provision in
the articles of incorporation. For example, many statutes
provide that a majority in interest of the shareholders shall
constitute a quorum of shareholders except that the quorum
may be reduced by specific provision in the articles of incorporation to a number smaller than a majority [MBCA (1984),
§ 7.25]. Many statutes provide that shareholders shall have a
preemptive right to acquire new shares (see § 7.18 of this
Nutshell) or to vote shares cumulatively (see § 9.6 of this
Nutshell) unless these rights are specifically negated by appropriate provisions in the articles of incorporation. Sections 6.30
and 7.28(b) of MBCA (1984) provide "opt in" (rather than
"opt out") provisions for these rights—i.e., a corporation's
shareholders do not have preemptive rights or the right to
vote cumulatively unless the articles of incorporation specifically provide for them. The statute of each specific state must
be consulted to determine the pattern adopted by that state in
connection with these rights.

Finally, corporations may elect to place optional provisions
relating to internal governance in the articles of incorporation
in order to make them more permanent, more difficult to
amend, and, hopefully, binding on persons who may not have
actual knowledge of them. Such provisions usually may also be

placed in the corporation's bylaws. However, many lawyers and judges expect important provisions, or unusual provisions denying customary rights to shareholders or others, to appear in the articles of incorporation. Such provisions are usually repeated in the bylaws to ensure that corporate officers are aware of them.

§ 4.6 Articles of Incorporation: The Corporate Name

Most statutes set up minimum requirements with respect to the corporate name. Typical provisions include:

(1) The name must contain a word indicating corporateness, such as "corporation," "company," or "incorporated," or an abbreviation of one of these words.

(2) The name may not contain a word or phrase indicating that it is organized for a purpose that it is not permitted to engage in. As a practical matter, with the development of general purposes clauses, the principal impact of this restriction is to preclude the use of names that suggest a purpose for which corporations may not be organized under the state business corporation act. Thus, "bank," "bank and trust," "certificate of deposit," "title guaranty," or "insurance" may not appear in corporate names in many states since there are special regulatory requirements in statutes relating to formation of corporations for such purposes. These limitations have been relaxed in many states.

(3) The name may not resemble too closely the name of any other corporation formed or qualified to transact business in the state. The precise statutory test varies. Older versions of the MBCA prohibited a name that was the "same or deceptively similar" to any other corporate name, and many state statutes embody this test. Section 4.01 of MBCA (1984) substitutes the test that the name be "distinguishable upon the

records of the secretary of state" from any other corporate name. This language was taken from the Delaware statute. The primary purpose of this requirement, however it is phrased, is to make sure that each corporation has a unique name. States that adopt the "same or deceptively similar" standard involve the Secretary of State in making decisions in part on the basis of unfair competition, a policy which (for reasons discussed below) the Secretary of State usually is not be well equipped to enforce.

(4) Some states add another layer to the name availability rules. Texas, for example, provides that if the name is "similar" (as contrasted with the "same or deceptively similar") to any other corporate name, it may be used only if a "letter of consent" is obtained from the owner of the similar name. The purpose of this requirement appears to be the prevention of confusion and unfair competition.

Secretaries of State usually maintain lists of corporate names that are in use and therefore not currently available, and check proposed new names against that list. This list is usually stored on a computer to provide instant access, and in some states may be searched by members of the public. This list is usually the sole standard applied by the Secretary of State who typically has neither the staff nor the resources to make an independent investigation of whether the use of the name may constitute unfair competition. It was for this reason that § 4.01 of MBCA (1984) rephrases the test of name availability as "distinguishable upon the records of the secretary of state." However, the decision as to name availability (whether the test be "the same," "distinguishable," or "deceptively similar") involves questions of judgment; some Secretaries of State have developed regulations or "house rules" to guide the exercise of discretion or judgment by office employees. As a practical matter, the issue whether or not a specific name is available is rarely litigated. Even if an attorney strongly disagrees with the Secretary of State as to the availability of a name, it is simpler and cheaper to select another name than to litigate over name availability. However, when two corporations or businesses have used similar names in the past, the right to the continued use of such name may have become so valuable as to lead to bitter litigation over whether the use of the name constitutes unfair competition. Secretaries of State are usually directed by statute to accept the results of such litigation in establishing name availability.

The discussion so far deals only with "official names," that is the name of the corporation that appears in its articles of incorporation and in the records of the Secretary of State. A corporation, like an individual, may do business under an assumed name so long as the purpose is not fraudulent and does not constitute unfair competition. Many states have "assumed name statutes" that require a person, whether an individual or a corporation, that is conducting business under an assumed name to file a statement (usually at the county level) disclosing who is actually conducting business under that name. The possible use of an assumed name by a corporation reduces significantly the importance of the name availability determination by the Secretary of State. A corporation named ABC Corporation, for example, may do business under the name XYZ Corporation upon complying with the assumed name statute (if the state has one). If there happens to be another corporation that has the official name XYZ Corporation, it can enjoin ABC Corporation from using that name as an assumed name only if there is unfair competition, typically name confusion. If the two corporations are not competing against each other because they are in different geographic locations or in totally different businesses, there is probably nothing that the "real" XYZ Corporation can do about it.

As a general proposition, the Secretary of State typically does not know what assumed name a corporation is using or plans to use, in what area of the state the corporation is operating, or even what the nature of the business of the corporation is. As a result the secretary of state is usually not in a position to make reliable judgments about questions of unfair competition.

Because official corporate names are handled on a first-come first-serve basis, many state statutes permit the *reservation* of a proposed corporate name for a limited time for a nominal fee. See MBCA (1984) § 4.02. Many states also authorize the *registration* of a name by a foreign corporation not transacting business in the state. See MBCA (1984) § 4.03. A registration of a corporate name allows a foreign corporation with long-term plans to expand into the state to reserve the exclusive use of its name and prevent a local corporation from using the same name as an "official name." A *reservation* of a name is for a brief period, usually three months, and may not be renewable. On the other hand, a *registration* of a name may be for a year or more and may be renewed indefinitely without any break in continuity of protection.

§ 4.7 Articles of Incorporation: Period of Duration

All business corporation acts now permit a corporation to have perpetual existence. In the past some statutes limited corporations to a fifty year or some other specified life span. These provisions are now obsolete. On the other hand, state statutes permit a corporation to elect a limited period of duration. It is probably unwise ever to designate a term less than perpetual. Even if it is contemplated that the corporation will be in business only for a limited period, plans may change and the articles of incorporation will have to be amended. A failure to amend may result in the corporation having uncertain status after the term expires. Why create a corporate structure that requires someone to remember to file an amendment if it can be avoided?

§ 4.8   Articles of Incorporation: Capitalization

Articles of incorporation must include information about the types or kinds of securities the corporation is authorized to issue. A separate chapter of this Nutshell is devoted to corporate securities, and the disclosure requirements applicable to articles of incorporation are discussed there. (See Chapter Seven of this Nutshell, particularly § 7.3.)

The required information about types or kinds of securities in articles of incorporation relates to securities the corporation is authorized to issue rather than the securities the corporation actually plans to issue. However, the statutes of several states require disclosure of what securities will actually be issued, either as a part of a tax return or a general information filing available to the public generally.

Minimum capital requirements in state statutes were practically universal twenty-five years ago. These statutes prohibited the corporation from commencing business unless it had received a specified minimum amount of capital and usually imposed personal liability on the directors if they permitted a corporation to commence business without the minimum capital. The most popular amount was $1,000, but some statutes required $500 or some other amount, and some required some specified percentage of authorized capital. Today all but a handful of states have eliminated such requirements on the theory that any minimum amount of capitalization is arbitrary and does not provide meaningful protection to creditors. The major problem with these minimum capital provisions was that they took no account of the specific capital needs of the particular business. It made no difference whether a corporation needed $1,000,000 or $100 to start up the contemplated business; both needed an initial capitalization of $1,000. Also, the requirement of $1,000, while perhaps meaningful in the 1950's or 1960's, had become the victim of inflation and was much less significant by the 1990's. The old Model Business Corporation Act eliminated its minimum capitalization requirement in 1969, and the trend is definitely in the direction of eliminating all such requirements. Thus, in most states today it is theoretically possible (as it is under the MBCA (1984)) to form a corporation with a capitalization of one cent.

In states with a minimum capital requirement, the principal enforcement mechanism is to make directors who assent to the corporation commencing business before it has received the required capital liable jointly and severally for that part of the capital not actually received. Usually this liability terminates when the required consideration is received. At one time, a few states had *in terrorem* statutes that made the directors personally liable for *all* corporate obligations incurred before the minimum capital was paid in, even if the shortfall of capital was small and the liabilities incurred were large. None of the remaining states with minimum capital requirements appear to fall within this category.

§ 4.9 Articles of Incorporation: Registered Office and Registered Agent

Every corporation must maintain a registered office and a registered agent at that office. Some states describe the registered agent as the "statutory agent." The registered office may but need not be the corporation's business office. The primary purpose of a registered office and registered agent is to provide an agent for service of process. The underlying idea is that it should be possible at all times to find a corporation and to have a person upon whom, and a place at which, any notice or process required or permitted by law may be served. A second purpose is to have an office to which tax notices and other official communications from the state may be sent. The original registered office and registered agent is specified in the articles of incorporation; if either is changed thereafter a statement describing the change must be filed with the Secretary of State.

Often a corporation designates its principal business office to be its registered office. In such a case, the registered agent is a corporate officer or employee. The principal disadvantage of this is the possibility that summons, legal documents, or other communications may be mixed in with routine business mail and not receive the attention they deserve. For this reason, many attorneys suggest that they be designated as the registered agent and their office be designated as the registered office.

Corporation service companies provide registered offices and registered agents for a modest fee. Corporations that are incorporated in a state in which they do not have a business office—Delaware is the most prominent example—often utilize this service provided by corporations service companies.

§ 4.10 Articles of Incorporation: Initial Board of Directors

The initial board of directors of the corporation must be named in the articles of incorporation in states in which the initial directors are to complete the formation of the contract. In states where the incorporators perform this function there is usually no requirement that initial directors be named in the articles of incorporation.

In states in which the initial board of directors is named in the articles of incorporation, there is no requirement that subsequent changes in membership be reflected by amendments to the articles of incorporation or in later filings with the secretary of state. Unlike the registered office and registered agent, the records maintained by the secretary of state do not indicate who are the current directors of a corporation.

Where the initial board of directors is named in the articles, it serves as the board only until the first annual meeting of shareholders or until the directors' successors are elected and qualify. The first annual meeting of shareholders may be set immediately after the organizational meeting of the initial board of directors so that elected directors take office almost immediately. It is possible in these states to name in the articles of incorporation persons who are nominal directors (that is, directors who have no continuing interest in the business and cease to serve as directors immediately after the organizational meeting). In this way all disclosure of the identity of the permanent board of directors in the articles of incorporation may be avoided. Whether or not this is desirable depends on the wishes of the clients.

Unlike incorporators, directors may sometimes incur liabilities by virtue of their office. Hence, it may be unwise for an attorney or his or her employees to serve as directors, nominal or otherwise, though the risk may be slight as a practical matter if the directorship is for a short period.

§ 4.11 Articles of Incorporation: Limitation of Directoral Liability

As a result of concern about the liability imposed on directors in the famous case of *Smith v. Van Gorkom* (Del.1985), the corporation statutes of many states have been amended to permit the shareholders to limit the personal liability of directors for monetary damages for violations of the duty of due care. See § 14.7 of this Nutshell. In 1994, the Model Act was amended to authorize corporations to grant obligatory indemnification of directors (see Chapter 15 of this Nutshell) with respect to all actions taken by a director except liability for "(A) receipt of a financial benefit to which he is not entitled, (B) an intentional infliction of harm on the corporation or its shareholders, (C) a violation of section 8.33 [relating to unlawful distributions], or (D) an intentional violation of criminal law." [MBCA (1984), as amended, § 2.02(b)(5)]

§ 4.12   Articles of Incorporation: Purposes and Powers

All state statutes now provide that a corporation may be formed for any lawful purpose. Many state statutes still require that the articles of incorporation specify what the corporation's purpose or purposes are, but usually permit a general statement that the corporation is formed "for lawful business purposes" or "to engage in any lawful business." The use of such clauses has become so common that the MBCA (1984) provides that all corporations have the "purpose of engaging in any lawful business unless a more limited purpose is set forth in the articles of incorporation."

The historical development of purposes clauses is interesting and is typical of basic trends in state corporation law. In the Nineteenth Century, corporations could only be formed for specific purposes, and in some states could only list a single purpose. These provisions were viewed as providing a significant regulatory component: Corporations were viewed with mistrust and permission to do business in corporate form was given only grudgingly. Application of these limiting principles often raised problems of ultra vires (discussed in § 4.13; literally, ultra vires means "beyond the purposes or powers of the corporation") and led to a large amount of litigation construing purposes clauses. The first major innovation was a superficially simple one: It permitted a corporation to state multiple purposes while preserving the rule that the corporation was organized only for whatever purposes were set forth in the articles of incorporation. This, however, opened the proverbial floodgates since there was no limitation on the number of purposes for which a single corporation may be formed. It was theoretically possible for a corporation to list every conceivable business in which a corporation may engage, including mining diamonds on the moon. Purposes clauses therefore became increasingly prolix, increasingly unreadable, and often completely uninformative as to what business the corporation actually planned to engage in. The next step permitted a corporation to use a very simple and general clause, e.g., "this corporation may engage in any lawful business." Since practically all corporations elected to take advantage of this innovation, the requirement of a purposes clause has been reduced to a formality, and the final step taken in the MBCA (1984) to eliminate the clause entirely seems to be natural and sensible.

Despite the modern freedom to use "any lawful business" clauses (or to omit the purpose clause entirely), articles of incorporation are sometimes filed with a narrow purposes clause as part of internal corporate planning. Like the limited duration clause, such a provision is apt to create more problems than benefits since a limited purposes clause does not actually limit the scope of the corporation's activities so that ultra vires conduct may occur.

Modern purposes clauses often specify the principal business or activity of the corporation and couple it with broader language such as, "and to engage in any other lawful business." This provides the reader of the articles of incorporation with information about the nature of the corporation's principal business without restricting the freedom of the corporation to engage in other businesses.

It may be necessary to use narrow purposes clauses in corporations that are to engage in businesses subject to specific state or federal regulation that require regulated corporations to have specified purposes.

Corporate "purposes" should be distinguished from corporate "powers." Every state business corporation act contains a list of corporate powers that every corporation organized under that act automatically possesses. In most states this list is broad and not exclusive. Section 3.02 of the Model Business Corporation Act (1984) is based on the long tradition of powers clauses in state statutes, but it contains additional language in the introductory clause, "and has the same powers as an individual to do all things necessary or convenient to carry out its business and affairs," that is designed to eliminate any historical remnant of doctrines of limited or enumerated powers. Section 3.02 is also broader than many state statutes in specific areas, such as section 3.02(15), authorizing the making of payments or donations or doing of other acts "not inconsistent with law, that furthers the business and affairs of the corporation." This language is independent of the power to make charitable donations [MBCA § 3.02(13)], and includes payments for political purposes or to influence elections.

A corporation with a narrow purposes clause may nevertheless possess broad powers under section 3.02 of the MBCA (1984) or similar state statutes, the broad powers to be exercised in furtherance of narrow purposes.

Where a state statute contains a broad list of powers, it is generally undesirable to include powers clauses in articles of incorporation since the inclusion of certain powers may be construed as negating the existence of non-enumerated ones.

Because of peculiar historical problems in some states, however, it may be desirable to refer to certain specific powers in the articles. Where this is felt necessary, the drafting should make clear that the clause relates to powers rather than purposes. A clause that permits a corporation, for example, "to enter into partnerships or joint ventures" states a "power" and not a "purpose." The corporation is utilizing the "power" to enter into a partnership to achieve a "purpose," e.g., a purpose of buying, selling, and trading in real estate.

§ 4.13   The Common Law Doctrine of Ultra Vires

The doctrine of ultra vires (literally beyond the scope of the purposes or powers of a corporation) is now largely obsolete in modern corporation law. In an earlier day, however, the doctrine had considerable practical importance and was given major attention. Before turning to the vestigial remnants of the doctrine in modern law, a brief description of the scope of the doctrine at common law should be given.

An ultra vires act was one beyond the purposes or powers of a corporation. The earliest view of the matter was that such acts were simply void. A corporation was formed only for limited purposes, the argument ran, and it could do nothing more than it was authorized to do. This early view, however, was unworkable and unrealistic. Carried to its logical conclusion it would permit a corporation to accept the benefits of a contract and then refuse to perform its obligations on the ground that the contract was ultra vires. (Indeed that may have been the view taken early by the English courts.) It would also impair the security of title to property in fully executed transactions in which a corporation participated. As a result, even though dicta supporting the view that ultra vires acts were totally void appeared in many cases, most courts actually adopted the view that such acts were voidable rather than void. The doctrine continued to be firmly grounded on the notion that a corporation possessed only limited purposes and powers, but a rather elaborate body of law developed defining when the defense of ultra vires might be asserted:

(a) An ultra vires transaction might be ratified by all the shareholders. Ratification could be express or implied, e.g., by the receipt of benefits without objection. Ratification, however, had to be by unanimous consent.

(b) The doctrine of estoppel usually precluded reliance on the defense of ultra vires where the transaction was fully performed by one party. In some cases, however, the corporation was held not to be estopped even where the other party had performed fully because the corporation had not received a "direct" benefit from the transaction. When benefits were classed as "direct" or "indirect" appeared to be erratic.

(c) A fortiori, a transaction which was fully performed by both parties could not be attacked. This principle was generally applied to assure security of land titles.

(d) If the contract was fully executory, the defense of ultra vires might be raised by either party.

(e) If the contract was partially performed, and the performance was held to be insufficient to bring the doctrine of estoppel into play, a suit in quasi-contract for recovery of benefits conferred was available.

(f) If an agent of the corporation committed a tort within the scope of his or her employment, the corporation could not defend on the ground the act was ultra vires. This conclusion was reached apparently because of the overriding necessity of protecting innocent third parties from corporate abuses over which they had no means of control.

These principles somewhat tamed the doctrine of ultra vires. That doctrine, however, continued to defeat legitimate expectations where the contract was still executory and possessed an unfortunate capacity to be applied in an erratic fashion in other situations as well. As a result, the modern trend has been to eliminate this doctrine from the law of corporations, or at least to sharply restrict its availability.

§ 4.14 The Modern Role of Ultra Vires

Modern developments relating to corporate formation reduce the probability that ultra vires acts will actually occur. Thus, the development of multiple purposes clauses and general clauses permitting corporations to "engage in any lawful business" indirectly limits the role of the doctrine. Further, it is now very simple to amend purposes clauses to broaden them to cover new activities if an ultra vires issue is presented. However, despite these factors, cases involving narrowly drawn purposes clauses still occasionally arise. In order to eliminate the complicated and arbitrary ultra vires rules in these cases, virtually all states have adopted statutes patterned on the following 1950 Model Act provision:

No act of a corporation and no conveyance or transfer of real or personal property to or by a corporation shall be invalid by reason of the fact that the corporation was without capacity or power to do such act or to make or receive such conveyance or transfer. (§ 7)

The Model Business Corporation Act (1984) says exactly the same thing in somewhat more elegant language: "The validity of corporate action may not be challenged on the ground that the corporation lacks or lacked power to act." [MBCA (1984) § 3.04(a)] However, both statutes permit the lack of capacity or power to be asserted in the following types of proceedings:

(1) In a proceeding by the corporation (or by a shareholder in a representative capacity) against the incumbent or former officers or directors of the corporation for exceeding their authority;

(2) In a proceeding by the Attorney General to dissolve the corporation, or to enjoin it from the transaction of unauthorized business; or

(3) In a proceeding by a shareholder against the corporation to enjoin the commission of an ultra vires act or the ultra vires transfer of real or personal property if all parties are before the court and circumstances make such an action equitable.

A limited purposes clause may be included because one or more of the participants desire to restrict the freedom of a corporation to go into new or different ventures. The possibility of enjoining a corporation from violating such a limited clause is recognized in clause (3), but only "if the circumstances make such an action equitable." However, the Official Comment to section 3.04 points out that rights of third persons who may be unaware of the restrictions must be taken into account in assessing equity; in view of the routine and pro forma nature of the modern incorporation process it is unlikely that a third person would be held subject to a limited purposes clause unless he or she was actually aware of it. The notion that a filing in a public office creates "constructive notice," whatever its merits in other contexts, probably should not extend to unusual provisions in articles of incorporation and, given the modern practice of virtual universal use of general purposes clauses, certainly should not extend to limited purposes clauses.

§ 4.15 Ultra Vires Problems in Connection With Corporate Powers

The concept of ultra vires may arise in one other modern context. As described in § 4.12 of this Nutshell, modern corporation statutes contain a list of powers that every corporation formed under the statute automatically possesses. Theoretically a corporation may do some act that is beyond its powers as set forth in this list. But the language of the Model Business Corporation Act (1984) is so broad that this is unlikely. However, the language of powers clauses vary and in some states corporations may not be specifically authorized to engage in certain actions even though they appear to be in furtherance of the stated purposes of the corporation. This problem is also declining in importance as the language of statutes are modernized, but the following kinds of activities may create ultra vires problems in some states.

(1) *Charitable or Political Contributions.* Under early decisions corporations did not have implied power to make donations to charitable, religious, or civic organizations. Most states now generally authorize such contributions though doubt may exist whether power exists to make gifts that are large in comparison to the income or assets of the corporation. A leading Delaware case, Theodora Holding Corp. v. Henderson (Del.Ch.1969), upholds such gifts so long as they are reasonable in amount given the corporate assets and do not exceed the maximum deduction allowed under the federal income tax law. Also a distinction may be drawn between gifts to established charities such as universities, hospitals, or the Red Cross, and gifts to organizations or foundations chartered by a controlling shareholder or director. Arguments may also be made that specific charitable gifts directly further the corporation's purpose and should be viewed as business rather than eleemosynary transactions.

Direct political contributions by corporations are unlawful and subject to civil and criminal sanctions in many states. In First National Bank v. Bellotti (S.Ct.1978), however, the United States Supreme Court held unconstitutional a Massachusetts criminal statute that prohibited corporations from making contributions or expenditures to influence a state referendum. In Austin v. Michigan Chamber of Commerce (S.Ct. 1990), the Court recognized that "narrowly drawn" limitations on corporate political speech were constitutionally permissible. In establishing First Amendment rights for corporations, the Supreme Court appears to be concerned with the rights of the hearer of the speech more than its source.

Sections 3.02(13) and 3.02(15) of the Model Business Corporation Act (1984) codify the power of corporations to make charitable contributions and other payments or donations in furtherance of the corporation's business and affairs.

(2) *Pensions, Bonuses, Stock Option Plans, Job Severance Payments, and Other Fringe Benefits.* These arrangements obviously serve legitimate business purposes, and it is clear that a corporation in an appropriate case may award these benefits without express statutory authority.

Most doubts about the propriety of these financial arrangements arise in either of two contexts: where the compensation appears to be excessive or based on self-dealing (discussed in § 14.11 of this Nutshell), or where arguably there is an absence of consideration. For example, consideration may be lacking where, as a humanitarian gesture, a corporation supplements the modest pension of a retired employee. Or a bonus may be paid to an employee at the end of the year without a prior agreement that a bonus would be paid. Or a voluntary payment may be made to the spouse of a deceased employee. Technically, the argument about lack of consideration is not based on lack of corporate power but on substantive contract law. In most cases consideration may be found if the court is willing to look for it. For example, a bonus in one year may lead to an inference that a bonus will be paid the following year; a promise to remain in the corporation's employment may be implied; or the payment of an apparently gratuitous pension may yield contemplated benefits to the corporation in the form of improved employee morale and a happier labor force. In the absence of excessive compensation or blatant self-dealing, courts generally strive to uphold rather than strike down compensation arrangements.

Section 3.02(12) of the Model Business Corporation Act (1984) expressly addresses the power of corporations to provide pension and similar benefits to present or former employees.

(3) *The Power to Enter Into a Partnership.* The statement that it is ultra vires for corporations to enter into partnerships appears in numerous cases. The concern is that the fiduciary duties owed to other partners may conflict with the directors' duties to the shareholders. Because of the prominence of these statements the Model Business Corporation Act (1984) specifically authorizes every corporation "to be a promoter, partner, member, associate, or manager of any partnership, joint venture, trust or other enterprise." [MBCA (1984) § 3.02(9)] The same language appears in the 1969 Model Act. Under such a statute there seems to be no doubt that a corporation has the power to become a partner. Most states have enacted this provision.

The major case dealing with the duties that directors of a corporation that is a general partner in a limited partnership has toward the limited partners is *In re USACafes* (Del.Ch. 1991).

(4) *The Power to Acquire Shares of Other Corporations.* The power of corporations at common law to acquire shares of

other corporations was sharply restricted on the theory that a general power to invest in shares of another corporation constituted an indirect way for corporations to avoid limitations in their own purposes clauses. These restrictions are obsolete; corporations today generally have power to purchase, sell, and hold shares or other interests in, or obligations of, other domestic or foreign corporations. This power is now codified in section 3.02(6) of the Model Business Corporation Act (1984); virtually identical language appeared in earlier versions of the Model Act.

(5) *Guaranty of Indebtedness of Another.* At common law, it was ultra vires for a general business corporation to guarantee the indebtedness of another person, e.g., a potential customer (an exception was made for corporations who were formed for the specific purpose of writing surety bonds for a fee). This principle, which has little to commend it as an abstract matter, gave rise to a considerable amount of injustice since third persons might readily rely on a corporate guarantee. Fortunately, it has been reversed by statutory provision or judicial decision; section 3.02(7) of the Model Business Corporation Act (1984), for example, authorizes corporations "to make contracts and guarantees [and] incur liabilities;" virtually identical language appeared in earlier versions of the Model Act.

(6) *Loans to Officers or Directors.* Section 3.02(11) of the Model Business Corporation Act (1984) provides that a corporation may elect directors, appoint officers, employees, and agents "and lend them money and credit." The MBCA (1984) recognizes that loans to officers or directors may be beneficial to the corporation, and imposes no special restraints or limitations on them. It was not always so, and it is not so in some states today.

The 1969 and earlier versions of the Model Business Corporation Act contained an unqualified prohibition against such loans: they stated that "no loans shall be made by a corporation to its officers or directors." In one form or another, restrictions on loans to officers or directors still appear in the statutes of many states; most of these restrictions are not total prohibitions (as in the 1969 Model Act) but permit loans, for example, that are approved by the shareholders or loans that are for the express purpose of permitting the individual to purchase shares of the corporation. Generally these restrictions have been construed as a "limitation on a specific power granted, not a positive prohibition." In other words, loans that violate these restrictions are ultra vires but not illegal. The 1969 version of the Model Act and the statutes of many states also provide that directors who vote for or assent to the making of an improper loan to an officer or director are jointly and severally liable for the amount of the loan until it is repaid. It may be argued that this specific provision constitutes the sole remedy for a violation of this restriction on the general powers of a corporation.

As originally approved, section 8.32 of the MBCA (1984) dealt specifically with loans by a corporation to a director. This section built off the more liberal state statutes, and permitted loans to directors that were (1) approved by a majority of the voting shareholders, (2) approved by the board of directors after a finding that the loan benefits the corporation, or (3) made pursuant to a general plan authorizing loans that was approved by the board of directors after a finding that the plan benefits the corporation. In 1988, however, the Committee on Corporate Laws adopted a new Model Act provision that dealt systematically with conflict of interest transactions between directors and their corporations. Viewing loans to directors as only a special case of conflict of interest transactions that did not require special treatment, the Committee repealed the original section 8.32. There is therefore now no special provision in the MBCA (1984) dealing with loans to directors.

Restrictions on loans to officers and directors are based on fear that loans to corporate decision-makers are peculiarly subject to abuse; in effect statutes like the 1969 Model Act address this fear by making ultra vires all loans to officers or directors whether or not they are in fact abusive. MBCA (1984) rejects this per se rule and treats such loans as merely one type of conflict of interest transaction. (See § 14.11 of this Nutshell for a discussion of the new MBCA (1984) provisions dealing with conflict of interest transactions.)

The early statutes prohibiting loans to officers or directors sometimes also included a general prohibition (which appears in the 1969 version of the Model Act) against loans "secured by shares of stock of a corporation." Apparently this provision was included to emphasize that from the standpoint of the corporation such a loan was in fact unsecured. (See § 7.15 of this Nutshell, discussing the role of treasury shares.) However, the desirability of including such a limitation on powers seems questionable and the clause was eliminated from the Model Act in 1969; it also has been eliminated from the statutes of most states.

§ 4.16 Completion of the Organization of the Corporation: In General

In addition to preparing and filing the articles of incorporation, the attorney usually handles a number of other routine details in connection with the formation of a corporation. Typically the lawyer:

(1) Prepares the corporate bylaws;

(2) Prepares the call of meeting of the initial board of directors or the incorporators, minutes of this meeting, and waivers of notice or consents if necessary;

(3) Obtains a corporate seal and minute book for the corporation;

(4) Obtains blank certificates for the shares of stock, arrange for their printing or typing, and ensure that they are properly issued;

(5) Arranges for the opening of the corporate bank account;

(6) Prepares the call of meeting of the shareholders, minutes of this meeting and waivers of notice, if necessary;

(7) Prepares employment contracts, voting trusts, pooling agreements, share transfer restrictions, and other special arrangements which are to be entered into with respect to the corporation and its shares;

(8) Obtains taxpayer and employer identification numbers from the Internal Revenue Service and from appropriate state agencies; and

(9) Ensures that the manner in which capital is proposed to be raised is in compliance with the requirements of the federal Securities Act of 1933 and the applicable state blue sky laws; and

(10) If the corporation qualifies for S Corporation tax treatment, discusses with the owners the question whether to make this tax election.

§ 4.17   Nature and Purpose of Bylaws

The bylaws of a corporation are a set of rules for governing the internal affairs of the corporation. They are adopted by the corporation and technically are binding only on intracorporate matters. They are often viewed as a contract between the corporation and its officers, directors and share-holders, and among those individuals themselves.

Bylaws are generally not filed with the secretary of state, and are not a matter of public record. They usually may be amended with considerable more facility than the articles of incorporation. In case of conflict between the articles of incorporation and the bylaws, the former, of course, control.

It is often optional whether a specific provision is included in the articles of incorporation or in the bylaws. If the provision is unusual or important, maximum legal efficacy is obtained by placing the provision on public record in the articles. On the other hand, corporate officers are much more likely to be conversant with the provisions of the bylaws. For this reason, procedural matters and mandatory provisions that appear in the articles of incorporation and even in the statute should be repeated in the bylaws. The bylaws should set out what amounts to an operating manual of basic rules for ordinary transactions, sufficiently complete to be relied upon by the directors and officers of the corporation as a checklist in administering the affairs of the corporation.

See § 8.10 of this Nutshell for a discussion of the power to amend bylaws.

§ 4.18   The Corporate Seal

In most states a formal corporate seal is no longer necessary. A handwritten facsimile seal has the same legal effect as a metal die, and some states have attempted to dispense entirely with the requirement of a seal. See MBCA (1984) § 3.02(2). Nevertheless, a seal is probably desirable since it helps to delineate corporate transactions from individual transactions. Also, title and abstract companies and attorneys in real estate work are accustomed to corporate conveyances being under seal, and it may be easier to satisfy them if a formal seal is available. No one need fight city hall unnecessarily.

The corporate seal is usually affixed to share certificates, bonds, debentures, evidences of indebtedness, corporate conveyances of land, certified excerpts from minutes of meetings, and important corporate contracts.

§ 4.19 Organizational Meetings

Most of the miscellaneous matters relating to the launching of a new corporation are accomplished at a meeting of the initial directors, or in some states, the incorporators. These matters may usually be handled by written unanimous consent if there is no dispute or controversy, thereby dispensing with the requirement of a formal meeting.

Typical actions include the acceptance of share subscriptions or contracts to purchase shares; the issuance of shares and the establishment of the consideration for them (see Chapter 7 of this Nutshell); the selection and election of permanent directors and officers; the approval of contracts, loans, leases and other business-related matters; approval of the bylaws and the seal; approval of the payment of the expenses of incorporation (see § 5.8 of this Nutshell); adoption of a resolution opening a bank account and designation of the officers authorized to sign checks; and numerous other possible business-related matters. Also, in some circumstances it may be necessary to have a meeting of the shareholders to elect permanent directors; a written unanimous consent may be used in lieu of this formal meeting also.

As a practical matter, the lawyer prepares not only the articles of incorporation and bylaws, but also the various minutes or written consents needed to complete the formation of the corporation. These documents are almost always prepared in advance of the actual formation. It may seem odd to prepare elaborate minutes for a meeting that has not yet taken place, but really it is not; the minutes serve as a script for the actual conduct of the meeting. Of course, if action is being taken by unanimous written consent, only signatures are required.

In states that require the organizational meeting to be held by initial directors named in the articles of incorporation, attorneys sometimes find it necessary, where the permanent parties in interest do not want their names to appear in the records of the secretary of state, to use nominal initial directors, hold a "meeting" of these initial directors to organize the corporation and issue stock, followed immediately by a "meeting" of shareholders to elect permanent directors, followed immediately by another "meeting" of the permanent directors to conduct other necessary business transactions.

If the permanent directors are willing to serve as the initial directors and be named as such in the articles of incorporation, it is simplest to name the permanent directors also as initial directors, since only a single "meeting" then suffices to complete the formation of the corporation.

It was because of scenarios such as these that the draftsmen of the Model Business Corporation Act (1984) decided to give each new corporation an option whether to have organizational meetings conducted by incorporators or by initial directors named in the articles of incorporation. As a practical matter, of course, this decision is made by the attorney forming the corporation as he or she contemplates the desires of the client and the steps needed to complete the formation of the corporation.

Where the unanimous written consent procedure is not available (as may be the case, for example, where one director is absent), the question sometimes arises as to whether it is necessary to actually hold meetings to reflect what the minutes describe. If the corporation is closely held and there is no disagreement about what is to be done, it seems to be a waste of time and silly play-acting to assemble several persons in a single room and actually hold a meeting at which the already-prepared minutes serve as a script. However, it is generally desirable to actually hold an informal meeting at which the actions referred to in the minutes are quickly approved. Such meetings do have a play-acting atmosphere but the validity of actions taken without a meeting may otherwise be questioned. Such a meeting may take only a minute or so if there is consensus as to what should be done.

[For unfamiliar terms see the Glossary]

CHAPTER FIVE

PREINCORPORATION TRANSACTIONS

§ 5.1 Introduction

The formation of a new corporation is often not a clean birth. Transactions on behalf of the corporation, or in the corporate name, may occur before the articles of incorporation are filed and the corporate existence begins. Such transactions may be entered into with full knowledge that the corporation is not yet formed (such as subscription agreements or contracts by promoters to ensure that the necessary business assets are available), or inadvertently, resulting from unexpected delays in the formation of the corporation. Preliminary transactions are usually classified under several different headings: promoters' transactions, de facto corporations, and so forth. They are, however, all closely related and often factual situations may be classified under more than one of these headings.

§ 5.2 Subscriptions for Shares

A "subscription" is simply an offer to purchase and pay for a specified number of theretofore unissued shares of a corporation. Subscriptions may be divided into "pre-incorporation subscriptions," that is, subscriptions for shares of a corporation that has not yet been formed, and "post-incorporation subscriptions," that is, subscriptions for unissued shares of an already existing corporation.

110

(1) Pre-incorporation subscriptions. Older texts devote a great deal of attention to pre-incorporation subscriptions as a device by which a new venture may be assured of adequate capitalization before it is launched. Typically, potential investors would be approached individually to determine whether they would be willing to purchase a specified number of shares; those that agreed to purchase shares signed a simple letter agreement stating that they had subscribed for and agreed to purchase at a specified price a specified number of shares. At common law, uncertainty existed whether a subscriber might withdraw from his subscription before the corporation came into existence and accepted it. The reason for this uncertainty was that pre-incorporation subscriptions were obtained individually and were usually viewed as independent offers running from each subscriber to the not-yet-formed corporation rather than as a contract among subscribers with the promise of each subscriber supporting the promises of other subscribers. There was no contract in this situation since one "party"—the corporation—was not in existence and could not be bound so that the other party—the subscriber— was not bound either. At the same time, there was a strong element of reliance on the part of the promoters of the corporation, and quite possibly also on the part of other subscribers.

This problem has largely faded away. Corporation statutes make pre-incorporation subscriptions irrevocable for a limited period (six months in § 6.20(a) of MBCA (1984)). During this period the formation of the corporation can be completed and the subscriptions accepted without regard to technical questions of consideration; until that period has expired, the statute makes the pre-incorporation subscription irrevocable by the subscriber. This six-month period is itself a matter of negotiation between promoter and subscriber, and a longer or shorter period of irrevocability may be agreed upon. Also, without regard to the period of irrevocability, all the subscribers to shares of a not-yet-formed corporation can agree to the revocation of a subscription by one or more specific subscribers.

A subscription may be conditioned on the occurrence of certain events, such as obtaining a specified amount of capital, or a specified loan, or a specified lease. The fulfillment of such conditions are conditions precedent to the obligation of the subscribers. The common law developed a rather confusing distinction between conditional subscriptions and "subscriptions on special terms" which constituted a type of condition subsequent. There was little practical difference, however, because failure of the corporation to comply with a "special term" also permitted the subscriber to rescind or withdraw from his or her subscription.

A subscription that is induced by fraud can be rescinded by the subscriber as any other contract. The fraud may be the act of an agent or a promoter of the corporation.

After the corporation is formed, its board of directors may call upon the subscribers to make payment on their subscriptions. Under MBCA (1984) § 6.20(b) the board of directors may determine the payment terms of pre-incorporation subscriptions, but calls for payment must be uniform among all subscribers of the same class of shares, "so far as practicable."

Modern distribution techniques for securities permit the meeting of all capital needs of publicly held corporations without resort to subscriptions. Indeed, the use of subscriptions in connection with a public offering is unattractive as a practical matter because the subscriptions themselves constitute securities under federal and state securities acts and must be registered. Since the underlying securities themselves also must be registered, the use of subscriptions results in two expensive registrations.

In closely held corporations where it is contemplated that there will be only a few shareholders, a contractual agreement among the contemplated shareholders to form a corporation and purchase specified shares is a binding agreement whether or not it is described as a "subscription agreement." Pre-incorporation contracts (described in the following section) have largely supplanted the common law subscription, though the wording in such agreements is usually that each investor "agrees to purchase *and subscribe* for" the securities he or she agreed to purchase. Pre-incorporation agreements are enforceable as multilateral contracts among the subscribers without reference to the special statutory provision relating to pre-incorporation subscriptions described above (which applies when each subscriber commits to a subscription individually and not in consideration of other subscribers' similar commitments).

A person who subscribes for or agrees to purchase shares does not become a shareholder until the subscription price has been fully paid, though some states permit shares to be issued for promissory notes for the unpaid portion of the purchase price.

(2) Post-incorporation subscriptions. An existing corporation may also seek to raise capital by obtaining commitments from potential investors to purchase shares. Subscriptions of this nature are normally cast in the form of a contract between the corporation and the investor, and are enforceable as any other contract by the corporation or the subscriber. See MBCA (1984) § 6.20(e).

It is customary in all modern subscription agreements or agreements to form a corporation to include a representation by purchasers of securities that they are purchasing for investment and not with a view toward resale.

§ 5.3 Agreements to Form Corporation

A "pre-incorporation agreement" is a contract among proposed shareholders to develop a business to be conducted in the form of a corporation. The contribution of each participant and the number of shares each is to receive are specified in this contract, which is a substitute for the common law pre-incorporation subscription. Because it is a contract among the participants, it is enforceable in the same manner as any other contract.

A pre-incorporation agreement may be a summary memorandum outlining the main points of an oral agreement, or a complete formal document. In a formal document, all aspects of the agreement between shareholders will usually be stated, as may understandings as to employment, capitalization, voting power, share transfer restrictions, who shall comprise the initial board of directors, or any other matter that is the subject of preliminary agreement. Copies of proposed articles of incorporation, bylaws, and minutes of proposed meetings may be attached as exhibits. The agreement may also designate who are to serve as officers of the corporation, but those designations should be subject to the authority of the board of directors after it is constituted to determine who should serve as officers of the corporation. See § 8.11 of this Nutshell.

Pre-incorporation agreements often impose restrictions upon the subsequent transfer of shares issued upon the formation of the corporation pursuant to the agreement.

One important issue with a pre-incorporation agreement is whether it is fully executed by the formation of a corporation as provided in the agreement or whether specific provisions survive the creation of the corporation. If it is desired to have certain provisions of the agreement survive and continue to bind the parties, the agreement should specifically so state, since otherwise a court may easily infer that only the provisions actually included in the articles of incorporation, bylaws, and minutes were intended to survive. If the agreement is to survive it should be specifically assumed by the corporation upon its formation. If the state in question has enacted § 7.32 of MBCA (1984) (discussed in section 12.9 of this Nutshell), the pre-incorporation agreement may also serve as a shareholders' agreement if it is appropriately described and executed by all of the shareholders of the corporation.

An agreement to form a corporation places the parties to the agreement in the relationship of joint venturers, the object of the venture being the formation of the corporation and the establishment of its business. If the agreement survives, there may be a conceptual difficulty since after the corporation is formed the parties are simultaneously being treated as having the rights of shareholders in the corporation and the rights of joint venturers in an underlying arrangement to form the corporation. To avoid possible conflicts, some courts have taken the position that when the parties adopt the corporate form, with the corporate shield to protect them, they necessarily "cease to be partners and have only the rights, duties and obligations of stockholders." Other courts however, have taken the position that the joint venture may continue after the formation of the corporation, at least where the parties' intention to this effect is clear. The question appears to be one of "intention" since there appears to be no reason why both relationships cannot exist simultaneously if that is what the parties desire.

§ 5.4   Promoters in General

A promoter is a person who takes the initiative in developing and organizing a new business venture. A promoter may act either alone or with co-promoters. The term "promoter" is not one of opprobrium; indeed, the promoter is often an aggressive, imaginative entrepreneur who fulfills the essential economic function of taking an idea and creating a profitable business to capitalize on the idea.

The role of a promoter is quite different than the role of an incorporator. The latter basically has the responsibility of signing a document that forms the corporation; the promoter is the person who has the responsibility of assuring that the corporation is an economic success. Obviously, promoters may also serve as incorporators.

The activities of promoters fall into two principal areas. (1) The promoter must arrange for the necessary capital for the corporation. He or she may invest only personal funds, or use personal funds plus loans from banks to obtain the necessary capital. Outside capital may be obtained from a small number of investors, who may be friends or neighbors. If so, the promoter must negotiate with the outside investors to determine their share in the forthcoming enterprise, and arrange either by contract or subscription to ensure that the capital will be forthcoming when needed. (2) The promoter must obtain the necessary assets and personnel so that the corporation may function. He or she may obtain a lease or an option to purchase needed land, or may enter into a contract to purchase with a view of assigning the contract to the corporation. He or she may negotiate construction contracts to build or remodel the necessary buildings. Arrangements must be made to secure the necessary employees which usually will include the promoter as an officer of the new enterprise. The necessary machinery, equipment, or fixtures must be secured; customers must be contacted; arrangements made for advertising; and so forth. Obviously, in this area, the kinds of activities promoters engage in are numerous and varied, depending on the nature of the business being promoted.

If the corporation is formed before the promoter commences his activities, subsequent contractual problems are usually minimized since all the necessary steps may thereafter be conducted in the name of the corporation, and there is little chance of confusion between the promoter's individual liability and the corporate liability on the arrangements being negotiated. Thus, actions may be taken in the corporate name and not in the name of the individual promoter. Of course, if a third person requests the personal liability of the promoter as well as the corporation, as may be the case with providers of debt capital, the promoter may execute an obligation individually or separately guaranteeing the corporation's performance.

Often, however, the formation of the corporation turns out to be one of the last steps in the promotional process. The promoter may begin investigation of the profitability of the proposed business, determine that the prospects of success are good, and proceed at once with business negotiations in the areas of capital formation, obtaining business assets, and entering into contracts without actually forming the corporation. In this situation there is greater likelihood of confusion and uncertainty, and most contractual litigation involving promoters arises in connection with not-yet-formed corporations.

§ 5.5 Promoters' Contracts

Let us assume that before the corporation is formed the promoter enters into a contract to purchase machinery for the new business being promoted, and consider whether the promoter is personally liable on that contract. No single, simple answer is possible. In some circumstances personal liability will exist, in other circumstances it will not. There are at least three different situations:

(1) *Contracts Executed in the Name of the Promoter.* If the promoter enters into a contract in his or her own name without referring to the corporation with the thought of subsequently assigning the contract to the corporation, personal liability on the part of the promoter clearly exists. The subsequent assignment of the contract to the corporation does not relieve the promoter of personal liability unless the creditor agrees, explicitly or implicitly, to release the promoter and look only to the corporation for performance. The release of a party to a contract when it is assumed by another is called a *novation.*

If the corporation wishes to adopt a contract entered into by the promoter, it typically does so by express resolution adopted by the board of directors.

(2) *Contracts Entered in the Name of the Corporation.* The promoter may execute a contract in the corporate name when in fact the corporation has not yet been formed. Many cases say that such a promoter is personally liable on the theory that a person acting as agent represents that a principal exists, and the promoter is liable because of a misrepresentation. Other cases rely on the agency principle that a person who purports to act as agent for a nonexistent principal thereby automatically becomes liable for the action. The latter theory is based on contract and the former on tort, though in most cases they should lead to the same result.

These cases often give the third person a windfall because presumably that person is not relying on the promoter's credit when entering into a contract in which a corporation is named as the other party; rather he or she is relying on the corporation's credit or, more likely, on the possibility that the corporation will do well and be able to pay off the obligations. However, virtually all courts in this situation hold the promoter personally liable despite the potential windfall.

If the corporation is thereafter formed and adopts the contract, the promoter may argue that the subsequent formation of the corporation corrected any misrepresentation or deception that may have occurred. Or he may argue that the manner of execution of the agreement indicates that the third person was content to accept the liability of the corporation, and that therefore the adoption of the contract by the corporation releases the promoter. In other words, the argument is that the transaction should be construed as a novation. Depending on the specific circumstances, other arguments may also be available to the promoter, but their probability of success is not very good.

To summarize: if the promoter enters into a contract with a third person in the name of the corporation without disclosing that it is not in existence, the promoter is personally liable on the contract. If the corporation is thereafter created and takes over the contract, the promoter has a chance of being relieved of liability but there is a substantial chance that a court will conclude that no novation was intended and the promoter remains personally liable.

(3) *Contracts Referring to the Fact the Corporation Is Not Yet Formed.* In this class of case the contract is executed by the promoter and the third party when both are aware that the corporation has not been formed. The contract itself usually reveals this fact, as for example when it is executed in a name such as "ABC Corporation, a corporation to be formed." Or the promoter may advise the third person that the corporation has not yet been formed when the contract is executed in the corporate name. It may be noted that this situation differs from situation (2) in that both parties are aware that the corporation is not yet in existence and there is no possible misrepresentation as to that fact.

This pattern may be analyzed in several different ways with widely divergent consequences. For example, it may be analyzed as an offer to the corporation which is revocable by either party and will result in a contract only if the corporation is thereafter formed and accepts the offer before it is withdrawn. Or it may be analyzed as an irrevocable option running to the corporation, with the consideration being a promise, express or implied, by the promoter to form the corporation and use best efforts to cause the corporation to adopt the contract. Or, it may be analyzed as a present contract between the third person and the promoter by which the promoter is bound, with the understanding that if the contract is adopted by the corporation the promoter will be released from liability under the contract. It is also possible that a court may conclude that the mere formation of the corporation did not constitute a novation.

Which of these various alternatives is the proper one in any specific situation depends on the elusive "intention of the parties." If an attorney is called upon to draft a pre-incorporation agreement it is relatively simple to ascertain the parties' intention and describe it in a written agreement in terms so precise that there can be no cause for misunderstanding. If the promoter is to be bound until the corporation adopts the contract, and then is to be released from liability, a contract that specifically so provides should avoid later disputes.

Litigation in this area generally involves agreements in which the intention is not clearly spelled out. The contract may have been negotiated by the parties without legal assistance, or the language chosen may not illuminate the specific problem one way or the other. Or the parties may have been unable to agree on their respective rights in the event of some remote contingency. Rather than forego a lucrative transaction, the parties use language such as "ABC Corporation, a corporation to be formed," hoping that the question of the liability of the promoter will not arise. In such situations, the search for intent is truly hopeless, though the courts must resolve the dispute one way or another.

Generalizations about tests which courts use to find "intention" are hazardous. Probably most courts feel that it is likely that the third person intended for *someone* to be liable. Hence, there is a strong probability that the promoter will initially be held liable, especially where the corporation is never formed. Indeed, many cases state without qualification that the promoter is personally liable in this situation unless there is specific agreement to the contrary. If the third person is to receive payments or partial performance before the corporation is formed, an intention to hold the promoter personally responsible may readily be inferred; presumably the promoter intends to make those payments or render the performance personally until the corporation is formed.

Professor Williston suggested that most persons assume that even if the promoter is initially liable, he or she is nevertheless to be released if the corporation is later formed and adopts the contract. In other words, there is to be a novation. The testimony of the plaintiff in Bradshaw v. Jones (Tex.Civ.App.1912) is representative of this understanding: "I understood that I was working for [Mr. Jones] personally until the railroad was organized; and after the railroad was organized, I was working for the railroad, of course." Not surprisingly, the court concluded that a novation was intended. There are, however, some holdings and a considerable amount of dicta to the contrary. One problem with the Williston approach is that it may encourage promoters to create "straw" corporations to take over contracts even after it is clear that the venture should be abandoned.

If the promoters are held liable, they are considered to be partners, and liable for all promotional contracts on a joint and several basis.

Where both parties are aware that the corporation has not yet been formed, several cases have held the promoter not personally liable on the contract. In Quaker Hill, Inc. v. Parr (Colo.1961), for example, the court concluded that on the facts the third party never intended to rely on the promoters' performance of the contract and therefore should not be able to hold the promoters personally liable. Later cases, however, have held that the burden of proving intention rests on the promoter, and that inferences about intention cannot be based merely on knowledge that formation of a corporation was contemplated. These recent cases demonstrate again the difficulty of prediction of result in this shadowy area, though it is probable in many cases that the third person in fact intended to look only to the corporation for performance of the contract.

§ 5.6 Liability of Corporations for Promoters' Contracts

It is quite possible that a promoter will enter into contracts in the name of the corporation that the corporation, after it learns of the existence of the contracts, will decide are not advantageous to it.

The corporation is not automatically liable on obligations incurred by its promoters before it is formed. The reason usually given is that the promoter cannot be the corporation's agent since the corporation is not in existence. This conceptualistic argument can be partially justified on the practical ground that the rule permits subsequent investors in the corporation an opportunity to consider and reject undesirable arrangements agreed to by the promoter. Of particular importance, it permits review and rejection by subsequent investors of contracts entered into between the promoters personally and the corporation (see section 5.7 of this Nutshell).

The theory on which corporations voluntarily become liable on pre-incorporation contracts negotiated by their promoters has been the subject of a great deal of confusing discussion. Assuming that the arrangement constitutes a contract between the promoter and third person in which it is understood that a corporation will be formed, the corporation "adopts" the contract. Technically, "ratification" is not the proper word to describe this situation because "ratification" assumes that the corporation was in existence at the time the contract was entered into. Courts nevertheless sometimes use the words "ratification" and "adoption" interchangeably. If the promoter is then relieved from liability, the "adoption" or "ratification" becomes a "novation."

In the last analysis, the legal words used are not particularly important. What is necessary is some form of assent by the corporation to the contract after it has been formed. The necessary assent may be express, or it may be implied from the circumstances. If a corporation takes the benefits of a contract made by its promoter, it will usually be concluded that it has assented to the burdens of the contract. For example, if a promoter negotiates a contract by which a third person agrees to become an employee of the corporation for a specified term, and a responsible officer of the corporation permits the employee to render services for the corporation after learning of the terms of the contract, the corporation has probably "adopted" the contract and cannot thereafter fire the employee without cause during the contract period.

Since the corporation becomes liable on the contract only when it assents, it has been held that the contract term begins when the assent occurs. This may be of importance for purposes of the statute of limitations or the one-year statute of frauds provision.

If the corporation is in existence, it will be responsible for obligations entered into by the promoter on its behalf if the promoter is an authorized agent of the corporation. The issue of authority may be a sensitive one, since either actual or apparent authority will bind the corporation. If the necessary agency relationship does not exist, the corporation may either disaffirm the contract or voluntarily assume it by adoption or ratification.

§ 5.7 Promoter's Fiduciary Duties

Co-promoters of a venture owe fiduciary duties to each other. In effect they are treated as partners in a venture to organize the business.

Difficult questions may be raised where a promoter enters into self-dealing transactions with the corporation before outside creditors, investors, or shareholders are brought into the venture. The transaction may involve the receipt of shares of the corporation by the promoter, or the creation of corporate indebtedness in favor of the promoter for services or property. The transaction may be entered into when the promoter is the sole shareholder, or with the approval of the then-shareholders. Later or subsequent creditors, investors, or shareholders may object to the transaction on the ground that the services or property were overvalued or the amount awarded to the promoter was excessive. In many cases of this kind the courts have used language of fiduciary duty in reviewing and setting aside transactions to the extent they are believed to be unfair. The leading case finding a fiduciary duty is Old Dominion Copper Mining & Smelting Co. v. Bigelow (Mass.1909), announcing the so-called "Massachusetts rule." Not all courts have agreed, however; see particularly Old Dominion Copper Mining & Smelting Co. v. Lewisohn (S.Ct.1908), involving the same transaction and announcing the "federal rule" that subsequent shareholders or investors may not set aside previously approved promoters' transactions.

As a practical matter, the issue in these cases is not so much whether or not a fiduciary duty exists as whether or not there has been full disclosure of the transaction to the subsequent interests. If there has been full disclosure, subsequent creditors, investors, or shareholders may readily protect themselves by refusing to deal with the corporation or by reducing the price at which they acquire shares to reflect the reduction in value caused by the promoter's transaction. Indeed, the fiduciary duty described above is basically a duty of full disclosure rather than a duty of fair dealing. Cases continue to arise, however, in which subsequent investors attack promoter's transactions, and some courts have set them aside on the basis of vague discussion of "fiduciary" duties.

Since failure to disclose may constitute a violation of federal or state securities acts, many cases that seventy-five years ago would have been analyzed as "promoter's fraud" cases may now be analyzed as "securities fraud" cases.

§ 5.8   Organizational Expenses Incurred by Promoters

Logically, expenses incurred in connection with the organization of a corporation should be treated no differently than other contracts entered into by promoters. For example, if an attorney is employed by promoters to draw up the articles of incorporation, the promoter should be liable for the attorney's fee unless the attorney agrees to look only to the corporation. If the corporation is formed and adopts the contract, it becomes liable for the fee, and whether or not the promoter is released from his or her obligation depends on whether the transaction is deemed a novation.

There are complications, however. Organizational expenses such as attorneys' fees are peculiar in that the mere corporate existence is in effect a use of the benefits of the contract by the corporation. Arguably, therefore, by its mere existence the corporation has agreed to pay whatever fee was negotiated by the promoter. The majority view, however, rejects this reasoning and holds that the corporation is not automatically bound. Rather the corporation—since it cannot refuse the services—can only be compelled to pay a reasonable fee under the circumstances.

Many states have statutes that permit the payment of reasonable charges and expenses of organization of a corporation out of the capital received by it in payment for its shares without impairing capital or rendering such shares not fully paid and non-assessable. See MBCA (1984) § 6.28. It is not clear whether such a provision is necessary in modern corporation statutes; it was retained by the draftsmen of the Model Business Corporation Act (1984) essentially because it could do no harm and might do some good.

The promoter or the attorney may suggest that the attorney take shares in the corporation for organizational expenses and services. There is nothing inherently wrong with this practice: indeed, it somewhat resembles a contingent fee which is based on the success of the business rather than on the outcome of litigation. The value of shares received by an attorney or promoter for services is, of course, taxable income to him or her and may be deducted by the corporation as an expense over a 60 month period.

Promoters naturally expect to be compensated for their efforts, and in view of the nature of their innovative efforts, they may legitimately expect compensation which would be considered generous by a salaried person. A promoter may form a corporation with nominal capital, and then seek outside financial support to make the promotion a success. The subsequent investors will usually purchase shares in the corporation at a higher price than the shares previously issued to the promoter. The investors' interest is thereby diluted and the promoters' interest increased in value. In a sense this increase in value represents partial compensation to the promoter; it is often a subject of negotiation between promoters and investors. However, both hope that the major portion of the promoter's compensation will result from the fact that the business does well so that the value of everyone's shares will be enhanced.

§ 5.9 Premature Commencement of Business and the De Facto Doctrine

At an earlier time, incorporation was not as simple as it is today. In addition to the basic filing requirement, there might be a requirement that a certain amount of capital be actually paid in and a certificate be filed reflecting that receipt, that shares be actually issued, that officers and directors be elected, and so forth. These additional requirements greatly increased the likelihood that there might be "premature commencement" of business, that corporate obligations might be incurred after some but not all of the necessary corporate steps for formation had been taken. What is the responsibility of directors, officers, or shareholders for these interim obligations?

The procedures required to form a corporation today under most corporation statutes are basically very simple. As a matter of fact, they are so simple and routine that attorneys may become careless and fail to comply with all the requirements that do exist. As a result, premature commencement problems may arise today. Mistakes may range from the trivial, such as using an incorrect address, to the more serious, where the attorney becomes so careless that he or she prepares but fails to file the articles of incorporation at all (this has actually happened). Delays in filing are not uncommon. Perhaps the secretary of state declines to accept the first filing because of some minor defect that the attorney subsequently corrects. In the meantime, the "corporation" has commenced business. Again the issue is whether directors, officers or shareholders have personal liability for the interim debts.

At common law, these problems were usually handled under the "de facto corporation" doctrine, though occasionally they appeared as promoters contracts; today many courts still apply common law concepts though they have been largely superseded by a statutory analysis.

A "de facto corporation" according to the common law was not a fully formed corporation (a "de jure corporation"), but was nearly as good since it was sufficiently formed to be immune from attack by everyone but the state. The usual test for de facto existence was threefold: there must be a statute under which incorporation was permitted, there must have been a "good faith" or "colorable" attempt to comply with the statute, and there must have been actual user of the corporate privilege. However, the cases arising under this doctrine were confusing, particularly with regard to the second requirement and legal commentators convincingly proved that the traditional tests provide little guidance for the decisions of concrete cases. After examining more than 200 de facto corporation cases arising prior to 1950, for example, the late Professor Frey concluded that the de facto doctrine was "legal conceptualism at its worst." In a later study, considering cases arising between 1950 and 1989, Professor Bradley reaches a similar conclusion.

At common law a "de jure corporation" might exist even though there were some minor defects in its formation. The common law drew a distinction between "mandatory" and "directory" requirements; failure to comply with the latter did not prevent the creation of a de jure corporation. An example of a "directory" requirement was the listing of addresses of directors or incorporators.

These problems today are usually resolved by reference to the specific language of the state's incorporation statute. Every state has a statute that provides in substance that the corporate existence begins either upon the filing of the articles of incorporation or their acceptance by the filing authority. See MBCA (1984) § 2.03(a). Most statutes add that acceptance of the articles is "conclusive proof" that all conditions precedent to incorporation have been complied with except in suits brought by the State. See MBCA (1984) § 2.03(b). Thus, if the Secretary of State accepts a filing, a de jure corporation is in existence despite mistakes or omissions in the articles of incorporation.

Another problem that arises under section 2.03(b) and similar statutes is whether a negative inference should be drawn that the corporate existence has *not* begun before the articles are accepted for filing. If this inference is accepted, personal liability exists for all pre-acceptance transactions. A few states have addressed this issue by adopting an additional statute that accepts the conclusion that liability exists with respect to transactions that occur during the pre-acceptance period. These statutes are based on section 146 of the 1969 Model Act, which states that "all persons who assume to act as a corporation without authority so to do shall be jointly and severally liable" for all debts and liabilities. However, even in states in which this statute is in effect, some courts have refused to hold participants personally liable on pre-incorporation transactions. One court construed the phrase "all persons who assume to act" as referring only to active participants in the venture, thereby immunizing inactive participants from liability. Timberline Equipment Co., Inc. v. Davenport (Ore.1973). All in all, the predictability of result under this statute was not much greater than under the de facto-de jure tests of common law.

The committee creating the Model Business Corporation Act (1984) took a fresh look at the standard to be applied to shareholder liability for pre-formation transactions, and came up with a somewhat different standard. Section 2.04 of MBCA (1984) provides that "all persons purporting to act as or on behalf of a corporation, *knowing there was no incorporation under this Act*, are jointly and severally liable for all liabilities created while so acting." (Italics added)

The basic problem with a simple rule conditioning the existence or nonexistence of a corporation on the acceptance of a filing by the filing office is that it has a substantial capacity for unfairness. Under such a rule, shareholders and promoters may be liable as partners for the pre-acceptance debts of the business. The result is that delay or negligence in filing on the part of A may cause crushing liabilities to be imposed on B who may have bought "shares" in the honest belief that the corporation's articles had been filed and accepted by the filing office. Of course, B might first check with that office, but most investors would not normally think to do so. The standard of section 2.04 of MBCA (1984), "knowing there was no incorporation under this Act," provides considerable protection to B in this situation.

§ 5.10   Corporations by Estoppel

Problems of the type discussed in the last section have sometimes been handled in the absence of statute under a related concept, a "corporation by estoppel." This phrase is not meaningful in and of itself. It is necessary to ask who is "estopped," under what circumstances, and for what reason. The classic requirements for equitable estoppel (or "estoppel in pais") are (1) there be a false representation to or concealment of a fact from a person ignorant of the truth (2) with the intention by the person making the representation of causing reliance, and (3) actual reliance by the innocent party on the basis of the false representation. "Corporations by estoppel" do not involve these principles.

Consider the following situation: A third person deals with what she believes to be a "corporation," relying on its assets and credit. When this "corporation" is unable to meet its obligations to her, she investigates and discovers that no filing had ever been made. She then sues the promoters and shareholders personally on the theory that they are liable as partners. The defendants, who also were unaware that no filing had been made, defends on the argument that the plaintiff is "estopped" by her prior dealings on a corporate basis (which shows that she was willing to rely solely on the assets and credit of the "corporation") from holding them personally liable. Some courts have accepted this argument. This is certainly not equitable estoppel in the classic sense, since the person who is being "estopped" never made any representation of any kind that was relied on by any other party. Rather, the person who herself relied is the one being estopped. In effect, courts are applying the label "corporation by estoppel" to reach a desirable result: used in this way "estoppel" is a conclusion, not an explanation. Nevertheless, there is a strong equitable argument for not allowing the plaintiff to recover from the personal assets of the defendants. The plaintiff receives a windfall if, after dealing and relying solely on the "corporation," she is permitted to hold the promoters or shareholders personally liable. Further, it is harsh, to say the least, to hold the defendants personally liable because of the negligence or neglect of some other person, particularly where they honestly and reasonably believed that the articles of incorporation had been filed and accepted. For these various reasons, some courts have held that the third person is "estopped" from suing the promoters or shareholders on the theory that there is a "corporation by estoppel."

It should be noted that this reasoning has some force even in the situation where the defendants were, or should have been, aware that no filing had been made. The reliance by the plaintiff is unaffected by this fact. However, if an estoppel principle were universally recognized promoters might seriously consider saving the filing fee by not filing anything and routinely conducting business in the corporate name. That proves too much. The principle of "estoppel" should be limited to situations where (a) the plaintiff dealt with the "corporation" as such, and (b) the defendant believed that the articles of incorporation had been properly filed and was not personally negligent in failing to make sure of that fact. This result is contemplated by § 2.04 of the Model Business Corporation Act, and appears to do justice to all parties. Furthermore, it does not seriously undermine the statutory policy requiring filing of articles of incorporation, since persons knowing that the articles have not been filed would have unlimited liability under all circumstances.

Not all the reported courts have agreed that "estoppel" should be applied in these types of cases, though the variations in decisions possibly may be explained by factual variations and variations in statutory wording.

§ 5.11   A Unified Conception of "Defective Incorporation"

In theory, "corporations de facto" and "corporations by estoppel" are alternative theories. The first relates to the extent to which the incorporator has sought to comply with the incorporation statute, while the second relates to the extent the plaintiffs have dealt with the defendants as a corporation. In fact, however, these two factors are not mutually exclusive.

A recent article, McChesney, Doctrinal Analysis and the Statistical Modeling in Law: The Case of Defective Incorporation, 71 Wash.U.L.Q. 493 (1993) suggests that "both factors affect judges' decisions in common-law defective incorporation situations." At the margin, "courts will more likely accord defendants limited liability when they have tried to comply and plaintiffs have treated the firm as a corporation. * * * Evaluated by what they do, not by what they say, judges apply one unitary doctrine—that of defective incorporation. * * * The apparent confusion shown by many judges in distinguishing the two doctrines reflects the fact that they are really not two doctrines at all." (71 Wash.U.L.Q, at 530–31)

[For unfamiliar terms see the Glossary]

CHAPTER SIX

"PIERCING THE CORPORATE VEIL" AND RELATED PROBLEMS

§ 6.1 "Piercing the Corporate Veil" In Context

Assume for a moment that a corporation has been properly and fully created in accordance with state law so that a "de jure corporation" has been created in the fullest sense of that phrase. The basic question discussed in this Chapter is whether and to what extent the separate existence of that corporation should be ignored in order to do basic justice or avoid the frustration of some clearly articulated public policy. At first blush, the basic concept that a corporation is a fictitious person or separate legal entity seems to dictate the answer that the separate existence of such a duly formed corporation should never be ignored. The law has not taken this extreme position, however, and courts often refuse to recognize the separate existence of a duly formed corporation. To put the matter into perspective, however, it should be added that this is the exceptional case, that in most cases courts respect the separate existence of corporations despite arguments that they should not do so. The corporate fiction is a basic assumption that underlies commercial transactions and there must be compelling reasons for a court to ignore that assumption.

When the separate existence of the corporation is ignored, courts often use colorful metaphors: "piercing the corporate veil," "alter ego" or "mere instrumentality," to name a few. These phrases shed little light on why the corporate existence is being ignored; they are statements of the conclusion, not reasons.

§ 6.2 Shareholder Responsibility for Corporate In-debtedness: Introduction

A shareholder may become liable for corporate indebtedness in a variety of ways. She may voluntarily guarantee the performance of the corporation's obligation—acting as a surety. She also may become personally liable by executing a document, such as a promissory note, in a way that makes it appear that she is acting as a co-obligor rather than as an agent acting on behalf of the corporation. She may also incur personal liability by failing to describe accurately the name of the corporation when dealing on behalf of the corporation, though case law tends to be generous to shareholders in these cases. For example, in one case a Mr. Pinson executed a lease in the name "Pinson Air Freight, Inc." when in fact his corporation's name was "Pinson Air Freight of Chattanooga, Inc." The court held the corporation and not Mr. Pinson liable on the lease. Pinson v. Hartsfield Int'l Comm. Ctr., Ltd. (Ga.App.1989). These are not true "piercing the corporate veil" cases.

In considering cases involving shareholder responsibility for corporate indebtedness, there should also be put aside cases where liability is imposed upon shareholders under conventional theories of contract, agency, or tort law. In other words, if individual A is personally liable for something individual B did under principles of agency, the same result should be reached if B is a corporation rather than an individual. To argue that the corporate veil is "pierced" in such cases is both unnecessary and confusing. Where the shareholder is actually acting as a principal in his own name and the corporation is acting as his agent, there is clearly liability on the obligation under simple principles of contract law. Similarly, if the shareholder is personally involved in the commission of a tort while acting as an agent for his or her corporation, she is personally liable for the tort because of her own actions and again it is unnecessary to discuss piercing the corporate veil. In this situation, usually both the actor and the corporation are personally liable as joint tort feasors.

The balance of this chapter assumes that liability is sought to be imposed on shareholders because of their ownership interest in the corporation and not because of their own conduct or the conduct of their agents.

§ 6.3   The Rhetoric of "Piercing the Corporate Veil"

The question of the status of a corporation usually arises in situations where a liability has clearly been incurred in the name of a corporation, but the corporation has become insolvent. The creditor, seeking to find a solvent defendant, may sue some or all of the shareholders, arguing that for some reason they should be called upon to pay the corporation's debts. In this situation the creditor may also sue directors, officers, and anyone else in any way connected with the corporation. The possible liabilities of directors, officers, or employees are discussed in later chapters (see particularly Chapters 11 and 14 of this Nutshell); this Chapter is limited to the possible liability of shareholders.

When the corporation is insolvent and unable to respond in damages, recovery may be sought from the shareholders. The court is then faced with the basic issue of piercing the corporate veil cases: Should the loss be imposed on third persons or on the shareholders; there is a loss and someone must pay. A blind application of the "artificial entity" approach would mean that the creditor always suffers the loss; certainly that result is often reasonable but it is not inevitable.

Most opinions by courts shed little light on the considerations governing how the piercing the corporate veil issue should be resolved. The traditional statement of the piercing corporate veil doctrine, taken from the leading case of Bartle v. Home Owners Cooperative (N.Y.1955), is that:

> The law permits the incorporation of a business for the very purpose of escaping personal liability. Generally speaking, the doctrine of "piercing the corporate veil" is invoked "to prevent fraud or to achieve equity." But in the instant case there has been neither fraud, misrepresentation nor illegality.

Such statements are unhelpful because they essentially restate the issue by using terms of uncertain content—equity, misrepresentation, fraud, or illegality.

Other tests for piercing the corporate veil also have support in the cases. Some courts have suggested that if the shareholder has exercised excessive control over the corporation and there is wrongful or inequitable conduct by the corporation, the corporation has become the "instrumentality" of the shareholder, and liability is imposed on the shareholder. Other courts have looked to see whether the corporation and shareholder have such unity of ownership and interest that they are "alter egos" and as a result "the separate existence of the corporation has ceased and recognition of the separate entity might lead to an inequitable result." Technically, "alter ego" means "other self." The problem with these tests is that they too rely on words of uncertain content: "excessive control," "wrongful or inequitable conduct," and "unity of ownership and interest."

Still other cases utilize a variety of different perjoratives (e.g., "shell," "dummy," or "fiction") rather than analysis; all of this name-calling asserts a conclusion without giving much clue as to the reasons underlying it. As early as 1926, Justice

Cardozo complained that the whole problem "is still enveloped in the mists of metaphor" and that the appropriate tests should be "honesty and justice." Berkey v. Third Avenue R. Co. (N.Y.1926).

§ 6.4 Piercing the Corporate Veil in Contract and Tort Cases

In the great bulk of cases in which piercing is sought, the corporation has virtually no assets. In these cases, a major consideration in determining whether the shareholders should be liable for losses or injuries suffered by a third party is whether the third party dealt voluntarily with the corporation or whether he or she is an involuntary creditor, typically a tort claimant. The general standards are quite different in these two types of cases.

In a contract case, the third party has usually dealt in some way with the corporation and should be aware that the corporation lacks substance. In the absence of some sort of deception, the creditor thus more or less assumed the risk of loss; if the creditor was concerned that the corporation might not be able to pay the obligation, he should insist that some solvent third person guarantee the performance by the corporation. If such a guarantee is requested and refused, the creditor may either simply forego the transaction or consciously assume the risk that the corporation may not be able to discharge its obligation by entering into the transaction anyway. Where a request for a personal guarantee is made and refused, the parties have in effect agreed upon the allocation of risk (at least in the absence of deception) and the court should not interfere with that allocation. Much the same analysis is true when no request for a guarantee is made, but the creditor simply enters into the transaction without investigation. Everyone assumes a risk when he enters into a transaction without investigation. Thus, in most contracts cases, the loss should be placed on the third person—the result actually reached in the great bulk of the contract cases by not "piercing the corporate veil."

In a tort case, on the other hand, there is usually no element of voluntary dealing (e.g. the plaintiff was trying to get out of the way of the defendant's truck). The question in these cases is whether it is reasonable for owners of a business to transfer a risk of loss or injury to members of the general public through the device of a marginally financed corporation. This logically should depend on whether the corporation was adequately financed to cover the reasonably foreseeable risks incident to the particular business the corporation is in. If the corporation was not adequately financed in this sense, there is objectionable risk shifting to members of the general public. In this regard, liability insurance should count as "capitalization" if the risk is an insurable one, since insurance makes funds available to injured tort victims just as much as equity capital does. The issues of public policy raised by tort claims thus bear little relationship to the issues raised by contract claims. This fundamental distinction, however, has not always been perceived by courts, which sometimes indiscriminately cite, and purport to apply, tort precedents in contract cases and vice versa.

These general policies do not explain all cases, but they do explain most of them. Some contracts cases involve a naïve or unsophisticated plaintiff who is duped into entering into the contract without making an investigation. Some cases of this type impose liability on the presumption that the plaintiff should be entitled to assume that a corporation has a reasonable amount of assets. Some tort cases may involve willful deception of a party to a contract; these cases are usually resolved as fraud cases, not as cases involving piercing the corporate veil.

Another class of piercing case that arises with frequency involves a corporation that conducts it business in a way that will clearly cause injury to creditors. The most common example is when the shareholders regularly make distributions of assets to themselves for their personal use, thereby rendering the corporation unable to meet its obligations to creditors. Since these cases involve direct shareholder enrichment at the expense of creditors, it is not surprising that judicial rhetoric in such cases is strong and plaintiffs usually win. Such transactions should be subject to attack as fraudulent transfers or as fraud on creditors, but in close cases courts may prefer to analyze the situation in terms of the rather vague tests of piercing the corporate veil.

Other types of misconduct by shareholders may be remedied by reliance on piercing the corporate veil theories. For example, the shareholder may mislead a third person regarding the financial status of the corporation so that the third person enters into a transaction believing the corporation has more capital than it actually has. Again this might be attacked as fraud, but shareholder liability may also be imposed on a theory of piercing the corporate veil. A similar principle may be applied if a shell corporation is substituted—without overt misrepresentation—at the last minute and the other party. is tricked into dealing with the shell corporation. Other situations involving manifest unfairness arising from unequal bargaining power but not reaching the level of unconscionability or other types of inequitable, unfair, or fraudulent conduct may also be envisioned. In the absence of any other clearly applicable theory, a court may rely on the piercing the corporate veil doctrine.

Several cases involve an oral promise by a shareholder to guarantee payment by the corporation's debt, a guarantee which itself is unenforceable under the statute of frauds. Some courts have held the shareholder liable on his promise on the theory that the "main purpose" exception to the statute of frauds is applicable. Others have imposed liability in part on a piercing the corporate veil theory.

Opinions in many cases accept the basic distinction between contract and tort, and rely on "inadequate capitalization" in holding shareholders liable for corporate tort obligations while talking about "risk assumption" in contracts cases. Cases, in either tort or contract often talk about piercing whenever recognition of the separate corporate existence will lead to "fraud" or an "unfair result" or "cause harm to innocent parties." Many cases, however, are not entirely consistent in following this distinction. Many courts, for example, list "adequate capitalization" as a factor to be considered in contracts cases. Some courts may apply a laundry list of factors to all cases indiscriminately and expressly disavow any distinction between the tests applicable in contract cases and those applicable in tort cases.

The common feature in all piercing cases is that courts agree that piercing is appropriate only when recognition of the separate corporate existence will lead to injustice or an unfair or inequitable result. This is a necessary but not a sufficient condition for imposing liability on shareholders.

There has been one empirical study of the actual outcomes of litigated piercing cases (Thompson, Piercing the Corporate Veil: An Empirical Study, 76 Cornell L.Rev. 1036 (1991). This study indicates that the corporate veil was pierced in 42 percent of the contracts cases and 31 percent of the tort cases; undercapitalization was a factor in 19 percent of the contracts cases and 13 percent of the tort cases. In this study, the results in 779 contracts cases and 226 tort cases were examined. It is likely that these results were skewed by the fact that liability insurance is often present in tort cases, and that insurance usually facilitates a settlement that involves some compensation to the injured plaintiff rather than litigation.

§ 6.5 Inadequate Capitalization

As indicated above, inadequate capitalization should be relevant primarily in tort cases, though it is often referred to (and sometimes relied upon) in contracts cases as well. The phrase "inadequate capitalization" has more than one possible meaning.

A few states require a corporation, before commencing business, to have received some minimum amount of capital, usually $1,000, for the issuance of shares. In a sense, a corporation in these states that begins business with less than $1,000 is inadequately capitalized, but that is not the usual meaning.

In the piercing area, "inadequate capitalization" usually means a capitalization that is very small in relation to the nature of the risks the business of the corporation necessarily entails. In other words it is based on likely economic needs rather than legal requirements. Thus, while the corporation need not be capitalized so as to ensure that all conceivable liabilities will be discharged, a corporation should be reasonably capitalized in light of the nature and risks of the business. This argument was accepted in the leading California case of Minton v. Cavaney (Cal.1961), and traces of it appear in opinions in several other jurisdictions. Minton v. Cavaney, like many other cases in this area, also involved another factor: a failure to complete the formation of the corporation, and the court may have been partially influenced by that factor as well. Whether a corporation is under-capitalized in the sense used here obviously presents a question of fact that turns on the nature of the business of the particular corporation.

As mentioned earlier, logically, in a tort case, liability insurance should "count" as equity capital, since it is available to compensate injured members of the general public. The leading case recognizing this principle is Radaszewski v. Telecom Corp. (8th Cir.1992). A corporation engaged in a hazardous business (such as, for example, a truck delivery service) that fails to purchase liability insurance may well thereby subject shareholders to massive personal liability on a piercing theory.

There is a serious question as to when the adequacy of capital should be measured. A corporation may be adequately capitalized initially, but then suffer unavoidable economic losses that renders the capital inadequate. Normally, adequacy should be measured at the time of formation of the corporation or perhaps at the time an existing corporation goes into a new capital-intensive or risky line of business. Assuming that an adequately capitalized corporation has suffered unavoidable losses, the general rule arguably should be that it should not be viewed as being undercapitalized. However, there appears to be scant authority, one way or the other. In any event, courts often simply evaluate the adequacy of capital at the time the transaction or accident occurred. This implicitly assumes that corporations have a duty always to maintain adequate capital for the nature of their operations, and failing to do so risks the imposition of liability on shareholders.

A particularly powerful policy argument may be made if assets that might be used for the purchase of insurance or retained in the business to increase the "creditor's cushion" are siphoned off through dividends, salaries or similar payments. This conduct is sometimes referred to as "stripping" a corporation of its assets. Stripping of assets may create the impression that corporate affairs are being conducted so as to minimize rather than maximize the assets available for tort claimants. The bounds of this policy argument are totally undefined, and as a result it seldom appears in court opinions. Indeed, it was apparently rejected in the majority opinion in a leading New York case, Walkovszky v. Carlton (N.Y.1966). Its influence, however, should not be underestimated: courts are much more likely to pierce the corporate veil and hold shareholders liable in tort cases when stripping of assets appears to have occurred. Conversely adequate capitalization and clear evidence that the corporation "did the best it could" to provide a "cushion" for creditors are likely to protect shareholders against tort claims based on the corporation's acts.

The taxicab industry has been an important source of new cases concerning shareholder responsibility for corporate tort liabilities. Particularly in New York City the practice has developed of separately incorporating one or two taxicabs in a large fleet and establishing a separate corporation to operate a central garage (and perhaps yet another corporation to run the dispatching service). Each operating taxicab company has the minimum required capitalization (usually invested in the taxicab itself) and carries the minimum liability insurance required by state law. A major cost of operating a taxicab in New York City is the cost of the medallion; medallions may be rented or leased. The taxicab while operating on the streets will almost always have a hired driver for at least part of the time. Hired drivers are almost always judgment proof. This is true even in the case of a one taxicab corporation with a single shareholder who also drives the cab. In order to make ends meet, single-owner taxicabs must usually be operated day and night. In this environment seriously injured victims of such marginal operations are usually limited in recovery to the minimum mandatory liability insurance since the corporation, the shareholders, and the hired drivers are all judgment-proof.

Not surprisingly, taxicab accident victims have often looked to the assets of shareholders who own a fleet of taxicabs even though they have separately incorporated each vehicle. The theory of "enterprise entity" discussed in section 6.8 of this Nutshell dictates that the separate existence of each minimally capitalized taxicab corporation should be ignored and the entire fleet of taxicabs should be treated as a single economic entity. The more difficult question is whether a claim may also be made asserted against the personal assets of the shareholders. In Walkovszky v. Carlton the court refused to hold a shareholder personally liable in the absence of allegations that he or she was conducting business in his or her individual capacity, and "shuttling * * * personal funds in and out of the corporations 'without regard to formality and to suit their immediate convenience.' " However, after the complaint was amended to add this specific allegation, it was upheld on a motion to dismiss and the case thereafter settled. The reluctance of the defendants to go to trial in cases of this character is understandable; most of the litigation arises on a motion to dismiss, and the cases are settled if the complaint survives that motion.

§ 6.6 Failure to Follow Corporate Formalities

Anyone reading cases dealing with shareholder liability for corporate obligations will be struck by the emphasis placed by courts on the failure to follow the requisite corporate formalities as a ground for imposing shareholder liability in both contract and tort cases. In many opinions, the court describes the failure to follow normal corporate procedures and then concludes that the corporation is the "alter ego" or "instrumentality" of the shareholder or that the "corporate veil should be pierced." There is a substantial risk that the separate existence of a corporation will be ignored if: (a) business is commenced without completing the organization of the corporation or without issuing shares and receiving the consideration therefor, (b) if shareholders' meetings or directors' meetings are not held (or consents are not signed), (c) if decisions are made by shareholders informally as though they were partners, (d) if shareholders do not sharply distinguish between corporate property and personal property, (e) if personal funds are used for corporate expenses without proper accounting, or (f) if complete corporate and financial records are not maintained. And this is only a partial list.

It is difficult to see, as a matter of logic, why comingling, confusion and informality of the types described in the preceding paragraph have been given the importance that they have. In most cases, these actions are not directly related to the claim advanced by either tort or contract plaintiffs. As a matter of fact, evidence of them is usually first found during discovery long after the transaction giving rise to the particular litigation took place. To hold shareholders personally liable because of activities that are almost always unrelated to the plaintiff's claim, creates a windfall for the plaintiff. For this reason, some courts have refused to pierce the corporate veil despite considerable evidence of confusion. One arguable justification for piercing the corporate veil in these cases is that the shareholder should not be permitted first to ignore the rules of corporate behavior and then later to claim the advantage of the corporate shield. In the absence of harm to anyone or to the state, however, it is difficult to see why the premise should lead to this conclusion.

The importance given to compliance with corporate formalities as a test for determining whether the corporation's separate existence will be recognized tends to create a trap for unwary shareholders. Shareholders in a small corporation often find managing the business a full-time occupation; formal corporate affairs such as meetings and the like are put off or ignored because there is full agreement in fact by all interested parties regarding what should be done and who should do it. The play-acting aspects of corporate meetings, elections, and the like in a closely held corporation may also strike businessmen as rather silly. Insistence by an attorney that formal corporate procedures be followed may be dismissed as a subtle attempt to obtain an additional fee. This attitude invites disaster.

When failure to follow appropriate corporate procedures tends to injure third persons, there is little objection to holding the shareholder liable. Procedures within the corporation may be so undifferentiated that a person may believe he or she is dealing with a shareholder individually rather than with the corporation. Similarly, intermingled personal and corporate assets may disappear into the personal coffers of the shareholder to the detriment of corporate creditors. Corporate assets may be used to pay personal obligations of the shareholders. These factors, however, are present in only a small minority of cases involving failure to follow corporate formalities.

§ 6.7   Parent–Subsidiary Cases

Many cases in which shareholder liability has been found concern shareholders that are themselves corporations. In these cases, a parent corporation is being held liable for the debts of a subsidiary. They have a somewhat different flavor than cases in which the shareholder defendant is an individual, and some cases even suggest that different tests are being applied depending on whether the defendant is an individual or a corporation. When a corporation is the defendant, only another business is being held responsible for the debt; when an individual is the defendant, however, personal liability extending to non-business assets is being imposed. There is therefore a widespread belief that piercing may be easier when the shareholder is a corporation rather than an individual. However, the one empirical study of the actual results reached in litigated cases indicates that this belief may be mistaken; that study indicates that corporate shareholders were held liable in 28 percent of the litigated cases while individual shareholders were held liable in about 40 percent of the litigated cases.

Many corporations create subsidiary corporations to operate and manage separate businesses without giving serious thought about limiting liability. However, that is often not true. If the new business involves significant risks, the parent corporation may well decide to form a subsidiary in an effort to assure that its core assets will not be subject to additional risks.

It may be observed that an overly-generous application of the piercing doctrine in parent/subsidiary cases may deter the creation of new businesses if the parent corporation cannot be reasonably assured that the separate corporate entity of the subsidiary will be respected.

Corporate shareholders have been held liable for subsidiary obligations in a number of situations:

(a) When the subsidiary is being operated in an "unfair manner," e.g., the terms of transactions between parent and subsidiary are set so that profits accumulate in the parent and losses in the subsidiary;

(b) When the subsidiary is consistently represented as being a part of the parent, e.g., as a "division" or "local office" rather than as a subsidiary;

(c) When the separate corporate formalities of the subsidiary are not followed;

(d) When the subsidiary and parent are operating essentially parts of the same integrated business, and the subsidiary is undercapitalized; and

(e) When there is no consistent clear delineation of which transactions are the parent's and which are the subsidiary's.

The maintenance of a consistent delineation between the parent's affairs and the subsidiary's affairs may be somewhat complex as a practical matter. Often the individual acting for the subsidiary is also acting as an agent of the parent in the same or related matters. If the "hat" the agent is wearing is not clear, the argument may be made that she was actually acting on behalf of the parent rather than on behalf of the subsidiary or, quite possibly, on behalf of both corporations. These cases may impose liability in terms of agency rather than piercing the corporate veil. In any event it is clear that the probability of parental liability increases significantly whenever there are close relationships, informality of operation, and overlapping of personnel employed by the corporations.

In many instances, ties between parent and subsidiary are inherently very close. Not only does the parent own all the shares of the subsidiary, but the two corporations may be housed in the same plant or offices. They often have common officers, employees, auditors and attorneys. They may file consolidated returns for federal income tax purposes. Such close ties of course are not necessarily inconsistent with the separate existence of the subsidiary. Problems arise from carelessness and casualness. Transactions between parent and subsidiary may not be adequately documented on the theory that "the money goes to the same place anyway." Common officers and directors may not specify on whose behalf specific action is taken. Independent books and records may not be maintained for each corporation. The parent may not recognize that the subsidiary is theoretically an independent entity with its own board of directors and managers. Very commonly, the board of directors of the parent may make detailed decisions on behalf of the subsidiary when in theory the decisions should have been made by the board of directors of the subsidiary.

Of course, in some cases the failure to delineate between operations of the parent and the subsidiary may actually mislead third persons into believing they are dealing with the parent corporate entity when in fact they are dealing with a subsidiary. Cases, however, tend to impose liability whenever intermingling is present on a wide scale without inquiring specifically whether the plaintiff was actually misled. As a result it is important in every "family" of corporations to maintain the maximum possible degree of separation.

Intermingling of assets on an informal basis is particularly dangerous. Separate accounts may be maintained, but informal transfers or unrecorded "loans" may be made from time to time to meet the day-to-day needs of the subsidiary's business. Such conduct unnecessarily increases the risk that the two corporations will be treated as a single entity. If funds owned by the parent are needed by the subsidiary, the proper procedure is to establish a formal loan, preferably using a promissory note, and then to transfer the funds to the subsidiary's bank account. The corporate books of both parent and subsidiary then reflect the transaction accurately and the risk that the intermingling of assets will result in the two corporations being treated as one is reduced.

Many large corporations with numerous subsidiaries have established centralized cash management plans. Each subsidiary is required to transfer all cash on a daily or overnight basis to a central account managed by the parent. Cash management plans permit the centralized management and investment of funds. It also permits the parent corporation to obtain a more favorable return than the subsidiaries could obtain individually and eliminates the possibility that funds may be kept in non-interest bearing accounts. Each subsidiary may draw on its funds deposited in this account on a daily basis as needed for its operations. If the cash management plan is properly approved and accurate records of all transfers of cash in both directions are kept, these plans do not involve the kind of intermingling that gives rise to potential liability. The leading case so holding is Fletcher v. Atex, Inc. (2d Cir.1995).

Other common features of a parent/subsidiary "family," are participation in a single employee retirement plan, a centralized accounting and legal staff, and centralized control over the raising of capital. These features also should not give rise to an inference that the separate existence of corporate subsidiaries should be ignored.

§ 6.8　The Concept of "Enterprise Entity"

"Enterprise entity" refers to the economic unity that is a single business enterprise. Courts are suspicious of attempts to divide what is essentially a single economic enterprise among several different corporations with the intention of minimizing the assets subject to claims of creditors of each enterprise. Perhaps this is because it is not "playing fair" with creditors who may reasonably believe that a single economic enterprise is the corporate entity; in any event, courts may well "put the enterprise back together" despite the shareholders' attempt to segregate it into separate corporate entities. In this kind of case, a "brother-sister" corporate relationship may be ignored as readily as a parent-subsidiary relationship. Indeed, an empirical study of litigated cases discovered a number of instances in which brother-sister enterprises were combined into a single unit for liability purposes.

Many large corporations are conglomerates consisting of several essentially discrete and independent businesses. The concept of enterprise entity does not apply to these operations. What is dangerous is taking a single business and separately incorporating its component operations. Of course, if one or more independent businesses are conducted as divisions of the parent corporation and are not separately incorporated, the parent is liable in all events for the debts of those divisions.

§ 6.9 Choice of Law and "Piercing the Corporate Veil"

Until about 1980, the law of "piercing the corporate veil" appeared to be independent of the state in which the case arose. Courts resolving piercing cases freely cited cases from other jurisdictions without inquiry into whether different states were more liberal or less liberal in imposing, or had different rules about, shareholder liability for corporate obligations. Indeed, the tests and rhetoric used by courts were so vague and amorphous that differences in formulation, even if they had existed, would have had little or no effect on the results reached. Thus, in the few cases in which courts did discuss whether the law of the state of incorporation or the law of the state in which the activities giving rise to the claim should apply, a definitive resolution of this conflicts issue was found to be unnecessary.

In recent years different state policies or philosophies with respect to the imposition of shareholder liability have appeared. Some states now seem clearly to be more "liberal" than others in imposing such liability. Some states have accepted the distinction between tort and contract cases suggested above while others have not. Texas has partially codified its law of piercing the corporate veil by enacting a statute that provides that (1) in contract cases "actual fraud" for the personal benefit of the shareholder is required for the imposition of liability, and (2) failure to follow corporate formalities or procedures is never an independent ground for imposing such liability. A number of states have created a "laundry list" of factors to be considered in piercing the corporate veil cases, and apparently have adopted a mechanical test of piercing the corporate whenever the number of factors favoring piercing exceed the number of factors that do not. The development of such identifiably different principles by specific states means that the conflicts of law issue must be addressed.

Many corporations are of course incorporated in Delaware and conduct their business primarily or entirely in other states. The Delaware position with respect to "veil piercing" has been described as very conservative: Persons seeking to pierce have a "heavy burden," and the separate existence of corporations will be recognized in the absence of fraud.

A plausible argument may be made that the law of the state of incorporation should apply to the piercing issue under the generally accepted rule that "internal affairs" of corporations are to be governed by the law of the state of incorporation. The scope of shareholder liability for corporate obligations plausibly seems to involve "internal affairs." Indeed, Texas has a statute that states explicitly that the responsibility of shareholders for corporate obligations of foreign corporations qualified to transact business in Texas is to be governed by the state of incorporation.

On the other hand, there may be a strong policy in favor of applying the law of the state with the most significant contacts with the litigation, particularly in torts cases. The Restatement of Conflict of Laws sets forth this as the applicable general principle. Consider, for example, a Delaware corporation that is wholly owned by Illinois residents; the corporation's entire business is conducted in Illinois, and a resident of Illinois is injured because of the negligence of the agents of the corporation who are Illinois residents. Certainly a plausible argument may be made that Illinois law rather than Delaware law should be applied since all the important contacts are with Illinois and not with Delaware. If Illinois law would permit "piercing" under the circumstances, it is probably unlikely that an Illinois court would deprive an Illinois resident of a remedy against another Illinois resident merely because the corporation was formed in Delaware and that state has a very conservative piercing rule.

§ 6.10 The Federal Law of "Piercing the Corporate Veil"

An issue that is related to the choice of law issue discussed in section 6.9 is whether there is a federal law of piercing the corporate veil that is applicable in suits in which the United States is a party.

Clearfield Trust Co. v. United States (S.Ct.1943), held that federal law should govern questions involving the rights of the United States arising from nationwide federal programs. Federal courts have held, for example, that in a suit to recover overpayments from a provider of services under the Medicare Program, a federal law of piercing the corporate veil should be fashioned to determine whether shareholders of the provider are personally liable for such overpayments. Other cases agree with this general approach. In fashioning federal law in this area, courts have generally relied on piercing cases that were in the federal courts because of diversity of citizenship. As a result, the federal law of "piercing" probably does not differ significantly from state law in most respects.

Mention should also be made of the Comprehensive Environmental Response, Compensation and Liability Act (CERCLA). This statute imposes broad responsibility for cleaning up toxic waste sites on both present and former "owners" and "operators" of the site. Early cases were in basic conflict over the relationship between the piercing the corporate veil doctrine and the liability of "owners" and "operators." There were three different approaches. (1) The "actual control" test stated that a parent corporation could be held liable as an "operator" of a facility owned by its subsidiary where the parent was "actively involved in the regular operations" of the site. (2) The "authority to control" test imposed liability upon the parent corporation more broadly whenever it had a sufficient ownership interest in the subsidiary that gave it authority to control the operation. In some cases, courts imposed liability under this test only where there was some "nexus" between this authority and the actual operation of the site. (3) The pure "piercing the corporate veil" test imposed liability on the parent only when the subsidiary's corporate veil could be pierced under traditional, i.e. non-CERCLA, principles.

The Supreme Court of the United States gave much needed guidance in this area in its opinion in United States v. Bestfoods (S.Ct.1998). This opinion reaffirmed that CERCLA liability could be imposed on the parent corporation if the corporate veil of its subsidiary could be pierced under applicable state law principles. The opinion then addresses the possibility that a parent corporation might be liable as an "operator" of the site. Such a liability may be imposed, the Court concluded, only if the parent corporation was involved in the operation of the site itself. It was not sufficient that the parent corporation was involved only in the operation of the subsidiary itself. Thus, no parental liability would arise if the parent's activities do not go beyond the normal relationships between parent and subsidiary. If the parent becomes involved in the operation of the site itself, it becomes an "operator" under CERCLA.

§ 6.11 Reverse Piercing

Most cases involve efforts by a creditor to hold the shareholder responsible for corporate obligations. In some cases, the shoe is on the other foot. A shareholder argues in a suit against a third party defendant that the separate existence of their own corporation should be ignored. The classic case is Cargill, Inc. v. Hedge (Minn.1985), where a farming family created a corporation to own the land and buildings that comprised their farm. When the Hedge family ran into financial difficulty, a creditor obtained a judgment and sought to execute on the land. Minnesota has a statute that provides an exemption from execution of farm property owned by individual farmers. In order to avoid the forced sale of their farm, the Hedges argued that the separate existence of their corporation should be ignored, and they should be entitled to the exemption. Based on the strong Minnesota public policy favoring protection of family farms from execution sale, the Minnesota court applied a "reverse pierce" principle to protect the family, but the court cautioned that this principle should be available only in "carefully limited circumstances." Other examples of "reverse piercing" exist.

Some courts have expressed skepticism about the reverse pierce doctrine, arguing in effect that if a person forms a corporation, he should be expected to "take the bitter with the sweet," and not be able to disclaim the corporate existence when it is in his interest to do so. In Sims v. Western Waste Industries (Tex.App.1996), the court refused to allow a parent corporation to take advantage of the immunity to direct suit that the Workmen's Compensation statute provided to its wholly owned subsidiary. The court stated, "we are persuaded that the legislature never intended parent corporations, who deliberately chose to establish a subsidiary corporation, to be allowed to assert immunity under the Texas Worker' Compensation Act by reverse piercing of the corporate veil they themselves established. WWI has accepted the benefits of establishing a subsidiary corporation in Texas and will not be allowed to disregard that entity now that it is to their gain to do so."

All in all, this doctrine should be viewed to have doubtful validity.

§ 6.12   "Piercing the Corporate Veil" to Further Public Policy

Yet another type of piercing the corporate veil case involves the claim that a separate corporate existence should not be recognized because to do so would violate a clearly defined statutory policy.

To take an illustrative case, the statutes of several states formerly prohibited branch banking. In other words in these states a banking corporation had to stick to a single location and could not open branches around the state. Accepting this statutory policy, may a banking corporation own the voting stock of another bank? Or, may a single holding corporation own a majority of, or all, the voting stock of several banks? Answers to questions such as these must be based on an evaluation of the strength of the state policy against branch banking rather than on policies underlying the separate existence of corporations. If the policy is a strong one, the recognition of a separate corporate existence may provide an unacceptable method of circumvention, and the separate corporate fiction must yield to the state policy. On the other hand, if the policy against branch banking was not a strong one, there was no reason for courts to find a fundamental conflict between the statute and the corporate form and hold invalid relationships that conform to the notion of separate corporate existence.

Public policy is also the critical question in cases involving family corporations organized to obtain social security or unemployment benefits for owners who would not be eligible for such benefits if the business had continued to be conducted in noncorporate form. Several federal decisions have held that social security benefits may not be denied to a person who "incorporates" his or her business assets and becomes an employee of the corporation for the sole purpose of qualifying for the benefits. Decisions at the state level concerning temporary disability insurance, workmen's compensation, and unemployment compensation, however, are split. A clearer example involves the unemployment compensation statutes that provide for an exemption from the tax for employers having fewer than some designated number of employees. May a single business be divided into several separate corporate units each employing less than the statutory minimum to obtain the exemption for each? Courts have held, not surprisingly, that the state unemployment commissions may disregard the separate corporations, treat the business as a single unit, and impose the tax on it.

Generalization is difficult in such cases. Sometimes, assistance may be gained from statutory language that indicates that the policy should be applied to "direct or indirect" relationships. Nevertheless, delicate judgments are required in these cases, for the policies underlying regulatory statutes must be weighed against the policies supporting the concept of the corporate entity.

§ 6.13 "Piercing the Corporate Veil" in Taxation and Bankruptcy

Given the broad social and governmental policies involved in the federal income tax laws and the federal bankruptcy act, it is understandable that specialized tests have evolved under these statutes for determining when the separate corporate existence will be disregarded.

Under the Internal Revenue Code of 1954 there is a need to preserve tax revenue and to set aside fictitious transactions that have as their sole purpose the minimization of taxes. A corporation's separate existence generally will be recognized for tax purposes if it is in fact carrying on a bona fide business and is not merely a device created for the purpose of avoiding taxes. The taxpayer, however, must accept any tax disadvantages of the corporate form if he or she has elected to choose that form. Further, even if the corporate form is adopted and carefully followed, the Commissioner has broad powers to disallow deductions or exemptions, or reallocate items of income to clearly reflect income.

Entirely different policies are involved in the bankruptcy area. Bankruptcy courts have considerable flexibility in dealing with controlling or dominant shareholders of bankrupt corporations. The bankruptcy court may:

(1) "Disregard the corporate entity" and hold the shareholder personally liable for the corporation's debts if the shareholder's conduct permits the court to pierce the corporate veil. The effect of this conclusion is that the controlling shareholder may be personally responsible for all corporate obligations; all payments made by the corporation to the

shareholder before bankruptcy may also be recovered by the trustee since essentially the corporation and shareholder are treated as a single unit.

(2) Refuse to recognize claims by shareholders against the corporation as bona fide debts provable in bankruptcy. If the claim is based on services or intangible benefits provided to the corporation, the claim may be disallowed in its entirety as fictitious or "not proved." If it involves infusions of capital or tangible property through loans, the bankruptcy court may consider them as contributions to capital rather than as debt. This treatment of shareholder debt is usually limited to loans made at or shortly after the formation of the corporation when the corporation is inadequately or thinly capitalized, and simply reflects that what in fact was equity capital should be treated as equity capital in bankruptcy proceedings. A number of decisions follow this approach and there are analogous holdings in the tax field. Yet the application of this principle is elusive. There is no easy way to determine when a corporation is in fact under-capitalized. Most courts have treated the issue on an "all or none" basis and reclassified all the debt as equity even though it is arguable that the court should reclassify only that portion necessary to make the capitalization adequate.

As a general matter, the original capitalization of a corporation should be viewed to be adequate if it is able to borrow the balance of the needed capital from independent sources of funds. Similarly, if the shareholder rather than a bank makes the loan under identical circumstances, the transaction should also be viewed as a bona fide loan.

(3) Under the "Deep Rock" doctrine (named for the Deep Rock Oil Corp., the subsidiary involved in the leading case of Taylor v. Standard Gas & Electric Co. (S.Ct.1939)), the bankruptcy court may subordinate claims presented by a control-

ling shareholder to claims of other creditors or preferred shareholders if the shareholder acted inequitably or unfairly. Examples of inequitable claims include taking unreasonable amounts as salary, manipulation of the affairs of the corporation in disregard of standards of honesty, or selling assets to the corporation at inflated prices. The type of conduct that will result in subordination under the Deep Rock doctrine can only be stated in general terms since the doctrine is based on general principles of equity and fair dealing. It is not necessary to show that the indebtedness was a sham or fiction, since technically what is involved is only "the order of payment of debts" and not an outright rejection of a claim. The theory is that a person who has acted unfairly in his or her management of the corporation should step aside so that other creditors may be first satisfied. Of course, the assets of a bankrupt estate will be inadequate to satisfy all claims; subordination therefore usually results in the shareholder receiving nothing on his or her claim. Despite this underlying theory, in at least one case the Deep Rock doctrine was applied when the controversy was between innocent creditors of the bankrupt subsidiary and the equally innocent creditors of the bankrupt parent.

The type of conduct that triggers these doctrines differs only in degree rather than kind. In a sense these are alternative weapons in the bankruptcy court's arsenal.

§ 6.14   Other Generalizations About "Piercing the Corporate Veil"

Three final observations should be made about the confusing and result-oriented doctrines discussed in this chapter. First, there is no inherent reason to assume that ignoring the separate corporate existence must be an all-or-nothing affair. Particularly if the dominant question does not involve public statutory policies but merely liability for corporate obligations, a corporation may be viewed as existing for some purposes but not for others. There is some case authority, for example, for piercing the corporate veil to hold shareholders active in the business personally liable, but recognizing the same corporation's separate existence to protect passive investors from the same liabilities. Second, there is a strong judicial feeling that when a person elects to do business in corporate form he or she must take the bitter with the sweet, and cannot later argue that the separate corporate existence should be ignored when it is to his or her benefit. Except in the rare "reverse pierce" cases (see § 6.11) the doctrine of piercing the corporate veil is not available for the benefit of shareholders, but only against shareholders. This view is particularly strongly developed in the tax cases. Finally, where the considerations are not strongly weighted one way or the other, a presumption of separate existence of the corporation should be respected. The fiction of separate corporate existence, in other words, should be the rule not the exception.

[For unfamiliar terms see the Glossary]

CHAPTER SEVEN

FINANCING THE CORPORATION

§ 7.1 Introduction

Perhaps no other area of corporation law is more confusing and mysterious to law students without prior business backgrounds than corporate securities and related subjects: shares of "common" and "preferred" stock, par value, "watered" stock, preemptive rights, bonds, debentures, and so forth. The language is new and unfamiliar, the concepts seem mysterious and sometimes illogical, and everything seems to build on historical concepts of dubious relevance today.

This chapter attempts to dispel the mystery. It deals with several basic topics. The first is the issuance of common shares by a corporation. Historically, this has been a relatively complex subject but the Model Business Corporation has greatly simplified the process. The second deals with the use of debt in the capitalization of the corporation. This is part of a subject that is often described as "corporation finance," a description of the ways modern business obtains the capital it needs in order to operate. The latter subject can become exceptionally complex; only a general introduction to basic concepts is discussed in this chapter. The third principal topic is an introduction to the world of senior securities: Preferred stock, bonds, and debentures.

§ 7.2   Common Stock: The Basic Definition

Shares of common stock are the fundamental units into which the proprietary interest of the corporation is divided. If a corporation issues only one class of shares, they may be referred to by a variety of similar names: common shares, capital stock, common stock, or, possibly, simply "shares" or "stock." Whatever the name, they are the basic proprietary units of ownership and are referred to here as simply common stock.

Section 6.01(b) of the MBCA (1984) defines the two fundamental characteristics of common stock. They are (1) the right to vote for the election of directors and on other matters, and (2) the right to receive the net assets of the corporation (after making allowance for debts and senior securities) when distributions are to be made. One innovation of the MBCA (1984) is that it permits these two fundamental characteristics to be divided or split among different classes of stock (so there may not be a single class that has both of these residual characteristics and, therefore, no class of stock that is unambiguously common stock). However, section 6.03(b) requires that at least one share of each class with these basic attributes be outstanding at all times. It is relatively uncommon to divide these basic attributes; the typical arrangement is that there is a single class of common shares that possess both of the described characteristics.

Traditionally, shares of stock of all types are represented by certificates issued by the corporation in the names of the owners. Stock certificates and modern substitutes are described in Chapter Nine of this Nutshell.

§ 7.3 Common Stock: Authorized and Issued Shares

Assuming that a new corporation is going to have only a single class of shares, the articles of incorporation must state the number of shares of stock the corporation is authorized to issue. This number is known, not surprisingly, as the corporation's "authorized capital" or "authorized stock." (In states with older statutes, the articles of incorporation must also set forth the "par value" of the authorized shares or a statement that the shares are "without par value." The significance of "par value" is discussed in sections 7.5–7.8 of this chapter.)

There is no statutory limitation on the number of shares that may be authorized by a corporation and no requirement that all or any specific fraction of the authorized shares be actually issued. Why, then, doesn't every corporation simply authorize millions or billions of shares, and then issue only the number desired? There are practical constraints. Some states impose franchise or stock taxes on the basis of authorized shares; in these states to authorize many more shares than there is any intention to issue simply increases taxes with no offsetting benefit. Also, authorizing a large number of shares may create concern on the part of prospective investors since authorized shares may be later sold at bargain prices set by the board of directors without shareholder approval. On the other hand, it is generally believed desirable to authorize at least some additional shares over and above what is immediately planned to be issued to take into account unexpected contingencies and to avoid the need for amending articles of incorporation if more shares are later needed.

The "capitalization" of a corporation is based on the number of shares actually issued and the capital received therefor, not on the number of authorized shares. Capital received in exchange for common shares is usually referred to as the corporation's invested capital (or sometimes its "contributed" or "permanent" capital) and is viewed as being invested in the corporation indefinitely.

§ 7.4   Common Stock: The Price at Which Shares Are Issued

Let us first consider the simplest possible situation: A newly formed corporation is authorized to issue 1,000 shares of common stock and it has been agreed that the two investors, A and B, will each contribute $5,000 for 50 percent of the stock. How many shares should be issued and at what price? Decisions relating to the initial capitalization of a new corporation are typically made in advance by the promoters, the incorporators or the initial board of directors of the corporation. After the corporation is formed, subsequent decisions to sell additional shares at specified prices are almost always made by the board of directors. Many state statutes authorize the shareholders to reserve this power to themselves by appropriate provision in the articles of incorporation. See MBCA (1984) § 6.21(a). As a practical matter, it is unusual for the shareholders to reserve this power to themselves; the board of directors normally determines how many additional shares should be sold and sets the prices at which they are to be issued.

Within a broad range, the number of shares and price per share initially can be set at any level. For example A and B might purchase one share each for $5,000, or 10 shares each for $500 per share, or 100 shares each for $50 per share. It is important, of course, that A and B each pay the same amount for each share and receive the same number of shares; however, as between themselves it makes no difference what that amount is per share. It would be undesirable, however, to issue 500 shares each at $10 per share, since that would exhaust the entire authorized capital and would require an amendment to the articles of incorporation if more capital was needed at a later date.

In this simple example it is assumed that the two shareholders have agreed in advance each to contribute $5,000 in cash. Either or both might contribute property or even services so long as the parties agree as to the value of that property or services. However, it is not essential that all shares be issued at the same price. If A were issued 100 shares at $50 per share and B 100 shares at $40 per share each would own 50 percent of the outstanding shares of the corporation. However, A's interest has been "diluted," since the corporation has only $9,000 of assets, so that A has paid $5,000 for an interest that is worth only $4,500. Why might A agree to do this? One possibility is there may be a side agreement under which B has agreed to provide services or other benefits to the corporation in the future that are difficult to value, and which the parties believe will be roughly worth the $1,000 difference.

The possibility of inadvertent dilution is obviously increased when one or more investors are contributing property or services rather than cash. After a corporation has commenced business it may need additional capital. If it decides to raise this capital by selling additional common shares, the pricing of the shares becomes more sensitive. If too low a price is set, the interest of the original shareholders will be diluted. However, as a practical matter if a corporation can sell additional shares shortly after commencing business, it is likely that its prospects will be bright and the new shares may therefore command a premium.

If only common sense were involved, the pricing of common shares would end at this point. However, the par value statutes in effect in many states impose an elaborate system of additional rules relating to the issuance of common shares. Even in states where par value is optional, many lawyers continue to use traditional par value concepts when forming a corporation. Par value rules have substantive as well as accounting implications even for apparently simple transactions. These rules dealing with par value are the subject of the following six sections.

One of the major innovations of the 1984 Model Business Corporation Act was the elimination of par value and the numerous consequences of this concept. These innovations simplified the capitalization of a new corporation to the point where it is often no more complex than the example given above. As of January 1, 1998, twenty-eight states have adopted the Model Act approach in this regard. However, many commercially important states, including Delaware, New York, Illinois, Texas, and California, retain par value concepts.

§ 7.5 Common Shares: Par Value and "Watered" Stock

Older state statutes assume that all shares will have a "par value" or "stated value" (which is the same thing). [Most of these traditional statutes also authorize a corporation to issue shares that are expressly "no par" shares or shares "without par value;" these shares, however, when issued under a par value regime are governed by complex rules very different from the simple principles established by the 1984 Model Act. See § 7.7.]

Par value of a share of common stock is simply a dollar amount designated as par value by the draftsman of the articles of incorporation. It may be one hundred dollars, ten dollars, one dollar, ten cents, one cent, one mil, whatever the draftsman designates. The par value designation is made in the articles of incorporation and is part of the fundamental description of the shares of stock. A typical provision describing par value stock is "The number of shares the corporation is authorized to issue is 1,000 shares of common stock with the par value of $10.00 per share and 500 shares of preferred stock with the par value of $100 per share."

To emphasize the basic nature of par value, each stock certificate issued by a corporation refers conspicuously to the par value of the shares. Indeed, certificates usually describe the type of stock, e.g. "common shares," and the par value in large and conspicuous type.

The use of par value goes back to medieval times. Originally par value was widely viewed as the amount for which the shares would be issued. Shares with a par value of one hundred dollars per share could be subscribed for at one hundred dollars per share with confidence that all other identical shares would also be issued for $100 per share. Par value was particularly useful in situations where a promoter was dealing with potential investors one by one. If the investor paid the par value of $100 per share, he could be confident that other investors will have paid the same amount, and his interest will not be diluted.

Today, par value serves a different function. It is in no way an indication of the price at which most shares are issued. However, it creates one basic rule about setting the price for shares of common stock with a par value: *the price per share must always be equal to or greater than the par value.* It is common today to use a "nominal" par value, say one dollar per share, and then issue shares for a price considerably higher than par value, say ten dollars per share.

Stock issued for less than par value is called "watered" stock. In most states an investor who purchases watered stock is automatically liable to the corporation for the difference between par value and what he actually paid. This "watered stock" liability is discussed in greater detail in § 7.9 of this Nutshell and is clearly a trap for the unwary or unsophisticated. Many investors are not aware of this potential liability until long after they purchased "watered" shares, and discover, to their regret, that they are personally liable to the corporation for some additional amount.

Par value can be viewed as a public representation that shares will be issued for not less than that value. The public nature of this representation means that anyone who purchased shares from the corporation for less than par value can later be called upon by corporate creditors to make good his representation and pay in the additional amount needed to equal par value. This is true even though the "contract" between the corporation and the shareholder may have been to the contrary.

There are several reasons why modern practice has moved to the use of nominal par value and away from the older practice of treating par value as the purchase price of shares. One factor is that it reduces the risk of inadvertently issuing watered stock. Another is that a high par value limits flexibility in the subsequent pricing of shares. If a public market for shares of the corporation develops, the corporation, when raising additional capital by selling shares, in effect competes with that market. If a high par value of $100 per share, say, is established, the corporation would have to stop selling shares when the market price of the previously-issued shares drops below $100 per share. At that point potential investors can get a better price in the public market than they can from the corporation which is locked into the $100 price by the par value. A third factor of largely historical importance was the federal documentary stamp tax on issuance of corporate securities (since repealed) which was based on the par value rather than the sales price or actual value of the shares. A nominal par value thus reduced federal stamp taxes. State franchise and stock transfer taxes also were (and to a limited extent still are) based on par or stated value; in these states a low par value again reduces the corporation's tax liability. High par value also creates a problem where property of uncertain value is being contributed by an investor. If high par value shares are given in exchange for such property, arguments may later arise that the property was in fact not worth the par value of the shares received and the recipients may have received watered stock. See § 7.9 of this Nutshell.

These various reasons provide adequate practical justification for always using nominal par value rather than high par value shares. Further, there is very little to be gained from using high par value shares; one arguable advantage is possible benefits to the corporation because psychologically investors or creditors may feel more secure dealing with a corporation with a high par value stock. Such an advantage is not very persuasive, however, since there is no reason to believe that investors or creditors pay much attention to par value one way or the other. In any event there has been a virtually universal shift by sophisticated corporation lawyers away from the use of high par value shares in favor of nominal par value shares.

§ 7.6   Common Shares: Par Value and the Capital Accounts of the Corporation

Par value serves an important function in addition to establishing a price floor below which shares may not be issued: It is an essential ingredient in determining the capital accounts of the corporation. In this and the following sections, the terminology of the 1969 Model Business Corporation Act will be followed. While not all states with par value statutes use this terminology, most states do (and those that do not embody similar concepts).

In order to understand "stated capital" and "capital surplus" and the issues that evolve from them, a brief excursion into fundamental accounting concepts is necessary. The basic syllogism or truism on which financial statements are based is that *net worth* equals *assets* minus *liabilities*. That syllogism is obviously true for an individual such as you or me; it is equally applicable to a corporation that is treated as an entity or fictitious person. By simple arithmetical manipulation of the basic syllogism, *assets* also equal *liabilities* plus *net worth*. This is the formula used in a "balance sheet" where the assets are placed on the left side and liabilities and net worth are placed on the right side of a ledger.

Assets	Liabilities + Net Worth

A balance sheet balances because it is simply a restatement of the basic equation.

Let us examine a balance sheet for a new corporation immediately after it has sold 100 shares of stock for 1,000 dollars in cash. The balance sheet shows:

Assets		Liabilities	–0–
Cash	$1,000	Net Worth	
	_____	Common Stock	$1,000
	$1,000		$1,000

The concepts of stated capital and capital surplus relate to how the common stock item is shown on the right hand side of the balance sheet. "Stated capital" is defined to be the aggregate par value of all issued shares (plus or minus certain adjustments not relevant for present purposes) while "capital surplus" is defined to be the excess (if any) of capital contributed over the par value. Thus, if in our hypothetical the 100 shares of common stock had a par value of $1 per share and were sold at $10.00 per share the balance sheet would be as follows:

Assets		Liabilities	–0–
Cash	$1,000	Capital Accounts	
		Stated Capital	$ 100
		Capital Surplus	$ 900
	$1,000		$1,000

In this balance sheet, the phrase "capital accounts" has been substituted for "net worth" to somewhat more closely reflect accounting terminology, but its meaning is the same.

Under par value statutes, there is no requirement today that any specific minimum amount be put in in the form of stated capital. Several states establish a minimum capitalization requirement of $1,000 (or some other amount), but these states require only an aggregate capital of the specified amount without differentiating between how much should be stated capital and how much should be capital surplus. Thus, it is theoretically possible to create a corporation with $0.01 of stated capital and $999.99 of capital surplus.

Now, a logical question that may be asked is what difference does it make if the capital contribution is recorded as stated capital or capital surplus? Rather surprisingly it does make a difference, which can best be appreciated if we first draw up a balance sheet after the corporation (1) has borrowed $1,000 from a bank and (2) has had two years of operations during which it has earned and accumulated an aggregate of $2,000 over-and-above all costs, taxes, etc. Further, for simplicity we will continue to assume that all of the assets are held by the corporation in the form of cash. The balance sheet looks like this:

Assets		Liabilities	$1,000
Cash	$4,000	Capital Accounts	
		Stated Capital	100
		Capital Surplus	900
		Earned Surplus	$2,000
	$4,000		$4,000

At this point the shareholders decide they want to distribute to themselves some or all of the $4,000. If the balance sheet is to continue to balance, every dollar taken from the left-hand column must obviously be reflected by the reduction of a right-hand column entry. The right-hand entries thus in effect limit or monitor the distribution of assets from the left-hand column. For example, as described in a later chapter, under the 1969 Model Act dividends may be lawfully paid only "out of" earned surplus. This means that amounts may be paid from the cash of the corporation as dividends up to the maximum amount shown in the right-hand column under "earned surplus," or $2,000 in the above example. Of course, a dividend of, say, $500 paid out of earned surplus would in the above example result in the reduction of cash by $500 to $3500, a reduction of earned surplus to $1,500, and the balance sheet still balances.

So far as distributions from capital is concerned, corporations have greater freedom to make distributions from capital surplus than from stated capital. The basic concept is that stated capital is "locked in" the corporation and cannot be distributed at all except upon the liquidation of the corporation; however, assets may be distributed to the extent of capital surplus simply with the approval of the holders of a specified fraction of the common shares. Such a distribution is not a dividend in the normal sense of the word but is called by various names, e.g., "liquidating dividend," "distribution in partial liquidation," or the like. (See § 18.1 of this Nutshell.) In addition, capital surplus (but not stated capital) may be used to repurchase or redeem outstanding shares previously issued by the corporation. (See § 18.6 of this Nutshell.)

If all the capital is put in the form of stated capital (i.e. the par value of the issued shares equals the consideration received) all the capital is "locked in;" if the bulk of the capital contributed is recorded as capital surplus rather than stated capital there is greater flexibility to distribute unneeded capital to shareholders or reacquire outstanding shares at a later date. In other words, there is greater flexibility in a corporation with this balance sheet:

Cash	$1,000	Liabilities	–0–
		Capital Accounts	
		Stated Capital	$ 100
		Capital Surplus	900
	1,000		1,000

than there is in a corporation with this balance sheet:

Cash	$1,000	Liabilities	–0–
		Capital Accounts	
		Stated Capital	$1,000
		Capital Surplus	–0–
	1,000		1,000

From the corporation's standpoint such flexibility is a mildly positive feature and is an additional reason for the widespread use of nominal par value which leads to low stated capital and high capital surplus. Of course, a subsequent creditor would prefer that all of the initial capital be in the form of stated capital so that no capital distributions could be made. The permanent capital of the corporation forms a "cushion" for creditors and increases the probability that the corporation will be able to repay loans when they come due. One should not make too much of this point, however, because lenders usually do not rely on the corporation statutes for protection against unwise distribution policies; they usually insist on contractual restrictions on distributions of assets to shareholders. (See § 18.7 of this Nutshell.) These restrictions are required so routinely by lenders that they have become the principal operative restriction on the freedom of corporations to distribute their capital to their shareholders.

§ 7.7 Common Stock: No Par Shares in a Par Value Regime

Historically, corporations were only permitted to issue shares with par value. No par shares in a par value regime are a relatively recent innovation, first permitted in New York in about 1915. The rules relating to no par shares were developed in the context of the established rules for accounting for par value shares. Obviously, the consideration for which no par shares are issued may be set without any reference to a minimum imposed by a par value. However, the capital received must still be allocated between stated capital and capital surplus. When no par shares are issued under most state statutes based on the old Model Business Corporation Act, the entire consideration fixed by the corporation for the shares constitutes stated capital. However, statutes generally permit the directors to allocate some portion or all of the consideration to capital surplus. Before 1969, the old Model Business Corporation Act limited this power to 25 per cent of the consideration received for shares, but par value states have generally eliminated this restriction. Most states today permit allocation of "any part" of the consideration received for no par shares to either stated capital or capital surplus. Under such a provision it is possible to create a corporation with as little stated capital by using no par shares as by using nominal par value shares.

For many years no par shares suffered from a tax disadvantage in that federal stamp taxes were computed on no par shares based on the issue price while the tax on par value shares was based on par value. Where this valuation structure is in effect (and it may continue to be in effect in some states) nominal par value shares obviously continue to offer a tax saving over no par shares. Perhaps this historical pragmatic reason explains why no par shares are not the dominant practice in par value states.

State statutes provide that the board of directors has the power to fix the consideration for which no par shares are issued but the articles of incorporation may expressly reserve this power to the shareholders. This option was originally based on the long since discredited idea that par value ensures equality of treatment of shareholders while no par shares may be issued at varying prices leading to dilution of some interests. In the modern context, the option for shareholders to set the issuance price of no par shares does not differ in any significant way from the similar election that is available with respect to nominal par value shares. It is doubtful if either is ever elected today.

§ 7.8   Common Stock: Shares Issued for Property or Services

This section deals with the issuance of shares for property (other than cash) or services under both the older par value statutes and the Model Business Corporation Act (1984).

If shares are issued for cash, the price is usually fixed by the board of directors, subject only to the limitation that the price must equal or exceed the share's par value, if any. If the shareholder-to-be is contributing property or services, however, the situation is more complicated.

In the first place, under traditional par value statutes not all types of property or services may serve as acceptable consideration for the issuance of shares. As of January 1, 1998, state constitutions or statutes in some twenty-six states provided, in varying language, that payment for shares must be "in whole or in part, in cash, *in other property, tangible or intangible, or in labor or services actually performed for the corporation.*" This quotation is taken from § 19 of the old Model Business Corporation Act, but it is common language in these states. In addition, many of these states specifically provide that promissory notes or the promise of future services do not constitute permissible consideration for the issuance of shares. Shares issued for ineligible consideration under these statutes are not validly issued and may be canceled or suit brought by other shareholders; or alternatively, persons receiving such shares may be compelled in a suit by creditors to pay in additional consideration on the theory the shares are "watered." (See § 7.9 of this Nutshell.)

These "eligible consideration" statutes are not part of the par value structure but are independent requirements. A state may eliminate the par value requirements and yet elect to retain these limitations on the types of eligible consideration for shares (as, indeed, California has done).

There is a fair amount of case law under these statutes that provides additional gloss on what is eligible consideration. Services performed before incorporation are "services actually performed" and thus qualify. Patents for inventions, "good will" of a going and profitable business, contract rights, or computer "software" all also qualify as permissible "intangible property." On the other hand, a lease or contract right that is subject to a substantial condition may not constitute "property" at all. Secret formulas, processes or plans that lack novelty or substantial value have also been held not to constitute "property." A note secured by a mortgage on real estate is usually considered to be eligible "property" rather than an ineligible "promissory note." Further, one case holds that if shares are issued partially for services previously rendered and partially for services to be rendered in the future, the entire issue of shares is invalid since the court will not apportion the consideration if the directors do not. Thus, shares to be issued to employees for services may be validly issued only if the issuance takes place at the end of the employment period. However, one decision, Rooney v. Paul D. Osborne Desk Co., Inc. (Mass.App.1995) holds that an employee who actually performs services is entitled to receive the promised-for stock on a theory of promissory estoppel. The court made the plausible argument that the statute's purpose is to protect creditors and existing shareholders, and those purposes do not require the invalidation of the agreement to issue stock where the services have been performed.

A second requirement under traditional statutes is that the "value" of the property or services must be determined at the time the stock is issued. Section 18 of the 1969 Model Act required the board of directors to "fix" the "consideration, expressed in dollars" that the corporation is to receive, and many state statutes have identical or analogous language. However, section 20 of the old Model Act provided that "in the absence of fraud in the transaction," the judgment of the board of directors as to the value of the consideration "shall be conclusive." This section took much of the potential sting out of a good faith but erroneously high valuation. These provisions are equally applicable to par and no par value shares. Under these provisions, the resolution of the board of directors accepting property for shares must do two things: it must specify the specific property involved, and it must express or fix the value of the property in dollars. Of course, the value so expressed must exceed the par value of any shares being issued if watered stock liability is to be avoided. The purposes underlying section 18 largely are to assure compliance with par value requirements and to enable existing shareholders to determine whether their interests are being diluted. The purpose of the "in the absence of fraud" language of section 20 is to give certainty to purchasers of shares. They can purchase shares in exchange for property without concern that the validity of the transaction may be attacked because the property was overvalued. Of course, from the perspective of existing shareholders, the language of section 20 might prevent attack on non-fraudulent transactions that significantly diluted their interest.

The Model Business Corporation Act (1984) essentially rejects all of these limitations on eligible consideration. Under section 6.21(b) eligible consideration may consist of "any tangible or intangible property or benefit to the corporation, including cash, promissory notes, services performed, contracts for services to be performed, or other securities of the corporation." This major change in policy was based on a recognition that the traditional rules often led to anomalous results and that "in the realities of commercial life" there is sometimes a need for the issuance of shares for contract rights or intangible property or benefits. Assume, for example, that Jane Fonda agrees to make a film in exchange for a twenty-five per cent interest in the film. Even though a bank might well be willing to lend $10,000,000 to a new corporation to make the Fonda film, the traditional rule would not permit the corporation to issue Jane Fonda her shares until after she has performed the requisite services. Similarly, John D. Rockefeller would not be able to give his promissory note for shares even though his promissory note is "as good as gold." However, the prohibition against promissory notes presumably would not prevent a third person from using Rockefeller's promissory note or the promissory note of a much less wealthy person as consideration for the issuance of the very same shares to the third person.

One consequence of the provisions of the MBCA (1984) is that corporations may issue shares immediately for promises of future service, promissory notes or future benefits. What happens if things do not work out as contemplated and the services are never performed, the notes are not paid, or the future benefits are never received? The answer is simple: The shares are still outstanding and validly issued; the corporation simply has whatever claims it can put forward for the future benefits or under the contract for services or on the promissory notes. If the corporation is not happy with this result, section 6.21(e) permits the corporation to escrow the shares until the services are performed, the benefits received, or the notes paid, and cancel them if there is a default. Alternatively, the corporation may restrict the transfer of the shares until the desired benefits are received.

The MBCA (1984) also changes the rules substantially with respect to the determination of the value of property received as consideration for the issuance of shares. The board of directors does not have to determine the actual value of property that is received; it need only determine "that the consideration received or to be received for shares to be issued is adequate." [MBCA (1984) § 6.21(c)]. Further, that determination "is conclusive insofar as the adequacy of consideration for the issuance of shares relates to whether the shares are validly issued, fully paid, and nonassessable." This language is designed to limit the non-rebuttable nature of the directors' determination to the issue whether the shares are validly issued to begin with.

§ 7.9   Common Stock: Liability for Watered Shares

This section deals primarily with problems arising under the par value statutes. To a limited extent, however, a similar problem may arise under the Model Business Corporation Act (1984).

The term "watered stock" is a colorful common law phrase describing the situation where shareholders receive shares without paying as much for them as the law requires. The common law defines three classes of such shares:

1) "Bonus" shares, are par value shares given to a shareholder "for nothing" when the shareholder purchases and pays for shares of another class;

2) "Discount" shares, are par value shares issued for cash for less than par value;

3) "Watered" shares are par value shares issued for property that is worth less than the par value of the shares.

All three of these types of shares are usually indiscriminately referred to as "watered shares," a convenient generic phrase.

Liability for watered stock only involves the initial purchaser or subscriber of shares from the corporation. Once shares have been issued they may be sold to subsequent purchasers at whatever price is set by the market or is agreed upon by the purchaser and seller. The original par value of the shares is relevant only with respect to the original issue of the shares.

Much of the early common law relating to watered shares concerned the liability of shareholders receiving watered shares to pay the additional consideration needed to "squeeze out the water." Two alternative theories by which creditors might hold shareholders liable for watered stock appear in the early cases.

The "trust fund" theory in effect treats the stated capital of the corporation as being a trust fund available for the payment of creditors, and failure to pay in the proper amount is therefore actionable by any creditor. As pointed out in Hospes v. Northwestern Mfg. & Car Co. (Minn.1892), this theory is to a large extent a fiction since corporate capital lacks virtually all the elements of a true trust.

The "holding out" theory in effect presumes (usually contrary to fact) that creditors rely on the stated capital of the corporation when extending credit. On this theory, creditors with claims arising prior to the wrongful issuance, or subsequent creditors who were aware of the wrongful issuance, cannot compel additional payments by the shareholders on account of the watered stock.

Early courts wavered between these two theories, often referring to a trust fund theory, but reaching decisions more consistent with the holding out theory.

Modern par value corporation statutes change these common law principles. They define the liability of shareholders in connection with the issuance of shares in precise though not always unambiguous terms. A widely adopted provision of the 1969 Model Business Corporation Act states that "a holder of * * * shares of a corporation shall be under no obligation to the corporation or to its creditors with respect to such shares other than the obligation to pay to the corporation *the full consideration for which such shares were issued or to be issued.*" [MBCA (1969) § 25.] This section must be read along with section 18 of the 1969 Model Business Corporation Act which authorizes par value shares to be issued "for such consideration expressed in dollars, not less than the par value thereof, as shall be fixed from time to time" by the directors. The provision for no par shares is essentially the same with the omission of the phrase "not less than the par value thereof." Read literally, these provisions (1) substitute a statutory obligation running in favor of both the corporation and its creditors for the trust fund or holding out theories of common law, and (2) measures the extent of the liability on the basis of "the consideration for which such shares were issued or to be issued" rather than par value.

Under this statute a shareholder is liable to the corporation if he or she pays less for the shares than the consideration fixed by the directors. This liability is measured by the difference between the consideration fixed and the amount actually paid for the shares. The use of nominal par value shares does not avoid this potential liability and the same risk of liability exists when no par shares are used. Under these statutes there is thus no difference in potential liability between par and no par shares.

Ambiguity may exist under these statutory provisions where property at an arguably excessive valuation is contributed in exchange for either par value or no par value shares. Under § 25 of the 1969 Model Act, shareholders have no liability to the corporation with respect to shares "other than the obligation to pay to the corporation the full consideration for which shares were issued or to be issued." The key phrase in this section, the "full consideration" for which shares were issued may conceivably refer either to the designated property itself or to the dollar value placed on the property by the directors when it expresses the consideration "in dollars." These provisions create a serious practical problem whenever a previously unincorporated business with lots of different kinds of property of uncertain values is incorporated. The same problem arises if either nominal par or no par shares are used. To take an example, assume that the directors authorize the issuance of 1,000 shares of $1.00 par value stock for specified property that they value at $10,000. Assume further the valuation of $10,000 is fraudulent and the property is actually worth only $5,000. After the shares are issued, the balance sheet of the corporation looks like this:

Assets		Liabilities	–0–
Property	$10,000		
		Capital Accounts	
		Stated Capital	$1,000
		Capital Surplus	9,000

At common law the rule in this kind of situation was that the shares were not watered at all since the value of the property received exceeded the aggregate par value of the shares issued.

Under modern par value statutes that require the directors to express the value of the consideration "in dollars," the shareholder would be liable for an additional $5,000 since the "full amount of the consideration fixed as provided by law" was $10,000 and he contributed property with a value of only $5,000.

At common law the issuance of watered, bonus, or discount shares gave rise to liability on the shareholders receiving the shares, not liability on the directors authorizing such shares. It is possible to devise various common law theories of liability by which directors could be held personally liable for authorizing watered shares, particularly in suits brought by other shareholders or creditors who relied on the financial statements thereby created. Yet another possibility is a suit brought by existing shareholders to cancel watered shares as not being lawfully issued. In many states this appears to be the most common way in which watered stock questions arise.

Section 6.22(a) of the MBCA (1984) is superficially similar to section 25 of the old Model Business Corporation Act. It provides that a purchaser of shares from a corporation is not liable to the corporation or its creditors "with respect to its shares except to pay the consideration for which the shares were authorized to be issued." Under this Act the consideration may consist of a promissory note or a contract to perform services in the future (see § 7.8 of this Nutshell). The Official Comment states that the phrase "with respect to its shares" was included to make clear that the shareholder remains liable on the promissory note or contract to perform services without regard to this section.

Section 6.22(b) of the Model Business Corporation Act (1984) states that "a shareholder is not personally liable for the acts or debts of the corporation" with two exceptions. The two exceptions are, first, that the articles of incorporation may expressly provide for such personal liability, and second, that the shareholder "may become personally liable by reason of his or her own acts or conduct." This latter clause is designed to cover both consensual assumption of liability for specific obligations and principles by which shareholders may inadvertently become liable for corporate obligations under the doctrine generally known as "piercing the corporate veil," discussed in chapter six of this Nutshell, or possibly other doctrines as well.

§ 7.10   Common Shares: Options, Warrants and Rights

Options to purchase shares may be used by a corporation as a capital-raising device, to provide employee incentives, and to a lesser extent as part of control devices. Of course, shares under option are not deemed issued and may not be voted until the options are exercised and the purchase price paid, or in some states, a firm commitment to pay the purchase price in the form of a promissory note has been delivered to the corporation.

Many state corporation statutes contain provisions that authorize the issuance of shares in connection with employee stock purchase or stock option plans by the board of directors, and provide that in the absence of fraud the determination by the board of the consideration for such shares shall be conclusive. (MBCA (1984) § 6.24).

"Warrants" are transferable options issued by the corporation that enable holders to acquire shares from the corporation at a specified price. Warrants may be publicly traded; warrants issued by a number of corporations are listed from time to time on the New York Stock Exchange or other securities exchanges. These warrants have many of the characteristics of an equity security since their price is a function of the market price of the underlying shares and the specified issuance price. Warrants frequently are issued as "sweeteners" in connection with the distribution of a debt or preferred stock offering; they may be issued in connection with a public exchange offer, or as compensation for handling the public distribution of other shares. Sometimes they are issued in a reorganization to holders of a class of security not otherwise recognized in the reorganization.

"Rights" are in effect short term warrants. Rights may be issued in lieu of a dividend, or in an effort to raise capital from existing shareholders.

There are also active public markets in "puts" and "calls" which are options to purchase or to sell publicly traded securities or indexes of publicly traded securities or commodities. These options are created by ("written by" is the "real world" description) securities traders as speculation on price movements and do not directly involve the corporation's capitalization. They are therefore quite unlike the options discussed in this section.

§ 7.11   Common Stock: Non–Voting Shares

State statutes authorize corporations to create various classes of common or preferred shares. (Preferred shares are discussed in § 7.21 of this Nutshell.) The power to create classes of common shares permits corporations to create classes of non-voting shares that do not have preferential distribution rights. These shares typically have the economic characteristics of common stock but lack the power to vote for directors. However, they have the right to vote on amendments to the articles of incorporation and on proposed mergers, share exchanges, and other extraordinary events that may affect the class of nonvoting shares as a class.

Classes of non-voting common shares differ depending on whether the corporation is closely held or publicly held.

In the closely held corporation, non-voting shares typically serve a planning role. For example, the right to elect the board of directors may be vested exclusively in the holders of one class of common shares. These holders may be the founders or managers of the corporation while the class of non-voting shares may be held by non-participating family members. In closely held corporations there seems to be no inherent reason why a specific exclusion of voting should not be part of the shareholder's overall "contract" with the corporation.

In publicly held corporations, non-voting shares have been treated with greater suspicion. Such shares are somewhat analogous to perpetual voting trusts, and have been criticized on policy grounds for this reason. (See § 9.13 of this Nutshell.) Corporations with non-voting shares held by the public are ineligible for listing on the New York Stock Exchange, and may suffer market and other disadvantages as well. In the early years of this century, many corporations were capitalized by the issuance of non-voting shares to the general public while the voting shares were held by the members of the family that founded or controlled the corporation. This practice has declined in recent years. Several corporations that originally issued non-voting shares for this reason later converted the non-voting shares into voting shares. This decision itself creates subtle issues as to the relative value of the right to vote and the fairness of the terms on which the privilege to vote is granted to the previously non-voting shares.

A corporation with a class of non-voting shares must also have outstanding a class of common shares with full voting rights.

§ 7.12   Common Stock: Classes of Common Shares in Closely Held Businesses

State statutes also give corporations broad power to create classes of common stock with different voting or economic rights or privileges. Such classes are usually designated by alphabetical notations: "Class A common," "Class B common," and so forth. In closely held corporations, classes of common stock are primarily used to effectuate control, voting, or financial arrangements of the type described in the preceding section. The following examples illustrate the variety and flexibility that classes of common stock may provide for closely held corporations:

(a) A Class A common may be created that is entitled to twice the dividend per share of Class B common, but in all other respects the two classes are identical.

(b) A Class A common may be created that has two votes per share while Class B common has one vote per share (this is permitted under the MBCA (1984) and in most but not all states; some states still have a "one vote per share" principle).

(c) A Class A common may be created that has the power to elect two directors; the holders of Class B common may have the power to elect one, two, or more directors, irrespective of the number of shares of each class outstanding.

(d) It may be required that the president of the corporation be a holder of Class A shares and the vice-president and treasurer be holders of Class B shares.

A classic case involving the use of different classes of shares in a closely held corporation that is planning to make a public offering of non-voting shares and wishes to ensure a a permanent control arrangement is Lehrman v. Cohen, discussed in §§ 9.16 and 12.6 of this Nutshell.

Closely held corporations that have classes of shares outstanding are ineligible for the attractive S corporation tax election except where the classes differ only in connection with voting rights.

§ 7.13 Common Stock: Classes of Common Shares in Publicly Held Businesses

Classes of common stock may also be used to solve financial, control, or dividend problems in publicly held corporations, though such use is not as common as in closely held businesses. When the Ford Motor Company went public in 1946, it created a special class of common shares to be held by the Ford Foundation. The special shares were convertible into regular common shares when sold by the Foundation. These shares were nonvoting so long as they were owned by the Foundation. Thus, they permitted control of the corporation to be vested in the public without requiring the Foundation to abruptly liquidate its huge interest in the corporation.

Several publicly held corporations in which specific families have long been associated in a control capacity have sought to combat potential takeover attempts by creating a special class of shares with super voting rights to be issued solely to family members. The terms of this special class provide that shares lose their special voting privileges if they are sold or conveyed to non-family members. Among the corporations adopting this device are the publishers of the New York Times and the Wall Street Journal. The special class assures that voting control resides in the family (so long as it remains reasonably cohesive) even though most of the shares are publicly held. In 1988 the SEC adopted rule 19c–4 (usually known as the "one share one vote" rule) designed to prevent such unequal divisions in voting power in the future, though the rule "grandfathered" existing capital structures. This rule was held invalid in The Business Roundtable v. SEC (D.C.Cir.1990), on the ground that it exceeded the powers of the Securities & Exchange Commission, but most securities exchanges have voluntarily adopted similar rules as prerequisites for listing shares for trading.

In Williams v. Geier (Del.1996), a sharply divided Delaware Supreme Court upheld a somewhat similar "tenure voting" plan for a publicly traded corporation. In order to preserve family control of the corporation, each shareholder became entitled to ten votes for each share he or she owned. However shares that were sold or transferred thereafter were immediately reduced in voting power to one vote per share for a period of three years, when they reacquired ten votes per share. The purpose of the plan was obviously to deter family members from selling shares into the public market.

§ 7.14   Common Stock: Tracking Shares

Several publicly held corporations have experimented with a simultaneous dual issue of publicly traded shares representing different components of the same corporation. A classic example was General Motors Corporation that at one time had three classes of common stock outstanding: (1) General Motors common shares, (2) General Motors Class E common shares that tracked the performance of its wholly-owned subsidiary, Electronic Data Systems Holding Corporation, and (3) General Motors Class H common shares that tracked the performance of another wholly-owned subsidiary, Hughes Electronic Corporation.

Tracking stock is sort of peculiar. It is issued by the parent corporation, General Motors, but its economic characteristics, including its market performance, dividend policy, and the like is based solely on the economic performance of the subsidiary. The major drawback of tracking stock is that it may create divisions between shareholders that can place one group or the other at a disadvantage and complicate board-level decisions. For example, any use of Hughes' assets by General Motors was sure to be objected to by the Class H shareholders and is likely to lead to litigation. After several years of experience with tracking stock, General Motors decided to dispose of the two subsidiaries and make them free standing, a decision that itself led to litigation that is unresolved in 2000.

§ 7.15   Common Stock: Treasury Shares

Treasury shares are shares of the corporation that were once lawfully issued but have been reacquired by the corporation (and theoretically held in its treasury, hence their name). However, it is important to recognize that from an economic standpoint treasury shares are no different from authorized but unissued shares. It is also important to recognize that there is no "treasury." Certificates for shares that are repurchased are cancelled. However, for the reasons discussed below a corporation has an incentive to preserve those shares as "treasury shares." This is done simply by maintaining a separate ledger in the stock transfer records for treasury shares.

The status of treasury shares is an uneasy one under traditional par value statutes. They are viewed as being issued for some purposes and unissued for other purposes. They are not viewed as being issued or outstanding for purposes of voting, quorum determinations, or dividends. Any such recognition would create obvious problems of circularity and dilute the votes of existing shareholders. On the other hand, they also are not subject to the restraints on issuance or new shares described in the previous sections, and to that extent are viewed as being issued. In other words treasury shares can be resold or reissued without regard to the par value of the shares or the nature of the consideration being received for them.

While all aspects of these anomalous results may not be accepted in all jurisdictions, it is generally recognized that treasury shares are not subject to the restrictions applicable to original issuance of shares. As a result, many corporations maintain a supply of treasury shares in part to permit the issuance of shares in transactions the consideration for which might not qualify under traditional rules.

Treasury shares are quite unlike shares of other corporations that the corporation may own. Shares of other corporations acquired by a corporation are investments by the acquiring corporation. In contrast, the acquisition of a corporation of its own shares is a distribution, not an investment. When a corporation acquires some of its own shares, the assets of the corporation are reduced by the amount of the purchase price and all the other owners of shares have a somewhat increased proportional interest in the reduced assets. In this respect, treasury shares are economically indistinguishable from authorized but unissued shares. Thus, it is never meaningful to treat the acquisition of its own shares by a corporation as anything but a disproportionate distribution of corporate assets to the selling shareholders, or better, a disproportionate dividend. See § 18.4 of this Nutshell.

The MBCA (1984) eliminates the concept of treasury shares. It treats all shares reacquired by the corporation as authorized but unissued shares [§ 6.31(a)]. This change was made on the theory that the relaxation of the rules relating to issuance of new shares made obsolete the concept of treasury shares.

§ 7.16 Common Stock: Circular Ownership of Shares

As indicated above, treasury shares have an intermediate status in many states. They are treated as issued but not outstanding and may not be voted or counted in determining the number of shares outstanding.

Shares that are owned by a wholly- or majority-owned subsidiary of the issuing corporation are called circularly owned shares. Even though they are not technically treasury shares, they are treated in an analogous fashion. They may not be voted or considered as outstanding for purposes of a quorum. See MBCA (1984) § 7.21(b). In other words, circular control of a corporation is prohibited. On a similar theory, shares held by the issuing corporation in a fiduciary capacity also have sometimes been barred from being voted or counted in determining the existence of a quorum, though MBCA § 7.21(c) and the statutes of a number of states permit voting of shares held in a fiduciary capacity.

§ 7.17 Common Stock: Current Trends Regarding Par Value

When all is said and done, the concepts of par value and stated capital have relatively little to commend them in the modern era. At best they are historical oddities that provide little real protection to creditors and have been twisted by sophisticated attorneys to squeeze out the maximum flexibility for their corporate creations. At worst, they are confusing if not misleading to unsophisticated persons.

The Model Business Corporation Act (1984) eliminates both the concept of par value (except to the limited extent discussed below) and the distinction between stated capital and capital surplus. The validity of corporate distributions to shareholders is measured by new insolvency and balance sheet tests. (See § 18.6 of this Nutshell.) Further, the MBCA (1984) eliminates the restrictions on eligible consideration discussed in § 7.8 of this Nutshell as well as the concept of treasury shares discussed in § 7.15. The elegance and simplicity thereby created has much to commend it since it returns the issuance of common shares back to a simple, common sense set of rules.

The MBCA (1984) permits a corporation to elect to create optional par value for shares. [MBCA (1984) § 2.02(b)(iv)] In effect the corporation may elect to be governed by par value provisions as a matter of contract if it so desires. The Official Comment suggests that election of an optional par value may be useful if the corporation is likely at some time in the future to transact business in a state in which franchise or other taxes are computed on the basis of par values rather than actual value of the shares.

Most practicing attorneys, of course, are familiar with par value statutes, having studied them in law school and practiced under them. In the twenty-odd states that have adopted all or significant portions of the MBCA (1984), some attorneys follow familiar patterns and continue to use optional par value. As time goes on, however, it is likely that more attorneys will take advantage of the flexibility and simplicity provided by the MBCA (1984) provisions.

§ 7.18　Common Stock: Preemptive Rights

"Preemptive rights" refers to the power often granted to existing shareholders of an on-going corporation to purchase a proportionate part of new issues of common shares. Preemptive rights are designed to permit existing shareholders to retain their relative ownership interests in the corporation when the corporation issues additional stock.

The issuance of additional common shares by a going concern must meet the same requirements as to kind and amount of consideration as on the original formation and capitalization of the corporation. The number of shares to be sold and the consideration therefor is set by the board of directors. In addition, however, since the issuance of new shares may affect the financial and voting rights of existing shareholders, additional legal requirements may be applicable.

If shares are issued to the current shareholders in strict proportion to their shareholdings, the relative position of each shareholder is obviously unaffected though the aggregate capital invested in the corporation has increased. However, if shares are issued to third persons or to existing shareholders not in strictly proportional amounts, the voting power of some shareholders will necessarily be reduced. Further, if the shares are issued disproportionately and for less than current value (a term that need not here be precisely defined), both the voting power and the financial interest of some shareholders in the corporation will be diluted.

The common law recognizes a "preemptive right" as a protection for existing shareholders in many circumstances. This right is now usually codified in corporation statutes, and is also subject to significant limitations or qualifications. Most importantly, modern statutes make preemptive rights permissive rather than mandatory; corporations may limit or deny preemptive rights by appropriate provisions in the articles of incorporation. However, even if preemptive rights are excluded, equitable principles may limit the power of corporations to dispose of new shares on an unfair basis.

Shares sold by a going corporation may come from three sources. They may be shares that are newly authorized by the corporation by an amendment to the articles of incorporation. Or, they may be shares that were previously authorized in the articles but never previously issued. Or they may be "treasury shares," shares that had been issued at one time but have been subsequently reacquired by the corporation. Even though the issue of any additional shares, no matter what the source, has exactly the same dilutive effect, different legal principles may be applicable depending on the source of the shares and the precise language of the state statute defining the shareholder's preemptive right.

At common law and under the statutes of many states the preemptive right does not extend to the following types of transactions:

(1) *Shares that were originally authorized but unissued.* The rationale for this exception is that an implied understanding exists between the original subscribers that sale of the remaining authorized shares to obtain necessary capital may be completed. However, this rationale is not persuasive today in light of the modern practice of authorizing additional shares

that are not sold as part of the original capitalization. As a result some states do not recognize this exception.

(2) *Treasury shares.* The rationale for this exception is that shareholders are not injured since the shares were previously issued and their reissuance simply restores a dilution that existed previously. Again this may not be persuasive, depending on the particular factual situation under consideration.

(3) *Shares issued for property or services rather than cash, or shares issued in connection with a merger.* The theory underlying these exceptions is that preemptive rights in such situations would frustrate or render impractical desirable transactions. For example, issuing shares in exchange for property would be impossible to work out if some but not all of the existing shareholders owned the property.

(4) *Shares issued to satisfy conversion or option rights.*

(5) *Shares issued pursuant to a plan of reorganization or recapitalization under court supervision.*

Some recent decisions have refused to apply these exceptions mechanically and have looked to the realities of the particular situation. One court, for example, held that preemptive rights should be available when property is the consideration for shares except where (a) the corporation has great need for the particular property, and (b) the new shares are the only practical and feasible method by which the corporation can acquire the property. In most situations, the corporation can pay cash to acquire the needed property; it can sell shares preemptively to shareholders for cash and use the cash to acquire the desired property. Permitting the corporation to issue shares only to the owners of the desired property defeats the preemptive right that would admittedly have existed if shares first had been sold for cash and the cash then used to acquire the property.

Modern state statutes change the common law preemptive right in several other respects:

(1) At common law it was generally held that a shareholder's preemptive right was an integral part of the ownership of shares. However, as indicated above, all modern statutes give corporations the privilege of dispensing entirely with preemptive rights if they so choose. The choice must be made by a specific provision in the corporation's articles of incorporation. Statutes granting the preemptive right, furthermore, are of two types: They may grant preemptive rights unless they are specifically negated in the articles (an "opt-out" clause), or they may preclude preemptive rights except to the extent specifically granted in the articles (an "opt-in" clause). Section 6.30 of MBCA(1984) adopts an "opt in" clause, but simplifies the drafting problem faced by an attorney desiring to create preemptive rights by establishing a "standard form" for electing preemptive rights in section 6.30(b). This standard form covers such matters as the scope of the preemptive right, waiver, and the duration of the right, but may be modified as desired.

(2) Some statutes give preemptive rights more broadly than the common law, e.g., they may extend the right to authorized but unissued shares, treasury shares, and securities convertible into common shares, all types of shares to which the common law preemptive right does not extend.

(3) Statutes usually provide specifically that preemptive rights do not exist between different classes of shares, e.g., holders of preferred stock do not have a preemptive right to acquire common shares. The MBCA (1984) standard form of preemptive rights, however, seeks to protect against dilution of voting power by providing that common shareholders have a preemptive right to acquire preferred shares that are enti-

tled to vote for directors or that may be converted into voting shares.

(4) Some statutes provide that shares issued pursuant to employee incentive or compensation plans are not subject to preemptive rights if the plan was originally approved by the shareholders. The MBCA (1984) standard form of preemptive rights does not include this proviso.

What considerations enter into the decision to limit or deny preemptive rights? The argument in favor of preserving preemptive rights is simple: A shareholder who purchases a given percentage of the original issue of the shares of a corporation should be entitled to maintain his or her percentage interest. This sounds like a democratic principle and undoubtedly it is in many cases. There are situations, however, in which preemptive rights are more a nuisance than anything else. Suppose for example that a corporation with a fairly large number of shareholders is in need of immediate funds and can obtain them only by a prompt sale of additional shares to bankers or underwriters. It may well find that compliance with and satisfaction of the preemptive rights of its existing shareholders will be expensive, time-consuming, and only partially successful.

If it is anticipated that the corporation will for some time remain a close corporation, preemptive rights may be retained so as to give each shareholder the maximum protection against dilution, though it is safer to provide such rights by shareholder agreement than by reliance on statutory preemptive rights.

Preemptive rights are usually eliminated where it is contemplated that corporation will in the near future engage in public financing or seek to acquire other companies or properties by the issuance of its shares. Elimination of preemptive rights in these situations avoids legal complications when the time arrives for the sale of additional shares or the acquisition of other companies or properties. And, in any event, preemptive rights serve little purpose where shares are publicly traded, since additional shares can be bought on the open market or additional shares sold into that market if desired.

Where preemptive rights have been specifically excluded, directors may nevertheless voluntarily decide that it is sensible to offer additional shares pro rata to existing shareholders. Indeed, in many corporations, existing shareholders may be the most logical purchasers, and therefore the ones contacted first when shares are being sold by the corporation.

§ 7.19 Oppressive Issuance of Shares

Additional shares of stock may be issued oppressively to dilute the interests of other shareholders in the corporation. Misuse of this power is often referred to as a "squeeze out" or "freeze out."

A number of cases attest that corporate management has a fiduciary duty of taking corporate action according to the best interests of the corporation rather than for personal advantage. This principle amply covers situations where, in the absence of preemptive rights, management dilutes the interests of shareholders simply by issuing additional shares to itself at a bargain price. This principle may also cover situations where management issues shares to itself at a fair price to ensure retention of control without offering the shares more broadly. In the first situation there is dilution of both financial and voting interests; in the second there is only dilution of the voting power.

Much more difficult are cases involving a combination of legitimate and self-serving purposes. Shares may be issued to friendly persons for apparently worthwhile purposes and entirely in accordance with statutory requirements, but the minority shareholders complain that the real purpose and principal effect of the transaction is to freeze them out or dilute their interest. Most cases have permitted such transactions to stand, at least where the ostensible purpose does seem to have substance. Courts are naturally reluctant to second guess decisions by directors and interfere in intracorporate disputes, but will do so if they feel that the ostensible purpose is a sham, and the real purpose of the transaction is simply to benefit management.

Preemptive rights give shareholders considerably less protection against such tactics than is often thought. Indeed, as a practical matter, the protection provided by preemptive rights is often illusory. A minority shareholder may be frozen out if he or she lacks the financial ability to exercise the preemptive right and purchase the additional shares in order to protect his or her proportionate interest. Often, the majority or dominant shareholders may purchase their allotment by offsetting indebtedness owed to them by the corporation (thereby exercising their preemptive rights without further financial investment) while other shareholders have to invest substantial amounts of cash just to stay even. In one case, for example, the court refused to intervene when a shareholder was given the choice of investing an additional $136,000 to preserve his twenty per cent interest or permitting his interest in the corporation to be diluted to less than one per cent. Hyman v. Velsicol Corp. (Ill.App.1951). In another case, where the reduction was from about 32 per cent to less than one per cent, the court applied the test whether the issuance of shares seemed to serve a substantial corporate purpose or whether it was designed simply to benefit management, and over one dissent, concluded that the issuance of shares should be set aside. Browning v. C & C Plywood Corp. (Or. 1967). The issue in these cases may come down to an evaluation of the existence of a valid business purpose for the transaction: e.g., the need of the corporation for the additional capital, or where indebtedness is canceled and the corporation receives no additional cash, whether the improvement in the balance sheet caused by the cancellation of indebtedness is a bona fide purpose. There appears, however, to be a trend toward giving minority shareholders protection against the unfair issuance of shares despite the presence of a nominal business purpose on the theory that the majority shareholder owes a fiduciary duty to the minority. See § 12.11 of this Nutshell.

§ 7.20　A Cautionary Postscript: The Risk of Violating Securities Acts While Raising Capital

The Federal Securities Act of 1933 and state statutes, called "blue sky laws," require corporations to register issues of securities with governmental agencies before they are sold publicly. (A significant part of state regulation of new issues was preempted by the federal National Securities Market Improvement Act ("NSMIA") in 1996.) Initial registration under these statutes, considered at length in advanced courses on securities regulation, is expensive, difficult, and time consuming. Further, selling shares without required registration gives rise to substantial civil liabilities and may lead to criminal prosecution as well.

When corporations raise capital by selling shares, it is important that the offering not become inadvertently a public one, thereby triggering the registration requirements of these statutes, or that some exemption from registration under these statutes is available. The definition of a "public offering" and the scope of exemptions from registration are often complex legal issues. As a result, the risk of an inadvertent violation of these statutes is often a real one.

When a corporation first registers securities under these statutes it is often said to "go public."

§ 7.21   Preferred Shares

The distinguishing characteristic of preferred shares is that they have a preference over common shares in the payment of dividends and/or a preference in the receipt of the assets of the corporation upon the voluntary or involuntary liquidation of the corporation. Usually preferred shares are non-voting shares that have a fixed and limited dividend that is not dependent on the earnings of the corporation. "Preference" simply means that the preferred shares are entitled to receive the specified payment (either a dividend or a liquidating distribution, or both) before the common shares are entitled to anything.

Many corporations issue several different classes of preferred shares. These different classes are often designated by letter: "Class A preferred," "Class B preferred," and so forth.

State corporation statutes give corporations almost complete flexibility in establishing terms of preferred shares. Preferred shares may be structured so that they closely resemble either debt or common shares. Through the device of preferred shares, a corporation may create securities with novel provisions that resemble neither debt nor equity.

Because of this flexibility, preferred shares are widely used to create innovative means of raising capital from third parties and to effectuate intracorporate agreements in closely held corporations. For example, a preferred stock may be made redeemable at the option of the holder at a specified price. Such a stock has the general economic characteristics of a demand promissory note. On the other hand, since it is denominated a preferred stock it lacks the same priority in payment that a promissory note possesses. At the other extreme, a preferred stock may be non-callable and entitled to a fixed dividend plus a right to share in a specified proportion of future earnings each year. Such a preferred has the general economic characteristics of common stock with a right to the stated dividend if the corporation has earnings or profits. This kind of stock may be described as a "participating preferred" but essentially the same characteristics may be created by creating a special class of common shares.

The following discussion describes traditional characteristics of preferred shares often seen in publicly held corporations. The characteristics of such preferred stock include the following:

1. Dividend Preferences. As indicated above, a dividend preference simply means that the preferred stock is entitled to some distribution before any dividends may be paid on the common shares. A dividend preference may be described either in terms of dollars per share (the "$3.20 preferred") or as a percentage of par or stated value (the "five per cent preferred"). A dividend preference does not mean that the preferred is entitled to the payment in the same way that a creditor is entitled to payment from his or her debtor. A preferred dividend is still a dividend, and the directors may decide to omit all dividends, common and preferred, and this decision is in no way dependent on whether or not there is current income. However, the dividend preference of preferred means that the corporation cannot declare a dividend on the common without also declaring dividends on the outstanding classes of preferred shares.

Shares preferred as to dividends may be *cumulative, noncumulative,* or *partially cumulative.* These terms relate to what happens if a dividend on the preferred is omitted in one year. If the dividend is cumulative, it is carried forward to subsequent years, and in any subsequent year all prior unpaid cumulative dividends plus the current year's preferred dividends must be paid in full before any dividend may be declared on the common shares. Noncumulative dividends disappear each year if they are not paid. Partially cumulative dividends are usually of the "cumulative to the extent of earnings" type. The dividend is cumulative to the extent of earnings (so that the preferred shares continue to have first claim to actual earnings), but noncumulative to the extent earnings fail to cover the dividend.

Unpaid cumulative dividends are not debts of the corporation, but a continued right to priority in future distributions. Directors (who are elected by the common shareholders) may defer preferred dividends indefinitely if the directors are willing to forego dividends on the common shares as well. However, many corporations include a provision giving the preferred shareholders the right to elect a specified number of directors if preferred dividends have been omitted for a specified period. In this respect preferred shareholders vote as a separate class independent of the common shareholders . .

2. Participating Preferred. Most preferred shares are entitled to a stated dividend and nothing more, no matter how profitable the corporation. Such shares are "non-participating." "Participating" preferred shares are entitled to the original dividend, and after the common receives a specified amount, they may share with the common in any additional distributions. Participating shares are sometimes referred to as "Class A common" or a similar designation reflecting that their right to share in dividends is open-ended.

Preferential rights to distributions are strictly construed. The preferred shareholders have those rights only to the extent they are specifically provided for by the governing documents of the corporation.

3. Redeemable Preferred. Shares of any class, including preferred shares, may be made redeemable by the corporation at a specified price so long as there remains outstanding one class of common shares with full voting powers. The price is usually set in the articles of incorporation but may also be set by resolution of the board of directors in Delaware and other states.

The power to cause the redemption of redeemable shares is vested in the board of directors. Upon exercise of that power, the rights of the preferred shareholders are automatically changed to a contractual right to receive the redemption price.

4. Convertible Preferred. Preferred shares may be convertible into common shares at a specified price or specified ratio. Typically, the original conversion ratio is established when the class of preferred is created; the conversion price is usually set at a level that requires the common to appreciate substantially in value before it becomes profitable to convert the preferred. When the price of the common rises above the conversion price, the preferred shares will thereafter fluctuate in price in tandem with price fluctuations of the common.

Conversion and redemption provisions often appear together in preferred stock issues. The redemption privilege usually does not limit the price of the convertible preferred since the privilege to convert customarily continues for a limited period of time after a call for redemption.

5. "Forced" Conversions. A conversion is said to be "forced" when shares are called for redemption at a time when the value of the shares obtainable on conversion exceeds the redemption price. Also like convertible debt securities discussed below (see § 7.28, convertible preferred issues usually contain elaborate provisions protecting the conversion privilege from dilution in case of stock dividends, stock splits, or the issuance of additional common shares.

6. "Downstream" Conversions. The statutes of some states prohibit the creation of preferred shares which are convertible into shares having superior rights and preferences as to dividends or upon liquidation. In other words, a common may not be made convertible into preferred or into debt, and a junior preferred may not be made convertible into a more senior preferred. Such conversions, where they are permitted, are called "upstream" conversions. A "downstream" conversion is the typical convertibility provision that authorizes preferred shareholders to convert their shares into common shares. State statutes also may limit the redemption privilege to securities that have a liquidation preference or permit redeemable common shares only if there is another class of common shares that are not subject to redemption. These limitations are virtually the only substantive statutory restrictions on the issuance of classes of preferred shares in most states. The Model Business Corporation Act (1984) does not contain either of these limitations. See § 6.01, and particularly the Official Comment.

7. Miscellaneous Provisions. The high interest rates of the early 1980s led to the development of many novel financing devices, many of which involved the use of preferred stock. For example, many corporations issued preferred stock that was redeemable at the option of the holder, or that was redeemed upon the occurrence of some external event, such as a change in interest rates or the lapse of a specified period of time. Still other corporations issued preferred with floating or adjustable dividend rates that varied with interest rates or with some similar measure. Such adjustments would normally be made periodically by the board of directors.

Most of these novel classes of preferred shares were designed to give corporate holders of the preferred the benefit of the exclusion for intercorporate dividends while at the same time giving the holders most of the benefits of traditional debt. Classes of preferred shares with "PIK" ("payment-in-kind") and "reset" provisions that varied either the number of shares outstanding or the economic terms of the class of preferred also were created. The validity of some of these novel types of preferred may be questionable under some state statutes; the Model Business Corporation Act (1984) contains provisions designed specifically to assure their validity. See § 6.01(c).

8. *Series of Preferreds.* Articles of incorporation may also authorize preferred shares to be issued in *series* created by the board of directors without shareholder approval. The articles of incorporation in effect creates a class of shares without any substantive terms and authorizes the board to create (or "carve out") "series" from within that class from time to time. Such shares are also called "blank shares" because none of the terms are specified in the provisions creating the class. The board may vary the substantive terms of each series to take into account changing economic conditions. Blank shares can be very advantageous in corporations where preferred shares in substantial amounts are to be sold by the corporation from time to time to raise capital. The privilege to adjust the terms of the preferred simplifies such financing since the price, dividend, liquidation preference, sinking fund provision, voting rights, and other terms of each series may be tailored to then-current market conditions. Shares of different series have identical rights except for the specified economic terms that may be varied. Before a new series of preferred shares is created, a public filing with the Secretary of State describing the terms of the new series is required.

The importance of the power to create series of preferred shares escalated in the 1980s with the development of the so-called "poison pill" defensive tactic against unwanted takeover attempts. See § 13.26 of this Nutshell for a discussion of "unfriendly" takeover attempts. A "poison pill" involves the creation of one or more series of preferred shares that have powers dependent on external events, typically the acquisition of some percentage of the corporation's voting shares by an outside aggressor. Upon the occurrence of such an event, the poison pill is "triggered" and a massive amount of new securities may be distributed to existing shareholders but not to the aggressor. The purpose is to dilute the interest acquired by the aggressor and make the takeover impractical. Poison pills are discussed further in § 13.28 of this Nutshell.

There is little or no difference between a "series" or a "class" of preferred shares except their manner of creation— by the articles of incorporation in the case of a class and by action of the board of directors in the case of a series. In recognition of this, section 6.02 of the MBCA(1984) and the statutes of a few states allow the creation of either "classes" or "series" by the board of directors if authority to do so is given in the articles of incorporation.

The various provisions defining the rights of preferred shareholders, which may appear in the corporation's articles of incorporation, bylaws, or directors' resolutions are referred to as the preferred shareholders' "contract" with the corporation and with other classes of shareholders. Rights of preferred shareholders are generally limited to those expressly set forth in this "contract."

§ 7.22   The Distinction Between "Equity" and "Debt"

Securities issued by a corporation may be broadly classified into "equity" securities and "debt" securities. "Equity" in this sense is roughly synonymous with "net worth" or "ownership" and is derived from the following, quite common usage: if one subtracts a business's liabilities (its debts) from its assets, what remains is the owners' "equity" in the business. Equity securities therefore refer to all securities that represent ownership interests in the corporation, and encompass both common and preferred shares. Debt securities, typically bonds or debentures, represent obligations that must ultimately be repaid, usually on or before a specific date.

Both debt and equity are right hand entries on the traditional balance sheet. However they are sharply separated into two separate categories, with debt traditionally appearing as a "liability" above the equity securities.

The distinction between "equity" and "debt" underlies much of the modern law and practice relating to corporation finance. At the simplest level the distinction is easy to grasp. A "debt" is something that must be repaid: It is the result of a "loan," the person making the loan is a "creditor," and if periodic payments are made, they are "interest" and not "dividends." On the other hand, "equity" represents an ownership interest in the business itself. One thinks in terms of shareholders, shares of common or preferred stock, voting rights, and "dividends." It is sometimes not realized, however, that as a matter of economics, there is no sharp distinction between debt and equity. For example, a subordinate debenture that matures in 100 years with interest payable solely from income if and when earned, and repayment subordinate to other specified liabilities of the business, is much more like an equity security than a traditional debt security. Yet it may be structured as a subordinated debt security.

Corporations often create mixed or "hybrid" securities which have some of the characteristics of debt and some of equity. Despite the lack of clear distinction between debt and equity in these situations, legal consequences vary substantially depending on how a particular hybrid security is classified.

A hybrid security may be treated as a debt security for some purposes and as an equity security for other purposes, e.g., for income taxation purposes, rights on bankruptcy or insolvency, and the right to participate in management. The classification of hybrid securities for tax purposes, in particular, has given rise to litigation.

§ 7.23 Equalizing Capital and Services When Forming a Corporation

A recurring problem in financing a close corporation involves the situation where investors have agreed to contribute capital or provide services in varying amounts, and shares are to be issued in some different agreed ratio. Assume, for example, that A and B have agreed to go into business with A providing the necessary capital of $100,000 with B to work exclusively for the new venture for at least three years. The parties have also agreed that A is to receive 60 per cent and B 40 per cent of the voting shares. The state in question has eliminated par value from its statute but has retained the restrictions on the types of eligible consideration for shares described in § 7.8 of this Nutshell. How can the arrangement be worked out?

(1) B cannot be issued shares immediately upon the execution of a long-term employment contract, since "future services" are not valid consideration for shares.

(2) There is no obstacle, however, to issuing shares for past services. Hence the arrangement may be worked out by issuing A 60 shares for $100,000 immediately, and issuing B 40 shares when the period of employment ends three years from now. There are disadvantages with this solution. Until B has completed the services, A is the sole shareholder with total power over the corporation and he may exclude B at any time (though such an exclusion may constitute a breach of con-

tract). B also will have to provide services for an extended period without receiving dividends or a salary to live on. And, he will have to pay income tax on the value of the shares when he receives them and will have to pay this additional tax from other financial resources.

(3) B may propose that he sign a promissory note for $66,667, have the 40 shares issued to him or her immediately in exchange for that note, and pay off the note by rendering services under the employment contract. Most states that prohibit contracts for future services serving as consideration for shares also prohibit the use of promissory notes for this purpose. Hence, this plan is not likely to succeed.

(4) Another solution is to issue shares at different prices. A may be issued 60 shares for $100,000 and B 40 shares for $40.00. There is no statutory requirement that all shares of the same class be issued for the same consideration. However, this suggestion is manifestly unfair to A if the business does not do well and the parties desire to liquidate since B in effect has an immediate 40 per cent claim upon A's capital.

(5) A more reasonable solution is to create two classes of common stock with identical rights on dissolution:

(a) Class A common, one vote per share; 6,000 shares issued to A for $100,000 in cash (or $16.67 per share).

(b) Class B common, one hundred votes per share, 40 shares issued to B for $667.00 (or $16.67 per share). If dividends are to be paid on a 60–40 ratio, the dividends on each share of class B stock would have to be set at one hundred times the dividend on each share of class A stock.

This solves the premature liquidation problem. However, multiple votes per share are not permitted in some states. Essentially the same pattern could be created by giving A shares with a fraction of a vote per share, if that is permitted under the specific state statute.

(6) Another solution is to issue A 60 common shares for $60 and B 40 common shares for $40, and have A lend the corporation $99,940. This solves the corporate law and premature dissolution problems but creates others. A corporation with such a capitalization is likely to be viewed as a "thin" corporation for tax and liability purposes. An attempt by the corporation to deduct interest payments on the $99,940 "debt" would be probably be disallowed under the tax laws. A also would probably not be able to maintain creditor status in a bankruptcy proceeding under the "Deep Rock" doctrine. B might also object that A should not have a creditor's claim with respect to his capital while B is contributing services for which he has no claim at all.

(7) Perhaps the best solution is this: A receives 60 common shares, for $60.00 ($1 per share) and B receives 40 common shares, for $40.00 ($1 per share). A also receives 500 preferred shares for $50,000 ($100 per share) and "lends" the corporation the remaining $50,000. Since the aggregate capitalization is now $50,100 (combining all the consideration received for the common and preferred), debt is less than 50 per cent and the debt/equity ratio is about 1:1. The chances of applying the "thin" corporation or "Deep Rock" doctrines are therefore greatly reduced. This pattern was essentially upheld in the Maryland case of Obre v. Alban Tractor Co. (Md. 1962), involving a state insolvency proceeding. It may be noted that the dividend preference of the preferred is not specified. Under the circumstances, that is a matter of negotiation between A and B.

If this problem were to arise in a state with a par value requirement, the shares of stock would have to be assigned a par value that is less than the lowest consideration for which the shares are to be issued.

In the solution suggested above, the corporation would not be eligible for the S corporation election for tax purposes. See § 1.19 of this Nutshell.

§ 7.24   The Advantages of Debt Financing

It is usually advantageous for a corporation to engage to some extent in debt financing. The notion that the best business is a debt-free business, while sounding attractive, is not consistent either with the minimization of income taxes or with the maximization of profits.

(1) *Tax Advantages of Debt.* There are tax advantages for individual shareholders to lend a portion of their investment in the corporation rather than to contribute it outright. Where the shareholders are individuals, such debt reduces the double taxation problem of C corporations discussed earlier. (See § 1.19 of this Nutshell.) Interest payments on such debt are deductible by the corporation while dividend payments on equity securities are not. Further, repayment of a debt may be a non-taxable return of capital, while a purchase or redemption of equity securities from a shareholder by the corporation is ordinarily a taxable event. When a shareholder lends a portion of a contemplated investment to the corporation, he or she is hopefully reserving the option of recovering this portion tax free at some later date if the corporation is successful.

There is no tax advantage in debt owed to individuals other than shareholders. However, the deductibility of interest payments to third persons may significantly reduce the cost of borrowed capital as compared to the cost of capital raised through the sale of equity securities. Indeed, the systematic cost advantage that borrowed capital has in the modern American economy has significantly affected the capital structure of all domestic corporations.

Where the contributor of capital is another corporation, different tax rules apply. The receiving corporation may exclude 70 per cent or more of intercorporate dividends, and such dividends of course are not deductible by the paying corporation. If the same arrangement were created in the form of debt and the payment of interest, the income tax treatment is reversed. The paying corporation deducts the interest payments which constitute taxable income to the receiving corporation. The way an intercorporate transaction is structured for tax purposes is determined by the bargaining power of the two corporations. The general rule is the corporation providing the capital initially is able to dictate the tax structure. As a result many intercorporate "loans" are structured as capital contributions.

The principle that the capital contributor can usually dictate the structure of the transaction is encapsulated in this modern version of the "golden" rule: "He who has the gold rules."

The tax advantages of debt financing have been so substantial for small closely-held corporations in the past that a substantial amount of case law has developed dealing with the question when debt in the corporate structure is excessive. If it is, the Internal Revenue Service may treat the debt as a kind of equity, and disallow interest deductions or treat the repayment of the debt as a taxable dividend. This problem has diminished in importance with the increased popularity of the S corporation election.

(2) *Non-tax Advantages of Debt.* In the non-tax area debt owed both to third persons and to shareholders may be advantageous to a corporation, but for entirely different reasons.

(a) Debt owed to third persons is desirable because of the factor of *leverage.* Leverage arises when the corporation is able to earn more on the borrowed capital than the cost of the borrowing. The entire excess is allocable to the equity accounts of the corporation, thereby increasing the rate of return on the equity invested in the corporation. An example should help to make this clear. Let us assume that a person is considering the purchase of a business that will yield $25,000 per year over and above all taxes and expenses. The purchase price is $200,000. If the person simply buys the business using only his or her own capital, the annual return is 25,000/200,-000 or 12.5 per cent.

Let us assume that the same person can borrow 80 per cent of the purchase price at an interest cost of 10 per cent per year. The person will then invest $40,000 of his or her own capital (20 per cent of $200,000), and borrow the remaining $160,000 (80 per cent of $200,000). The interest cost of the loan is $16,000 per year (10 per cent of $160,000). Since the business still makes $25,000 per year, the net profit after interest costs is $9,000 on a net investment of $40,000, and the return on the investment is 9,000/40,000 or 22.5%. In other words, by borrowing 80 per cent of the purchase price, the return per equity dollar invested is increased from 12.5 per cent to 22.5 per cent. If there were five such simultaneous opportunities, a rational investor would take his or her initial $200,000 and invest $40,000 in each of the five businesses rather than buying only one debt-free business. By buying five businesses with 80 per cent loans, he or she will make $9,000 x 5 = $45,000 rather than $25,000. This is leverage, a device well understood by real estate syndicates and promoters who seek to obtain the largest possible mortgage and the smallest possible equity investment of their own.

The reason that it is desirable to leverage in this hypothetical is that each dollar invested earns 12.5 per cent but the cost of borrowing is only 10 per cent. The 2.5 per cent difference on every borrowed dollar is allocable to the equity investment—the 20 per cent—thereby increasing the overall return on the equity. The risk involved with the extensive use of leverage, of course, is that the income from the project may not be sufficient to cover the fixed interest charges. The investor would then quickly see his or her return reduced to zero and it is possible that an over-leveraged position will generate a "negative cash flow," which means the investor would have to invest additional capital to cover the shortfall of income over expenses. Certainly, an at-risk investor will be wiped out much more quickly in a leveraged investment than an unleveraged one.

Since World War II, the United States has suffered an inflationary spiral, particularly in the years before 1990. Since 1990 the rate of inflation has diminished significantly. High levels of inflation encourage debt financing because the loans will ultimately be repaid with inflated dollars. Of course, the competition for loans in such circumstances may well cause higher interest charges (as actually occurred during much of the period between World War II and the 1990s) that will offset, either wholly or partially, the benefits of inflation.

The Miller–Modigliani theorem states (with certain simplifying assumptions) that the aggregate value of a corporation's securities (the market value of its equity securities plus the market value of its debt securities) is independent of the amount of debt in the corporation's capital structure. In other words, in a perfect world any enhanced value of common stock because of the advantages of leverage is precisely offset by a decline in the market value of the indebtedness.

Among the factors that affect the Miller–Modigliani thesis is the fact that in its simplest form set forth above it does not take into account the tax effects of debt as contrasted with equity investments.

(b) Leverage can be obtained only by the use of other people's money. Nevertheless, it is often advantageous for non-tax business reasons for shareholders to advance a portion of their investment in the business in the form of loans rather than capital contributions. As a creditor, a shareholder may have greater rights upon bankruptcy or insolvency than she would have as a mere shareholder. However, if the loans are made as part of the original capitalization of the company, there is a substantial risk that such loans will be subordinated to the claims of general creditors in a bankruptcy proceeding. (See §§ 6.13, 7.27 of this Nutshell.) The basic test in this area is whether the capitalization is such that a third person would have made an arms length loan. If so, the loan by the shareholder should be treated as a loan for bankruptcy purposes. Loans for subsequent business needs also may fare better and stand a good chance of being recognized as bona fide loans.

§ 7.25 Tax Consequences of Excessive Debt Capitalization in C Corporations

The substantial tax advantages of shareholder debt financing in C corporations have led to a large amount of tax litigation as to whether ostensible debt should be reclassified as equity for tax purposes. The judicial decisions in this area do not establish a simple, easily understood test as to when a reclassification from debt to equity is proper. The diversity of possible factual situations is substantial, and there is less than total agreement in the cases as to the applicable legal principles. Perhaps Judge John R. Brown was being somewhat ironic when, in the leading Fifth Circuit case on the question, he stated: "Although the results are diverse, sometimes favoring the taxpayer, sometimes the Government, the cases are in accord in applying with an even hand the controlling legal principles for determining the outcome * * *." Tomlinson v. 1661 Corp. (5th Cir.1967).

Two interrelated ideas appear to underlie the judicial reasoning in the numerous cases in this area: First, are the legal incidents of the relationship between corporation and shareholder more similar to an equity investment or to a debt relationship? And second, even where the principal incidents of debt exist, is there some paramount policy of federal tax law that requires that particular debt interests be treated as equity investments?

Certainly, many cases may be explained on the ground that despite the label "debt" attached to an interest, the shareholder really holds an equity interest in the corporation. Some of these cases adopt a test of the "intention" of the shareholder in making the investment, but state that this "intention" may be inferred from the provisions of the debt instrument itself or from surrounding circumstances. The following factors have been held to indicate an "intention" to make an equity or capital contribution:

(a) use of initial payments, both capital and "loans," to acquire capital assets;

(b) proceeds used to start up the corporate life;

(c) subordination to other indebtedness;

(d) an "inordinately postponed due date;"

(e) provision for payment of "interest" only out of earnings; and

(f) an express or implied agreement not to enforce collection of the "debt."

At one time it was thought that the talismanic test was the ratio between debt and equity. It was intimated in the Supreme Court decision in John Kelley Co. v. Commissioner

(S.Ct.1946) that a ratio of 4:1 (debt equal to four times equity) or more automatically led to the reclassification of the debt as equity. A corporation with a high debt/equity ratio is often called a "thin" corporation. Later cases, however, have rejected the suggestion that the test is a mechanical one based on an arithmetic calculation. In other words, courts have rejected in strong terms the argument by the United States that a high ratio of debt to equity automatically indicates an objectionable avoidance of taxes, and therefore grounds for treating the debt as equity. However, high debt/equity ratios are relevant and it is not surprising that most cases in which debt has been reclassified as equity involve debt/equity ratios higher than 4:1, and often higher than 10:1.

§ 7.26 Debt as a Second Class of Stock in S Corporations

In order to qualify for the S corporation tax election, the corporation may not have more than one class of stock outstanding (except classes that differ only in voting rights). A number of early tax cases considered the question whether debt might constitute "a second class of stock," thereby causing the loss of the S corporation election.

After the Internal Revenue Service won several such cases, Congress enacted a definition of "straight debt," the inclusion of which in a corporate capital structure does not cause loss of the S corporation election. In general terms, the definition of straight debt requires a market interest rate and the inclusion only of terms typical of arms-length debt transactions. The test, however, is basically an objective one.

§ 7.27 The Deep Rock Doctrine Revisited

The so-called Deep Rock doctrine applied in bankruptcy cases has been discussed in a previous chapter (see § 6.13 of this Nutshell). It permits subordination of shareholder-owned debt to the claims of general creditors when the court believes it is fair to do so. It is, therefore, the bankruptcy analogue to the "thin corporation" problem in tax law described in § 7.25. The shareholder claims that are subordinated may be either secured or unsecured: Under this doctrine the court may treat secured shareholder claims either as on a parity with general unsecured claims or as inferior to all other claims. Obviously, this doctrine, when applied, has the effect of eliminating one major advantage of shareholder indebtedness.

The doctrine has generally been applied in Federal bankruptcy cases, and it has also been recognized in some state insolvency proceedings.

Some cases have held that a mere showing of inadequate capitalization is not enough for disallowance or subordination in the bankruptcy area and that there must be some additional showing of unfairness, fraud, or misrepresentation. The shareholder involved may have the burden of showing "the inherent fairness and good faith of the transactions involved." One court has suggested that "[i]t is only where the conduct of a stockholder or officer toward his or her corporation can be challenged as being detrimental to the creditors that there is any duty on behalf of the [bankruptcy judge] or the courts to recast the voluntary acts of the corporation into something different from what they have in good faith undertaken to engage in." Wages v. Weiner (5th Cir. 1967). As a practical matter, however, if the initial capitalization is grossly inadequate, some other element of unfairness can usually be found that will permit the court to subordinate the shareholder indebtedness. Also the case law is in disagreement as to whether the adequacy of the initial capital is to be judged in the light of the needs of the particular business, or on some abstract basis of substantiality.

As in the case of tax controversies, subsequent loans needed to keep the business afloat are likely to be accepted by the courts as true loans for bankruptcy purposes, though unfair attempts to obtain security for such loans may still be attacked under the Deep Rock doctrine.

§ 7.28   Publicly Traded Debt Securities

Debt is obviously an important source of capital for both publicly held and closely held corporations. Debt may range from very short "overnight" bank loans to term loans for periods of up to a year or more to lines of credit established with banks or other institutional lenders that may be available indefinitely. This section, however, deals only with long term debt instruments that are usually publicly traded and viewed as securities in their own right. They are often called "fixed-income securities," here called "debt securities."

There are two principal types of debt securities: debentures, and bonds. Technically a "debenture" is an unsecured corporate obligation while a "bond" is secured by a lien or mortgage on some part (or all) of the corporate property. However, the word "bond" is often used indiscriminately to cover both bonds and debentures and is so used hereafter. Typical debt securities are issued in multiples of $1,000, pay interest at a fixed rate for the life of the security, and have a specified maturity date that may be many years in the future.

Debt securities are created by an indenture, a formal contract between the issuer, the trustee (usually a bank or financial institution), and either the financing source or the underwriter who will purchase the securities with a view toward reselling them to the investing public. The provisions of the indenture define the rights of holders and the duties of the trustee; a summary of the principal provisions may appear on certificates issued to purchasers.

A "private placement" of an issue of debt securities means that the entire issue has been sold to a single institutional investor or to a relatively small number of such investors. A "public offering" of debt securities means that the issue is being sold to members of the investing public through an underwriter. A public offering of debt securities must be registered under the Securities Act of 1933.

Bonds and debentures historically were reflected by certificates that usually were printed on heavy paper with elaborate and intricate designs, lettering, and figures. The purpose was to deter forgeries. They were bearer instruments, negotiable simply by delivery of the certificate. Indeed, in a sense the certificates *were* the bonds. Future interest payments were represented by coupons. Each coupon was itself a tiny negotiable instrument payable to bearer that reflected one interest payment due on some date in the future. These coupons were "clipped" with scissors as they matured, and submitted to the issuer or trustee for payment, usually through a bank or broker. Because these were bearer instruments, there was a potentially serious theft risk, and bonds were usually kept in safe deposit boxes at banks or in safes in commercial or residential buildings.

The anonymity of bearer instruments turned out to be a handy device for hiding income from the Internal Revenue Service. Congress amended the Internal Revenue Code in 1982 to deny deductions for interest paid on bearer bonds. As a result, bond ownership today is reflected either by certificates registered in the name of the owner and transferable only by endorsement, or increasingly by book entries on the records of brokerage firms and issuers.

Interest payments on debt securities are usually fixed obligations, due in any event, and expressed as a percentage of the face amount of the security. A "six percent" bond means that a $1,000 bond will pay $60 per year. Since the $60 payment is fixed for the life of the bond, the market value of the bond will move inversely with interest rates.

Not all bonds carry a fixed coupon rate. Some corporations have issued "income bonds," in which the obligation to pay interest is conditioned on adequate corporate earnings. Somewhat rarer are so-called participating bonds, where the amount of interest payable on the bonds increases or decreases with corporate earnings. The 1980s saw the development of novel interest provisions for bonds similar to novel preferred stock provisions. "PIK" ("payment in kind") bonds pay interest in the form of promissory notes or additional bonds rather than cash for a stated period of years; cash interest payments begin on a specified date. "Reset" bonds contain provisions that require the issuer to adjust ("reset") the interest rate at a specified date in the future in the event the bonds are selling below face value so as to return the bonds' market value to their face value. These novel provisions have created difficulties for borrowers; in several instances, for example, reset bonds were selling at such a low price as the reset date approached that no adjustment in the interest rate could return the bonds' market price to their face value. In the case of such bonds, default or renegotiation of their terms was inevitable.

Debt securities may have rights analogous to those provided for preferred shares discussed in § 7.21. For example, they are usually subject to redemption by the issuer: The corporation reserves the power to call in the securities and pay them off before the maturity date, usually at a premium over the face value. New issues of bonds usually provide that they are nonredeemable for a stated period. If less than the entire issue is being redeemed, bonds selected for redemption may be chosen by lot or by some other system. "Sinking fund" provisions in bonds may require the corporation to set aside cash to redeem a part of the issue each year (or to purchase bonds on the open market and retire them). In some instances, sinking funds accumulate until the entire issue matures when the proceeds of the fund are used to pay off the entire principal.

Many debentures are made convertible into equity securities, usually common stock, on some predetermined conversion ratio. This ratio is usually adjusted for stock splits, dividends, and the like. In effect, these provisions protect the conversion privilege from dilution. When convertible debentures are converted, they, and the debt they represent, disappear and the new equity securities (the "conversion securities") take their place.

When the market value of the conversion securities exceeds the redemption price, the convertible debentures will be priced at or near their conversion value rather than at their inherent value as a debt security. If a convertible debenture is called for redemption when it is selling at its conversion value, it is obviously to the holders' advantage to convert before the debentures are actually retired. Such a conversion is described as a "forced" conversion. Conversion in such situations is possible because a redemption privilege is exercisable only after notice is given as specified in the indenture while the conversion privilege continues to exist until the instant of redemption. Where debentures are widely held by members of the general public, litigation has arisen over the adequacy of the notice of redemption, the issue typically being whether the issuer need only give the minimum notice called for in the indenture or whether broader public notification must be given.

Some states authorize holders of bonds to participate in the selection of the board of directors either generally or upon specified contingencies, such as default in payment of interest.

The inclusion of such powers, of course, blurs the distinction between debt and equity securities. The MBCA (1984) does not permit debenture holders to be given the power to vote (though several state statutes authorize corporations to give the power to vote to bond holders).

A few debt securities are publicly traded and listed on the New York or American Stock Exchanges. Most transactions in debt securities, however, take place over the counter, at prices negotiated by and between brokers or dealers. Quotations for bond trading appear regularly in financial and general newspapers.

Many states, municipalities and state agencies issue debt securities. These state issues are often attractive because the interest paid by them may not be subject to the Federal income tax. Not all bonds issued by state agencies are tax-exempt, but those that are provide a much lower yield than analogous taxable debt securities as the price of the security incorporates the value of the tax exempt status of the distributions. Some state issues are also exempt from state or local income taxes. These are called "double tax exempt" or "triple tax exempt" bonds.

[For unfamiliar terms see the Glossary]

CHAPTER EIGHT

THE DISTRIBUTION OF POWERS WITHIN A CORPORATION: SPECIAL PROBLEMS

§ 8.1 The "Statutory Scheme" in General

Traditional state business corporation acts envision a particular model or norm of management and control within the corporation. The traditional model assumes that shareholders elect directors who "manage" the business and affairs of the corporation and who select the officers to carry out the board's directions. This model is referred to as the "statutory scheme," or "statutory norm." This model assumes that every corporation has certain characteristics even though, manifestly, many corporations in the real world do not possess these characteristics.

The traditional statutory model assumes that a corporation has several (or many) shareholders when it provides that the shareholders will hold meetings to select directors pursuant to a notice given a certain number of days in advance of the meeting date. These requirements do not make sense in a corporation with only a single shareholder. A "meeting" of one person is not very much of a meeting, and the requirement that all shareholders be given ten days' notice of that meeting is slightly ridiculous.

Further, rather surprisingly, a large, publicly-held corporation also does not fit all aspects of the traditional model. In these corporations, shareholders are usually so diverse and poorly organized that their principal participation in business affairs is ratifying the selection of directors made by persons who control the day-to-day operations (and who are collectively referred to as the "management"). Further, the board of directors does not of itself "manage" the business of a large publicly held corporation; that is done by the corporate executives and officers (the "management"). The board of directors participates in corporate affairs through its selection of the chief executive officer and to some extent through the exercise of other functions, including oversight, the provision of advice to management, establishment of compensation levels, perhaps approval of major transactions, and so forth. See Chapter 13 of this Nutshell. The large publicly held corporation model fundamentally is quite unlike the traditional corporate model which assumes that the board of directors in fact manages the business.

It is probable that the traditional statutory scheme more or less accurately describes control relationships in many intermediate corporations in the continuum between the very small and the very large.

§ 8.2   The Power to Vary the Statutory Scheme

A question that is critically important is the extent to which the traditional statutory requirements relating to management and control may be varied in corporations that do not closely resemble the traditional model. In connection with closely held corporations, as late as the 1930s it was accepted dogma that the statutory scheme could not be varied or relaxed by agreement of the shareholders in any significant way even though the number of shareholders was small. Since then, however, a more liberal and relaxed view of what is permitted has become generally accepted.

A small, closely held corporation in practice more closely resembles partnerships than publicly held corporations. A person not versed in corporation law might well conclude that in the absence of harm to some class of persons, businessmen should be permitted to vary the statutory norms to fit the needs of their particular business relationship. Such freedom is generally available in partnerships, and there seems to be no reason why it should not be equally available in closely held corporations. While the trend mentioned above is clearly in the direction of providing increased freedom within the corporation, it is still not available to the same extent as it is in a partnership.

The principal reason the development in closely held corporations has been slower than in partnerships is the theory that the privilege of limited liability is a concession by the State. The State may grant or withhold permission to conduct business in the name of a fictitious entity. In order to gain that permission one must follow the procedures and rules set forth in the business corporation statutes. (See generally § 2.1 of this Nutshell). Despite criticism of this theory as pure formalism, vestiges of it remain embedded in the thinking of judges, and it is therefore unsafe to attempt by simple agreement of the shareholders to make substantial variations from the statutory norm that are not expressly authorized by statute.

This chapter essentially describes the traditional statutory norms. Chapter 12 of this Nutshell discusses the legislative changes that have specifically relaxed these statutory norms for closely held corporations. As described in chapter 12, there are two different but overlapping approaches: (1) the enactment of special close corporation elections that provide rules for internal management quite different than those discussed in this Chapter, and (2) the enactment of general statutes authorizing variations from the statutory norm without limitation.

Chapter 13 describes the general structure of management of publicly held corporations.

§ 8.3   The Statutory Scheme: Shareholders

The shareholders in the traditional statutory scheme are the ultimate owners of the corporation, but have only limited powers to participate in management and control. The statutes contemplate that they may act through four main channels:

(1) Election and removal of directors;

(2) Approval or disapproval of corporate operations that are void or voidable unless ratified;

(3) Approval or disapproval of amendments to articles of incorporation or bylaws constituting the ''contract'' between the corporation and its shareholders; and

(4) Approval or disapproval of fundamental changes not in the regular course of business (e.g. mergers, compulsory share exchanges, dissolution, or disposition of substantially all the corporate assets).

This list does not fully exhaust the shareholders' powers. Statutes also grant shareholders miscellaneous incidental powers, perhaps the most important of which is the right to inspect corporate books and records. See, for example, Chapter 16 of the Model Business Corporation Act (1984), discussed in Chapter 19 of this Nutshell. The MBCA (1984) and state statutes also authorize shareholders to file derivative suits on behalf of the corporation (MBCA (1984) §§ 7.40—7.47) or suits to enjoin ultra vires acts (MBCA (1984) § 3.04). Also, § 8.03 of the MBCA (1984) requires shareholder approval for certain major changes in the size of the board of directors. State statutes that embody the traditional par value corporation finance concepts grant shareholders additional powers, including a veto power over repurchases of corporate shares out of capital surplus or dividends payable in shares of the corporation, and a power to approve the consideration for which no par shares are issued.

It is also well established that shareholders may adopt resolutions making recommendations to the board of directors, and because of the power to select and remove directors, it is probable that the directors will listen carefully to the views of a majority of the shareholders. (See § 8.8 of this Nutshell.)

The selection of independent accountants in publicly held corporations is vested in the shareholders by tradition and by regulations adopted by the Securities and Exchange Commission.

Nevertheless, the fact remains that in the traditional corporate model the shareholders have only limited powers to participate in management and control: their principal function is to select other persons—the directors—to manage the business of the corporation for them.

§ 8.4 The Statutory Scheme: Directors

The traditional language of business corporation statutes defining the role of the board of directors is that "the business and affairs of a corporation shall be managed by the board of directors." The verb "shall be managed" has a mandatory ring. In the statutory scheme, directors are "free spirits" entitled to make management decisions without regard to orders or suggestions from shareholders. Indeed, courts have sometimes struck down, as against public policy, agreements among shareholders that purport to dictate how persons shall vote as directors.

In the very large corporation with billions of dollars of assets, it is not realistic to expect the directors actually to manage the day-to-day affairs of the business. That is management's responsibility. In recognition of this, § 141(a) of the Delaware General Corporation Law and § 8.01(b) of MBCA (1984) (as well as the statutes of many other states) have modified the basic description of the directors' role. Essentially it now reads: "all corporate powers shall be exercised by *or under the authority of,* and the business and affairs of the corporation *shall be managed under the direction of,* its board of directors * * *" subject to any limitation set forth in the articles of incorporation. The italicized language authorizes corporations to vest actual management authority in the executive officers of the corporation under the general oversight or direction of the board of directors. The final "subject to" clause, it may be noted, authorizes limitations on the scope of the traditional power of directors to be placed in the articles of incorporation.

The scope of the phrase "business and affairs" is not defined in the statutes. Generally, in closely held corporations directors formulate the policy of the corporation, and authorize the making of important contracts. They may delegate details of the actual daily operation of the corporation to officers and agents, but they closely oversee those activities. In the publicly held corporation, most management decisions are delegated to corporate officers subject to general oversight by the board of directors.

Directors have specific statutory authority in numerous areas. For example, the decision to declare dividends is specifically a directorial function, as is the determination of the consideration for which shares are to be issued. Even in the case of important corporate changes (such as mergers or amendments to articles of incorporation that require shareholder approval) the directors have the responsibility to formulate the proposed change, approve it, and submit it to the shareholders for approval or disapproval. The directors thus serve a "gatekeeper's role" with respect to many transactions.

The power of directors with respect to the business and affairs of the corporation in the traditional model flows from the statute rather than from the shareholders who elected them. It is granted to the directors by the statute and not delegated to them by the shareholders in the electoral process. As a result, directors may, at least in theory, disregard the expressed desires of a majority of the shareholders and act as they think best—subject of course, to the ultimate power of the shareholders to select different directors next time. However, there are only a few recorded illustrations of the exercise of this independent power in the teeth of expressed disapproval by a majority of shareholders. As a practical matter, the power of selection and removal of directors is a powerful brake on boards of directors acting independently of the expressed wishes of a majority of the shareholders. In addition, there is perhaps a partially articulated notion that complete independence of action is inconsistent with shareholder democracy in publicly held corporations. This problem occasionally arises immediately after a successful corporate takeover where the new majority shareholders do not possess the power to remove sitting directors without cause.

Perhaps the clearest illustration of the directors' independence from shareholders is their gate keeping function in connection with mergers and amendments to articles of incorporation. Under the MBCA (1984) and the statutes of many states, if the directors do not approve a proposal and recommend that it be submitted to the shareholders, the shareholders are without power to act on the proposal on their own.

The relationships between directors, shareholders and the corporation are *sui generis*. The shareholders elect directors who are granted broad authority with respect to the corporation and its property. Further, responsibility accompanies power. The directors owe fiduciary duties and a duty of care to the corporation and to the shareholders. Directors who violate these duties may incur specified statutory liabilities for their misconduct. They also may be subject to common law or statutory duties in connection with self dealing, usurpation of corporate opportunities, and the like. A director may conceivably be liable for misconduct even though he or she is following the wishes of a majority of the shareholders of a corporation. Because of this risk of directorial liability, cases involving the role of directors place great importance on their unimpaired independence of decision. Shareholder agreements on matters that are reserved to the discretion of directors are often described by courts in antagonistic terms: they are against public policy because they "fetter" the discretion of directors, or in extreme cases, "sterilize" the board of directors.

§ 8.5   The Statutory Scheme: The Power to Remove Directors

At common law, a director had considerable security of office for the period of his or her election. He or she could be removed by shareholders only "for cause," after following a procedure technically known as "amotion." A director, threatened with removal for cause, was entitled to elements of due process including notice of charges, an opportunity to be heard, and a hearing. In a corporation with shares widely held by the general public, the "trial" of a director by the shareholders at a meeting was unwieldy and impractical. The number of shareholders eligible to vote on the fate of the director could easily be in the tens or hundreds of thousands. Decision would be made in fact by the granting or withholding of proxy appointments by individual shareholders executed before the formal hearing would occur. Courts recognized this reality and required that the imperiled director be given access to the proxy machinery to conduct his or her defense at the proxy solicitation level. There is also case law questioning the power of a court to remove a director even for cause if a majority of the shareholders refused to do so. These common law rules were, of course, basically consistent with the principle that directors' independence of judgment cannot be restricted or interfered with by shareholders.

These common law rules have been virtually totally superseded by statute. Modern corporation statutes permit shareholders to remove directors without cause [see MBCA (1984) § 8.08], though in a few states such a power exists in all circumstances only if specifically reserved to the shareholders in the articles of incorporation. Furthermore, a number of states expressly permit a court to remove directors upon a judicial finding that the director "engaged in fraudulent or dishonest conduct, or gross abuse of authority or discretion," and that removal is in the best interest of the corporation. See MBCA (1984) § 8.09. The power to remove a director by judicial act is appropriate in two circumstances: (1) where the director possesses sufficient voting power as a shareholder to prevent removal, and declines to vote for his or her own removal, and (2) in publicly held corporations where the director refuses to resign despite requests to do so, and the cost of an amotion proceeding to remove him or her is substantial.

The statutes permitting the removal of directors without cause subtly change the relation between shareholders and directors. The power to remove for policy or personal reasons not involving "cause" in the legal sense may be important in several situations, for example:

(1) Where a person has recently acquired a majority of the outstanding shares (or at least working control) and desires to put "his own people" in control of the corporation immediately;

(2) In closely held corporations where a majority (or sole) shareholder may wish to elect friends as directors but ensure their continued loyalty. An unlimited power of removal without cause goes a long way toward ensuring that loyalty.

Under modern statutes a corporation may voluntarily elect to grant directors the broader tenure they possessed at common law. Such provisions are not uncommon. For example, some publicly held corporations have granted directors security as part of a defensive plan to make takeovers more difficult. The theory was that a potential purchaser of a working majority of the corporation's voting shares might be deterred if the purchaser is unable to obtain immediate control of the corporation's board of directors. In closely held corporations, similar provisions may be part of a plan to assure continued minority shareholder representation on the board of directors over the possible opposition of the majority shareholders.

A question may exist as to whether an amendment to bylaws granting (or restoring) the power to remove directors without cause may be made effective against incumbent directors who were elected under bylaws that guaranteed them greater security of office. A court may be tempted to argue in this situation that a change in the bylaws during the term of a director is an invalid deprivation of a vested right.

§ 8.6   Elimination of the Board of Directors

Until relatively recently it was an accepted premise of the statutory scheme that every corporation had to have a board of directors. The first important exception to this principle occurred in the special close corporation statutes described in Chapter 12 of this Nutshell. The theory underlying the decision to permit closely held corporations to dispense with a board of directors and have their affairs conducted directly by shareholders runs along the following lines. Why should a corporation with a few shareholders—perhaps only one or two—have to have a board of directors? Why should not such a corporation be permitted to dispense with a board of directors entirely and simply conduct business directly through shareholders? In fact, that is what almost always happens, with the shareholders donning their "director hats" when their lawyer tells them to. There seems to be no good reason why such a corporation should not be able to have its formal structure reflect the reality of the way the business is run. This reasoning is persuasive, and a number of states have enacted close corporation statutes authorizing direct shareholder management.

The close corporation statutes generally require an election by the corporation to adopt all aspects of those statutes. But why should the option to dispense entirely with the board of directors be limited to corporations that have made the close corporation election? If a non-electing corporation has only one or two shareholders, why should it not also be entitled to dispense with its board of directors without getting involved with the close corporation election? It was on the basis of reasoning implicit in these questions that the original draftsmen of the Model Business Corporation Act (1984) added section 8.01(c) that permits any corporation with 50 or fewer shareholders to elect to dispense with or limit the authority of the board of directors. In 1992, this privilege was broadened even further to permit any corporation to adopt non-traditional governance rules, including dispensing with a board of directors, by a simple written agreement executed by all of the shareholders. MBCA (1984) § 7.32. It is too early to tell whether this innovative provision will be widely used; certainly it represents a sharp departure from the traditional mores of the corporate form.

§ 8.7   The Statutory Scheme: Officers

Corporation statutes generally do not attempt to define the authority and role of officers. A typical statutory provision merely states that each officer of the corporation "has the authority and shall perform the duties set forth in the bylaws or, to the extent consistent with the bylaws, the duties prescribed by the board of directors or by direction of an officer authorized by the board of directors to prescribe the duties of other officers." [MBCA (1984) § 8.41] In theory, corporate officers administer the day-to-day affairs of the corporation subject to the direction and control of the board of directors. In fact, of course, their authority is often considerably greater, particularly in larger publicly held corporations. Further, the precise scope of the implied authority of officers vis á vis third persons—particularly the president—is somewhat broader, but apparently varies from state to state. (For a discussion see § 11.6 of this Nutshell.) The basic point for present purposes, however, is that corporate officers are visualized in the traditional statutory model as agents carrying out policies established by the board of directors.

In modern statutes, the board of directors is given complete discretion as to the titles for persons filling specific corporate offices. Older statutes designate that each corporation must have a "president," a "secretary," a "treasurer" and one or more "vice presidents." However, the board of directors is given authority to create additional offices and designate the titles for persons holding those offices.

§ 8.8 Shared Responsibility With Respect to Corporate Operations

As indicated previously, in the traditional corporate governance model, the directors have responsibility for the management of the business and affairs of the corporation. In real life shareholders also have clearly defined roles on certain business matters. Many corporate decisions involve the participation of both directors and shareholders.

Shareholders of publicly held corporations may be called upon to review and approve the selection of accountants, auditors or attorneys who are to evaluate the stewardship of the directors. Also, shareholders are sometimes called upon to approve or refuse to approve specific corporate operations or corporate transactions that directors have authorized or approved. Shareholder ratification usually involves transactions in which management is personally interested (see § 14.21 of this Nutshell) or requests by officers or directors for indemnification against liability or litigation costs (see § 15.4 of this Nutshell).

It is standard operating procedure today for publicly held corporations to submit incentive compensation plans for officers and high level employees (profit sharing plans, stock option plans, "phantom stock" plans, and the like) to shareholders for approval. Approval of these transactions by shareholders does not totally immunize them from attack since a court may subsequently decide that a plan involves waste or a gift of corporate assets. Approval by shareholders, however, probably prevents shareholders who vote to approve the plan from later attacking it; approval may also prevent other shareholders from attacking the fairness of the transaction or shift the burden of proof or persuasion from the directors to the attacking shareholders. Ratification or approval of transactions, however, does not validate fraudulent, oppressive or manifestly unfair transactions involving officers or directors.

Shareholders are sometimes asked to approve a blanket resolution covering all business and other transactions by management during the period since the last meeting. Such resolutions are of questionable utility since they do not validate improper transactions of which the shareholders have no knowledge.

Independent of statute, shareholders also make recommendations to the board of directors on corporate matters. While without legal effect, such resolutions express the views of the ultimate owners of the corporation, and are usually followed. For example, in one leading case, Auer v. Dressel (N.Y.1954), it was held proper for shareholders to vote upon a resolution approving the administration of an ousted president and demanding his reinstatement. The Court said, "The stockholders, by expressing their approval of Mr. Auer's conduct as president and their demand that he be put back in that office, will not be able, directly, to effect that change in officers, but there is nothing invalid in their so expressing themselves and thus putting on notice the directors who will stand for election at the annual meeting."

§ 8.9   Shared Responsibility: Approval of Fundamental Corporate Changes

Shareholders have the specific statutory power to approve or disapprove certain fundamental changes in the corporation's structure proposed by the board of directors. In a few states, shareholders have the power both to propose and to adopt such changes, but in most states directors must first approve the action and recommend it to the shareholders before the shareholders may act. While the types of changes that require formal shareholder approval vary to some extent from state to state, most states require shareholder approval of the following:

(1) Amendments of articles of incorporation.

(2) Mergers and consolidations.

(3) Dissolution.

(4) Sale of all or substantially all of a corporation's assets not in the ordinary course of business.

(5) Statutory share exchanges where the decision is binding on all owners of shares.

In most states, a majority of all the outstanding voting shares must approve the proposed transaction, though several states retain the older requirement (almost universal thirty years ago) that two-thirds of the outstanding shares (both voting and nonvoting) must approve the proposed transaction.

As noted earlier, under the MBCA (1984) and the statutes of many states, the board of directors has a "gate keeping" function with respect to these types of transactions. The board of directors must approve the transaction before the shareholders may consider it. If the board of directors refuses to recommend the transaction to the shareholders, they may not approve the proposal on their own motion. Thus, decisions on fundamental matters in most states are shared between shareholders and directors, and there is a requirement that both must concur in the proposal. In a handful of states, including Massachusetts, shareholders have power to effectuate basic corporate changes without the concurrence of the directors, but that is the exception rather than the norm.

In addition to these fundamental changes, state statutes may provide for shareholder approval of less substantial transactions, including distributions in partial liquidation out of capital, reductions of stated capital, or the purchase of corporate shares out of capital surplus.

§ 8.10   Shared Responsibility: Bylaw Amendments

In most states, the initial bylaws of a corporation are adopted by the board of directors or incorporators, whichever group completes the organization of the corporation. Thereafter, the power to amend or repeal bylaws may be vested in either the shareholders or the directors, or very commonly in either group. The 1969 Model Act contained a skeletal and rather ambiguous provision that still appears in the statutes of many states. The second sentence of MBCA (1969) § 27 states that the power to amend bylaws is vested in the board of directors "unless reserved to the shareholders by the articles;" the section also provides that the shareholders may "repeal or change" bylaws adopted by the directors.

The MBCA (1984) devotes three different sections to bylaw amendments. Section 10.20 provides that directors may adopt, amend, or repeal bylaws unless (a) the bylaw deals with a subject that the statute or the articles of incorporation reserve exclusively to the shareholders, or (b) the shareholders have previously amended or repealed a bylaw on the same subject and have provided expressly that their action is not subject to change by the directors. Further, section 10.20(b) makes it clear that the shareholders' power in this area is primary since the directors may not declare any bylaw off-bounds to the shareholders in the same way that shareholders can with respect to future action by the directors. Section 10.21 deals with bylaw provisions increasing quorum or voting requirements for shareholders while section 10.22 deals with bylaw provisions relating to quorum or voting requirements for directors.

There are wide variations in the state statutes dealing with the power to amend or repeal bylaws. Generally, the power is shared but the primacy of shareholders in this regard is usually recognized. In a few states directors may not repeal or amend bylaws adopted by shareholders; in others the shareholders may designate bylaws that may not be amended by the board of directors.

§ 8.11   Restrictions on Directors in Close Corporations

Experience has shown that in the real world the participants in a business venture often wish to divide up the powers of management and control in a way that is difficult to fit within the traditional statutory scheme. Great strain on the statutory scheme may occur in closely held corporations if the parties wish to allocate authority in a way that is not consistent with the statutory scheme. But similar problems also occur in joint venture corporations and even in publicly held corporations. This section considers the developing case law as to the extent to which the broad authority of directors can be limited or varied by agreement.

A not uncommon situation arises when two or three persons own a business that is being conducted in corporate form. A minority participant wishes to have a veto power over some specific corporate action. Is such a power consistent with the statutory scheme? As with many other corporate issues, there are ways that a veto power may be formally created. For example, the corporation statutes of many states permit a corporation to increase voting requirements up to and including unanimity. It may be possible to give a single director a veto power over specific transactions through modification of the voting requirements in the articles of incorporation or the bylaws. Similarly, a provision that the treasurer of the corporation must be a holder of a certain class of stock is enforceable in most states. It may be possible to create classes of shares that will ensure that a specific person will be named as treasurer. Also, nothing would apparently prevent the corporation from creating a non-statutory office such as "comptroller" and assign virtually all duties of the treasurer to that new office. Doubtless other devices may be invented by ingenious counsel to make enforceable specific management arrangements in states that closely follow the traditional management norm.

The risk in these arrangements is that a veto power in a single shareholder is potentially inconsistent with the statutory scheme since it is a restriction on the broad discretion granted the board of directors by statute. As a result it is possible that a court may invalidate these types of arrangements on broad public policy grounds.

A case from the 1960s well illustrates this danger. In Burnett v. Word, Inc. (Tex.App.1967), a minority shareholder in each of two closely held corporations desired to retain a veto over the corporation borrowing money. The shareholders entered into a written agreement that the corporations would not borrow more than $10,000 and $40,000 respectively, except by unanimous approval of the shareholders. The agreement also stated that each party "binds himself to vote as stockholders and directors in such a manner as to carry out bona fide the purposes and intent of this agreement." This agreement obviously fettered to some extent the business discretion of the board of directors, and thereby departed from the statutory scheme. The court invalidated the portion of the agreement relating to the directors: "An agreement by which directors abdicate or bargain away in advance the judgment the law contemplates they shall exercise over the corporation is void. The agreement of the parties to bind themselves as directors is void." In a more recent case, the New York Court of Appeals upheld by a closely divided vote a similar provision. Zion v. Kurtz (N.Y.1980). Cases such as these, whether or not correctly decided, illustrate the pervasive impact of the statutory scheme on judicial thought and the danger of assuming that simply because all parties in interest agree to a variation in the statutory scheme, the variation is automatically valid. It may be noted in passing that the agreement in Burnett v. Word, Inc. was upheld to the extent it constituted an agreement by shareholders to vote as shareholders in a specified manner. Agreements of this type are discussed in § 9.12 of this Nutshell. In other words, the danger of invalidity lies in agreements that prescribe what the board of directors will do, not agreements among shareholders as to what shareholders will.

Some courts have upheld variations on the statutory scheme, and the modern trend distinctly appears to be running in the direction of upholding such agreements and away from the strict position of Burnett v. Word, Inc. The classic line of cases with respect to agreements fettering the discretion of directors arose in New York. In McQuade v. Stoneham (N.Y.1934), the Court invalidated an agreement between the majority shareholder and two minority shareholders that one minority shareholder would be retained as treasurer of the corporation at a specified salary. There was a falling out, and the board of directors failed to reappoint the shareholder to the office of treasurer and discontinued his salary. The Court said, "We are constrained by authority to hold that a contract is illegal and void so far as it precludes the board of directors, at the risk of incurring legal liability, from changing officers, salaries or policies or retaining individuals in office, except by consent of the contracting parties. On the whole, such a holding is probably preferable to one which would open the courts to pass on the motives of directors in lawful exercise of their trust." (An independent ground for this decision also existed.)

Two years later the same problem again came before the highest New York court in the case of Clark v. Dodge (N.Y. 1936). Clark owned 25 per cent and Dodge owned 75 per cent of the stock of two corporations manufacturing medicinal preparations by secret formulae. Dodge did not actively participate in the management of the business; only Clark, who actively managed the business, knew the secret formulae. In 1921, Dodge and Clark entered into an agreement by which Dodge agreed to retain Clark as general manager of the business and to pay him one-fourth of the income either in the form of salary or dividends. The agreement was to continue so long as Clark remained "faithful, efficient and competent to so manage and control the said business." Clark, in turn, agreed to disclose the secret formulae to Dodge's son and upon Clark's death without issue to bequeath his 25 per cent interest in the corporation to the wife and children of Dodge. This entirely sensible business arrangement appears to run afoul of the McQuade principle, since Dodge was in effect agreeing that the board of directors would retain Clark as general manager and pay him twenty-five per cent of the earnings in the form of salary or dividends. The Court nevertheless upheld the agreement:

Are we committed by the *McQuade* case to the doctrine that there may be no variation, however slight or innocuous, from [the statutory] norm, where salaries or policies or the retention of individuals in office are concerned? There is ample authority supporting that doctrine * * *. [S]omething may be said for it, since it furnishes a simple, if arbitrary, test. Apart from its practical administrative convenience, the reasons upon which it is said to rest are more or less nebulous. Public policy, the intention of the Legislature, detriment to the corporation, are phrases which in this connection mean little. Possible harm to bona fide purchasers of stock or to creditors or to stockholding minorities have more substance; but such harms are absent in many instances. If the enforcement of a particular contract damages nobody—not even, in any perceptible degree, the public—one sees no reason for holding it illegal, even though it impinges slightly upon the broad provision [vesting directors with the sole powers of management]. Damage suffered or threatened is a logical and practical test and has come to be the one generally adopted.

Where the directors are the sole stockholders, there seems to be no objection to enforcing an agreement among them to vote for certain people as officers * * * .

If there was any invasion of the powers of the directorate under that agreement it is so slight as to be negligible; and certainly there is no damage suffered by or threatened to anybody. The broad statements in the *McQuade* opinion, applicable to the facts there, should be confined to those facts.

This decision arguably can be distinguished from *McQuade* on two different grounds:

(1) The Court emphasized that in *Clark* all the shareholders were parties to the agreement. In *McQuade*, some shareholders were not parties to the agreement. Certainly, non-consenting shareholders may be injured if directors fail to exercise their "honest and unfettered" judgment, and hence it seems reasonable to reconcile the two cases on this ground. On the other hand, the agreement in *McQuade* was not being attacked by a non-consenting shareholder, but by a person who was a party to the arguably unenforceable agreement. No

emphasis was placed on the presence of non-consenting shareholders in the *McQuade* decision.

(2) The *Clark* opinion stresses that the arrangement harmed no one, and that "damage suffered or threatened" is a logical and practical test. The *McQuade* court, on the other hand, could foresee possible injury if courts were called upon to evaluate the motives of directors when they change officers, salaries or policies.

If "damage suffered or threatened" were in fact the sole test for evaluating impingements on the statutory norm, the courts might accept very substantial variations. However, subsequent cases in New York indicate that this is too expansive a reading of Clark v. Dodge and that stress should be placed on the statement that the impingement in that case was "slight" or "innocuous" as well as the language that no damage was "suffered or threatened." In Long Park, Inc. v. Trenton–New Brunswick Theatres Co. (N.Y.1948), all the shareholders agreed that (1) one shareholder should have "full authority and power to supervise and direct the operation and management" of certain theaters, and (2) that shareholder could be removed as manager of those theaters only by arbitration. The court invalidated this arrangement under *McQuade*: "We are not confronted with a slight impingement or innocuous variance from the statutory norm, but rather with the deprivation of all the powers of the board insofar as the selection and supervision of the manager of the corporation's theaters, including the manner and policy of their operation, are concerned."

In 1982, the New York Court of Appeals put a rather bizarre twist on these cases, which, if accepted generally, may eliminate most of the problems in this area. Zion v. Kurtz (N.Y.1980), involved a complex financing arrangement in which the creditor obtained a minority interest in a closely held corporation as part of the security for a loan. He also received a commitment from the dominant shareholder that the corporation would not enter into transactions or new business without the consent of the creditor. Under the law of Delaware, such an agreement might validly be entered into by a corporation if it elected to be a statutory close corporation. See § 12.8 of this Nutshell. However, to make this election the corporation had to expressly elect close corporation status in its articles of incorporation and also to refer specifically to the agreement limiting the discretion of directors. The corporation involved in Zion v. Kurtz had done neither. The court nevertheless viewed these omissions as "technical" defects and within the power of the court to correct by an order of reformation. Three justices dissented vigorously on the ground that the whole theory of close corporation election was that public notice should be provided in the articles of incorporation, and the reasoning of the majority vitiated this important principle.

Delaware rejected the underlying premise of *Kurtz* in Nixon v. Blackwell (Del.1993). The Delaware Supreme Court held that it was improper to apply special close corporation provisions to a non-electing corporation, "because the provisions of the statute relating to close corporations and other statutory schemes preempt the field in their respective areas." 626 A.2d, at 1380.

Section 620 of the New York Business Corporation Law was added in 1961 to overrule the *McQuade* principle in limited circumstances. That section basically provides that a restriction on the discretion of the board of directors is enforceable if it appears in the corporation's certificate of incorporation and is approved by all of the shareholders. While this section would not validate the agreements reached in the cases described above, it does provide a road map for making enforceable agreements restricting the discretion of directors in New York.

Galler v. Galler (Ill.1964) is a leading case that rejects the rather narrow view of *McQuade* and similar New York cases. *Galler* enforced a complex shareholders' agreement containing numerous "impingements" of varying degrees of seriousness on the statutory scheme. Among them was a mandatory dividend requirement. The court upheld the arrangement in its entirety. After drawing a sharp distinction between closely held and publicly held corporations, the Court called for statutory recognition of the special problems of the closely held corporation. It concluded that "any arrangements concerning the management of the corporation which are agreeable to all" should be enforced if (1) no complaining minority interest appears, (2) no fraud or apparent injury to the public or creditors is present, and (3) no clearly prohibitory statutory language is violated. While this decision has generally been approved and applauded, a subsequent Illinois case refused to extend *Galler* to validate a shareholders' agreement that more or less squarely contradicted a specific statutory provision relating to the amendment of bylaws. Because of the qualification in the *Galler* opinion about violating "clearly prohibitory statutory language," there is some lingering doubt as to the breadth of the court's holding in this leading case.

§ 8.12   Ameliorating Trends

The most important ameliorating trends are statutory provisions that permit non-traditional management forms for certain corporations. Many modern state statutes permit the participants in a corporation to adopt non-traditional forms of governance. For example, section 8.01(b) of MBCA (1984) originally provided that the power of the board of directors to direct (or oversee the direction of) the business and affairs of the corporation was "subject to any limitation set forth in the articles of incorporation." This "subject to" clause arguably authorized all variations to the statutory scheme discussed in the previous sections so long as the appropriate provision appeared in the articles of incorporation. In 1992, this clause was eliminated and replaced by a much broader authorization in section 7.32 of the Model Act. This section, which is discussed in § 12.9 of this Nutshell, eliminates the requirement that provisions be included in the articles of incorporation and substitutes the much simpler requirement that the provisions be approved unanimously by the shareholders.

As a result of the *Galler* decision discussed above, about 20 states have enacted opt-in close corporation statutes. See § 12.8. These statutes also permit electing closely held corporations to adopt non-traditional forms of governance.

§ 8.13 Delegation of Management Powers and the Statutory Scheme

Interference with the discretion of directors has also been used as a basis for attacking broad management agreements by the corporation that appear to take the sole power of management away from the board of directors and vest it in a manager. There seems to be no inherent reason why a corporation should not be able to appoint a general manager with broad powers over day-to-day affairs subject to a very general power of oversight by the board. The management agreement cases appear to depend on whether the court believes that the board has retained a sufficiently general power of oversight. Similar arguments have been applied to invalidate agreements that grant a shareholder the sole power to manage a portion of the corporation's assets without review by the board of directors. Potentially over-broad delegation to an executive or other committee of the board of directors may also be attacked on a similar ground, though that question is now usually dealt with by specific statutory provision. (See § 10.10 of this Nutshell.) The test in all these cases is whether the agreement "sterilizes" the board so that it has no managerial role at all or whether reasonable powers of oversight are preserved to the board.

[For unfamiliar terms see the Glossary]

CHAPTER NINE

SHARES AND SHAREHOLDERS

§ 9.1 Annual and Special Meetings of Shareholders

Every state statute contains more or less routine provisions about meetings of shareholders. The Model Business Corporation Act (1984), for example, provides that a meeting shall be held "annually at a time stated in or fixed in accordance with the bylaws," [MBCA (1984) § 7.01(a)], that notice of an annual or special meeting shall be given not less than ten nor more than sixty days before the meeting [MBCA (1984) § 7.05(a)], and so forth. The failure to hold an annual meeting does not "affect the validity of any corporate action" [MBCA (1984) § 7.01(c)], though any shareholder may obtain a summary court order requiring the corporation to hold an annual meeting if one is not held "within the earlier of 6 months after the end of the corporation's last fiscal year or 15 months after its last annual meeting" [MBCA (1984) § 7.03(a)(1)]. So far as notice is concerned, statutes permit written waivers that may be executed before, at, or after the meeting in question [MBCA (1984) § 7.06(a)]. These provisions rarely give rise to litigation, though one recent Delaware case ordered a newly formed corporation that delayed its initial meeting to hold the meeting within the time specified by the court.

The principal purpose of an annual meeting obviously is the annual election of directors, but the annual meeting may act on all matters that are within the ambit of shareholder control. It is a general meeting and not limited to the purposes set forth in the notice. Indeed, no statement of purposes at all need appear in the notice of annual meeting. [MBCA (1984) § 7.05(b)]

A special meeting is any meeting other than an annual meeting. It may be called by the persons specified in the statute or in the bylaws of the corporation. Such a meeting may be called by the board of directors, the holders of some specified percentage of the outstanding shares of the corporation, or by certain officers. The 1984 Model Business Corporation Act authorizes holders of ten per cent of the votes eligible to be cast at the meeting to compel the holding of a special meeting. [MBCA (1984) § 7.02(a)(2)] This is somewhat controversial since it may result in a shareholders' meeting being held on matters that management would prefer not be considered or on matters on which there is no chance of passage. There is also the possibility that repetitive or unnecessary meetings might be called by small factions of shareholders. The Official Comment to MBCA (1984) § 7.02 suggests that the board of directors has some discretion in calling special meetings at the request of shareholders to meet this last problem.

Unlike the annual meeting, the only subjects that may be considered at a special meeting are matters described in the notice of meeting. [MBCA (1984) §§ 7.05, 7.02(d)]

A quorum consists of a majority of the outstanding shares, except that the quorum requirement may be increased or decreased by provisions in the articles or bylaws. Statutes usually prescribe a minimum below which the quorum may not be reduced. The most popular figure is one-third, based on old MBCA § 32; the 1984 Model Business Corporation Act does not contain any statutory minimum. Statutes do not prescribe a maximum number to constitute a quorum, and it is therefore possible to require the presence of all outstanding shares to conduct business at a shareholders' meeting. Unanimous quorum requirements are sometimes adopted in close corporations as a planning device, even though it increases the risk of a deadlock since a single shareholder, no matter how small his or her holding, may prevent the holding of the meeting.

Statutes typically provide that if a quorum is present, the affirmative vote of a majority of that quorum is sufficient to bind the corporation. Such statutes may lead to questionable results in situations where shares are present (and counted toward the quorum) but their owners abstain from voting on an issue. Abstentions are in effect counted as negative votes since an action can be adopted only if a majority of all the shares that are present vote in favor of the measure. The 1984 Model Business Corporation Act changes the traditional rule: It provides that if a quorum is present a measure is approved "if the votes cast * * * favoring the action exceed the votes cast opposing the action." [§ 7.25(c)] The example used in the Official Comment to explain why this is preferable posits a meeting of a corporation with one thousand shares outstanding. A quorum is, of course, 501 shares in the absence of a specific provision in the articles of incorporation. Assume that 600 shares are represented at the meeting and the vote on an action is 280 in favor, 225 opposed, and 95 abstaining. Under the traditional statute, the measure fails since 301 votes are necessary (a majority of the quorum); under the MBCA (1984), the action is approved, 280–225. It may be noted that if the owners of the 95 abstaining shares had not been present at all, the action would have been approved under both types of statutes.

Somewhat different rules of shareholder voting are often applicable to elections of directors. These rules are discussed in § 9.6 of this Nutshell.

If a quorum is initially present, a disgruntled faction may fear that it will lose a vote, and leave the meeting seeking to "break" the quorum and thereby prevent the victorious faction from voting on the issue. The general rule is that a quorum, once present, is deemed to be present during the entire meeting, and the withdrawal of a faction does not disable the remaining shareholders from continuing. See § 7.25(b) of the MBCA (1984). Because of this rule, a faction that knows it will be in the minority but believes that a quorum will not exist without their presence, should stay away entirely rather than appearing and later withdrawing.

§ 9.2 Shareholder Action by Consent

Statutes today authorize shareholders to conduct business by unanimous written consent without holding a meeting. Unanimous consent is particularly helpful in closely held corporations, where most shareholders' decisions are unanimous, and the formality of a meeting may be dispensed with (though to be valid under these statutes the consent must be evidenced by a signed writing).

About a dozen states, including Delaware, have gone a step further and authorized holders of the number of shares needed to act on a matter to act by written consent without a meeting. (Del. Gen. Corp. Law, § 228) As discussed in the chapter on proxy voting in publicly held corporations, elimination of the unanimity requirement in corporations with numerous shareholders is not as radical a proposal as might first be thought. Most shareholders vote by proxy in any event, and the same information must be provided for either a vote by proxy or an action by consent. (See section 13.14 of this Nutshell.) In closely held corporations, however, majority consent provisions do not contain the same built-in safeguards. And even in publicly held corporations, the majority consent provision has had some unexpected consequences since it enables a successful aggressor that acquires a majority of the target's voting shares to make immediate changes in management without holding a meeting of shareholders. The majority consent provision in Delaware has led to a fair amount of litigation, because corporations have attempted to blunt its force by imposing procedural obstacles on the power to act by majority written consent.

One recent Delaware case holds that a consent vote does not satisfy the statutory requirement that an annual meeting be held.

§ 9.3 Record and Beneficial Ownership of Shares

Every corporation retains records of the persons in whose name shares have been issued and every share certificate that is issued refers by name to that person. This person is called the "record owner" and generally the corporation may deal with the record owner as though he were the sole owner of the shares. The theory is that when the record owner sells shares, he hands over the certificate to the purchaser with the endorsement on the reverse side of the certificate properly executed. The purchaser then submits the endorsed certificate to the corporation with a request that a new certificate be issued in the name of the purchaser. The old certificate is canceled (and retained with the records of the corporation) and a new certificate is issued in the name of the purchaser (or in another name designated by the purchaser) who then becomes the new record owner.

While modern practice in the transfer of shares of publicly held corporations is quite different from this theory, record ownership concepts continue to apply in all corporations. The corporate records of the names and addresses of record owners are called the "stock transfer books" or "share register" (though they may consist simply of stubs from which share certificates were detached).

The corporation deals only with record owners on matters such as dividends, voting, and notices of meetings. A purchaser who does not follow the procedure described above to become a record owner is the "beneficial owner" of those shares. While corporations do not recognize beneficial owners (since they deal only with record owners), the beneficial owner is the "real" owner of the shares. He or she can compel the record owner to turn over dividends or to execute appropriate documents to permit the beneficial owner to exercise the power to vote or to become the record owner.

Many state statutes authorize a corporation to issue certificateless shares. In these corporations, records of share ownership are maintained by the corporation and new owners are provided with a written statement of the information otherwise required on certificates. See MBCA (1984) § 6.26. Apparently certificateless shares are not widely used today in closely held corporations.

Obviously every publicly held corporation with active trading in its shares must have available new certificates to issue to transferees. It must also take steps to ensure that transfers are properly recorded, that new certificates refer to the same number of shares as old certificates, and so forth. These mechanical functions of registering share transfers are handled by "transfer agents" who keep exact records of all shareholders, their names, addresses and number of shares owned. Transfer agents are usually independent businesses that perform these critical functions pursuant to a contract with the issuer. Publicly held corporations also use "registrars," whose function is to make sure the corporation does not inadvertently over-issue shares. In closely held corporations, the Secretary of the corporation usually serves as the transfer agent.

In an earlier era, the mechanical functions of registration of transfer of shares were quite onerous. However, the modern "book entry" system of recordation and transfer of ownership interests of publicly held corporations described in § 13.12 of this Nutshell simplify the keeping of records and have greatly reduced the practical problems faced by transfer agents and registrars.

§ 9.4   Record Dates

When shares are in the process of being sold or transferred, some rule must be established to determine whether the buyer or the seller is entitled to vote or to receive the distribution. This is usually done today by establishing a "record date" in advance of the meeting or distribution. The person in whose name shares are registered on the record date is entitled to vote, to receive the dividend, or what have you, even if he or she is no longer the owner of the shares. The record date is established for the convenience of the corporation. A record date may be established directly by bylaw provision, but it is more customary to authorize the board of directors to set record dates.

With respect to voting, section 7.07 of the MBCA (1984) requires that a record date be established in advance and that it be not more than seventy days before the date of the meeting. The record date is usually specified in the resolution of the board of directors calling the meeting. If a record date is established, the corporation continues to register transfers and issue new certificates to transferees, but the persons eligible to vote are those in whose name the shares were registered on the record date. If a person purchases shares after the record date but before the meeting and wishes to vote at the meeting, he must obtain a proxy appointment from the record shareholder. Normally the seller will voluntarily give such an appointment to the buyer (because, after all, the seller no longer owns the shares), but if for some reason he refuses to do so, the buyer can obtain a court order commanding the seller to give him such an appointment.

If the board of directors does not formally set a record date (which often occurs in closely held corporations) the corporation is deemed to set a record date as of the date the notice of the meeting is mailed, and eligibility to vote is determined as of that date. [MBCA (1984) § 7.05(d)]

Older statutes permit the board of directors, rather than establishing a record date, to order the stock transfer books closed for a stated period of at least ten days but not more than fifty days before the meeting. [MBCA (1969) § 30]. While the stock transfer books are closed, the corporation refuses to register transfers of shares and eligibility to vote is determined by who was the record owner on the date the books were closed. In effect the corporate records are frozen, though, of course, individual shareholders may sell shares and deliver certificates to purchasers during the period. This alternative is apparently obsolete, though it may be followed in isolated instances by closely held corporations. The MBCA (1984) does not refer to closing the transfer books as an alternative to setting a record date.

The record date provisions are obviously for the benefit of the corporation. They permit the corporation to give proper notice of the meeting, to prepare a voting list, and to establish precisely who is entitled to vote. They also permit management and other shareholders to solicit votes informally before the meeting. If the action involves the payment of a dividend, the record date determines in whose names checks are issued.

With respect to entitlement to dividends in publicly held corporations, see § 18.5 of this Nutshell.

Analogous record date provisions are authorized by the Model Business Corporation Act (1984) for other shareholder actions, e.g., who may demand a special meeting. In the case of a proposal based on the written consent procedures which involves solicitation of numerous shareholders (see § 9.2 of this Nutshell), the record date for determining validity of consents is the day the first written consent is filed with the corporation. A record date for consent solicitations is necessary because the corporation may receive hundreds or thousands of signed consent forms.

§ 9.5   Preparation of Voting List

A voting list of shareholders eligible to vote must be prepared before each shareholders meeting. Section 7.20 of the Model Business Corporation Act (1984) is a typical provision. It contains fairly detailed rules about how this list should be compiled and where it must be kept before and during the meeting. It also requires that this list be available for inspection by shareholders before the meeting beginning two business days after the notice of meeting is given, and during the meeting itself. (The theory is that the corporation must compile a list of shareholders entitled to receive notice of the meeting before the notice is actually given and so it is no burden to prepare the voting list at the same time.) Some states require that the voting list be available only at the meeting itself.

While the failure to prepare the voting list does not affect the validity of any action taken at the meeting [MBCA (1984) § 7.20(e)], such a failure may lead to a summary court order to create the list and to postpone the meeting.

Every shareholder has an absolute right to inspect the voting list. This right is not subject to the qualifications imposed upon a shareholder's right to inspect other books and records of the corporation. (See Chapter 19 of this Nutshell).

At the meeting, the share transfer books of the corporation determine who are the shareholders entitled to vote. In other words, a mistake in the creation of the list does not affect who is entitled to vote at the meeting.

§ 9.6   Election of Directors: Cumulative or Straight Voting

All directors are usually elected each year at the annual meeting of shareholders. (The exception is for "classified" or "staggered" boards discussed in § 9.7.) The most common statutory provision is simply that directors are elected by a vote of the owners of a majority of the shares (1) present at the meeting and (2) entitled to vote, assuming that a quorum is present. This formulation does not address the situation of three or more factions contending for election (in which case it is quite possible that no faction will obtain a majority of the votes present at a meeting). Section 7.28(a) of the Model Business Corporation Act (1984) handles this possibility by making the standard for election "a plurality of the votes cast by the shares entitled to vote in the election at a meeting at which a quorum is present." Many states have adopted this sensible modification to a basic voting rule.

Generally, shareholders may only vote in favor of candidates. As in the case of elections of public officials, they may not cast negative votes against candidates.

The articles of incorporation (and in some states, the by-laws), may increase, but may not decrease, the percentage of the shares required for election. In close corporations it is not uncommon to exercise this privilege and require unanimity as a planning device, even though the possibility of a deadlock in the election of directors is thereby obviously increased.

An important question relating to the election of directors is whether shares may be voted "cumulatively" or must be voted "straight." The workings of straight and cumulative voting can be most simply described by an illustration. Let us assume a corporation with two shareholders, A with 26 shares, and B with 74 shares. Further, let us assume that there are three directors and each shareholder nominates three candidates. A critical point is that candidates run "at large" and do not run for specific places. The three candidates with the most votes in this election are the winners. If only "straight" voting is permitted, A may cast 26 votes for each of any three candidates, and B may cast 74 votes for each of any three candidates. The result, of course, is that if they do not agree on any candidates, all three of B's candidates are elected. If cumulative voting is permitted, the total number of votes that each shareholder may cast is first computed and each shareholder is permitted to distribute these votes as he sees fit over one or more candidates. In the example above, A is entitled to cast a total of 78 votes (26×3) and B is entitled to cast 222 votes (74×3). If A casts all 78 votes for herself, she is assured of election because B cannot divide 222 votes among three candidates in such a way as to give each candidate 79 or more votes and preclude A's election. (If B gives 79 votes to himself and 79 votes to B_1, he will only have 64 votes left for B_2.) Obviously, the effect of cumulative voting is that it increases minority participation on the board of directors. In straight voting, the shareholder with 51 per cent of the vote elects the entire board; in cumulative voting, a relatively small faction (26 per cent in the above example) obtains representation on the board.

The difference between cumulative and straight voting may be vividly illustrated by the deadlock situation where all shares are owned equally by two shareholders—say fifty shares each. If only straight voting is permitted and each shareholder votes only for his or her own candidates, a deadlocked election is inevitable. If there are two places to be filled A will vote 50 shares for herself, and 50 shares for A_2; B will vote 50 shares for himself, and 50 shares for B_2. Thus, four candidates will each have 50 votes for two positions, and the result is that no one is elected. If cumulative voting is permitted on the other hand, A may cast 100 votes for herself and she will be guaranteed election (since B obviously cannot give two candidates more than 100 votes each.) If there are an odd number of directors to be elected (say 3) straight voting still leads to deadlock: A_1–50, A_2–50, A_3–50, B_1–50, B_2–50, B_3–50. If cumulative voting is permitted, A and B may each elect one director but the situation is unstable: a deadlock will be created if each tries to elect the tie-breaking director and the other votes rationally. However, the strategy and counter-strategy can become complex. If A gives A_1 76 votes, A_1 will be guaranteed of election since B has only 150 votes and obviously cannot prevent A_1's election; similarly, if B gives B_1 76 votes, A cannot prevent B_1's election. If both shareholders follow this conservative strategy, the result will be A_1–76, A_2–74, B_1–76, B_2–74, with A_1 and B_1 each being elected and a tie existing between A_2 and B_2. However, if B knows that A will follow this strategy in voting, B might be tempted to divide his vote equally between two candidates in order to elect two of the three directors: A_1–76, A_2–74, B_1–75, B_2–75, with A_1, B_1, and B_2 all being elected. A may counter this strategy by also giving her two candidates 75 votes each, thereby creating a four way tie and electing no one. Indeed, it is disastrous if either shareholder deviates from these very precise voting patterns. If B decides to vote only slightly illogically, for example, by giving B_1–77 votes and B_2–73 votes, he delivers control of the corporation over to A even if A follows the conservative strategy of guaranteeing the election of one director: B_1–77, A_1–76, A_2–74, B_2–73, with B_1, A_1 and A_2 elected.

In these and the following illustrations it is assumed that A or B, once they have adopted a strategy and cast their votes, cannot thereafter change them. This is true to a limited extent in the real world. Balloting for directors is usually by written ballot rather than voice vote so that each shareholder must establish his or her voting strategy without being sure of an opponent's strategy; however, until the vote is announced, a shareholder may be able to recast his or her votes and thereby improve his or her position. The traditional rule is that votes may be changed before the results of the election are announced, though this probably depends on whether the person presiding at the meeting permits a change to be made.

As the preceding discussion illustrates, one undesirable aspect of cumulative voting is that it tends to be a little tricky. If a shareholder casts votes in an irrational or inefficient way, he or she may not get the directorships a different voting strategy would have guaranteed; when voting cumulatively it is relatively easy to make a mistake in spreading votes around. The most graphic illustration of this are the cases where a majority shareholder votes in such a way that he or she elects only a minority of the directors. This is most likely to occur when one shareholder votes "straight" and another votes cumulatively. For example, if A has 60 shares and B only 40, with five directors to be elected, B may nevertheless elect a majority of the board if A votes "straight," and B knows that A is doing so. The result might look like this:

A_1–60, A_2–60, A_3–60, A_4–60, A_5–60, B_1–67, B_2–66, B_3–65, B_4–1, B_5–1.

This strategy is daring of B because he is spreading his vote over three persons when he can be sure only of electing two. If A knows that B will try to elect three persons, A, by properly cumulating her votes, can elect four directors, in effect "stealing" one of B's. The results of such an election might be as follows:

A_1–73, A_2–74, A_3–75, A_4–76, A_5–2, B_1–67, B_2–66, B_3–65, B_4–1, B_5–1.

A minority shareholder generally should not create tie votes among his own candidates. If he does so, and the tied candidates come in fifth and sixth in an election for five directorships, say, the tie may be broken by a new election for only the fifth seat. In this run-off election, the majority shareholder may be able to vote his shares in the run-off election for his own candidate and thereby cause the other shareholder to lose a seat.

Section 7.28(d) of the Model Business Corporation Act (1984) and the statutes of many states require shareholders to give advance notice before the meeting if they plan to vote cumulatively. Such a requirement seems plainly desirable because, as the last illustration graphically demonstrates, election results are illogical if some shareholders vote cumulatively while others do not.

The following formula is useful in determining the number of shares needed to elect one director:

$$\frac{S}{D + 1} + 1.$$

Where S equals the total number of shares voting, and D equals the number of directors to be elected. The analogous formula to elect n directors is:

$$\frac{nS}{D + 1} + 1.$$

A minor modification may sometimes be necessary. The first portion of the formula, $\frac{S}{D + 1}$, establishes the maximum number of shares voted for a single person that is insufficient to elect that person as a director. Any share, or fraction thereof, in excess of that amount will be sufficient to elect a director. The formula set forth in the text ignores fractional shares that sometimes may lead to a one share-error. For example, where there are 100 shares voting and five directors to be elected, the first portion of the formula is $\frac{100}{5 + 1}$, or $\frac{100}{6}$. In this example, 16 shares will not elect a director, but 17 shares will, since the first part of the formula yields $16\frac{2}{3}$. The above formula mechanically yields an answer of $17\frac{2}{3}$.

In several states cumulative voting is mandatory by state constitution or provisions in the state corporation statute. Most states today, however, permit a corporation to exclude cumulative voting; usually this option requires a specific exclusion in the articles of incorporation (an "opt out" election) though in some states, cumulative voting is not permitted unless specific provision for it is made in the articles of incorporation (an "opt in" election). The Model Business Corporation Act (1984) adopts the latter course [MBCA (1984) § 7.28(c)].

Cumulative voting has historically had a strong emotional appeal. The states that mandate cumulative voting by constitutional or statutory provision believe that it is more democratic than straight voting. Persons with large (but minority) holdings, it is argued, should have a voice in the conduct of the corporation. Also, arguably, it may be desirable to have as many viewpoints as possible represented on the board of directors. Further, the presence of a minority director may discourage conflicts of interest by management since discovery is considerably more likely.

There is also no shortage of arguments against mandatory cumulative voting. (1) The introduction of a partisan on the board is inconsistent with the notion that the board should represent all interests in the corporation. (2) A partisan director may cause disharmony that reduces the efficiency of the board. (3) A partisan director may criticize management unreasonably so as to make it less willing to take risky (but desirable) action. (4) A partisan director may leak confidential information. (5) Cumulative voting is usually used to further narrow partisan goals, e.g. to give an insurgent group a toehold in the corporation in an effort to obtain control.

As a practical matter, cumulative voting in a factionalized, close corporation may be of considerable importance. It is irrelevant, of course, in one-shareholder corporations or corporations in which the parties are in amity and agree upon the persons who should be on the board of directors. In the large, publicly held corporation, cumulative voting is traditionally considered more of a nuisance than anything else because it complicates voting by proxy, and usually does not affect the actual outcome of an election. It should be observed, however, that where large boards are involved, cumulative voting may permit institutional investors or "public interest" or other groups to obtain representation on the board. It also may simplify the task of a person seeking to take over the corporation by giving the aggressor a "toe hold" on the board of directors, though that is debatable. While some groups have advocated that public corporations be required to adopt cumulative voting, management of such corporations tends to oppose cumulative voting, stressing the mechanical and technical complexities of such voting.

In a closely held corporation, representation of minority interests on the board of directors may be ensured by using different classes of common shares that have identical financial rights but are entitled to vote separately as classes for the election of specified numbers of directors. It is generally preferable to use different classes of shares when the business plan contemplates that holders of minority interests in the corporation are to have representation on the board of directors than relying on cumulative voting. Cumulative voting tends to be a bit tricky and may be eliminated or minimized by a variety of devices discussed in this and the following sections.

§ 9.7   "Classified" Boards of Directors

Many states permit a board of directors consisting of nine or more directors to be "classified" or "staggered" so that approximately one-third of the directors are elected each year, and each individual director is elected for a three year term. In states where cumulative voting is mandatory, and sometimes in corporations formed in other states as well, it is not uncommon to employ this device to minimize the impact of cumulative voting. Classification minimizes the impact of cumulative voting because it takes a larger minority interest to elect one of three directors than it does to elect one of nine directors. For example, if there are nine directors elected each year, ten per cent of the stock can elect one director; if the nine directors are classified and three are elected each year, it takes twenty-five per cent of the stock to elect one director. (If you do not believe these percentages, try them out on the formulas set forth above.)

The theoretical justification for classification is that it ensures "experience of service" on the board, since only one-half or one-third of the board will be elected each year. However, experience of service is usually not a major motivating factor for classifying a board, since as a practical matter, experience is provided simply by reelecting the same persons as directors year after year.

One consequence of a classified board in which only one-third of the directors are elected each year is that directors elected by the prior shareholders are continued in office for one or two years even though an aggressor has acquired a majority of the outstanding shares or a controlling interest in a corporation has been sold to outsiders. Where the board consists of three classes, a person becoming a majority share-holder cannot be assured of electing a majority of the board for two full years. This effect of classification is of course independent of its impact on cumulative voting, and in some instances classification has been proposed in publicly held corporations primarily for this reason. However, a majority shareholder may have power to remove directors without cause, and where that power is available, a majority share-holder can replace directors at will, no matter who elected them.

Classifying or staggering the board of directors thus has two basic effects:

(1) It makes it more difficult for a minority faction to elect a director when there is cumulative voting.

(2) It makes take-over attempts more difficult when directors can be removed only for cause.

Section 8.06 of the MBCA (1984) and many state statutes permit variations of the classification scheme. A board of directors with nine or more members may be divided into two or three classes of as nearly equal numbers as possible with one class being elected each year. Thus, each director serves for two years (if there are two classes) or three years (if there are three classes). Some states permit a board to be classified only if the corporation does not provide for cumulative voting. These statutes may make takeovers more difficult but prohibit classification solely to minimize the impact of cumulative voting.

§ 9.8   Other Devices to Minimize Cumulative Voting

Other devices also limit the impact of cumulative voting. If cumulative voting is not required by statute or constitutional provision, it may be eliminated by an amendment to the articles of incorporation in the same way as any other attribute of shares. (See § 20.2 of this Nutshell.)

Reduction of the size of the board of directors has much the same effect as staggering the election of directors. Such a reduction may require an amendment to the articles of incorporation, but many states permit corporations to have variable size boards of directors, and the size of the board may be varied by the directors without shareholder approval. [MBCA (1984) § 8.03] Shares may sometimes be tied up in voting trusts or voting agreements; in many states non-voting shares also may be used consistently with a cumulative voting requirement.

It may be possible to remove a minority director without cause and replace him or her with a more congenial person, at least until the next election. Section 8.08(c) of MBCA (1984) and the statutes of many states, however, prohibit the removal of a minority director elected by cumulative voting unless the votes in favor of removal would have been enough to prevent the original election of the director in an election for directors.

The influence of minority directors elected through cumulative voting may also be minimized by having informal discussions in advance of meetings, scheduling board meetings at inconvenient times or places, and delegating functions to committees composed entirely of management directors. While a few instances of the use of such tactics have been reported, they do not appear to be very common. That may be because cumulative voting and the election of minority directors is not required in most states, and corporations generally do not elect voluntarily to have cumulative voting.

§ 9.9 Voting by Proxy

A proxy is a person who is authorized by a record shareholder to vote his or her shares. The relationship is one of principal and agent. Some confusion may arise in terminology since the single word "proxy" may interchangeably be used to designate the document that creates the authority, the grant of authority itself, and the person granted the power to vote the shares. The Model Business Corporation Act (1984) limits the use of the word "proxy" to the person with the power to vote; it refers to the grant of authority as the "appointment" of a proxy, and the document creating the appointment as an "appointment form."

The law of proxy regulation rather neatly divides itself into two areas. On the one hand is the skimpy—almost nonexistent—state law dealing with the legal requirements and duration of a proxy appointment. Under state law, perhaps the most lively issue is whether a proxy appointment that is stated to be irrevocable is in fact irrevocable. See § 9.10 of this Nutshell. That this is not an earth shaking issue is attested to by the virtual absence of reported litigation on this question. On the other hand is the burgeoning law of federal proxy regulation in publicly held corporations subject to the reporting requirements of section 12 of the Securities Exchange Act of 1934. This is discussed in a later chapter of this Nutshell (see § 13.4).

The standard state statutory provision relating to proxies merely states that a shareholder may vote either "in person or by proxy." MBCA (1984) § 7.22(a). No particular form of proxy appointment is required under this section. Proxy appointments have been ruled valid despite omission of the name of the proxy, the date of the meeting, or the date the proxy appointment was executed. However, the proxy appointment must be in writing, a provision of obvious benefit to the inspector of elections and the corporation. A proxy need not be a shareholder.

The usual state statutory provision relating to duration of a proxy appointment states that an appointment "is valid for 11 months unless a longer period is expressly provided in the appointment form." MBCA (1984) § 7.22(c). Some state statutes limit all proxy appointments to a period of eleven months. The theory of the eleven-month provision is that a new appointment form should be executed before each annual meeting. However, under the MBCA (1984) there is nothing to prevent the parties from agreeing that a much longer period shall be applicable to a specific proxy appointment. Since a proxy is an agent, his or her appointment is normally revocable at the pleasure of the record owner. Thus, even if a long period is designated as the duration of the proxy appointment, it may be revoked at any time.

A proxy appointment may be revoked either expressly or by implication. For example, the execution of a later proxy appointment constitutes a revocation of an earlier, inconsistent appointment. Personal attendance at a meeting may also constitute revocation of an earlier proxy appointment, though this depends on the intention of the shareholder. Since later proxy appointments revoke earlier ones, it is important that appointment forms be dated. Inspectors of election, where there is a contest, must determine which is the latest appointment form executed by a specific shareholder in order to determine how the shares are to be voted.

§ 9.10   Irrevocable Proxy Appointments

Certain proxy appointments may be irrevocable. Generally a mere recitation that a proxy appointment is irrevocable does not make it so; such an appointment is usually as revocable as any other agency appointment. The general rubric for determining whether a proxy appointment is truly irrevocable is whether it is "coupled with an interest." This phrase, which has its origin in the agency case of Hunt v. Rousmanier's Adm'rs (U.S.1823), has no inherent meaning of itself and must be fleshed out with examples and further analysis.

It is not enough that the proxy appointment merely be supported by consideration. The clearest example of this is an outright purchase of a proxy appointment for cash by a shareholder seeking to obtain control of the corporation. Such a purchased vote almost certainly would be held to be against public policy and unenforceable; rather than being irrevocable, such a proxy appointment might not be enforceable at all. On the other hand, if a person lends money to a shareholder and takes a lien on the shares as security, an irrevocable appointment of the creditor as proxy almost certainly would be enforced against the shareholder. What is the difference between these two situations? A person who purchases a vote presumably intends to recoup his or her investment in the vote by exercising the power to vote in some way. This power may very well be exercised in a manner adverse to the corporation. The proxy's interest is in recouping his payment for the vote, and in a sense he is antagonistic to the corporation. The creditor's interest, on the other hand, is to preserve or increase the value of the shares that constitute the security for the loan. Thus the creditor has a financial interest fundamentally consistent with the best interest of the corporation while the vote purchaser does not. While this explanation may not justify all irrevocable proxies, it does illustrate the policy considerations that justify recognizing some forms of irrevocable proxy appointments.

To express the same thought in another way, an irrevocable proxy appointment separates the ownership from the voting power. There is possibility of injury to the corporation and its shareholders by the abuse of a naked voting power unconnected with a financial interest in the well-being of the corporation. For this reason, courts have generally refused to recognize the irrevocability of a proxy appointment except where there appears to be little likelihood that the power to vote will be abused. This is the nub of the concept of "a proxy coupled with an interest." The following types of proxy appointments are "coupled with an interest:"

(1) A proxy appointment given to a pledgee under a valid pledge of the shares.

(2) A proxy appointment given to a person who has agreed to purchase the shares under an executory contract of sale.

(3) A proxy appointment given to a person who has lent money or contributed valuable property to the corporation.

(4) A proxy appointment given to a person who has contracted to perform services for the corporation as an officer.

(5) A proxy appointment given in order to effectuate the provisions of a valid pooling agreement (described in the following section).

Some courts have upheld irrevocable proxies in specific situations that do not squarely fall within any of the above categories.

There appears to be a slow trend toward statutory codification of the common law proxy appointment "coupled with an interest" doctrine. New York and California have statutes that define the five situations described above as those in which an irrevocable proxy appointment should be recognized [N.Y. Bus. Corp. Law, § 609(F); Cal. Corp. Code, § 705]. These statutes resolve possible future disputes very simply, but there is some danger that a reasonable irrevocable proxy appointment might be invalidated because it does not fit squarely into any of the above categories. It was for this reason that section 7.22(d) of the MBCA (1984), while based generally on the language of the New York statute, makes the list non-exclusive.

§ 9.11 Vote Buying

It was pointed out in the previous section that the purchase of a proxy appointment may be against public policy. Are all purchased proxy appointments against public policy and unenforceable? Most courts that have considered the question appear to view purchased votes as invalid *per se*. The one case that arguably reached the opposite result, Schreiber v. Carney (Del.Ch.1982), concluded that a purchased vote should be viewed as a "voidable transaction subject to a test of intrinsic fairness." In that case, a shareholder agreed to withdraw its opposition to a proposed merger in exchange for a favorable loan from a participant in the merger. The loan transaction was disclosed to the other shareholders who voted overwhelmingly in favor of the merger. The court concluded that the loan transaction was entered into primarily to further the interests of the remaining shareholders and upheld the proxy appointment.

§ 9.12   Shareholder Voting Agreements

A shareholder voting agreement is a contract among the shareholders, or some of them, to vote their shares in a specified manner on certain matters. Such an agreement is usually called a "pooling agreement" because it results in the shares of the participants being voted as a pooled unit. The purpose may be to maintain control, or to maximize the voting power of the shares where cumulative voting is permitted, or to ensure that some specific objective is obtained. The manner in which the shares are to be voted, i.e. for or against a specified proposal or motion, may be specified in the agreement itself. More commonly, the pooling agreement provides for subsequent negotiation and decision by the shareholders with some method of determining how the shares are to be voted in the event of a failure to agree. A shareholders' pooling agreement extends only to voting on matters that are within the province of shareholders, such as the election of directors, and should be sharply distinguished from agreements that attempt to resolve matters that are vested in the discretion of directors. The latter type of agreement raises serious questions of validity (see § 8.11 of this Nutshell). The pooling agreement does not.

In a pooling agreement, the shareholders retain all the indicia of ownership of shares except the power to vote. In this respect, a pooling agreement differs from a voting trust (discussed in § 9.13 of this Nutshell) which contemplates that legal title to the shares be transferred to the trustees. Generally, the advantages of a pooling agreement over a voting trust are that it is less formal, easier to establish, and there is no disruption of other ownership attributes.

The pooling agreement is generally recognized as a valid contract, subject only to the rules applicable to the validity of contracts in general. A few states have adopted statutes regulating pooling agreements, often limiting the period during which a pooling agreement may continue (e.g. to ten years), requiring that copies of the pooling agreement be deposited at the principal office of the corporation, and so forth. However, in most states, the pooling agreement is essentially an unregulated contractual voting device that may continue for long periods of time. Section 7.31 of MBCA (1984) basically codifies the common law rules applicable to pooling agreements.

A basic part of a pooling agreement is the manner of resolution of possible disagreements in the future. While the parties to the agreement are presumably in complete accord as to how their shares should be voted today, there is no assurance that they will be in accord tomorrow. Pooling agreements usually specify that participants will consult in advance of the meeting as to how the pooled shares should be voted, and that the shares will be voted as a majority or some other percentage specify. For example, in an important Delaware case, the agreement provided that the six participants in the pool could select eight agents (most selecting one, some two) and the shares would be voted as any seven agents specified. Abercrombie v. Davies (Del.1957). Arbitration was provided for in the event seven agents were unable to agree. While this agreement ultimately was held to constitute an invalid voting trust rather than a pooling agreement, the method of dispute resolution is interesting in that it required a high degree of consensus by the participants. Resolution of disagreements may be by arbitration or by a decision of some person mutually trusted by all the participants. However, if the pooling agreement covers enough shares to constitute working control of the corporation, arbitration may in fact vest control of the corporation in the hands of the arbiter, a person with no financial interest in the enterprise. A "runaway" arbiter is unlikely because the shareholders may, by agreeing among themselves, retake control over the voting of the pooled shares. Pooling agreements also often provide that the participants in the pool may substitute arbiters by mutual agreement. Instead of arbitration, a pooling agreement may give a participant the option of withdrawing his or her shares if disagreement continues over a period of time. Such a provision, of course, in a sense defeats the original purpose of a pooling agreement.

Enforcement of a pooling agreement creates special problems since the shares are registered in the names of the individual shareholders. Many courts will enforce a pooling agreement by decreeing specific performance. It is not always certain, however, that specific performance will be available. In Ringling Bros.-Barnum & Bailey Combined Shows v. Ringling (Del.1947), the leading Delaware case involving pooling agreements, the agreement itself did not specifically appoint anyone to vote the shares of an objecting shareholder who refused to follow the arbiter's instructions. Nevertheless, the Chancellor found by a process of implication that a proxy appointment existed in favor of the other shareholder. On appeal, the Supreme Court held that the proper remedy was simply not to count votes cast in contravention of the instructions of the arbiter. Under the circumstances, the result was to defeat utterly the purpose of the pooling agreement, since the minority shareholder who was not a party to the pooling agreement had a majority of the remaining shares after giving effect to the disqualification.

Some state statutes specifically address the enforcement issue either by authorizing irrevocable proxy appointments in connection with pooling agreements or by stating expressly that pooling agreements are specifically enforceable. New York, for example, validates and makes irrevocable a proxy granted in connection with a pooling agreement [N.Y. Bus. Corp. Law §§ 609(e), 620], while section 7.31(b) of MBCA

(1984) simply states that a pooling agreement "is specifically enforceable." The New York statute is less desirable since, to take advantage of that statute, the agreement probably should specifically appoint a proxy. Enforcement of pooling agreements under the New York statute might also create practical problems for inspectors of corporate elections who must decide who is entitled to vote shares based on the pooling agreement rather than on the corporate records. In these circumstances, an inspector probably would insist that a court decree be first obtained determining how the shares should be voted—a result that the MBCA (1984) formulation clearly contemplates.

§ 9.13   Voting Trusts: Purpose, Operation, and Legislative Policy

A voting trust differs from a pooling agreement primarily in that legal title to the shares is vested in trustees, and the shares are registered in the names of the trustees on the books of the corporation. Voting trust agreements usually provide that all dividends or other corporate distributions are to be passed through to the equitable owners of the shares. The trustees may also issue transferable voting trust certificates representing the beneficial interests in the shares and these certificates may be traded much as shares of stock are traded.

Voting trust agreements may limit the power of trustees to vote on certain matters. They may also limit the power of the trustees to convey shares held in the trust to third parties without the consent of the beneficial owners. Despite these limitations, the legal title to the shares in a voting trust, and usually the entire power to vote, are separated from the equitable ownership of the shares.

At common law there was great suspicion of voting trusts. One commentator described a voting trust as "little more than a vehicle for corporate kidnapping." This attitude has largely disappeared. State statutes now uniformly recognize the validity of voting trusts and they have received a more hospitable judicial reception. MBCA (1984) § 7.30 states that a voting trust may be created subject to minimal requirements:

(1) The agreement may not extend beyond ten years.

(2) The agreement must be in writing and signed by one or more shareholders who transfer their shares to the voting trustee on the books of the corporation.

(3) The voting trustee must prepare a list of the persons with beneficial interests in the voting trust and deliver that list and a copy of the agreement to the corporation at its principal office. These documents are thereafter available for inspection by shareholders.

Section 7.30(c) deals with the matter of extending a voting trust beyond its ten year maximum life. The statutes of several states permit an extension during the last year of the life of a voting trust. Section 7.30(c) adopts the somewhat simpler rule that a voting trust may be extended at any time during its life for a period of ten years running from the date the first shareholder signs the extension of a voting trust. Of course, an extension is binding on shareholders who agree to the extension; a person objecting to the extension is entitled to a return of his or her shares upon the termination of the original term of the voting trust.

A minority of states have imposed a further substantive requirement on voting trusts that the essential purpose of the trust must be a proper one. It is unlikely that a trust would ever expressly state an improper purpose, e.g. securing lucrative employment of a shareholder with the corporation. Proof of motive or purpose usually depends on subjective testimony; the cautious, close-mouthed creator of a voting trust in these states may create an enforceable voting trust despite wrongful motives, while a garrulous person with basically good motives may inadvertently make damaging statements about the underlying purpose of the trust. However, in a majority of the states, the purpose of a voting trust is simply not inquired into; a voting trust is valid if it complies with all statutory requirements.

A voting trust agreement that fails to comply with all statutory requirements is considered invalid in its entirety in most states. Even though formal requirements are basically simple ones that may be easily complied with, a number of cases have arisen in which these requirements have not been complied with. The most common failing is not filing a copy of the voting trust agreement with the records of the corporation. In addition, some states take the position that a voting trust that is not by its terms limited to ten years is invalid from the outset because it does not meet the statutory requirements. The MBCA (1984) adopts the more sensible rule that a trust that contains no specified term is valid for ten years only.

Courts generally treat voting arrangements that have the essential characteristics of a voting trust to be subject to the formal statutory requirements of a voting trust even though the arrangement is not formally a voting trust. The leading case in this respect is Abercrombie v. Davies (Del.1957). Another case, Hall v. Staha (Ark.1990) holds that a limited partnership formed in order to obtain voting control over the corporation was in effect an unenforceable voting trust.

§ 9.14   Voting Trusts: Use in Public Corporations

A voting trust, unlike most of the other control arrangements discussed in this Chapter, may be used in publicly held corporations as well as in closely held corporations. For example, a voting trust may be used in connection with the capitalization or reorganization of a corporation to provide for temporary stability of management. A temporary voting trust may be ordered where as a result of the reorganization the voting power is lodged in a large, unorganized group of bondholders who previously had no power to control the corporation. Another possible use is in connection with divestiture orders under the Federal antitrust laws, where the court desires to order an immediate termination of control, but where the financial details of the divestiture may take a long time to work out. A voting trust may also be used by creditors of a publicly held corporation to remove holders of large blocks of stock whom the creditors mistrust from the control of the corporation. An outstanding example of this use was a 1960 loan of $165,000,000 to Trans World Airlines by a consortium of banks. As a condition to the loan, Hughes Tool Co., then wholly owned by Howard Hughes, was required to place its shares of TWA (amounting to 75 per cent of the outstanding shares) into a voting trust with the banks designating the trustees. In this way, Mr. Hughes was isolated from the actual management of TWA.

§ 9.15   Voting Trusts: Powers and Duties of Trustee

Voting trusts usually contain precise provisions defining the powers and duties of the trustees. Voting trustees may have working control of the corporation for extended periods of time, but may have little or no financial interest in the corporation. Problem areas that have arisen include:

(1) May the trustees elect themselves as directors and/or officers? The wisdom of permitting dual offices is debatable since it is unlikely that a voting trustee would vote to remove himself or herself as a director.

(2) May the trustees remaining in office fill a vacancy in the trustees? Trustees are often given this power, though it may also be vested in the holders of voting trust certificates.

(3) May the trustees vote on major corporate changes, such as mergers, dissolution, or the sale of substantially all of its assets? Arguably, consent of the holders of voting trust certificates should be obtained on such major matters, but voting trust agreements often provide that the trustees may vote on such matters as they see fit.

(4) May the trustees dispose of the shares subject to the voting trust? Voting trust agreements often provide that no sale of underlying shares may be effected without the prior consent of all, or a designated percentage, of the holders of voting trust certificates.

(5) Should the trustees be relieved of liability for errors in business judgment or nonfeasance? Trustees typically desire broad exculpatory clauses in the modern litigious environment. Courts may decline to enforce broad exculpatory clauses applicable to fiduciaries or read such clauses narrowly.

(6) What deductions, if any, may the trustees make from dividends received by them before paying them over to the equitable owners?

(7) Are the trustees entitled to compensation, and if so, in what amount?

(8) What provision, if any, should be made for the eventuality that the trustees may disagree among themselves as to how the shares should be voted? Normally, the rule should probably be that majority vote controls, but it is possible that

the creators of some voting trusts might prefer a rule allocating the voting power proportionately among the ownership interests represented by the voting trustees. Provision may also be made for the eventuality that the voting trustees might themselves deadlock on some specific issue.

Generally, courts tend to construe voting trust agreements narrowly or to imply a broad fiduciary duty by which trustees' actions may be tested.

§ 9.16 Creation of Floating Voting Power Through Different Classes of Shares

The common law treated with some suspicion various devices that effectively divorce the privilege of shareholder voting from the ownership of shares. They include irrevocable proxies (§ 9.10 of this Nutshell), shareholder pooling agreements (§ 9.12 of this Nutshell), and voting trusts (§§ 9.13–9.15 of this Nutshell). While these devices are all valid and enforceable within their respective spheres, they are hedged with restrictions or limitations.

One device that apparently permits the effective divorce of voting power from ownership of a significant financial interest in the corporation is the creation of classes of shares with disproportionate voting and financial rights. In most states, no limitation is placed on the creation of classes of shares without voting rights, with fractional or multiple votes per share, with power to select one or more directors, and with limited financial interests in the corporation. As a result it is possible to vest control over the corporation in a person with a nominal financial interest in the corporation. The leading case is Lehrman v. Cohen (Del.1966). Two families, the Lehrmans and the Cohens, owned equal quantities of the voting stock of a major grocery chain. The shares were divided into two classes, denominated AL and AC, and each could elect two directors. Because of internal disputes and disagreements that could not be resolved because of the makeup of the board, both families agreed to the creation of a third class of voting stock, AD stock, consisting of one share with the power to elect one additional director, making five directors in all. The par value of the one share of AD stock was $10; this stock was not entitled to receive dividends, and on liquidation was entitled to receive back only its $10 par value. Further, the AD stock could be redeemed or called at any time upon the vote of four directors upon the payment of the par value to the holder. The AD stock was clearly a tie-breaking mechanism in case of disagreement between the holders of the AL and AC stock.

For several years, this tie-breaking mechanism worked well. The holder of the one share of AD stock, Mr. Danzansky, was at the time the attorney for the corporation. He elected himself director and participated actively in the meetings of the board. Eventually, Mr. Danzansky allied himself with the Cohen family and, by a vote of 3–2, he was elected the chief executive officer of the corporation and given a long term employment contract. Despite the fact that the AD stock was little more than a floating vote or tie-breaking mechanism with only a nominal financial interest in the corporation, its validity was upheld against the contentions that it constituted a voting trust or an invalid voting arrangement. A plausible justification for this result is that it seems impossible to draw a line between permissible and impermissible classes of shares. When the statute gives virtually total freedom to vary voting and financial interests of any class of stock; one cannot say that $10 is too little, but that some other financial interest is enough.

§ 9.17   Share Transfer Restrictions: Purposes, Operation, and Effect

In the absence of specific agreement, shares of stock are freely transferable. However, restrictions on free transferability of shares may be of vital importance in both closely held and publicly held corporations.

A.   *Closely Held Corporations.* In the closely held corporation share transfer restrictions typically constitute contractual obligations to offer or to sell shares either to the corporation or to other shareholders, or to both successively, on the death of the shareholder or when he or she decides to retire or leave the venture. The principal types of restriction may take various legal forms:

(1) An option exercisable by the corporation or shareholders to purchase shares at a designated or determinable price.

(2) A mandatory buy-sell agreement obligating the corporation or shareholders to purchase the shares at a designated or determinable price.

(3) A right of first refusal, giving the corporation or the shareholders an opportunity to meet the best price the shareholder has been able to obtain from outsiders.

The choice between these three forms of share transfer restrictions depends on the business needs of the shareholders. Obviously, an option or a right of first refusal does not guarantee the shareholder a specified price, whereas a buy-sell agreement does. Since investors or participants wish to avoid being "locked in" to an investment, most closely held corporations adopt buy-sell agreements.

In closely held corporations, share transfer restrictions usually benefit all shareholders. They enable participants in the venture who wish to leave to liquidate their interests at an acceptable price. They also enable the continuing participants to decide who shall thereafter participate in the venture.

The right of "exit" is particularly important to minority shareholders in a closely held corporation since otherwise their interest is largely at risk of actions taken by the controlling shareholders. There is no external market for minority shares in closely held corporations. In effect share transfer restrictions achieve the corporate equivalent of the partnership notions of dissolution-on-demand and *delectus personae.*

Share transfer restrictions also may ensure a stable management and protect the corporation and its other shareholders against an unexpected change in the respective proportionate interests of the shareholders that might occur if one shareholder is able to quietly purchase shares of other shareholders.

A further advantage of share transfer restrictions in a closely held corporation is that if properly prepared they may materially simplify the estate tax problems of a deceased shareholder. If the corporation or other shareholders are obligated to purchase the shares owned by the deceased shareholder (a buy-sell agreement) the estate may be assured that a large, illiquid asset will be reduced to cash. Further, either an option or a buy-sell agreement, if properly prepared, will be accepted by the Internal Revenue Service as establishing the value of the shares for federal estate tax purposes, thereby avoiding a potentially serious dispute with the tax authorities.

Since closely held shares have no market on which value can be based, in the absence of a binding agreement the Internal Revenue Service is apt to take a very optimistic attitude as to the value of such shares.

Share transfer restrictions in closely held corporations may also be imposed to ensure the continued availability of the S corporation election (see § 1.19 of this Nutshell). Restrictions on transfer for this purpose may be necessary to ensure that the seventy-five shareholder maximum is not exceeded and that shares are not transferred to an ineligible shareholder (such as a corporation or trust) that would cause the loss of the election.

B. *Publicly Held Corporations.* In a publicly held corporation, share transfer restrictions are often used to prevent violations of the Federal Securities Act where the corporation has issued unregistered shares, e.g., in connection with the acquisition of another business. In order to prevent the unregistered shares from immediately being resold into the public market, share transfer restrictions are imposed on the unregistered shares and instructions may be placed with the transfer agent to refuse to accept unregistered shares for transfer unless accompanied by an appropriate attorney's opinion. Share transfer restrictions may also be used to ensure the continued availability of an exemption from registration that may be lost, for example, if the shares are offered for resale to nonresidents. The availability of several exemptions from registration created by the Securities and Exchange Commission are expressly conditioned upon the corporation imposing restrictions on the transfer of shares issued in reliance upon the exemption.

Share transfer restrictions in publicly held corporations differ in nature as well as purpose from share transfer restrictions in closely held corporations. In the latter, restraints usually are of the option or buy-sell variety that require the shareholder to offer or sell his or her shares to the corporation or to other shareholders. In the publicly held corporation on the other hand, restrictions usually take the form of flat prohibitions on transfer unless the transferor can establish that the transfer is consistent with the securities laws or regulations. This may require an opinion of counsel, affidavits by a purchaser or transferee, and the acceptance of further restrictions on transfer by the purchaser or transferee. Such uses of share transfer restrictions are considered fully in courses on securities regulation.

§ 9.18 Share Transfer Restrictions: Scope and Validity

Many early judicial decisions take the position that share transfer restrictions are restraints on alienation and should therefore be strictly construed. As a result it is important to specify clearly and unambiguously the essential attributes of the restrictions and the events that trigger the restraint. In option or buy/sell agreements for example, the death, divorce, or bankruptcy of a shareholder normally trigger the restriction. A plan to sell or donate the shares to a third person will also usually trigger the restriction but a transfer by gift to children or grandchildren may be permitted. Careful drafting on such matters is essential. Restrictions are usually construed narrowly since they constitute restraints on alienation. It has been held, for example, that a restriction against sales "to the public" does not prohibit a sale to another shareholder, or that a prohibition against sale to an "officer-stockholder" does not cover a sale to a corporation owned by an officer-stockholder. Obviously, such holdings may tend to defeat rather than further the basic purpose of share transfer restrictions, depending on the circumstances.

The common law legal test as to the validity of a share transfer restraint is that it must "not unreasonably restrain or prohibit transferability." Under this test, an outright prohibition on transferability would certainly be held invalid. Also dangerous are restrictions that prohibit transfers unless consent of directors or other shareholders is first obtained; the possibility that consent may be arbitrarily withheld may invalidate the restraint. Language that consent "will not be unreasonably withheld" may validate a restriction of this type, though such language increases the vagueness and ambiguity of the restriction. Other questionable types of restrictions include restrictions barring transfers to competitors or to an arbitrary class, such as aliens; restrictions imposing a penalty, such as a loss of vote or loss of dividend as a consequence of the transfer; or a grant to the corporation of the power to repurchase shares at the election of the corporation.

The niggardly common law view about the enforceability of share transfer restrictions reflected in the preceding paragraphs has caused several states to adopt legislation broadening the types of restrictions that may be enforced. MBCA (1984) § 6.27 builds on these provisions; it attempts to eliminate most of the undesirable restrictive features of the common law. It distinguishes between the purpose of a restriction (subsection (c)) and the type of restriction (subsection (d)). Section 6.27(c)(3) provides that generally the purpose of a restriction must be "reasonable," but creates a "safe harbor" for restrictions described in subparts (1) and (2)—to maintain the status of the corporation when it is dependent on the number or identity of shareholders and to preserve exemptions under federal or state securities law. Such restrictions are valid without investigation into their reasonableness. Phrased differently, the purposes set forth in subparts (1) and (2) are conclusively presumed to be reasonable. Section 6.27(d) lists two types of restrictions—consent restrictions, and prohibitory restrictions that are valid if "the requirement is not manifestly unreasonable." This last clause is taken directly from section 202 of the Delaware statute. (Del. Gen. Corp. Law, § 202.) Several other states have adopted similar statutes.

Restrictions are sometimes imposed after the corporation has been created and shares issued. In these situations the question may arise whether the shares previously issued are subject to a restraint that is later inserted in the articles of incorporation or bylaws. In the absence of statute, the case law has split on whether the restrictions may be imposed retroactively. MBCA (1984) § 6.27(a) provides that restrictions may not be applied to previously issued shares unless the holders of the shares are parties to the agreement creating the restrictions or voted in favor of imposing them.

§ 9.19 Share Transfer Restrictions: Duration of Restraints

Unlike voting trusts that usually have a statutory duration of ten years or less, there is no express restriction on the duration of share transfer restrictions. So long as the type of restriction is limited to traditional option or buy-and-sell agreements, it is probable that the restriction remains enforceable without regard to the rule against perpetuities or equitable notions of "reasonableness." Less orthodox types of valid restraints presumably continue so long as a need or justification for them can be established.

Share transfer restrictions may terminate prematurely in one of two ways: by express agreement of the shareholders involved (e.g., when all decide to sell their shares to an outside purchaser despite a restriction against such a sale), or by abandonment or disuse. If shares are sold or transferred without compliance with the restrictions and without objection by the various parties, a court may conclude that the restrictions have been abandoned and are no longer enforceable. Isolated sales in violation of the restriction may not be sufficient to support such a conclusion, though a person objecting to the current sale may be estopped if he or she participated in an earlier transaction. A policy of selective enforcement of share transfer restrictions—enforcing them in some instances and waiving them in others—probably will result in the restrictions being invalidated.

§ 9.20 Share Transfer Restrictions: Procedural Requirements

In creating share transfer restrictions it is important that the proper formalities be followed and that the requirements of the relevant business corporation act be complied with. Most restrictions appear in the articles of incorporation or bylaws of the corporation, though some may be imposed by simple contract between the corporation and shareholders or among the shareholders themselves. Statutes generally require that a reference to any restriction imposed in corporate documents also be placed or "noted" on the face or back of each share certificate that is subject to the restriction. [MBCA (1984) § 6.27(b)] Generally, however it is not necessary that the full text or a complete description of the restriction appear on the certificate. Section 6.27(b) also requires that the notation be "conspicuous," a term that is defined in § 1.40 as meaning "so written that a reasonable person against whom it is to operate ought to have noticed it. For example, printing in italics or boldface or contrasting color, or typing in capitals or underlined, is conspicuous. A printed heading in capitals * * * is conspicuous. Language in the body of a form is 'conspicuous' if it is in larger or other contrasting type or color." The requirement of conspicuous notation also appears in Article Eight of the Uniform Commercial Code, and in many states that is the only place where a "conspicuous" requirement appears.

Unless the procedural requirements described in the previous paragraph are complied with, the restriction is unenforceable against a shareholder who is unaware of the restriction. A person who is aware of the restriction at the time the shares are acquired is bound by the restriction whether or not these procedural requirements have been met.

§ 9.21   Option or Buy/Sell Agreements: Who Should Have the Right or Privilege to Buy?

Share transfer restrictions that constitute option or buy/sell agreements to purchase the shares may run either to the corporation or to some or all the other shareholders. The choice is a matter of convenience, though usually it is preferable for the restriction to run to the corporation. There are three principal advantages. (1) The corporation may be able to raise the necessary cash more easily than the shareholders individually. (2) The relative proportionate interests of the remaining shareholders are unaffected by a corporate purchase. (3) A corporate purchase is usually advantageous from a tax standpoint.

A repurchase of shares by a corporation is a distribution of assets to the selling shareholders that must meet certain legal requirements. In par value states, the purchase may be lawfully made only if the corporation has the necessary earned or capital surplus at the time the purchase is to be made. Under the MBCA (1984), such a transaction must meet the tests of of a distribution under MBCA (1984) § 6.40. See § 18.6 of this Nutshell. In order to take care of the possibility that the corporation may be legally barred from acquiring the shares, buy/sell agreements may require the shareholders or some of them to agree to buy the shares if the corporation may not lawfully do so.

If the corporation purchases all the shares owned by one shareholder, that transaction is treated as a ''sale or exchange'' of the stock by the seller, and gain is taxed at the favorable tax rates applicable capital gains. Furthermore, the transaction is not treated as an indirect dividend to the remaining shareholders even though their proportionate interests in the corporation have changed. Thus, a repurchase transaction provides favorable tax treatment for the seller and a tax-free benefit to the remaining shareholders. These tax advantages are so substantial that it is standard operating procedure to retire a shareholder's interest through a corporate repurchase of the shares whenever that is practicable.

If the share transfer restrictions run to the other shareholders and not to the corporation, a problem arises if one or more of the shareholders are unable or unwilling to purchase their allotment of shares. Agreements usually provide that in that situation any shares not purchased should then be offered proportionately to the remaining shareholders who may or may not be obligated to purchase the shares. The proportionate interests of the shareholders will necessarily be changed if one shareholder is unable or unwilling to purchase his or her allotment. It is possible that a shareholder may not desire that shares be offered proportionately to the other shareholders. For example, a majority shareholder with a son and daughter may wish to provide that all shares be first offered to his or her son and then to his or her daughter (or vice versa) rather than be offered proportionately to all shareholders.

If the number of shareholders is large—more than four or five, say—the mechanics of having the restrictions run to the shareholders become complicated, and it usually is preferable for the restrictions to run to the corporation. Many share transfer restrictions provide that the shares be offered first to the corporation, and then, if the corporation is unable to purchase them, proportionately to the other shareholders.

It is very common to fund share repurchase plans triggered by the death of a shareholder with life insurance. The proceeds of the life insurance policy provide funds to purchase shares on the death of the shareholder. In these arrangements, it is usually simplest to have the corporation pay the premiums and own the policies on the lives of each shareholder. The alternative is to have each shareholder insure the life of every other shareholder. If there were 25 shareholders, a complete cross-purchase arrangement with life insurance would require 600 policies!

§ 9.22 Option or Buy/Sell Agreements: Establishment of Purchase or Option Price

The price provisions of shareholder option or buy-sell agreements often raise the most difficult and important problems in drafting these arrangements. Since closely held shares by definition have no market or quoted price, one simply cannot refer to a "fair," "reasonable," or "market" price; some definite method of valuation must be provided. Further, since it usually is impossible to know whose shares will be first offered for sale under such an agreement, everyone's goal in establishing a mechanism to determine the price is usually to be as fair as possible. (Of course, this is not universally true; individualized circumstances may well exist which make it reasonably clear that one shareholder's interest will be retired first, and the other shareholders may be tempted to act opportunistically when creating the pricing mechanism.)

The following methods are often used to establish a purchase price usually stated on a per share basis:

(1) A stated price;

(2) Book value;

(3) Capitalization of earnings;

(4) Best offer by an outsider;

(5) Appraisal or arbitration, either by expert, impartial appraisers or arbitrators, or by directors or other shareholders; or

(6) A percentage of net profits to be paid for a specified number of years following the event which triggers the sale.

It is impossible to state definitively which is the most desirable method, since it depends on the nature of the business and assets being valued. The simplest method is for the parties to fix a definite price in the agreement itself. This may be par value, original purchase price, or a price established by negotiation. In the absence of fraud or overreaching, courts have enforced agreements where the price is well below the value of the shares, though there is always a possibility that a court may deem a grossly inadequate price to constitute an unreasonable restraint on alienation or to be "unconscionable."

Generally, it is desirable to provide for periodic reevaluation of the fixed price as the fortunes of the corporation rise or fall. One problem that may arise is what happens if the parties fail to agree on a new price, or if they fail to revise the price from time to time as contemplated by the agreement. A willful refusal by a younger shareholder to renegotiate the price under such an agreement might be considered a breach of contract or even fraudulent, as might be a convenient "forgetfulness" on the part of such a shareholder. It is also possible that a court might conclude that there are sufficient fiduciary relationships among the shareholders to justify a court-ordered price reevaluation, whether or not specific provision therefor was made.

By far the most popular method of valuation is "book value," which may be computed by a simple division of a balance sheet figure by the number of outstanding shares. Indeed, it is probable that book value is often used without serious consideration as to its advantages or disadvantages in connection with the specific business. Book value is based on the application of certain accounting conventions to corporate transactions and whether or not book value is a realistic estimate of value depends on the circumstances. It may be appropriate to provide that book value be adjusted in certain specified ways before being used to establish a purchase price. For example, a basic accounting convention requires assets to be valued at cost and not be reappraised upward or downward to reflect current market values. Thus, a corporation that owns real estate acquired decades earlier at low prices may have a book value that greatly understates the true value of the assets. Similarly investments in readily marketable securities may be shown on the books at cost even though current market values may be obtained from the financial tables of any newspaper. In these instances, a restatement of the value of assets in terms of current market or appraised values may be more appropriate than "pure" book value.

Accounting conventions also allow corporations to include certain things as assets that may never be realized; for example, costs of initial formation or of "good will" acquired in connection with the purchase of another business. When adjusting book values, it may be appropriate to eliminate such non-asset "assets" from the balance sheet before computing book value.

A number of accounting techniques have been developed for federal income tax purposes, and it may be undesirable to have a shareholder's interest in a corporation be valued using tax accounting principles. For example, if the corporation utilizes accelerated depreciation schedules for tax purposes, it may be desirable to specify that straight line depreciation should be used to compute book value for valuation purposes. Or, if inventory is valued on a LIFO basis, it may be desirable to require the inventory to be valued at a more realistic figure before computing book value.

Appraisal of the values of closely held stock has its own difficulties. In the past, appraisers tended to rely on historic earnings and book values of assets owned by the corporation. A typical analysis would identify historical trends and project them into the future. Modern finance generally rejects reliance on historic accounting data and current book values. Rather, businesses are valued on the basis of estimates of future cash flows. The most widely accepted method of valuation today is the discounted cash flow method, in which the appraiser in effect seeks to determine the maximum hypothetical dividend that the company can pay each year over the next five years without affecting its ability to function as a continuing going business. The appraiser determines how much cash hypothetically could be available for distribution each year and then calculates the present value of that hypothetical distribution based on an appropriate discount rate. The "residual" value of the firm (the present value of its operations after the fifth year (is also calculated using projections based on trends during the five year period. The value of the firm then is the sum of the present values of the five hypothetical distributions plus the residual value of the firm.

In addition to discounted cash flow analysis, many appraisers also consider traditional valuation techniques based on book earnings and estimated liquidation values if assets were sold. They may examine the market value of common stocks of publicly traded firms in the same business. The final value determined by the appraiser may be influenced by, or be an average of, these various methods of valuation. However, the logic of averaging the results of discretely different techniques is doubtful, since if a corporation, for example, is worth more as a going concern than it is liquidated, it should be valued as a going concern without regard to the lower liquidation value.

After the value of the overall business is obtained, the per share value is usually obtained by a simple division by the number of outstanding shares. However, complications may involve the basis on which senior securities are valued and whether a further discount from the per share value should be taken because the shares are an isolated minority block with no chance of sharing in control. There is an extensive body of decisions (and law review commentary) on the priority of specific discounts and premiums in the valuation process.

§ 9.23 Option or Buy/Sell Agreements: Life Insurance

The unexpected death of a shareholder may cause serious disruption or catastrophe in a close corporation. If the decedent were the key person in the operation of the corporation's business, it might be best to sell the business outright or dissolve and liquidate it. If the business is to be continued, two things are essential if the corporation is to pass smoothly through such difficult periods: planning and money. A properly drafted buy-and-sell agreement or option may provide the former; life insurance is often the simplest way of providing the latter. It is possible, of course, to provide that the estate of a deceased shareholder is to be paid out over a period of time from anticipated future earnings. This may not be satisfactory from the standpoint of an estate, faced with large tax liabilities and a desire to wind matters up promptly. Life insurance, usually owned by the corporation, may provide the necessary funds to allow the estate's interest to be retired promptly. Of course, this assumes that the shareholder is insurable, that his or her age is not such that the cost of premiums is prohibitive, and the corporation's cash flow will support the necessary premiums without adversely affecting business operations.

§ 9.24 Selection of the Purchaser in Deadlock Buy-outs

A mandatory buy-sell arrangement is often recommended as the best solution in possible deadlock situations, where (usually) two equal shareholders operate the business but fear that there may be disagreements in the future. As described in some detail in a later chapter, (Chapter 12 of this Nutshell), the judicial remedies for deadlock in the absence of agreement are not entirely satisfactory. In the event of significant, unresolvable disagreement, it seems much neater and cleaner that one shareholder should buy out the other. In addition to important questions about price and timing, a serious question may be who is to buy out whom if both desire to continue the corporate business. Often the senior should buy out the junior, though if the age discrepancy is large, it may be more sensible to reverse the order and have the junior buy out the senior. One variation, that somewhat resembles roulette (or the classic family device when children are cutting up a pie evenly) is to have one shareholder set a price at which he or she is willing to buy the stock of the other shareholder, who in turn has the election to sell or buy at that price. While there is nothing inherently improper with this device, it should be utilized with caution since it may be necessary to persuade a court of its reasonableness in order to obtain judicial enforcement by a decree of specific performance. Another issue is precisely what events trigger the power to buy? Some kind of objective standard is usually desirable, such as the failure to agree on a slate of directors for some specified period. Yet another issue is which of the various pricing formulas should be used and which should be avoided? In light of the deadlock it seems important to choose a formula that does not rely on a cooperative effort to set the price. On the other hand, it also seems desirable to use a formula that will yield as "fair" a price as possible rather than one that creates a bargain for one faction or the other.

§ 9.25   Deferred Payment of the Purchase Price

Many share transfer restrictions provide that the purchase price of shares is to be paid in annual or more frequent installments extending over several years following the retirement of a shareholder or his or her separation from the firm. The theory is that these provisions enable the business to pay for the shares out of future profits or cash flow without incurring indebtedness. The withdrawing shareholder may or may not be entitled to interest on the deferred payments. Under modern statutes such debts are on a parity with general trade creditors. See § 18.10 of this Nutshell.

Where payments of the purchase price are deferred, the parties may also agree that the aggregate amount of the price may be adjusted upward or downward depending on the profitability of the business in the years following the exercise of the share transfer restriction. In effect, this is a form of "work out," widely used in connection with the purchase of businesses to adjust the purchase price to reflect the future success of the business. A "work out" may avoid an impasse over valuation of the business where the seller believes a high valuation is appropriate while the buyer is much more pessimistic. A "work out" permits the actual operation of the business to determine which estimate was more reasonable.

[For unfamiliar terms see the Glossary]

CHAPTER TEN

DIRECTORS

§ 10.1 Number and Qualifications of Directors

Historically, virtually all statutes required that a board of directors have at least three members. Many statutes also required that each director must have certain qualifications, such as being a shareholder or a resident of the state. Mandatory qualification requirements have been almost universally eliminated and most states now permit boards of directors to consist of one or more directors.

The privilege of having a board of one or two directors in a few states is limited to corporations with one or two shareholders. The notion that only corporations with one or two shareholders may have boards of directors consisting of one or two members seems superficially plausible. Presumably the shareholders will be the directors. In some situations, however, these statutes create unnecessary problems. Consider, for example, a corporation that is owned entirely by one person, who is the sole shareholder and sole director. Assume further that the shareholder desires to make gifts of shares of stock to his two minor children. Under these statutes, the board of directors would have to be increased to three members after the gifts are made since there are technically three shareholders!

Under section 8.03(a) of the Model Business Corporation Act (1984) and the statutes of more than 40 states, any corporation may have a one-person or two-person board without regard to the number of shareholders.

Even though mandatory qualifications for directors have been abolished, corporations are free to provide for special qualifications, such as requiring each director to be a shareholder or to be a holder of shares of a specific class. Qualifications for directors may appear either in the articles of incorporation or the bylaws.

The number of directors of a corporation may be "specified in or fixed in accordance with the articles of incorporation or bylaws." [MBCA (1984) § 8.03(a)] Many corporations permit the board of directors to vary its own size. The bylaws may expressly give this power to the board, or the original number of directors may be fixed in the bylaws but the board of directors may be given the general power to amend bylaws. (See § 8.10 of this Nutshell.) However, § 8.03(b) of MBCA (1984) restricts the power of the board of directors to make major changes in board size. Shareholders must approve changes in the size of the board of directors that increase or decrease it by 30 per cent or more. Alternatively, the articles of incorporation or bylaws may create a variable range size for the board of directors and the board of directors may set the size of the board within that range. Again, shareholder approval is required for changes in the outer limits of that range or for a change from a fixed to a variable size board, or vice versa. [MBCA (1984) § 8.03(c)] The purpose of these provisions is to give the board of directors power to add desirable members to the board without shareholder approval, or to decide not to fill a vacancy, but to prevent the board from manipulating its own size in a substantial way without shareholder approval. These provisions were added because of policy considerations; only a few states restrict the power of the board of directors to alter its size in this manner.

Some cases have recognized that bylaws setting the number of directors may be amended informally, as for example by the shareholders electing four directors when the bylaws specify that the board shall consist of only three directors. However, that is not a desirable practice, injecting future uncertainty as to the number of directors to be elected and reducing the certainty of the written bylaws.

In the United States, only "individuals" may serve as directors. [MBCA (1984) § 8.03(a)] In some countries, corporations or other artificial entities may serve as directors; this practice has never taken root in the United States. In countries that permit artificial entities to be directors, an individual must be designated to represent the corporate director at board meetings and for voting purposes. However, that individual is an agent of the corporate director and does not have the obligations and personal responsibilities of a director in his or her own right.

§ 10.2 Directors' Meetings: Notice, Quorum, and Similar Matters

Detailed provisions relating to directors' meetings typically appear in corporate bylaws. Only skeletal provisions are set forth in business corporation statutes or articles of incorporation.

The chairman of the board of directors presides at meetings of the board. The chairman often is also the senior executive officer of the corporation, the "president" or "chief executive officer." He may or may not also be a major shareholder. The duties of the chairman of the board of directors may be described in the bylaws of the corporation but are largely determined by tradition and practice. He presides at meetings of the board. He usually determines the agenda of the meeting and may also be involved in the preparation of the information books distributed to directors before the meeting. He has power to call special meetings of the board of directors. He may have power to determine who will serve on committees of the board of directors. A vice-chairman may be named to perform these functions when the chairman is absent. The chairman is elected annually by the board of directors, but that is often a formality.

Regular meetings of the board of directors may be held weekly, monthly, quarterly, or at any regular interval. The bylaws specify when such meetings are to be held, or authorize the directors themselves to specify, by resolution, when regular meetings are to be held. It is customary to hold a regular meeting of directors immediately after the annual meeting of shareholders. The boards of directors of publicly held corporations usually meet infrequently: less than twelve regular meetings per year is the norm.

Special meetings are meetings other than regular meetings. The principal difference between regular and special meetings is that a regular meeting may be held without notice while a special meeting "must be preceded by at least two days' notice of the date, time, and place of the meeting." [MBCA (1984) § 8.22(b)] However, all notice of meetings may be dispensed with if an appropriate provision is placed in the articles of incorporation or bylaws. Directors may also waive notice (if such notice is required at all) in writing before, at, or after the meeting. [MBCA (1984) § 8.23(a)] In many corporations, it is routine to have directors sign waivers of notice at every meeting.

Unlike a shareholders' meeting, any relevant business may be transacted at a special meeting of directors even though not referred to in the notice. The theory behind this distinction is that directors' meetings routinely consider a variety of business matters under varying degrees of urgency whereas shareholders meet only to consider a limited number of important matters. As a result the only practical difference between regular and special meetings of directors is the notice requirement.

In a board of directors with a fixed size, a quorum consists of a majority of the number so fixed. If the board does not have a fixed size (e.g. a board with a variable range), a quorum consists of a majority of the directors in office immediately before the meeting. [MBCA (1984) § 8.24(a)] The articles of incorporation or the bylaws, however, may authorize a quorum to consist of as few as one-third of the number described in the preceding sentence. [MBCA (1984) § 8.24(b)] This provision is patterned after § 707 of the New York Business Corporation Law; in most states, a quorum of directors may not be set at less than a majority. MBCA (1984) § 8.24(a) and the statutes of every state permit the articles of incorporation or bylaws to specify that any number greater than a majority, including all directors, may constitute a quorum.

Where a quorum is present, the act of the majority of the directors present at the meeting is the act of the board, again unless the articles of incorporation or bylaws require a greater number. [MBCA (1984) § 8.24(c)] Under this section, the quorum must be actually present when the action is taken; many state statutes are silent on the question whether a quorum must be present throughout the meeting in order to take action. It may be recalled that a different rule is applicable to meetings of shareholders. Once a quorum is present at a shareholders' meeting it is deemed to exist throughout the meeting even if some shareholders withdraw. (See § 9.1 of this Nutshell.) The opposite rule was made applicable to boards of directors in view of their management and fiduciary responsibilities. The quorum rule for directors also encourages management to present important issues early in the meeting when a quorum is more likely to be present rather than toward the end of the meeting when some directors may have left.

Provisions that a quorum consists of all directors often appear in articles of incorporation of closely held corporations. Unanimity requirements for voting also may appear in these documents. These provisions are obviously intended as control provisions to grant a veto power to a single director; as a practical matter, they create potential deadlocks at the directorial level since the refusal of a single director to attend or vote affirmatively on a matter prevents the corporation from acting.

With a single exception, if a quorum is not present the board of directors may not act. The only exception is where the directors are filling a vacancy under section 8.10(a)(3) of MBCA (1984). This section provides that "if the directors remaining in office constitute fewer than a quorum, they may fill the vacancy by the affirmative vote of a majority of all the directors remaining in office."

Many state statutes contain a provision based on the language of the 1969 Model Act that states that a vacancy "may be filled by the affirmative vote of the remaining directors *though less than a quorum.*" An ambiguity hides in this italicized language. That ambiguity involves a board of directors that has one or more vacancies, but the number of directors in office is greater than a quorum. If two factions are vying for control, the smaller faction may stay away from a meeting called by the larger faction to prevent a quorum from being present to fill the vacancies with persons favorable to the majority. At this meeting the number of directors present is less than a quorum even though the number of directors in office is greater than a quorum. The cases are split as to whether the faction present at such a meeting, "though less than a quorum," may fill the vacancies. In Tomlinson v. Loew's (Del.1957), bylaw language similar to the phrase "though less than a quorum" was held to refer to the directors in office rather than to the directors present at the meeting. Several other cases, however, adopt the opposite construction.

§ 10.3 Compensation of Directors

The traditional view is that a director is not entitled to compensation for his or her ordinary services as director unless the board of directors determines otherwise. The general theory is that directors are either acting as trustees or are motivated by their own financial interest in the corporation. However, a director may be entitled to compensation if agreed to in advance or if he performs extraordinary services beyond normal directorial functions. He may also be compensated if he serves as a corporate officer or agent as well as a director. These principles were based generally on tradition, not legal rules.

Modern state statutes expressly authorize compensation for directors. The Model Business Corporation Act, for example, provides that "unless the articles of incorporation or bylaws provide otherwise, the board of directors may fix the compensation of directors." [MBCA (1984) § 8.11] In the early years of this century the practice developed in many corporations of paying small honoraria to "outside" or "nonmanagement" directors for attending meetings. This practice has grown significantly, and it is now virtually universal to provide substantial compensation to nonmanagement directors serving on boards of publicly held corporations. Compensation to outside directors in many cases is quite generous, often exceeding $100,000 per outside director per year. Many corporations also provide retirement plans for outside directors.

Directors' compensation traditionally has been paid in cash. However, the National Association of Corporate Directors proposed in the 1990s that directorial compensation should be paid largely in common stock or options to purchase common stock in order to better align the interests of outside directors with those of shareholders generally. This proposal has been widely adopted by publicly held corporations. Some individuals may serve as outside directors on more than one publicly held corporation; at one time, an outside director might serve on four or five boards. In recent years, this practice appears to have diminished; most outside directors today serve only on one board of directors.

Corporations obviously believe these compensation plans improve the quality and interest of outside directors, though shareholder-oriented groups have sometimes complained that these plans are too generous.

§ 10.4   Filling Vacancies

Modern statutes authorize vacancies in the board of directors to be filled either by the shareholders or by the board of directors. [MBCA (1984) § 8.10(a)] Directors elected to fill vacancies must stand for election at the next annual meeting of shareholders even if the term otherwise would continue beyond that meeting. [MBCA (1984) § 8.05(b)] Some states follow earlier versions of the Model Act that provided that directors elected to fill a vacancy remain in office for the term of their predecessor. This question has application only if the terms of the board are "staggered" so that each director is elected for a two-or three-year term. See § 9.7 of this Nutshell.

Some older statutes distinguish between "old" and "new" vacancies. An "old" vacancy is created by the death or resignation of a director and may be filled by the remaining directors. Under these statutes, a successor director in an "old" vacancy serves the unexpired term of his or her predecessor. A "new" vacancy, on the other hand, is created by an increase in the number of directors by amendment of the bylaws or articles of incorporation. A "new" vacancy may be filled only by the shareholders and not by the directors. The distinction between "old" and "new" vacancies arose in decisions in the State of Delaware, and was included in the 1950 version of the Model Act. However, it was eliminated by an amendment in 1962. This history explains why § 8.10(a) of the MBCA (1984) expressly states that a "vacancy resulting from an increase in the number of directors" may be filled in the same way as other vacancies. Many but not all statutes reflect this simpler and more sensible approach.

A common device to ensure minority representation on boards of directors of closely held corporations is to provide that separate classes of shares are entitled to elect specified numbers of directors. MBCA (1984) § 8.10(b) provides that in such corporations, if vacancies are to be filled by the shareholders, only shareholders authorized to vote for the original election to that position are authorized to vote in the election to fill the vacancies. If such vacancies are to be filled by the board of directors, all directors, including those elected by other classes of shares, may vote. However, the damage this might do to the interests of a class of shares entitled to elect the original directors is limited because directors elected to those positions may be thereafter removed without cause solely by the class of shares entitled to vote in the original election. [MBCA (1984) § 8.08(b)] Section 8.10(c) adds that a vacancy that will occur in the future (as by a post-dated resignation) may be filled immediately, with the resigning director being entitled to vote. This provision may preserve the status quo in corporations with closely divided or deadlocked boards of directors when one director wishes to resign but does not want thereby to change the balance of power within the board of directors.

§ 10.5 Hold–Over Directors

Statutes provide that despite the expiration of his term, a director continues to hold office until his successor is "elected and qualified." [MBCA (1984) § 8.05(e)] As a result, the failure to hold annual meetings of shareholders does not affect the power of a corporation to continue to transact its business since directors presently in office continue in office with power to act.

The hold-over director provision is particularly important in situations where shareholders are deadlocked in voting power and unable to elect successors to directors whose terms have expired. In this situation, those who are "in" remain as directors apparently forever; however, the ultimate solution is the involuntary dissolution of the corporation (or a mandatory buyout of one faction's shares at a judicially determined price) if the deadlock cannot be broken. See § 12.10 of this Nutshell.

§ 10.6 Necessity for Meeting and Personal Attendance

Numerous early cases establish the principle that the "power invested in directors to control and manage the affairs of a corporation is not joint and several, but joint only." Basically, that means that action by directors must be taken "as a body at a properly constituted meeting." The underlying theory is that the shareholders are entitled to a decision reached only after group discussion and deliberation. Views may be changed as a result of discussion, and the sharpening of minds as a result of joint deliberation improves the decisional process. Several corollaries arise from this theory. (1) The independent, consecutive approval of an act by each director acting individually and not at a meeting is not effective directorial action. (2) Directors may not vote by proxy. (3) Formalities as to notice, quorum, and similar matters must be strictly adhered to.

These corollaries make very little sense when applied to a close corporation where all the shareholders are active in the business. In that situation, even the requirement of a formal meeting of the directors is likely to be considered a meaningless formality. Further, rigid application of the doctrine often permits a corporation to use its own internal procedural defects as a sword to undo plausible transactions that turn out to be injurious to the corporation. The potential for basic injustice created by these "rules" is heightened because persons dealing with the corporation usually have no way of verifying that formalities have been in fact followed.

As a result, the historical principle that required group decision-making by boards of directors was gradually vitiated by judicially created exceptions even as it was being articulated. The basic exceptions are "estoppel," "ratification," and "acquiescence." Even though informal directorial action may be ineffective to formally authorize a transaction, it may be considered acquiescence in and ratification of the transaction. "Ratification" or "acquiescence" is usually implied where the corporation accepts the benefit of a contract without objection or where all the shareholders are aware of the contract and voice no objection. "Estoppel" is usually applied where the secretary of a corporation certifies that a meeting took place when it in fact had not; the corporation is "estopped" from questioning whether the requisite formalities were followed or the described action was not validly approved. It may also apply where responsible corporate officers accept the benefits of a transaction that they later regret. While it is dangerous to assume that the historical principle that directors may act only at meetings is totally obsolete, it is probable that one or more of the exceptions will be found applicable in most situations.

§ 10.7 Telephonic Meetings

The Model Business Corporation Act (1984) authorizes members of the board of directors (or a committee of the board) to participate in a regular or special meeting through the use of a means of communication "by which all directors participating may simultaneously hear each other during the meeting." [MBCA (1984) § 8.20] Most states have similar statutes that at least extend to that most ubiquitous "means of communication:" the conference telephone call. Participation through one of these "means of communication," the statute adds, "constitutes presence in person at a meeting." The articles of incorporation or bylaws may prohibit this use of modern technology, but it is unlikely that corporations will elect to do so.

Telephone meetings are of considerable practical importance. Modern technology permits directors who may be in different cities distant from the location where the meeting is held to participate without physically travelling to the meeting site. As technology improves, one can easily imagine electronic meetings where no two of the participants are in the same room. Nevertheless, the fact that specific statutory authorization was felt to be necessary for a common sense idea such as telephonic meetings illustrates the persistence of the common law notion that directors can act only in meetings and through communal participation.

§ 10.8 Action Without a Meeting

Section 8.21 of MBCA (1984) permits directors to act by unanimous written consent without a formal meeting "unless the articles of incorporation or bylaws provide otherwise." Most states have similar statutes. It is unlikely that corporations will elect to prohibit decisions by unanimous written consent, since that is an efficient way to dispose of noncontroversial matters.

Action by written consent has the same effect as a unanimous vote and may be described as such in any document. [MBCA (1984) § 8.21(c)] This modest and sensible provision solves most problems created by the rule requiring actions to be taken at directors' meetings. Problems still may arise, however. For one thing, obtaining a written consent signed by all the directors is itself a formality that may be overlooked by a careless attorney. For another, there is the problem of timing; action by consent is effective only when the last director signs the consent. [MBCA (1984) § 8.21(b)] It is difficult to argue under this language that written consent can be effective retroactively. While arguments may then be made based on the doctrine of ratification, it is always possible that by the time the last director signs, one or more other directors may have changed their minds. And, of course, the procedure is simply inapplicable if one of the directors is out of the country or objects to the transaction in question and refuses to execute the consent. A formal meeting is then essential. All in all, it may be simpler to set a relatively low quorum level and act only through called meetings on all except the most trivial matters.

§ 10.9 Directors' Objections to Actions

Directors are sometimes faced with the difficult problem of what to do when a majority insists on authorizing a transaction that the director feels to be precipitate, risky, a breach of fiduciary duty, or outright illegal. The concern of such a director is not theoretical, since in some circumstances all acquiescing directors may be held personally liable even though some of them may have had serious mental reservations about the action. To avoid this result a director must file a written dissent or make his objection known in one of the ways set forth in section 8.24(d) of MBCA (1984). He may request that his objection be noted in the minutes or he may deliver written notice of dissent or abstention "to the presiding officer of the meeting before its adjournment or to the corporation immediately after adjournment of the meeting." If he fails to do so, he is deemed to have assented to the action taken.

Filing a dissent not only eliminates liability, but also obviates later questions of proof. It also may have a desirable psychological effect upon the other directors who realize that at least one director considers the conduct sufficiently questionable as to require legal protection. And it gives notice to shareholders or others examining the corporate records that at least one director seriously questioned the propriety of the specific decision.

Rather than filing a notice of dissent, directors may take other steps to delay an action believed to be unwise. For example, they may request that the corporation obtain an opinion of counsel as to the propriety of the proposed transaction. While directors may rely in good faith on the opinion of counsel [MBCA (1984) § 8.30(b)(2)], an unqualified reliable opinion may be difficult to obtain as a practical matter if the transaction is questionable. Another option is resignation from the board before the action is taken; if the resignation occurs after the transaction is approved, liability may be avoided only if the director files the appropriate written dissent. Presumably, a written resignation because of disagreement over an action taken by the board of directors would be viewed as a dissent from that action.

Even though a meeting is called without proper notice, a director waives any objection to the notice by attending the meeting and participating in it. Indeed, any participation by a director in an improperly called meeting is likely to be considered a waiver even though the director objects at the outset to the lack of notice. Section 8.24(d)(1) also addresses this issue in part by providing that such a director must object "at the beginning of the meeting (or promptly upon his arrival) to holding it or transacting business at the meeting."

§ 10.10   Committees of the Board of Directors

Many corporations utilize committees of the board of directors to consider in detail technical matters, to consider corporate transactions that in some way affect the personal interests of one or more directors, and to make directorial decisions during periods when the board does not meet. In addition to the committees discussed here, some corporations have utilized committees that may be composed of directors (and sometimes outsiders) to provide advice and perspective to the board of directors or to corporate management. Corporations also may form committees of management personnel to consider business-related problems; these committees form part of executive management rather than part of the decisional structure of the board of directors. The committees discussed here are not all purely advisory or part of management; they are committees of directors that may have the power to act to some extent in lieu of the board or directors.

Where a board of directors meets relatively few times per year, it may be convenient to appoint an executive committee

to perform the functions of the board of directors between
meetings of the full board of directors. Executive committees
are usually composed of inside directors who are officers or
employees of the corporation (or at least are likely to be
available upon call or upon short notice). The executive committee is probably the best known type of committee of
directors; the earliest corporation statutes that recognized the
need for committees of the board of directors apparently had
this type of committee in mind. The scope of the authority of
an executive committee is discussed below.

In the last thirty years, a strong trend has developed toward
creating additional committees within the boards of directors
of publicly held corporations. The three most popular standing
committees are the audit committee, the compensation committee, and the nominating committee. Their use has become
virtually universal as a result of strong encouragement by the
Securities and Exchange Commission. These committees are
primarily or exclusively composed of outside directors who are
not affiliated with management. Other committees that may
predominantly be composed of outside directors include strategic planning, public policy, environmental compliance, management development, technology, and employee benefits.

In addition to these standing committees, special ad hoc
committees may be created to consider the merits of specific
sensitive issues: e.g., derivative litigation filed by shareholders
on behalf of the corporation, requests for indemnification for
expenses incurred by directors or officers in connection with
that litigation, or the ratification of conflict of interest transactions between a director and the corporation.

Many state statutes permit committees of directors to be
formed only if there is express authorization to do so in the
articles of incorporation. The MBCA (1984) and modern statutes generally permit the creation of committees unless ex-

pressly prohibited by the articles of incorporation or bylaws. Many statutes require that the creation of a committee be approved by an absolute majority of the directors (as contrasted with a majority of the directors present at a meeting at which a quorum is present, the test applicable to normal directorial decisions). The Model Act provides that the creation of a committee requires the approval of the greater of a majority of all directors in office or the number of directors required by the articles or bylaws to take action on a matter. [MBCA (1984) § 8.25(b)] The MBCA (1984) and the statutes of many states require that a committee consist of at least two directors, though some statutes permit a committee to consist of one or more members.

A question that has received a fair amount of legislative attention is whether limits should be imposed on the delegation of power to directorial committees. The early statutes dealing primarily with executive committees limited the authority of committees to "routine matters" relating to the business of the corporation. Many statutes also expressly negated the power of committees to act on behalf of the board on such important or extraordinary matters as approving mergers, declaring a dividend, or authorizing the sale of shares. The concerns apparently were to obviate the possibility of a "runaway" committee and ensure that the full board of directors considered important matters.

Section 8.25(e) of the Business Corporation Act (1984) contains a list of prohibited functions that was developed on a somewhat different theory. It was believed that delegation of authority to committees should be restricted in only three types of situations. (1) The actions substantially affect the rights of shareholders among themselves as shareholders and are irrevocable when completed. (2) The actions are likely to become irreversible within a brief period of time. (3) The actions are likely to involve significant changes of position by third persons that cannot be rectified. In other words, the test basically is to prohibit delegation of important actions that cannot be overruled or overturned by the board of directors.

Among the nondelegable matters listed in section 8.25(e) are authorizing distributions, filling of vacancies on the board of directors, amending bylaws, authorizing the repurchase of shares, authorizing the issuance of shares, and recommending approval of transactions that the statute requires be approved by the shareholders.

[For unfamiliar terms see the Glossary]

CHAPTER ELEVEN

OFFICERS

§ 11.1 Statutory Designations of Officers

Traditional corporation statutes require every corporation to have certain designated officers. Typically, these statutes require that each corporation have a president, one or more vice presidents, a secretary, and a treasurer. The apparent need for four different officers in even small corporations is significantly tempered by the further provision that any two offices (other than secretary and president) may be held by the same individual. The requirement that the president and secretary be different individuals is apparently based on the perceived need for two officers to execute contracts and other formal documents; some statutes that require designated officers allow all the offices without limitation to be held by a single individual. Even though these statutes designate the titles of the offices, most of them do not purport to define what the roles of these officers are or what the inherent powers of the various offices are.

The Model Business Corporation Act (1984), following the Delaware statute, eliminates all mandatory titled officers. Section 8.40(a) provides simply that each corporation shall have the officers described in its bylaws or appointed by its board of directors. The reasons for this change are that some corporations desire to have officers with different titles, and there seems to be no good reason to require all corporations to fit into a fixed statutory mold in this regard. Also, there was some concern that implications of authority may be drawn

322

from the statutory titles that may be inconsistent with the corporation's desires.

The MBCA (1984) did find it necessary to define the duties of one corporate officer in section 8.40(c). The responsibility for preparing minutes of meetings and authenticating records referred to in that section are traditionally viewed as part of the responsibility of the secretary of a corporation, and the MBCA uses the designation "secretary" in the statute when referring to the officer with those responsibilities. [MBCA (1984) § 1.40(20)] However, it is not necessary that a corporation actually use this designation for the officer with this responsibility. The definition of "secretary" in the MBCA is intended to be used only for internal cross references within the statute itself.

Closely held corporations tend to use traditional descriptions for specific offices. Thus, in such a corporation, the senior executive officer is very likely to be designated as the "president," and the principal financial officer as the "treasurer."

Publicly held corporations typically use a different nomenclature for senior officers. Officers are usually given titles such as chief executive officer (CEO), chief operating officer (COO), chief legal officer (CLO), and chief financial officer (CFO). The chief executive officer is generally viewed to be the individual ultimately in charge of the management of the business; that person is often, but not always, also designated as the "chairman of the board of directors." See § 10.2 of this Nutshell. Publicly held corporations in traditional states that designate the titles of officers usually use this designation and may assign the statutory office of president to an intermediate management position rather than the CEO.

§ 11.2　An Introduction to Principles of Agency Law

The law of agency is intimately associated with the role of corporate officers and employees since a corporation is an artificial entity and can act only through agents. A partnership is also an artificial entity that can only act through agents, but partnership statutes usually state that each general partner is an agent of the partnership. Agency relationships within a corporation are more complex.

Agency involves a tripartite relationship. In the corporate context, the corporation itself is the "principal" on whose behalf an officer or employee, the "agent," acts. The agent may be any person authorized to act on behalf the corporation. The "third person" is the person who enters into a transaction with the corporate principal by dealing with the agent.

"Authority" is the power of an agent to affect the legal relations of the principal by acts done in accordance with the principal's manifestations or directions. Authority in this context may be conferred expressly or by implication and is often referred to as "express" or "actual" authority. "Inherent" authority is authority that arises by virtue of an office or position held by an agent with or in the principal. Persons holding the office of "president" or "secretary" of a corporation, for example, have authority to enter into certain types of transactions on behalf of the corporation by virtue of the offices they hold.

"Apparent" authority is not actual authority. It is created by conduct of the principal that creates the impression in the mind of the third party that a person is authorized to act on behalf of the principal when in fact that person does not have authority. It is based on a concept of estoppel and not on "authority" in the sense that word is used in the previous paragraph.

Corporations may also expressly ratify or adopt unauthorized transactions. Even where corporations do not desire to ratify a specific transaction, amorphous doctrines of "implied ratification," "estoppel," or "unjust enrichment" may sometimes allow third persons to hold corporations responsible for actions by officers despite the absence of actual or apparent authority when the action occurred.

Concepts of apparent authority, ratification, adoption, estoppel, and unjust enrichment are further discussed in § 11.7 of this Nutshell.

§ 11.3 Sources of Authority of Corporate Officers

The authority of corporate officers to act on behalf of the corporation may arise from several different sources. The source may ultimately be the state's business corporation act or the corporation's articles of incorporation. However, these two sources rarely shed light on the specific authority of corporate officers. Even the older statutes that require every corporation to have certain designated officers rarely shed light on what authority persons holding those offices have. Section 50 of the 1969 Model Act is a typical statutory provision. It simply states that each designated officer "shall have such authority and perform such duties in the management of the corporation as may be provided in the bylaws, or as may be determined by resolution of the board of directors not inconsistent with the bylaws." Section 8.41 of the Model Business Corporation Act (1984) restates this provision in somewhat different language and adds the important concept that officers may have power to delegate authority to subordinates. Section 8.41 also provides that officers "shall perform the duties set forth in the bylaws, or, to the extent consistent with the bylaws, the duties prescribed by the board of directors or by direction of an officer authorized by the board of directors prescribe the duties of other officers."

Modern articles of incorporation usually do not refer at all to the authority of corporate officers. However, article 2.02 of the MBCA (1984) states that "articles of incorporation may set forth * * * provisions not inconsistent with law regarding * * * managing the business and regulating the affairs of the corporation." Closely held corporations may include in their articles of incorporation provisions implementing negotiated agreements as to the management of corporate affairs. These individually negotiated provisions may contain grants of authority or limitations on authority of designated persons or officers.

The most important sources of authority for corporate officers are (1) the bylaws and (2) express resolutions of the board of directors authorizing the officers to enter into specific transactions approved by the board. Bylaw provisions are described in the following section; they give little specific or reliable practical guidance so that, as a practical matter, express authority is most likely to be found in authorizing resolutions of the board of directors. These resolutions are discussed in § 11.5 of this Nutshell.

§ 11.4 Bylaw Provisions Describing Roles of Corporate Officers

The following descriptions of roles of corporate officers are drawn from model bylaws intended for use under a statute that requires designated officers, and therefore represent normal "boilerplate" descriptions usually used in closely held corporations.

(1) The president is "the principal executive officer of the corporation" and, subject to the control of the board, "in general supervises and controls the business and affairs of the corporation." He or she is the proper officer to execute corporate contracts, certificates for securities, and other corporate instruments.

(2) The vice president performs the duties of the president in the absence of that officer or in the event of his or her death, incompetence, or inability or refusal to act. Vice presidents act in the order designated at the time of their election, or in the absence of designation, in the order of their election. Vice presidents may also execute share certificates or other corporate instruments.

(3) The secretary has several functions. He keeps the minutes of the proceedings of shareholders and the board of directors. He sees that all notices are duly given as required by statute and the bylaws. He acts as custodian of the corporate records and of the corporate seal. He makes sure that the seal of the corporation is properly affixed on authorized documents. He keeps a register of the names and post office addresses of each shareholder. He signs, along with the president or vice president, certificates for shares of the corporation. He is in general charge of the stock transfer books of the corporation.

(4) The treasurer has "charge and custody of and is responsible for" all funds and securities of the corporation, and receives, gives receipts for, and deposits, all moneys due and payable to the corporation. The treasurer may be required to give a bond to ensure the faithful performance of his or her duties.

Traditional statutes also usually provide that the board of directors may assign additional duties to any statutory corporate officer, and the president may also assign additional duties to any vice president, the secretary, or the treasurer. Statutes also provide that corporations may create assistant secretaries, assistant treasurers, and other officers not specifically referred to in the statute.

In publicly held corporations, the roles of CEOs, COOs, and the like are usually not described in the corporation's fundamental documents. They may be described in organization manuals or the like that describe the management structure for the specific corporation. These manuals typically are prepared by management and may be approved by the board of directors.

§ 11.5   Express Authority Created by the Board of Directors

When a person negotiates with a corporation, he or she deals with a flesh-and-blood human being. That person may represent, either expressly or by implication, either that she is authorized to bind the corporation, or that approval of a more senior officer has been obtained. How does one make certain that the corporation—a fictional entity—is in fact bound by a specific transaction? It is possible, of course, to trust to appearances, implied authority, the representation by the person as to the scope of her authority, general descriptions of authority set forth in the previous section, blind luck, and the like. However, that is very dangerous since litigation may be necessary to prove that the person in fact had authority to bind the corporation, and, because agency principles tend to be vague and amorphous, it is always possible that one may lose.

The most foolproof way to ensure that the corporation is bound by a specific transaction is to require the person purporting to act for the corporation to deliver a certified copy of a resolution of the board of directors authorizing the specific transaction in question. The resolution should direct a named officer to enter into the transaction on behalf of the corporation. How can one be sure that the person executing the certificate was authorized to do so and that the facts stated in the certificate are true? If the certificate is executed by the corporate secretary or an assistant secretary and the corporate seal is affixed, the corporation is estopped to deny the truthfulness of the facts stated in the certificate. The reason is that keeping and certifying corporate records is within the actual authority of the secretary so that the act of certification binds the corporation without more. Since the binding nature of such a certificate rests on an estoppel theory, an inquiry into the background behind the certificate is therefore not only unnecessary but may possibly destroy the basis of the estoppel.

A third person who knows or has reason to know that facts recited in a certificate are not true is not able to rely on a theory of estoppel. However, in the absence of such knowledge, one can deal with a corporate officer with confidence upon the production of a duly executed secretarial certificate. This procedure is fine, so far as it goes, but it does not cover many small transactions that are never taken before the board for review and approval. Of course, if the corporation accepts the benefit of a contract it will be bound on a theory of ratification even if the transaction was not specifically authorized by an office or senior employee.

Attorneys required to give an opinion that a major transaction has been duly approved by a corporation will normally review articles of incorporation and bylaws, and will inspect the minutes of the meeting of the board of directors at which the action was approved. However, they will primarily rely on the certificate of the secretary of the corporation that the minutes accurately reflect who was present and what action was taken; reliance on the secretary's certificate is entirely consistent with the attorneys' obligation to investigate with due diligence.

§ 11.6 Inherent Power of the Corporate President

Most non-lawyers are apt to think that the person holding the office of president of a corporation is the most important single person within the corporation. They may believe that the president has authority not only to enter into normal business transactions but also extraordinary transactions as well. These widely held views are erroneous: The present state of the law in many jurisdictions is that the president has only limited authority which may not extend beyond minor, ordinary, routine transactions. Essentially, the focus of power to approve significant transactions is in the board of directors, not the president.

This narrow construction of the president's authority is based primarily on older cases and may readily lead to injustice. Persons relying on reasonable appearances may discover that their reliance was ill-advised, and that the corporation is not obligated on a relatively routine transaction authorized by the corporate president. Persons aware of the rule are forced virtually to insult the president by demanding an exhibit of his actual authority.

Some courts have broadened the implied authority of the president, and there appears to be a general trend in this direction. Broader authority of the president is most likely to be found in cases where the corporation later regrets the transaction and seeks to hide behind the lack of authority of its nominal chief officer. Based on these cases, some courts have suggested that a president presumptively has any powers which the board could give him or her. Others have given that officer authority to enter into transactions "arising in the usual and regular course of business," and construe that phrase broadly. This may include, for example, the power to hire or discharge employees.

However, the inherent authority test is at best uncertain in its application to specific facts so that all unusual or extraordinary contracts should be authorized by the directors. This includes, for example, lifetime or long-term employment contracts and the settlement of material litigation.

§ 11.7 Implied Authority, Ratification, Estoppel, and Unjust Enrichment

Where an officer is purporting to act on behalf of a corporation and the transaction has not been authorized by a previous action of the board of directors, the doctrines of ratification, estoppel, implied actual authority, or apparent authority may be available. These various doctrines, described below, are closely interrelated.

(a) *Ratification and Related Doctrines.* The board of directors of a corporation may learn that an officer has entered into a transaction in the past without being specifically authorized to do so. If the board does not promptly attempt to rescind or revoke the actions previously taken by the officer, it is probable that the corporation will be bound on the transaction on a theory of "ratification." Ratification may arise merely from knowledge of the transaction by responsible corporate officers or the board of directors and failure to disaffirm or rescind it.

Usually, however, there are additional elements of retention of benefits by the corporation and/or known reliance by the third party on the presumed existence of the corporate obligation. "Estoppel" or "unjust enrichment" might equally well be applied in many cases. Estoppel differs from ratification mainly in that attention is focussed on the reliance by the third person, and the inequitableness of permitting the corporation to pull the rug out from under a person who reasonably relied on the corporation's silence.

(b) *Implied Authority.* Problems involving implied authority of corporate officers arise when the third person seeks to hold the corporation on a current transaction by showing that the directors routinely accepted or ratified prior similar transactions. The argument is that the acquiescence of the board of directors indicates that there was an informal grant of actual authority. The same facts that support a finding of ratification of transaction A_1 may be used to conclude that a later similar transaction, A_2, was impliedly authorized. This is, of course, a conclusion that actual authority exists.

(c) *Apparent Authority.* Apparent authority bears somewhat the same relationship to the concept of estoppel as implied authority bears to ratification. As described in § 11.2 of this Nutshell, apparent authority requires proof of such conduct on the part of the principal as would lead a reasonably prudent third person, using diligence and discretion, to believe that the agent has the authority he or she purports to exercise. A third person, knowing that an officer has exercised authority in the past with the consent of the board of directors, may continue to rely on the appearance of authority, and the doctrine of apparent authority may protect that reliance. It is essential to recognize that for apparent authority to exist, there must be some conduct on the part of the principal, i.e., the corporation, that creates the appearance of authority; a mere representation by an agent that he or she possesses the requisite authority is not sufficient. However, "conduct" may consist of silence by the principal if it is aware that the agent has represented the existence of authority. It may also consist of acquiescence in, and ratification of, acts performed by the putative agent in the past.

The principal difference between apparent authority and implied actual authority is that the former requires the third person to show that he or she was aware of the prior acts or holding out. Implied actual authority, on the other hand, may be found to exist even in the absence of knowledge or reliance on the part of third persons. This conduct may often be cited to prove the existence of either implied actual authority or apparent authority.

In view of the close interrelationship between the various doctrines discussed in this section, it is not surprising to find that courts sometimes appear to slip from one doctrine to another, sometimes perhaps not being fully aware of the differences.

The various doctrines discussed in this section may be applicable to affirmative conduct as well as silence and acquiescence. For example, a corporation may be estopped to deny that a transaction was authorized if it expressly creates the appearance of authority but withholds actual authority. Similarly, implied authority or apparent authority may arise from a variety of affirmative circumstances as well as silence.

Courts may be reluctant to find ratification of an unauthorized act by an officer where the act is fraudulent, unfair to shareholders, or against public policy. Often, in such situations, the court may conclude that the corporation lacked the requisite full knowledge to ratify the act. Of course, to avoid liability for such an act the corporation must return any benefits obtained by it from the act.

§ 11.8   Fiduciary Duties of Officers, Employees and Agents

Corporate officers, employees and agents owe a fiduciary duty to the corporation. The common law standard imposed involves a high degree of honesty, good faith, and diligence when acting on behalf of the corporation. An officer, employee or agent should act for the sole benefit of the corporation and give to it his or her best uncorrupt business judgment. Full disclosure of possibly conflicting transactions may be required, and the officer, employee or agent may be found to hold in trust for the corporation profits made personally in competition with, or at the expense of, the corporation. When all is said and done, however, general statements about the scope of fiduciary duties rarely decide specific cases.

Corporate officers typically have broad authority when making decisions on behalf of the corporation. Section 8.42(a) of the MBCA (1984) as amended in 1999, requires officers to act (1) in good faith, (2) with the care that a person in like position would reasonably exercise under similar circumstances, and (3) in a manner the officer reasonably believes to be in the best interests of the corporation. Section 8.42(b) permits a officer, when making decisions on behalf of the corporation, to rely on corporate information and regularity of actions by other corporate agents so long as the officer has no reason to believe that such reliance is unwarranted. This section is similar to the duties imposed on directors under the Model Act.

A corporate officer, employee or agent may be liable to the corporation for losses suffered if he or she knowingly exceeds his or her actual authority and binds the corporation to a transaction with a third person. Such a transaction, of course, must be within the officer's or agent's apparent authority if the corporation is to be bound at all.

§ 11.9   Liability of Officers and Agents to Third Parties

A corporate officer, employee or agent who acts within the scope of his or her authority as the corporation's representative in a consensual transaction is not personally liable on the transaction. The corporation is liable on the transaction but the agent negotiating it is not. This is a basic principle of agency law. However, there are ways in which a corporate officer, employee or agent may become personally liable on a corporate obligation despite this general principle.

First, an agent may expressly guarantee the performance by the corporation, intending to be personally bound on the obligation. Such a guarantee may be written or oral, and must be supported by consideration or reliance if it is to be enforceable. Whether or not it must also be in writing depends on the proper scope of the provisions of the statute of frauds dealing with promises to answer for the indebtedness of another. For example, an oral promise by the president of a corporation to a supplier that, if necessary, she will personally assume the obligation of payment for goods delivered to the corporation presumptively is unenforceable under the suretyship provisions of the statute of frauds. However, it might be enforced either on the theory that the president was a "primary obligor" or that the "main purpose" or "leading object" of the transaction was to benefit the president personally.

Second, an agent may not intend to be personally bound, but may in fact bind herself by creating the impression that she is negotiating on an individual rather than corporate basis, or by executing an agreement in such a way as to indicate personal liability. Even if the existence of the corporation is disclosed, joint liability of the corporation and the agent may be created because of informality in the manner of execution. The proper manner for a corporate officer or agent to execute a document in the name of, and on behalf of, a corporation is as follows:

ABC Corporation

By: _____.
           President

Any variation from this form is dangerous, since the mere designation of the corporate office may be deemed to be an identification of the signing party rather than an indication that he or she signed as agent. For example, the following form of execution:

ABC Corporation

_____,
President

is ambiguous since the corporation and the president may be either joint obligors or the president may have intended to sign only in a representational capacity as an agent of the corporation. The word "president" does not resolve the ambiguity since it may be either an identification of an individual co-obligor or an indication that he or she signed only as an agent of the corporation. Particularly dangerous is the execution of a promissory note in this ambiguous form, since a court may view the form as establishing conclusively that a joint obligation was involved. Courts appear to be more willing to allow corporate officers to testify about the "real intention of the parties" when executing general contracts than when executing promissory notes.

Third, if an officer negotiates a transaction without disclosing she is acting solely on behalf of the corporation, the officer is personally liable to the third person on general agency principles relating to undisclosed principals.

Fourth, if the agent is acting beyond the scope of her authority she may be personally liable on the transaction unless the corporation takes the agent off the hook by ratifying the transaction. A person acting as an agent generally implicitly warrants she has authority to bind the principal to the transaction. However, this principle does not apply if the third person is aware the agent lacks authority and the transaction must be submitted to the principal for approval.

Finally, liability may arise because imposed by statute. Failure to pay franchise taxes or to publish a notice of incorporation in some states may, in some circumstances, lead to individual as well as corporate liability on corporate obligations. In addition, the federal income tax statutes provide for a penalty of one hundred per cent of the tax for failing to pay over income taxes withheld from employees. This penalty tax may be imposed on "any person required to collect, truthfully account for, and pay over" the tax. (IRC § 6672.) There are perhaps other statutes as well that impose personal liability for failing to comply with statutory obligations.

§ 11.10 Imputation of Knowledge to Corporation

In the foregoing discussion, there have been several references to "corporate knowledge" or "notice" to the corporation that appear to ignore the fictional nature of a corporation. Of course, a corporation can "know" or "have notice of" something only if one or more persons who represent the corporation know or have notice of the thing. Usually, knowledge acquired by a corporate officer or employee while acting in furtherance of the corporate business or in the course of his or her employment is imputed to the corporation. Thus, if the president knows of a transaction, the corporation ratifies it if the corporation accepts the benefits of the transaction, even though some or all of the directors or other officers may not know of the transaction. Similarly, service of process on an authorized agent of the corporation supports a default judgment against the corporation even though the agent fails to forward the papers to the corporation or its attorney.

Difficult problems arise when it is sought to impute knowledge of an agent to the corporation if the agent is acting adversely to the corporation. Generally information or knowledge of an agent who has ultimate responsibility for the transaction may be imputed to the corporation even if the agent is acting adversely to or in fraud of the corporation. Similarly, if a corporate officer learns that an employee is stealing from or defrauding the corporation, the officer's knowledge is imputed to the corporation even though the officer does not disclose the information to directors or other responsible officers.

Generally, an agent's wrongful intention may be imputed to a corporation so that a corporation is subject to civil or criminal prosecution, even including prosecution for traditional crimes such as murder or rape. While there are some examples of corporations being indicted for such "personal" crimes, actual prosecutions are not very common. For a corporation to be prosecuted for such conduct, the conduct itself must have been connected with, or in furtherance of, the corporation's business and the agent's position with the corporation must have been such as to justify imputation of the agent's criminal intent to the corporation.

§ 11.11 Tenure of Officers and Agents

Corporate officers and agents generally serve at the will of the person or board having authority to elect or appoint the officer or agent. Corporate officers are elected or appointed by the board of directors, and corporation statutes generally permit their removal by the board of directors with or without cause. [MBCA (1984) § 8.43(b)] So far as agents appointed by the president or chief executive officer are concerned, the power to discharge is implicit in the power to employ. Corporate bylaws often explicitly grant the power to remove or discharge as part of the power to appoint.

An officer or agent may be given an employment contract, and premature removal of that officer or agent may give rise to a cause of action for breach of contract. Typically, the remedy for breach of an employment contract is damages and not reinstatement. Further, the mere election or appointment of an officer or agent, even for a definite term, does not of itself give rise to a contract right. [MBCA (1984) § 8.44] The validity of employment contracts in light of special corporate bylaw provisions is discussed in the following section.

Many state statutes refer to the "election" or "appointment" of officers. The Model Business Corporation Act (1984) uses only the word "appointment," reserving the word "election" for the selection of directors. In a sense, of course, corporate officers may be "elected" by the board of directors.

§ 11.12 Long–Term Employment Contracts

Long-term or lifetime employment contracts have given rise to litigation primarily in the context of closely held corporations.

(1) *Validity.* Corporate bylaws usually provide that officers are to be elected or appointed by the board of directors for a term of one year. Does that bylaw restrict or limit the power of a corporation to grant an officer an employment contract extending beyond the term of that office? Generally, the answer is "no" since an officer or employee may be relieved of

his duties at any time even if he has an employment contract. Of course, the corporation may be liable for breach of contract for the premature termination of the employment period. [MBCA (1984) § 8.44(b).]

Another argument may also be made if the board of directors has power (as most boards do) to amend the bylaws. An employment contract for more than one year may be viewed to be an implied amendment of the bylaws by the board. Presumably, the board could first amend the bylaw to eliminate the one year term limitation and then enter into the long term employment contract. While some courts have accepted this argument, there is a potential problem with implied amendments to bylaws since one cannot then rely on the written bylaws as being the current and complete rules governing the corporation's internal affairs.

On a parity of reasoning, long-term leases or contracts are upheld despite the fact that they "bind" subsequent boards of directors.

(2) *Lifetime Employment Contracts.* The claim that a person has been given a lifetime employment contract by a closely held corporation is treated with hostility by courts. A claim that a lifetime employment contract was created is usually based on oral statements within the context of a family-run business. While such a contract is not within the statute of frauds, courts often feel that the factual basis for such an open-ended and long-term commitment is inherently implausible. Also, lifetime contracts may subject a corporation to a substantial liability that may run for a long and indefinite period during which circumstances may materially change. Where the promise of lifetime employment was unambiguous, courts may nevertheless refuse to enforce it on the ground the person authorizing the arrangement lacked actual or apparent authority to do so. However, there is nothing inherently illegal

about a lifetime contract if in fact it was authorized by the board of directors.

(3) *Discharge for Cause.* It is clear that an officer or employee with a valid employment contract may be discharged for cause without breaching the contract. "Cause" may consist of acts of dishonesty, negligence, refusal to obey reasonable orders, refusal to follow reasonable rules, or a variety of other acts such as engaging in sexual harassment or an unprovoked fight. In effect, such conduct constitutes a breach of an implied covenant in the employment contract.

Employees or agents of the corporation that do not have term employment contracts are at will employees and may be discharged at any time without cause.

(4) *Basis of Compensation.* Employees or agents sometimes request that they be compensated on the basis of a percentage of sales or corporate earnings or profits rather than at a flat rate. No particular legal problem is raised by these arrangements, though questions sometimes arise as to how earnings and profits are to be measured. Simple phrases such as "net profits" or "gross revenue" may be ambiguous and their meaning elusive.

(5) *Miscellaneous.* Employment contracts for highly paid personnel in publicly held corporations often provide for deferred compensation, pension plan benefits, options to purchase shares at bargain prices, reimbursement of business expenses, and other tax-related benefits. The high levels of compensation for CEOs of public corporations was a matter of political controversy during the 1990s. Congress limited income tax deductions for salaries in excess of $1.0 million dollars per year in certain situations, but that limitation has been largely ineffective, and may actually have had the unintended consequence of encouraging higher levels of compensation.

In the closely held corporation, employment contracts may be an integral part of the basic planning arrangement among shareholders. Terms relating to employment may be placed in shareholders' agreements so that they will be binding on all the other shareholders as well as on the corporation. There is a greater possibility of specific performance of shareholders' agreements than of simple employment contracts. It is therefore possible that a court may order reinstatement of a shareholder/employee who has been improperly discharged from employment rather than simply awarding him damages for breach of contract. Specific enforcement may be significant in a close corporation where the right to participate in management is an important aspect of the control arrangement agreed to by the shareholders. As a result, contracts within the closely held corporation sometimes specifically state that the remedy of specific performance should be available in the event of a breach of contract.

[For unfamiliar terms see the Glossary]

CHAPTER TWELVE

THE CLOSELY HELD CORPORATION

§ 12.1 The Meaning of "Closely Held" and "Publicly Held"

The phrase "closely held corporation" normally signifies only that the corporation has a few shareholders. This simple definition of "closely held" seems intuitively satisfactory, but creates a serious problem at the margin. When corporations are classified solely by the number of shareholders, they form a continuum from one-owner corporations, at one end of the spectrum, to corporations with hundreds of thousands of shareholders at the other. It is not possible to define precisely what is meant by a "few" except on a purely arbitrary basis. Whatever number is chosen to define "few", there will always be indistinguishable corporations that have precisely one more shareholder than whatever number has been chosen.

A more useful definition is obtained by isolating the essential characteristic of a "publicly held" corporation and then defining a "closely held" corporation negatively as a corporation that is not "publicly held." This approach leads to a more useful classification system, though it does not eliminate the basic classification problem at the margin. A "publicly held" corporation may be defined as one that has a sufficiently large number of shareholders that there exists an active established market in which its shares are traded. The existence of an active trading market for shares means that investors have a power to "enter" or "exit" simply by buying or selling shares in this public trading market. In contrast, where an active trading market for shares does not exist, the power to "enter" or "exit" is necessarily circumscribed and may not exist at all. The unique problems of closely held corporations arise because there is no power to "enter" or "exit" through an active trading market.

Under the definition suggested here, most closely held corporations are small and are owned by one or a few persons. However, some corporations that do not have an active trading market may be large in terms of assets and some may have a substantial number of passive shareholders. Corporations with a hundred or more shareholders may be classified as "closely held" for purposes of this chapter even though a limited market of sorts for their shares may exist. Indeed, there are a fair number of these "in between" corporations. A reporting service, the "pink sheets," publicly lists many inactively traded stocks along with price quotations and the name of the broker who has placed the listing. Many offerings on the pink sheets list a "bid" price but no "asked" price and in any event there is no assurance that actual purchases or sales at or near the quoted prices will take place.

While these infrequently traded stocks may be viewed as "closely held" under the definitions set forth above, they are not the focus of this chapter, which concentrates on the special problems of corporations that have relatively few shareholders. Chapter 13 discusses publicly held corporations.

§ 12.2   The Economic Importance of Closely Held Corporations

Chapter 1 of this Nutshell discusses recent developments with respect to unincorporated business forms that provide virtually complete protection from liability for owners. Chapter 1 points out that the current federal income tax treatment of these new business forms may be more attractive to owners than the current tax treatment of corporations. As a result, there appears to be a decline in the use of the corporate form for closely held businesses. However, the closely held corporation will undoubtedly continue to be an important business form so long as the present tax and legal regimes continue to exist.

For one thing, the number of closely held corporations in existence today is very large. Data collected by the Internal Revenue Service for the tax year 1995 (the latest year for which data is available) reveals that 4,474,000 corporate income tax returns were filed. Of this number, 2,153,000 returns elected Subchapter S tax treatment. Subchapter S in 1995 was available only for corporations with 35 or fewer shareholders—closely held corporations in every sense of the word. Thus, about 48 percent of all corporations filing separate returns in 1995 were clearly closely held. In addition, many closely held corporations do not elect Sub S tax treatment for one reason or another. Sources estimate that the number of publicly held corporations with widely traded securities is in the range of 10,000 to 15,000 corporations. Obviously many of the roughly 2,300,000 C corporations are closely held.

Closely held corporations usually retain that business form for their entire period of existence. The reason lies in part in the current Internal Revenue Code. An existing corporation can usually convert to an unincorporated business form only at a significant tax cost. Such a conversion is viewed as a dissolution and sale of all corporate assets for tax purposes and results in the immediate taxation of all unrealized appreciation of assets. Therefore, movement from corporation to unincorporated business form occurs rarely. In contrast, conversions in the opposite direction, from unincorporated business forms to corporations usually have no tax cost and occur frequently.

Many newly formed businesses elect the corporate form at the outset despite the possible loss of tax flexibility. Data collected by state filing authorities reveal that the number of new incorporations remains substantial despite the development of unincorporated business forms that provide limited liability and more favorable tax treatment for owners.

The most spectacular new businesses in the late 1990s have been the so-called "dot-com" high technology companies that hope to have an initial public offering (an "IPO") that will make the founders and employees into paper millionaires (or billionaires) overnight. These new businesses are formed as corporations since both interim financing from venture capital firms and the subsequent IPO are available as a practical matter only to business entities formed as for-profit corporations. See § 13.2 of this Nutshell.

§ 12.3 The Reality of Management, Control and Participation in a Closely Held Corporation

It is useful to first consider issues of management, control and participation in closely held corporations in which there has been no advance planning. There are typically two or more shareholders. One shareholder (or an allied group of shareholders) owns a majority of the shares of the corporation while other shareholders own a minority of the shares. There is thus a "majority shareholder" (or a controlling group of shareholders) on one hand, and "minority shareholders" on the other.

A special case involves corporations with two shareholders or factions owning precisely the same number of shares. Deadlock is likely to arise in this situation if the two shareholders or factions have a major disagreement. This situation is discussed in § 12.10 of this Nutshell.

So long as majority and minority shareholders are in amity, the corporation is likely to function smoothly. However, when disagreements arise, the difference between these two groups becomes great. Disagreements may arise because of lack planning for contingencies such as death, divorce, or personal quarrels between former friends and allies. They may arise because controlling shareholders conclude that other shareholders are not making an appropriate contribution to the welfare of the corporation, and seek to eliminate them from the enterprise.

In the absence of planning, when disagreement arises the management and control of a closely held corporation will be governed by the "default" provisions of the corporation statutes or, as it is sometimes phrased, the "standard model" of the corporation. This standard model in effect turns management of the corporation over to the majority shareholders. They have the power to elect whomever they wish to serve on the board of directors. In the absence of cumulative voting (see § 9.6 of this Nutshell), the majority shareholders name the entire board of directors. The board of directors in turn has total power over management and financial decisions. It includes the power to exclude minority shareholders from all participation in management and deny them all financial benefits. The majority may, for example:

(i) Exclude the minority shareholders from having any "voice" in the management of the enterprise by not electing them as directors or officers of the corporation;

(ii) Decide not to pay dividends or make distributions to shareholders;

(iii) Provide the controlling shareholders and their allies with jobs with the corporation at generous salaries while refusing to employ minority shareholders in any capacity; and

(iv) Arrange for the corporation to provide a variety of benefits or "percs" to the controlling shareholders and their associates: corporate automobiles, country club memberships, first class airplane tickets, computers for home use, and the like, while providing no similar benefits at all to the minority shareholders.

The standard model does not provide minority shareholders with a power to "exit." They cannot compel dissolution of the corporation (except in limited circumstances described in § 12.14); they cannot compel the corporation or the controlling shareholders to redeem or purchase their shares. These matters are all subject to the control of the majority shareholders. As a result, minority shareholders can be "locked in" a situation from which there appears to be no escape.

§ 12.4 Advance Planning in Closely Held Corporations

Corporate law long imposed restrictions on the power of participants in a corporation to modify or vary the formal requirements of the standard corporation model. However, these restrictions generally did not prevent participants in closely held corporations from voluntarily entering into agreements or contracts that effectively changed the characteristics of this model. And that is what many closely held corporations do. For example, a minority shareholder has no power of "exit" in the standard corporation model with a few shareholders. A person willing to participate in a corporation as a minority shareholder but unwilling to accept the "lock in" of the standard model might negotiate a contract by which he can sell his shares back to the corporation at his election at a specified price in specified circumstances. Such a contract is usually called a "put." The terms of this "put" would undoubtedly be carefully negotiated. An unrestricted put allows the minority shareholder to act opportunistically by threatening to exercise it àt a time most inconvenient to the corporation. An overly restrictive put may not be acceptable to the incoming shareholder because it might not be effective to prevent the shareholder from being frozen into an unacceptable minority position. But a mutually acceptable agreement might be reached.

Another example involves the concern on the part of a minority shareholder/employee that the controlling shareholder might fire him at some later date and deprive him of his livelihood. A solution is to have the corporation and the shareholder/employee enter into an employment contract guaranteeing the employee his position and his salary. Again the contract would have to be carefully negotiated to assure that the employee cannot "shirk" his duties while enjoying his contractual salary. A personal guarantee by the controlling shareholder may also be required to ensure that the controlling shareholder does not strip assets from the corporation and render it unable to meet its financial obligations under the employment contract.

Contractual provisions do not have to appear in the articles of incorporation or bylaws of the corporation. They may appear in employment agreements, stock purchase agreements, or in letters or memoranda. In some instances arrangements may be oral. However, in the aggregate they can spell out a relationship that differs significantly from the standard corporation model and indeed may resemble a partnership.

Recognition that the standard corporation model was a default model and not descriptive of actual arrangements in many closely held corporations was the insight of several legal scholars of the "law and equity" school. It is helpful to consider briefly the typical negotiation model contemplated by these scholars. In this model, a person is considering whether to accept employment with a closely held corporation. He also may make a capital investment by purchasing some shares and may be given options to purchase additional shares. He thus may be both an employee and a minority shareholder. The potential employee/investor has alternative investment opportunities and is therefore free to "walk" away from the negotiations if a satisfactory deal with the majority shareholders cannot be reached. Presumably, the corporation is able to attract other similarly situated investors if this specific investor cannot be satisfied; it is perhaps somewhat less likely that the corporation will be able to find an employee with identical skills and the financial resources to make an equity investment in the enterprise. There is thus an arms length negotiation by parties who are under no compulsion to enter into the transaction and who are rational and adequately informed. In this model the parties may be trusted to hammer out a mutually acceptable arrangement with adequate protections for the investor/minority shareholder. If an acceptable arrangement cannot be worked out, there will simply be no transaction. In this model, judicial or legislative intervention is rarely justified after the fact since whatever arrangements are agreed to by the consenting parties should be respected.

The insight that closely held corporations are usually largely contractual in nature helps to explain why problems of oppression and freeze-out do not occur more often than they do, given the large number of active closely held corporations in existence. Problems of oppression and freeze-outs in closely held corporations, once viewed as the principal problem of closely held corporations, are not viewed as seriously today.

While rational investors may readily obtain protection against oppressive and freeze-out tactics by contractual provisions negotiated in advance, cases involving such tactics continue to arise with some regularity. The reason is that not all minority shareholders and employees in a closely held corporation negotiate effectively. Regrettably every corporation lawyer encounters situations in which for one reason or another minority shareholders do not have adequate contractual protection against oppressive conduct by controlling shareholders. Some of these situations may be the consequence of ineffective negotiation. An unsophisticated potential employee may be overly trusting of the controlling shareholder. He may not realize that he will be an employee at will and that he will not be able to withdraw his investment if he is unexpectedly fired. If he has been promised a generous savings and retirement plan plus stock options, he may be unaware that these benefits do not vest for an extended period or that the corporation may be disabled from providing them when they become due. The attitude towards these kinds of problems by law and economics scholars generally is that they provide no basis for judicial intervention and revision of the contractual terms agreed upon, whatever they are. Courts, on the other hand, tend to be somewhat more willing to intervene to protect minority shareholders than those scholars would like.

Another common problem involves unexpected changes in circumstances. An investor who is in amity with the controlling shareholders at the outset may see no reason to negotiate for detailed protections. However, over a period of time changes in personnel through deaths or withdrawals may result in distinctly adverse and hostile interests obtaining control of the closely held corporation.

Finally, in some situations, particularly those involving family corporations, no advance planning may take place at all.

The paradigm situation is the unexpected death of a controlling or sole shareholder of a successful business before he has made plans with respect to the corporation following his death. If he has three or more heirs who are consumed by former sibling rivalries, they may promptly form controlling and minority factions in a standard corporation model. Another recurring problem involves a two-shareholder corporation in which the two shareholders have long worked amicably. One dies unexpectedly leaving a widow and family, none of whom are capable of assuming the role of the deceased husband. If the widow wishes to sell her husband's shares, she will have to negotiate with the surviving shareholder who may be able to negotiate from the position of a controlling shareholder. A buy-sell agreement would have eliminated a significant controversy; life insurance purchased by the corporation on both shareholders would also have provided considerable protection for the widow in this type of case. But in the absence of planning, the widow's position is a very weak one.

A surprisingly large number of oppression and freeze-out cases involve family corporations similar to those described in the previous paragraph. While perhaps controlling shareholders should be criticized for not planning for succession, these cases nevertheless are not uncommon.

§ 12.5 Limitations on the Power to Contract Within Closely Held Corporations

Oppression and freeze-outs obviously may be avoided through a variety of contractual devices. Other control devices discussed in chapter 9 of this Nutshell may also be used. However, care must be taken that a chosen control device will be enforced by a court and that it will effectively protect the non-controlling shareholders.

A potential trap for the unwary is the common law principle discussed in § 8.11 of this Nutshell that invalidates shareholders' agreements *inter se* that restrict the discretion of directors. That principle, to the extent it remains valid, obviously limits the usefulness of simple contractual arrangements among shareholders as a control device. However, alternative arrangements may usually be created in the form of pooling agreements, voting trusts, irrevocable proxies, election of statutory close corporation status, and classes of shares.

In addition, some modern state corporation statutes may expressly validate shareholder agreements that eliminate or restrict boards of directors. Other state statutes, however, validate agreements only if the corporation has made the special close corporation election discussed in § 12.8 of this Nutshell. Other state statutes validate these agreements if they are in writing and agreed to by all the shareholders. Section 7.32 of the Model Business Corporation Act (1984), approved in 1991, also validates contractual arrangements generally. This section is discussed in § 12.9 of this Nutshell.

§ 12.6   Classes of Shares

A flexible and fool-proof device to establish representation on the board of directors of a corporation or a veto power over certain types of decisions is the use of different classes of shares, usually different classes of common shares. (See generally §§ 7.12 and 9.16 of this Nutshell). Classes of common shares may be used effectively to create a variety of different control devices independent of the financial interests in the corporation. The following examples illustrate the flexibility of this device:

(1) A corporation is to have two shareholders, one putting in $100,000, the other $50,000. They desire to share equally in

control but in the ratio of their contributions (2:1) for financial purposes. The attorney suggests that an equal number of shares of two classes of common stock, Class A common and Class B common, be authorized. Each class is entitled to elect two directors, but the dividend and liquidation rights of each Class A share are twice those of each Class B share. The corporation then issues all the Class A common to one shareholder for $100,000 and all the Class B common to the other shareholder for $50,000. In this structure, the S corporation election would be unavailable because of the two classes of stock but the desired financial relationship is ensured.

(2) Alternatively, if shares with multiple votes per share are authorized in the particular state, the shares may be identical in financial respects but one class may have two votes per share and the other class one vote per share. The shares are then issued in proportion to the different financial contributions. In this structure, the S corporation election is available, since different classes of stock do not disqualify a corporation if the classes differ only in voting rights.

(3) A minority shareholder wishes to be assured of being treasurer of the corporation and to have a veto over all amendments to the articles of incorporation. The attorney suggests that a special class of common shares be created and issued to the minority shareholder. Rights of this class include (1) the treasurer must be a holder of that class of shares, and (2) the articles may be amended only by an affirmative vote of two-thirds of each class of shares, voting by classes. In other respects the classes have equal rights.

(4) There are three shareholders, each contributing the same amount of capital, but C is also contributing the basic idea and wants the same voting power as A and B combined. The attorney suggests that the corporation issue voting and

non-voting common shares (with equal dividend and liquidation rights) in the following amounts:

	Voting	**Non-voting**
A	50	50
B	50	50
C	100	–0–

Somewhat the same result may be obtained by the use of nonvoting preferred shares or indebtedness rather than nonvoting common shares. If the classes of shares differ other than in voting rights the S corporation election is unavailable.

(5) A, B, and C each plan to contribute the same amount of capital, but A wants to be sure that B and C will not combine to oust her and cut off her income. The attorney suggests that A execute a five-year employment contract with the corporation guaranteeing her the specified income. At A's option, the contract may be renewable for a second five year term. In addition, to assure that A has a permanent right to participate in board deliberations, the attorney suggests that three classes of stock be created with identical financial rights but each class has the power to elect one director. The S corporation election is available to a corporation with this capital structure. B and C may object to this structure because of the duration of A's guarantee of employment.

These suggested arrangements all increase the possibility of deadlock within the corporation.

There seems to be little doubt about the validity of control arrangements based on different classes of shares. While there has been litigation on the outer bounds of the power to create specialized classes of shares, recent decisions are uniformly favorable. In perhaps the most startling case, Lehrman v. Cohen (Del.1966), the Delaware Supreme Court upheld a class of common shares that consisted of one share having a par value of $10. This class could elect one of the five directors. (The other four directors were elected by two equal faction, each with the power to elect two directors.) The one-share class was not entitled to receive dividends and could share in the proceeds of dissolution only to the extent of $10. Finally, the one share class could be redeemed by the corporation at any time by paying the shareholder $10 but this action required approval of four of the five directors. The one-share class comes close to a naked vote completely divorced from ownership. It was clearly designed to avoid a potential deadlock between the two other equal shareholders. The subsequent history is interesting and reveals potential problems that may arise in any control arrangement. The one share with virtually no economic rights was issued to the attorney representing the corporation who became actively involved in the management of the corporation. After several years, he and one of the other two shareholders combined forces to take over working control of the corporation to the exclusion of the third shareholder. This solution was made permanent by a long-term employment contract given to the attorney by the board of directors by a vote of 3–2. The Delaware Supreme Court upheld this arrangement in its entirety. (See § 9.16 of this Nutshell for a discussion of the same case in a somewhat different context.)

§ 12.7   Increased Quorum and Voting Requirements

Another useful device in planning shareholder control arrangements is increased quorum and voting requirements that give minority interests a veto power. This veto power may be applicable at the shareholder level, at the board of directors level, or both. It is possible to increase the percentage needed to take some action by the shareholders or directors to any desired number. Usually unanimity is imposed, but in some circumstances a lesser percentage may be sufficient to have the same effect. While a unanimity requirement was invalidated in Benintendi v. Kenton Hotel (N.Y.1945), the language of that statute was promptly amended, and the language of modern statutes is broadly permissive. There is therefore little doubt today about the validity in all states of increasing voting requirements up to and including unanimity.

It is usually necessary to increase both the quorum requirement and the minimum vote requirement in order to assure that it is impossible for the corporation to act without the assent of all shareholders or all directors. The provision creating the increased voting requirement (either in the bylaws or the articles of incorporation) should itself be made non-amendable except by the increased voting requirement. Some state statutes provide this protection automatically, but many do not. See MBCA (1984) § 7.27(b).

Where the voting requirement has not been increased to require unanimity, it is sometimes possible for a minority shareholder or director to prevent action by staying away from the meeting if that makes it impossible to obtain a quorum. That may be particularly important if death or retirement has given one faction a temporary majority. In one case, refusal to attend a meeting was held to constitute a breach of fiduciary duty. Gearing v. Kelly (N.Y.1962). This decision seems questionable given the dynamics of the closely held corporation.

Increased quorum and unanimity requirements increase the possibility of a deadlock within the corporation.

§ 12.8   Special Close Corporation Statutes

Some 18 states, including California, Delaware, and Texas, have adopted special statutes designed specifically for closely held corporations. The genesis of these special statutes is the famous decision in Galler v. Galler (Ill.1964), in which the court upheld an highly unorthodox shareholder's agreement in a two person corporation. The opinion contains a strong plea to state legislatures to consider the unique problems of closely held corporations and the need to permit relaxation of traditional restrictions on corporate structure.

The special close corporation statutes vary widely from state to state. They have the common characteristic that they are optional and must be specifically elected by an eligible corporation by inclusion of a statement in the articles of incorporation that "this corporation is a statutory close corporation" or a similar statement. Eligibility is usually based solely on the number of shareholders. A corporation is eligible for the close corporation election if it has fewer than some maximum number of shareholders: 25, 30 or 35 are popular numbers.

These statutes have rather elaborate provisions dealing with how the election is to be made, how notice that the election has been made is to be publicly communicated, how the election may be revoked, and so forth. They also deal with what happens when the number of shareholders increases so that it exceeds the maximum number permitted by the election.

Special close corporation statutes permit an electing close corporation to adopt informal internal procedures. They authorize corporations to dispense entirely with a board of directors and have the business conducted by the shareholders either following the partnership format or by adopting some other system of governance. Bylaws, meetings, and elections of managers may be dispensed with. Shareholders' agreements are validated even if they interfere with the discretion of boards of directors. Some statutes include a provision expressly prohibiting the application of the piercing the corporate veil doctrine for informal conduct by electing corporations. A variety of judicial remedies for oppression, dissension or deadlock are specifically authorized. In the event of a deadlock at the directorial level, courts are specifically empowered to break the deadlock by the appointment of one or more impartial "provisional directors." This provision is designed to provide a simpler, more flexible and less drastic solution to deadlocked corporations than the traditional remedies of the appointment of a receiver or involuntary dissolution under court supervision. Some statutes make this remedy applicable to all electing close corporations and with no provision for opting out by a specific corporation. In the event of deadlock at the shareholders' level or oppressive conduct, courts are invited to fashion remedies that are suitable for the circumstances. Some statutes list as many as eleven different remedies that a court may invoke, including removal from office of any director or officer or the appointment of an individual as a director or officer. Special dissolution provisions also may be included.

These special close corporation statutes have been widely praised by commentators but rather surprisingly they do not appear to be widely used "on the ground" by corporate practitioners. Studies in various states indicate that exercise of the close corporation election is relatively uncommon. This may indicate only that old habits of corporate lawyers die hard. It may also indicate, however, either that the need for special treatment of close corporations has been overstated or that corporate managers are reluctant to grant courts the broad authority to intervene in the corporation as contemplated by these statutes.

The attractiveness of these special close corporation statutes may also have been reduced in part because states generally have eliminated needless restrictions on all corporations. Most states today authorize any corporation to permit action by written consent, increases in quorum and voting requirements, reduction of the size of the board of directors to one person, and traditional directorial functions to be performed by the shareholders.

The Committee on Corporate Laws developed a "Close Corporation Supplement" at approximately the same time as it approved the 1984 Revised Model Business Corporation Act. This Supplement was largely based on these special close corporation statutes. In part reflecting skepticism about the value of special close corporation statutes, the Committee decisively rejected a proposal that this "Supplement" be formally made a part of the Model Act. In 1991, the Committee withdrew this "Supplement" entirely when it approved § 7.32, a much simpler provision broadly validating all unanimous shareholder agreements relating to management within closely held corporations. This provision is discussed in the following section of this Nutshell.

§ 12.9   Section 7.32 of MBCA (1984)

Section 7.32 of the Model Act, approved in 1991, is a broad provision authorizing shareholders' agreements that departs completely from the traditional statutory scheme. Under this section, an agreement entered into by all the shareholders of a corporation that affects or changes the governance process of a corporation is broadly effective. A § 7.32 agreement may, among other things, eliminate the board of directors, authorize distributions not in proportion to share ownership, establish who shall be directors or officers, specify their manner of selection, delegate the authority of the board of directors to one or more shareholders or other persons, and require dissolution on the demand of one or more shareholders or upon the occurrence of a specific contingency. The Official Comment states that these provisions are illustrative and not exclusive.

A further example given in that Comment approves a system of weighted voting for directors based on shareholdings.

However, there are outer limits. The Official Comment suggests that a shareholder agreement that provides that the directors of the corporation have no duties of care or loyalty to the corporation or the shareholders is beyond the purview of this section. Also, if the powers of directors are vested in persons other than directors, traditional directorial duties must be imposed on those other persons.

Shareholder agreements valid under section 7.32 are not automatically binding on the state, on creditors, or on third parties. For example, a shareholders' agreement that provides that only the president has authority to enter into contracts would not preclude a third person from relying on other corporate officers under general principles of agency. Special rules are also provided for persons who subsequently acquire shares in the closely held corporation while unaware of the agreement. A purchaser of shares who is unaware of the existence of the agreement is bound by the agreement, but she is granted an unqualified power to rescind the purchase upon discovering the agreement. However, if the shares are represented by certificates that contain a proper legend the purchaser is presumed to have knowledge of the existence of the agreement and cannot rescind. Persons acquiring shares through gift or bequest also are bound by the agreement and have no power to rescind unless the contrary is provided in the agreement itself.

Agreements under this section are valid for ten years unless the agreement provides otherwise. Section 7.32 also provides that the agreement terminates automatically if the corporation makes a public offering of its shares.

It remains to be seen whether this innovative provision will be more widely used than the special close corporation statutes that remain in effect in many states.

§ 12.10 Deadlocks

A "deadlock" involves situations in which a closely held corporation finds itself on dead center and unable to act. Deadlocks may readily be avoided by advance planning. The fact that cases involving deadlocks continue to arise with some regularity simply demonstrates that planning sometimes does not occur when it should.

A corporation is potentially subject to deadlock in a variety of circumstances.

(1) A deadlock may arise when two shareholders or factions each own fifty per cent of the outstanding shares. Equal ownership may be preplanned, e.g., by two equal partners deciding to incorporate their ongoing business, or by two entrepreneurs deciding they wish to share equally in all aspects of the business. The same situation may arise from planning decisions by a prior shareholder, e.g. a sole shareholder bequeathing one half of her holdings to each of two descendants or from a lack of planning, where an entrepreneur dies intestate leaving two children but no spouse.

(2) A deadlock may arise if there are an even number of directors, and two factions each have the power to select the same number of directors.

(3) A deadlock may arise if a minority shareholder has retained a veto power through the device of increased quorum or voting requirements and there is a substantial disagreement at a later time.

A deadlock may occur either at the shareholders' level or at the directors' level, or at both levels at the same time.

A deadlock does not mean that the corporation is unable to continue to conduct its business. If the shareholders are deadlocked and unable to elect new directors, the corporation may continue to operate indefinitely under the management of the board of directors in office when the deadlock arose. Statutes provide that "despite the expiration of a director's term, he continues to serve until his successor is elected and qualifies * * *." [MBCA (1984) § 8.05(e)]

A deadlock at the directorial level may arise if there are an even number of directors who divide into two equal factions, and the shareholders are so divided that they cannot resolve the deadlock. Such a deadlock also may not prevent the corporation from continuing to function. It is quite possible that some corporate officers, e.g. the president, secretary and chief financial officer, can continue to operate the business either alone or in cooperation with each other despite the deadlocked board of directors.

The most practical solution for the deadlocked corporation is usually for one faction to buy out the other in a negotiated transaction. If they cannot agree on a sale, they may be able to agree voluntarily to dissolve the corporation. However, it is almost always preferable to preserve a going corporation rather than to dissolve it. The business assets of a corporation, including intangible good will, are ordinarily worth more as a unit than when they are fragmented and sold separately.

If a sale cannot be agreed upon, the ultimate solution is involuntary dissolution, a solution provided by statute in all states. See § 12.14 of this Nutshell.

§ 12.11 Resolution of Disputes by Arbitration

Mandatory arbitration may be used as a device to resolve internal corporate disputes and deadlocks. In most states today, arbitration is generally available to resolve future disputes without regard to their justiciability. Arbitration, of course, requires either a current willingness to arbitrate a dispute or a pre-existing agreement to submit a dispute to arbitration. In considering the desirability of arbitration for internal corporate disputes, two questions should be considered: first, what kinds of controversies is the arbitrator likely to face, and second, what kinds of solutions will he be permitted to adopt?

The advantages of arbitration are speed, cheapness, informality (as contrasted with a court proceeding), and the prospect of a decision by a person with knowledge and experience in business affairs. Where the reason for deadlock is a question not involving a basic personal or policy matter, arbitration may satisfactorily resolve a dispute and permit the corporation to continue. For example, in Vogel v. Lewis (App.Div. N.Y.1967), the issue was whether a corporation should exercise an option to purchase contained in a lease of real property. The court held that this issue should be submitted to arbitration, a result that seems reasonable under the circumstances.

However, many close corporation disputes involve economic issues, personality conflicts, or irreconcilable differences in policy. An arbitrator may have no criterion for resolving such disputes, and even if he or she does resolve a specific dispute, it is unlikely that the decision will have cured the basic disagreement that led to the dispute. In Application of Burkin (N.Y.1956), a well-known New York case, a minority shareholder in a corporation sought arbitration of a claim that the majority shareholder should be removed as director. The corporation's governing documents required unanimity but the majority shareholder not unnaturally refused to vote in favor of his own removal. The court refused to order arbitration on the theory that the dispute was not arbitrable, a result which was later overruled by statute. It is certainly doubtful that arbitration is a suitable remedy for a dispute such as this.

§ 12.12 "Oppression," "Freeze–Outs" and "Squeeze–Outs"

"Oppression," "freeze-outs" and "squeeze-outs" are terms that describe various abusive tactics by controlling shareholders that limit or exclude minority shareholders from participation in the management of the business and deprive them of significant economic return on their investment. The words are not precise synonyms, and all abusive tactics are sometimes described in general terms as "oppression" of minority shareholders.

The term "oppression" may describe a situation in which a minority shareholder originally had rights of participation that she has been deprived of by the controlling shareholders. That term may also refer to transactions that involve non prorata distributions of corporate assets. Typically, the controlling shareholders enter into a transaction with the corporation by which they receive assets from the corporation but no similar opportunity is offered to the minority shareholders. In these situations, the transaction is almost always structured so that the controlling shareholders remain in full control of the corporation following the transaction.

A typical "freeze-out" involves the use of control to deprive the minority of all participation rights and benefits of share ownership in an effort to persuade the minority to sell their shares to the controlling shareholders at an unfavorable price.

A "squeeze out" is a transaction that involves the issuance of additional shares by the corporation on a non-proportionate basis that dilutes the interest of minority shareholders. A typical squeeze-out in a closely held corporation occurs when the controlling shareholder, having previously made loans to the corporation to finance operations, causes the corporation to offer to sell shares at a specified price to all existing shareholders. The controlling shareholder "pays" for his additional shares by canceling a portion of his debt claims while minority shareholders are compelled to pay cash to the corporation if they wish to preserve their percentage ownership interest in the corporation. If they decline to purchase the new shares, their existing holdings are diluted by reason of the new shares issued to the controlling shareholder. Other types of transactions also may be used to dilute the interests of minority shareholders.

Sections 12.14 and 12.17 of this Chapter describes a variety of statutory and judicially created principles that are designed to monitor and control abusive transactions. These principles reflect the extent to which courts are willing to limit the total control that majority shareholders may possess. However, the power of majority shareholders to manage and control the closely held business is generally accepted in the absence of serious abuses of that power. In the absence of advance planning, minority rights are extremely limited in the closely held corporation.

§ 12.13   Share Transfer Restrictions and the "Market" for Shares in a Closely Held Corporation

This section discusses the possibilities of sales of shares in a closely held corporation in which no contractual right of exit exists.

As described above, abusive transactions are possible in closely held corporations primarily because of the absence of a guaranteed right of "exit." Of course, in theory shares of every corporation are freely transferable. Shares of publicly held corporations are traded in large and active securities markets and therefore are usually salable simply by a telephone call to one's broker. The reality is far different when one is dealing with shares of a closely held corporation. Because there are no other potential purchasers, the controlling shareholder can set the price he chooses pretty much on a take-it-or-leave-it basis. Controlling shareholders furthermore may "soften up" minority shareholders by denying that they have any interest in purchasing their shares while depriving them of any return on them. The controlling shareholders typically are in no hurry. Time is on their side since the minority shareholders are locked in.

Why should controlling shareholders offer minority shareholders anything at all for their shares? Typically the controlling shareholder does not need the additional shares to retain his position of control. Acquisition of minority shares at a favorable price, however, does have benefits to the controlling shareholder. For one thing, minority shareholders do have some statutory rights that may prove troublesome in practice. For example, they have the power to inspect corporate books and records in limited circumstances. Elimination of these rights is a benefit to controlling shareholders. Of more importance, minority shares provide a platform for bringing lawsuits against the corporation and the controlling shareholders. Shareholders may bring derivative lawsuits in the name of the corporation charging controlling shareholders with improper transactions or breach of fiduciary duty. The elimination of this litigation base is potentially important to controlling shareholders. Finally, elimination of minority shareholders increases the freedom that controlling shareholders have to make subsequent radical changes in the corporation. For example, elimination of minority interests permits controlling shareholders to dissolve the corporation voluntarily without making any proportionate payment to those interests.

Viewed from the perspective of the controlling shareholders, the value of minority shares has little to do with the intrinsic value of the corporation. Rather, controlling shareholders value minority shares primarily based on their nuisance or blocking value. And that may have little or no relationship to the economic value of the shares calculated as a fraction of the entire corporation.

If controlling shareholders purchase minority shares personally, they reduce the amount of their personal liquid assets by the purchase price. Controlling shareholders who decide to purchase minority shares therefore usually do so by arranging for the corporation to make the purchase, in effect using corporate assets to complete a transaction that is beneficial to them personally.

There are other possible purchasers of minority shares. Other minority shareholders are a possibility. However, they usually have little interest in purchasing additional minority shares since the purchase does not generally improve their position significantly vis á vis each other or the majority shareholder. In effect they become larger minority shareholders. Their financial investment in the corporation increases but their influence does not.

Sales of minority interests to third parties also are conceivable. However, they are unlikely to occur unless the purchaser is acceptable to the controlling shareholders and is able to negotiate an arrangement with them before making the purchase. In the absence of such an arrangement, a purchaser of minority shares will find himself in exactly the same position as the minority shareholder from whom he purchased.

Thus, while there is a market of sorts for minority shares, it is a distress market not at all like a market involving the traditional willing buyer and willing seller contemplated by economic theory.

§ 12.14   Receivership   and   Involuntary   Dissolution: The Traditional Solutions to Oppression and Deadlock In Closely Held Corporations

Today, statutes in every state provide a remedy of the appointment of a receiver or involuntary dissolution at the request of a minority shareholder in specified situations. The language of § 14.30(2) of MBCA (1984) is typical of the situations in which these remedies may be available:

(1) The directors are deadlocked in the management of the corporate affairs, the shareholders are unable to break the deadlock, and "irreparable injury to the corporation is threatened or being suffered, or the business and affairs of the corporation can no longer be conducted to the advantage of the shareholders generally, because of the deadlock;" or

(2) The directors or those in control of the corporation "have acted, are acting, or will act in a manner that is illegal, oppressive, or fraudulent;" or

(3) The shareholders are "deadlocked in voting power," and have failed, for a period that includes at least two consecutive annual meeting dates, to elect successors to directors whose terms have expired; or

(4) The corporate assets are being "misapplied or wasted."

One problem with these statutes is that they grant the court discretion whether or not to order dissolution in cases that fall within these categories. They state that a court *"may dissolve"* a corporation in a proceeding brought by a shareholder if the shareholder establishes that one or more of the conditions described above exist. Further, since there was no right of involuntary dissolution at common law, courts may construe these statutes strictly and require strong showings of potential or actual abuse or harm before ordering relief.

This early attitude toward a narrow construction of these statutes seems to be disappearing since a more flexible attitude has been demonstrated by some courts. "Oppressive conduct," for example has been virtually equated by some courts with "fair dealing" or "fair play." Conduct has been found to be "oppressive" upon a showing that the action taken was inconsistent with the expectations of the shareholders as to their roles in the corporation. Another definition equates "oppression" with "burdensome, harsh and wrongful conduct," or "a visible departure from the standards of fair dealing, and a violation of fair play on which every shareholder who entrusts his money to a company is entitled to rely." These last quotations are taken from Baker v. Commercial Body Builders (Or.1973).

Involuntary dissolution is also not an ideal remedy for oppression or deadlock. Involuntary dissolution is not attractive if it leads to the destruction of a valuable and profitable business. It would be more sensible to auction off the business to the highest bidder and distribute the proceeds or arrange for a buyout at a fair price.

Involuntary dissolution also may cause significant hardship to participants on an erratic basis. For example, if a single shareholder's personal abilities largely explain the corporation's current success, she may well desire to dissolve the corporation in order to capitalize on her abilities to the exclusion of other shareholders. However, these other shareholders may have made substantial contributions to the corporation at an earlier time in the form of research, good will and dedicated service. If the corporation were dissolved, presumably the dominant shareholder could capture the fruits of the good will that has been generated by others within the existing corporation. A classic example of the attempted use of dissolution by a dominant shareholder in this manner is In re Radom & Neidorff, Inc. (N.Y.1954). In this case, the court refused to exercise its discretion to order dissolution; the probable result was to require the dominant shareholder to offer his estranged sister a fairer price for her fifty percent interest. Whether or not dissolution unfairly benefits a shareholder in these situations appears to be fact-dependent; in some situations it does while in other situations it does not.

§ 12.15   Court–Ordered Buy–Outs

As a result of concerns about the draconian nature of a court-ordered dissolution, courts began to develop alternative or supplemental remedies even in states with statutes that refer exclusively to receivership or involuntary dissolution as the remedies for oppression or deadlock. The most common remedy is that a court orders a mandatory buyout of the interest of a minority shareholder at a judicially determined price. If the controlling shareholder is unwilling to purchase the interest, the court may then order involuntary dissolution. In the case of deadlocked corporations, the court may determine not only the price for the shares but who is to buy out whom. Courts were influenced in their development of these non-statutory remedies by the flexible remedies provided in the special close corporation statutes discussed in § 12.8 of this Nutshell, and in effect extended these remedies by analogy to all closely held corporations.

Several states have adopted statutes supplementing the traditional involuntarily dissolution remedy by expressly authorizing a judicially imposed buy-out at an appraised or judicially determined price.

The judicial decisions and statutes discussed in this section led to the development of section 14.34 of the Model Business Corporation Act (1984), discussed in the following section.

§ 12.16   Section 14.34 of MBCA (1984)

In 1991, the Committee on Corporate Laws, recognizing the trend away from exclusive reliance on involuntary dissolution under traditional statutes, adopted § 14.34 of the Model Business Corporation Act (1984), creating an explicit buy-out remedy in deadlock or oppression cases. However, § 14.34 is less flexible than the remedies devised by the courts.

A major limitation in § 14.34 is that it is triggered only if a shareholder brings suit for involuntary dissolution under the traditional statute. Further, when such a suit is filed, the only option available to the court is to give the corporation or the remaining shareholders an election to purchase the shares owned by the plaintiff. There is no reciprocity or discretion here; the shareholder who files a suit seeking involuntary dissolution must be the seller if the corporation or the remaining shareholders make the election to purchase. As a result, a lawsuit requesting involuntary dissolution becomes a high risk enterprise. In the case of a deadlocked corporation with two fifty percent shareholders, in particular, it is easy to visualize a situation where neither party is willing to file the suit and thus assent to be the seller. In this situation, paradoxically, the effect of MBCA § 14.34 may be to chill attempts to obtain judicial assistance in resolving permanent deadlocks.

Section 14.34 gives little guidance as to how fair value should be determined. It is clearly an issue of fact on which expert testimony may be appropriate. The section does authorizes the court to order the purchase price to be paid in installments and to allocate or apportion purchased shares among the various shareholders of various classes in order "to preserve the existing distribution of voting rights among holders of different classes insofar as practicable." If the price and other terms determined by the court are unacceptable to the corporation or its controlling shareholders, dissolution the corporation should follow.

§ 12.17   Fiduciary Duties of Controlling Shareholders

Until relatively recently it was generally accepted that shareholders generally did not owe fiduciary duties to other shareholders, and that directors of closely held corporations did not owe special fiduciary duties to minority shareholders. The first indication of change in this attitude occurred in early judicial opinions and law review articles that concentrated on problems of oppression and deadlock; they referred to closely held corporations as "incorporated partnerships" and argued that partnership-type duties should be imposed on managers of such corporations. The decision in Galler v. Galler (Ill.1964) was particularly influential in this regard.

Donahue v. Rodd Electrotype Co. (Mass.1975) is the leading case imposing a broad fiduciary duty on controlling shareholders of closely held corporations. The duty created in that case is similar to the duty partners in a partnership owe to each other. The case involved a non pro rata distribution to a controlling shareholder, a distribution in which minority shareholders were not permitted to share. The court created a general principle of "equal opportunity" for minority shareholders in such cases. Many state courts have cited *Donahue* approvingly. The principle of *Donahue* can be easily extended to other types of oppressive or unfair conduct. For example, courts have also applied a fiduciary duty to controlling shareholders who negotiate to purchase shares of minority shareholders without disclosing relevant information to them. The information may relate to the value of the shares or to the fact that the controlling shareholder has a commitment from outsiders to purchase the shares at a higher price.

While the *Donahue* principle may prevent many instances of oppression and unfairness, experience has also demonstrated that it has a significant capacity for mischief. It often leads to judicial review of the validity of business decisions. For example, several Massachusetts decisions after *Donahue* have involved the discharge from employment of minority shareholders who were also employees at will. It is of course possible that a firing of a minority shareholder may be part of a planned freeze-out. Indeed, the classic freeze-out entails cutting minority shareholders off from any distributions by the corporation. However, the decision to fire the employee also may have been because he regularly drank too much alcohol at lunch and was ineffective for the rest of the day. It may have been because the nature of the corporation's business has changed and the skills of the minority shareholder were no longer needed by the corporation. It may have been because the corporation has hired a younger person who turns out to have superior skills so that the minority shareholder has become superfluous or redundant. The consequence of a broad application of the *Donahue* principle is that these clear business decisions become litigable issues under a fiduciary duty principle. Law and economics scholars have strongly criticized the Donahue principle on this ground.

In Wilkes v. Springside Nursing Home, Inc. (Mass.1976) the court recognized that an "untempered application of the strict good faith standard" of *Donahue* might impose undesirable "limitations on legitimate action by the controlling group * * * which will unduly hamper its effectiveness in managing the corporation in the best interests of all concerned." The court concluded that majority shareholders "have certain rights to what has been termed 'selfish ownership' in the corporation which should be balanced against the concept of their fiduciary duty."

Law and economics scholars have also criticized the *Donahue* principle on the ground that it imposes an *ex post* duty that the parties to the transaction almost certainly would not have agreed to if they were negotiating independently in their respective self interest.

In Nixon v. Blackwell, (Del.1993), the Delaware Supreme Court refused to adopt the *Donahue* principle. It took the position that it was inappropriate to create special judicially-created duties for closely held corporations in the absence of some legislative direction. It may be suggested, however, that the traditional duties of directors in Delaware, particularly the restrictions against self dealing (see § 14.10–14.14 of this Nutshell) may cover many of the more egregious transactions invalidated under the *Donahue* principle.

[For unfamiliar terms see the Glossary]

CHAPTER THIRTEEN

THE PUBLICLY HELD CORPORATION

§ 13.1 The Publicly Held Corporation in Perspective

As described in § 12.1 of this Nutshell, the most important difference between a publicly held corporation and a closely held corporation is that there is a public market for shares of publicly held corporations. A shareholder of a publicly held corporation who desires to sell his or her shares may do so simply by calling a securities broker. An investor who decides to become a shareholder of a specific publicly held corporation or increase his investment in that company may do so simply by calling a broker and placing an order to buy.

Many publicly held corporations are huge economic entities with billions of dollars of assets, tens or hundreds of thousands of employees, and millions of shares outstanding owned by tens of thousands of shareholders. These very large corporations differ from closely held corporations in several fundamental respects. The bulk of this chapter is devoted to these very large publicly held corporations. Sections 13.4 through 13.10 describe the unique aspects of these very large companies.

In addition to these huge economic entities, the population of publicly held corporations includes a very large number of mid-sized and smaller corporations. Many of these corporations are also very substantial business entities in their own right though smaller than industry leaders. As one moves downward through the hierarchy of publicly held corporations, they generally become smaller, less profitable and with less public interest in their securities. A few publicly held corporations are quite small while a few closely held corporations rival the larger publicly held corporations in size. However, these corporations are exceptional and unusual cases.

As described in § 12.1 of this Nutshell, the "Pink Sheets" represent the dividing line between publicly held and closely held corporations. The number of publicly held corporations has been estimated to be in the range of 10,000 to 15,000. In contrast there are more than four million closely held corporations. Nevertheless, in terms of wealth, power, and economic importance, publicly held corporations dwarf closely held businesses of all types; in the United States the 10,000 or so publicly held corporations own over 90 percent of all business assets.

Technological changes in the last decade, particularly developments in computer technology and the Internet, have led to the creation of many new "high tech" companies that have experienced spectacular growth. New technology is also causing radical changes in the securities industry and the manner in which publicly held shares are traded. See §§ 13.2 and 13.3 of this Nutshell.

§ 13.2   The "High Tech" or "Dot.com" Company

Some high tech companies that were created in the 1980s have reached the size of the largest traditional corporation in a very brief period. Examples include Microsoft, Dell, and America Online. Newer companies in some instances have gone public and made their owners millionaires or billionaires on paper overnight. Many of these newer companies rely on the Internet to develop more efficient methods of distribution of products and services to consumers and to businesses, to facilitate trading in securities, or to make further improvements in technology. This section describes briefly how new "high tech" public companies, mostly creations of the 1990s, develop and grow so rapidly.

The original concept behind a new high tech company obviously comes from one or more imaginative individuals. They attract other people to take the original concept and develop it to the point where it appears to have some commercial possibility. The new corporation with a fashionable high tech name is usually incorporated at this stage in the process. At this point the company is called a "start-up." Money is required to translate a start-up into a viable business. Additional employees are needed; equipment must be purchased; an assembly plant must be rented or purchased; and so forth. Shortly advertising, demonstration models, salesmen, and other market-generating activity will be needed.

At this point "venture capital" firms enter the picture. These firms provide capital, often in the millions of dollars, to the start-up in order to permit it to complete the economic development of the business. They work in close cooperation with the start-up in major ways. They provide technical and business advice relating to the development of the product or service. They help to formulate business strategy. They serve as a sounding board for the entrepreneurial team, assisting them in the formulation of marketing plans and in the resolution of crises. They obtain additional and alternative financing as needed from other venture capital firms and other sources. They help in the recruitment of additional management personnel, vendors and suppliers. The legal relationships between the venture capital firm and the start-up are complex, with the venture capital firm receiving a substantial slice—often 40 percent or more—of the equity interest in the start-up.

The goal of the cooperative efforts between venture capital firm and high tech start-up is to permit the latter to reach the stage where it can "go public" through an "initial public offering" (an "IPO"). An IPO requires the company to complete a complex registration process before the Securities and Exchange Commission ("SEC"). The sale of shares to members of the public is handled by one or more professional underwriting firms. However, shares that are to be distributed to the public may be allocated by the start-up and the venture capital firm; it may be impossible for members of the general public to purchase shares at the initial offering price. Typically, prior to the IPO, the start-up will have issued many shares or options to purchase shares to entrepreneurs, employees and suppliers of capital. Public sale of these shares is prohibited by SEC regulation and contract for a specified period following the IPO.

The price at which shares are to be publicly sold in the initial public offering is set by the underwriters. A trading market for the shares begins immediately after the IPO. It is not uncommon for the initial offering price to be set at $15 or $20 per share but almost immediately the shares are valued in the public trading market at five or seven times the initial offering price. However, it is also not uncommon for the after-market price to decline below the initial offering price.

Once the IPO is completed, investors often talk in terms of the "market cap" of the company. The "market cap" is the theoretical market value of the firm obtained by multiplying the current market price of the publicly traded shares by the number of shares, registered and unregistered, previously issued or optioned by the high tech firm. It is at this point that newspaper articles begin to talk about instant millionaires and billionaires. These statements are somewhat misleading, however, because the market price of the high tech shares is often affected by the fact that there are only a relatively few shares being publicly trading. The market presumably would decline if many new shares entered the public market. There is an air of unreality to many of these IPOs and a widespread belief by experienced securities analysts that there will eventually be a shake-out of many of these companies.

One interesting aspect of high tech companies with astronomical valuations per share is that they have the ability to use shares as currency to purchase other companies. Thus, even though the long term valuation of many of these companies may be suspect, so long as the current valuation holds up, the companies are able to grow quickly through mergers with other companies involving exchanges of stock. In describing the value of these mergers, typically the number of shares involved in the acquisition is multiplied by the current market price of shares of the acquiring corporation.

Why are investors willing to purchase shares of an IPO where the company has never shown a profit? As this is written, shares of Amazon.com are valued at a high price even though the company has incurred continuing losses, and there is no immediate prospect of profits. How can that be? The answer is in part psychology and in part the fact that Amazon.com is involved in a major gamble on a new, highly promising method of retail selling. Certainly some of these new high tech companies will in the long run justify their current market prices. The problem is to determine which ones they will be.

§ 13.3 The Impact of Technology on Public Trading of Securities

Historically, virtually all securities trades by members of the general public were handled through professional securities brokerage firms. Transactions were executed either over a securities exchange—the New York Stock Exchange, the

American Stock Exchange, or one of the regional exchanges—
or "over the counter" through a dealer who was a member of
the National Association of Securities Dealers. Fees, commissions, and "spreads" (the difference between prices dealers
charge when they buy and sell a specific security) were relatively high. Securities firms kept "bankers' hours" (as did the
major securities exchanges) and provided investment advice
and a variety of financial services to individual customers.

Recent technological developments have shaken up this
rather traditional and conservative industry. Computerization
made feasible the development of "discount brokerage firms"
that execute transactions for customers at a much lower cost
than traditional brokerage firms. Discount brokers often do
not provide ancillary services to customers. In the early 1990s,
"on line trading" developed by which individual speculators
can enter securities transactions on their own through the
Internet at a nominal cost or on a flat fee basis for unlimited
trading rights. On line trading of the stock of high tech
companies is particularly widespread. On line trading in turn
has led to a phenomenon known as "day trading." Day traders
are speculators who execute numerous transactions during the
day in an effort to capture profits from modest variations in
securities prices; day traders usually "zero out" their positions at the end of the day and do not carry a securities
position overnight.

Another important development has been the creation of
securities "chat rooms" on the Internet, in which anyone may
post information, rumors, recommendations about securities
transactions, and future developments. A fair amount of "hyp-
ing" specific stocks of dubious reliability appears to occur in
these chat rooms.

Traditional securities exchanges and securities brokerage
firms have felt compelled to respond to these changes. Trading

hours have been extended into the evening to compete with Internet trading. Commissions and fees have declined. Traditional "white stocking" securities firms have created unlimited on line trading systems for customers who trade actively. Historic restrictions on the market in which specific securities are traded are being eliminated. The Securities & Exchange Commission is taking steps to require greater price transparency for less frequently traded securities. A national system of showing price quotations for each specific security on a single bulletin board may be developed. A digital global stock market is likely to be developed in the future.

Also, several proprietary computerized securities exchanges have been created that are limited to large trades by institutional investors. The largest of those proprietary exchanges are Instinet, POSIT, the Crossing Network, and the Arizona Stock Exchange. The costs of trading on these private exchanges are considerably lower than trading on the established exchanges.

These are significant changes for an industry that has the reputation of being rather staid and traditional (and very profitable). It is probable that even greater changes will occur in the future.

§ 13.4 Description of The Very Large Publicly Held Company

Many publicly held corporations are huge economic entities with billions of dollars of assets, tens or hundreds of thousands of employees, and millions of shares outstanding. These corporations differ from closely held corporations and high tech start-ups in several fundamental respects:

(a) *Economic Power.* The largest publicly held corporations wield immense economic power in the United States and world-wide. They decide what products to develop, what safety devices to incorporate in them, what environmental pollutants to create and how to handle them (subject of course, to overriding governmental regulation), who to employ, where to locate plants, whether to move production facilities to Mexico or the Pacific Rim, and so forth. The manner in which such decisions are made and the relationship between such private, presumably profit-oriented decisions and the broader goals of social and governmental policy have been the subject of intense speculation and analysis for nearly a century.

(b) *Diffusion of Ownership.* The ownership of very large corporations is divided up among hundreds of thousands of different investors and there is no cohesive group of persons that can be described as the "owners." Investors typically are passive and have no voice in management except indirectly by voting for directors. Even though shares are widely owned by thousands of different investors, a significant fraction of the outstanding shares may be held by relatively few institutional investors. See § 13.11 of this Nutshell.

(c) *Professional Management.* The managers of the business are professionals who receive the bulk of their compensation from their managerial services and not from share ownership. While managers are encouraged to own shares, and may well be given options to purchase shares at below-market prices, they own typically a fraction of one percent of all the voting shares. Even in corporations whose names are associated with specific individuals or families, it is uncommon to find that management control is based on share ownership. Possible exceptions involve corporations that are relative newcomers to the public scene; they are often the modern success stories in which, after the corporation goes public, the founders of the business have retained control of the enterprise. William Gates and Michael Dell are possible examples.

(d) *Bureaucratic Structure.* The management structure within the business is highly bureaucratic in nature, with very substantial amounts of discretion with respect to ordinary business transactions lodged in individuals below "the top."

(e) *Public Availability of Information.* Because the corporation is publicly held, it is required by federal law to make publicly available a considerable amount of information about its affairs, including periodic audited financial statements and interim disclosure of important developments that materially affect the business. It has been stated that the senior management of a publicly held corporation operates in a goldfish bowl; that is an overstatement, but certainly these corporations have an obligation to make public disclosure of significant developments, both good news and news that the management would probably prefer not be widely disseminated.

(f) *Sources of Capital.* Very large corporations may readily obtain substantial amounts of capital either through the public sale of securities to individuals and sophisticated institutional investors or through the placement of loans with banks and other financial institutions.

§ 13.5   The Internal Structure of Very Large Corporations

Very large publicly held corporations are so large that they almost defy imagination; they rival many governments in terms of wealth, size, and economic power. One large corporation may have hundreds of plants and offices, a dozen or more discretely different lines of businesses, and tens of thousands of products. Hundreds of thousands of employees and their dependents may depend directly or indirectly on the continued success of the corporation for their livelihoods. If one counts suppliers and their employees, customers, communities and even entire states, the success or failure of a large corporation affects millions of persons.

A large corporation may have operations in foreign countries that rival in size their American operations. Manufacturing plants may be located in Mexico, Malaysia, Taiwan, England, and a number of other countries. Sales offices numbering in the thousands may be located in all major countries and in many minor ones as well. The most intense competition may come from foreign enterprises rather than domestic ones.

A large publicly corporation may have scores or hundreds of subsidiaries that are owned and controlled by the corporation. Subsidiaries are usually wholly owned by the parent corporation. As described below, there is a sharp legal difference, but little economic difference, between a wholly owned subsidiary and a division of the corporation itself. There may be minority shareholders in some subsidiaries. Two independent publicly held corporations may enter into a joint venture to develop a new line of business through a new corporation fifty percent owned by each of the parent corporations. Commonly known as ''joint venture corporations,'' these businesses may grow to the point where they rival in size their parent entities.

Since the total number of employees of a very large business is in the tens or hundreds of thousands, the mere keeping of personnel records is a daunting task. Among the employees may be a legal staff of hundreds of lawyers—staffs larger than many major law firms. General Electric's legal staff consisted of 637 lawyers at the end of 1998. Consider also the obligation of a large corporation to file a tax return each year with the federal government. A tax return for such a large entity is certainly going to be complex. The 1998 tax return for one major corporation, Citibank, alone ran to 30,000 pages. More than 200 tax professionals participated in the preparation of this return. Such a corporation is under almost continuous audit by Internal Revenue Service agents assigned exclusively to review its transactions, and a cadre of tax attorneys, accountants, and tax specialists are employed by the company to make sure that its activities are reported in a way most favorable to the company. Control over such a large and complex entity involves a hierarchy of employees, a private bureaucracy so to speak.

As with any bureaucracy, the very large corporation may be slow to react to changes in technology and innovation, to changes in consumer tastes, and to the development of competitive products. This may be a product of simple inertia: The bureaucratic structure may resist change and simplification, accumulating rust, as it were. However, it may also reflect imperfect markets that fail to react promptly to economic changes. The changes in computerization and technology that have occurred during the 1980s and 1990s (and appear likely to continue to develop at an accelerated pace in the future) appear to pose the greatest challenges to established large businesses in the coming years.

§ 13.6   Profit Centers

A large corporation is built around organizational charts, targeted goals, and delegated responsibilities. Generally, successively higher levels of management are given increasingly broad discretion and responsibility. The bureaucratic structure is complicated, however, because large corporations are involved in numerous activities and product lines, and decision-making is diversified and diffused. Several large internal hierarchical structures may exist simultaneously within the lower levels of the bureaucracy. Starting at the lowest level of business management, such as shop foreman or a similar position, successive layers of broader responsibility can be traced up through successive levels of management. If this process is followed, it may culminate in a single person or, in rare instances, a small committee, that has responsibility for one or more areas of operations. A single person may be "President of the Plastics Division" or "Manager of the Chemicals Sector" of a large corporation. That person may have virtually complete responsibility for a multi-plant business with sales of billions of dollars per year. At the same time, that person may be several hierarchical levels below the highest management level within the corporation itself. This intermediate manager may have broad discretion with respect to the management of the division or sector on a day-to-day basis; however, commitments and decisions above a stated level may be made only with the approval of more senior managers.

A "profit center" may be structured as a separate wholly owned business entity, typically a corporation, or they may legally be a division or department of the corporation itself. The words "department" or "division" usually connote that the profit center is not a separate corporation while the word "subsidiary" connotes that the profit center has independent legal existence. However, usage is not uniform, and one sometimes sees references to a "division" when the word "subsidiary" would have been more accurate, and vice versa.

The typical profit center functions as a largely autonomous business having wide discretion over research, product development, advertising, sales policies, and other matters. The head of the profit center has the ultimate responsibility for the operations of that profit center. If the profit center does poorly or has internal difficulties or problems, that person may be demoted or lose his job. A profit center is usually sufficiently discrete and self-standing that it can be bought as a unit by a third party without causing a major reshuffling of assets, employees, and records.

Even though there is considerable decentralization of management and day-to-day control within large corporations, the results of operations are reported on a company-wide basis. The financial statements of all components are "consolidated" into a single financial statement for the entire enterprise. For internal purposes, however, accounting statements for individual profit centers may be created on an annual, monthly, weekly, or even daily basis.

§ 13.7 The Home Office

Above profit centers there is an "umbrella organization," that may be defined as the "home office" or "corporate headquarters" of the corporation itself. In this home office there is a central bureaucracy that has general oversight of all the various profit centers. In addition, the home office handles a number of core operations such as accounting, capital raising, and investment of surplus funds common to all profit centers. The home office may be located in any state without regard to where the corporation is incorporated. Usually it is in a city or state in which the corporation has some historic tie. While Delaware is the most popular state of incorporation, very few large corporations have their home offices in that small state.

The home office is also hierarchical in form. At the highest levels are managers, usually with responsibility for specific functional areas; these managers have ultimate authority over broad areas of business activities. They have titles that describe their areas of responsibility: "chief legal officer," "chief operations officer," "chief financial officer," "chief accounting officer," and so forth. These officers are often referred to by their acronyms: "CFO," "COO," "CAO," and "CLO." The senior management official, the top of the management pyramid to which all the functional managers report, is the chief executive officer, or the "CEO." See § 13.8 of this Nutshell

Many state corporation statutes require that every corporation have certain specified officers: e.g. a president, a secretary, a treasurer, and one or more vice presidents. In order to comply with these statutory requirements the statutory title may be appended to a specific office: the CFO may have the title "chief financial officer and treasurer," for example, and the CEO may have the title "President and Chief Executive Officer." By and large functional titles are used and little attention is paid to statutory titles. However, titles of "vice president," "assistant secretary," and "assistant treasurer" may be given to numerous employees in various offices and plants around the country in order to permit contracts to be entered into and other corporate actions performed locally without involving home office personnel.

The home office selects top operating managers for individual profit centers and monitors and reviews their performance. In this way, good performance may be rewarded and consistent compensation levels for managers may be maintained across the entire business of the corporation. A centralized system of employee classification may be used to assure equity in salary schedules throughout lower levels of the corporation.

The home office also provides a variety of centralized services that experience demonstrates is more efficiently provided on a centralized basis than by allowing each profit center to develop its own system. Areas of central direction and control typically include the provision of auditing and legal services; the raising of capital; the maintenance of employee benefit plans for all employees; and the provision of incentive compensation plans for top managers. The home office makes major decisions as to the long-term direction of the enterprise, and may also review proposed plans developed by profit centers that involve significant investment.

The home office may also have the responsibility of assuring the overnight investment of available funds and minimizing borrowing costs. A "cash concentration" system requires that all funds available throughout the entire enterprise be deposited on a daily basis in accounts handled by the home office. Profit centers, in other words, may not have their own bank accounts or banking connections, but may have access to funds deposited in these central accounts. One advantage of this system from the standpoint of the enterprise is that borrowing costs are minimized. Excess funds generated by one profit center may be "lent" to another profit center, thereby avoiding the possibility that one profit center may be seeking a bank loan when another profit center has excess funds invested in low yielding or non-interest bearing bank deposits.

Another function generally handled by corporate headquarters is raising capital from various sources and allocating it among the various profit centers. While many profit centers have the capability of borrowing funds on their own from commercial sources, the main office is able to borrow on more favorable terms than any single profit center. Concentrating capital raising at the home office also permits centralized review of proposed capital investments by individual profit centers. This, in turn, permits the corporation to divide its huge—but ultimately limited—resources among competing proposals in a rational manner in order to maximize overall return.

The home office is "the corporation" for purposes of shareholder relations, interaction of the board of directors with management, dividend payment decisions, and the like.

§ 13.8   The Chief Executive Officer

At the apex of managerial control within a large corporation is an individual referred to almost universally as the "chief executive officer" or "CEO." The CEO has responsibility for the management team that directs the enterprise, and is ultimately responsible for the success of the enterprise. If, for example, the CEO loses confidence in the CFO, the CEO must replace him and find a more satisfactory one. In theory, the CEO has power to call the shots in the corporate bureaucracy on narrow issues as well as broad ones, where and when he wishes. In practice, the CEO, as the head of a large bureaucratic organization, cannot hope to run details of the business operations. To be effective, he must delegate authority over day-to-day operations, including personnel, financing, advertising, and production. The CEO should concentrate on the broadest issues relating to the business.

The typical CEO is a professional manager. Rarely does he own an appreciable fraction of the corporate stock. His power arises from his position at the top of the bureaucracy rather than from his ownership interest or voting power at the shareholder level. His tenure is ultimately determined by the board of directors of the corporation.

Because the CEO has ultimate responsibility for the success or failure of the corporation, he—and quite possibly he alone—may make the final decision on whether to embark upon a radical change in business strategy. The CEO may decide, for example, to close fifteen plants in order to redirect the primary emphasis of the corporation, or to develop a new product such as a state-of-the-art airplane or modern computer that will strain the economic resources of any very large corporation. If unsuccessful, such a strategy may call into question the long term viability of the enterprise and cause the CEO to lose his job. These decisions are usually made by the CEO following discussions with the board of directors. The board has the power to reject the CEO's proposal. In rare instances, the board of directors may actually exercise this power and reject a major proposal by the CEO. Within the corporate culture, this is evidence that the CEO has lost the confidence of the board of directors and his resignation is the normal consequence. This is well understood both by the CEO and the members of the board of directors. Thus, where the CEO has the confidence of the board of directors, the board will usually approve a proposal even though individual directors may have serious reservations about its wisdom.

During the early part of the Twentieth Century, the CEO's power was viewed by most observers as virtually absolute. Whether or not the power of the CEO was truly absolute in the past, it was certainly greater in the past than it is today. There are many indications that the power of the typical CEO has declined in the 1980s and 1990s for a variety of reasons, and that increased power has been assumed by the board of directors.

§ 13.9   Compensation of Senior Executives

One visible and controversial aspect of modern corporation law is the level of compensation of senior executives, particularly the CEO. In the 1990s the average salary of CEOs and other senior executives of Fortune 500 corporations was in the high six or low seven figures; but this was usually supplemented by stock options, bonuses, and incentive compensation arrangements. The aggregate compensation paid to some CEOs was in the tens or even the hundreds of millions of dollars in a single year. A survey of 350 corporations in early 1995 revealed that levels of CEO compensation had increased by 8.1 per cent from 1992 to 1993 and an additional 11.4 per cent from 1993 to 1994. During the same two years, white collar salaries generally had increased by only a total of 4.2 per cent, and in many instances work forces had been "downsized" or salary levels reduced by changing the work force from employees to "contract workers." Senior executive salary levels in the United States are much higher than the salaries of their European or Asian counterparts. Compensation thus has become a major political issue. Visible consequences of this controversy include the following:

1) The Revenue Reconciliation Act of 1993 limits the income tax deductibility of salaries in excess of one million dollars per year. Covered employees include the CEO and the four other highest compensated officers. However, since the provision excludes "performance-based" compensation, it appears to have had only minimal effect on actual levels of compensation. Some corporations have continued paying compensation in excess of $1,000,000 per year despite the loss of the tax deduction; others have apparently *increased* the levels of compensation from the high six figures to the million dollar level.

2) Other parts of the Revenue Reconciliation Act affect rules of corporate governance as well as tax law. The definition of "performance-based" payments requires the creation of a compensation committee consisting only of outside directors. The tax regulations contain a definition of an "outside" director. The compensation committee must develop performance criteria at the beginning of the performance period. The compensation arrangement must be adequately disclosed to, and approved by, the shareholders before compensation is paid. In addition, the outside directors must certify in writing that the performance criteria have been met before compensation may be paid.

The SEC requires the compensation committee to discuss the corporation's policies with respect to the one million dollar cap in its proxy statement.

Corporations have exhibited some reluctance in seeking approval of performance compensation plans by shareholders. They are perhaps concerned about the possible use of this information in later class action or derivative suits brought by shareholders.

3) The Securities and Exchange Commission requires elaborate and complete descriptions of compensation levels in proxy statements, including a "specific discussion" of compensation levels compared with profitability and shareholder return.

4) The SEC requires corporations to place shareholder proposals with respect to compensation levels in proxy statements. See § 13.23 of this Nutshell.

5) The SEC requires footnote disclosure of the value of stock options granted to senior executives. A continuing controversy exists about the common practice of repricing options downward following a decline in the price of the stock.

§ 13.10   Shareholders as "Investors" or "Owners"

Assume you buy one hundred shares of stock of General Motors Corporation. In January, 2000, such a purchase would have cost about $8,000, including brokerage commissions. In one sense you are now a partial owner of a major automobile business; or at least that is how the New York Stock Exchange has historically wanted small investors to view their own roles. However, that is not a very realistic way of looking at your role. General Motors has some 655 million odd shares outstanding; your one hundred shares is not a very large percentage interest in General Motors. Also, there certainly is not very much you can do to influence what GM does. Why does someone such as yourself invest $8,000 in this way? Almost all investors view the purchase of shares of stock as purely a financial one: Will I make money if I invest my $8,000 in General Motors? The sources of potential gain are two-fold. First, the investor will receive dividends (in 1999, GM was paying a dividend of $2.00 per share per year, or $200.00 per year on a $8,000 investment). Second, if GM does well, the price of the stock will go up and the investor may profit by selling it for more than he paid for it. A quick calculation shows that the dividend yield on GM stock in 1999 was a little over 3 per cent per year. The possibility of price escalation is obviously a very important consideration since an investor at the same time can obtain a yield of 5 percent or more in a totally riskless savings account.

If GM stock turns downward or management does something you do not like, the sensible thing to do is simply to sell your GM stock and invest the funds somewhere else. This is known as "exercising the Wall Street Option."

Of course, shareholders do have the right to vote for the election of directors and from time to time they may have limited additional rights to participate in management. For example, shareholders are entitled to vote for or against the appointment of a specific accounting firm to audit GM's books and report the result of the audit. They may vote on other proposals that appear in proxy statements. They also have some additional rights, for example, to bring derivative suits, to vote on mergers and other fundamental transactions, and so forth. However, it does not take a genius to see that the actual participation in corporate decision-making by small shareholders in large corporations is nominal at best. The interest of the average small shareholder in a publicly held corporation is purely economic.

Of course, exercising the Wall Street Option is not a neutral act, particularly if a large number of shareholders decide to do so at about the same time or if several large investors conclude at about the same time that they no longer want GM in their portfolios. The price of GM stock will go down, a result which management is not going to be happy about. Low stock prices harm management since compensation is to some extent incentive-based and usually measured by increases in stock prices. More seriously, the loss of investor confidence may reflect itself in loss of confidence in top management within the board of directors, and the CEO and top management may be in danger of losing their jobs.

In light of the truly nominal role that most shareholders play in managing the corporate enterprise, it is questionable whether small investors should be viewed as the "owners" of the business at all. Indeed, as described in § 2.4 of this Nutshell, modern economic theory visualizes the very large business as a "nexus of contracts" and rejects the assumption that investors—shareholders in publicly held corporations, typically—should be viewed as "owners" at all. Rather they are viewed as contributors of capital having the right to receive the residual cash flow and capital of the business, and being the first to suffer the consequences of losses. Implicit in this analysis is the assumption that the managers of the business—the CEO, his subordinates, and the board of directors—are the central organizers and the central component of a business with investors being contributors of capital much like commercial lenders. Capital is of course only one of numerous inputs in a business (albeit a very important one) and there is no inherent reason to denominate the contributors of this input as "owners."

§ 13.11   Institutional Investors

In the early 1930s, Berle and Means published a seminal book entitled *The Modern Corporation and Private Property.* Its principal thesis was that fragmented ownership carries with it none of the control that ownership normally provides. Berle and Means drew from this thesis the conclusion that the managers of publicly held corporations had dictatorial power over the corporation and shareholders were without power. This picture was probably never completely accurate, but certainly modern trends in securities ownership and the role of boards of directors are moving strongly away from the Berle and Means model.

Since Berle and Means wrote, there has been an important—almost revolutionary—change in the patterns of ownership of publicly held corporations. Today, "institutional investors," a group that was unimportant sixty years ago, dominate stock ownership of many corporations and transactions on major securities markets. The principal categories of institutional investors are private pension funds, public employee pension funds, mutual funds, banks, university endowments, life and casualty insurance companies, and private investment funds. As of August, 1999, institutional investors owned about 60 percent of all the stock of the one thousand largest corporations in the United States. It is not uncommon for the hundred largest shareholders in a very large corporation—all institutional investors—to own more than 50 percent of the voting shares of that corporation. In some very large corporations that are highly popular investment vehicles, institutional investors as a group may own 80 percent or more of all the voting shares of that corporation.

In one respect institutional investors differ from the typical small individual investor. Most institutional investors are in effect investing other people's money in a fiduciary capacity.

Pension funds manage money set aside for the retirement of specific individuals. Insurance companies manage the proceeds of insurance premiums that ultimately will have to be paid out to beneficiaries. Mutual funds make investment decisions on behalf of individuals who have opted to have other people invest their money for them. All of these institutional investors owe fiduciary duties to third persons. They therefore may be required to make short term decisions with respect to portfolio securities in response to those duties rather than on the basis of long term investment goals of maximizing the gain from ownership of specific stocks.

Clearly the holdings of institutional investors today could lead to control over much of American industry if they work together as a group. Even where control is not in fact exercised, their collective influence on management can be great. Collective effort, however, has not been easy to obtain. There are legal impediments to any one institutional investor (or any one investor of any kind, for that matter) owning more than five percent of the voting stock of any issuer. Most institutional investors as a matter of policy limit their holdings to less than this percentage. Furthermore, most institutional investors diversify their portfolios by spreading their capital around among many different investments and many different companies. As a result, the stock of any one issuer is always a relatively small part of each institutional investor's portfolio even though the aggregate number of dollars invested by all institutional investors in a single issuer may be very large. An investor with a diversified portfolio has little incentive to participate actively in management (since changes in the price of any one stock will have a small effect on its aggregate wealth). Rather they tend to vote their shares in support of management and the status quo. Indeed, many institutional investors delegate their voting of portfolio shares to outside companies subject to general instructions.

Before 1992 the SEC proxy regulations also discouraged cooperative institutional investor involvement in corporate governance by imposing substantial disclosure requirements on any group of more than ten shareholders working cooperatively together to elect directors or influence management. The principal change made in 1992 permits institutional investors to communicate directly with each other with respect to voting of shares so long as they do not actually solicit the proxies of others. Today, institutional investors are free to communicate their collective dissatisfaction with the performance of specific portfolio companies to management or to specific directors. A corporation with fifty percent or more of its stock owned by institutional investors can hardly ignore such a communication.

Activism by institutional investors has also increased in part because many of them recognize that they are long term, locked-in investors. It may be difficult for individual institutional investors to exercise the "Wall Street option" if they are dissatisfied with the performance of a portfolio company. Large blocks of shares as a practical matter may be salable at an acceptable price only if other institutional investors are willing to buy them. The market power of institutional investors is now so great that a decision to sell by several of them can have a dramatic (and traumatic) negative effect on the price of that stock. Issuers take seriously indications that several institutional investors are dissatisfied with their economic performance and are considering removing the stock from the investors' portfolios.

§ 13.12 Street Name Registration of Securities; Book Entry

Most stock certificates today are registered in the names of nominees and not the equitable owners of the shares. The practice of using nominees apparently arose early in the Twentieth Century in connection with banks and financial institutions. Faced with onerous transfer requirements applicable to shares registered in a fiduciary capacity, these institutions began to record ownership interests in the name of one or more partnerships of employees with names such as "Abel & Company." However, registration under these names continued to be made in the stock transfer books of the issuer.

Until the 1960s, transfers of shares of publicly corporations were executed by the transfer of certificates that were registered in nominee name and endorsed in blank and delivered to the purchaser or his broker. As the volume of securities transactions increased in the 1960s, a serious "back office" problem arose as the clerical staffs of brokerage firms were unable to keep up with the increased volume. Brokerage firms were awash in stock certificates of uncertain ownership. As a result, a new system of executing securities transactions and recording share ownership was developed. This new system may be described as a "book entry" system or "street name registration."

In the book entry system stock certificates are largely immobilized. Ownership of securities is recorded in the records of brokerage firms and not in the share transfer books of the issuers. (Some owners of publicly traded shares do not use the book entry system and arrange to have shares recorded in their names as described in § 9.3 of this Nutshell; however relatively few holders of publicly traded shares follow this procedure today.) Most physical certificates are permanently stored in vaults at the Depository Trust Company (DTC) and other clearing offices. Most of these shares are registered in the name of "Cede & Co." Cede is the registered owner of more than 70 percent of all shares traded on the major securities exchanges. DTC maintains accounts for securities owned by hundreds of brokerage firms while the firms maintain accounts for individual customers. Transfers of securities are recorded in the records of the brokers representing the buyer and seller and, if necessary in adjustment of the brokerage firm records maintained by DTC.

The book entry system involves two sets of intermediaries between the owner of shares and the issuer. The system is extremely efficient not only for trading but also for the distribution of dividends, which are transferred by wire from the issuer to brokerage firms on the day the dividend is payable, and deposited into the accounts of customers on the same day. There may be problems, however, in communicating through two sets of intermediaries for various types of shareholder actions, particularly actions that must be taken within narrow and clearly defined time limits.

Article 8 of the Uniform Commercial Code has been revised to provide rules for book entry transfers. Considerable protection against insolvency of brokerage firms is provided by the Securities Investors Protection Corporation, a federal corporation that insures against securities losses of up to $500,000 for each brokerage firm customer of a brokerage firm that becomes insolvent owning fewer securities than reflected in its customer records. This protection is essential for the success of the book entry system, since ownership of all shares of customers of a brokerage firm are recorded in the name of the firm at DTC, and therefore can be sold by the firm without the prior consent of the customer.

With further developments in computerization, the SEC has authorized a variation of a book entry system that permits direct book entries of ownership in the records of the issuer. These shares are certificateless, but readily transferable by the owner. Brokerage firms have resisted this development because the current book entry system closely ties brokerage firm customers to the specific brokerage firm. Book entry maintained in the issuer's records would permit an owner to use any brokerage firm to effect any securities transaction.

§ 13.13   The Board of Directors of Large Publicly Held Companies: Theory and Reality

The board of directors serves an essential function in corporation theory. As with many other areas of corporate law, one has to separate the theory from the reality when discussing the roles of directors in publicly held corporations. The board of directors in theory has plenary power over management. Under the unambiguous directive of § 8.01(b), the board certainly has the power to manage the business and affairs of the corporation and reduce the CEO and his or her staff to little more than an errand boy. The board of directors unquestionably can reverse management decisions on any specific issue that it chooses to involve itself with. In real life, however, it is very unusual for a board of directors in a large publicly held corporation to actually become involved directly in business management.

Modern boards of directors are composed primarily of outside directors who are busy and successful persons often with their own businesses to run. Furthermore, the typical board of directors is a part-time board. It may meet six or eight times a year, for perhaps an average of three hours. Much of that time is devoted to routine matters dealing with the board's activities, discussion of financial results, and reports of committees. Of course, board member involvement is not limited to formal meetings. There may be periodic communications to board members, informal discussions, and meetings of committees. Nevertheless it is not realistic to expect that the board of directors of a large publicly held corporation is going to have exhaustive continuous involvement in corporate affairs.

The 1999 revision of section 8.30 of the Model Business Corporation Act identifies (but does not define) two basic roles of directors: A "decision making function" and an "oversight function." A director must "become informed" in connection with the decision making function and "devote attention" to the oversight function. In either event each director must exercise "the care that a person in a like position would reasonably believe appropriate under similar circumstances."

The most important function of a board of directors is monitoring the performance of the CEO. and, when necessary, selecting a replacement. The relationship between a CEO and the corporation's board of directors is complex. Historically CEOs had a major voice in deciding who should serve on the board. Even today, the views of the CEO may be sought about who should be invited to serve on the board of directors. Thus, the manager may be involved in the selection of his overseers while the shareholders can only vote for or against the overseers so selected. Clearly, the relationships between the CEO, the board of directors, and the shareholders are more complicated than theory suggests.

There are other important management functions that the board of directors must perform. There must always be in place a command structure for the business of the corporation and some one must be in command. Some provision must be made for the catastrophic event in which the bulk of the senior management of the firm is wiped out in an accident. There must always be in place an accounting and reporting system that assures that transactions are being appropriately recorded and monitored by responsible managers. Indications that there are breakdowns in the accounting and reporting system must be taken as seriously as breakdowns in the command structure. Finally, there must be an information system in place that assures that responsible officers or employees are informed about problem areas as they develop.

In short, boards of directors of publicly held corporations do not "manage"; the management "manages." It is misleading to suggest that there is actual management "by" a board of directors in a large publicly held corporation. Monitoring of management is a more accurate description of the board's function.

§ 13.14 The Election of Directors

Again it is useful to separate theory from the reality. In theory, individual members of the board of directors are elected by the shareholders at meetings. Each director must be nominated and must receive, depending on the specific statute involved, either a majority or a plurality of all votes cast in the election. The theory thus is that shareholders select directors. The reality is quite different.

Virtually all shareholders in publicly held corporations vote by proxy; only a handful of them actually attend meetings in person. (Indeed, there is no building in the world large enough to hold all the shareholders of, say, GM). The decision as to who is to be elected is not made by the vote taken at the shareholders meeting. The decision is *really* made some time earlier when owners of shares fill out proxy forms. These proxies are mailed in and tabulated, and the result is announced at the meeting. Actually, the decision is *really* made some time before the proxy forms are distributed. Shareholders voting by proxy do not normally have the right to select who to vote for from a list of candidates. In almost all proxy solicitations, only candidates that have been selected by the corporation are listed, and the only choice the shareholder has is to vote for those persons or withhold their vote entirely. A shareholder voting by proxy cannot direct that his vote be cast for himself or some other person not identified as a candidate in the proxy form. Proxies signed and returned without making a selection will nevertheless be voted for the management candidates unless the proxy specifically directs that the vote is being withheld.

In short, new directors are selected by the corporation before proxies are solicited. Today, candidates for the board of directors are usually selected by a committee of the board of directors. At an earlier time this century they were usually selected by the CEO.

It is possible for an outside group of shareholders to organize and solicit proxies in competition with management—a "proxy fight." However, because of the substantial cost of soliciting thousands of shareholders it is unusual for any competing group to make a serious solicitation in an effort to elect a majority of the directors in opposition to management. Further, a solicitation of proxies from more than ten shareholders requires compliance with the complex SEC proxy regulations, itself a costly process. As a result, genuine proxy fights for control occur in only a small handful of publicly held corporations every year. Much more likely is a negotiated take-over, though it is not uncommon for a proxy fight to be threatened as part of the negotiation process.

§ 13.15   "Inside" and "Independent" Directors

A useful classification of directors is between "inside" directors and "outside" or "independent" directors. "Inside" directors consist of directors who are high level employees of the corporation or who have a significant economic relationship to the corporation. Examples include a banker affiliated with the major bank used as a depository by the corporation, a lawyer who is a partner in the law firm used by the corporation as its principal source of outside legal assistance, or executives of corporations that are suppliers to the corporation. "Outside" or "independent" directors are directors who do not have an employment or other significant economic relationship with the corporation. Today, boards of almost all publicly held corporations consist primarily of outside directors, and as a result their degree of independence from management dominance is increasing.

In some classifications of directors, a distinction is made between "affiliated outside directors"—outside directors with significant economic or familial relationships with the corporation—and "inside" directors. In the discussion that follows "affiliated outside directors" are treated as inside directors.

§ 13.16   Historic Dominance of the Board by the CEO

Prior to about 1970, most publicly held corporations had management-dominated boards composed primarily of inside directors and the CEO.

In corporations that as a matter of policy included some independent directors on the board, the CEO would interview candidates he did not personally know and develop a social and personal relationship with them. The CEO also could usually drop independent directors from the board at the next election simply by not including them. A CEO might therefore limit outside directors to friends, college roommates, fraternity brothers, and the like. Such a board was stacked with "yes men," good friends of the CEO, and inside directors whose jobs were subject to CEO review. Some literature from this period comments acidly that management believed the best kind of director was one who could be expected to reliably say "yes" or "no" on cue. Members of the board of directors acted independently only when faced with a dire emergency such as the unexpected death or disability of the CEO when there was no clear heir apparent or a financial disaster of such a magnitude that it threatened the continued viability of the corporation.

While this picture is undoubtedly overdrawn in some respects, it was quite plausible since the CEO had such a dominant role in the selection of individual directors that the board was largely viewed as "his" board of directors. Hence it is not surprising that Berle and Means, writing before World War II, viewed the typical board of directors as being dominated by the CEO and impotent or irrelevant in monitoring the enterprise—the aspic on the fish, to use one graphic phrase of that era.

Another important aspect of CEO dominance of corporate boards was the fact that the CEO was usually also chairman of the board of directors. He therefore was physically present at meetings of the board of directors and controlled both the agenda and whatever information was circulated before or at the meeting. In this environment significant external input and oversight was difficult to obtain, and frank discussion and review of the CEO's performance was virtually impossible. A secret meeting of the outside directors in the absence of the CEO was viewed as high treason. A decision to request the CEO to resign involuntarily required a "palace coup," a conspiracy by persons whose positions on the board, and sometimes their jobs, were at stake if the plot was revealed prematurely.

A principal catalyst for adding truly independent directors (though many corporations had added some independent directors many years earlier) was the Watergate-related scandals of the early 1970s. Disclosure during this period revealed that many corporations had engaged in illegal conduct in the United States and abroad. As a result of those scandals, the

SEC required all publicly held corporations to create audit committees composed of independent directors to review financial reporting, the relationship with outside auditors, and controls over unlawful conduct within each corporation. Corporations found it necessary to add independent directors to meet this requirement. The New York Stock Exchange, the National Association of Securities Dealers and the American Stock Exchange amended listing requirements to require that a majority of directors be independent directors.

By 1995, conservative organizations such as the Business Roundtable and the Business Law Section of the American Bar Association had recommended that boards of directors of all publicly held corporations should be predominantly composed of outside directors. In addition, they recommended that the critical function of selecting candidates for the board of directors be vested in a nominating committee composed predominantly of independent directors.

Even though new directors are selected by the nominating committee today, the CEO usually has some involvement in the work of that committee. He may be a member of the committee or his views solicited regularly. The theory is that he must be able to work effectively with all outside directors. However, the CEO's influence in the actual selection process has declined dramatically.

§ 13.17 The Modern Board of Directors

The average board of directors today may consist of 9 or 11 individuals; large boards of 15 or 17 persons are uncommon and the trend appears to be towards smaller boards. Today boards of 5 or 7 members are not unusual. Less than one-third of the directors of a typical board will be inside directors, and again the trend appears to be reducing the number of inside directors.

Boards with a majority of outside directors—the typical board today—are sometimes referred to "majority independent" boards. A number of corporations have created "super-majority independent boards" consisting only of independent directors and the CEO. Recent empirical studies have questioned the efficacy of super-majority independent boards. These studies suggest that the quality of business decisions is improved if there are one or two inside directors who are intimately familiar with corporate operations on the board in addition to the CEO. Inside directors also may become aware that the CEO is aging or becoming less effective before independent directors. The issue of succession or replacement may be quietly raised with independent directors before the issue becomes acute. Members of management who serve as inside directors are also likely to be leading candidates to succeed the incumbent CEO. The presence of inside directors on the board therefore permits independent directors to become familiar with likely future candidates for CEO.

Typical independent directors are (1) CEOs of other publicly held corporations, (2) retired CEOs or high level executives of other publicly held corporations, (3) a university president or high academic officer, (4) a former public official, (5) a successful small businessman, and (6) one or more independent investors. Most corporations have one or more female directors; many have at least one minority director as well.

CEOs and former CEOs of other corporations are the most popular independent directors. It is believed that they understand the complexities of managing a large enterprise and appreciate the complex relationships between the CEO and the board of directors. They also understand the need of the CEO for both support and disinterested recommendations and advice and the broad discretion that the CEO must have to run the enterprise. Also, CEOs and former CEOs have practical experience and background. This may be a weakness as well as a strength. CEOs of other companies may sympathize with the incumbent's problem and give him the benefit of the doubt on a "there but for the grace of God go I" theory.

In any event, the modern CEO deals with a board of directors composed of persons with considerable business sophistication who are not employed by the corporation and are whose positions are not dependent on the CEO.

These changes in board composition in the last few decades have had dramatic impact. Illustrative is the fact that the 1990s have seen the abrupt dismissal of a large number of CEOs of under-performing or marginal corporations. Between 1992 and 1996, 125 CEOs of Fortune 500 corporations were replaced, including General Motors, Compaq Computer Corporation, General Electric, American Express, Apple Computing Company, and others. There was no similar period of CEO dismissals even during the depths of the Great Depression. Economic factors during the early 1990s undoubtedly contributed to these dismissals. However, there has also been a clear shift of power away from CEOs and toward the board of directors.

In many corporations, independent directors now meet separately from the CEO and inside directors at least once a year to discuss the performance of management. In some corporations the chairman of the board of directors is an outside director and not the CEO. Such an arrangement would have been unthinkable a few decades ago. General Motors, perhaps the most traditional corporation in the automobile industry, has publicly released a "GM Board Guidelines for Corporate Governance Issues" which embodies and approves many of the developments discussed above. Similar guidelines for directors have been issued by the Business Roundtable (an association of CEO's), and by Calpers and TIAA/CREF (two major institutional investors).

Another factor affecting corporate governance is the increased activism of large institutional investors. Direct communication between independent directors and institutional investors is common today. See § 13.8 of this Nutshell. Large shareholders today may prefer to talk with independent directors rather than with the CEO about problems. Institutional investors have also created monitoring programs to evaluate portfolio corporations. For example the New York State Retirement Fund screens the economic performance of about 900 companies, each year and makes governance recommendations for companies viewed to be underperforming. CalPERS and TIAA/CREF also have created extensive screening programs for over a thousand portfolio companies each; companies that fail to meet guidelines are contacted by the staff of the institutional investors. Implicit is the threat that the institutional investor will divest itself of investment in companies that refuse to consider making changes in governance procedures.

The magazine *Business Week* publishes each year a list of the 20 "Best Boards" and the 20 "Worst Boards". These evaluations are based on "objective" guidelines, including (1) not having more than two inside directors on the board, (2) having only outside directors on the audit, nominating, and compensation committees, and (3) having no interlocking directorships (a director of company A serving as a director on the board of company B while a director of company B is serving as a director on the board of company A).

Modern boards periodically review the performance of the CEO and senior executives, typically in connection with compensation issues. A modern board of directors will have a compensation committee composed entirely of independent outside directors to deal with compensation matters for high level employees in general, and the CEO in particular. There may also be a separate committee to consider periodically the CEO's overall performance. However, the difficult and painful process of replacing the CEO if his stewardship of the business is unsatisfactory is largely independent of the committee review process. Basically, the CEO's continued tenure today is dependent on his ability to retain the confidence of the board of directors as a whole, particularly the independent directors on the board. Today the CEO is viewed as the highest level employee more than as the leader of the enterprise.

§ 13.18 The "Chicago School" of Law and Economics

In the last three decades there has developed a law and economics analysis of the publicly held corporation that challenges many of the traditional beliefs about the role of management, the importance of takeover attempts by outsiders, and the efficacy of many legal rules. This analysis has come to be associated with scholars at the University of Chicago and will be referred to here as the "Chicago School;" it is appropriate to point out, however, that scholars with this analytic approach today teach at many different law schools. Central to the Chicago school analysis is the treatment of the corporation described in § 2.4 of this Nutshell as a "nexus of contracts" in which the shareholders are viewed as contributors of capital rather than ultimate owners of the business.

From a common sense viewpoint, it should be obvious that the interests of the CEO and top management are likely to diverge from the interests of shareholders generally. The professional managers of the corporation—the CEO and his subordinates—are interested in keeping their positions, the power they have to direct a huge enterprise, their "percs," and their compensation. Shareholders on the other hand are interested in high dividends and high stock prices. During the

last half of this century an analysis has developed that ana-
lyzes and rigorously identifies this divergence. As presented by
Jensen and Meckling, Theory of the Firm: Managerial Behavior, Agency Costs, and Ownership Structure, 3 J. Fin. Econ.
305 (1976), this demonstration begins with discussion of an
arrangement under which one or more persons (the principals) engage another person (the agent) to perform some
function that requires delegation of decision-making authority
to the agent. Each party in the relationship is assumed to be a
rational utility maximizer, that is, that each attempts to
obtain the most beneficial mix of (1) his own personal wealth
to the extent he lawfully may do so and (2) the various non-
pecuniary benefits that he prefers. Non-pecuniary benefits
might include "the physical appointments of the office," "the
level of employee discipline," "the kind and amount of charitable contributions," "personal relations ('love,' 'respect,' etc.)
with employees," "a larger-than-optimal computer to play
with," and "purchase of production inputs from friends."
These non-pecuniary benefits of course are a cost to the
enterprise; they are not free. If one first assumes that the
owner of the business is also the manager, the owner will
operate the business at a level and in a manner that the
marginal utility to the owner of the benefits he obtains from
his ownership interest in the business equals the cost. If the
manager owns 50 percent of the residual equity interests in
the business, on the other hand, a divergence from this
optimal point will occur. The manager will again rationally
maximize his utility, but since he bears only one half of the
cost of the non-ownership benefits he will increase his con-
sumption of those benefits proportionally. As one posits that
the residual interest of the manager declines (to less than one
percent), the emphasis by the manager on non-ownership
benefits increases. In other words, professional managers seek
to maximize their own utility by increasing personal benefits

that are charged to the entire enterprise and rely less on their proportional interest in the ownership of the business. The tendency of management to overconsume is described in the literature as "shirking" by top management.

The divergence between goals of professional managers and goals of shareholders is described by economists as being part of a larger problem of "agency costs." Agency costs arise because of the separation of ownership and control: Because of management's tendency to consume available perquisites, take excessive compensation, and shirk their responsibilities in search of maximizing their own personal utility. Jensen and Meckling define "agency costs" as the sum of (1) the "monitoring expenditures" by the principal, (2) the "bonding expenditures" by the agent, and (3) the residual loss (equal to the dollar loss caused by the manager's decisions that do not optimize the wealth of the owners). "Monitoring expenditures" include budget restrictions, compensation policies, operating rules, and so forth, imposed by the owners to limit the power of the manager to obtain non-pecuniary compensation. "Bonding expenditures" include contractual guarantees that the accounts will be audited by a public auditor, explicit bonding against malfeasance on the part of the manager, and contractual limitations on the decision-making power of the manager. In response, owners must spend resources to increase the fidelity of the managers to the enterprise and to the owners. These expenditures reduce the value of the enterprise and are the third part of agency costs associated with the separation of management from ownership.

Agency costs are reduced by aligning the interests of managers with the owners. This may be done by increasing the manager's financial interest in maximizing share prices by grants of options to purchase stock. Incentive compensation plans based on earnings or the return to shareholders have the same effect. Thus long term incentive compensation plans in the tens or hundreds of millions of dollars for a very successful CEO may be in the interests of shareholders because they may reduce agency costs by a greater amount. Recent proposals that have received some degree of acceptance are (1) to pay directors in shares rather than cash and (2) eliminate pension or retirement plans for directors.

Certainly a major contribution of economic analysis to the law of corporations has been this rigorous analysis of how the interests of management may be more closely aligned with the interests of the shareholders.

Other aspects of economic analysis of legal rules should be briefly mentioned. When approaching legal rules, members of the Chicago school do not usually start with an already-existing problem and seek to devise a rule that does substantial justice to the persons involved in that problem. This approach is usually referred to as an "ex post" establishment of rules; the Chicago school prefers to adopt an "ex ante" approach that assumes the rule is already in place and asks how the presence of the rule will affect prospective transactions or behavior.

In a few articles or books written by law and economics scholars, there are references to the "shareholders" in publicly held corporations deciding to do X (or not doing X), where X is a management decision that affects the value of the corporation's shares. These are usually references either (1) to decisions rational shareholders would make if they were actually voting in their own self-interest, or (2) to decisions made by managers of the corporation who are rationally acting in the best interest of shareholders generally. In some instances, they may be references to market consequences when shareholders exercise their "Wall Street Options." These decisions also may be referred to as "implicit decisions," which are defined as decisions that a rational investor would make if given a free choice as to alternatives, not real ones.

A final important contribution of the Chicago school is recognition of the importance of the securities markets as a disciplining device for management. Decisions by shareholders to sell their shares is in a sense a vote. A poor operating performance by management causes shareholders to sell shares, thus depressing share prices and, unless corrected, leading ultimately to the ouster of management.

Non-economic sources of pressure against under-performing corporations also exist. The threat of shareholders' derivative suits produces pressure. Disclosure requirements of federal law may exercise a cautionary effect on management. Widespread publicity in the financial press produces pressure on outside directors to take steps to correct current problems. While the threat that management will be turned out by an irate band of voters—as often occurs in political elections—is largely illusory, there is a very real possibility that incumbent management may lose the confidence of a majority of independent directors and be forced to resign. The possibility of being ousted from a position of power for poor performance is in the modern scene quite real.

§ 13.19 Share Prices and The Changing Body of Shareholders

One feature of publicly held corporations is that the composition of the body of shareholders is changing every day. Modern computerized securities trading programs permit investors to sell their entire holdings instantaneously in order to capture an additional 25 or 50 cents per share. Many shareholders, particularly some institutional investors, have short term profit horizons. An aggressive growth fund may turn over its entire portfolio in a twelve month period. Management has an incentive to keep the shareholders happy by making short term share prices as high as possible and preserving the flow of dividends at all costs even though the actions may not be in the long term best interest of the enterprise. Indeed, management sometimes may adopt strategies designed solely to bolster the market price of the stock. A common strategy is the announcement of a planned share buy-back by the corporation. The announcement of a plan to reduce the number of publicly traded shares through a buy-back almost always has a positive effect on share prices even if the plan is never fully effectuated in the form it is announced.

Modern economic analysis suggests that management should act to maximize the intrinsic value of shares, acting as though it is "blissfully ignorant" of the effect of various decisions on the stock's market price. The phrase "blissfully ignorant" is taken from Hu, Risk, Time, and Fiduciary Principles in Corporate Investment, 38 U.C.L.A. L.Rev. 277 (1990). However, it is likely that many managers make decisions with an eye on their effect on the stock, and it is understandable that they do so given the importance that share prices have in the eyes of sophisticated investors.

§ 13.20   The Takeover Movement of the 1980s

The 1980s saw a wave of third party offers to purchase for cash control of large corporations at premium prices significantly above the then current stock price. (This wave ended abruptly in about 1990 and a new wave of takeovers based on negotiated mergers began later in the decade.)

Law and economics scholars suggest that these takeover transactions in the 1980s constituted a market device that disciplined a management that was not maximizing sharehold-

er value. The theory was that anyone willing to invest billions
of dollars to purchase control of a large corporation must
believe that he or she can produce greater shareholder value
than was currently being produced by the incumbent management. Most economics scholars appear to accept this analysis
as the most plausible explanation for transactions of that
period. However, other less optimistic explanations have also
been put forth. The takeover movement has been described as
an example of speculative excess with little social value similar
to the tulip boom in Holland or the American stock market in
the late 1920s. Still other explanations suggest that the takeover movement of the 1980s was largely driven by the benefits
of substituting tax-deductible interest payments for taxable
distributions. But economists believe that some takeovers in
fact did improve efficiency and therefore provided significant
benefits to corporate governance by automatically eliminating
less efficient managers. Therefore the takeover movement, to
that extent at least, was beneficial from an efficiency standpoint.

Many economists viewed the end of this era in 1990 as a
most unfortunate development. This concern, however, turned
out to be premature, because after a brief hiatus a different
powerful merger movement developed. See § 13.30 of this
Nutshell.

§ 13.21 Proxy Regulation in Publicly Held Corpora-
tions

In this and the following sections, the word "proxy" is used
to designate the person to whom a power to vote is granted.
The word "appointment" is used to describe the grant of
authority by a registered owner to another to vote. And the
words "appointment form" are used to describe the document

that makes the appointment. This usage follows that of § 7.22 of MBCA (1984).

Most modern law of proxy regulation is of federal rather than state origin. Section 14(a) of the Securities Exchange Act of 1934 is a broad grant of authority to the SEC to develop regulations "necessary or appropriate in the public interest or for the protection of investors" in connection with the solicitation of proxy appointments for securities registered under section 12 of the Act. Section 14 makes it unlawful for any person to use the mails or any means or instrumentality of interstate commerce or the facilities of a national securities exchange "in contravention of" such regulations. Congress gave the SEC this broad and undefined grant of rulemaking authority because in 1934 it was concerned about abuses in the proxy process but was uncertain about remedies. The SEC has issued comprehensive and detailed regulations that not only define the form of proxy solicitation documents but also require the distribution of substantial information about the issuer, the backgrounds of candidates for directorships, and information about other issues to be voted upon by shareholders.

Regulations under § 12 of the Securities Exchange Act require the following corporations to register securities: all corporations a) with shares registered on a national securities exchange or b) having assets in excess of $10,000,000 and a class of equity securities held of record by 500 persons or more. It is not the total number of security holders that is significant, but the number of holders of the specific class of security for which registration is required. For example, a corporation with 400 shareholders of record holding common stock, and another 400 shareholders of record holding preferred stock is not required to register either class under section 12. It therefore is not subject to proxy regulation (unless, of course, one of the classes of shares is registered on a national securities exchange). However, once a corporation is required to register under section 12, its registration may be terminated only if (a) the number of shareholders of the class drops below 300, or (b) the assets drop below $10,000,000 and the number of shareholders of the class drops below 500 for a period of three consecutive years.

As a practical matter, it is impossible to solicit proxies in connection with a security registered under section 12 without using the mails or facilities of interstate commerce.

The SEC proxy rules may be broken down into four broad categories:

(1) Requirements of disclosure of full information to shareholders relating to (a) proposals for shareholder action presented by management through the proxy solicitation machinery, and (b) to a lesser extent, general information about the operation of the corporation.

(2) Prohibitions against fraud or deceptive nondisclosure in proxy solicitation material.

(3) Requirements that appropriate proposals submitted by shareholders be included in the proxy solicitation materials prepared by management and shareholders be given an opportunity to consider them.

(4) Special requirements applicable only to proxy fights.

§ 13.22 Disclosure Requirements in Connection With Proxy Solicitations

Rule 14a–3 of the SEC proxy regulations provides that with certain exceptions each solicitation of a proxy appointment must be accompanied by a proxy statement setting forth detailed information. Proxy statements are one of the principal sources of shareholder information about corporate affairs. If management is making the solicitation, information must be furnished about the corporation's affairs, about the background of directors and nominees, about their remuneration, about other transactions with management and with others, and about any matter on which the vote of shareholders is sought. Proxy statements are not required for solicitations that involve less than ten persons or solicitations by brokers to beneficial owners to determine how to vote shares held in street name.

The term "proxy statement" has been broadly construed to include newspaper ads and informal communications among shareholders with respect to voting plans. In 1992, the SEC narrowed its regulations to permit communications that specify how the writer plans to vote but do not actually solicit proxies. (This is the provision that has permitted institutional investors to take an increased role in corporate governance.)

Before 1992, the SEC conducted a presolicitation clearance and review process for proxy documents. This process has been discontinued and currently the SEC only requires that preliminary forms of proxy statements be filed before a solicitation begins, and that no proxy be actually solicited until after the filing of a definitive proxy statement. SEC staff informally reviews preliminary proxy statements to ensure proper disclosure; in this respect it is a "neutral umpire" in the proxy process.

The SEC proxy rules also indirectly require the distribution of annual reports. Rule 14a–3(b) provides that if a solicitation is made on behalf of management relating to an annual meeting of shareholders at which directors are to be elected, the proxy statement must be accompanied or preceded by an annual report of the corporation. The annual report is the other major informational document provided to shareholders.

Corporate management usually must solicit proxy appointments in order to assure that there is a quorum at the meeting. As a practical matter, the number of shares voted by shareholders who appear personally plus the number of shares owned by management is likely to be numerically insignificant and much less than the minimum required for a quorum. In some corporations subject to registration under section 12, however, major shareholders present in person at the meeting may own enough shares to constitute a quorum without any solicitation of public shareholders. The Securities Exchange Act of 1934 requires that section 12 corporations that plan to conduct a shareholders' meeting without first making a qualified proxy solicitation must supply shareholders with the same information that would have been required if a proxy solicitation had been made. This section graphically illustrates that a major purpose of SEC proxy regulation is to ensure that significant information is made available to shareholders, whether or not they are requested to act on some matter. It may be noted in passing that while state corporation statutes require notice of a shareholders meeting, they usually do not require the disclosure of specific information.

Section 13.12 of this Nutshell discusses the practice of holding shares in book entry form in the names of nominees. This practice creates a problem for the SEC proxy disclosure process since the beneficial owners of such shares do not directly receive proxy statements or annual reports and are not entitled to vote directly (since they are not record owners). SEC regulations require that brokers and dealers transmit proxy material to beneficial owners of shares. This material must either (i) provide executed proxy appointment forms in blank so that the beneficial owners can vote, or (ii) contain an agreement to vote the shares as the beneficial owners direct.

The distribution of proxy statements and appointment forms is now usually handled by private companies specializing in that activity. The counting of votes (particularly if a controversial issue is under consideration) also may be undertaken by specialized firms. Studies by the SEC have concluded that these indirect methods of distribution of proxy information and the counting of votes work reasonably effectively. Nevertheless, § 7.23 of MBCA (1984) sets forth an alternative (and experimental) device that permits corporations to establish procedures to treat beneficial owners of shares as traditional registered owners. Such procedures have been discussed but apparently have not been widely implement.

SEC regulations also require record holders and intermediaries to disclose the names of beneficial holders directly to the issuer (unless the beneficial holder objects) so that the issuer may communicate directly with the beneficial owners. Some brokerage firms recommend that customers object to the disclosure of their identities. Beneficial owners who permit their identities to be disclosed are called "NOBOs" (nonobjecting beneficial owners).

SEC regulations also prescribe the proxy appointment form itself and prohibit certain devices such as undated or postdated proxy appointment forms or broad grants of discretionary power to proxies. Shareholders must be given the option to vote for or against candidates for directors, and proxies must actually vote the shares as shareholders direct for the election of directors and on other issues presented for decision to the shareholders.

Non-compliance with the SEC's proxy regulations entails significant risks. The SEC has authority to assess monetary penalties for non-compliance with its regulations under the Securities Enforcement Remedies and Penny Stock Reform Act of 1990. It may also issue cease and desist orders.

§ 13.23 Shareholder Proposals

Rule 14a–8 establishes a procedure by which shareholders may submit proposals for inclusion in the registrant's proxy solicitation material. If the proposal is an appropriate one for shareholder action, and is timely, the issuer must include the proposal even if opposed to it. This is one of the few ways that minority shareholders may communicate with fellow shareholders. Users of this device include church, public interest, and advocacy groups seeking to obtain support for their views on public issues. Shareholder proposals may address levels of executive compensation, discrimination, affirmative action, the treatment of minority groups, the use of nuclear power, and environmental concerns. Many of these proposals are openly political in nature.

Shareholder proposals are almost never approved by a majority of the shareholders. However, that is not the point. The process does require the corporation to address the concerns of groups submitting proposals. It is therefore widely believed that defeated proposals relating to corporate matters have an indirect educational effect. They call management's attention to some problem area that exists in the corporation's activities. Certainly some shareholder proposals decisively rejected at the polls have been subsequently quietly accepted and implemented by management. Nevertheless, concern has also been expressed that the costs imposed by the shareholder proposal rule may outweigh the benefits of that rule.

Institutional investors have sometimes utilized shareholder proposals in their effort to influence management decision-making. Proposals presented by institutional investors usually deal with issues of direct concern to the electorate: secret ballot procedures, the adoption of cumulative voting, rotating the location of annual meetings, and actions with respect to "poison pill" defenses implemented by the board of directors without shareholder vote. These proposals not uncommonly receive substantial support, and have been approved in some instances. At the present time, however, most institutional investors prefer to discuss problems with independent directors directly on an informal basis rather than utilize the shareholder proposal device, though a few institutional investors continue to use the rule 14a–8 process.

When a corporation receives a serious shareholder's proposal, it will usually respond and seek to reach a mutually acceptable accommodation. (In the past, many corporations as a matter of policy refused to discuss matters with shareholders on the theory that business decisions were for management and the board of directors; this attitude is changing.) Many proposals are settled at a preliminary stage before the filing of a formal shareholder's proposal. For example, in 1994, the New York City pension funds were able to persuade corporations to adopt 13 of their proposals without submitting them to shareholders.

If agreement is not possible, management may seek to omit the proposal from its proxy statement. To do so, it normally seeks a "no action letter" from the SEC. A "no action letter" reflects a decision by the SEC staff that it will recommend to the Commission that no action be taken if the proposal is omitted because the proposal falls within one or more of the permissible exclusions described below. The Second Circuit has held that a "no action letter" is not formal agency action that may be subject to immediate judicial review.

If a proposal opposed by management must be included in the proxy statement, the proposing shareholder may include a statement of not more than 500 words in support of the proposal. A shareholder may submit only one proposal in a proxy statement. Even though the proponent is limited to 500 words, management may explain the basis of its opposition without limitation.

Because shareholders may seek action on proposals of dubious relevance or propriety, or simply for personal publicity, the SEC has imposed specific requirements and limitations on topics that may be the subject of shareholder proposals. These requirements and limitations have generated a substantial body of administrative rulings by the SEC, and not uncommonly lead to judicial review. The SEC has also issued policy statements from time to time with respect to issues raised by shareholder proposals.

Under present SEC regulations, a shareholder's proposal may be omitted in a variety of circumstances. The most important reasons for omission are:

(1) It is not a proper subject for action by security holders under the law of the issuer's domicile;

(2) It relates to the enforcement of a personal claim or the redress of a personal grievance, against the issuer, its management, or any person;

(3) It deals with a matter that is not significantly related to the issuer's business;

(4) It deals with a matter relating to the ordinary business operations of the issuer;

(5) It relates to an election to office;

(6) It is substantially the same as a proposal by another shareholder that will be included in the proxy materials;

(7) Substantially the same proposal has previously been submitted to the shareholders within the previous five years and failed to receive specified percentages of the vote, depending on the number of times it was submitted previously; and

(8) It relates to specific amounts of dividends.

Over the years the SEC has issued numerous rulings applying many of these exclusions; as a result, phrases such as "proper subject" or "ordinary business operations" have been given considerable practical content, and the tests are not as open-ended as the language might indicate. For example, the SEC has ruled that important business related proposals are "proper subjects" for shareholder action under state law if they are phrased as recommendations to the board rather than as specific directions. See the discussion of state law on this subject in § 8.3 of this Nutshell.

In 1998 the SEC revised Rule 14a–8 into a simpler and more understandable plain English question-and-answer format. The theory was that this rule is often used by individuals without legal backgrounds.

§ 13.24 Private Actions for Violations of Federal Proxy Rules

Rule 14a–9 makes it unlawful to distribute proxy solicitation information that contains "any statement which, at the time and in the light of the circumstances under which it is made, is false or misleading with respect to any material fact, or which omits to state any material fact necessary in order to make the statements therein not false or misleading." This broad prohibition was held to create a private cause of action by shareholders. J.I. Case Co. v. Borak (S.Ct.1964). The Court justified this holding on the theory that "private enforcement of the proxy rules provides a necessary supplement to Commission action. As in antitrust treble damage litigation, the possibility of civil damages or injunctive relief serves as a most effective weapon in the enforcement of the proxy requirements."

It should be noted that subsequent decisions by the United States Supreme Court have refused to extend this reasoning to other statutory provisions. However, despite occasional criticism, the Court appears to be unwilling to reconsider the holding in *Borak* itself.

Since *Borak* there has been a substantial volume of private litigation under rule 14a–9. This litigation is within the exclusive jurisdiction of the Federal courts so that state "security for expenses" statutes are inapplicable (see § 16.8 of this Nutshell).

Rule 14a–9 litigation has largely been shaped by three subsequent decisions by the United States Supreme Court. In TSC Industries, Inc. v. Northway, Inc. (S.Ct.1976), the Court stated that an omitted fact is "material" "if there is a substantial likelihood that a reasonable shareholder would consider it important in deciding how to vote." The competing test that was rejected would have defined material facts to include all facts "which a reasonable shareholder *might* consider appropriate." While this difference in phrasing may seem primarily semantic, the Court's distinction constituted a warning to lower courts to limit rule 14a–9 to substantial misstatements. Prior to this decision some courts had tended to find relatively minor misstatements or omissions to be "material" and therefore violations of rule 14a–9.

The other two important cases are Mills v. Electric Auto–Lite Co. (S.Ct.1970) and Virginia Bankshares, Inc. v. Sandberg (S.Ct.1991). These two cases look in opposite directions. *Mills* involved the question of the required nexus between a material misstatement or omission and the approval of the proposal. It held that it was unnecessary to show a direct causal relationship between the violation and the vote; it was only necessary to show that the proxy solicitation was itself an essential step in the transaction under attack. It therefore concluded that examination of reliance by individual shareholders on a specific misstatement should not be inquired into, and that reliance should be presumed if the vote was necessary for the completion of the merger under consideration. *Mills* also discusses at some length the remedies available for a violation of rule 14a–9 after the transaction in question has been consummated, and establishes the right of the plaintiffs' attorney to recover attorneys' fees in rule 14a–9 cases. *Virginia Bankshares* involved two issues. The first was whether the following statement was a statement of fact or a statement of opinion (that could not be made the basis of a 14a–9 claim): "The plan of merger has been approved by the Board of Directors because it provides an opportunity for the Bank's public shareholders to achieve a high value for their shares." Since the directors did not in fact believe that the price offered was a "high" price, the statement was viewed as a statement of fact and not of opinion. The second issue involved in *Virginia Bankshares* was whether a rule 14a–9 claim can be maintained if the shareholders eligible to vote do not have a sufficient number of votes to block the transaction in question. The court narrowed the scope of rule 14a–9 by holding by a majority vote that such a claim could not be maintained.

§ 13.25   Proxy Contests

A traditional proxy contest is a struggle for control of a public corporation in which the high cards are typically held by management. A non-management group (usually referred to as "insurgents") compete with management in an effort to obtain sufficient proxy appointments to elect a majority of the board of directors and thereby obtain control. Management has several advantages in a traditional proxy fight. (1) It has the current list of shareholders, while the insurgents may have to go to court to get it. This was a major advantage at an earlier time, but the growth of book entry and street name registration makes this of less importance today. (2) Within a broad range, management may finance its solicitation from the assets of the corporation, while the insurgents must finance their campaign from outside sources. (3) For the reasons discussed earlier, shareholders unhappy with management tend to sell rather than fight. See § 13.10 of this Nutshell. For many years, these advantages appeared to be overwhelming and relatively few proxy fights were instituted. Insurgents wishing to take over another company preferred to use cash tender offers or to negotiate a friendly takeover. With the growth of the shareholdings of institutional investors and their increased activism (see § 13.11 of this Nutshell), however, there has been a resurgence in interest in proxy fights as a device to get management's attention, if not to oust it outright. In these modern proxy fights, the roles of institutional investors are usually critical. The willingness of institutional investors to support insurgents in specific instances undoubtedly contributed to an increase in the number of such contests during the late 1980s.

Perhaps the most significant indication of the increasing importance of proxy fights in mid-size corporations is the 1998 proxy fight conducted by TIAA/CREF that ousted the entire board of directors of Furr's/Bishop, Inc., a struggling publicly-held restaurant chain. Previously, the most successful effort by institutional investors had led only to the election of a minority of new directors.

Proxy fights usually occur in relatively small publicly held corporations. Today, they are more likely to be used (or threatened) as a tool to encourage the incumbent board to consider negotiating a consensual merger. They may also be used in conjunction with tender or exchange offers. For example, an aggressor may acquire a substantial minority position in the target by purchase and then use a proxy contest to obtain sufficient additional votes to replace incumbent management. This tactic has sometimes been used when the aggressor lacks sufficient resources to acquire a majority of the target's shares outright. It may also be used when management's defenses against a purchase-type takeover appeared to be impregnable, and the aggressor feels compelled to seek proxy appointments to force the dismantling of those defenses.

Proxy fights for public corporations subject to section 12 of the Securities Exchange Act of 1934 are subject to regulation by the Securities and Exchange Commission. Regulations promulgated by the SEC require "participants" (other than management) in a proxy contest to file specified information with the SEC and the securities exchanges at least five days before a solicitation begins. "Participant" is defined to include anyone who contributes more than $500 for the purpose of financing the contest. The information that must be disclosed relates to the identity and background of the participants, their interests in securities of the corporation, when they were acquired, financing arrangements, participation in other proxy contests, and understandings with respect to future employment with the corporation.

In addition, the Williams Act, an amendment to the 1934 Act, requires any person or group that acquires more than five percent of the voting stock of a publicly held corporation to file a disclosure statement within ten days thereafter. It is not uncommon for an aggressor to purchase more than five percent of the target's shares in a series of transactions and then announce his intention to conduct a proxy fight when the Williams Act filing is made.

The general philosophy of the proxy contest regulations is well expressed by the court's opinion in SEC v. May (2d Cir.1956): "Appellants' fundamental complaint appears to be that stockholder disputes should be viewed in the eyes of the law just as are political contests, with each side free to hurl charges with comparative unrestraint, the assumption being that the opposing side is then at liberty to refute and thus effectively deflate the 'campaign oratory' of its adversary. Such, however, was not the policy of Congress as enacted in the Securities Exchange Act.''

State law on the subject of proxy fights tends to be rudimentary and there are very few reported state cases dealing with them. However, issues such as the validity of proxy appointments and the propriety of allocating expenses to the corporation may be governed by state law, presumably the law of the state of incorporation under the "internal affairs" rule. The cost of a proxy fight is typically born by the corporation. There appears to be no doubt that the corporation should pay for printing and mailing the notice of meeting, the proxy statement required by Federal law, and the proxy appointments themselves. These are legitimate expenses because without the solicitation of proxy appointments it is unlikely that a quorum of shareholders may be obtained. Most courts have gone further, however, and allowed the corporation to be charged for the reasonable expenses of defending against the aggressor. The theory is that such expenses are for the purpose of educating shareholders when the controversy involves a "policy" question rather than a mere "personal" struggle for control. Since virtually every proxy fight may be dressed up as a "policy" rather than "personal" dispute, the net effect is that all management expenses are paid by the corporation.

If the insurgents are successful, they may seek to have the corporation reimburse them for their expenses. Reimbursement of successful insurgents has been permitted if (a) approved by the shareholders and (b) the dispute involved "policy" rather than "personalities." Where these tests are met, the corporation ends up paying for the expenses of both sides since losing management will normally reimburse itself before leaving office. Again, there is a strong undercurrent of judicial opinion that would sharply limit or totally preclude insurgents' reimbursement, but this view has not prevailed.

Law review writers have sometimes suggested that reimbursement should be permitted for all unsuccessful insurgents since they perform a socially useful function but there is apparently no authority for doing so. Most economists view proxy fights as basically desirable phenomena that help rid corporations of inefficient or ineffective management.

§ 13.26 Cash Tender Offers During the 1970s and 1980s

The development of cash-oriented takeover techniques is perhaps the most spectacular development in corporate and securities law since World War II. See § 13.20 of this Nutshell. Cash purchases of publicly held corporations became feasible as a result of the growth of very large pools of capital. This takeover movement not only shook the complacency of management to its core but also enriched the vocabulary of corporate law, led to statutory enactments at both the federal and state levels, and raised important issues of state and federal power. It also led to the development of extremely effective defensive tactics by incumbent management.

An appropriate starting point is the classic cash tender as it evolved in the 1960s. A cash tender offer is a public invitation to the shareholders of the "target" corporation to tender their shares to the "aggressor" corporation for purchase at a specified price, originally about 20 percent in excess of the then current market price, but later 50 percent or more above that price. In the late 1960s, there were numerous cash tender offers based on the element of surprise, virtually blitzkrieg tactics. Incumbent management would awaken one morning to discover that some outside group was making a public offer to purchase a controlling interest in their corporation at a significant premium over the closing share market price the previous day. If management had not previously put into place effective defenses, it usually lost.

The success of takeover bids, however, was primarily due to the large premiums over market price offered by aggressors rather than the element of surprise. These premiums virtually assured that profit-conscious institutional investors would tender into the takeover bid. When a cash offer to purchase shares was made, the open market price for the shares immediately increased dramatically so that it was close to the tender offer price. (Whether it equaled or exceeded the tender offer price depended on a complex variety of factors, including the probability that a competing offer at a higher price might be made, whether the offer was likely to be over-subscribed, and so forth.) Persons owning shares had the choice of selling their shares in the open market or tendering them into the offer. However, most shares sold on the open market were ultimately tendered as a group of speculators, known as "arbitrageurs," purchased shares in the open market at prices below the tender offer price in order to tender them and profit by the difference between the two prices. In several spectacular incidents, competing bids from different aggressors were forthcoming. If another bidder entered the battle, the arbitrageurs would accumulate shares to await the ultimate winner and then tender the shares, profiting even more. The volume of transactions effected by arbitrageurs during this period was very substantial.

A company that was made the target of a takeover attempt was said to be "in play." Once in play, Wall Street wisdom went, the company was sure to be taken over by somebody, though this was not invariably true.

The element of surprise was partially eliminated by the enactment of the Williams Act in 1968 (and amended in 1970). Under the Williams Act, any person who makes a cash tender offer for a registered corporation must disclose information about the following: the source of funds used in the offer, the purpose for which the offer is made, plans the aggressor have for the target, if successful, and any contracts or understandings with respect to the target corporation. The issuer must respond publicly to the offer. The Act also imposes miscellaneous substantive restrictions on the mechanics of these offers, as well as including a broad prohibition against the use of false, misleading, or incomplete statements. Similar requirements are also imposed upon (1) issuers making an offer for their own shares, or (2) issuers in which a change of control is proposed to be made by seriatim resignations of directors. These requirements largely eliminate the element of surprise.

In Piper v. Chris–Craft Industries, Inc. (S.Ct.1977), the Court held that a defeated tender offeror did not have standing to sue for damages under the false statement provision of the Williams Act.

Public takeover activity reached its peak in the 1980s. Aggressors were able to obtain access to billions of dollars of capital to purchase publicly held companies. Multi-billion dollar cash transactions became common-place. The Delaware courts developed new rules for these transactions, as aggressor and target sought to use the courts to further their goals.

The 1980s saw the development of a new kind of transaction, the "leveraged buyout" (LBO) in which funds to purchase the outstanding shares of a publicly held corporation were raised by the issuance of "junk bonds" to institutional investors and others, and through temporary or "bridge" loans from commercial banks. Assuming the takeover was successful, the expected source of repayment was the earnings and cash flow of the target corporation, which was required to assume the repayment obligation for the junk bonds and loans. LBOs are "bootstrap" acquisitions: The acquired business provides the funds to finance its own purchase. In many instances, incumbent management participated in the buyout, and managed the business after the public shareholders were eliminated. The fear of becoming the target of such a takeover led many publicly held corporations to reduce their attractiveness as an LBO candidate by distributing excess cash and by incurring indebtedness and distributing the loan proceeds, in effect voluntarily restructuring their capitalization by substituting debt for equity. This might also be done by making a distribution of debt instruments directly to shareholders. Whether or not all this was desirable from a social or economic perspective is questionable.

In LBOs, a successful aggressor almost always planned to restructure the target company in a way that required the aggressor to own 100 percent of the outstanding shares of the target. Following a purchase offer, there was always a handful of shareholders who did not sell into even the most attractive and successful offer. These remaining minority interests were eliminated by a "cash out merger" of the type described in chapter 20 of this Nutshell.

§ 13.27 Combination Strategies Involving Proxy Fights and Cash Tender Offers

Proxy fights never totally disappeared even during the 1980s when cash offers were the dominant takeover device. Initially, proxy fights became increasingly difficult to justify. Shareholders were inclined to withhold votes from aggressors on the theory that "if you think you can run the company better than us, put your money into the company by buying our stock. Don't just ask us to turn the company over to you."

When leveraged buyouts began to fail in the late 1980s, funds for cash buyouts began to dry up. In addition, defensive strategies against cash buyouts were improving steadily in the 1980s. See § 13.28 of this Nutshell. As a result, proxy fights again began to look attractive, and many aggressors adopted a strategy of combining the proxy fight and cash takeover bid. In one dramatic example, a $6 billion takeover of National Cash Register by AT & T in 1991 successfully combined a proxy fight and cash takeover bid.

A proxy fight may be either an adjunct to a cash tender offer or it may be a substitute for such an offer. Increasingly it has become the former. An initial "toe-hold" may be obtained by a proxy fight and followed by a cash tender offer to all remaining shareholders. Alternatively, the "toe hold" may be obtained by a private or public purchase of shares from a limited number of shareholders and followed by a proxy fight to obtain control of the target.

§ 13.28   Defensive Tactics

With the increasing success of cash tender offers and leveraged buy-outs during the 1970s and 1980s, attention turned to defensive tactics designed to make takeover bids more difficult. These tactics, varying from the blunt to the sophisticated, clearly increased in sophistication over time.

Popular tactics included: finding a more congenial suitor (a "white knight"); buying a business that increased the chances that the threatened takeover will give rise to anti-trust problems; adopting voting procedures that made it difficult for an offeror who acquires a majority of the voting shares to replace the board of directors; instituting suit to enjoin the offer for violations of the Williams Act, the antitrust laws, or on other grounds; issuing or proposing to issue additional shares to friendly persons to make a takeover more difficult (a "lock-up"); increasing the dividend or otherwise driving up the price of shares to make the takeover price unattractive; amending the basic corporate documents to make a takeover by even a majority shareholder more difficult; buying off the aggressor; buying up the corporation's own shares in the market to drive up the price; creating new classes of stock that increase in rights if any person acquires more than a specified percentage of shares ("poison pills"); and imposing restrictions in connection with the creation of debt that thwart attempted take-overs.

Of these varying devices, the poison pill has developed into the most effective defensive tactic. A "poison pill" (also called a "shareholder rights plan") provides that upon a specified triggering event (usually the acquisition by an outsider of some designated percentage of the voting shares of the corporation) the corporation will issue debt or equity securities to the remaining shareholders at a bargain price, thus significantly diluting the interest purchased by the outsider. The dilution is usually so great that it is not practical for the outsider ever to obtain control of the target by market purchases. Poison pills also provide that the board of directors of the target corporation may voluntarily disarm the poison pill before it is triggered. This ingenious device in effect compels the aggressor to negotiate with the incumbent management of the target corporation.

It is theoretically possible for an aggressor to purchase shares slightly below the number that "triggers" the pill, and then seek by a proxy fight to replace sufficient directors to cause the target to voluntarily disarm the poison pill. To prevent this maneuver, shareholder rights plans have added a "dead hand" provision that provides that only the directors in office at the time the plan is approved may vote to redeem the rights granted by the plan. In a significant decision, the Delaware Supreme Court held that the "dead hand" feature was unenforceable because it violates the basic principle that the current board of directors has control over corporate affairs. *Quickturn Design Systems v. Shapiro,* (Del.1998). Some decisions in other states, however, have upheld the validity of "dead hand" plans. Some corporations have adopted a "no hands" pill which cannot be disarmed by anyone. Another variation is a "chewable poison pill" that gives the incumbent board a period of time to negotiate before the pill becomes effective. Experimentation continues with other devices to assure that corporations have an effective poison pill that courts will accept.

Many cases have considered the validity of defensive tactics in different contexts. Of particular importance are a series of classic Delaware cases that have largely shaped the permissible area of takeover defenses. Moran v. Household International, Inc.(Del.1985), upholds under Delaware law the adoption of the basic concept of a "poison pill" as a defensive tactic in advance of a specific takeover attempt. Unocal Corp. v. Mesa Petroleum Co. (Del.1985), sets forth the basic test for evaluating defensive tactics: To be protected by the business judgment rule, a defensive tactic must be reasonable in relation to the threat posed to the corporation. This evaluation requires "enhanced judicial scrutiny" over and above the traditional business judgment rule standard. See § 14.7 of this Nutshell. Revlon, Inc. v. MacAndrews & Forbes Holdings, Inc. (Del.1985), holds that if the board of directors concludes that the sale of the business is inevitable, its role shifts from a participant in the contest to an auctioneer ensuring that the shareholders get the best possible price for their shares. Paramount Communications, Inc. v. Time, Inc. (Del.1989) modifies the Revlon/Unocal test and adopts a "range of reasonableness" test. Paramount Communications, Inc. v. QVC

Network, Inc. (Del.1994) holds that the lower court should apply the "enhanced scrutiny" test to determine whether defensive measures are "draconian," defined as either "coercive or preclusive." Finally, Unitrin, Inc. v. American General Corp. (Del.1995) requires the lower court to consider, first, whether the defensive measures adopted were draconian, and if not, whether they were reasonable responses to the threat presented.

The application of these decisions by the Delaware Supreme Court, elaborating the basic rules relating to defensive tactics, have been difficult to predict in advance, holding in some cases that the defensive tactic was proper and in others that it was not.

§ 13.29 State Intervention in the Takeover Movement

Some publicly held corporations that become targets of takeover attempts are incorporated in states other than Delaware. These corporations often are economically important to the state and as a result have considerable political power within the state. Thus, from the outset of the takeover movement, some individual states, believing that domestic corporations were threatened by takeover attempts by outside interests, enacted statutes that were in effect defenses for their corporations.

The first wave of antitakeover statutes, called Business Take–Over Acts, required a pre-offer notification period, a filing of a registration statement, review and a public hearing by the Secretary of State or other state official, and approval or disapproval by that official if it concluded the transaction was fair to domestic shareholders. In Edgar v. MITE Corp. (S.Ct.1982), the Supreme Court held the Illinois statute of this type to be unconstitutional under the Commerce Clause.

States promptly turned to other statutory devices to protect local corporations against unwanted takeover attempts. In CTS Corporation v. Dynamics Corp. of America (S.Ct.1987), the Supreme Court upheld the Indiana Control Share Acquisitions Act, a statute clearly enacted to make unwanted acquisitions of Indiana corporations more difficult. Under this statute, a person who purchased shares that increased his percentage of ownership above specified limits was prohibited from voting the additional shares without the prior approval of the remaining shareholders. The opinion of Justice Powell in *CTS* is particularly noteworthy because it carved out a broad area of state regulation in the takeover area, rejecting the argument that there was a "market for control" that was protected from state interference by the Commerce Clause. The Court also rejected an argument that state-created defenses for domestic corporations were preempted by the Williams Act. Since *CTS*, more than forty states have adopted statutes designed to make more difficult the acquisition of publicly held corporations incorporated in that state.

States have also enacted "business combination" statutes. These statutes restrict the power of persons who acquire more than a specified percentage of stock from engaging in certain transactions with the corporation for a specified period without the prior consent of the pre-acquisition board of directors. In 1988, Delaware adopted § 203 of its General Corporation Law. This statute provides that if a person acquires 15 percent or more of a corporation's stock it may not engage in a variety of transactions with the corporation for a period of three years, with several exceptions. These exceptions include (1) a transaction in which the purchaser increases its ownership from below 15 percent to over 85 percent in a single transaction (the "85% ownership out" exemption) or (2) a transaction that is approved by the target's board of directors and is approved by two-thirds or more of shareholders other than the aggressor (the "vote out" exemption). Because of the importance of Delaware as the state of incorporation of publicly held corporations, § 203 has had wide impact in the way takeover attempts are structured. This statute has been upheld on the basis of the broad language of *CTS*.

§ 13.30   The Takeover Movement in the 1990s

The era of leveraged buyouts and unsolicited takeover attempts came to a crashing halt at the end of the 1980s with the collapse of the Drexel Lambert securities firm and the drying up of sources of capital to finance cash transactions. In this period, a number of LBOs went into bankruptcy, the cash flow not being sufficient to carry the load of debt added by the LBO. "Junk bond" offerings had to be withdrawn because of lack of interest. Some banks and other lenders that had made "bridge" loans to finance an LBO discovered that they had in fact become permanent lenders rather than interim ones.

Following this collapse, the takeover movement remained quiescent for about four years. In late 1993, takeover transactions began again, and the volume has increased significantly thereafter. The new era of takeovers differ both qualitatively and quantitatively from the transactions of the 1980s. By and large, they are not financially-driven hostile takeovers or leveraged buyouts. Rather, they involve the acquisition by major United States corporations of smaller companies through negotiated mergers. In part, the goal is to assure that companies have the size and resources to compete in the United States and abroad with major foreign competitors. Size hopefully assures the ability to invest in new technology, to develop new products, and to guarantee access to world-wide markets. In part the goal is to permit traditional businesses to position themselves to take advantage of the new computer and Internet technology. This trend is also fueled by the high price of stock of computer and Internet companies that make stock purchases attractive. Computer hardware and software companies, banks, entertainment companies, and oil companies, "dot Com" companies have been the most visible participants in this new movement: for example, Chase Bank and Chemical Bank, Disney and American Broadcasting Company, Time Warner and Turner Broadcasting Company, followed by Time Warner and America On Line. However, mergers are also appearing in diverse industries, including drugs, paper products and consumer products. This trend is still in full swing as of the time this is written.

Proxy contests for smaller corporations also have continued during the 1990s. In 1998, about 20 proxy contests involving smaller companies took place. A few aggressors combined these contests with tender offers.

[For unfamiliar terms see the Glossary]

CHAPTER FOURTEEN

DUTIES OF DIRECTORS

§ 14.1 Directors, Controlling Shareholders and Senior Officers as "Fiduciaries"

This chapter deals principally with the duties of directors, controlling shareholders, and senior officers of publicly held corporations. The duties of all three are similar, a consequence of their broad power to control, manage and direct the enterprise. For purposes of simplicity, in most of this chapter all three types of controlling persons are lumped together under the single word "directors."

Duties of directors may be divided into two broad categories: a duty of care and a duty of loyalty. The duty of loyalty is referred to in the American Law Institute's *Principles of Corporate Governance* as a duty of "fair dealing." The duty of care relates to the *quality of decision-making* by directors, controlling shareholders, and senior officers while the duty of loyalty involves an assessment of the *propriety of specific transactions.*

Directors owe duties of fidelity and loyalty to the corporation in connection with their actions. These duties are generally referred to as "fiduciary duties," and directors are sometimes referred to as "fiduciaries" and their duties are analogized to those of a trustee of a trust. Indeed, some early cases specifically state that directors are "trustees." However, it is important not to carry this analogy very far: Directors of corporations are not strictly trustees, and their duties and liabilities are not identical with those of other fiduciaries. Directors are expected and indeed encouraged to commit the enterprise to risky ventures in order to maximize the return to shareholders; trustees are usually charged with preservation and maintenance of the assets under their control. Indeed, trustees of a trust may be surcharged if they commit the trust assets to speculative ventures. Acts that might be considered breaches of trust by other fiduciaries are therefore often not so regarded in cases of directors. The relationship between director and corporation, in short, is a unique one that should not be analyzed by making analogies to other types of fiduciary relationships.

In most instances, directors owe duties to the corporation as a whole rather than to individual shareholders or to individual classes of shareholders. However, if a director deals with a shareholder directly, or acts in a way that injures the economic interest of a specific shareholder, the director may become directly liable to that shareholder.

§ 14.2   Duties of Shareholders and Junior Officers

Since shareholders as such have no power to manage the business and affairs of the corporation, it is not surprising that the relationship of a shareholder to the corporation differs from the relationship of a director or senior officer to the corporation. It is often said that a shareholder owes no duty to the corporation or the other shareholders. These statements, however, are too broad. While shareholders may usually vote as their own self-interest dictates, they may owe a duty to the corporation or their fellow shareholders in some circumstances. Controlling shareholders, in particular, owe duties to creditors, holders of senior securities and minority shareholders when they transfer control of the corporation to a third party. See § 14.37 of this Nutshell. Many cases have found fiduciary duties akin to those existing in a partnership in closely held corporations.

The relationship between corporate officers or employees who are not in a control position and the corporation depends to some extent on the position occupied by the officer or employee and the type of liabilities that are being imposed. Officers or employees in subordinate positions typically owe a correspondingly lesser degree of duty, though even the lowest agent owes the principal certain minimum duties of care, skill, propriety of conduct, and loyalty and honesty in all matters connected with his or her employment. The duties owed by junior officers and employees are largely defined by work rules, union rules, specific instructions from more senior officers or employees, job descriptions, organizational charts, and the law of agency. See § 11.7 of this Nutshell.

§ 14.3 Sources of Law Relating to Duties of Directors—Common Law, State and Federal Statutes

The basic relationship between a corporation and its directors is common law in origin. The duties of care and loyalty (and a subdivision of the general duty of loyalty, the prohibition against usurping business opportunities belonging to the corporation) all clearly have their origin in common law and tradition. These common law duties have given rise to a great deal of litigation; they define fundamental obligations in a complex relationship.

Some modern state corporation statutes address certain aspects of these common law duties, and also supplement them by imposing liability on directors for certain specific acts, such as paying dividends when the corporation may not lawfully do so or making loans to directors in certain circumstances. Directorial liability to the corporation is the principal or exclusive method by which many statutory prohibitions are enforced.

Federal statutory law is also an important source of legal principles relating to duties and obligations within a corporation. The Federal securities acts are the genesis of this development with much of it based on Rule 10b–5 promulgated by the Securities and Exchange Commission under the Securities Exchange Act of 1934. Rule 10b–5 is the source of law with respect to insider trading (§§ 14.29–14.33 of this Nutshell) and the "fraud on the market" theory by which misleading corporate publicity affecting securities prices is regulated. See § 17.3 of this Nutshell. While based on federal statute, these duties are virtually completely defined by judicial decision.

§ 14.4 Duty of Care

A director owes a duty to the corporation to exercise proper care in managing the corporation's affairs. More than forty states have a partial statutory definition of this duty. Most state statutes are drawn from or are similar to § 8.30(a) of the 1984 Model Business Corporation Act: "A director shall discharge his duties as a director * * * (1) in good faith; (2) with the care an ordinarily prudent person in a like position would exercise under similar circumstances; and (3) in a manner he reasonably believes to be in the best interests of the corporation." However, many variations exist. Virginia, for example, substitutes for parts (1), (2), and (3) a standard of decisions "in accordance with his good faith business judgment of the best interests of the corporation." Va. Code Ann. § 13.1–690. Pennsylvania eliminated the statutory definition entirely in 1990 and relies on case law that provides that directors should exercise the degree of diligence, care, and skill "which ordinarily prudent men would exercise under similar circumstances in their personal business affairs." Selheimer v. Manganese Corp. of America (Pa.1966). There probably is little practical difference in these formulations; general language of this sort rarely helps to resolve concrete cases.

In 1999, § 8.30 of the Model Act was amended by eliminating clause (2) and the reference to an "ordinarily prudent person." This reference was felt to imply a standard of caution and avoidance of undue risk in decision-making, whereas in fact directors should be encouraged to take major business risks when they believe that is in the best interest of the corporation. Also, this phrase might imply that the "correctness" of the decision should be evaluated, when in fact the proper criterion should be the manner in which the decision was made under the business judgment rule. See § 14.5 of this Nutshell.

Section 8.30(b) was amended to read "when becoming informed in connection with their *decision-making function* or devoting attention to their *oversight function*," directors are to discharge their duties "with the care that a person in a like position would reasonably believe appropriate under similar circumstances." The "oversight function" refers to the monitoring of decisions by management while the "decision-making function" refers to specific matters delegated to the directors, such as authorizing distributions or selecting corporate officers. The decision-making function may also refer to a board of directors in a closely held corporation that is itself performing the management function.

In In re Caremark International, Inc. Derivative Litigation (Del.Ch.1996), Chancellor Allen imposed a heightened standard of good faith in the area of oversight of a corporation's personnel and business activities. The directors must make a good faith effort to establish procedures to protect the corporation's interests from malfeasance by employees. A sustained or systematic failure to assure that a reliable information and reporting system is in place constitutes a violation of the duty of care. An earlier case, Graham v. Allis–Chalmers Mfg. Co. (Del.1963), adopting a more lenient standard, was viewed as obsolete and inconsistent with modern views as to the appropriate roles of directors.

A critical and sometimes misunderstood principle is that § 8.30 is not the operative test for determining whether directors are liable for damages for failing to exercise reasonable care. The proper test for liability is the "business judgment rule" described in the following section of this Nutshell. The 1999 amendments to the Model Act make this crystal clear: The revised § 8.30 is entitled "Standards of Conduct for Directors," while a completely new § 8.31, entitled "Standards of Liability for Directors," is added. Essentially, § 8.31 codifies the "business judgment rule" described in the following section.

Directors regularly make complex decisions on the basis of partial, incomplete, or inaccurate information. There is also always the possibility that unexpected events may occur thereafter that change a plausible decision into a disastrous one. Evaluation of a substantive decision after the fact should take into account the reasonableness of the process that was followed by the directors in making the decision and not by assessing the decision that was made with the benefit of hindsight.

Furthermore, a specific business decision may involve hundreds of millions of dollars; to impose personal liability on decision-makers too readily will deter desirable persons from serving as directors of publicly held corporations. Because of the latter concern, most states have enacted statutes limiting the liability of directors for monetary damages under broad circumstances. See § 14.7 of this Nutshell.

In a word, one should not look at the provisions of revised § 8.30 of MBCA (1984) to determine whether directors are personally responsible for bad decisions.

Most of the case law that has developed in the last few decades with respect to the liability of directors is consistent with this approach. While there are a few cases in which the court appears to have imposed liability based on a review of the substantive decision itself, most cases in which liability for damages has been imposed involve an element of self-dealing or egregious misconduct not consistent with good faith. The strongest kind of case for imposing personal liability on a director is where the director knowingly participates in a wrongful act. Thus, personal liability has been imposed on directors where they authorize the improper use of corporate funds, knowing that the use is not in furtherance of corporate affairs. Personal liability may also be imposed where directors authorize the corporation's use of a financial statement to obtain credit knowing that it is false or fraudulent. On the other hand, attempts to hold directors or officers personally liable for antitrust fines imposed on the corporation or for bribes or improper payments made by the corporation have generally been unsuccessful. This is true despite evidence in some cases of the directors' or officers' personal involvement in the conduct or personal knowledge of the payments in question.

A few cases in which liability has been imposed involve situations where the directors failed to do anything at all even in the face of some evidence of wrongdoing. These cases typically involve directors who view themselves as "figure-heads" or "honorary directors" without any real obligation or responsibility to the corporation. They may involve a spouse who agrees to be a director in order to meet a statutory requirement that the board consist of at least three directors as a favor to the other spouse. Some directors may erroneously believe that since they are a minority of the board they have no responsibility for what is happening. A failure to direct at all is a serious violation of the duty of care.

One well-known case imposing liability because of the failure of a director to direct is Francis v. United Jersey Bank (N.J.1981). The sons of the deceased founder of the corporation, an "insurance reinsurance" firm, siphoned large sums of money from the corporation in the form of unsecured loans and other improper payments to family members. Ultimately the corporation became insolvent, and suit was brought by the bankruptcy trustee against the estate of Mrs. Pritchard, the widow of the corporate founder, who had been a director during the period the improper payments and loans were made. Mrs. Pritchard had not been active in the affairs of the corporation during this period; she was elderly and alcoholic, and stricken at the loss of her husband. She was also unfamiliar with the insurance reinsurance business generally and the affairs of the corporation in particular. Even though the improper transactions were clearly reflected in the financial statements prepared by the corporation, Mrs. Pritchard was unaware of them since she did not examine the financial statements. The court upheld a judgment against her estate for more than $10,000,000 since "she never made the slightest effort to discharge any of her responsibilities as a director." The court further concluded that her failure to fill the minimal responsibilities of her office was a proximate cause of the loss, since consultation with an attorney and threat of suit would have deterred the misconduct. A failure to respond to obvious problems, in short, is one way for a director to be held personally liable for losses suffered by the corporation.

What should a director who is aged, ill, resident of a distant state, or merely lazy or unduly trusting, do in order to avoid liability? As an abstract matter the answer is plain: When a person agrees to be a director she accepts certain responsibilities and obligations, and if these are too burdensome, the proper course is to resign rather than fail to meet them.

The issue of causation discussed in Mrs. Pritchard's case is sometimes a difficult one. Barnes v. Andrews (S.D.N.Y.1924), is the leading case holding that a direct causal relationship must be shown between the director's failure and the specific loss. If this is correct, the burden of proof will often be difficult if not insuperable, since in most cases it may be plausibly argued that the loss would have occurred even if the director had met his or her responsibility. The 1999 revision of the Model Act requires a party seeking to hold a director personally liable for money damages to show that harm to the corporation or its shareholders occurred because of the improper or negligent conduct and that "the harm suffered was proximately caused by the director's challenged conduct." MBCA (1984) § 2.31(b)(1), as amended.

Also helpful to defendants in duty of care cases are principles set forth in revised §§ 8.30 and 8.31 of the Model Act. For example, directors "who [do] not have knowledge that makes reliance unwarranted" may rely on persons "whom the director reasonably believes to be reliable and competent." This may include an assumption that persons are honest, that information, opinions, reports or statements are accurate, and that professionals have expert competence. MBCA (1984) §§ 8.30(c), (d), (e), as amended. The standard of good faith reliance, however, does not permit a knowledgeable director "to bury his head in the sand" and rely on information or advice he or she should know was erroneous. An attorney who is a director cannot ignore his or her legal background; the same is true of an accountant or banker. On the other hand, a person without specialized knowledge may rely on specialists if acting in good faith, and be immune from liability if she does so.

The revised § 8.31 sets forth specific situations in which liability may be imposed on directors. For example, the action was not taken "in good faith," the "director did not reasonably believe [the action] to be in the best interests of the corporation," or "the director was not informed to an extent the director reasonably believed appropriate in the circumstances." Also a party asserting liability will prevail if he establishes "a lack of objectivity due to the director's familial, financial or business relationship" with another person, "a sustained failure of the director to be informed about the business and affairs of the corporation, or other material failure of the director to discharge the oversight function," or receipt of a "financial benefit to which the director was not entitled * * *." MBCA (1984) § 8.31(a)(2), as amended.

These principles reduce significantly, but do not eliminate entirely, the risk of liability of directors for breaches of the duty of care.

§ 14.5   The "Business Judgment Rule"

The phrase, "the business judgment rule" is a helpful shorthand description of a basic principle applicable to business decisions by boards of directors. Decisions made by the board of directors upon reasonable information and with some rationality do not give rise to directorial liability even if they turn out badly or disastrously from the standpoint of the corporation. A related principle is that such decisions are valid and binding upon the corporation and cannot be enjoined, set aside, or attacked by shareholders. In the balance of this section both of these principles are collectively referred to simply as the "business judgment rule."

Most statements of the business judgment rule add the further qualification that a decision is not protected if the directors making it have "a disabling conflict of interest" or are involved in self-dealing transactions. The rule thus has its principal application to claims based on alleged mismanagement or misjudgment unaffected by any claim that personal gain was sought.

In a broad sense, the revised Model Act restates the basic principles of the common law business judgment rule. Directors are granted discretion with respect to the management of the corporation and the rational exercise of that discretion is generally not subject to judicial review. Also perhaps relevant is the belief that most judges are not businessmen capable of second-guessing effectively the exercise of that discretion.

The ALI's Principles of Corporate Governance also sets forth the principle underlying the business judgment rule in traditional language. Section 4.01(a) sets forth the general duty of care. Section 4.01(c) states that a "director or officer who makes a business judgment in good faith fulfills his or her duty" under § 4.01(a) if (1) he or she "is not interested in subject of the business judgment," (2) he or she "is informed with respect to the subject of the business judgment to the extent the director or officer reasonably believes to be appropriate under the circumstances," and (3) he or she "rationally believes that the business judgment is in the best interests of the corporation."

It should be noted that the business judgment rule involves a "decision," a "judgment" or "conduct." Doing nothing without more can never be protected by the business judgment rule. However, a *positive decision* to do nothing is clearly protected by the business judgment rule if in fact the directors meet the standards for decision-making under that rule.

A basic aspect of the business judgment rule is that it does not involve a court in the substantive evaluation of the business judgment. Rather, the court examines the process or procedure by which the judgment was made, though the "rational belief" portion of the test may be viewed as in some part substantive.

The business judgment rule protects directors from liability for many types of actions that turn out badly from the standpoint of the corporation. Examples include:

(1) A reorganization of a subsidiary company, including a distribution of surplus, reduction of capital, and distribution of a share dividend;

(2) Election of a manager and president;

(3) A sale of part of the assets of a company;

(4) Acceptance of a note for a judgment rather than enforcing it by execution;

(5) The closing down of an unproductive mine; and

(6) The determination of the adequacy of information and reporting systems pursuant to the Caremark decision described in § 14.4.

§ 14.6   The Famous Case of Smith v. Van Gorkom

The most controversial case that tested the scope of the business judgment rule is Smith v. Van Gorkom (Del.1985). The court's opinion in *Van Gorkom* sets forth the facts in great detail, and the correctness or incorrectness of its holding depends in large part upon how one categorizes the facts. The majority opinion adopts this categorization: Van Gorkom was the chief executive officer of Trans Union Corporation, a publicly held corporation. Van Gorkom owned 75,000 shares out of 20,000,000 outstanding. During review of the future of the corporation, the possibility of taking the company private through a leveraged buyout or selling it outright was discussed. Van Gorkom, who was close to retirement age, stated that he would accept $55 per share for his stock; during this period the stock was trading in the $24–$39 range. The $55 figure was apparently an intuitive judgment by Van Gorkom of what he thought an attractive price was based on his knowledge of the corporation's business. Studies were made by management to determine whether the cash flow of the corporation at the present level of operations could support the debt needed to support a $55 price in a leveraged buyout. (See § 13.26 of this Nutshell for a description of a "leveraged buyout.") On the basis of projections run by the corporation's chief financial officer, it appeared that the cash flow might be adequate for this purpose. Without further investigation into the value of the company, and without seeking other possible buyers, Van Gorkom contacted Pritzker, "a well-known corporate takeover specialist and a social acquaintance" and pointed out that a leveraged buyout of Trans Union might be feasible at $55 per share. Pritzker promptly offered to buy the corporation in a straight purchase at $55 per share with a decision required within three days. Some members of Trans Union management opposed the proposed sale on the grounds that the price was too low and not supported by adequate appraisals. The board of directors was then presented with the $55 proposal as an emergency matter with a strict three day deadline for approval. Van Gorkom urged approval of the transaction based on the argument that the company would consider other offers for a period of months as a "market test" of the adequacy of the price. The chief financial officer stated that the price was "fair but at the beginning of the range." The board then approved the transaction without asking questions or without extended discussion. Van Gorkom thereafter actively worked to obtain shareholder approval of the transaction without considering other possible alternatives, and the transaction was eventually completed at $55 per share. At one stage, a preliminary feeler was received from a third party offering $60 per share, but was not investigated.

The documents for the Trans Union sale were executed by Van Gorkom while attending an opera. Apparently he signed them without personally reviewing them. The transaction subsequently was submitted for approval of Trans Union shareholders. Approximately 69.9 percent of the shares were voted in favor of the transaction with 7.25 opposed, and the balance not voting.

Based essentially on these facts, the Delaware Supreme Court by a 3–2 vote concluded that the directors had not adequately informed themselves about the value of the company and the proposed transaction and therefore were not entitled to the protection of the business judgment rule. The basic test of the duty of care, the court stated, was "gross negligence." The dissenters, and much of the subsequent critical commentary about the case, argued that the directors should be able to evaluate a proposed sale of the company on the basis of their own financial experience, and in reliance on Van Gorkom's experience and background. Other factors relied upon by the critics of the decision as indicating that the directors had acted properly include the substantial difference between the $55 offering price and the market range within which Trans Union stock had traded in the recent past. Emphasis also was placed on the general financial sophistication of the outside directors of the corporation. The mathematics of the court's holding also received attention: If the measure of damages is $5 per share (not an unreasonable conclusion considering that Trans Union received an apparently serious "feeler" of $60 per share), then the joint and several liability of the directors is $5 times approximately

12,700,000 shares, or a cool $63,500,000. Following the Delaware Supreme Court decision, the case was apparently settled for a payment of approximately $22,000,000 from insurance proceeds and funds supplied (apparently voluntarily) by the purchaser in the transaction under attack. The fees payable to the attorneys for the plaintiffs were about $18,000,000.

A decision to sell the business of a publicly held company is the most important decision that ever comes before a board of directors. It may be argued that *Van Gorkom* was basically correctly decided because such an important decision should not be made without investigation and in blind reliance on the judgment of a single person who will benefit significantly from the transaction. This should be true no matter how confident the directors are in that person's abilities and objectivity.

A person considering this scenario in light of the discussion above about the business judgment rule might well raise the question why the outside directors should be liable when Van Gorkom and the other members of his management team appear to have been the persons primarily responsible for the decision. A plausible argument might be made that the outside directors relied upon Van Gorkom and other members of management, and that that reliance was reasonable and met the requirements of the business judgment rule. The Supreme Court of Delaware was itself aware of possible distinctions among the defendants and at least twice asked the defendants' attorney during oral argument whether a difference in treatment for the outside directors might be justified. Apparently for strategic reasons, however, the defendants adopted a "one for all and all for one" strategy and refused to address the question whether some defendants might have defenses not available to other defendants.

The immediate consequences of the Van Gorkom decision on the business community were disturbing. Lawyers and law firms sent out memoranda to their clients warning them of the risk of liability in the absence of a careful investigation. The memoranda recommended that experts be hired and a "paper trail" be created to demonstrate that a sufficient investigation was made to comply with the requirements of the business judgment rule. Also, some outside directors began to reassess their decision to be directors, and isolated instances of resignations were reported. The number of lawyers serving on the boards of directors of their clients declined. And some people reported that it was becoming increasingly difficult to persuade desirable persons to serve on boards because of the potential risks involved, despite the level of compensation and the availability of indemnification and insurance.

§ 14.7　Section 102(b)(7) of the Delaware GCL

Delaware quickly responded to the decision in *Van Gorkom* and the subsequent developments. In 1986, § 102(b)(7) of the Delaware General Corporation Law was added to authorize corporations to amend their certificates of incorporation to eliminate or limit the personal liability of directors for monetary damages, with certain limited exceptions. These exceptions are (i) for breach of the director's "duty of loyalty" to the corporation, (ii) for acts or omissions "not in good faith or which involve intentional misconduct or a knowing violation of law," and (iii) for any transaction from which the director derived an improper personal benefit. Thousands of Delaware corporations promptly amended their articles of incorporation to take advantage of this new provision, which was quickly copied in many other states. Section 102(b)(7) requires a vote of shareholders to implement the limitation since it is an "opt in" election. Some states "improved" upon the Delaware statute either by making a similar amendment automatically applicable to all corporations unless rejected by the corporation (an "opt out election") or by narrowing or eliminating some of the exceptions, thereby broadening the protection accorded to directors by the statute.

One major effect of this statute was to permit individuals to become directors with additional peace of mind, and hence effectively it reversed trends created by a broad reading of *Van Gorkom*. In terms of the effect on suits for due care violations, the statute probably has encouraged suits to enjoin transactions before they are consummated rather than seeking damages after the transaction has taken place. This is arguably desirable because the imposition of monetary damages on individual directors is often out of proportion to the nature of the wrongful conduct. Suits to enjoin transactions are not affected by section 102(b)(7), since they do not involve the imposition of personal monetary liability. Further, claims based on self-dealing or breach of the duty of fair dealing are also not covered by § 102(b)(7) since they involve the "duty of loyalty."

§ 14.8 The Business Judgment Rule in Takeover Contests

The business judgment rule has been involved in numerous cases brought against directors of corporations that face unwanted takeover attempts and adopt defensive tactics designed to defeat the takeover. See the discussion of defensive tactics in § 13.28 of this Nutshell. In Panter v. Marshall Field & Co. (7th Cir.1981), Marshall Field, a department store chain, successfully fended off an unwanted takeover bid by another retail chain primarily by acquiring or opening additional stores that created serious antitrust problems for the aggressor. Following the withdrawal of the offer because of the legal complications created by the expansion policy, the price of Marshall Field shares dropped precipitously, and minority shareholders brought suit against the directors for damages. The court applied the business judgment rule in a broad and expansive manner, and exonerated the defendants. There was a vigorous and forceful dissent that argued that the majority's opinion permitted incumbent management to entrench themselves in office without limitation to the detriment of the public shareholders.

The leading cases arise in Delaware, which has taken a narrower and more variable approach. The leading Delaware case permits directors to adopt a "poison pill" (see § 13.28 of this Nutshell) in advance of any takeover attempt as a matter of business judgment [Moran v. Household International, Inc. (Del.1985)]. In addition, a selective stock repurchase plan that was designed solely to defeat an aggressor who was making an "inadequate and coercive two-tier tender offer" was upheld as a valid exercise of business judgment in the circumstances [Unocal v. Mesa Petroleum Co. (Del.1985)]. In this case, the Delaware Supreme Court recognized that selective stock repurchases (excluding the aggressor but including all other shareholders) had the capacity to defeat every tender offer, and adopted a modified business judgment rule: "A further aspect is the element of balance. If a defensive measure is to come within the ambit of the business judgment rule, it must be reasonable in relation to the threat posed. This entails an analysis by the directors of the nature of the takeover bid and its effect on the corporate enterprise." Shortly following the *Unocal* decision, the Securities and Exchange Commission adopted rule 14d–10 under the Williams Act, generally known as the "all holders rule" that prohibits selective stock repurchases. Nevertheless, the standard of "balance" set forth in *Unocal* continues to be applied by the Delaware courts to a wide variety of defensive tactics.

The Delaware Supreme Court adopted yet another twist to the business judgment rule in Revlon, Inc. v. MacAndrews & Forbes Holdings, Inc. (Del.1985). In this case, the directors of Revlon vigorously fought an attempted takeover, but eventually it became clear that the sale of the company to one aggressor or another was inevitable. In this situation, the Supreme Court stated, the directors no longer may exercise business judgment to prefer one bidder over another, but instead they have the duty of obtaining the best possible price for the company. A decision to use a "lock up" to defeat a higher bidder and favor a lower bidder violates this duty and thus cannot be protected by the business judgment rule. This last holding, in particular, is broadly consistent with the rationale underlying *Van Gorkom* that when the company is being sold, the directors must try to get the best price rather than simply selecting one bidder and dealing exclusively with it. The general principle of *Revlon* has been considered and applied by the Delaware Supreme Court and Chancery Court in an important series of cases that address a number of subsidiary issues, such as whether this duty requires an auction, and if so, how long it must continue.

The application of the business judgment rule in connection with defensive tactics in takeover situations raises a broad question as to whether the directors, or at least some of them, should be viewed as having a "disabling conflict of interest" and therefore not protected by the business judgment rule. Incumbent management, of course, has lucrative positions with the corporation that are likely to disappear if the aggressor is successful and takes over the target. When they propose strategies to defeat the aggressor, is that a conflict of interest? The answer is "probably yes." Theoretically, outside directors have positions that carry with them considerable prestige as well as financial benefits, all of which would almost certainly disappear if the aggressor is successful. But to disqualify all of the incumbent board in this manner may well be counterproductive, since the shareholders may then receive no informed advice as to the desirability of the takeover.

In cases where the court has concluded that the board has gone too far in protecting the position of its members, the court is likely to talk about decisions that tend to "entrench management." Such decisions therefore involve a conflict of interest and are not entitled to the protection of the business judgment rule. Delaware opinions indicate that approval by independent directors of defensive tactics will be given greater deference by courts then decisions in which inside directors participate.

§ 14.9   The Business Judgment Rule in Derivative Litigation

The application of the business judgment rule in connection with the dismissal of derivative litigation has also been controversial. Basically the question is whether the business judgment rule should be applied to decisions by an "independent" committee of the board of directors to discontinue derivative litigation (see § 16.10 of this Nutshell). Such litigation, brought by shareholders seeking recovery in favor of the corporation against one or more officers or directors, is very common. Typically, the decision whether or not to seek to discontinue such litigation is initially delegated to a "Litigation Committee" composed of outside directors who are not themselves principal defendants or involved in the acts complained of. The recommendation to discontinue the litigation is made following an investigation by the committee into the merits of the litigation and the advantages and disadvantages to the corporation of pursuing it.

If decisions by litigation committees are protected by the business judgment rule, the decision to discontinue litigation is binding on the plaintiff shareholder. He is thereafter foreclosed from litigating the merits of the case because of the binding nature of the impartial directors' business judgment. The plaintiff, however, may litigate issues such as the independence and lack of involvement of the members of the committee recommending discontinuance of the litigation, or of the adequacy of the underlying investigation.

At first blush it is somewhat startling to put forward the proposition that a court should dismiss litigation involving claims of wrongful conduct without considering its merits on a decision by a group of independent directors. However, decisions to discontinue or pursue litigation involve business considerations quite as much as decisions such as whether to go into a new business or to hire a new executive officer. On the other hand, there is a real risk that independent directors will have a "structural bias" in favor of their co-directors, that they "will look out for their own" or take the attitude that "there but for the grace of God go I." It may perhaps be no coincidence that in virtually every instance in which there has been a referral to an independent litigation committee, the committee has concluded that it was in the best interest of the corporation not to pursue the matter.

Early decisions, including decisions by the United States Supreme Court and the Court of Appeals of New York, uncritically applied the business judgment rule to litigation committee decisions. The approach taken by the Delaware courts has been more cautious. The scope of the business judgment rule in Delaware is determined by whether the case is initially classed as a "demand required" or a "demand excused" case. A case is "demand excused" if the plaintiff has pleaded "particularized facts" that "tend to show that the decision complained of is not protected by the business judgment rule." If the decision appears to be protected by the business judgment rule, it is a "demand required" case. Otherwise, the case is a "demand excused" case.

The first decision by the Delaware Supreme Court, Zapata Corp. v. Maldonado (Del.1981), involved a situation where virtually all the directors then in office benefited from the board decision. Therefore it was a "demand excused" case. By the time the litigation was filed, changes in the board had occurred and several directors who had not participated in the earlier decision were on the board. A litigation committee drawn from these new board members recommended that the suit be discontinued as "inimical to the Company's best interests." The court held that before applying the business judgment rule in a "demand excused" case a court should (1) consider the independence and good faith of the "Independent Litigation Committee" and (2) exercise its own "independent business judgment" as to whether the litigation should proceed.

However, the Delaware Supreme Court subsequently held in Aronson v. Lewis (Del.1984) that this dual principle only applies in "demand excused" cases. In all "demand required" cases a straight business judgment rule should be applied and courts are not to apply an "independent" business judgment. In a "demand required" case, the plaintiff must make a demand on the board or his case will be dismissed for failing to exhaust his remedies. If a demand is made, moreover, that is a concession by the plaintiff that the case is in fact a "demand required" case, and the plaintiff's case is lost if the committee determines that the decision is protected by the business judgment rule. The plaintiff cannot thereafter argue that the case was really a "demand excused" case all along. As a result, demand is virtually never made in Delaware cases today.

The Delaware approach has been criticized on the ground that it places excessive importance on the demand requirement and requires a decision at the pleading stage when there has been no discovery. Further, because making a demand concedes the application of the business judgment rule, a demand is virtually never made and an interlocutory appeal is almost certain to follow the dismissal for failing to make a demand. In any event the case is likely to be resolved solely on the pleadings without any discovery. In subsequent cases, Delaware courts have held that in "demand required" cases, the plaintiff should use the "tools at hand," including shareholder inspection rights, to obtain access to critical facts if he believes more information is necessary. The adequacy of this source of information is problematic.

Dissatisfied with the Delaware approach, both the American Law Institute and the ABA Committee on Corporate Laws have put forward alternative approaches. Both plans require that a demand be made in all cases, and then provide separate standards for the scope of review of litigation committee decisions. Section 7.43 of MBCA (1984), added in 1989, provides that the litigation committee decision is final where the directors making the decision are truly independent. MBCA (1984) § 7.44(a). The American Law Institute's *Principles of Corporate Governance* Project provides a more flexible scope of judicial review and oversight based on the nature of the derivative claim and not solely on the independence of the directors.

Most decisions involving litigation committees have arisen under Delaware law. However, there are several decisions in other states. These decisions have generally not adopted the demand required/demand excused distinction of Delaware law. While the stated tests vary, most courts appear to judge the validity of litigation committee decision in part on whether the decision appears proper and reasonable on the record before the committee and the court.

§ 14.10 The Duty of Loyalty

The duty of loyalty has produced a steady stream of litigation in which transactions have been set aside or directors and officers have been held liable for breach of duty. These cases may be divided into five broad types:

(1) Cases involving transactions between a director and the corporation (self-dealing);

(2) Cases involving transactions between corporations with one or more common directors;

(3) Cases involving a director taking advantage of an opportunity which arguably may belong to the corporation;

(4) Cases in which the director competes against the corporation in its business; and

(5) Cases in which directors distribute false or misleading information to shareholders, usually in connection with some transaction that requires shareholder approval.

Virtually all states have statutes that deal with some aspects of the duty of loyalty.

§ 14.11 Self Dealing

The danger of self-dealing transactions between a corporation and one or more of its directors is the risk that the corporation may be treated unfairly in the transaction. Since these transactions are usually voluntary, it is not surprising that in a self-dealing case the burden is typically placed on the director to prove the propriety of the transaction and not on the plaintiffs. The form the transaction takes is not significant. The courts apply essentially the same test to transactions involving the sale of corporate property to a director, the sale of property to a director's spouse, the sale of property by a director to a corporation controlled by the director, a contract between the corporation and a director for the director to perform services (such as selling stock or managing the business), or a transaction between the corporation and a child or close relative of the director. Self dealing is also involved if a director who is also an officer participates in the determination of his salary or other emoluments.

The early common law took the position that all self-dealing transactions were automatically voidable at the election of the corporation. It was eventually recognized, however, that a black-and-white rule of this type did not fit business needs. Even though self-dealing transactions may be potentially injurious to the corporation, many of them are in fact entirely fair and reasonable. Indeed, in many situations directors may give their corporations benefits that are more favorable to the corporation than it could obtain elsewhere. For example, loans by directors to the corporation may be made when the corporation itself could not borrow at all on its own credit. Transactions of this type should obviously be encouraged and not invalidated. The modern case law on self dealing transactions basically recognizes that transactions approved by disinterested directors or shareholders are presumptively enforceable and that transactions involving interested directors should not be voidable if the director establishes that they are fair.

Since 1975, a number of states have adopted statutes dealing with conflict of interest transactions. The Model Business Corporation Act, as adopted in 1984, contained a section based on these state statutes [old § 8.31], but in 1988 that section was repealed and a new subchapter F [§§ 8.60 through 8.63] was added to deal more precisely with conflict of interest transactions. It is important to consider old § 8.31 first because most state corporation statutes have provisions similar to this section. As of January 1, 1998 only eleven states had adopted provisions similar to or identical with §§ 8.60 through 8.63.

Old § 8.31 provided that a conflict of interest transaction is not voidable "solely" because of the conflict of interest if any one of three requirements is met:

(1) The transaction was ratified or approved by the board of directors or a committee of the board after full disclosure and without the participation of interested directors,

(2) The transaction was ratified or approved by the shareholders as provided in old § 8.31(d) (which required the exclusion of shares owned by or voted under the control of the interested directors), or

(3) The transaction was fair to the corporation.

There is a linguistic trap in this language (a trap that also appears in most similar statutes). The "or" at the end of paragraph (2) is not intended to limit paragraphs (1) and (2) to transactions that cannot meet the test of "fairness," i.e. only to unfair transactions. Rather, these three methods of "sanitizing" a self-dealing transaction are intended each to be an independent way to establish a transaction's validity. Thus, a transaction may be sanitized under paragraphs (1) or (2) without going into the question of fairness at all. This makes sense once it is realized that a judicial inquiry into fairness may involve a difficult and expensive hearing on complex business issues.

Put another way, ratification by disinterested corporate participants creates a "safe harbor" that "sanitizes" self-dealing transactions without the necessity of a judicial inquiry into the fairness of the transaction.

Furthermore, old § 8.31 and similar statutes do not establish that "sanitization" automatically and conclusively validates all transactions. Rather, it simply removes a possible impediment arising from the fact that a director was involved in the transaction. Again put another way, ratification under old § 8.31(a)(1) or (a)(2) does not validate transactions that involve waste, fraud, or actions in excess of authority. However, if the transaction is "sanitized" under (a)(1) or (a)(2), the burden of proving fraud or waste is on the plaintiff attacking the transaction. This important principle was clearly set forth in the Official Comment and is implicit in the language of the statute itself.

The new subchapter F is a much more ambitious undertaking than old § 8.31. Its basic structure is similar: a conflict of interest transaction is not voidable by the corporation if (1) it has been appropriately approved by disinterested directors or shareholders, or (2) the interested director establishes the fairness of the transaction. Unlike old § 8.31, however, subchapter F creates a series of "bright line" principles that increase predictability and enhance practical administrability of the "safe harbor." Thus it defines with some precision (1) the transactions to which subchapter F is applicable, (2) the types of "interests" that constitute "conflicting interests," and (3) the directors that may vote on other directors' conflict of interest transactions.

Only persons who are "qualified directors" may vote on other directors' conflict of interest transaction. A "qualified director" is one that does not have (1) a direct financial interest or (2) "a familial, financial, professional, or employment relationship with a second director who does have a direct financial interest, which relationship would, in the circumstances, reasonably be expected to exert an influence on the first director's judgment when voting on the transaction."

[MBCA (1984) § 8.62(d), as amended in 1988.] In addition subchapter F gives preclusive effect—i.e. there is to be no judicial review—to decisions by directors qualified to act under Subchapter F if those decisions satisfy the requirements of the business judgment rule. However, the Official Comment adds an unusual caution:

"If the directors who voted for the conflicting interest transaction were 'qualified directors' under subchapter F, but approved the transaction merely as an accommodation to the director with the conflicting interest, going through the motions of board action without complying with the requirements of section 8.30(a), the action of the board would not be given effect. * * * Board action on a director's conflicting interest transaction provides a context in which the function of the 'best interests of the corporation' language in section 8.30(a) is brought into clear focus." Official Comment to § 8.61(b).

Let us assume that a self-dealing transaction is ratified by the board of directors (or a committee of the board) pursuant to subchapter F. The transaction does not involve fraud or waste, but nevertheless is attacked as being unfair to the corporation and unnecessarily favorable to the interested director. Since the transaction was ratified by the directors, a full fairness inquiry is not necessary. Further, if all directors who vote to ratify are "qualified directors" (and the process followed meets the standards of the business judgment rule), the transaction is totally binding on the corporation. There is simply no further judicial review available of the decision itself or the process by which it was reached.

Is this degree of finality and immunity from judicial review desirable, or should the court make some kind of residual fairness inquiry before accepting the decision? Or to put the issue in another way, does the act of ratification by "qualified" directors "sanitize" the transaction entirely from judicial scrutiny? The answer provided by subchapter F is "yes." The American Law Institute's *Principles of Corporate Governance* addresses the same issue but permits judicial inquiry into the directors' decision to the extent of determining that "it could reasonably be believed to be fair to the corporation at the time of such authorization." The question of the scope of judicial inquiry into director-approved conflict of interest transactions was immensely controversial within the American Law Institute, and to a lesser extent within the Committee on Corporate Laws of the American Bar Association. The differences in these two formulations, however, may not be as great as might first appear. Under the Official Comment to subchapter F quoted above, the court can always inquire into whether the standards of the business judgment rule have been met. Among those standards is the requirement that the directors rationally believe that the action is in the best interests of the corporation.

Old § 8.31 was patterned after § 144 of the Delaware GCL. Under § 144, the Delaware courts permit broader judicial scrutiny of transactions than subchapter F of the MBCA. The leading case is Fliegler v. Lawrence (Del.1976), which involved ratification by interested shareholders. The court stated that § 144 of the Delaware General Corporation Law does not provide a "broad immunity," but "merely removes an 'interested director' cloud when its terms are met and provides against invalidation of an agreement 'solely' because such a director or officer is involved. *Nothing in the statute sanctions unfairness* to Agau [the complaining shareholder] *or removes the transaction from judicial scrutiny.*" (emphasis added)

A footnote dictum in another case, Marciano v. Nakash (Del.1987) states that "approval by fully-informed disinterested directors * * * permits invocation of the business judgment rule and limits judicial review to issues of gift or waste with the burden of proof upon the party attacking the transaction." However, Kahn v. Lynch Communication Systems (Del.1994), holds that compliance with the terms of § 144—ratification by disinterested shareholders or directors—only has the "effect of shifting the burden of proof of unfairness to the plaintiffs." The self-dealing transaction is not to be validated merely because the ratification decision itself was made consistently with the business judgment rule. The court stated, "Nevertheless, even when an interested cash-out merger transaction receives the informed approval of * * * an independent committee of disinterested directors, an entire fairness analysis is still the only proper standard of judicial review."

In Cooke v. Oolie (Del.Ch.1997) the Court applied these principles, concluding that the directors involved were disinterested and had engaged in a process that entitled them to the safe harbor of § 144(a)(1). The Court also concluded that the undisputed facts reflected that the terms of the transactions were entirely fair.

Two critical issues in this area are (1) who should be considered disinterested for purposes of determining who may act on a self-dealing transaction? (2) What degree of specific knowledge or notice of the underlying facts (and, indeed, of the existence of the conflict of interest itself) is required to prevent an effective authorization or ratification? These issues are discussed with some precision in MBCA (1984), § 8.60 but are not addressed directly in the other statutes discussed in this section.

§ 14.12 Interlocking Directors

Transactions between corporations with common directors may lend themselves to the same evil as self-dealing transactions between a director and the corporation. The interest of a common director may be very small in one corporation and very large in the other. Common law decisions relating to transactions between corporations with common directors applied a simple test of manifest unfairness to one corporation. The role of the common director in approving the transaction also was inquired into. If the corporation on the losing side of the transaction relied on the views of the common director without a full evaluation of the risks, or without disclosure that the director was interested in the other corporation, the chances that the transaction would be set aside were greatly improved. The stated test, however, was an objective one of fairness, not a procedural test based on the degree of the common director's participation.

Section 8.60(1)(ii) of MBCA (1984), as amended, treats a transaction between corporations with a common director as a conflict of interest transaction if "the transaction is brought (or is of such character and significance to the corporation that it would in the normal course be brought) before the board of directors of the corporation for action." This provision recognizes that routine business transactions between large corporations should not be subject to attack simply because the two corporations happen to have a common director. Even transactions that involve millions of dollars may be routine transactions not considered by the board of directors of large corporations. The quoted language is designed to limit conflict of interest transaction to those that are of sufficient importance that they should be considered by the board of directors.

§ 14.13   Executive Compensation

The compensation of directors who also serve as corporate officers or agents is a specific application of the principles relating to self-dealing. Many publicly held corporations have sought to avoid these problems through the use of compensation committees composed of independent directors to monitor compensation levels. Amendments to the Internal Revenue Code have encouraged the use of such committees. See § 13.9 of this Nutshell.

In publicly held corporations, independent directors usually receive compensation in the form of directors' fees, and also may be eligible to participate in various deferred compensation or retirement plans. Some corporations pay independent directors in stock rather than in cash, a practice encouraged by the National Association of Corporate Directors. Section 8.11 of MBCA (1984) allows the board of directors to establish compensation programs for directors. Presumably, the fairness of these amounts may be inquired into under Subchapter F.

Much modern law relating to executive compensation is directly or indirectly related to federal income tax rules. The Internal Revenue Code allows deductions for ordinary and necessary business expenses, including a "reasonable allowance" for services actually rendered. Thus, the standard for self-dealing transactions and for deductibility of compensation for tax purposes is not the same. The issues differ in publicly owned corporations and in closely held corporations. Within closely held corporations, the S corporation election creates further strategic considerations.

(1) In a closely held corporation, all the shareholders may be employees of the corporation. If so, and the corporation does not elect S corporation tax status, the salaries paid to the shareholders are likely to be set so as to minimize the aggregate tax liabilities imposed on the corporation and the shareholders combined. A salary payment may be deductible by the corporation while payment of the same sum in the form of a dividend is not, so there is strong incentive in a C corporation

to set shareholders' salaries as high as possible. In a closely held C corporation, the Internal Revenue Service routinely reviews the reasonableness of corporate salaries and may disallow deductions for unreasonably large salaries or for salaries that are being paid in proportion to shareholdings. The total amount paid by the corporation to the shareholders is still taxable to the shareholder-recipients either as a dividend or as compensation; the issue is the deductibility of the payments at the corporate level. To the extent the payments are deductible, the double tax regime of the C corporation is avoided. The same tax-minimization motive is not present in S corporations where earnings are allocated automatically to shareholders for tax purposes.

If some shareholders of a closely held corporation are not employed by the corporation, they are adversely affected by the payment of generous salaries to other shareholders. Obviously they would prefer that the same sum be distributed pro rata in the form of a dividend payable to all shareholders, even though the combined tax obligations of the corporation/shareholders may thereby be higher. The adverse effect of generous salaries to some but not all shareholders is independent of the S corporation election. The fact that a salary payment is a dividend for tax purposes does not necessarily mean that it should also be treated as a dividend under corporation law. However, the disallowance by tax authorities of a salary deduction may suggest to minority shareholders that the payment was also improper under general corporate fiduciary principles as well.

In an S corporation, all shareholders must pay tax on corporate earnings allocated to them, whether or not actually distributed. Corporations usually distribute an amount at least equal to the increased taxes owed by shareholders; the failure to do so for all shareholders places a considerable burden on individual shareholders not receiving a salary from the corporation and may give rise to claims of breach of fiduciary duty.

(2) In publicly held corporations, executive compensation is not usually viewed as a manner of distributing earnings. The executive is receiving "other people's money," and the effect of his or her compensation on earnings per share is likely to be minimal. However, compensation in public corporations may be very substantial and the question has arisen as to the circumstances under which a court may set aside compensation on the ground that it is excessive and therefore improper. The tests applied by the courts to determine whether compensation is excessive in a publicly held corporation is whether the payments constitute "spoilation or waste." Rogers v. Hill (S.Ct.1933). Courts, however, have been reluctant to conclude that executive compensation is excessive, particularly if procedures are adopted which minimize the appearance of self-dealing. As a result, there apparently has been no recent case applying the test of Rogers v. Hill. The rationale for "refusing to enter this thicket" is set forth in an often-quoted statement from the leading New York case of Heller v. Boylan (N.Y. 1941):

"Yes, the Court possesses the power to prune these payments, but openness forces the confession that the pruning would be synthetic and artificial rather than analytic or scientific.

"If comparisons are to be made, with whose compensation are they to be made—executives? Those connected with the motion picture industry? Radio artists? Justices of the Supreme Court of the United States? The President of the United States? Manifestly, the material at hand is not of adequate plasticity for fashioning into a pattern or standard.

"Courts are ill-equipped to solve or even to grapple with these entangled economic problems. Indeed, their solution is not within the juridical province. Courts are concerned that corporations be honestly and fairly operated by its directors, with the observance of the formal requirements of the law, but what is reasonable compensation for its officers is primarily for the stockholders. This does not mean that fiduciaries are to commit waste or misuse or abuse trust property, with impunity. A just cause will find the Courts at guard and implemented to grant redress."

Total compensation must bear at least some minimal relation to the services rendered. If it does not, the payment constitutes waste of corporate assets.

Rogers v. Hill is the classic case. It involved a compensation plan for executives of the American Tobacco Company that used a formula based on profits in excess of a fixed number. This formula yielded the president of the corporation more than $680,000 of extra compensation in 1929 and more than $1,300,000 in 1930. At the time, these payments were shockingly large. The United States Supreme Court held that these payments were so excessive as to be subject to examination and revision by the courts. Even though the formula was reasonable when it was approved by the shareholders in 1912, subsequent developments had led to payments so large as to raise the question whether they constituted waste.

§ 14.14   Corporate Opportunities In General

The corporate opportunity doctrine requires a corporate director to render to Caesar at the best possible price that which is Caesar's. As a fiduciary, a director owes a duty to further the interest of the corporation and to give it the benefit of his uncorrupted business judgment. He may not take a secret profit in connection with corporate transactions, compete unfairly with the corporation, or take personally the profitable business opportunities that belong to the corporation.

Very often the application of the doctrine of corporate opportunity to a specific situation comes down to a judicial evaluation of business ethics. Serious problems of definition and evaluation lie close to the surface—when is an opportunity a corporate opportunity? When may a director take advantage of a corporate opportunity on the ground that the corporation is unwilling or unable to take advantage of it? Under what circumstances may a director enter into a business that competes directly with the corporation? These questions are considered below.

§ 14.15   What is a Corporate Opportunity?

The test established by modern cases as to when an opportunity is a corporate opportunity usually combines a "line of business" test with the more pervasive issue whether it is unfair for the director under the circumstances to take advantage personally of the opportunity. Some courts have in effect collapsed the "line of business" requirement into the fairness test and stated that the single test is simply whether it is fair under all the circumstances for the director to take advantage of the opportunity. It is probably helpful, however, to recognize that there are two issues: does the corporation have a legitimate interest in the opportunity at all (the "line of business" test) and, second, if it does, under what circumstances may the director nevertheless take advantage of it (the "fairness" test).

The "line of business" test typically compares the closeness of the opportunity to the types of business in which the corporation is engaged. The closer it is, the more likely it is to be a corporate opportunity. Some earlier decisions articulated narrower tests as to the necessary relation between the opportunity and the corporate business. One test is that the opportunity must involve "property wherein the corporation has an interest already existing or in which it has an expectancy growing out of an existing right." This is a very narrow test. Another test is that the opportunity must in some sense arise out of the corporation's business as it is then conducted. Each of these tests are narrower than the modern "line of business" test, but in the last analysis, the verbal formulation of the test is less important than the court's sensitivity to reasonable business ethics as to what belongs to the corporation and what does not.

Other factors may also be important in determining whether an opportunity is a corporate opportunity. For example, weight might be given to whether or not there were prior negotiations with the corporation about the opportunity or whether the opportunity was originally offered to the corporation or to the director as an agent of the corporation. Another factor might be whether the director learned of the opportunity by reason of his or her position with the corporation. Another factor is whether the director used corporate facilities or property to take advantage of the opportunity. Finally, it may be relevant to assess how substantial was the need of the corporation for the opportunity. These factors may be considered as sufficient separately or in combination. For example, an opportunity may be viewed as a corporate opportunity if it was originally offered to the corporation whether or not the opportunity is within corporation's current "line of business."

Section 5.05(b) of the American Law Institute's Corporate Governance Project defines a "corporate opportunity" as any one of the following: (1) The director reasonably believes the opportunity was offered to the corporation. (2) The director reasonably believes that the opportunity would be of interest to the corporation. (3) The opportunity is "closely related" to a business in which the corporation is engaged or expects to be engaged. This test is specifically adopted in the leading case of Northeast Harbor Golf Club, Inc. v. Harris (Me.1995).

Corporate opportunities bear a similarity to self dealing transactions discussed in § 14.11 of this Nutshell, and there is some confusion in judicial decisions about which test to apply. The interested director statute should apply where a director seeks to transact business with the corporation while a corporate opportunity analysis is appropriate where a director seeks to capitalize on an opportunity offered to the corporation.

§ 14.16   When May a Director Take Advantage of A Corporate Opportunity?

Even if an opportunity is a corporate opportunity, officers or directors are not necessarily precluded from taking advantage of it. The corporation may voluntarily relinquish it and permit the directors to take advantage of it. Such a relinquishment is a form of self-dealing transaction subject to the tests described in § 14.11 of this Nutshell. A persuasive policy reason for the relinquishment, e.g., a decision that under the circumstances it would be unwise to expand the corporation's business, may establish that the corporation voluntarily decided not to pursue the opportunity.

Directors may also take advantage of a corporate opportunity if the corporation is incapable of taking advantage of the opportunity. Examples include claims that a corporation may not take advantage of the opportunity, because the third person has refused to deal with the corporation, or that the corporation is not financially able to capitalize on the opportunity. This last defense, particularly, is a troublesome one, since directors may be tempted to refrain from exercising their strongest efforts on behalf of the corporation if they wish to take advantage personally of a profitable opportunity. There is thus some support for a "rigid rule" prohibiting directors from taking advantage of a corporate opportunity on this ground. One can argue that the directors should lend or contribute the necessary funds to the corporation to permit it to take advantage of the opportunity or entirely forego the opportunity. Case law, however, does not support such a strict rule. Courts have permitted directors to utilize corporate opportunities upon a convincing showing that the corporation indeed lacked the independent assets to take advantage of the opportunity without considering the possibility that the directors might lend funds to the corporation.

An important case involving this issue, Klinicki v. Lundgren (Or.1985), concludes that a director may not rely on financial inability of the corporation to justify taking a corporate opportunity unless the opportunity is first presented to the corporation for its consideration. A director who secretly takes advantage of an opportunity obviously has greater difficulty justifying his conduct than one who advises the corporation of the existence of the opportunity, and the corporation takes no steps to capture the opportunity.

§ 14.17   Must a Director First Offer the Opportunity to the Corporation?

Section 5.05(a) of the ALI's *Principles of Corporate Governance* states that "A director or senior executive may not take advantage of a corporate opportunity unless * * * the director or senior executive first offers the corporate opportunity to the corporation * * *." Recent case law has not fully accepted this principle, though courts do recognize that such an offer, if coupled with full disclosure of the director's interest, may be a conclusive factor in evaluating the propriety of the director's conduct.

Some courts have held that an offer of the corporate opportunity to the corporation is required in every case. Demoulas v. Demoulas Super Markets, Inc. (Mass.1997). Other courts have held that circumstances may exist in which it is proper for the directors to take advantage of the opportunity without first offering it to the corporation. The leading cases are Broz v. Cellular Information Systems, Inc. (Del.1996) and Ostrowski v. Avery (Conn.1997). These courts hold that a corporate fiduciary may be able to establish by clear and convincing evidence that his action did not deprive the corporation of the opportunity without making a formal proffer of the opportunity to the corporation. However, the burden of establishing this is on the director. Furthermore, making a formal offer with full disclosure creates a safe harbor for the director, immunizing him from subsequent claims that he wrongfully usurped a corporate opportunity.

§ 14.18 Competition with the Corporation

Directors generally may engage in a similar line of business in competition with the corporation's business if it is done in good faith and without injury to the corporation. A number of cases, however, have found a competing director guilty of a breach of fiduciary duty on various theories: conflict of interest, corporate opportunity, misappropriation of trade secrets or customer lists, or wrongful interference with contractual relationships. In this area, tort concepts of unfair competition are closely related to fiduciary duties.

Unfair competition with the corporation may involve business activities generally, or may involve specific corporate transactions, such as the director who competes with the corporation in selling shares of stock or who acquires at a discount claims against the corporation when the corporation could have done so. Again, judicial notions of fairness or fair play seem dominant, and a close appraisal of the fiduciary's conduct in light of ethical business practice may be decisive.

§ 14.19 Fairness to Minority Shareholders

The preceding sections dealing with the director's fiduciary duties to the corporation demonstrate that a test of fairness is an important criterion for evaluating the propriety of specific transactions. This test is explicitly a criterion in evaluating transactions between corporations with common directors. It is also the principal test used in determining whether a director may take advantage of corporate opportunities or evaluating the propriety of self-dealing transactions generally (at least in the absence of approval of the transaction by independent directors under the business judgment rule).

The test of fairness generally protects the interests of the corporation, since well-meaning officers and directors should not be discouraged from dealing with the corporation and reasonable transactions should not be set aside merely because of some formal or technical defect in corporate procedure. Further, the fairness test protects shareholders and creditors alike from overreaching or unwise transactions. The major problem with a fairness test is that it tends to be subjective and elastic; a judicial proceeding testing the fairness of a transaction may be broad-ranging and complex.

The test of fairness is also applicable to a variety of transactions that defy precise categorization. For example, it may be unfair for a controlling shareholder to redeem a portion of his holdings at a higher price than offered to minority shareholders. It may be unfair in the absence of preemptive rights for a controlling shareholder to cause the corporation to issue to him new or treasury shares at a fair price if the motive is to affect or preserve voting control.

Fairness principles often apply to transactions affecting different classes of stock. In Zahn v. Transamerica Corp. (3d Cir.1947), for example, the directors of the Axton–Fisher Tobacco Company knew that the inventory of the corporation had appreciated greatly in value over its value shown on the books of the corporation. To obtain the greatest portion of this appreciation for itself, the majority shareholder, Transamerica Corporation, caused the corporation to redeem a senior convertible security without disclosing the inventory appreciation to the holders. As a result, most of the holders of the senior securities permitted their holdings to be redeemed at $80.80 per share rather than converting them into common shares that were worth considerably more. Directors are required to treat fairly each class of stock and must provide holders with accurate information about the transaction.

It is important, however, that the fairness principle be put into context. Directors elected by the common shareholders may declare extra dividends on common shares so long as required provision is made for senior securities. Directors may redeem a senior security with limited rights simply to improve the position of the common shareholders. Thus, in *Zahn*, the holders of senior securities would have had no complaint if accurate information had been provided to them even though the effect of the redemption was to greatly benefit the common shareholders. The original opinion in *Zahn* contained language that intimated that the call for redemption itself constituted a breach of fiduciary duty, but on a subsequent appeal on the issue of damages, the Third Circuit adopted the theory that the only breach was the failure to disclose relevant information. Speed v. Transamerica Corp. (3d Cir.1956).

§ 14.20 "Fairness" and the Merger of a Subsidiary into Its Parent

There is overlap and possible conflict between the cases in which the fairness test described in the previous sections is applied and the cases described in §§ 14.5 through 14.9 of this Nutshell dealing with the business judgment rule. This is illustrated by two cases involving transactions between parent corporations and their subsidiaries.

Sinclair Oil Corp. v. Levien (Del.1971) involved transactions between a parent corporation and its 97 per cent owned subsidiary. The minority shareholders of the subsidiary attacked several transactions between parent and subsidiary. They included decisions (1) to pay large dividends by the subsidiary solely to meet the cash needs of the parent, (2) to limit oil development in other countries to different subsidiaries, and (3) to cause the subsidiary not to pursue claims for breach of contract against the parent. The alternative rules potentially applicable, the court stated, are "intrinsic fairness," on the one hand or "business judgment" on the other. Under the latter, actions are upheld unless there is a showing of "gross or palpable overreaching."

The court concluded that the issues involving the excessive dividends and limiting of business opportunities should be evaluated by the "business judgment rule" while a refusal to enforce the contract claim should be evaluated under "intrinsic fairness." The basic distinction, the court stated, is whether the transaction involves self-dealing, that is, whether the parent received something from the subsidiary "to the exclusion and detriment of the minority shareholders" of the subsidiary. Since the dividends were paid proportionally to all shareholders, there was no self-dealing and the business judgment rule was applicable. So far as the business opportunities were concerned, there was no showing that they were corporate opportunities of the subsidiary and thus were not taken improperly by the parent. Giving up a contract claim that the subsidiary had against the parent, however, constituted self-dealing since the minority shareholders did not participate and that issue should therefore be judged by "intrinsic fairness."

The requirement that transactions between parent and subsidiary must be evaluated on the basis of "intrinsic fairness" often limits the power of the parent to utilize the subsidiary's assets most efficiently in connection with its overall operations. For this reason, parent corporations often eliminate minority shareholders from the subsidiary in a "freeze-out" or "cash-out" merger. Modern statutes permit the involuntary elimination of minority shareholders (see § 20.7 of this Nutshell) but such a merger is itself a conflict of interest transaction that requires proof of "intrinsic fairness."

Weinberger v. UOP, Inc. (Del.1983) involved the cash-out merger of a partially owned subsidiary. In that case, the court held that the merger failed to meet the standard of intrinsic fairness. Intrinsic fairness, the court stated, has two basic aspects: "fair dealing" and "fair price." Fair dealing means fairness in the initiation, structuring, negotiation, and disclosure of the transaction to the minority shareholders of the subsidiary. Fair price requires an examination of all economic and financial considerations that affect the intrinsic or inherent value of the subsidiary's stock. Fair dealing and fair price are not to be considered separately; the test is "not a bifurcated one" and "and all aspects of the issue must be examined as a whole since the question is one of entire fairness." Further, the burden to establish intrinsic fairness is on the parent corporation.

In an important footnote the court states that "the result here could have been entirely different" if the subsidiary had appointed an independent negotiating committee of outside directors to deal at arms length with its parent. The court added that "fairness in this context can be equated to conduct by a theoretical, wholly independent, board of directors acting upon the matter before them." In a parent-subsidiary context this requires a showing that the action taken would have been entered into if each of the contending parties had been unrelated and in fact exerted its arm's length bargaining power. Such a result, the court concluded, would be "strong evidence" that the transaction meets the test of fairness.

The message of *Weinberger*, is that independent directors should be added to the boards of partially owned subsidiaries to permit arms-length bargaining if the parent wishes to enter into a transaction with the subsidiary that implicates intrinsic fairness. Of course, if independent directors are available, their decision must be consistent with the business judgment rule if their action is to have any effect. In Cinerama, Inc. v. Technicolor, Inc. (Del.1995), the Court stated that in this context the business judgment rule has both procedural and substantive aspects. It is "procedural" because it places the initial burden of proof on the defendants to establish that the business judgment rule is applicable. If the defendants establish that the business judgment rule was satisfied, the burden of proof shifts and the transaction is approved unless the plaintiff can affirmatively prove the lack of intrinsic fairness. If the business judgment rule has not satisfied the burden does not shift and the defendants must establish the intrinsic fairness of the transaction.

In these cases involving cash out mergers of partially owned subsidiaries, Delaware case law strongly suggests that it is appropriate and desirable to add the additional requirement that the transaction be approved by a majority of the minority shareholders after full disclosure of all material facts.

§ 14.21   The Effect of Shareholder Ratification

Ratification by shareholders of a transaction between a director and his corporation will sometimes validate a transaction that otherwise might be invalid. Clearly, many self-dealing transactions cannot be ratified by majority vote. Transactions that involve fraud, undue overreaching, or waste of corporate assets (e.g., a director using corporate assets for personal purposes without paying for them) can only be ratified by a unanimous vote, and even then may be attacked by representatives of creditors if the corporation becomes insolvent. Any individual shareholder may object to a clearly improper use of corporate assets even though a majority of the shareholders are in favor of that use.

The test of transactions that may be ratified by shareholder action is traditionally phrased in terms of whether the transaction is "voidable" or "void." Only the former may be ratified. However, as discussed in *In re Wheelabrator Technologies, Inc. Shareholders Litigation* (Del.Ch.1995), the rules are more complicated than a simple "go"/"no-go" test. The term "ratification" may apply to transactions that the board of directors could theoretically have approved on its own without shareholder action or to transactions that are valid only if they are approved by shareholders and directors, e.g., a merger. A distinction furthermore may be drawn between cases where shareholder approval is required by statute and cases where approval is required by contract, e.g., the "majority of the minority" approval discussed in the Delaware parent-subsidiary merger cases. *Wheelabrator* holds that the effect of independent shareholder approval (1) in duty of care cases is to validate actions, but (2) in duty of loyalty cases is to shift the burden of proof of fairness (or lack thereof) to the corporation. Duty of loyalty cases involve both parent/subsidiary mergers and interested transactions between the corporation and a director.

§ 14.22 Provisions That Exonerate Directors

Provisions are sometimes placed in articles of incorporation of a corporation that purport to validate transactions between directors and the corporation that otherwise might be voidable. These clauses do not validate fraudulent or manifestly unfair acts or significantly modify the legal rules discussed in earlier sections. They may (1) permit an interested director to be counted in determining whether a quorum is present, or (2) exonerate transactions between corporation and director "from adverse inferences which might be drawn against them." Clauses that go even further and provide that self-dealing transactions are not subject to rescission or that no liability may be imposed on directors arising from them are probably ineffective. Despite these clauses, courts examine with care transactions that involve conflicting loyalties on the basis of the standards described in §§ 14.10–14.21.

§ 14.23 Statutory Duties and Statutory Defenses

Business corporation statutes expressly impose liability on directors for certain transactions. Liability under these statutes usually does not require a finding of bad faith or wrongful conduct. While provisions vary from state to state, statutory liability is typically imposed for the following:

(1) Paying dividends or making distributions in violation of the statute or of restrictions in the articles of incorporation. MBCA (1984) § 8.33. Liability is usually limited to the excess of the amount actually distributed over the amount that could have been distributed without violating the provision or restriction.

(2) Purchasing its own shares in violation of statute. The liability again is usually limited to the amount paid for shares that exceeds the maximum amount that could have been paid without violating the statute. The Model Business Corporation Act (1984) in effect treats this prohibition as part of (1) since a "distribution" under MBCA (1984) is defined to include both dividends and repurchases of shares.

Klang v. Smith's Food & Drug Centers, Inc. (Del.1997) holds that in applying the prohibition against repurchasing shares out of capital, a corporation may revalue assets in good faith and the test is not to be applied simply to the book numbers shown on financial statements.

(3) Distributing assets to shareholders during the liquidation of the corporation without paying and discharging, or making adequate provision for the payment and discharge of, known debts, obligations, or liabilities of the corporation. The Model Business Corporation Act does not directly address this kind of misconduct. See MBCA (1984) § 14.05(a)(3).

(4) Permitting the corporation to engage in business if it does not have the minimum required capital. With the elimination of minimum capital requirements in MBCA (1984) and in most states, this provision is of little practical importance today. In states that continue to require minimum capital, the liability is limited to the unpaid part of the minimum capital, and the liability terminates when sufficient additional capital is received. Earlier statutes in some states extended liability to all debts or liabilities incurred before the required capital has been paid in but these provisions, which created a serious trap for the unwary director, apparently have been repealed.

(5) Permitting the corporation to make a prohibited loan to an officer, director, or shareholder of the corporation. MBCA (1984) has eliminated all restrictions on loans to officers,

directors or shareholders; in states where these restrictions continue to exist, liability of directors who approve the loan is usually imposed up to the unpaid amount of the loan.

Business corporation acts also usually impose joint and several liability on all directors present at a meeting at which a transaction giving rise to a statutory liability is approved. A director who is held liable may be entitled to contribution from other directors who assented to the transaction. In addition shareholders that receive an unlawful distribution may be compelled to return the distribution. See MBCA (1984) § 8.33(b). Under the MBCA (1984), however, only shareholders who "[know] the distribution was made in violation of the Act or the articles of incorporation" are liable. Shareholders receiving a distribution in ignorance of its illegality are entitled to keep it. In this situation, of course, the possibility of detrimental reliance by innocent shareholders is quite high.

The directorial liabilities imposed by these statutes are not all automatic. Some may be subject to defenses available to directors generally. For example, in some states it may be a defense that the directors met a standard of care or relied in good faith upon financial statements or advice given by appropriate corporate officials, attorneys, or others. However, in most states directors may be personally liable for violation of statutory duties even though they acted in good faith and with due care. The Model Business Corporation Act (1984) further reduces the significance of these statutory liabilities by making all general statutory defenses applicable to them.

There has been very little reported litigation seeking to impose liability under these statutory provisions, and virtually no litigation over the scope of possible defenses.

§ 14.24   Purchase or Sale of Shares or Claims Under State Law

This and the following sections deal with the potential liability of directors and officers when buying or selling shares of the corporation. These transactions may involve either state or federal securities law. State law on this topic, until recently, has been overshadowed by the growth of federal law, particularly rule 10b–5, discussed in the following section of this Nutshell. However, there are indications that state law rules may become more important in the future.

(1) *Purchase or Sale of Shares by an Officer or Director on the Basis of Undisclosed Information.* An officer or director of the corporation may have knowledge about corporate affairs that is unknown to the general public or to other shareholders. He may be tempted either to purchase or to sell shares in order to make a personal profit, depending on the nature of the information, without disclosing the information. These transactions may be effected either through personal negotiation or by anonymous transactions over a securities exchange. An officer or director who uses inside corporate information for personal gain violates rule 10b–5 and most cases of this type are currently brought in federal court under that rule.

The common law did not develop a simple test for handling these situations. If an affirmative misrepresentation was made in direct negotiations, normal fraud principles dictate that the defrauded person can rescind the transaction. Furthermore, in personal dealings, some courts found an affirmative duty on the part of the insider to disclose specific facts that were of critical importance and peculiarly within the knowledge of the insider. The leading case is Strong v. Repide (S.Ct.1909). The Supreme Court stated that there was a duty to disclose "special facts" without attempting to define which facts are "special." In this case, the insider was held liable because he concealed his identity from the purchaser and failed to disclose material facts about the value of the shares being purchased.

In a related line of cases, Kansas adopted a general fiduciary duty to disclose relevant facts on the part of officers or directors when entering into transactions with shareholders. This position, sometimes described as the "minority" rule, appears in fact to have become the majority rule in cases involving closely held shares and personal dealings with corporate directors. A good recent example is Van Schaack Holdings, Ltd. v. Van Schaack (Colo.1994).

Diamond v. Oreamuno (N.Y.1969) holds that a publicly held corporation may recover "profits" made by insiders in a "bad news" situation. The insiders sold their shares into the public market on the basis of internal corporate information that costs would increase materially in the future and the value of the corporation's securities would therefore decline. Relying on analogies with the federal securities laws, the court in effect concluded that inside information was corporate property and an insider should not be permitted to profit from the use of that corporate property even though the corporation was not injured by the transaction. This view has been accepted by some courts and rejected by others.

(2) *Purchase at a Discount of Claims Against the Corporation.* A corporate officer or director may purchase claims against a *solvent* corporation at a discount, and enforce them at face value, though in some circumstances the opportunity to acquire a claim at a discount may itself be a corporate opportunity. Persons who validly purchase claims at a discount when a corporation is solvent may share at face value in a subsequent distribution in insolvency or bankruptcy.

A different rule is applicable to claims purchased at a discount when the corporation is insolvent or in bankruptcy or liquidation. The theory is that in cases of insolvency, liquidation, or reorganization, directors have a duty to settle or discharge claims against the corporation on the best possible terms from the corporation's standpoint. In other words, in this situation, the directors' duty is to protect creditors and shareholders generally, rather than seeking to profit personally.

(3) *Purchase or Sale of Shares in Competition With the Corporation.* In some circumstances an officer or director may attempt to sell his or her personal shares when the corporation itself is attempting to raise capital by selling additional shares. Such conduct is actionable if the opportunity to sell shares to a third person is itself a corporate opportunity. The same principle should be applicable to corporate opportunities to repurchase its own shares as well.

(4) *Purchase or Sale of Shares by a Corporation in a Struggle for Control.* If outsiders or insurgents are seeking to wrest control of a public corporation away from incumbent management, the incumbents may cause the corporation to make open market purchases of its own shares to drive up the stock price and reduce the available supply of shares. Their purpose obviously is to defeat the takeover attempt. Or they may cause the corporation simply to buy out or pay off the insurgents at a premium price. (This strategy is called "green mail.") Similarly, they may issue additional shares at a low price to themselves or to friendly persons in order to defeat the takeover attempt.

In a variation of these themes, majority shareholders in a closely held corporation, may decide to have the corporation purchase the shares owned by a particularly obstreperous minority shareholder at a generous price in order to get rid of him.

The general test of propriety adopted by the courts to evaluate all of these various strategies is one of underlying purpose:

> "[I]f the actions of the board were motivated by a sincere belief that the buying out of the dissident stockholder was necessary to maintain what the board believed to be proper business practices, the board will not be held liable for such decision, even though hindsight indicates the decision was not the wisest course * * *. On the other hand, if the board has acted solely or primarily because of the desire to perpetuate themselves in office, the use of corporate funds for such purposes is improper."

Cheff v. Mathes (Del.1964). This test may be criticized on the ground that it is possible to dress up virtually every transaction as a "proper business practice." However, a number of cases have invalidated transactions of the types described above, so that the test obviously has some teeth. In addition, a special penalty tax enacted by Congress discourages green mail transactions; several states have also enacted statutes relating to these uses of corporate assets.

In the early 1980s, the purchase of a block of shares by a potential aggressor pursuant to a plan to compel the issuer to repurchase shares at a higher price was viewed as a serious evil. Such a strategy in Delaware today is evaluated under the *Cheff* standard or the *Unocal* standard of "proportionality." See § 13.28 of this Nutshell. Heckmann v. Ahmanson (Cal. App.1985) holds that the seller of shares to the corporation in this strategy may be liable as an aider and abettor if the transaction is found to be a breach of the directors' fiduciary duties.

§ 14.25   Duties of Directors of Financially Distressed Corporations

In general terms, officers and directors owe duties of care and fiduciary duties of loyalty to the corporation itself and not to its creditors. They are expected to act in good faith and with the honest belief that the actions they take are in the best interests of the corporation and are designed to maximize the wealth of the shareholders. Indeed, if directors take discretionary steps to favor creditors at the expense of shareholders, they may be liable to shareholders for breach of duty to them.

These duties immediately shift when a corporation files for reorganization under Chapter 11 of the Bankruptcy Code. Under the Bankruptcy Code management has a duty to protect the interests of creditors. Since court approval of many actions by the corporation is required, directors usually take close or difficult questions of fiduciary duty to the court for approval before action is taken. Hence it is unusual for directors of a corporation in Chapter 11 to be surcharged for actions taken that benefit the shareholders rather than creditors.

If the corporation becomes insolvent, the sole recourse of a corporate creditor normally is against the corporation or its estate, and not a direct suit against a director or officer. If permitted, such suits would obviously permit one creditor to obtain a priority or other advantage over other creditors.

Geyer v. Ingersoll Publications Co. (Del.Ch.1992) holds that directors owe fiduciary duties to the creditors if the corporation is "in fact" insolvent though not formally in bankruptcy or reorganization. Insolvency "in fact" is defined as "a corporation in which the value of its assets has sunk below the amount of its debts."

In Credit Lyonnais Bank Nederland, N.V. v. Pathe Communications Corp. (Del.Ch.1991), the Court held that directors of a corporation "in the vicinity of insolvency" owe fiduciary duties to both shareholders and creditors. Their responsibility is to "maximize the corporation's long-term wealth-creating capacity" for the benefit of both shareholders and creditors. In a famous footnote (footnote 55), the Court described why directors of a corporation "in the vicinity of insolvency" may be tempted to engage in more risky transactions than directors in solvent corporations. The "vicinity of insolvency" is obviously a difficult concept to apply in real life.

§ 14.26 Disclosure Obligations Under State Law

Traditionally, disclosure obligations of corporations are based on federal securities law discussed in the immediately following sections, and not state law. This is particularly true with respect to corporations whose shares are publicly traded.

In Malone v. Brincat (Del.1998), the Delaware Supreme Court identified an area in which state fiduciary duties may require affirmative disclosure in the context of a publicly held corporation. The case involved an action against the directors complaining that the directors had intentionally overstated the financial condition of the corporation throughout a four-year period in its disclosures to shareholders. The Chancery Court dismissed on the ground that this claim only implicated federal law. The Supreme Court ordered that court to give the plaintiffs an opportunity to replead because a state claim of improper disclosure existed in some circumstances.

The court pointed out that directors provide information to shareholders in publicly held corporations in three different contexts:

1) When the board is seeking shareholder action on some specific matter;

2) When directors speak to the securities markets about the corporations activities and prospects; and

3) When the directors speak to the shareholders about corporate affairs generally but not in respect to any specific shareholder action.

In the first context Delaware law has long recognized a fiduciary duty of the directors to disclose all material information reasonably available with respect to the specific matter on which action is sought. With respect to the second category, the court stated that federal securities law provides detailed regulation, and there is no room or need for state involvement. With respect to the third category, however, the court held that state fiduciary duties of loyalty and good faith apply. Basically, they require directors to deal honestly with shareholders when they provide information. The knowing dissemination of false information to shareholders is therefore an actionable breach of fiduciary duty under state law.

A significant issue that arises in connection with this new fiduciary duty is whether the injury is to the corporation itself or to the shareholders individually. Injury to the corporation must be prosecuted in a derivative action. Injury to the shareholders individually may lead to a recovery by the plaintiff of money damages. The case before the court was properly dismissed, the court held, because the complaint did not articulate which theory the plaintiffs were pursuing. However, an opportunity to amend should be provided to permit the plaintiffs to identify whether they were pursuing a direct or a derivative claim.

§ 14.27 Rule 10b–5

Rule 10b–5, promulgated by the Securities and Exchange Commission under section 10(b) of the Securities Exchange

Act of 1934, is the source of most law relating to transactions in securities by officers, directors, and others. Rule 10b–5 has some of the attributes of a roller coaster: A dizzying growth followed by a sudden decline as the United States Supreme Court sharply limited the growth of the jungle of case law. The deceptively simple language of rule 10b–5 deserves quotation:

> "It shall be unlawful for any person, directly or indirectly, by the use of any means or instrumentality of interstate commerce, or of the mails or of any facility of any national securities exchange,
>
> (1) to employ any device, scheme, or artifice to defraud;
>
> (2) to make any untrue statement of a material fact or to omit to state a material fact necessary in order to make the statements made, in light of the circumstances under which they were made, not misleading, or
>
> (3) to engage in any act, practice, or course of business which operates or would operate as a fraud or deceit upon any person,
>
> in connection with the purchase or sale of any security."

Rule 10b–5 is a federal regulation and claims arising under it are federal claims. Thus, there is no need for diversity of citizenship, suit must be brought in a federal court, and state security-for-expenses statutes (see § 16.8 of this Nutshell) do not apply.

While many Rule 10b–5 cases probably can be brought in state court on state fiduciary or fraud principles, the federal forum was traditionally preferred by plaintiffs for several reasons. The procedures are simpler and discovery procedures broader. There is nationwide service of process and broad venue provisions. The enactment of statutes in 1995 and 1998 tightening the procedural requirements for class actions under

Rule 10b–5, has simultaneously limited the attractiveness of the federal forum and preempted state courts from trying certain class action cases. See §§ 17.5–17.17 of this Nutshell.

In the early 1990s the Supreme Court decided two securities cases that narrowed the scope of Rule 10b–5. The first of these opinions held that a private action for "aiding and abetting" liability did not exist under Rule 10b–5, since the text of the language of that Rule was controlling of its scope. Central Bank of Denver, N.A. v. First Interstate Bank (S.Ct.1994). This decision was startling because all prior lower courts had found that such liability did exist. The second held that the word "prospectus" has a narrow meaning in § 12(2) of the Securities Act of 1933 despite the fact that the Act itself defines "prospectus" very broadly. Gustafson v. Alloyd Co. (S.Ct.1995). Again the decision was startling because prior lower court cases had all construed the word "prospectus" in § 12(2) very broadly. It is not clear, however, that these decisions indicate that the Supreme Court has firmly resolved to narrow the scope of modern federal securities law.

The present contours of Rule 10b–5 can be briefly stated. A private cause of action exists for violations of the Rule. Only persons who are purchasers or sellers of securities may be plaintiffs and take advantage of Rule 10b–5. Defendants may be liable under Rule 10b–5 even though they themselves neither purchased nor sold securities. The plaintiff must establish that defendants acted with "scienter," usually defined as "intentional wrongdoing" or a "mental state embracing intent to deceive, manipulate or defraud." However, in some circumstances recklessness may satisfy the scienter requirement. Finally, Rule 10b–5 only prohibits deception, not unfairness. In other words, a transaction (e.g., a merger) that is adequately disclosed cannot be attacked under Rule 10b–5 even though its terms may be unfair.

Rule 10b–5 is triggered by the use of facilities of interstate commerce. This jurisdictional requirement is broadly construed. To use a classroom example, a violation of Rule 10b–5 occurs if the president of a small Denver corporation offers over the telephone to purchase shares owned by a shareholder also living in Denver on the basis of a misrepresentation. Because the telephone is a facility of interstate commerce, the president has violated Rule 10b–5 without ever leaving his Denver office.

Rule 10b–5 proscribes not only affirmative misrepresentations but also half-truths. In addition, in limited circumstances a failure to disclose "material facts" may be misleading. Mere silence may constitute a violation, e.g., by failing to correct a statement that was accurate when made but is now false. The test of "material" is whether a reasonable person would attach importance to the information in determining his or her course of action—in other words, if the information would, in reasonable and objective contemplation, affect the value of the securities, it should be considered "material." Examples of material information are a significant ore strike, a resale contract for the shares or corporate assets, or a merger opportunity.

Rule 10b–5 has been applied in a variety of different contexts described in the following sections.

§ 14.28   Rule 10b–5 as an Anti-fraud Provision

Rule 10b–5 is applicable to private transactions that involve closely held shares if the jurisdictional requirements have been met and a misrepresentation or half-truth has occurred. Rule 10b–5 thus provides a federal cause of action for private transactions involving securities that is often an alternative to fraud claims under state law.

Rule 10b–5 is also involved in numerous class actions involving claimed fraud or misrepresentation relating to information about publicly traded shares. These lawsuits became so numerous and controversial that Congress in 1995 enacted the "Private Securities Litigation Reform Act" ["PSLRA"] to deal with this type of litigation. President Clinton's veto of this legislation was overridden by Congress. One effect of this legislation was to encourage suits to be brought under state law in state courts, and in 1998 Congress enacted another statute, the Securities Litigation Uniform Standards Act ("SLUSA") to return this litigation to Federal court. PSLRA and SLUSA are described in detail in Chapter 17. See §§ 17.5–17.17 of this Nutshell.

§ 14.29   Insider Trading: The Beginnings

Rule 10b–5 has been applied to transactions in which persons with non-public information have sought to capitalize on that information by entering into securities transactions before the information becomes public. Insider trading is perhaps the most important area of Rule 10b–5 jurisprudence today. However, the subject is not specifically mentioned in the language of Rule 10b–5 and in fact its regulation is almost entirely based on judicial decisions.

The first statement that trading on the basis of inside information in the anonymous securities markets might violate Rule 10b–5 appears in In the Matter of Cady Roberts & Co. (1961), an SEC broker discipline case.

Insider trading was first widely-publicized by the decision in Securities and Exchange Commission v. Texas Gulf Sulphur Co. (2d Cir.1968). The court held that purchases of common shares and call options on common shares of Texas Gulf by officers and employees based on an undisclosed mining discovery violated Rule 10b–5. In addition to direct trades by persons affiliated with Texas Gulf, Rule 10b–5 was also held to have been violated by transactions entered into by "tippees" of those persons—persons who had been told of the discovery by officers or employees of Texas Gulf. Rule 10b–5 was also held to have been violated by transactions that occurred shortly after the news of the mining discovery was released at a press conference but before the market had had a chance to react to the information. The court held that persons with inside information may not trade until after the market has had an opportunity to digest the information.

The purpose of Rule 10b–5, the court held, was to assure that all traders had relatively equal access to information. This was presumably based on intuitive notions of fairness in the great trading markets.

The New York Stock Exchange thereafter published guidelines as to when it was appropriate for an insider to trade in shares of the corporation. These guidelines suggest periodic investment purchases (e.g., buying a few shares every month) or limiting transactions to brief periods after public information is released. Where a development of major importance has occurred, uncertainty may exist under these guidelines as to when an insider may trade even after the information has been released. It is usually impractical for an insider himself to publicly disclose material facts (since that is a corporate function). Insiders with material information about corporate matters must simply abstain from trading until after the facts are made public and have been reasonably disseminated.

§ 14.30   Insider Trading: The Defining Case Law

The modern law of insider trading has been largely shaped by four decisions of the Supreme Court of the United States.

(1) Chiarella v. United States (S.Ct.1980). In this case, the Court set aside the criminal conviction under Rule 10b–5 of a blue collar printing plant employee. The plant produced documents for securities transactions, including tender offers by aggressor corporations. While the names of both aggressors and targets were left blank (or false names were substituted) in the material submitted, Chiarella was able to ascertain the identities of the corporations involved and he used this information to profit on trades of shares of the target corporations. A majority of the Supreme Court held that Chiarella owed no duty to the general public to disclose the information he obtained since he was not an insider and received no information from the target corporation. There was, furthermore, no general rule that required a person with inside information to disclose that information before trading. Hence his criminal conviction was overturned.

Chief Justice Burger filed a dissenting opinion arguing that Chiarella should be convicted under Rule 10b–5 because "a person who has misappropriated nonpublic information has an absolute duty to disclose that information or to refrain from trading." The majority of the Court declined to consider this theory because it had not been considered by lower courts.

Shortly after *Chiarella* was decided, the SEC adopted Rule 14e–3 relating specifically to tender offers. The Rule prohibits trading by anyone on the basis of undisclosed information about pending tender offers. Thus, even an eavesdropper who overhears discussion of a tender offer at a restaurant or while walking in the street violates this Rule if she trades on the basis of the information. Chiarella's conduct would have violated Rule 14e–3 even though it did not violate Rule 10b–5. The Supreme Court upheld the validity of Rule 14e–3 in United States v. O'Hagan, (S.Ct. 1997).

Chiarella was the first person prosecuted criminally for violating the insider trading rules. While the prosecution was unsuccessful, he was not to be the last.

(2) Dirks v. SEC (S.Ct.1983). Dirks, a broker, was given non-public information by an insider about a major fraud that was occurring within Equity Funding Corporation, a life insurance and mutual fund corporation. Dirks publicly "blew the whistle" on the fraud only after advising his clients to sell their Equity Funding stock. Dirks was therefore a "tippee," a person who receives information from a person (the "tipper") with nonpublic information. In *Dirks,* the Court held that a tippee was subject to Rule 10b–5 only if the tipper breached a fiduciary duty in giving information to the tippee. This question, in turn, is to be resolved on the basis of whether the tipper received a direct or indirect personal benefit from the disclosure, such as a pecuniary gain or a "reputational benefit." In a footnote, the Court also suggested that persons such as underwriters, accountants, attorneys, or consultants working for the corporation who receive corporate information in a legitimate manner should be viewed as temporary insiders and not as tippees. Hence, if they disclose confidential information it is as a tipper and not a tippee.

The requirement of *Dirks* that a tippee is liable under Rule 10b–5 only if the tipper obtains an improper benefit from the disclosure, has lead to unusual allegations. In one case, for example, the former CEO of a major corporation was charged with providing inside information to several friends and his mistress; the SEC charged that the former CEO received a direct personal benefit from his "close personal relationship" with the mistress!

(3) Carpenter v. United States (S.Ct.1987) offered the Court another opportunity to consider the "misappropriation theory" first suggested by Chief Justice Burger in *Chiarella*. In

this case, Winans, a reporter for the *Wall Street Journal*, wrote a daily column called "Heard on the Street" that discussed specific stocks. Favorable mention of a stock in this column usually led to a run-up in price of that stock. Winans gave information about which stocks would be featured in future columns to his associates who purchased stock in advance of the column and thereby profited from the run-up in price. The parties in this scheme made significant efforts to hide their relationship with each other.

This case involved the misappropriation theory because Winans received no information from the issuer itself. The information he was using belonged to the *Wall Street Journal*, not to the companies referred to in his column. Winans was convicted of criminal violations under the mail fraud statute, § 10(b) and Rule 10b–5. The convictions were upheld by the Second Circuit. The Supreme Court affirmed the conviction under Rule 10b–5 by an equally divided court, thus leaving the status of the misappropriation theory in doubt. However, at the same time the Court by a vote of 8–0 upheld the mail fraud convictions. With this holding, criminal prosecution of insider trading suddenly became a very serious matter, since the mail fraud statute carries substantial penalties and conviction usually leads to imprisonment.

(4) United States v. O'Hagan (S.Ct.1997) also involves the misappropriation theory. This case involved a tender offer by Grand Met, an English company, to purchase Pillsbury Company. Grand Met was represented by the Minneapolis law firm of Dorsey & Whitney. O'Hagan was a partner in Dorsey & Whitney but did not work directly on the Pillsbury acquisition. However, he learned of the proposed tender offer from conversations within the firm, and he made huge purchases of Pillsbury stock and options before the takeover attempt was announced. When the takeover occurred, O'Hagan sold his

positions in Pillsbury stock, at a profit of more than $4.3 million.

O'Hagan himself received no information from Pillsbury, the issuer of the shares he purchased. He therefore violated no duty to Pillsbury. Rather, he misused information that belonged to the Dorsey firm and its client, Grand Met. Any injury that O'Hagan's transactions caused was to the law firm or to Grand Met. In one sense, what O'Hagan did was a violation of the duty he owed not to misuse law firm information. The District Court nevertheless convicted O'Hagan on 57 counts under the mail fraud statute, § 10(b), Rule 10b–5, and Rule 14(e)(3). The Eighth Circuit reversed the convictions on all counts, holding that no violation of the securities acts had occurred, and that criminal liability cannot be grounded on the misappropriation theory.

The Supreme Court reversed, reinstating the convictions and holding by a majority vote that insider trading violation occurs when a person misappropriates confidential information for securities trading purposes in breach of a duty owed to the source of the information. See § 14.33 of this Nutshell for a discussion of the policy justification for this decision.

Rule 10b–5 case law has also considered the liability of a tipper who gives his tippee knowingly false information, and as a result the tippee lost money trading. In Bateman Eichler, Hill Richards, Inc. v. Berner (S.Ct.1985), the Court held that *in pari delicto* should be applied only where "the plaintiff bears at least substantially equal responsibility for the violations he seeks to redress," and refused to dismiss the case. ITSFEA, discussed in the following section of this Nutshell makes both tipper and tippee jointly liable for profits made by the tippee. Under this statute, the SEC has accepted settlements based on the assumption that the conduct of the tipper is as reprehensible as the conduct of the tippee who knowingly trades on proprietary information.

§ 14.31   Insider Trading: Statutory Recognition and SEC Enforcement Policies

In the 1980s, Congress enacted two statutes that assume that there is a lawful prohibition against insider trading, but do not attempt to define the scope of that prohibition.

The Insider Trading Sanctions Act of 1984 (ITSA) authorizes the SEC to impose civil penalties for insider trading violations up to three times the profit gained or loss avoided.

The Insider Trading and Securities Fraud Enforcement Act of 1988 (ITSFEA) increases the criminal penalties for willful violation of the securities acts from a maximum of $100,000 and five years imprisonment to $1,000,000 and ten years imprisonment for individual violators and a fine up to $2.5 million for artificial entities. ITSFEA adds a bounty provision for informants who locate insider trading violations and creates a cause of action by "contemporaneous traders" against persons trading on inside information. ITSFEA also imposes civil penalties on "controlling persons" who directly or indirectly control a person (a "controlled person") who engages in insider trading. The test for liability of a controlling person is whether he "knew or recklessly disregarded the fact that * * * [the] controlled person was likely to engage" in unlawful insider trading or "knowingly or recklessly failed to establish, maintain or enforce" policies or procedures designed to prevent such trading. Under this section, law firms, accounting firms, issuers, financial printers, newspapers and magazines, and others, are required to implement policies designed to prevent insider trading.

Both of these statutes clearly assume that there is an effective legal prohibition against insider trading, though they make no attempt to define the scope of that prohibition.

The SEC makes the enforcement of the prohibition against insider trading one of its major priorities. Where trading in advance of a major transaction indicates that persons may have been trading on information before it was released publicly, the SEC has consistently investigated even relatively small transactions. The SEC appears to have a policy of "zero tolerance" for insider trading violations. Most investigations are terminated by settlements or consent decrees in which the person trading, as well as persons who provided the information, admit their violation, agree to restitution of profits (to the SEC) and pay an additional civil money penalty that may be two-or three-times the profits. In more egregious situations, criminal prosecutions have led to guilty pleas and the assessment of criminal penalties.

§ 14.32 Insider Trading: The Possession/Use Debate

The Securities and Exchange Commission has long defined the insider trading prohibition as involving trading "while in knowing possession of" inside information. An alternative test, adopted in SEC v. Adler (11th Cir.1998), was that insider trading was unlawful only if the insider "used" inside information when making trades. The difference between "possession" and "use" becomes relevant primarily as defenses against liability. For example, can a defendant who clearly possessed material nonpublic information when he traded avoid liability by establishing by persuasive evidence that he had firm plans to enter into the transaction before he learned of the information? If so, he "possessed" the information when he traded but he did not "use" the information to make the trade. The leading case supporting the SEC's position is United States v. Teicher (2d Cir.1993).

In 2000, the SEC promulgate a new Rule 10b5–1 that would make illegal securities trades "on the basis of material non-public information about that security or issuer, in breach of a duty of trust" owed to the issuer, to shareholders, or "to any other person who is the source" of the information. However, the Rule provides for affirmative defenses, including "instances in which a person had a binding agreement to buy or sell or had given instructions to another to execute a trade" prior to acquiring inside information. Also excluded are transactions made pursuant to a written plan (created before the acquisition of inside information) specifying the purchases or sales that are to be made or establishing a plan for trading securities that is designed to track or correspond to a market index, market segment or group of securities.

A new Rule 10b5–2 was also promulgated would extend insider trading liability to family members or personal friends of corporate insiders.

§ 14.33   Insider Trading: The Policy Justifications

The justification of the insider trading prohibition of Rule 10b–5 has itself shown a considerable capacity for growth and development.

The original articulations of the policy underlying the insider trading prohibition in *Cady Roberts* and *Texas Gulf* were "equal access" and "fairness." An insider in possession of material nonpublic information must either disclose that information, thereby giving the public access to the information, or abstain from taking advantage of it. As indicated above, as a practical matter disclosure was usually impractical so the rule was really one of abstention.

The court's opinion in *Chiarella* states that the disclose or abstain rule is not triggered merely because the trader possesses material nonpublic information; for there to be fraud, there must be silence when there is a duty to speak and the duty arises out of a fiduciary relationship. Further, in the case of trading by a tippee, liability arises only if the tipper has breached a fiduciary duty when disclosing the information to the tippee, and the tippee should know that he received the information in violation of a fiduciary duty. Thus the theory shifted from equal access to information and fairness to prevention of breaches of fiduciary duty.

The misappropriation theory requires the development of yet another theory. Liability is imposed on any person who misappropriates material non-public information through a breach of fiduciary duty owed to a person unconnected with the issuer, and uses the information to enter into a securities transaction without disclosing the proposed trade to that person. Disclosure to the person on the other side of the trade is irrelevant. The breach of duty under this theory is the failure to disclose the proposed trading to the person with the proprietary right to the information. In other words, O'Hagan would not have committed a serious criminal violation if he had advised the Dorsey law firm and Grand Met that he proposed to speculate in Pillsbury stock.

An argument may be made that the most plausible goal of the insider trading prohibition is protection of the right to ownership of information. While this is a plausible and desirable purpose (that justifies the misappropriation theory), it does seem a bit odd to use securities fraud as its basis.

§ 14.34 Rule 10b–5 as a Protector of the Issuer

Rule 10b–5 is potentially applicable when a corporation issues or acquires its own shares. In other words, the phrase "purchase or sale" literally covers transactions by the corporation in its own shares as well as transactions by third persons. If shares are issued or acquired by a corporation as a result of deception or the failure of a person to disclose material facts to the corporation, the corporation may have a claim under Rule 10b–5. Presumably, this claim may be asserted derivatively by a minority shareholder. For example, stock options granted to officers of Texas Gulf Sulphur Corporation who knew of the major ore strike were canceled since the recipients did not advise members of the Texas Gulf option committee of the material information (the mining discovery). Similarly, a Rule 10b–5 violation occurs if the corporation is fraudulently induced to issue shares for inadequate consideration even though such conduct also may constitute a violation of state-created fiduciary duties. Of course, in all cases of this type, there must be both deception and scienter in order to meet the fundamental requirements of Rule 10b–5.

§ 14.35   Rule 10b–5 as a General Prohibition Against Wrongful Conduct

For a brief period courts permitted Rule 10b–5 in civil cases to be cast adrift from all of its moorings and applied to any situation in which bad conduct occurred and there was some relationship either to the securities market or to trading in securities. The leading case involving this free wheeling approach is Superintendent of Ins. of New York v. Bankers Life & Cas. Co. (S.Ct.1971), where the United States Supreme Court found a Rule 10b–5 violation when the proceeds of a arms-length bond sale were fraudulently diverted to third parties. Thus, for a relatively brief period Rule 10b–5 appeared to have an apparently limitless growth potential. However, in the 1970s, the United States Supreme Court eliminated this possibility when it held that the last clause of Rule 10b–5 ("in connection with the purchase or sale of any security") requires the plaintiff to be a purchaser or seller of securities. This doctrine is called the "Birnbaum doctrine" based on the name of an earlier Court of Appeals decision that limited Rule 10b–5 plaintiffs to actual buyers or sellers of securities.

§ 14.36 Section 16(b) of the Securities Exchange Act of 1934

Section 16(b) of the Securities Exchange Act of 1934 is an *in terrorem* provision designed to prevent specified persons from trading in a corporation's securities on an in-and-out basis on the strength of inside information. The following comments outline the scope of this statutory liability:

(1) Unlike Rule 10b–5, section 16(b) is only applicable to corporations with a class of securities registered under section 12 of the Securities Exchange Act. Corporations must register if (i) they have securities traded on a national securities exchange or (ii) they have assets of more than $10,000,000 and more than 500 shareholders of record of any class of equity security.

(2) Section 16(b) is only applicable to specified persons, namely officers, directors, and ten per cent shareholders of the issuer. In contrast, Rule 10b–5 is potentially applicable to "any person."

(3) Section 16(b) is applicable only if there is an offsetting purchase-and-sale or sale-and-purchase of an equity security within a six-month period. For example, if there is a sale on January 1, § 16(b) is applicable if there is an offsetting purchase made at any time from six months before to six months after the sale. The sequence of the transactions or the fact that different certificates are sold, is irrelevant. However,

a transaction on July 2, six months and one day after the original transaction on January 1, is not a violation of § 16(b).

(4) The words "purchase" and "sale" are construed broadly. A gift may be a sale, as may be a redemption, a conversion, or a simple exchange of shares pursuant to a merger or consolidation. The grant of a warrant may be a purchase. The conversion of a convertible security may be a sale of the convertible and the purchase of the conversion securities, and so forth. The test is that a transaction will be considered a "purchase" or a "sale" for purposes of section 16(b) if it is of a "kind that can possibly lend itself to the speculation" encompassed by § 16(b). Under this test, commentators and lower courts have struggled with whether all sorts of transactions, such as recapitalizations, exchanges, conversions, mergers, puts, or calls should be considered "purchases" or "sales."

(5) Actual use of inside information is not a prerequisite for § 16(b) liability. Even a sale for entirely justifiable reasons— e.g., unexpected medical expenses—will trigger § 16(b) if there has been an offsetting transaction within the six-month period.

(6) Profits are payable to the corporation. However, if the corporation fails to take steps to recover the profit, any shareholder may bring suit. It is not necessary that the shareholder have owned shares when either of the transactions took place.

(7) Profits are computed by comparing the highest sale price with the lowest purchase price during the relevant six month period, the next highest sale price with the next lowest purchase price, and so forth. In this computation, all loss transactions are ignored and any individual transaction may be matched only once (though a single large purchase may be broken up and partially matched against two or more sales

that occurred at different times). The purpose is to squeeze out all possible profits from the transaction. It is possible to have a substantial loss in a trading account and yet have an equally substantial § 16(b) profit under this method of computation. The United States Supreme Court has never specifically passed on this rather draconian measure of recovery.

(8) Transactions involving options to buy or sell (puts or calls) are covered by section 16(b) if they have the effect of a purchase-and-sale or sale-and-purchase.

(9) Section 16(a) requires persons subject to § 16 to report holdings, and changes in holdings, of covered securities to the SEC. Changes in holdings must be reported within ten days after the end of the month in which the change occurred. This information is publicly available and one may review these filings to locate possible § 16(b) violations. Attorneys' fees are awarded in a successful § 16(b) suit brought in the name of a nominal plaintiff (who need not have been a shareholder at the time either of the purchase or of the sale). Much of this § 16(b) litigation may be champertous, but it is the principal enforcement device of section 16(b).

(10) Like Rule 10b–5, the jurisdiction of section 16(b) suits is exclusively federal.

Because liability under § 16(b) is automatic, people do not knowingly violate it. Persons subject to § 16(b) regularly receive periodic warnings and general memoranda from issuers describing this liability. Despite all this, inadvertent violations of § 16(b) continue to occur from time to time. Most violations are inadvertent and do not involve actual misuse of inside information. Many of these violations are a result of the failure to appreciate how broadly the words "purchase" and "sale" may be construed. The number of § 16(b) cases has declined over the years, in part because of increased sophistication on the part of covered persons.

The Securities and Exchange Commission has authority to exempt classes of transactions from § 16(b). Historically, this power was exercised sparingly, creating exemptions that tended to be narrowly drawn to cover specific situations. In 1991, however, the SEC issued regulations that are broader and more comprehensive, and designed to avoid most arbitrary aspects of § 16(b) jurisprudence. Of particular importance to corporate management are provisions relating to executive compensation, particularly stock options and incentive plans. In addition, regulations rationalize the application of § 16(b) to derivative securities as well as offsetting transactions in shares of different classes. These regulations also have contributed to the decline in the number of § 16(b) cases.

In the 1970s, a number of § 16(b) cases arose in takeover situations where an unsuccessful aggressor acquired over ten per cent of the target's shares and then sold his shares to the successful bidder within six months. In Foremost–McKesson, Inc. v. Provident Securities Co. (S.Ct.1976), the Court "solved" the application of § 16(b) to the unsuccessful tender offeror by holding that the initial purchase that puts an aggressor over ten per cent was not itself a § 16(b) purchase. An earlier case, also of general interest, is Blau v. Lehman (S.Ct.1962), holding that a partnership not itself a ten per cent holder may violate § 16(b) if one of its partners is a director of the issuer and the partnership has "deputized" the partner to represent the partnership on the board.

§ 14.37 Transfers of Control

For purposes of this section, a "controlling shareholder" is a person who owns either (1) an outright majority of the shares of a corporation or (2) a substantial minority of the shares with the balance so fragmented that the shareholder is able to designate the senior corporate officers. A group of individuals working cooperatively together may also constitute a "controlling shareholder." A controlling shareholder, by selling his shares to a third person thereby delivers the power to manage the corporation to the purchaser. The usual method of "delivering" control in this sense is by the seriatim resignation of existing directors and their successive replacement by nominees of the purchaser. Alternatively, the new controlling shareholder may wait until the next meeting and elect "his" directors at that meeting.

The price a controlling shareholder receives when he sells his interest to third persons includes a "control premium" as well as the inherent value of his interest in the business. Other persons not participating in this transaction, particularly minority shareholders, senior security holders, and creditors have a substantial interest in this transaction and may be injured if the purchaser turns out to be dishonest.

Generally a controlling shareholder may sell his shares for whatever price he can obtain for them. He has no obligation to minority shareholders to offer them the opportunity to sell proportionate parts of their holdings or otherwise to share in the control premium. As a result the price the controlling shareholder receives is usually not available to other shareholders. In many instances, the purchaser will offer to buy minority interests in the corporation at the same time but at a price lower than he is offering to the controlling shareholder. In this situation, the controlling shareholder may have an obligation to disclose to minority shareholders all facts he knows with respect to the transaction.

A few cases have suggested that the controlling shareholder owes a fiduciary duty to the corporation and to the minority shareholders. E.g., Perlman v. Feldmann (2d Cir.1955). This possibility is called the "equal opportunity doctrine" and has not been generally accepted. Scholars have put forward theoretical arguments both for and against this doctrine. One view is that all control premiums in good conscience should be shared with all shareholders because shares of stock are fungible and the control premium represents a corporate asset owned proportionally by all shareholders. Other commentators, particularly law and economics scholars, argue that most sale of control transactions are beneficial from the standpoint of the buyer, the seller, the minority interests that remain, and the economy in general. A mandatory sharing requirement is undesirable because it would discourage desirable transactions and render impractical most transfers of control.

Case law today clearly rejects the equal opportunity doctrine and permits the controlling shareholder to capture the entire premium. However, some cases have imposed liability on the controlling shareholder on a negligence theory, that before he sells control to third parties he should investigate their reputation and background. He is negligent if he fails to do so and it turns out that the purchasers convert assets of the corporation to their personal use and to the detriment of the remaining shareholders. These cases are called "looting cases."

It is important to put the looting problem in context. Most sale-of-control transactions appear to be beneficial to minority interests. Fresh and imaginative leadership may be the tide that lifts the value of all shares. It is possible that inordinate attention has been paid to the relatively infrequent looting cases. But the cases do exist.

Because the seller and buyer are not the only persons interested in the transaction, it is reasonable to impose some duty on the selling shareholder that he not sell the corporation to thieves. The scope of this duty is controversial. The American Law Institute's Principles of Corporate Governance impose a disclosure duty on the selling shareholder when "it is apparent from the circumstances that the purchaser is likely to violate the duty of fair dealing * * * in such a way as to obtain a significant financial benefit for the purchaser or an associate.''

Some looting cases however, appear to impose a greater obligation on a controlling shareholder than the mere requirement to speak where "it is apparent" that the purchaser is likely to violate basic duties. If there is indication or suspicion that a potential purchaser intends to loot the corporation, the controlling shareholder may have a duty to make a reasonable investigation and refuse to transfer control if there is doubt as to the purchaser's plans. A variety of danger signals may exist. The purchasers may be willing to pay an excessive price and have an excessive interest in the liquid and readily salable assets of the corporation. An insistence by the buyer that readily-salable assets be made available in negotiable form, as by the delivery of negotiable certificates endorsed in blank at the closing is another danger signal. Courts have not evolved a consistent or precise theory about the scope of this duty. For example, it would certainly be sensible for the controlling shareholder to make simple credit checks on the potential purchasers, but there does not appear to be a requirement that the shareholder actually do so.

A controlling shareholder who is found to have violated a duty to minority interests upon the sale of control may be liable for the entire damage suffered, i.e., the amount looted, rather than for the purchase price paid or for the amount of the control premium.

Control premium issues have also arisen in a few other cases. In Honigman v. Green Giant Co. (8th Cir.1962), holders of the class of voting shares agreed to share the voting power with holders of a larger class of previously nonvoting common shares. The price was a bigger slice of the "equity" being allocated to the original voting shares. The test for transactions of this type is the inherent fairness of the transaction.

Jones v. H. F. Ahmanson & Co. (Cal.1969), arguably involves a control premium, though the case may also be viewed as an unfair freeze-out or squeeze-out. In this case, the majority shareholders of a savings and loan association created a holding company and exchanged their shares for all the holding company shares. Minority shareholders in the association were not permitted to participate in the exchange. The holding company then made a public offering of its shares and an active market developed for holding company's shares. The minority shareholders of the S & L remained locked into a minority position in a subsidiary that was salable only to the holding company. The court held that this reorganization violated the majority's fiduciary responsibility to the minority and that recovery might be based either on the appraised value of the savings and loan shares when the holding company was created, or on the value of a "derived block" of the holding company shares on the date litigation was commenced, calculated on the assumption that convertibility had been originally provided for.

A few older cases require the sharing of a control premium on a theory of "corporate action" or usurpation of corporate opportunity. The paradigm case is the situation where the purchaser first offers to buy the assets of the corporation, but the controlling shareholder suggests that the transaction be recast in the form of a purchase of the controlling shares but not the shares of minority shareholders. In this situation, a reasonable argument may be made that the favorable sale opportunity was a corporate opportunity belonging to all the shareholders and not merely an opportunity to sell controlling shares. The facts of Perlman v. Feldmann mentioned above arguably present this pattern.

A few cases adopt the theory that the control premium is for the sale of a corporate office rather than the sale of stock. Since a sale of office as such seems clearly to be against public policy, the payment, to the extent it reflects a sale of office, may be recovered by the corporation for the benefit of the minority shareholders. The problem with this argument is that it simply proves too much, since all sales of control stock at a premium accompanied by a transfer of control may be analyzed as involving a sale of office. This argument is most likely to be accepted in two types of situations: Where the additional payment is conditioned on the immediate transfer of offices or where the selling shareholders own a minuscule proportion of the outstanding shares and the sales agreement provides for a seriatim resignation of directors. Petition of Caplan (N.Y.App.Div.1964) is the leading case accepting this argument. In that case the controlling shareholders owned only 3 per cent of the outstanding shares and sought to capture the entire control premium.

Liability for a portion of the control premium has also sometimes been based on a theory of nondisclosure or misrepresentation. In these cases a controlling shareholder contracts to sell more shares than she owns, planning to purchase the additional shares from other shareholders without disclosing the existence of the resale contract. The controlling shareholder may be liable under state or federal law (though an argument may also be made that the resale opportunity is not material since it was only made to the controlling shareholder). However, frontal attacks on sale of control premiums under Rule 10b–5 have been unsuccessful because of the *Birnbaum* principle that the plaintiff must be a purchaser or seller of securities. (See § 14.35 of this Nutshell.)

Courts have permitted either the corporation or the minority shareholders to recover a control premium, depending on the theory adopted. In a few cases, courts have required that a corporate recovery be paid over proportionally only to the minority shareholders in order to avoid part of the recovery falling under the control of a wrongdoer.

[For unfamiliar terms see the Glossary]

CHAPTER 15

INDEMNIFICATION AND INSURANCE

§ 15.1 Definitions of Terms

"Indemnification" by the corporation simply means the corporation reimburses a defendant who is a corporate officer or director for (a) expenses incurred in defending against a claim or prosecution, particularly legal fees but including other expenses as well, and (b) amounts paid in settlement of suits or to satisfy a judgment entered against (or fines imposed upon a conviction of) the defendant officer or director. Indemnification raises obvious issues of public policy. The permissible scope of indemnification is discussed in sections 15.3 and 15.4 of this Nutshell.

"Advances for expenses" are payments by the corporation to officers or directors who are named as defendants in a lawsuit to cover their expenses as they arise. Advances for expenses are discussed in section 15.5 of this Nutshell. They are governed by many of the same principles and limitations that govern indemnification by the corporation.

"Directors and officers liability insurance" (usually called "D & O insurance") is third party insurance written by insurance companies that insures the corporation and individual officers and directors against expenses incurred in connection with litigation. D & O insurance may also cover amounts paid in settlement of suits or to satisfy a judgment against insured parties. D & O insurance is discussed in section 15.6 of this Nutshell.

§ 15.2 The Need for Protection of Directors and Officers

There are persuasive policy justifications in modern society for limiting the exposure of officers and directors to the risks and costs of litigation: (1) it encourages innocent directors to resist unjust charges, (2) it encourages responsible persons to agree to serve as director, and (3) it discourages groundless shareholder litigation. However, the most important justification for indemnification protection for directors and officers today unquestionably is that it is essential in order to attract desirable persons to serve in these positions. The possibility of derivative or direct litigation which is groundless or of doubtful validity is great and the costs of successfully defending such suits are high. Concern about being ensnared in litigation is so great today that most persons of wealth or property will refuse to consider serving as a director or officer of a publicly held corporation unless they are guaranteed the maximum possible protection against such litigation.

Maximum protection today for directors typically involves three levels or layers of protection: (1) provisions in articles of incorporation and bylaws that minimize the exposure of the director to personal liability (see § 14.7 of this Nutshell), (2) indemnification protection provided by the corporation, and (3) D & O insurance in substantial amounts provided by and paid for by the corporation.

While corporations today generally seek to provide the maximum possible protection to its directors and officers, not all corporations desire to provide this protection. A corporation with minimal capitalization may prefer to husband its resources for business purposes even though it thereby leaves its directors and officers exposed to some extent to liability. The Model Business Corporation Act therefore also authorizes a corporation to limit or exclude all indemnification obligations if it expressly does so in its articles of incorporation [MBCA (1984) § 8.58(c)]. Most publicly held corporations do not elect to limit indemnification.

§ 15.3   Public Policy Limitations on Indemnification

Indemnification may violate basic tenets of public policy if it permits management to use corporate funds to avoid the consequences of improper conduct. Directors who intentionally inflict harm on the corporation or seek to line their own pockets by the misappropriation of corporate assets should not receive corporate funds to assist them in avoiding the consequences of their wrongful conduct. Indemnification of expenses incurred by such directors in defending unsuccessfully against valid claims is clearly against public policy. [The director or officer engaged in significant misconduct should be required to pay out of his own pocket any judgments entered against him and the costs of his defense.]

Equally strong policy considerations may apply in criminal prosecutions, agency investigations or administrative proceedings. Any director or officer that is involved will need legal advice and thus will incur costs even if he is ultimately exonerated.

Doubt may arise about the propriety of indemnification in certain situations. For example, what if the director is absolved of liability on the basis of a defense, such as the statute of limitations, which is not on the merits? What about amounts paid or expenses incurred in connection with the settlement of a dispute? A settlement is fundamentally ambiguous. It may reflect a small payment to settle a nuisance suit that is without merit or it may reflect the fact that the defendant realizes that there is a high probability that he will lose on the merits. Finally, indemnification of judgments or settlements of derivative suits brought by or on behalf of the corporation creates obvious problems of circularity if indemnification payments are made by the corporation to the defendant who pays the funds back to the corporation to resolve the claim.

As phrased by one commentator, the goal of indemnification statutes is to "seek the middle ground between encouraging fiduciaries to violate their trust, and discouraging them from serving at all."

State statutes work out a compromise of these competing considerations. A number of states have only very general statutes authorizing indemnification that give little indication of the outer limits, so that courts must address directly the public policy issues. The indemnification provisions of Chapter 8 of the Model Business Corporation Act (1984) (which were substantially modified in 1994) have been particularly influential. The discussion below is based on these provisions as amended in 1994.

§ 15.4 Statutory Treatment of Indemnification

Indemnification statutes may be either "exclusive" or "non-exclusive." An exclusive statute defines the outer limits of the power to indemnify in the statute itself. Non-exclusive statutes define certain areas in which indemnification is required or authorized, but corporations may increase the scope of indemnification by provisions in articles of incorporation or, more commonly, in bylaws or resolutions of the board of directors or shareholders. The New York BCL, § 721, is a typical non-exclusive statute. It states "the indemnification and advancement of expenses granted pursuant to * * * this article shall not be deemed exclusive of any other rights to which a director or officer * * * may be entitled to" by other corporate action. The outer limits of non-exclusive indemnification are set by principles of public policy, sometimes summarized in the statutes themselves. The New York statute, for example, prohibits indemnification to a director or officer "if a final adjudication adverse to the director or officer establishes that his acts were committed in bad faith or were the result of active and deliberate dishonesty * * * or that he personally gained in fact a financial profit or other advantage to which we has not legally entitled."

The following discussion deals with statutes of both the exclusive and non-exclusive types.

Indemnification may be either "mandatory" or "discretionary." Mandatory indemnification is created by statute. The basic test is that the defendant must have been "successful on the merits or otherwise." [MBCA (1984) § 8.52] Under this provision, a defendant who prevails because of the statute of limitations or because of pleading defects is as entitled to indemnification as the defendant who prevails on the merits. This result is justified on the theory that otherwise a defendant with a valid procedural defense would have to go to the expense of litigating the merits of the claim in order to establish his right to indemnification; it may also be based on the implicit premise that a defendant with a valid procedural defense has a high probability of winning on the merits as well.

Permissive indemnification is authorized as a matter of discretion, not as a matter of right. The general test set forth in § 8.51(a) of MBCA (1984) is that indemnification is permitted only if the defendant director has "(1) conducted himself in good faith and (2) reasonably believed (i) in the case of conduct in his official capacity with the corporation, that his conduct was in the best interests of the corporation; and (ii) in all other cases, that his conduct was at least not opposed to the best interests of the corporation." [MBCA (1984)

§ 8.51(a)(1)(i) and (ii).] Further, indemnification may be permitted against criminal fines if the defendant "had no reasonable cause to believe his conduct was unlawful." [MBCA (1984) § 8.51(a)(2)]

Authority to make discretionary indemnification is limited by MBCA (1984) § 8.51(d), which prohibits indemnification:

(a) in suits brought by or in the right of the corporation (except that expenses of such litigation may be indemnified if it is determined that the director met the relevant standards of conduct set forth in § 8.51(a)), and

(b) in any proceeding in which the director was adjudged liable "on the basis that personal benefit was improperly received." However, as a further qualification to this qualification, any director denied indemnification at any time may seek a court order that "in view of all the relevant circumstances, that it is fair and reasonable." [MBCA (1984) § 8.54(a)(3).]

Settlement of litigation or a plea of *nolo contendere* does not of itself create a presumption that a person acted in bad faith. Even a judgment or a criminal conviction entered against a director is not conclusive that the defendant is ineligible for permissive indemnification. [MBCA (1984) § 8.51(c)] Of course, a criminal conviction or civil judgment usually involves a determination of bad faith that prevents indemnification.

A determination whether an office or director should be given permissive indemnification under these standards may be made (a) by disinterested directors either as a board or as a committee, (b) by the shareholders, or (c) by special legal counsel. [MBCA (1984) § 8.55.] Precise rules as to how these decisions are to be made and who may select a committee of the board or name the independent legal counsel are set forth. The Model Act also recognizes a distinction between decisions *determining* that a director has met the standards for discretionary indemnification (a quasi-judicial determination of good faith, etc.) and decisions *authorizing* such indemnification (a business determination that limited corporate resources should be expended for indemnification rather than for other purposes). [MBCA (1984) § 8.55.]

The Model Act also deals with technical questions about the scope of indemnification of officers and agents, and the peculiar problem of the rights of a director who is also an officer or agent. [MBCA (1984) § 8.56.]

Another important provision of the Model Act is that a corporation may commit itself in advance to provide indemnification "to the fullest extent permitted by law" [MBCA (1984), § 8.58], and authorizes courts to enforce that obligation at the request of a director or officer. [MBCA (1984) § 8.58] This provision ensures that indemnification will be available in situations where a change in corporate control may have occurred or the defendants have had a falling out with the persons in control of the corporation. Many corporations make this election because it ensures that all defendants who may be indemnified consistently with public policy under the statute receive indemnification.

Section 16.22(b) of the Model Act requires that discretionary indemnification of directors and officers be reported to shareholders.

§ 15.5 Advances for Expenses

Section 8.53 of the Model Act, and the statutes of most states, authorize (but do not require) a corporation to advance funds to pay expenses of directors and officers prior to the final termination of a legal proceeding. As a practical matter, the right to make advances may be as important as the grant of indemnification itself, since many directors find it difficult or impossible to advance sizable sums out of their own pockets for their own defense. Further, an effective defense usually requires employment of counsel at the commencement of the proceeding. To deny all advances might therefore create an invidious discrimination against less wealthy directors.

The basic problem with advances is that they are made early in the proceeding before very much is known about the merits of the litigation. The persons authorizing an advance usually have limited information about whether the persons seeking advances will ultimately be eligible for or entitled to indemnification.

If the director is ultimately found not to be entitled to indemnification, he must repay amounts advanced. MBCA (1984) § 8.53(a) requires a director, before any advance is made, to give a written affirmation of his good faith belief that he is eligible for indemnification. He must also file a written undertaking to repay the funds advanced if it is ultimately determined that he is not entitled to indemnification. However, this undertaking "need not be secured and may be accepted without reference to the financial ability of the director to make repayment." The theory is to avoid unintentional discrimination between affluent and poorer directors (who may not be able to post security or establish financial ability to repay amounts advanced). However, the lack of security makes it less likely that repayment will actually be made. In any event, there does not appear to be recent examples of repayment actually occurring or of a corporation actively seeking to recover advances for expenses.

Corporations may make advances for expenses mandatory by an appropriate provision in the articles of incorporation or bylaws, or by action by the directors or shareholders. Many corporations do so in an effort to give the maximum protection possible to prospective directors and officers. These provisions, however, may have unexpected and undesirable consequences. In one case, a corporation conducted an investigation of certain transactions on its own and concluded that two officers had enriched themselves improperly in connection with transactions with the corporation, a charge that the officers denied. Because of the mandatory advance for expenses provision, the corporation found itself in the position of having to advance funds to pay the expenses of both the plaintiff and the defendants in a complex trial. In another case, two officers charged with racketeering and theft from the corporation requested advances for expenses before any determination of liability. Even though they clearly appeared to be entitled to advances under the corporate documents, a court refused to order advances, relying on broad public policy and fiduciary duties of the remaining directors. Fidelity Fed. S & L Ass'n v. Felicetti (E.D.Pa.1993). A later court of appeals opinion in a similar case, refused to follow this decision, stating that "it is not the province of judges to second-guess" the policy determinations made by the corporation in approving mandatory advances for expenses provisions. Ridder v. CityFed Financial Corp. (3d Cir.1995).

Section 16.22(b) of MBCA (1984) requires decisions granting advances for expenses be reported to shareholders.

§ 15.6 D & O Insurance

Insurance against directors' and officers' liabilities (usually called "D & O" insurance) provides additional meaningful protection to corporate directors. First of all, it provides a source for payments; a director or officer entitled to indemnification is therefore assured that payments would be made even if the corporation is in financial difficulty or is in reorganization. It may also cover claims which the corporation elects not to indemnify. Insurance is also important to the corporation because it pays amounts that the corporation otherwise might be obligated to pay under the indemnification statutes or provisions in articles of incorporation or bylaws.

Companies writing D & O liability insurance are not eleemosynary institutions; they cover only insurable risks and establish premiums in light of the magnitude of the contemplated risks. They cover claims based on negligence, misconduct not involving dishonesty or knowing bad faith, and false or misleading statements in disclosure documents. Wrongful misconduct, dishonest acts, acts in bad faith with knowledge thereof, or violations of statutes such as section 16(b) are not insurable events. Also excluded are actions entered into for personal profit or gain and suits based on claims of libel or slander. There are numerous express exceptions and exclusions in D & O policies, which may vary significantly from one policy to the next.

D & O insurance is not cheap: In 1993, the median premium was $228,000 per year for an average liability limit of $30.7 million.

Unlike some other types of insurance, the language of D & O policies varies considerably from issuer to issuer. There is no standard-form policy for D & O insurance. Competition among insurers may be in terms of improving policy language or enhancing coverage rather than by reducing premiums. Changes or enhancement of policy language or coverage typically must be requested by the insured and negotiated individually. They do not occur automatically.

During the middle 1980s there was a "D & O insurance crisis" as payments to insureds increased dramatically. Premiums skyrocketed while maximum limits of coverage were reduced. Many companies declined to write or renew D & O policies at all. During this period, policy language was revised to narrow provisions that proved open-ended or that permitted claims to be made that were not contemplated by the insurer. One example is the "insured against insured" exception, that excludes coverage for claims asserted voluntarily by the corporation against an insured officer or director. This was viewed as being the equivalent of "found money," since the corporation in effect was suing itself. While the crisis of the 1980s has ended, many of the exclusions and exceptions in current policies were developed during this period.

D & O policies are written on a "claims made" basis so that each year's policy covers only claims actually asserted during the year in question (though extensions for the period of reporting claims arising in a year that has ended may be negotiated). Policy applications require extensive disclosure of contingent or possible claims and a failure to disclose known claims may permit the insurer to void the entire policy. Policies also provide that expenses advanced by the insurer reduce the amount of insurance coverage provided.

Many state statutes specifically permit corporations to purchase D & O insurance. [MBCA (1984) § 8.57.] Where there is no statutory authorization, the power to purchase insurance is probably implicit in the corporate power to provide executive compensation. During the 1980s "crisis" some states enacted legislation to enable marginal corporations to provide protection to outside directors independently of the traditional D & O insurance policy—"captive" insurance companies, for example, that insure only a single company, or escrow or trust arrangements for the benefit of officers and directors. Energy companies, in particular, had difficulties in obtaining D & O insurance during this period.

[For unfamiliar terms, see the Glossary]

CHAPTER SIXTEEN

DERIVATIVE LITIGATION

§ 16.1 Direct and Derivative Suits in General

Litigation brought by shareholders against the corporation may be divided into two basic categories: direct and derivative.

A *direct* suit involves the enforcement by a shareholder of a claim belonging to the shareholder on the basis of his ownership of shares. These are suits involving contractual or statutory rights of the shareholder, the shares themselves, or rights relating to the ownership of shares. Classic examples of direct suits are suits to recover dividends, to examine corporate books and records, and to compel the registration of a securities transfer. The most controversial type of direct suit today are class actions brought by shareholders under Rule 10b–5. See Chapter 17 of this Nutshell. A *class* action is a direct suit in which one or more shareholder plaintiffs purport to act as a representative of a larger class of shareholders for injuries to the interests of the class.

A *derivative* suit is an action brought by one or more shareholders to remedy or prevent a wrong to the corporation. In a derivative suit, the plaintiff shareholders do not sue on a cause of action belonging to themselves as individuals. Rather, they sue in a representative capacity on a cause of action that belongs to the corporation but which for some reason the corporation is unwilling to pursue; the real party in interest is the corporation. In effect, the shareholder is suing as a champion of the corporation. The derivative suit itself is controversial and raises a number of procedural and substantive questions that are the topic of this chapter.

A derivative suit usually has a class aspect, and is subject to the same potential abuses as a class action. In a derivative suit the plaintiff shareholder is in effect representing the interest of a class consisting of some or all of the other shareholders in the corporation. Derivative suits are equitable in nature, a categorization that may be significant in resolving procedural questions. In Ross v. Bernhard (S.Ct.1970), the United States Supreme Court held that a right to jury trial may exist in derivative suits brought in federal courts where the issue is of a "legal" (as contrasted with an "equitable") nature.

Derivative suits provide a device by which shareholders may enforce claims of the corporation against managing officers and directors of the corporation. Persons who are in control of the corporation are unlikely to authorize the corporation to bring suit against themselves personally. The derivative suit permits a shareholder to prosecute these claims on behalf of the corporation.

Derivative suits involve shareholder enforcement of corporate obligations and as a result may intrude on the traditional management powers of the board of directors. In recent years, there have been significant efforts by the board of directors to reassert control over derivative litigation, and these efforts, described in § 16.10 of this Nutshell, have had considerable success.

§ 16.2   Derivative and Direct Claims Distinguished

Different procedural and substantive rules are applicable to direct and derivative claims. As a result, there is a fair amount of litigation over whether a specific claim must be pursued as a direct or as a derivative suit. Unfortunately the line between the two types of injury is sometimes hazy. In one sense anything that harms the corporation also harms shareholders by reducing the value of their shares. However, a shareholder may not automatically transmute a derivative claim into a direct one simply by alleging a direct reduction in value of his shares because of injury to the property or business of a corporation. The justifications for requiring that injury to the corporation be remedied through derivative litigation are (1) it avoids multiplicity of suits, (2) it insures that all injured shareholders benefit proportionally from the recovery, and (3) it protects creditors and preferred shareholders against diversion of corporate assets directly to shareholders.

Many cases have considered whether a claim is derivative or direct. A few examples: A suit charging officers and directors with misapplication of corporate assets or other breaches of duty is derivative in character. Suits to recover improper dividends or to require a controlling shareholder to account for a premium received on the sale of his shares are also derivative in nature since the benefit inures to the corporation.

Examples of direct claims include failure to permit a shareholder to vote his shares on a proposed transaction or to honor his employment contract with the corporation. A claim that it was improper for a controlling shareholder to vote on a resolution authorizing the corporation to issue additional shares to him is direct in character since it prevents the dilution of the voting power of the complaining shareholder's shares. A claim alleging a conspiracy by the directors to use their powers to depress the market price of the shares so that minority shares may be bought at less than fair value also states a direct claim.

As these examples indicate, not only is the line between direct and derivative sometimes hazy, but careful pleading may affect the categorization. A suit claiming a denial of preemptive rights seems direct; however, it may also be considered derivative if it is alleged that the corporation was induced to issue the shares for inadequate consideration through fraud or a violation of federal securities law. In some situations a single injury may give rise to both a direct and a derivative claim; in these situations the plaintiff may be able to proceed with two suits simultaneously.

The American Law Institute's Corporate Governance Project includes a sensible provision that authorizes courts to treat derivative claims as direct claims in cases involving closely held corporations if it determines that to do so would not unfairly expose the defendants to multiple actions, prejudice the interests of creditors, or interfere with the fair distribution of the recovery among all interested persons. Typically, this is sensible if all shareholders are party to the suit and creditors will not be affected by the outcome.

§ 16.3 Alignment of Parties in a Derivative Suit

In derivative suits, the shareholder is aligned as a nominal plaintiff and the corporation is aligned as a nominal defendant even though recovery usually runs exclusively in favor of the corporation. The corporation in a sense is an involuntary plaintiff, and a necessary party in a derivative suit; without it, the action cannot proceed. The plaintiff shareholder brings suit on behalf of and as champion for the defendant corporation and not as an individual. As a result, the plaintiff shareholder usually may not combine individual or direct claims with a derivative action in the same suit. Similarly, the traditional view is that counterclaims against the plaintiff shareholder individually may not be asserted by the corporation or the individual defendants in a derivative suit. See § 16.11 of this Nutshell.

Derivative litigation is essentially three-sided: In addition to the plaintiff shareholder and the corporation, the defendants include the persons who are alleged to have caused harm to the corporation or who have personally profited from corporate action. The claim of wrongdoing by these defendants is of course the central core of the derivative suit and the interest of the corporation in the litigation is usually directly adverse to the interest of these defendants. Therefore, it is customary today for the individual defendants to be represented by their own attorneys and not the attorneys for the corporation. The corporation may, but need not be an active party in the litigation. It may side with the individual defendants and argue that their conduct did not harm the corporation.

In rare instances a recovery in a derivative suit may be paid directly to the injured shareholders rather than the corporation. See § 16.12 of this Nutshell.

§ 16.4   Role of the Plaintiff's Attorney

Typically, the plaintiff in a derivative suit is self-selected. If shares are widely held, thousands of potential plaintiff shareholders may exist. It is not infrequently alleged that an attorney is the principal mover in filing a derivative suit, that he locates a possible derivative claim and then finds himself an eligible shareholder to serve as plaintiff. Such conduct may be essentially champertous but is quite common in both derivative and class litigation discussed in Chapter 17. Also, there is no requirement that the plaintiff shareholder have a significant financial stake in the litigation. As a result, the plaintiff shareholder may be a purely nominal participant in the litigation, with his attorney having a much more direct and substantial financial interest in the case and its outcome.

Since a derivative suit has class as well as derivative aspects, multiple derivative suits may be filed by several different shareholders; in the absence of other considerations, the suit first filed is generally permitted to proceed while later actions may be stayed, dismissed, or consolidated with the initial suit. Intervention by other shareholders is permitted and indeed may be encouraged if for some reason the original plaintiff shareholder is considered unrepresentative. The court has discretion to designate an attorney for another sharehold-er as the principal counsel for plaintiffs. In some circum-stances, the corporation itself may be permitted to take over a derivative suit and prosecute it directly, though that is not very common in the modern era. The selection of lead counsel is of importance not only because of his control over litigation strategy but also because it may be critical in the apportion-ment of fees at a later date. In all such matters, the trial court has "great discretion."

Most derivative suits are settled and do not go through trial and appeal. The lead attorney for the plaintiff has the major voice in determining whether a proposed settlement is accept-able. Historically, the secret settlement of shareholders' suits was a serious evil. "Strike" suits were thereby encouraged, and the plaintiff shareholder sometimes received substantial sums which in fact were a payment to ignore a corporate wrong. Courts have held that where a secret settlement has led to a payment to the shareholder plaintiff, other sharehold-ers may bring a derivative suit in the name of the corporation against the plaintiff shareholder to recover the amount of the secret settlement.

The fee to be paid the lead counsel for the plaintiff share-holder is usually negotiated as part of an overall settlement of a derivative suit. However, all aspects of the settlement is subject to judicial review and approval. The Federal Rules of Civil Procedure provide that derivative actions may "not be dismissed or compromised without the approval of the court, and notice of the proposed dismissal or compromise shall be given to shareholders or members in such manner as the court directs." A similar provision is applicable to class suits. Many state statutes (as well as section 7.45 of MBCA (1984)) contain similar requirements. In reviewing proposed settlements, courts consider several factors, including: (1) The size of the potential recovery and the size of the suggested settlement; (2) The probability of ultimate success; and (3) The financial position of the defendants. Shareholders may also appear at the hearing on a proposed settlement and object to its terms. However, if the attorneys for the plaintiff shareholder, the corporation, and the individual defendants all appear and support a proposed settlement, the court is very likely to accept the settlement.

If the plaintiff is successful or the case is settled, the plaintiff may be awarded his expenses, including attorneys' fees by the court, if they are not specified in the settlement agreement. Since most derivative suits are taken on a contingent or open fee basis, the plaintiff's attorney will receive compensation only if the suit is successful on the merits or the case settles. Such a recovery is justified on the theory that it encourages meritorious shareholder suits. The expenses and fees may be paid out of the funds obtained by the corporation as a result of the termination of the suit; however, expenses may be required to be paid by the corporation even where the corporation receives no money so long as the result of the suit "was of some benefit to the corporation." Thus, expenses and fees may be awarded in a suit that results only in an injunction against the officers and directors of a corporation from engaging in improper conduct. A settlement under which the corporation agrees to amend bylaws or make some procedural changes also may justify an award of expenses, including payment of a fee to the attorney. These rules may encourage the filing of marginal suits on a contingent fee basis as much as they encourage the filing of meritorious actions.

Theoretically, a payment of the plaintiffs' expenses by the corporation does not compel the "losing party" to pay the other's expenses since both the corporation and the plaintiff are winning parties.

The size of the attorneys' fee to be awarded depends on a variety of factors—the nature and character of the litigation, the skill required, the amount of work actually performed, the size of the recovery, the nature of the harm prevented, and other factors. The size of the fee is a question of fact. To choose one example more or less at random, a fee of $200,000 in a suit leading to a $1,025,000 settlement was upheld. Of course, in cases that are settled, the fee is usually a matter of direct negotiation among the parties.

§ 16.5   Derivative Litigation as Strike Suits

There have been numerous complaints of long standing that derivative litigation is often abused. These complaints go back to before World War II, and have continued until this day. The principal complaint is that most derivative litigation is brought at the instigation of entrepreneurial attorneys who first find a potential violation and then find a plaintiff shareholder who is qualified to maintain the derivative suit. The objective of these suits is to obtain a settlement with the principal defendants and the corporation that provides the attorney with a generous attorney's fee. From the standpoint of the corporation and the individual defendants the benefit of a settlement of a marginal or unjustified claim is that the plaintiff "goes away," and the decision is *res judicata*, preventing the filing of other suits on the same claim. See § 16.13 of this Nutshell.

One consequence of the concern about strike suits is that states have established elaborate criteria to ensure that the plaintiff shareholder is an appropriate representative, and (in many states) that if he has a small financial interest in the outcome he be required to post security-for-expenses. These requirements are discussed in §§ 16.6–16.9 of this Nutshell. These devices, however, essentially have not prevented the filing of strike suits.

In the 1980s, a new device was created to handle perceived abuses of the derivative suit. This device, the litigation committee discussed in § 16.10 of this Nutshell, has provided for an expeditious disposition of many doubtful derivative claims, and possible some meritorious ones as well.

§ 16.6   Contemporary Ownership

Section 7.41(1) of MBCA (1984) and most state statutes dealing with derivative litigation require the plaintiff to have been a shareholder when the cause of action arose and continuously since that time. A handful of states, most notably California, permits a shareholder to serve as a plaintiff even though not a shareholder when the cause of action arose if the shareholder acquired the shares in ignorance of the existence of the claim. This is called the "contemporaneous ownership" requirement.

The ostensible purpose of the contemporaneous ownership requirement is to prevent the purchase of a lawsuit, or to put the matter somewhat differently, to prevent an attorney from creating an instant plaintiff simply by having someone purchase shares in the defendant corporation. Of course, if "buying a lawsuit" were the real concern, the contemporaneous ownership requirement might be safely liberalized to allow suit by plaintiffs who discover the facts giving rise to the lawsuit only after becoming a shareholder. Since most states do not permit such shareholders to act as plaintiff, contemporary ownership requirement in fact appears to be largely grounded in antipathy to derivative litigation.

The Federal Rules of Civil Procedure contain a contemporary ownership requirement primarily to prevent the collusive establishment of diversity of citizenship. The state statutes described in the previous paragraph appear to be based primarily on notions of preventing "the buying of a lawsuit."

§ 16.7 Demand on Directors and Shareholders

Section 7.42 of the Model Act requires that a demand must be made on directors in every case before a derivative suit is filed. About sixteen states have similar provisions. The balance of the states generally require a demand but excuse it in limited situations. A typical provision is rule 23.1 of the Federal Rules of Civil Procedure: "The complaint shall also allege with particularity the efforts, if any, made by the plaintiff to obtain the action he or she desires from the directors or comparable authority and the reasons for his or her failure to obtain the action or for not making the effort."

Typically demand is excused if the plaintiff can show that a majority of the board is interested in the transaction or made no effort to inform themselves about the transaction. Demand may also be excused where the transaction complained of is sufficiently egregious that it could not have been the product of reasonable business judgment. An example might be an allegation that "the wrongdoers are in complete control of the management of the corporation." Cases in which demand is excused are called "demand futile" or "demand unnecessary" cases. The more typical case in which a demand is required, is called "demand required" or "demand necessary" case.

In most states, if a demand is required but not made the court will dismiss the case and the plaintiff can make a demand and refile his law suit without suffering a detriment. Delaware, however imposes significant substantive consequences to the "demand required"/"demand excused" distinction. Because Delaware is such an important state for purposes of corporation law, the special Delaware rules are discussed in § 16.10 of this Nutshell.

In addition to a demand on directors, a minority of states require either that a demand be made on shareholders before a derivative suit is filed or give an "adequate reason" for not making the effort. MBCA (1984) does not require a demand on shareholders.

Because making a demand on shareholders is expensive when the number of shareholders is large, most attention has been paid to acceptable reasons not to make this demand. Adequate reasons for omitting a demand on shareholders include the following: (1) The wrongdoers own a majority of the shares and hence favorable shareholder action is impossible. (2) The number of shareholders is so large that it is unreasonable to require the plaintiff to incur the expense of what is essentially a proxy solicitation when there is little chance of success. (3) The acts complained of cannot be ratified by the shareholders, so that action by the shareholders is useless. While some cases have required a demand on shareholders even when the cost would be substantial, many cases have held that a demand on shareholders may be omitted when the number of shareholders make the cost prohibitive. Massachusetts appears to have adopted a stringent rule, requiring a demand in every case where a majority of shareholders are not wrongdoers without regard to the cost. Other state courts have proceeded on a case-by-case basis, not requiring a demand when there are thousands of shareholders, and apparently taking into account the motives of the plaintiff, the number of shareholders joining in the action, and the proximity to the next shareholders meeting.

§ 16.8 Security–For–Expenses Statutes

Some eight states currently require certain plaintiff shareholders in derivative suits to give to the corporation "security for the reasonable expenses, including attorneys' fees" that the corporation or other defendants may incur in connection with a derivative suit. The 1969 version of the Model Act included such a provision but it was omitted from MBCA (1984) because of increasing doubts about its efficacy and fairness.

Security-for-expenses statutes apply only to plaintiffs. Shareholders required to post security are usually defined in terms of the size of their holdings: the 1969 Model Act provision, for example, required security from plaintiffs whose ownership was less than one per cent of the outstanding shares or the value of the shares was less than $25,000. Virtually all plaintiff shareholders seek exemption under the dollar requirement. Other states had similar provisions though the dollar and percentage limits varied from state to state. In a few states, a security-for-expenses filing is required only upon a judicial finding that the suit was apparently brought without reasonable cause or seems patently without merit.

Where security must be posted, it is usually in the form of a bond with sureties, though it also may be in the form of cash or marketable securities. The size of the bond required depends on the estimated expenses of the corporation. Since they may include not only the direct expenses of the corporation, but also the expenses of other defendants for which the corporation may become liable by indemnification or otherwise, it is relatively easy for a substantial corporation to justify security running into the hundreds of thousands of dollars. The requirement of posting security of this magnitude obviously may result in the litigation being abandoned.

Security-for-expenses statutes usually do not define when the corporation may actually look to the security for reimbursement; rather they usually state in effect that "[t]he corporation shall have recourse to such security in such amount as the court having jurisdiction shall determine upon the termination of such action." (This quotation is taken from the 1969 Model Act, § 49, last par.) Thus, security-for-expenses statutes have a secondary effect of also creating a right of reimbursement in favor of the defendant against the plaintiff where none existed before. As a further consequence, an unsuccessful shareholder-plaintiff who actually posts security-for-expenses may end up paying the expenses of both sides of unsuccessful litigation.

Security-for-expenses statutes are applicable under the *Erie* principle to suits in federal court based on state-created causes of action. In other words, if a state has a security-for-expenses statute, the federal courts in that state must require security in cases arising under state law. However, security-for-expenses statutes are not applicable to suits in federal court based on federal law. Nor are they applicable to direct class actions brought either in the federal or state courts. These statutes therefore also have the incidental effect of encouraging suits to be brought under federal securities law rather than under state law.

One purpose of security-for-expenses statutes undoubtedly is to deter "strike" suits brought in the hope of securing a settlement profitable to the plaintiff shareholders and their attorneys. However, statutes generally do not distinguish between "strike" suits and bona fide shareholder suits. Rather, they are applicable to all shareholder suits, and thus have the effect of making all such suits more difficult.

Security-for-expenses statutes were held to be constitutional despite the arbitrary numerical limit in Cohen v. Beneficial Industrial Loan Corp. (S.Ct.1949).

Section 7.46 of MBCA (1984) authorizes a court to assess costs, including attorneys' fees, against a plaintiff or defendant if the court determined that the suit was brought without just cause. Many states have similar rules which deter the filing of groundless or marginal derivative suits.

§ 16.9 Verification of the Complaint

Many state statutes, as well as rule 23.1 of the Federal Rules of Civil Procedure, require complaints in derivative suits to be verified, i.e., sworn to. The purpose of this requirement is to provide some protection against groundless litigation without deterring suits brought in good faith. The leading case involving this requirement is Surowitz v. Hilton Hotels Corp. (S.Ct.1966), holding that a complaint in a derivative suit verified by the plaintiff should not be dismissed merely because the plaintiff did not understand the specific allegations in the complaint.

A verification requirement appeared in the 1984 MBCA (1984) but was eliminated by the 1990 amendments to that Act after doubt was expressed that a verification requirement was a meaningful check against unjustified litigation.

§ 16.10 Resolution of Derivative Litigation by Board Committees

Early derivative litigation cases established that a committee of the board of directors could act on behalf of the board to resolve derivative litigation brought by a shareholder involving only enforcement of claims against unrelated third parties. Evaluation of such claims appears to involve only business judgment since by definition no director or corporate officer is involved and the decision relates only to business relationships and presumably a natural desire on the part of the board to recover on valid claims.

Gall v. Exxon Corporation (S.D.N.Y.1976) was the first case to authorize a committee composed entirely of directors unrelated to the transaction to consider a derivative suit brought not against third parties but against other directors or officers of the corporation. The court relied on a case involving a suit against third parties. It rejected an argument that the committee was necessarily or inevitably involved "in a way calculated to impair their exercise of business judgment on behalf of the corporation." However, rather than permitting the derivative suit to proceed with the shareholder as plaintiff, the court scheduled a hearing on whether the committee members were in fact impartial. Prior to this decision it was generally believed that a derivative suit in which corporate directors or officers were the principal defendants could automatically be maintained by an eligible plaintiff shareholder. The concern was that even disinterested directors could not avoid being influenced by considerations of friendship or structural bias when they consider claims against co-directors and officers.

Because Delaware is the principal state of incorporation for publicly held corporations, most litigation involving derivative litigation arises in that state. Almost immediately following the *Gall* decisions, the corporate defendant in derivative litigation in Delaware used the independent litigation committee device in an effort to avoid a full-scale trial of the underlying substantive issues. Delaware courts quickly accepted the notion that a litigation committee consisting solely of disinterested and independent directors not involved in the questioned transactions had the power of an independent board of directors to dismiss litigation.

In a series of important decisions, the Delaware Supreme Court developed a set of rules that tie the power of independent litigation committees to dismiss derivative litigation on the basis of a business judgment that pursuit of the litigation is not in the best interests of the corporation. Furthermore, scope of the power of the litigation committee depends on whether the case is classified as a demand required case or a demand futile case. A case is "demand futile" (or "demand excused") only where facts are alleged with particularity which create a reasonable doubt that the directors' action was entitled to the protections of the business judgment rule. This requires that the particularized allegations create a reasonable doubt that the directors are disinterested and independent and the challenged transaction was otherwise the product of a valid exercise of business judgment. The classic demand futile case involves a transaction in which all the directors receive a personal benefit. All other cases are "demand required" cases. The rules with respect to the two types of cases are quite different:

(1) If the case is a demand futile case, it was by definition properly brought without making a demand on the board of directors. However, the corporation may thereafter impanel a litigation committee to consider the merits of the claim. Assuming the committee recommends that the litigation not be continued, a reviewing court should first ascertain that the litigation committee was independent and free from conflict of interest, second, whether the decision appears to meet the requirements of the business judgment rule, and third, whether in the court's own "independent business judgment" the dismissal recommendation should be accepted. The last inqui-

ry is not mandatory and may be dispensed with by the court under proper circumstances.

(2) If the case is "demand required" the plaintiff must make a demand on the board of directors. If he fails to do so the case will be dismissed for failure to exhaust available remedies. Assuming that a demand is made, the decision may be referred to a litigation committee and a decision by that committee that the suit should not be pursued is protected by the business judgment rule. If the decision meets the lenient standards of that rule, there is no basis for a court to apply its "independent business judgment" or a standard of "intrinsic fairness."

Subsequent Delaware cases establish additional principles in the demand required situation. (1) If the plaintiff makes a demand on the board, that is an admission that the case is a demand required case. (2) If a demand is made and rejected, the shareholder may obtain judicial review of the rejection only if he can allege particularized facts that indicates the decision rejecting the demand was not proper, i.e. not protected by the business judgment rule. (3) In determining whether to make a demand and in appealing from a decision rejecting a demand, the plaintiff is not entitled to discovery. He must formulate his particularized factual allegations on the basis of the "tools at hand" that permit a shareholder to secure limited information from the corporation. The principal "tool at hand" is the statutory right to inspect books and records. See chapter 19 of this Nutshell.

There is no question but that the development of these rules in Delaware has dramatically changed the handling of derivative litigation. Plaintiffs do not make demands; to do so is to concede control over the plaintiff's case to an unfriendly litigation committee. A Chancery Court decision dismissing a case for failing to make a demand is appealed to the Delaware

Supreme Court on the basis of a record that contains limited information about the background of the transaction and the merits of the claim. If the Supreme Court affirms the Chancery Court conclusion that demand was required, the case is over. If it concludes that demand was excused, the parties have a strong incentive to settle. It is perhaps no surprise that this Delaware procedure is widely viewed as being extremely favorable to defendants.

The litigation committee experience in Delaware has caused a rethinking of the desirability of the "demand futile" exception. In 1989 the Model Business Corporation Act (1984) was amended to make a demand a universal prerequisite for all derivative suits; the American Law Institute's Corporate Governance Project takes essentially the same position. In both of these codifications, the issue of the standard of review of dismissal recommendations is divorced from the demand requirement itself though the Model Act appears to accept a pure business judgment rule standard while the Corporate Governance Project assumes some level of review of the substance of the committee's decision.

Several state courts have also had occasion to consider the litigation committee approach to terminating derivative suits. Most of these cases accept the basic principle that independent litigation committees may resolve derivative suits involving officers and directors of the corporation. These opinions, however, appear to contemplate greater review of the reasonableness of the decision of the litigation committee than is contemplated by the Delaware cases.

§ 16.11   Defenses in a Derivative Suit

Defenses in derivative suits may be grouped into three broad categories. One category involves alleged failure to comply with requirements peculiar to such suits. A failure to make a demand on the directors, or a failure to post security when required to do so under the applicable security-for-expenses statute, for example, will result in the dismissal of the suit. A second category of defenses are those that would be available to the third party defendants if the corporation had sued directly on the claim that is the underlying basis of the derivative suit. If the action is barred by the statute of limitations or statute of frauds, for example, the derivative suit based on the same claim is also barred. Presumably, such defenses may only be raised by the third party defendants, not the corporate defendant. Somewhat similarly, a defense based on ratification of the transaction by directors or shareholders may be available if the transaction is voidable rather than void, or if it arguably falls within the ordinary business judgment of the directors.

Derivative suits basically involve two separate claims: the substantive claim by the corporation against a third person and the claim by the shareholder that he or she should be permitted to represent or champion the corporation. The particular category of defense may go to one claim or the other with quite different consequences. Laches, for example, may bar some shareholders but not others from acting as plaintiff. If the plaintiff shareholder actually participated in the wrongful transaction, or assented to it, she may be estopped from questioning the transaction. Shares owned by that person are called "tainted shares" or "dirty stock" and innocent transferees of such shares may be estopped from questioning the transaction. (Such a transferee may also be barred from maintaining suit under the contemporaneous ownership requirement.)

§ 16.12　Private Settlement of Derivative Suits

A recovery in a derivative suit is usually payable to the corporation rather than to individual shareholders on a pro rata basis. This principle normally protects fully the interests of shareholders and creditors alike, and does not involve the court in making a business judgment as to whether corporate funds should be distributed to some or all of the shareholders, or reserved for creditors.

If an individual wrongdoer is also a shareholder, a corporate recovery permits that wrongdoer to share in the recovery. In a few instances, courts have been persuaded to grant some shareholders a pro rata recovery in order to limit the recovery to "innocent" shareholders. For example, in Perlman v. Feldmann (2d Cir.1955), a control premium paid to a former controlling shareholder was held to be recoverable in the derivative suit but it was made payable to the non-selling shareholders pro rata on the theory that it was improper for the persons presently in control (who had paid the control premium to the defendants) to share in the recovery. Similarly, if the corporation is controlled by the wrongdoers, the court may order a pro rata recovery by the innocent shareholders on the theory that it is improper to permit the funds recovered to revert immediately to the control of the wrongdoers. Such situations, however, are uncommon, and a pro rata payment to innocent shareholders is therefore the exception rather than the rule. Part of the problem is that a pro rata recovery may create logical and practical problems. In the Perlman case, for example, the pro rata recovery by non-selling shareholders creates the possibility that the persons presently in control may themselves resell at a premium and then argue that the remaining shareholders have already been compensated for the loss of the control premium and should not be permitted to question the propriety of the second sale.

§ 16.13   Res Judicata Effect of Derivative Suits

A resolution of a derivative suit on the merits is *res judicata* and precludes other derivative suits on the same claim on the theory that the suit is brought on behalf of the corporation. In this respect, derivative litigation differs from other types of class litigation in which individual shareholders may opt out of the class. A court-approved settlement ordinarily has the same effect as a final judgment on the merits, though problems may arise as to whether shareholders are bound if they were not notified of the proposed settlement. In some situations, the court may order that notice be given to all other shareholders before a derivative action is settled or disposed of voluntarily. Such action may then be continued by intervening shareholders, if any appear.

The *res judicata* effect of a dismissal of a derivative suit depends on the reason for the dismissal. A voluntary dismissal, or a dismissal because the plaintiff shareholder is not a proper plaintiff (e.g., for not being a contemporaneous owner or for not posting security-for-expenses) does not bind the remaining shareholders. On the other hand, a dismissal on the merits will normally be given full *res judicata* effect.

[For unfamiliar terms see the Glossary]

CHAPTER SEVENTEEN

CLASS ACTIONS UNDER FEDERAL SECURITIES ACTS

§ 17.1 Securities Class Actions in General

This chapter deals with direct class actions brought by shareholders against publicly held corporations, their officers, directors, auditors or attorneys. Chapter 16 deals with derivative litigation in which the shareholder sues on behalf of a corporation on a corporate claim. This chapter deals with direct suits by shareholders on behalf of a class of shareholders similarly situated for an alleged wrong committed by the corporation. Many of the problems discussed in chapter 16 with respect to entrepreneurial attorneys and "strike suits" are also common in securities class actions.

The most common type of modern securities class action involves a claim that the corporation in one or more of its public statements knowingly made false or misleading statements that had an adverse effect on the price of the corporation's securities. As a result all shareholders who bought or sold shares in reliance on the price influenced by the false or misleading statements were injured by the false or misleading statements. These class action suits are usually brought under rule 10b–5, promulgated under the Securities Exchange Act of 1934. See §§ 14.27–14.35 of this Nutshell. They may also claim a violation of rule 14a–9 promulgated under the same statute if the false or misleading statements appear in proxy solicitation documents. See § 13.24 of this Nutshell.

There is a widespread belief that securities class actions of the type described above are primarily brought by entrepreneurial attorneys in order to obtain a negotiated settlement and a large fee. Congress has largely accepted this characterization of such actions. This is revealed by the enactment of two statutes: the "Private Securities Litigation Reform Act of 1995," ("PSLRA") and the "Securities Litigation Uniform Standards Act of 1998" ("SLUSA"). PSLRA was vetoed by President Clinton but his veto was overridden by Congress; SLUSA was signed into law by the President. This chapter specifically addresses these developments which are certainly a major, if not a radical, change in rules relating to securities litigation.

It is important to recognize that today the law of securities class actions for fraud is subject to federal standards established by PSLRA and that most state court actions for securities fraud have been preempted by SLUSA. See § 17.16.

§ 17.2   SEC Disclosure Requirements and the "Safe Harbor"

The SEC has long required corporations registered under section 12 of the Securities Exchange Act routinely to make public financial and other information about their activities. Periodic quarterly and annual disclosure is required as well as immediate disclosure of significant events affecting the issuer. These disclosure requirements are often referred to as creating a "goldfish bowl" atmosphere for publicly held corporations.

Prior to 1979, the SEC's general policy was to restrict disclosure to "hard" factual information of a historical character. However, it should be apparent that from the standpoint of investors forward looking information and projections are much more useful than purely historical data. In 1979, the SEC amended its disclosure policy to encourage dissemination of "soft" data, including projections of financial data, discussion of management objectives and goals for future performance, discussion of economic trends affecting the business, and information about the assumptions underlying the projections.

Because there is an obvious risk that projections and forward looking information might not in fact be borne out by events, the SEC at the same time adopted a "safe harbor" provision protecting issuers from liability. The original safe harbor protected projections and forward looking information except those that were "made or reaffirmed without a reasonable basis or disclosed other than in good faith."

Nevertheless, corporations were reluctant to make use of this freedom. Shortly thereafter, the SEC imposed a new requirement on issuers to prepare a "Management's Discussion and Analysis of Financial Condition and Results of Operations" (usually abbreviated as the "MD & A") each year. The MD & A regulations require management to make a frank assessment of its expectations for the short-term future and the factors that affect the ability of the business to meet those expectations.

As a result there is today a steady flow of forward-looking information from publicly held corporations that is publicly available and widely disseminated through financial services, newsletters, newspapers, brokers, analysts, and advisers.

An important additional factor is that in the 1980s and 1990s many high technology companies have registered and sold their securities to the investing public. The shares of these companies have tended to be very volatile and sharp fluctuations in price occur regularly. Companies in these developing industries have particularly complained about class actions being filed following a substantial unexpected variation in the price of their securities. It is in this environment that the class action litigation "crisis" was viewed, and which gave rise to legislative correction.

§ 17.3   The Growth of Class Action Securities Litigation

The basic elements of a securities fraud claim under rule 10b–5 are (1) a misstatement or omission, (2) that is material in that a reasonable person would attach significance to it in deciding whether to make or dispose of an investment, (3) made with scienter, and (4) causes injury to a plaintiff who relied upon the misstatement or omission.

Class action proceedings became practical on a broad scale for rule 10b–5 cases because of the "fraud on the market" rule. This rule makes it unnecessary to establish that each plaintiff specifically or individually relied on a specific misrepresentation or even that she was aware of the statement when she entered into a securities transaction. The "fraud on the market" rule is based on the premise that an investor trading in an "efficient market" may rely on the price established in the market as being set by free market forces unaffected by fraud or misstatements. In Basic Inc. v. Levinson (S.Ct.1988), a sharply divided Court concluded by a plurality vote that a rebuttable presumption exists that each investor relies on the accuracy of the going market price in deciding whether to buy or sell. From this presumption it follows that if a securities price was influenced by false statements, the investor necessarily has relied on those statements and was injured by them.

The growth and cost of securities fraud litigation based on the fraud on the market theory became an increasing concern to corporate managers, particularly "high tech" companies. Not surprisingly, members of Congress with companies in their districts were sympathetic to the complaint that much securities litigation under the fraud on the market theory had become a form of high level extortion. This led to the enactment of PSLRA in 1995.

The Committee Report proposing the 1995 legislation described a typical modern securities class action as involving "a high-growth, high-tech company that has performed well for many quarters, but ultimately misses analysts' expectations." Whenever an announcement is made that causes an unexpected change in stock prices, securities fraud actions are filed "immediately" complaining that some group of defendants "knew or should have known" about the negative information, and which should have been disclosed earlier. Both the corporation and individual defendants are named as defendants. The individual defendants have "deep pockets" and the damages sought amount to hundreds of millions of dollars based on estimates of the aggregate market loss suffered by all shareholders who traded during the period. The plaintiff shareholders themselves own only a few shares and many of them are " 'professional plaintiffs' " who work with the same law firm and file many complaints each year. The leading plaintiff law firms keep a "stable of professional plaintiffs" that permit suits to be filed within hours after the news of a stock price decline and with no evidence of actual wrongdoing, using complaints that allege fraud, "while citing a laundry list of cookie-cutter complaints."

The House Report continues by stating that in "the typical case" the court refuses to dismiss the complaint, "triggering the costly discovery process, and imposing massive costs on the defendant who possesses the bulk of the relevant information." Discovery requests are very broadly phrased and require the production of millions of pages of material as well as e-mail messages and other information stored on computers.

The cost of answering discovery requests is usually the largest single defense cost.

The costs of prosecuting the plaintiffs' claim are advanced by the plaintiff's law firm. As the costs of discovery rise, the pressure to settle "becomes enormous," and as a result of the settlement, "the plaintiffs' lawyers take one third of the settlement, and the rest is distributed to the members of the class, resulting in pennies of return for each individual plaintiff. There is no adjudication of the merits of the case."

While this picture may be overdrawn, it was the picture presented to the Congress that led to the enactment of PSLRA.

§ 17.4 Original Judicial Response to "New Era" Class Actions

Rule 10b–5 litigation is within the exclusive jurisdiction of the federal courts. As class action securities litigation grew, the federal courts exhibited increased impatience with suits that appeared to involve "cookie cutter" allegations and were filed within minutes after the facts were made public. This led to three developments:

First, both District Courts and Courts of Appeals appeared to be more willing to dismiss hastily filed complaints on motions to dismiss.

Second, rule 9(b) of the Federal Rules requires allegations of fraud to be plead "with particularity." Case law in the Second Circuit required not only that the plaintiff state facts with particularity but also these facts must give rise to a "strong inference" that the defendant's intent was fraudulent.

Third, circuits adopted a "bespeaks caution" principle that prevents reliance on forward looking statements (such as a forecast, projection, or statement regarding expectations of future performance) if the document includes sufficient cautionary warning statements that the investment was risky and results not guaranteed.

Nevertheless, these developments did not stem the flow of class action litigation, and in 1995 Congress acted by overruling the presidential veto of PSLRA.

§ 17.5   The Private Securities Litigation Reform Act of 1995

Serious efforts to curb private securities litigation began in about 1992, pushed primarily by major accounting firms and later joined by dozens of business corporations. However, these bills went nowhere until the Republican victories in the 1994 off-year election.

The PSLRA makes numerous substantive amendments to the Federal securities laws and includes a number of innovative provisions. The following sections summarize only the most important provisions of this complex litigation. Special provisions relating to the liability of issuers under the Securities Act of 1933 and RICO are omitted.

§ 17.6   PSLRA Class Action Provisions

PSLRA contains a number of provisions relating to "professional" and "lead" plaintiffs. Every lead plaintiff must file a sworn and certified statement that he has reviewed and authorized the filing and that he did not purchase securities at the direction of counsel or to qualify him to act as a plaintiff. Generally, a lead plaintiff may not serve as such more than three times in the previous five years. Restrictions are also placed on the compensation that a lead plaintiff may receive: his compensation generally may not exceed his proportionate share of any recovery, but he may be compensated for additional work and effort.

The general practice of allowing the first to file to serve as the lead plaintiff is discouraged. Within 20 days after filing, the plaintiff must give notice to all members of the class, identify the principal claims, and inform class members that they may move to serve as the lead plaintiff. In addition, courts are directed to select the lead plaintiff based on a presumption that the plaintiff with the "largest financial stake" should be selected. The intention was to encourage institutional investors to serve as lead plaintiff, though it is questionable whether these investors will desire to serve in that capacity. A recent study shows that institutional investors agreed to serve as lead plaintiff in only 9 of the 175 cases in 1997.

Class counsel is to be selected by the lead plaintiff. Attorneys who own shares of the class may be disqualified from serving as class counsel. A cap is also placed on attorney's fees that may be paid to class counsel. The amount is to be based on a reasonable percentage of the amount of damages and prejudgment interest recovered. Amounts paid to the corporation pursuant to disgorgement proceedings brought by the SEC may not be "dipped into" to pay or calculate the fee to be paid the class counsel.

§ 17.7   New Safe Harbor Provisions for Forward Looking Statements

The law prior to PSLRA contained two safe harbor provisions for forward looking statements: (1) the SEC's rule adopted in 1979 that protected statements made on a reasonable basis and in good faith, and (2) the judicially created "bespeaks caution" principle, some form of which had been adopted by most courts of appeals. The legislative history of PSLRA suggests that Congress believed that these protections were not sufficient and that issuers tended to say as little as possible about future predictions and forecasts. As a result PSLRA crafts a new statutory safe harbor provision that broadens the preexisting doctrines.

The statutory safe harbor is a bifurcated test. Branch one protects persons from liability for misrepresentations or omissions in forward-looking statements if they are (i) identified as forward-looking, and (ii) accompanied by "meaningful cautionary statements" identifying important factors that could cause results to differ materially from those protected in the statement. The cautionary statements must convey substantive information about factors that realistically could cause operating results to differ materially from projected results. "Important" factors are those that are relevant to the forward-looking statement and could actually affect the ability of the issuer to achieve the results predicted. The legislative history suggests that safe harbor protection should be available even though *all* important factors are not listed or even though the list does not include the factor that actually caused the results not to be realized. An *oral* forward-looking statement is protected by the safe harbor if it is identified as a forward-looking statement and it is stated that results may differ materially from the statement; it is not necessary to identify orally "important factors" if they are described in a readily available document.

Branch two of the statutory safe harbor test looks at the mind-set of the person making the forward-looking statement rather than the statement itself. A person is protected by the statutory safe harbor unless the plaintiff can show that the person made the statement with actual knowledge that it was false or misleading.

Several legislators voiced concern that the inter-relationship between these two branches might confer immunity from liability even for intentionally fraudulent forward-looking statements. The literal language of the section does not exclude this possibility, though one leading legislator supporting the bill stated that it does not give a "license to lie."

Several classes of securities transactions are entirely exempted from the safe harbor provisions, including going private transactions, partnership roll-ups, and other types of transactions that the Securities and Exchange Commission had found to involve numerous violations of the securities laws.

§ 17.8 PSLRA Discovery Provisions

As described above, excessive discovery costs were viewed as an important reason that compels defendant corporations to accept settlements even though the complaint may be without merit or frivolous. PSLRA addresses this concern by providing that courts must stay all discovery pending a ruling on a motion to dismiss except in exceptional situations where particularized discovery is necessary to preserve evidence that might otherwise be lost. At the same time, PSLRA makes it unlawful for any person named as a defendant to willfully destroy relevant evidence.

If the issue whether a forward-looking statement is protected by the statutory safe harbor provision (see § 17.7 of this Nutshell), a court must stay discovery (other than discovery directly related to the application of the safe harbor provision) until the issue of safe harbor protection is resolved.

§ 17.9   PSLRA Proportionate Liability Provisions

Most securities class actions involve multiple defendants. The current rule is that defendants are jointly and severally liable, so that each defendant who is found liable is automatically fully responsible for the entire judgment even though his conduct may have made only a minor contribution to the total loss. Congress believed this rule contributed to the negative aspects of securities class actions for three reasons. First, it encouraged plaintiffs to name as defendants as many persons with "deep pockets" as possible, including attorneys, auditors, underwriters, and directors. Second, it was wildly unfair because if a single defendant was found to be 1% liable he could be forced to pay 100% of the damages. Third, it contributed to settlements of marginal or groundless class actions because of the risk to deep pocket defendants of being exposed to liability for grossly disproportionate damages. Concern was also expressed that unlimited exposure had a chilling effect on the willingness of capable people to serve as directors of publicly held corporations.

PSLRA adopts several highly innovative provisions ameliorating the rules of traditional joint and several liability. It creates a distinction between "knowing violations" and all other violations. A person who commits a knowing violation has full joint and several liability while all other persons are subject to a new regime of "proportionate liability" discussed below. A "knowing violation" consists of making a material misrepresentation with actual knowledge that the statement is false and that persons are likely to rely on the information. Recklessness is not "knowing" behavior.

Defendants who are found liable but who have not engaged in knowing violations are liable only for the portion of damages that are attributable to their conduct. The jury is to be instructed to decide what each defendant's percentage of responsibility is, considering the nature of that person's conduct and its causal relationship to the damages caused. There are, however, two qualifications:

First, all defendants continue to be jointly and severally liable to plaintiffs whose damages are in excess of 10% of their net worth and their net worth is less than $200,000. Investors who may benefit from this exception are viewed as small, unsophisticated, and in need of special protection under the securities law. The legislative history indicates that $200,000 was chosen to ensure that the majority of investors would not be affected by the proportionate liability principle.

Second, defendants who have not engaged in knowing violations may also be called upon to pay an additional amount up to 50% of their personal liability to make up any shortfall in the plaintiff's recovery due to insolvency of other defendants. Defendants who settle before the verdict or judgment are not subject to this additional "anteing up" requirement to cover claims against insolvent defendants.

§ 17.10 PSLRA Settlement Provisions

Before a settlement agreement can be finalized, notice of the terms of the settlement must be given to all members of the class. The basic terms and other critical information about the settlement must appear in summary form on the cover page of the notice.

PSLRA provides that settlement agreements may not be filed under seal unless a party shows that "direct and substantial" harm, including reputational harm, would result from the open filing of the agreement.

§ 17.11 PSLRA Fee Shifting Provisions

Congress actively debated the desirability of adopting a "loser pays" structure in PSLRA as a device to discourage the filing of ungrounded or frivolous suits. In the end, Congress strengthened the application of Rule 11 of the Federal Rules of Civil Procedure, but did not impose a general fee shifting requirement.

PSLRA requires the court at the conclusion of a case to make specific findings as to whether counsel for both sides complied with all aspects of rule 11(c). If not, there is a presumption that sanctions should be imposed unless the violation is *de minimis.* However, the sanctions imposed on the plaintiff and the defendant for violations of rule 11 are not the same. The sanction to be imposed on the plaintiff is payment of all attorneys fees and costs incurred by the defendants. Sanctions to be imposed on the defendant are those specified by rule 11(b), which typically is limited to reasonable attorneys' fees incurred as a direct result of the violation. This disparate treatment appears to have been intended specifically to deter filings by plaintiffs in doubtful cases.

The court may require any party or attorney representing a party to post a bond to ensure that the person will be able to respond to a sanction that is imposed. The legislative history suggests that the bond requirement should usually be imposed on the plaintiff's counsel rather than on the plaintiff himself. Again this appears to have been intended specifically to deter filings by plaintiffs in doubtful cases.

§ 17.12   PSLRA Pleading Provisions

Rule 9(b) of the Federal Rules of Civil Procedure requires allegations of fraud to be made "with particularity." Prior to PSLRA and SLUSA, courts of appeals adopted varying standards as to how this requirement should be construed. The Second Circuit adopted the strongest standard, requiring allegations of fact "giving rise to a strong inference of fraudulent intent" on the part of the defendant. The First Circuit adopted a less stringent test, requiring the complaint to set forth specific facts making "it reasonable to believe" that the defendant knew that the statement was materially false or misleading. The Ninth Circuit stated that the "with particularity" requirement was satisfied merely by alleging specifically that scienter existed, arguing that the rule only requires particularity in the ultimate allegation and nowhere requires allegations to support inferences. The test set forth by the Second Circuit is usually referred to as the "strong inference" test while the test of the First Circuit is described as a "some inference" test.

PSLRA requires the allegation of scienter in a complaint to "state with particularity facts giving rise to a strong inference that the defendant acted with the required state of mind." There are indications in the legislative history that Congress intended this standard to be more stringent in some undefined way than the standard required by the Second Circuit. There are also indications in the legislative history that Congress did not intend to eliminate a cause of action for recklessness

PSLRA also contains other detailed pleading provisions. The plaintiff must specify each statement alleged to be misleading and the reason or reasons why the statement is misleading. If the allegation is made on information and belief, all information on which the belief is formed must be pleaded. However, rather surprisingly, the legislative history states that "[b]ecause the Conference Committee intends to strengthen existing pleading requirements, it does not intend to codify the Second Circuit's case law interpreting this pleading standard." A footnote appended to this statement adds that "[f]or this reason, the Conference Report chose not to include in the pleading standard certain language relating to motive, opportunity, or recklessness."

A plaintiff must also allege and prove that the misstatement "actually caused" the loss incurred by the plaintiff, though this may be shown if the plaintiff can prove the price at which he bought the stock was artificially inflated as a result of the misstatement.

Since the enactment of PSLRA there have been several opinions by courts of appeal establishing varying (and to some extent inconsistent) principles for pleading under PSLRA. It is likely that this issue will ultimately be addressed by the Supreme Court.

§ 17.13   PSLRA Damage Provisions

Estimates of damages in securities fraud class actions are usually based on the difference between the purchase price and the price of the security on the date the corrective information is disseminated to the market. The legislative history suggests that this method of calculation often overstates the actual damages caused by the misstatement.

PSLRA provides that damages should be calculated as the difference between the purchase price and the mean trading price of the security during the 90–day period after dissemination of the information correcting the misstatement, except that if the plaintiff sells the security during that 90–day period the price that should be used is the actual selling price.

The mean trading price is defined as the average of the closing prices of the security during the 90–day period.

§ 17.14   PSLRA Aiding and Abetting Provisions

In Central Bank of Denver v. First Interstate Bank (S.Ct. 1994), the Supreme Court held that rule 10b–5 did not authorize private suits against aiders and abettors. This ruling was surprising in that the Court on its motion directed that this issue be argued, and the decision was inconsistent with literally hundreds of decisions by the lower federal courts.

PSLRA reinstates aiding and abetting liability in suits brought by the Securities and Exchange Commission but does not reinstate it on behalf of private parties.

§ 17.15   PSLRA Auditor Disclosure Provisions

An innovative provision of PSLRA imposes new duties on independent public auditors. The general position of the auditing profession is that the discovery of fraud is not the central goal of outside auditors; rather, fraud should be detected by internal controls and internal audits. The role of outside auditors is to assure fidelity to generally accepted accounting principles and generally accepted auditing standards in the development of financial reports and financial statements.

PSLRA mandates a role for outside auditors in the detection of fraud. Audits by independent public accountants must include procedures designed to provide reasonable assurance of detecting illegal acts that would have a direct impact on the determination of financial statement amounts. In addition, procedures must be adopted that permit the identification of transactions with related parties that are material. Finally, procedures must be established that permit an evaluation of the issuer's ability to continue as a going concern. The power of the SEC to modify generally accepting auditing standards where necessary to effectuate these procedures is expressly confirmed.

The new statute also imposes a series of reporting requirements on the auditor who discovers fraud or illegal action. If an auditor detects or becomes aware of conduct that may be illegal (whether or not it is believed to be material), he must report that information to the appropriate level of management of the issuer and assure that the board of directors or the audit committee is provided with adequate information about the conduct (unless the act is "clearly" inconsequential). If the effect of the action is material, or if the senior management does not take timely remedial action when the failure to take such action would warrant action, the auditor must report its conclusions to the board of directors.

The board of directors upon receiving a report of illegal action must notify the SEC within one business day. A copy of this notice must also be given to the auditor; if the auditor does not receive this notice he must either resign or directly notify the SEC of the apparent failure of the board to take action. If he resigns, he must notify the SEC of that action and the reason therefor.

Auditors have no personal liability in private suits for failing to comply with these requirements. However, the SEC is specifically authorized to impose civil penalties on auditors who willfully fail to comply with these reporting requirements.

§ 17.16 The Securities Litigation Uniform Standards Act of 1998 (SLUSA)

The impact of PSLRA on securities fraud litigation is a classic example of the law of unintended consequences in action. After an initial decline in the number of newly filed securities class actions (while lawyers evaluated the new statute), plaintiffs' lawyers promptly found ways to avoid the impact of PSLRA. Indeed, following the initial decline, the number of new securities fraud cases filed increased significantly. There was a pronounced trend toward filing class actions in state courts under state blue sky or antifraud statutes. Filing suit in state courts apparently avoided PSLRA's stay on discovery, its pleading requirements, its fee shifting rules, the safe harbor for forward-looking statements, and the rules about proportionate liability. In some instances suits were filed simultaneously in state and federal courts; in these cases, discovery was pursued in state court while the federal suit remained inactive. In other cases, suit was filed only in state court apparently with the intention of filing a Federal suit at some late date. Indeed, state court litigation threatened to checkmate at the outset most of the major innovations of PSLRA.

Evidence indicated that the principal purposes of filing in state court were to avoid the stay on discovery and the more stringent pleading requirements of PSLRA. Simultaneous filing of lawsuits in state and federal courts also gave plaintiffs strategic advantages and significantly increased the problems faced by defense counsel. It is therefore not surprising that companies that originally persuaded Congress to enact PSLRA decided to go back to Congress for additional relief. The result was the enactment of the "Securities Litigation Uniform Standards Act of 1998" ("SLUSA"). Even though President Clinton had vetoed PSLRA, he decided to sign SLUSA. This new statute contains complex provisions that sharply limit recourse to state courts and is likely to have dramatic effects in the future on the roles of state and federal courts in class action litigation.

SLUSA applies to "covered securities" and "covered class actions." "Covered securities" are defined to be securities that are publicly traded on the NYSE, AMEX, and NASDAQ, while "covered class actions" are defined to be lawsuits in which more that 50 persons are actual or prospective class members and the suit involves common questions of law and fact. A covered class action may involve a suit brought in state court by a single plaintiff if other suits involving 49 other plaintiffs are pending in that state. A suit brought on behalf of an undefined class that may involve more than 50 plaintiffs is also a covered class action.

The federal preemption of state law mandated by SLUSA is set forth in 15 U.S.C. § 78bb(f)(1): "No covered class action based upon the statutory or common law of any State or subdivision thereof may be maintained in any State or Federal court by any private party alleging—

"(A) A misrepresentation or omission of a material fact in connection with the purchase or sale of a covered security; or

"(B) that the defendant used any manipulative or deceptive device or contrivance in connection with the purchase or sale of a covered security."

The critical point is that all covered class actions "based upon the statutory or common law of any State" are preempted and must be brought under Federal law in Federal courts. Other sections of SLUSA provide that a covered class action filed in state court is removable at any time to a Federal court and Federal judges are expressly authorized to stay discovery in any state court proceeding "when necessary in aid of its jurisdiction or to protect or effectuate its judgments."

The breadth of SLUSA is limited by two "carve-outs" from its exclusive coverage. The most important is the "Delaware carve-out" that has two prongs. One prong excludes from "covered class actions" suits involving breach of fiduciary duty claims arising from transactions taking place between the issuer and its securities holders. The second prong excludes cases involving breach of fiduciary duty claims arising from an issuer's recommendations or actions with respect to tender offers, freeze-outs, and mergers or other transactions requiring shareholder approval. This carve-out is limited to actions "based upon the statutory or common law of the State in which the issuer is incorporated." A second "carve-out" excludes from preemption suits in which the plaintiff is a state political subdivision. This carve-out permits suits brought by school districts, counties, cities or other local jurisdictions to continue to pursue their claims in state courts.

PSLRA and SLUSA together create an entirely new allocation of litigation responsibility between state and federal courts. Coupled with NMSIA (which preempts most traditional state blue sky regulation) these statutes significantly increase the exclusive jurisdiction of federal courts and correspondingly limit traditional state court involvement in securities regulation. The precise dimensions of this increased federal role in corporation law cannot be determined at the time this is written, but it appears to be substantial. As this chapter is written in May, 2000, there are only a handful of federal district court decisions construing SLUSA. However, academic writers have not hesitated to speculate about these changed relationships. See, for example, Thompson, Preemption and Federalism in Corporate Governance: Protecting Shareholder Rights to Vote, Sell, and Sue, 62 Law & Contemp. Prob. 215 (1999); Levine and Pritchard, The Securities Litigation Uniform Standards Act of 1998: The Sun Sets on California's Blue Sky Laws, 54 Bus.Law. 1 (1998).

CHAPTER EIGHTEEN

DIVIDENDS, DISTRIBUTIONS, AND REDEMPTIONS

§ 18.1 Cash or Property Dividends and Distributions

The profits of a business corporation—its purpose or goal—may be accumulated by the corporation or paid out, in whole or in part, in the form of dividends. The decision whether or not to pay dividends generally rests in the discretion of the board of directors of the corporation.

The dividend policy of a corporation depends in part on whether the corporation is publicly or closely held. In publicly held corporations, dividends are usually paid on a periodic basis, in amounts that remain stable from period to period. Stability of dividend policy is maintained by such corporations because frequent changes—and certainly any downward change—is interpreted by investors as indicating that the corporation has financial difficulties. Unpleasant surprises should be avoided. Many corporations maintain a stable dividend even though current earnings are not sufficient to support the dividend in the hope that operations will improve in the future. Public shareholders, without effective voice in the management of the business, may look in part to the history of dividends by the corporation to determine whether to purchase shares of the corporation. Probably greater attention, however, is paid to the prospects of dividends in the future and to the hope that the market price of the shares will rise (which itself may be a function of the business prospects of the corporation).

The term "dividend" refers to distributions of earnings; where a distribution of capital (which may be in partial liquidation of the business of the corporation or simply a distribution of excess capital not needed in current operations) is made, the term "distribution" is more accurate than "dividend," though this usage is not uniform—e.g. it is not uncommon to refer to a "liquidating dividend" rather than a "liquidating distribution." The MBCA (1984) does not use the word "dividend." Section 1.40(6) defines "distribution" to include all distributions of assets or debt by corporations to their shareholders on account of their shares without regard to their source. Also, as described below (see § 18.6 of this Nutshell), the Model Act provides a single test for the validity of all distributions. Statutes of many states, however, do establish different tests for determining the legality of distributions of current retained earnings on the one hand, and distributions of capital on the other.

Most discussions of dividends classify them into three categories: cash dividends, dividends-in-kind or property dividends, and share dividends (discussed in the following section). Cash and property dividends are true distributions by the corporation of assets or property whereas a share dividend is not. A cash dividend—the most common—as the name implies, pays cash (from legally available funds) to the shareholders in proportion to their holdings. The amount may be expressed either as so many cents or dollars per share or as a percentage of the par or stated value of the shares. A property dividend is a division of assets other than cash of the declaring corporation among the shareholders. For obvious reasons, the property so divided is usually fungible; it may consist, for example, of shares of a subsidiary corporation or of a corporation in which the declaring corporation has an investment, or undivided fractional interests in an asset or a fund. Corporations also may pay property dividends in the form of new debt instruments creating corporate obligations.

Most publicly held corporations that pay cash dividends do so on a quarterly or semi-annual basis. Such dividends are referred to as "regular" dividends. A "special" dividend is a one-shot, non-recurring payment that cannot be counted on to be paid again in a following year. Most property dividends are special dividends. A special dividend that accompanies the payment of a regular dividend is called an "extra."

An informal or irregular payment may be a "dividend" for some purposes. For example, excessive payments in the form of salary, rent, or interest may be treated as a dividend for tax purposes. Such payments, of course, usually will not be proportional to share holdings.

§ 18.2   Share Dividends and Share Splits

A share dividend distributes additional shares of the corporation among its shareholders. A share dividend is not a true dividend since no cash or property leaves the corporation; a distribution of additional shares does not reduce the real worth of the corporation or increase the real worth of the shareholder. Rather, a share dividend increases the number of ownership units outstanding without decreasing the corporation's assets. Share dividends, however, often adversely affect the rights of other classes of shares. A distribution of common shares to common shareholders does not affect the interest of any senior class of shares: the residual ownership is simply divided up into a larger number of units. The same may not be true of distributions of senior securities, since the increased number of shares may lead to a larger preferential right to cash or property dividends or a larger preference on liquidation, thereby adversely affecting the interests of holders of more junior securities.

Share dividends are usually paid to holders of the same class of shares: Additional common shares are distributed to the common shareholders and, less commonly, additional preferred shares are distributed to the preferred shareholders. However, this is not necessarily so; holders of common shares may receive a dividend in the form of preferred shares, or vice versa. Such interclass distributions almost always affect the interests of holders of both classes of shares.

Consider the practice of many publicly held corporations of declaring annual share dividends rather than paying cash dividends. Such dividends do not affect the aggregate assets of liabilities of the corporation. If a shareholder receiving such a dividend sells the new shares, she may view the transaction as involving essentially the same thing as a cash dividend, since she owns the same number of shares as before and has, in addition, the cash received from the sale of the new shares. However, the shareholder who sells the new shares thereafter owns a slightly smaller percentage of the enterprise than she owned before the dividend (since the number of outstanding shares has increased by the number of new shares distributed). The dilution in such situations may be so slight as to be unimportant. But it is nevertheless a dilution. It is surprising that many people apparently are unaware that a share dividend is unlike property or cash dividends in this regard.

Where shares are publicly traded, a share dividend, other things being equal, will reduce the market price for each share proportionately; however, other things usually are not equal, and other factors may cause a price change that masks the decline attributable to the dividend. If no decline occurs, a small shareholder may sell his or her dividend shares for cash and yet have a diluted investment with undiminished market value.

A share dividend is often expressed as a ratio. Thus, a 20 percent dividend means that a shareholder receives a 20 percent increase—one additional share for each five shares held; a shareholder who owns less than five shares or a number of shares not divisible by five, will receive either a fractional share or "scrip," or at the election of the directors the fair value of the fractional share in cash. [MBCA (1984) § 6.04] "Scrip" differs from fractional shares in that it grants no voting or dividend rights; it represents merely the right to a fraction of a full share that may be bought or sold so that a full share may be assembled. Fractional shares may also be created in other ways as well.

A share "dividend" and a share "split" are closely related. Indeed, a dividend can be readily envisioned as a small split. In states with par value statutes, however, these transactions are accounted for differently in the capital accounts of the corporation. A share dividend results in the transfer of an amount equal to the par value of the shares being transferred from earned surplus (or some other surplus) to stated capital and increases that account by the par value of the new shares. A "split" on the other hand simply divides the shares into a greater number of shares and reduces proportionally the par value of those shares so that there is no change in the aggregate stated capital of the corporation. MBCA (1984) and states that have eliminated the concept of par value generally do not distinguish between share dividends and splits. However, this distinction is recognized by the New York Stock Exchange in its *Listed Company Manual* which requires more realistic accounting treatment than provided in the corporation statutes. The *Manual* defines a "stock dividend" as the distribution of less than 25 per cent of the outstanding shares (calculated before the distribution) while a "stock split" is a distribution of 100 per cent or more of the outstanding shares. Distributions of between 25 per cent and 100 per cent are called "partial stock splits." The *Manual* also requires the capitalization of the full market value of share dividends (rather than merely the par value) but not of stock splits and warns against the use of the word "dividend" in connection with splits or partial stock splits.

A practical difference between share dividends and share splits may also exist in connection with the adjustment of dividend rates on shares on which a dividend or split has been announced. Since cash dividend rates are usually not adjusted following a share dividend, such a dividend increases slightly the effective rate of dividend pay-outs. In other words, the dividend rate remains the same but the total number of shares against which that rate is applied has been increased. The dividend rate is usually adjusted in a share split; for example, if a share of a corporation which regularly pays dividends of $1.00 per share is split two-for-one (i.e. each holder of 100 shares receives a certificate for another 100 shares and now owns 200 shares in all), the dividend on the split shares may be set at $0.55 cents per share, or an effective rate on the old shares of $1.10.

Shares may be split by publicly held corporations in order to keep the trading price within its historical range, or to broaden the market for the shares by decreasing the cost of a round lot for trading purposes. The New York Stock Exchange *Listed Company Manual* lists these as among the justifiable reasons for a corporation to split its shares.

§ 18.3 Distributions of Rights or Warrants

"Rights" or "warrants" are simply options to purchase additional shares at a price usually (through not invariably) below the current market price of the shares. Most "rights" are short lived (usually a period of weeks at the most); where they remain in effect for longer periods they are usually called "warrants." Rights or warrants when distributed to shareholders are also not true dividends, though they may be so regarded by recipients. The effect of a distribution of rights or warrants in proportion to existing shareholdings is that a shareholder must add new capital to the enterprise in order to retain his or her relative ownership interest in the corporation. Rights or warrants issued by publicly held corporations are themselves traded and often listed on securities exchanges, the price fluctuating with the price of the underlying shares. A shareholder who sells rights or warrants distributed as a "dividend" thereby dilutes slightly his or her proportionate interest in the corporation.

The price at which rights or warrants may be exercised is called the "strike price." The value of rights or warrants that are issued with a strike price below the current market price is based on two variables: the inherent value reflected by the difference between the market and strike price and the time value that reflects the possibility that the market price of the underlying shares will rise during the life of the right or warrant. Rights or warrants that are issued with a strike price above current market price may have a time value even though they have no inherent value.

§ 18.4   Share Reacquisitions as Distributions; Treasury Shares

The acquisition by a corporation of its own shares decreases the real worth of the corporation by the amount of the consideration paid for the shares. The shares so acquired are not assets of the issuing corporation any more than authorized but unissued shares are assets. As a result, a reacquisition of shares is a type of distribution, and is included within the MBCA (1984) definition of that term. If the corporation reacquires a proportional part of the shares owned by each shareholder, the result is the equivalent of a dividend. If the reacquisition is not proportional (the normal case), the interest represented by each share in the corporation that is not reacquired is increased proportionally to the shares reacquired.

Only reacquisitions of a corporation's own shares constitute distributions. If a corporation purchases shares of another corporation, that is an investment. The difference can be readily envisioned by considering how the transactions appear on a balance sheet. A purchase of shares of another corporation affects only the asset side of the balance sheet; a corporation that purchases its own shares, however, must account for the transaction by reducing both the "asset" and "equity" sides of the balance sheet.

Under older state statutes, shares issued by a corporation that are reacquired by that corporation are called "treasury shares." Treasury shares are viewed as having an intermediate status. They are not issued shares for purposes of quorum or voting purposes or for the payment of dividends. But they are also not viewed as having been canceled: they are in limbo, in an intermediate status of being neither issued nor canceled. One unique feature of treasury shares is that they may be resold by the corporation without regard to the restrictions on original issue of shares described in an earlier Chapter. (See § 7.5 of this Nutshell.)

Obviously if treasury shares are reissued through a share dividend, the assets and relative positions of the common shareholders are unchanged; if they are resold to third persons, the assets of the corporation will be increased by the resale price and the relative voting interests of the other shareholders will be diluted. If the treasury shares are resold at a bargain price to third persons, the financial interest of the remaining shareholders will also be diluted.

MBCA (1984) does not recognize the concept of treasury shares. Section 6.31(a) provides simply that reacquired shares have the status of authorized but unissued shares. This simplification was a byproduct of the elimination of the concepts of par value, stated capital, and eligible and ineligible consideration in the Model Act.

§ 18.5   Shareholders' Rights to a Dividend

A dividend is distributable to shareholders of record on a specific date called the "record date." Record dates may be determined in the same ways as record dates are established to make determinations of eligibility to vote at meetings. (See § 9.4 of this Nutshell.) If no record date for a distribution is fixed, the record date is the date the directors authorize the distribution. [MBCA (1984) § 6.40(b)] Generally, when a dividend has been declared it becomes a debt of the corporation and cannot be rescinded or repealed by the directors.

Where shares are transferred shortly before or shortly after the record date but before the dividend is actually paid, the purchaser and seller may agree between themselves as to who is entitled to the dividend. Such an agreement, of course, is binding between the purchaser and seller but generally not binding on the corporation, which will simply pay the dividend to whoever is the record owner on the record date. The date on which payment is actually made is called the "payable date," which in the case of a publicly held corporation may be set three weeks or so after the record date. Securities exchanges have promulgated conventions or rules dealing with whether the buyer or seller of publicly held shares is entitled to dividends. The "ex-dividend" date is the first date the seller becomes entitled to keep the dividend, i.e., the date that a purchaser of the shares buys the shares without the dividend. Under New York Stock Exchange rules, shares normally are traded ex-dividend on and after the third business day before the record date for the dividend. For example, a dividend may be made payable on March 28 to shareholders of record on March 14. The stock goes ex-dividend on March 11 according to the conventions of the New York Stock Exchange. A purchaser of the shares on March 10 is entitled to the dividend; a purchaser on March 11 is not. In either event the dividend will be paid on March 28 to whoever was the record owner on March 14. In contracts for the purchase and sale of shares after the ex-dividend date, the seller retains the right to the dividend, and the amount of the dividend is not included in the contract price. Since most transactions in publicly held shares involve brokers, the purchaser or seller is not directly involved in the mechanics of transferring the amount of the dividend if it is received by a selling party to a transaction occurring before the ex-dividend date.

The theory of the ex-dividend date is that it is tied to the traditional settlement date for transactions in publicly traded securities, which historically has been five business days after the trade (T + 5). In 1996, the SEC mandated a change in the settlement date to T + 3. The ex-dividend date changed at the same time.

The price of a stock usually declines when it goes ex dividend. It may or may not decline from the previous closing price by exactly the amount of the dividend; other factors may also affect the market price simultaneously and bring about a greater or lesser change than the adjustment due to the shares going ex dividend. Where the corporation issues rights, shares go "ex-rights" on the same basis as they go ex dividend.

§ 18.6   Statutory Restrictions on the Declaration of Dividends

Statutory restrictions on the distribution of dividends are basically designed to assure that payments to shareholders are made out of current or prior earnings and not out of corporate capital. These restrictions are rarely a problem in connection with publicly traded shares, but often must be taken into account when considering the legality of distributions by smaller, closely held corporations. MBCA (1984) has developed a simple set of rules for determining the validity of distributions.

(1) *Traditional Statutes.* Restrictions are phrased in accounting terms applicable to the right hand side of the traditional balance sheet. (If this reference is unclear read § 7.6 of this Nutshell.) Unfortunately the language of traditional state statutes varies widely, and an examination of the specific statute may be necessary to ascertain whether specific payments are prohibited. State statutory provisions usually address the following issues:

(a) *Solvency.* All states provide that the payment of a dividend is prohibited if the corporation is "insolvent" or the payment of the dividend will render the corporation insolvent. "Insolvency" is usually defined in the equity sense of being unable to meet corporate obligations as they mature, though a few states define insolvency in the bankruptcy sense of corporate liabilities exceeding corporate assets. A distribution in violation of the bankruptcy test may also constitute an act of bankruptcy under the Federal Bankruptcy Act.

(b) *Surplus Test.* A number of states permit distributions to be paid from "surplus" as contrasted with "capital." Under statutes of this type, dividends usually may be paid from earned surplus and capital distributions from capital surplus without special designation of the source. The statutes of this type may be phrased in terms of prohibitions against impairment of "capital" or "capital stock," but the net effect is that the available assets may be reduced down to the minimum core of "capital" that the corporation must maintain but no lower. California has an unusual surplus test that requires assets to be maintained at least equal to one and one fourth times specified liabilities.

Randall v. Bailey (Sup.1940) raised the question whether it was permissible for directors to write up the value of appreciated assets on the books of the corporation in order to increase its dividend paying ability. In holding that it was permissible to use asset write-ups for this purpose, the court relied in part on the language of the New York statute that only prohibited dividends that "impaired capital stock."

(c) *Earned Surplus Test.* This test, adopted in earlier versions of the Model Act, permits dividends to be paid only from "earned surplus." (As described in the following section, however, these statutes also usually permit distributions from capital accounts such as capital surplus but they are not called "dividends.") In these statutes earned surplus is defined to be a composite income item determined by adding together all net profits, income, gain and losses during each accounting period going back to the original creation of the corporation with reductions for expenses, prior dividends and transfers to other accounts. It is questionable whether write-ups of the *Randall v. Bailey* type are permissible to increase earned surplus available for dividends in these states, and if written up, it is also questionable whether they may thereafter have to be written down.

(d) *Distributions From Capital.* State statutes with an "earned surplus" test often permit distributions to be made from capital accounts when there is no earned surplus. A common provision permits distributions of capital surplus to common shareholders if the articles of incorporation so provide, or with the approval of the holders of a majority of the common shares. Distributions of capital surplus to holders of cumulative preferred shares in discharge of cumulative dividend rights are generally permitted in any event. The justification for permitting cumulative dividends to be paid from capital surplus is that it permits a corporation to avoid building up preferred arrearages during the early years of operation when there may be no earned surplus. As a result, dividends may be paid to common shareholders at an earlier time and in a greater amount.

A distribution to common shareholders is permitted only if all preferential cumulative dividends have been paid, and the capital remaining in the corporation is sufficient to cover all preferential rights on liquidation.

Most statutes require payments made from capital surplus to be identified as such when made to shareholders.

(e) *Net Profits Test.* Some states permit distributions from current profits even if there is an earnings deficit from operations for prior periods. These dividends are called "nimble dividends." The leading case holding that current earnings may be distributed without being used to eliminate prior deficits is Goodnow v. American Writing Paper Co. (N.J.1908). Some states do not permit nimble dividends.

(f) *Restrictions on Surplus.* Many statutes permit dividends to be paid only from "unrestricted" earned surplus and distributions of various kinds may be made only from "unrestricted" capital surplus. Restrictions on surplus arise from the acquisition of treasury shares by the corporation. When treasury shares are acquired, the earned or capital surplus used for their acquisition is restricted so that the same surplus cannot be used again for distributions or dividends. Restrictions on surplus rather than reductions of surplus are used in this situation because the treasury shares may later be reissued, in which event the restrictions are removed *pro tanto* to the extent of the consideration received for the treasury shares. If the treasury shares are canceled, the restrictions are changed to permanent reductions in the appropriate surplus accounts.

(g) *Reduction of Stated Capital.* Statutes generally permit a corporation to reduce its stated capital simply by amending the articles of incorporation to reduce the par value of outstanding shares. Stated capital represented by "no par" shares or by amounts previously transferred from other accounts to stated capital may be reduced by a simple resolution approved by the shareholders and directors.

Provisions permitting the reduction of stated capital make it clear that the par value structure in fact provides little protection for creditors, since it is possible for the shareholders acting alone to eliminate the "cushion" reflected by stated capital without the approval of creditors.

(h) *Restrictions on Distributions by Repurchase or Redemption of Shares.* Statutory restrictions on the power of a corporation to repurchase its own shares are generally analogous to statutory restrictions on the payment of dividends. For example, they are also phrased in accounting terms applicable to the right hand side of the traditional balance sheet. They are subject to insolvency prohibitions, or, in some states, the requirement that after such purchase or redemption, the fair value of the corporation's total assets must be less than the total amount of its debts. These restrictions may create problems for closely held corporations desiring to repurchase a substantial fraction of their common shares from a retiring shareholder.

Statutes dealing with share repurchases may permit repurchases from earned surplus or from capital surplus if authorized by the articles of incorporation or a vote of shareholders. They also permit shares to be purchased from stated capital (or any other capital account) for certain limited purposes, namely:

(i) To eliminate fractional shares;

(ii) To collect or compromise indebtedness owed by or to the corporation;

(iii) To pay dissenting shareholders entitled to payment for their shares under the Act; and

(iv) To effect the purchase or redemption of its redeemable shares in accordance with the provisions of the act.

(2) *The Model Business Corporation Act (1984).* MBCA (1984) drastically revises the financial provisions described above. The provisions relating to distributions in § 6.40 apply the same tests to all types of distributions: to distributions of cash or property, to corporate reacquisitions of shares, and to less common types of distributions, such as creating evidences of indebtedness and distributing them to shareholders. No distinction is made between distributions of capital or of earnings; all distributions are subject to the same tests. Section 6.40 also provides firm answers for a number of technical questions about the lawfulness of distributions that are not covered in most existing statutes.

Section 6.40(c) sets forth a dual test for the legality of distributions of all types: after giving effect to the distribution, (a) the corporation must be "able to pay its debts as they become due in the usual course of business," and (b) the corporation's total assets must exceed its total liabilities after making provision for the liquidation preferences of senior securities. The first test is usually referred to as the "insolvency" test (since it in effect defines equity insolvency) and the second "the balance sheet" test. Both must be satisfied if the distribution is to be lawful.

The balance sheet test presupposes the use of some kind of accounting conventions to determine "assets" and "liabilities." Section 6.40(d) permits the board of directors to base a determination either on "accounting practices and principles that are reasonable in the circumstances" or on a "fair valuation or other method that is reasonable in the circumstances." Because § 6.40 is applicable to all corporations, small as well as large, it was not thought appropriate to require the use of generally accepted accounting principles or some other accounting standard that might require the employment of an accountant. The Official Comment describes in some detail what the determination of solvency requires and also points out that in making all decisions under this section, the directors are liable for an unlawful distribution only if the directors fail to meet their duty of care under § 8.30. [MBCA (1984) § 8.33]

Section 6.40(e) also describes at what time the insolvency and balance sheet tests are to be applied. To some extent, the time is determined by the nature of the distribution, and to a lesser extent, the time of declaration in relation to the time of payment.

§ 18.7 Contractual Provisions Relating to Declarations of Dividends

Because of the great liberality of modern business corporation statutes in permitting distributions to shareholders from earnings and capital, much of the modern law of dividends is contractual in nature. Creditors of a corporation are naturally anxious that the assets of the corporation not be dissipated through unwise distributions. Provisions are therefore routinely inserted in loan agreements and similar contracts to prohibit or restrict the power of the corporation to make distributions to shareholders. Such restrictions vary widely. If the debtor is a publicly held corporation with an established history of regular dividend payments, the agreement may permit dividends of specified amounts provided that certain ratios are maintained between assets and liabilities, or between current assets and current liabilities. Other restrictions may permit any distribution so long as a minimum net worth and minimum cash balance are maintained. Similar agreements with closely held corporations may prohibit all dividends, and may even impose restrictions on salary payments, bonuses, and other distributions having the effect of a dividend.

Contractual provisions relating to dividends also may appear in articles of incorporation. Where classes of preferred shares are authorized, complex provisions relating to dividends may be negotiated. The preference rights of the senior security may be defined (e.g., cumulative, non-cumulative, or cumulative to the extent earned). See § 7.21 of this Nutshell. In addition, provisions may be inserted as part of the preferred shareholders' rights restricting the amount of common dividends that may be paid, requiring a portion of earnings to be set aside as a sinking fund to be used to retire a portion of the preferred each year, limiting senior indebtedness that may be created, and so forth. The preferred shareholder otherwise receives scant protection under most business corporation statutes since claims to preferential dividends, even if cumulative, are not corporate debts but a mere priority to possible future distributions and may be deferred indefinitely.

§ 18.8   Liability of Directors and Shareholders for Illegal Dividends

Directors who vote for or assent to a declaration of dividends or the distribution of assets to shareholders which are wholly or partially in violation of statutory limitations or a provision in the corporation's articles of incorporation, are jointly and severally liable to the corporation for the illegal portion of the dividend or distribution. This statutory liability is ameliorated in many states by possible defenses discussed earlier. See § 14.23 of this Nutshell.

Statutes and a common law "trust fund" theory may impose liability on directors if they authorize distributions or share repurchases at a time when the corporation is insolvent. See, e.g. Munford v. Valuation Research Corp. (11th Cir.1996).

Shareholders who accept a distribution knowing the distribution was made in violation of this Act or the articles of incorporation may be required to return the unlawful payment. This qualified provision in effect protects the probable reliance of an innocent shareholder upon receipt of a distribution; the directors authorizing the illegal dividend of course remain responsible to restore the unlawful payment. If the shareholder knows the payment was unlawful, she may be required to restore it to the corporation, and the liability of the directors will be reduced accordingly. Not all states extend similar protection to innocent shareholders. See § 14.23 of this Nutshell.

§ 18.9   Shareholders' Right to Compel a Dividend

In the absence of contractual protection, minority shareholders in closely held corporations are likely to be unhappy about the dividend policy established by the corporation. In a C corporation the shareholders in control of the corporation prefer to pay salaries to themselves or make other tax-deductible payments rather than pay the same funds in the form of dividends to all shareholders. In an S corporation, shareholders must include their pro rata share of corporate earnings in their own tax returns whether or not anything is distributed to them. A no-dividend policy in such a corporation may cause serious cash flow problems to minority shareholders who may lack the funds to pay the additional tax due to the allocation of S corporation income to them. A common provision in S corporation articles or bylaws requires the corporation, if it has eligible earnings, to pay a dividend at least equal to the amount of additional taxes incurred by each shareholder as a result of the allocation of S corporation income to them. These distributions are called "tax distributions."

Large distributions in the form of salaries to controlling shareholders have the effect of diverting corporate income to the controlling shareholders at the expense of the minority. In sufficiently egregious circumstances, a shareholder may petition a court for an order compelling the payment of a dividend to all shareholders. Historically, suits to compel the declaration of a dividend faced serious obstacles. The discretion of the board of directors with respect to business decisions was so broad that a strong showing of fraud, bad faith, or abuse of discretion was necessary. In short, an abuse of power or a clear failure to exercise it honestly for the corporation and all its shareholders had to be shown. Dodge v. Ford Motor Co. (Mich.1919) is a classic case in which minority shareholders were successful in compelling the declaration of a dividend, though the court there appeared to rely heavily on the unusual frankness of Henry Ford, the majority shareholder, and the court's own view of desirable social policy.

Other cases have also compelled the declaration of a dividend particularly where the defendant was outspoken as to his strategy of freezing out the minority, though in a "head count" of such cases, plaintiffs come off as net losers. A major concern of courts in ordering a dividend to be paid is that there appears to be no standard to guide the court as to how much may safely be paid out and how much should be retained by the corporation for contingencies and future growth. Judges usually have little knowledge or familiarity with the specific business before them. Hence even where a finding of bad faith may be made in connection with refusing to declare a dividend, a court is likely to be cautious in establishing the amount of any judicially-declared dividend.

§ 18.10   Corporate Repurchase of Its Own Shares: Installment Sale

The distributional aspect of repurchases by corporations of their own shares has previously been commented upon (see § 18.4 of this Nutshell). These transactions create several additional problems that are not present in the dividend area that deserve additional consideration.

Since redemptions are almost never proportional to shareholdings, the shareholders' relative positions are affected by the corporate repurchase, and it is often possible for managing shareholders in a closely held corporation to utilize a share repurchase for personal reasons. For example, a leading Massachusetts case held that it was a breach of fiduciary duty for the majority shareholder to cause the corporation to purchase a portion of a family member's shares at inflated prices while refusing to purchase shares owned by a non-family member at any price. Donahue v. Rodd Electrotype Co. of New England, Inc. (Mass.1975). In this case, the family member whose shares were redeemed was elderly and the effect of the redemption was to further the goals of an estate plan set up by him some time earlier. The court articulated the view that shareholders in a closely held corporation have fiduciary duties to each other that rival those that exist in a partnership. In effect this case recognizes a reverse preemptive right on the purchase of shares in some situations. While later Massachusetts cases have retreated to some extent from the broad fiduciary duty language of this opinion and not all jurisdictions have accepted the reasoning of this decision, it nevertheless is an important case describing duties that may arise in connection with transactions that favor some shareholders but not others without any apparent business justification.

In a closely held corporation, the usual reason to reacquire shares is to eliminate the interest of one or more shareholders in the enterprise who desire to leave. The reason for the elimination may be a death or desired retirement, or a negotiated withdrawal following disagreements over business policies. Usually, the remaining shareholders do not wish to increase their investment in the business by purchasing the shares personally (and may lack the liquid assets to do so). A repurchase by the corporation may be attractive because corporate assets are used to repurchase the shares and the transaction does not affect the relative voting power of the remaining shareholders. Hence acquisition by the corporation is logical. However, if the corporation has not been in existence for long or has suffered losses in the past, the legal restrictions on repurchase of shares discussed in a preceding section may be an obstacle.

If the corporation delivers promissory notes to the selling shareholder as part of the purchase price, the transaction is an "installment sale." Usually, an installment sale occurs because the corporation lacks the assets to buy the shares outright and it is contemplated that future payments will be made in whole or in part out of (hoped for) future earnings.

An installment sale raises the question whether the insolvency and availability of surplus requirements applicable to dividends should be applied only when shares are reacquired and the notes issued, or whether those requirements should be repetitively applied to determine the validity of each payment on the notes when it is made. The limited case law tends to apply the tests to each payment but § 6.40(e)(1) of the Model Business Corporation Act (1984) provides that the test should be applied only when the shares are acquired and the notes issued. The argument for this position is that the transaction should be treated no differently than if the corporation borrowed the purchase price from a bank in order to acquire the shares for cash. The alternative view would require at least the insolvency test to be applied at the time of each payment. A further question may arise as to whether the promissory notes issued by the corporation for the balance of the purchase price should be viewed as on a parity with general trade creditors or as subordinate to them. Section 6.40(f) provides that such notes should be on a parity with general unsecured creditors if the notes were validly issued to begin with; the theory is that the corporation could have used cash to buy the shares, borrowing if necessary from a third party, and there is no reason to treat the shareholder who accepts promissory notes from the corporation any differently from any third party lender.

In a public corporation, shares may be reacquired in order to have them available for stock options or other compensation plans, or for acquisitions of other corporations. Otherwise, the number of shares outstanding may increase substantially, causing significant dilution of the interests of public shareholders. Many corporations purchase their own shares for these purposes. Publicly held corporations may also repurchase their own shares for financial reasons, planning to retire them. In these situations the corporation has made the judgment that the market has for some reason under-priced the corporation's securities. Retirement of shares at bargain prices has the effect of increasing the price and earnings per share of the remaining outstanding shares; this assumes, of course, that the corporation has idle cash that is surplus to its reasonably anticipated business needs and its use to retire shares does not significantly reduce overall earnings.

A corporation may desire to purchase its own shares for improper purposes as well as for proper ones. Corporate management faced with the threat of a takeover by an outside corporation may cause the corporation to purchase its own shares as a defensive measure to entrench incumbent management. Purchases on the open market may drive up the price of the shares, thereby tending to defeat a cash tender offer or public exchange offer. A filing under the Williams Act may be required before such transactions are undertaken. Or the insurgent group may be willing to accept "green mail" and the corporation may be willing to buy out the insurgents to make them "go away."

§ 18.11 Redeemable and Convertible Securities

Corporations may issue shares that are redeemable at the option of the corporation if authorized by their articles of incorporation. [MBCA (1984) § 6.01(c)(2)] The statutes of many states permit redeemable *preferred* shares but not redeemable *common* shares, but the MBCA (1984) does not contain such a limitation. The concern with redeemable common shares is that management may use the redemption device to discipline or eliminate antagonistic shareholders. One commentator stated that even the suggestion of redeemable common shares is "corporate heresy." Such concerns, however, do not appear to be borne out in practice.

In modern financing practice within publicly held corporations, preferred shares are usually cumulative and redeemable, and in addition are often convertible into publicly traded common shares (the "conversion shares") on a predetermined ratio. Typically, the conversion ratio is established at a level that requires a significant increase in price of the conversion shares before conversion becomes economic. Thereafter, if the market price of the conversion shares does in fact rise to the point that the conversion shares are worth more than the preferred shares (priced without the conversion feature), the preferred will fluctuate in price in tandem with the common. If these securities are thereafter called for redemption, preferred shareholders should rationally elect to convert rather than permit the shares to be redeemed. Such conversions are called "forced conversions." The economic justification for a forced conversion is that usually the dividend payable on the conversion security is significantly lower than the dividend on the convertible preferred security.

In modern financing practice, shares may also be made redeemable at the option of the holder or upon the occurrence of some external event such as an increase in interest rates. Earlier statutes contemplated redemption only at the option of the corporation, but section 6.01(c)(2) of MBCA (1984) authorizes redemptions to be triggered by other events as well. Shares redeemable at the option of the holder have some of the same characteristics of a demand note.

See generally §§ 7.10–7.13 of this Nutshell.

[For unfamiliar terms see the Glossary]

CHAPTER NINETEEN

INSPECTION OF BOOKS AND RECORDS

§ 19.1 Inspection by Directors and Shareholders Compared

Both shareholders and directors have the right to inspect corporate books and records in certain circumstances. However, the inspection right of a director is considerably broader than the right of a shareholder and rests on an entirely different theoretical base.

A director is a manager of the corporation and owes certain duties to it and to all the shareholders. Indeed, a director may be liable for negligent mismanagement if he does not adequately acquaint himself with the business and affairs of the corporation. For this reason, some cases state that the directors' right to inspect books and records is absolute and unqualified. However, as with many supposedly absolute principles, there are exceptions. Courts have sometimes denied inspection rights to directors where it was clear that the director was acting with manifestly improper motives and adequate information prepared by unbiased persons was otherwise available to the director. Such cases, however, are exceptional and unusual.

The right of a shareholder to inspect books and records, on the other hand, is considerably narrower. A shareholder has a financial interest in the corporation, and the common law recognizes a right to inspect books and records to protect this interest. However, because the shareholder is not charged with management responsibility and is not subject to broad fiduciary duties, the right to inspect is available only for a "proper purpose," and is otherwise hedged with restrictions. The balance of this chapter deals exclusively with the "proper purpose" test and the more limited inspection rights of shareholders.

§ 19.2   Common Law and Statutory Rights of Inspection by Shareholders

A right of shareholders to inspect books and records of the corporation may arise from several different sources. Corporation statutes grant a right of inspection in some circumstances and these statutes form the bulk of the discussion in the balance of this chapter. In addition, a shareholder who is in litigation against the corporation may have the same rights of discovery as any other litigant. Some state statutes require corporations to make reports or submit tax statements that are then available for inspection by shareholders. And, of course, if information must be made publicly available, any shareholder may examine it. Finally, in some states there may exist a residual common law right of inspection that has not been superseded by the statutory right of inspection.

From the standpoint of the corporation, a shareholder's demand to inspect books and records is almost always viewed as a hostile and threatening act. Before the statutory right of inspection was created, the practice developed of denying all inspection requests out-of-hand and compelling the shareholder to litigate, relying on whatever pretext may be available for the denial. The first statutes defining a statutory right of inspection were enacted in an effort to combat this attitude. The most notable feature of these statutes was that they combined a restatement of the common law right of inspection with penalties imposed on corporate officers with custody of the books and records who arbitrarily refuse to permit proper

examination of books and records. These statutes retain the
"proper purpose" standard of the common law.

The statutory right of inspection in many states is available
to persons whose shareholdings meet certain objective criteria;
a typical provision extends the statutory right to persons (1)
who have been shareholders of record for at least six months
prior to the demand or (2) who own at least five per cent of
the outstanding shares of the corporation. As indicated above,
a person who meets these objective criteria must also state a
"proper purpose" for the inspection in a written demand.
However, under many statutes, the burden of proof as to
proper purpose shifts if the shareholder meets the objective
criteria and alleges a proper purpose, so that the corporation
then has the burden of showing the plaintiff did not in fact
have a proper purpose. Shareholders who fail to meet these
objective criteria continue to have the common law burden of
establishing that their purpose is a proper one.

A corporate officer who improperly refuses to grant a statutory right of inspection is liable for a penalty that may be
defined in various ways. Several states make the penalty one
or two per cent of the value of the plaintiff's shares, others
impose a maximum penalty of $500; still others impose a per
diem penalty of $25 or some other amount. Some states
require the officer to pay the litigation expenses, including
attorneys' fees, of the shareholder who is forced to sue in
order to vindicate his or her right to inspect. As a practical
matter, these provisions are rarely invoked, though there are a
handful of instances in which penalties of fairly substantial
amounts were actually imposed on recalcitrant officers. Of
course, the number of litigated cases may not describe the
informal impact that these penal provisions have, since the
potential of a substantial penalty may cause some corporate

officers to grant inspection rights they might otherwise have resisted.

The Model Business Corporation Act (1984) rejects the penalty approach, though it does contain provisions designed to assure that the right to inspect is made available on a timely basis. First, like the statutes of several states, § 16.02(a) requires a shareholder desiring to inspect books and records to give five days written demand in advance. Second, § 16.02(b) describes in considerable detail the types of records a shareholder may examine. Third, in an effort to reduce "fishing expeditions," § 16.02(c) requires the demand to be in "good faith" and for a "proper purpose" and that the shareholder define with reasonable particularity his purpose and establish that the records sought are "directly connected" with that purpose. Section 16.04(b) provides for direct judicial action to enforce a right of inspection under § 16.02; the court is directed to dispose of such a case on an "expedited basis." Further, if the court orders inspection, it must order the corporation to pay the shareholders' costs of the proceeding, including reasonable attorney's fees, unless the corporation can prove "that it refused inspection in good faith because it had a reasonable basis for doubt about the right of the shareholder to inspect the records demanded." [MBCA § 16.04(c)] This is a corporate obligation, not an obligation of the officer with custody of the books and records, as is the case under older inspection statutes.

§ 19.3   Corporate Records: What May Be Examined?

Business corporation acts require each corporation to keep minutes of meetings, books and records of account, and information about record shareholders so that an appropriate voting list of shareholders may be created. The language of these statutes varies widely from state to state. Section 16.01 of

MBCA (1984) is a carefully drafted provision that is designed not to impose unreasonable record-keeping requirements on corporations. In addition to a record of shareholders [§ 16.01(c)], it generally requires keeping of "records" of actions taken at meetings rather than "minutes" of meetings; it also requires only "appropriate accounting records" to be maintained rather than the older language of "books and records of account." [MBCA (1984) §§ 16.01(a), (b)] Of course, many corporations may find it necessary to keep much more detailed and elaborate records: § 16.01 sets forth the irreducible minimum. In a bow to the computer age, § 16.01(d) permits these records to be kept on tape or in machine-readable form capable of being converted into written form in a reasonable time.

Under most state statutes, the shareholder's right to inspect extends not only to enumerated records but to corporate records in general. Case law has tended to be expansive in this regard. One case authorized the examination of "records, books of account, receipts, vouchers, bills and all other documents evidencing the financial condition of the corporation." Another case authorized the examination of the books of a subsidiary controlled by the corporation. Corporate contracts and even the correspondence of the chief executive officer have been held to be subject to inspection in appropriate cases. The right generally extends to all relevant records necessary to inform the shareholder about corporate matters in which he or she has a legitimate interest. The corporation cannot defeat this right by offering summaries, substitute papers, or financial statements prepared by the corporation's auditors.

Section 16.02(b) of the MBCA (1984) is considerably more restrictive than most statutes, since it contains an exclusive enumeration of what records may be examined. Shareholders may inspect only excerpts of minutes, the accounting records, and the record of shareholders under this section. This does not mean, however, that all records not described in that section are immune from inspection. Rather the shareholder seeking such information must persuade the court that he or she has a non-statutory right to the documents under § 16.02(e)(2) which preserves "the power of a court, independently of this Act, to compel the production of corporate records for examination."

§ 19.4   What Is a "Proper Purpose"?

The basic test of inspection by shareholders is a "proper purpose." A "proper purpose" means a purpose that is reasonably relevant to the shareholder's interest as a shareholder. A purpose is proper under this definition if it is directed toward obtaining information bearing upon or seeking to protect the shareholder's interest and that of other shareholders of the corporation. A purpose to determine the worth of the shareholder's holdings is a proper purpose. So is a purpose of seeking reasons for a decline in profits. So is a purpose of ascertaining whether there has been mismanagement or alarming transactions.

A corporation cannot deny the right to inspect by arguing that the shareholder has an improper purpose simply because he is unfriendly to management. An improper purpose is one with ulterior or vindictive motives. Obvious examples are general harassment of management or a desire to obtain trade secrets for a competitor. Probably mere idle curiosity is not a proper purpose, though it is a rare shareholder who cannot allege a more specific purpose. Some courts appear to be more willing than others to countenance "fishing expeditions."

Obviously, substantial and difficult factual issues arise as to the shareholder's true purpose. The issue may come down to predominant motive and intent. The burden of proof, discussed earlier, may be significant. It is probably fair to conclude that it is always easy to couch an inspection demand in the form of a purpose that is proper, and that careful coaching of testimony may lead to the conclusion that the purpose for inspection is proper, while an outspoken or unusually forthright witness may run into difficulty. The mere fact that a shareholder making a demand to inspect books or records is a competitor of the corporation does not necessarily make the demand improper, though it may raise suspicions. In this type of situation, some courts have imposed restrictions on the use or distribution of information being produced, apparently without express statutory authority to do so. Section 16.04(d) of the MBCA (1984) expressly endorses this practice.

§ 19.5   Who Is Entitled to Inspect?

A person who is a beneficial owner of shares but is not the record owner has a common law right of inspection, and depending on the wording of the specific statute, may have a statutory right as well. See MBCA (1984) § 16.02(f). Pledgees, judgment creditors, and holders of voting trust certificates also have a statutory right to inspect under the statutes of many states.

Section 16.03 of the 1984 Model Act makes clear that an inspecting shareholder may be accompanied by an attorney or agent. Further, the right to inspect entails, if reasonable, the right to obtain copies of the inspected documents. The corporation may impose a reasonable charge for providing copies. While many courts doubtless would require corporations to provide copies as a matter of common sense, express provisions covering these commonly recurring issues seem desirable.

§ 19.6   Inspection of Shareholders Lists

Every corporation must maintain "a record of its shareholders, in a form that permits preparation of a list of the names and addresses of all shareholders in alphabetical order by class of shares showing the number and class of shares held by each." [MBCA (1984) § 16.01(c)] This is a list of record owners, not beneficial owners. This record is subject to the statutory or common law right of inspection possessed by every shareholder. In contrast, the voting list compiled immediately before the meeting (see § 9.5 of this Nutshell) is automatically open to inspection by any shareholder without any proof of proper purpose before and during the shareholders meeting. There has been a substantial volume of litigation over shareholders' lists in publicly held corporations since such lists have historically been, to quote a colorful phrase, "the line of scrimmage for contests involving incumbent management, dissident shareholders, acquisition-minded corporations, and those who have been described in current fiction as 'corporate raiders'." Of course, the widespread use of nominees, street names, and the book entry system for recording ownership (see § 13.12 of this Nutshell) all greatly reduce the value of such a list from the standpoint of a potential aggressor seeking to take over a publicly held corporation. On the other hand, many institutional investors regularly disclose their entire portfolios, so that considerable information about holdings of securities in specific companies by specific institutional investors is publicly available for anyone who is willing to collect the data.

A list of names and addresses of numerous well-to-do persons is itself valuable, and at least theoretically may be sought in order to sell it to mail solicitation firms. New York and several other states have statutes that provide that a shareholders' list need not be produced if the applicant has offered to sell or assisted another person in the sale or offering for sale of a shareholders' list within the preceding five years. The modern use of nominees, street names, and the book entry system in publicly held corporations largely deprive this list of commercial value and there appears to have been no recent case involving sales of lists of record shareholders.

Much of the litigation dealing with shareholders' lists involves closely held corporations and the "proper purpose" test. Generally it has been held that it is a proper purpose to desire to communicate with other shareholders about matters of corporate concern: To solicit proxies, to initiate a proxy contest, to publicize mismanagement, to discuss a derivative suit, to discuss proposals of management, to form a protective committee, and the like. It has also been held to be a proper purpose to communicate to other shareholders an offer to purchase the shares of the corporation. Courts probably tend to be more lenient in granting access to shareholders' lists than to other books and records.

In a Viet Nam war era case, it was held that a purpose to seek the list in order to communicate one's own social or political views to shareholders of a publicly held corporation was not a proper purpose. Where a corporation is large enough to be registered under section 12 of the Securities Exchange Act of 1934 (500 shareholders of record of any class and $10,000,000 of assets), the federal proxy regulations provide an alternative basis for inspection of the shareholders' list. Rule 14a–7 requires a corporation either to supply a shareholders' list or to mail solicitations to shareholders on behalf of a shareholder upon payment of the postage by that shareholder. The corporation usually elects the latter alternative.

One case that predates the creation of the book entry system for holding shares of publicly held corporations holds that a solicitation of shareholders asking them to join in a request for a shareholders' list (in order to meet the 5 per cent requirement of state law) is itself a solicitation under the proxy rules, and requires filing with the Securities and Exchange Commission if more than ten such solicitations are made. Studebaker Corp. v. Gittlin (2d Cir. 1966).

§ 19.7   Financial Reports for Shareholders

Corporations that have a class of securities registered under section 12 of the Securities Exchange Act of 1934 must provide shareholders with annual reports that contain audited financial statements. The annual proxy statement also contains considerable useful information, particularly in the "MD & A", described in § 17.2 of this Nutshell. Registered corporations also must file data with the SEC on a quarterly and annual basis that is immediately made publicly available, and is widely disseminated.

In many states, there is no requirement that corporations provide any financial information at all to shareholders, though some states provide that tax returns or annual reports filed with state officials may be inspected by shareholders.

Section 16.20 of the 1984 Model Act requires all corporations to provide at least some financial data to shareholders. Because many small corporations do not have auditors or accountants, the requirement is carefully phrased so as not to impose unreasonable burdens on small corporations. However, § 16.20(a) requires a corporation that prepares financial statements on the basis of generally accepted accounting principles to prepare annual financial reports to shareholders on the same basis.

[For unfamiliar terms see the Glossary]

CHAPTER TWENTY

ORGANIC CHANGES: AMENDMENTS, MERGERS, AND DISSOLUTION

§ 20.1 Introduction and Caveat

Transactions discussed in this chapter are often complex. State statutes dealing with them vary substantially from state to state. In addition, voting requirements with respect to approval of specific types of transactions also vary from state to state. This chapter gives only a general overview of organic changes within a corporation.

MBCA (1984) contains innovative provisions designed to simplify and rationalize the current law. The organic provisions set forth in MBCA (1984) have been adopted by about twenty-five smaller states, and have been influential to some degree in amendments to statutes in other states.

In November, 1999, the Committee on Corporate Laws approved substantial amendments to many of the provisions of MBCA (1984) discussed in this chapter. Because these changes are so recent, they have not been enacted anywhere but may be favorably considered in the future. Sections 20.2 through 20.13 describe the current MBCA (1984) while § 20.14 briefly summarizes the major changes made by the 1999 amendments.

§ 20.2   Amendments to Articles of Incorporation in General

Articles of incorporation may be freely amended subject only to the broad requirement that the amended articles of incorporation may contain only provisions that may be lawfully contained in original articles of incorporation at the time of the amendment. [MBCA (1984) § 10.01(a)] Additionally, if a change in shares or rights of shareholders, or an exchange, reclassification or cancellation of shares or rights, is to be made in connection with the amendment, either the articles of amendment, or the amendments themselves, must set forth the provisions necessary to effectuate the change, exchange, reclassification, or cancellation. [MBCA (1984) § 10.06(3)]

Under MBCA (1984) and most state statutes, the board of directors must first approve an amendment and recommend that it be adopted before it can be considered by the shareholders. The board thus has a "gate keeper" function in this regard. Its favorable recommendation is necessary before the shareholders may even consider a proposed amendment. The board of directors has a similar function in connection with mergers, sales of assets requiring approval of the shareholders, and other organic changes discussed in this chapter. However, in some states, shareholders may be able to act by unanimous or majority written consent without prior recommendation of the board of directors.

States require amendments to articles of incorporation to be approved by a super-majority vote. Older statutes generally require an affirmative vote of two-thirds vote of all outstanding shares, voting and non-voting. Most states today, however, follow the less restrictive requirement of MBCA (1984) and require amendments to be approved by an absolute majority of the voting shares. MBCA (1984) reduces this requirement in limited situations. [MBCA (1984) § 10.03(e)]

A broad equitable principle requires directors and majority shareholders to act in a fair way toward the corporation and minority shareholders. This principle may provide entry into the courthouse for minority shareholders who claim that an amendment serves no purpose other than injuring them. In other words, vindictive amendments and transactions that seem to serve no purpose other than to enrich the majority at the expense of the minority may be subject to attack on fiduciary principles. The test may be phrased as "good faith" or "reasonableness" or "conflict of interest." (See §§ 14.10, 14.19 of this Nutshell.) An obligation of full disclosure may also exist under the Federal securities laws if proxies must be solicited.

§ 20.3   Vested Rights

Under modern statutes no shareholder has a vested right in any specific provision in articles of incorporation. [MBCA (1984) § 10.01(b)] It is therefore possible for the majority of shareholders to adopt amendments that dramatically change or eliminate the rights of minority shareholders or the rights of holders of classes of nonvoting or senior securities. Shareholders may mistakenly believe that provisions of articles of incorporation that are significant to them can be changed only with their consent. That position is erroneous in most states. While it is possible that a court might give shareholders protection not found in the statute on the basis of self-dealing or fiduciary principles, one can hardly count on it. As a result, careful attention must be given to procedural protections provided in the corporation statutes, and if the statutory protections are not adequate, special voting requirements should be placed in the articles of incorporation to assure that necessary protection is available.

Some early judicial decisions evolved the theory that certain rights, such as accrued cumulative dividend rights of preferred shares, are "contractual" or "vested" rights and cannot be eliminated over the objection of a single shareholder. In order to reverse these decisions decisively and unambiguously the statutes of many states contain a non-exclusive "laundry list" of permissible amendments:

Amendments increasing or decreasing the number of shares a corporation is authorized to issue;

Amendments exchanging, classifying, reclassifying, or canceling any part of a corporation's shares, whether or not previously issued;

Amendments limiting or canceling the right of holders of a class of shares to receive dividends, whether or not the dividends or rights to receive the dividends had accumulated in the past;

Amendments creating new classes of shares whether superior or inferior to shares already outstanding, or changing the designations of shares or the preferences, limitations, or rights of classes of shares, whether or not previously issued; and

Amendments changing the voting rights of outstanding shares, including elimination of the power to vote cumulatively or assigning multiple or fractional votes per share, or denying the power to vote entirely to classes of shares, whether or not previously issued.

In MBCA (1984) and the statutes of most states there are two basic protections against abuse of the majority's power of amendment. First, is the right to vote by classes (described in the MBCA as voting by "voting groups") on specified kinds of amendments discussed immediately below. Second, is the statutory right of dissent and appraisal described in § 20.12 of this Nutshell.

It should be added parenthetically that not all statutes contain all of these broad provisions; in some states there may be specific limitations on the power of amendment.

§ 20.4   Voting by Classes

One major protection of shareholders against unacceptable amendments imposed by holders of other classes of shares is the right to vote by class (or by "voting groups") on specific amendments. The scope of this right depends on the specific statute, but generally, the objective is to require class voting on all amendments that are burdensome to a single class as such and beneficial to other classes. [MBCA (1984) § 10.04] Class voting may also be required by a specific provision in the articles of incorporation as part of that class's "contract" with the corporation. The discussion below is limited to the statutory protection of class voting.

The concept of class voting is quite simple. A class of shares is entitled to vote as a class if it is affected in one of the ways specified by statute. In most states amendments that require class voting must be approved by the required percentage (either an absolute majority or two-thirds) of each class voting as a separate class, and in addition, by the required percentage of all other voting shares in the aggregate entitled to vote on the amendment. Classes of shares that are nonvoting are nevertheless entitled to vote as a class if they are affected in one of the ways specified in the statute. [MBCA (1984) § 10.04(d)] This is "class veto" not individual shareholder veto. The basic idea is that if the specified percentage of a class of shares is willing to accept a real or potentially burdensome amendment, the balance of the class may not block it.

Dissenting members, however, may have the statutory right of dissent and appraisal.

In some situations, one class of shares may be counted in both the class election and the general election on the amendment by all shares entitled to vote generally. More typically, however, the class of shares that is entitled to vote as a class will not have been given the right to vote generally, and therefore they participate only in the class vote.

The concept of "voting groups" in MBCA (1984) is identical to traditional class voting. A new linguistic convention was necessary to distinguish between voting units and "classes" as set forth in the articles of incorporation. MBCA (1984) permits some series or classes of shares to vote separately in some circumstances [MBCA (1984) §§ 10.04(b)] but combines two or more classes or series in other situations as a single voting group. [MBCA (1984) §§ 1.40(26), 7.25, 7.26] The term "voting groups" is also less confusing linguistically and is used hereafter to describe the basic class voting concept.

Section 10.04(a) of MBCA (1984) lists nine types of proposed amendments that trigger the right of a class of shares to vote as a separate voting group on an amendment:

Amendments that would increase or decrease the number of authorized shares of that class; that would effect an exchange or reclassification (or create a right to exchange or reclassify) of shares of that class into shares of another class;

Amendments that would permit shares of some other class to be exchanged or reclassified into shares of the class;

Amendments that would change the designations, rights, preferences or limitations of all or part of the class; that would change some or all of the shares of that class into a different number of shares of the same class;

Amendments that would create a new class of shares having rights or preferences prior to, superior to, or substantially equal with the class;

Amendments that would change the rights of some other class so that they will then have rights or preferences prior to, superior to, or substantially equal with the class;

Amendments that would limit or deny an existing preemptive right of the class; and

Amendments that would cancel or affect cumulative dividends to which the class is entitled.

Each of these types of amendments that trigger the right to vote as a separate voting group has the characteristic of harming the class as such. Dissenting shareholders in these classes may also have the right of dissent and appraisal.

§ 20.5   Mergers and Consolidations

Business corporation statutes specifically authorize several types or kinds of corporate amalgamations:

(1) The merger of one domestic corporation into another domestic corporation;

(2) The consolidation of two domestic corporations into a new domestic corporation;

(3) The merger or consolidation of a domestic corporation and a foreign corporation, with the surviving or new corporation being either a domestic or a foreign corporation.

(4) In about a dozen states, the mandatory exchange of shares of one corporation for shares, cash, or other consideration provided by another corporation.

(5) In a handful of states, a conversion of a corporation into another business form, such as a limited liability company or

limited partnership, without undergoing a formal dissolution and reconstitution in the new business form.

Technically a "merger" of corporation A into corporation B means that corporation B survives and corporation A disappears, while in a "consolidation" of corporation A and corporation B, both corporations disappear and a new corporation C is created. MBCA (1984) does not recognize the consolidation as a separate amalgamation device. The Official Comment states that such a device is obsolete since it almost always is advantageous for one entity or the other to survive, and if it is not, it is always possible to create a new entity and merge the other corporations into it.

These statutory methods of amalgamations are described as "statutory mergers" to distinguish them from the asset-purchase and stock-purchase transactions described immediately below. Upon a statutory merger, the surviving or new corporation automatically has title to all assets of the disappearing corporations, and assumes all the liabilities of those corporations. Shareholders in all the corporations involved are entitled to receive whatever consideration is specified in the plan of merger.

A statutory merger or consolidation is only one of several possible ways of effecting a corporate acquisition or creating an amalgamated corporation out of formerly independent operations. The Internal Revenue Code has its own set of definitions that provide a useful summary of non-statutory amalgamation techniques. It describes a statutory merger or consolidation as a class "A" reorganization, and the most important alternative types as class "B" or "C" reorganizations.

A class "B" reorganization occurs when one corporation exchanges its voting shares for all or most of the outstanding shares of the other corporation, if the acquiring corporation has control of the other corporation immediately after the transaction. The distinguishing feature of a class B reorganization is that it involves an exchange of stock. Two possible disadvantages of a stock acquisition are that the acquiring corporation may have to deal with a fairly large number of sellers, and the acquired business remains liable for all undisclosed or unknown liabilities, such as income tax deficiencies of prior years. This transaction is referred to as a "stock purchase" or "stock acquisition" transaction.

A class "C" reorganization occurs when one corporation exchanges its voting shares for the assets of another corporation. The purchase may include all or most of the assets of the acquired corporation, or may include only the assets used in one line of business. After the transaction is completed, the acquired corporation remains in existence with assets consisting primarily of the stock of the acquiring corporation. It also remains liable for liabilities not expressly assumed by the purchaser. Usually such a corporation will thereafter liquidate after making provision for liabilities not assumed by the purchaser, distributing the remaining stock to its shareholders. Alternatively, such a corporation may continue in existence operating as a holding or investment corporation. This transaction is referred to as an "asset purchase" or "asset acquisition" transaction.

Another combination strategy is to structure an acquisition as a purchase of stock for cash or assets for cash. Those transactions differ from those described above because they are taxable events, involving the recognition of gain or loss, and the establishment of a new tax basis for the assets or stock acquired. The statutory mergers and reorganizations described above involve transactions that ordinarily are not taxable transactions, giving rise to taxable gain or loss.

The same basic economic result can be reached by casting a transaction in the form of a statutory merger, a Class B or C reorganization, a stock purchase, or an asset purchase. The question as to which form a particular transaction should take is a complex one, involving a variety of tax and non-tax considerations. Often the parties to a specific transaction will have different views on which form of transaction is most desirable.

Because of the similar economic effects of these acquisition techniques, there is a slight possibility that the selection of a particular form to achieve some goal (such as not assuming certain types of liabilities) will not be successful. A court may reject form, "look at substance," and recast the transaction into a different form. This is the "de facto merger" notion, adopted in Farris v. Glen Alden Corp. (Pa.1958), but generally rejected by later cases. The court held in that case that dissenting shareholders had appraisal rights provided by a statutory merger despite the fact that the transaction was cast as a non-statutory asset acquisition. In this transaction the "selling" corporation exchanged its assets for shares of the acquiring corporation and thereafter dissolved and distributed the shares it acquired to its shareholders. Because the "selling" corporation was much larger than the "acquiring" corporation, the selling corporation's shareholders dominated the combined entity. The court referred to this transaction as a "hybrid form of corporate amalgamation" and said:

> [I]t is no longer helpful to consider an individual transaction in the abstract and solely by reference to the various elements there in determining whether it is a "merger" or a "sale." Instead, to determine properly the nature of a corporate transaction, we must refer not only to all the provisions of the agreement, but also to the consequences of

the transaction and to the purposes of the provisions of the corporation law said to be applicable.

Several cases are contra to *Farris,* and most academic writing has been highly critical of the de facto merger doctrine, since it makes rational corporate planning difficult if not impossible in many situations.

§ 20.6   Triangular Mergers, Cash Mergers, Short Form Mergers, and Related Developments

Until about 1960, statutory mergers and consolidations contemplated the amalgamation of two independent businesses into a single entity. All shareholders in the disappearing corporation received shares in the surviving corporation in exchange for their shares in the disappearing corporation. These notions are now obsolete. Today the consideration in a statutory merger may consist in whole or in part of cash or property other than shares, and most mergers do not involve the amalgamation of corporations of approximately the same size with both sets of shareholders being involved in the combined enterprise. Rather, mergers usually involve (1) acquisition-type transactions, (2) the elimination of minority interests in corporations for cash, (3) the change in the state of incorporation of a corporation, or (4) some other unexpected transaction that at first blush has nothing to do with the traditional concept of a merger. These transactions are possible because modern merger statutes permit a merger agreement to be extremely flexible. MBCA (1984) and the merger statutes of most states now provide expressly that one or more parties to the merger may have their shares converted by the merger into "shares, obligations or other securities of the surviving corporation or any other corporation, or into cash or other property in whole or part." [MBCA (1984) § 11.01(a)(3)]

Also, many mergers today are "triangular" or "reverse-triangular" mergers involving three or more business entities.

In a triangular merger the acquiring corporation forms a wholly owned subsidiary, "drops" cash or its own shares into that subsidiary, and then merges the corporation being acquired into the subsidiary. The shareholders of the acquired corporation may receive cash or shares of the acquiring corporation (not, it should be noted, shares of the subsidiary into which the acquired corporation is merged). In this way, (1) the acquiring corporation acquires all of the shares of the acquired corporation, (2) the shareholders of the acquired corporation receive cash or marketable shares of the acquiring corporation, and (3) the acquiring corporation does not become individually responsible for liabilities of the acquired corporation.

A reverse-triangular merger is a more complex transaction. A new wholly-owned subsidiary is created by the acquiring corporation and merged *into* the corporation to be acquired. Shareholders of the acquired corporation theoretically receive shares of the newly created subsidiary; those shares are theoretically immediately exchanged for cash or for shares of the acquiring corporation. The acquired corporation therefore ends up being a wholly-owned subsidiary of the acquiring corporation while its former shareholders own cash or shares of the acquiring corporation. One benefit of this type of transaction is that non-assignable government contracts owned by the acquired corporation have not been assigned. Similarly, tax characteristics of the acquired corporation that are non-transferable are (hopefully) unaffected by the transaction. The critical point here is not the detail of the transactions: indeed, one commentator has stated that the "procedure is a magical one" and those who claim to understand it fully "are under an illusion." Rather, the critical point is that both triangular and reverse-triangular mergers involve three-way transactions by which corporation A becomes a wholly owned subsidiary of corporation B without there being a transfer or assignment. The acquired corporation's shareholders receive cash or shares of the acquiring corporation even though the merger is with a subsidiary of that corporation.

In these situations, the parent corporation is usually a publicly held corporation with widely traded shares; the newly created subsidiary exists solely for the purpose of facilitating the particular transaction.

Section 11.02 of MBCA (1984) creates a mandatory "share exchange" procedure as a substitute for a reverse triangular merger. This transaction is misnamed; it is not so much an exchange of shares as it is a device to compel a mandatory sale of shares. Under this procedure, a corporation adopts a plan of "share exchange" by which all of its shares are transferred to another entity upon approval by a majority of the shareholders. Shareholders who object to the sale are nevertheless bound by it but have a statutory right of dissent and appraisal.

The merger statutes of many states permit the vote of the shareholders of a surviving corporation to be eliminated when the number of outstanding shares is to be increased by no more than 20 percent when compared to the number of shares outstanding before the merger. Since there is no vote by the shareholders of the surviving corporation, there is also no right to an appraisal remedy. The theory is that an increase of 20 percent or less is likely to be relatively unimportant to the shareholders of the surviving corporation and an appraisal right is therefore unnecessary.

§ 20.7 Cash-out Mergers

These modern merger statutes permit another type of transaction, the "cash out merger." These transactions are also

called "freeze out" or "squeeze out" mergers. In these transactions, certain shareholders are compelled to accept cash or
property for their shares, and the merger is a device to force
out or chase out unwanted shareholders.

A typical cash out merger is structured as follows. A corporation merges into its own subsidiary with the majority shareholders receiving stock in the subsidiary and the minority
shareholders receiving a specified amount of cash for their
shares. This procedure may be used not only to force out
unwanted minority shareholders, but also to eliminate all
public shareholders in a "going private" transaction or to
"mop up" the non-selling shareholders following a successful
tender offer. It also permits a parent corporation to eliminate
unwanted minority shareholders in a subsidiary.

Transactions of this nature raise two basic questions to be
addressed in §§ 20.10 and 20.12 of this Nutshell. (1) May such
transactions be attacked on the ground that they lack any
business purpose or are unfair to the minority? (2) Are statutory appraisal rights an adequate protection for the frozen-or
squeezed-out shareholder?

§ 20.8 "Upstream" and "Downstream" Mergers

A merger between a parent corporation and its subsidiary is
called an "up stream" merger if the surviving corporation is
the parent corporation. It is a "down stream" merger if the
surviving corporation is the subsidiary.

A downstream merger is used to change the state of incorporation of a publicly held corporation. The corporation
creates a wholly-owned subsidiary in the new state of incorporation, and then merges itself into its subsidiary in a
downstream merger with all shares and financial interests of
the parent being mirrored in the shares and financial struc-

ture of the subsidiary. When the merger occurs, each shareholder and creditor of the old publicly held corporation incorporated in State A automatically becomes a shareholder
and creditor in a corporation incorporated in State B.

§ 20.9   Short Form Mergers

Many states have adopted statutes that provide a special
summary merger procedure for upstream mergers where the
parent owns a large majority (but less than all) of the shares
of the subsidiary. A "short form" merger permits a parent
corporation to merge its subsidiary into it without the vote of
shareholders of either corporation. To be eligible for a short
form merger, the parent must own a specified percentage (90
percent in the Model Act) of the subsidiary's shares. [MBCA
(1984) § 11.04] The theoretical basis of omitting both votes is
that (1) a vote of the subsidiary's shareholders is unnecessary
because the minority shareholders are, in any event, unable to
block the merger, and (2) a vote of the parent's shareholders is
unnecessary because the merger will not materially affect
their rights which already include a 90 per cent interest in the
subsidiary. The latter conclusion is based on the relatively
slight increase in the parent's interest in the subsidiary resulting from the merger.

The major practical justification for the short form merger
statute is that it effectuates a saving of the cost of proxy
solicitations and meetings where the parent corporation is
publicly held. The short form merger procedure creates no
appraisal rights on the part of dissenting shareholders of the
parent though it does for minority shareholders of the subsidiary who are "cashed out."

The most difficult theoretical problem with the short form
merger statute lies in its treatment of the minority shareholders of the subsidiary. In a merger between independent corpo-

rations, it is unlikely that the shareholders of a corporation will approve a merger that is unfair to them (if there has been full and accurate disclosure). However, in the merger of a subsidiary into its parent, no such automatic protection exists against terms unfair to the subsidiary's minority shareholders; indeed, terms that are unfair to the minority shareholders are advantageous from the standpoint of the majority shareholders of the parent. The short form merger statute addresses this problem by creating appraisal rights. See § 20.12 of this Nutshell.

§ 20.10 Fiduciary Duties in Mergers

The developments discussed above—cash mergers, going private transactions, short form mergers, and related practices—raise the question whether courts should have any role in judging or evaluating these transactions so long as the formal statutory procedural requirements have been complied with. Despite some academic argument that (1) courts should not judge motive or subjective fairness, and (2) judicial review should be limited to assuring that the minority protection devices granted by statute are made available, the case law has developed in the opposite direction.

Cases recognize that cash mergers and related practices are self-dealing transactions that must be judged by fiduciary principles applicable to those transactions. See § 14.11 of this Nutshell. The reason for this should be obvious when it is recognized that the price being offered minority shareholders in these types of transactions is being set exclusively by the majority. The first case clearly accepting this principle was Singer v. Magnavox Co. (Del.1977) which established a dual test: the transaction must have a "business purpose" and the transaction must meet a standard of "intrinsic" or "entire" fairness. Other states quickly followed the lead of Delaware in this regard. However, the Delaware court, after struggling in several cases with the meaning of "business purpose," eliminated the "business purpose" test in Weinberger v. UOP, Inc. (Del.1983) because it provided little or no protection to shareholders. The court, however, continued to apply a strict "intrinsic fairness" test that includes a requirement of full and meaningful disclosure. These cases are analyzed in § 14.20 of this Nutshell. The court also concluded that in the future the remedy in the event of a claim of inadequate price should be limited to a more generous appraisal remedy (see § 20.12 of this Nutshell) than was available in Delaware previously.

Some courts in other states continue to apply a "business purpose" test in evaluating cash out transactions. Both New York and Massachusetts, for example, apparently still impose the dual test derived from *Singer.*

Fiduciary duties and tests of "intrinsic fairness" have been made applicable to cash mergers and similar transactions by state courts applying state law. In Santa Fe Industries, Inc. v. Green (S.Ct.1977), the Supreme Court rejected a test of "fairness" in Rule 10b–5 cases, holding that the essence of a rule 10b–5 violation was nondisclosure or misrepresentation of material facts. As a result of this holding, judicial controls over the transactions described in this section are more fully regulated by state law than by Federal securities acts.

§ 20.11 Sales of All or Substantially All the Assets of a Corporation

A sale, lease, exchange, or other disposition of all, or substantially all, the property and assets of a corporation, not in the usual and regular course of business, must, under the statutes of most states, be approved by shareholders. [MBCA (1984) § 12.02] If the transaction is in the ordinary course of business (as may be the case with a corporation that is, e.g., in the business of buying and selling real estate), shareholder approval is not usually required. [MBCA (1984) § 12.01] Most states consider a pledge, mortgage, or deed of trust covering all the assets of the corporation to be within the ordinary course of business and therefore shareholder approval is not required. Section 12.01 also provides that deployment of assets through a wholly-owned subsidiary is not a transaction that requires shareholder approval.

The phrase "all or substantially all" has received varied judicial treatment. Most courts have construed this language flexibly, and required shareholder approval when significant components of a corporation are sold even though other significant components are retained. The Official Comment to § 12.01 of MBCA (1984) suggests that this phrase is synonymous with "all or nearly all" and "was added merely to make clear that the statutory requirements could not be avoided by retention of some minimal or nominal residue of the original assets." Most decisions have not adopted this stricter approach.

In most states, shareholders have a statutory right of dissent and appraisal in connection with transactions involving the disposition of substantially all the assets of the corporation not in the ordinary course of business. [MBCA (1984) § 13.02(a)(3)] See § 20.12 of this Nutshell.

When a corporation sells substantially all its assets not in the ordinary course of business, the purchaser of the assets normally continues to operate the business (though it may be broadened or narrowed in scope). The selling corporation usually thereafter dissolves and distributes the proceeds of the sale to its shareholders. The purchaser may assume specified liabilities that arise in the ordinary course of business, but typically will expressly not assume other liabilities of the enterprise, known or unknown. Following the sale, the selling corporation must discharge all known obligations before it distributes the remaining assets to its shareholders. However, provision usually is not made for unknown liabilities or liabilities that may arise in the future.

"Product liability" claims are claims by persons who are injured by products manufactured by the selling corporation. These injuries may occur many years after the selling corporation dissolved. The purchaser of the assets (that continued the business) is invariably sued in this situation, and typically argues that it is not liable because it expressly did not assume products liability claims. In recent years, some courts have evolved theories of de facto merger, continuity of business, or product line liability by which the purchaser may be held liable for such claims despite the provision expressly negating assumption of liability for them. Most courts, however, have declined to impose liability on the purchaser in this situation. If the purchaser is not liable, the injured plaintiff typically goes uncompensated.

A corporation that sells substantially all of its assets may remain in existence and continue in business. It may thereafter deploy its assets by purchasing or creating other businesses or it may simply invest the proceeds in marketable securities and continue in business as an investment company. Such a corporation is taxed as a personal holding company if the number of shareholders is small.

§ 20.12 The Right of Dissent and Appraisal

State statutes give shareholders the right to dissent from certain types of transactions and obtain the appraised value of their shares through a judicial proceeding. [MBCA (1984) ch. 13] Since this right is entirely the creature of statute, it is available only when the statute expressly provides that it is available. In a handful of cases, however, innovative courts have created appraisal-type remedies in non-statutory situations.

The remedy of dissent and appraisal was originally created as part of the liberalization of the rules relating to shareholder approval of fundamental transactions at the beginning of the 20th Century. Statutes in the Nineteenth Century usually required unanimous consent, a rule that permitted a single shareholder to block a decision desired by the majority. In exchange for eliminating this individual shareholder veto, objecting shareholders were given the option to be bought out at an appraised price. Today, this remedy primarily serves the purpose of assuring that controlling shareholders offer a fair price in cash-out and related transactions in which minority shareholders are compelled to accept cash for their shares.

The statutory appraisal remedy is surrounded by elaborate statutory procedures that must be followed by shareholders wishing to elect that remedy. The right may be lost if these procedures are not precisely followed. If the right is lost, the dissenting shareholder must go along with the objectionable transaction. These procedures advise the corporation of the number of dissenting shareholders, and hence the cost of proceeding with the transaction. These procedures tend to be a trap for the unwary frozen-out shareholder, who may well lose his right of dissent if mandatory notice and other requirements are not complied with.

Under § 13.02 of MBCA (1984) the appraisal right is available in regular mergers, short form mergers (shareholders of the subsidiary only), compulsory share exchanges, sales of substantially all corporate assets not in the ordinary course of business, and specific types of adverse amendments to articles of incorporation. The standards for determining when the right of dissent and appraisal is available differ to some extent from the standards (described in § 20.4 of this Nutshell) for determining when shares are entitled to vote by classes (or by voting groups) in MBCA (1984) § 10.04. The MBCA (1984) limits the right of dissent and appraisal basically to shares that are entitled to vote on the transaction, but many states do not impose this limitation and may permit nonvoting shares to elect to dissent from specific transactions.

Statutes usually make the statutory appraisal remedy exclusive in the absence of fraud, though some states purport to make it exclusive without exception, while others make it nonexclusive in all cases. Section 13.02(b) of MBCA (1984) follows the New York statute, which makes the appraisal remedy exclusive "unless the action is unlawful or fraudulent with respect to the shareholder or the corporation."

The Delaware Supreme Court in Weinberger v. UOP, Inc. (Del.1983) held that shareholders objecting to cash-out mergers solely on the basis of inadequate price must normally rely on the appraisal remedy rather than seeking recissory damages or an order setting aside the transaction. The court also relaxed the principles previously applicable in Delaware to determine the value of shares. This change was designed to make the appraisal remedy more attractive and easier to administer. However, the complexity of appraisal proceedings when applied to a large publicly held corporation should not be under-estimated. The appraisal proceeding involving minority shareholders of Technicolor, Inc. began with the original transaction in 1982; in early 2000, the case is still pending final resolution in the Delaware Chancery Court. It has been appealed twice to the Delaware Supreme Court and a third appeal seems likely.

Because appraisal claims may constitute serious cash drains, it is not uncommon in merger and other agreements to provide an "out" if an excessive number of dissents are filed. Following the affirmative vote on the proposal, the dissenting shareholders automatically have the status of creditor rather than shareholder. Unlike the Delaware statute, MBCA (1984) sets forth an elaborate procedure to determine value. The dissenting shareholders must designate in writing a price at which they are willing to sell and the corporation must respond by setting a written price at which it is willing to buy. If negotiation fails, a court proceeding to establish the appraised price follows. This appraised price is to be fixed as of the time immediately before the transaction in question is to occur, and no account is to be taken of the potential impact of the transaction on the value of the shares. Payment of the amount the corporation accepts as reasonable is required immediately in most cases.

The traditional appraisal remedy has a superficial appeal and plausibility. However, from the dissenting shareholders' point of view it is usually not an attractive remedy, and there has been litigation by parties seeking to avoid appraisal proceedings and suing for damages on other theories. The process involves potentially long delays, and litigation over the value of shares may be expensive and unrewarding. Since the corporation is an active participant in the judicial proceeding (seeking to establish the lowest possible valuation), the cards are to some extent stacked against dissenting shareholders. They must accept the judicially determined price that may be based primarily on evidence and materials presented by the corporation.

Chapter 13 of MBCA (1984) permits the court to award costs, including attorneys' fees, either for or against the corporation depending on the court's estimate as to whether valuations were made in good faith.

The statutes of many states contain a "market exception" to the appraisal remedy. Under these statutes, the right to dissent does not exist if there is a liquid market for the shares in question. Earlier versions of the Model Business Corporation Act contained such a provision, but it is not included in MBCA (1984). The theory behind the market exception is that the appraisal remedy is really necessary only for minority shareholders locked into the corporation. If a liquid market exists for the dissenters' shares there is no need for a statutory appraisal. The argument against such a restriction basically is that the modern purpose of the appraisal remedy is to protect shareholders against unattractive cash-out transactions. The "market exception" permits the corporation to time the transaction to minimize the cost of paying minority shareholders.

§ 20.13   Voluntary Dissolution

Most state statutes contain a variety of dissolution provisions. These include streamlined provisions for dissolution before commencement of business (by the incorporators or initial directors) and dissolution at any time with the unanimous consent of the shareholders.

The regular dissolution process involves the formal procedures required for organic changes: Adoption of a resolution to dissolve by the board of directors and approval of it by a majority (or some other percentage) of shareholders. Directors thus serve a gate keeping function with respect to the decision to dissolve. Some older states require the filing of a notice of intent to dissolve as the first step in the dissolution process. In these states, final articles of dissolution are filed only when the winding up process is completed. In MBCA (1984) and other states, only a single filing of articles of dissolution is required. This filing may be made at any time during the dissolution process. Irrespective of the type of statute involved, notice to creditors must be given, and final dissolution is permitted only after all franchise and other tax obligations have been satisfied. Directors are under a fiduciary duty to pay, discharge, or make provision for, all known liabilities of the corporation before making final liquidating distributions to shareholders.

State statutes provide that despite dissolution the existence of a corporation continues for a stated period (usually two years) so that the corporation may be sued on claims. A major problem in post-dissolution litigation is the status of product liability claimants arising after that period has expired.

For obvious reasons, there is no statutory right of appraisal in connection with a voluntary dissolution. There may be, however, equitable limitations on the power to dissolve. These involve situations where a voluntary dissolution is arguably unfair to minority shareholders or is a "freeze out" of minority shareholders. Cases have arisen where the objective of dissolution was apparently the elimination of some shareholders from sharing in the profits of a desirable business. In these situations, the business was not discontinued but turned over to a new corporation owned by some but not all of the previous shareholders. Were such behavior sanctioned, a minority could be ejected from a successful venture through the process of dissolution as readily as through a cash merger. If so, none of the statutory protections for minority shareholders presumably would be applicable. The test of "entire fairness" developed in the merger cases should logically apply to at least some statutory dissolutions as well.

§ 20.14 Changes Made by the 1999 MBCA Amendments

The significant revisions with respect to organic changes made by the Committee on Corporate Laws in 1999 means that the Model Act now diverges significantly from the actual law of any state. On the other hand, the net effect or spirit of the new provisions is quite consistent with the way the law actually works in most jurisdictions.

A fundamental change made in 1999 eliminates the right of shareholders in a surviving corporation to vote on many organic transactions. Thus in a traditional merger that combines the business of one corporation with another corporation, the shareholders of the surviving corporation do not automatically have the voting right and as a result they do not have an automatic appraisal right. However, another fundamental change gives shareholders the right to vote on every transaction that increases the number of shares issued by the corporation if the new shares carry 20 percent or more of the voting power and are issued other than for cash. [MBCA (1984) § 6.21, as amended] The 20 percent rule dramatically changes older rules; for example, the shareholders of the parent corporation in a triangular merger will have a right to vote if the transaction involves an increase in voting stock of 20 percent or more of the parent.

The 1999 amendments also change the voting rules to approve organic transactions. The new requirement is that a transaction is approved by a majority of the shares present at a meeting at which a quorum is present consisting of a majority of all shares. Prior law generally required a majority vote of all the outstanding shares (or in some states two-thirds of all shares) to approve an organic change. Under the 1999 amendments, a vote of a little over 25 percent of the outstanding shares may be sufficient.

The 1999 amendments also change significantly the rules relating to sales of assets by the corporation not in the ordinary course of business. The traditional rule is that shareholder approval is required when a transaction involves "all or substantially all" of corporate assets. As indicated in the preceding text, courts never applied this standard literally, and required shareholder approval of significant changes. The 1999 amendments adopt a more objective test. No vote is required if the corporation retains a "significant continuing business activity." Further, retention of a business activity that represents at least 25 percent of total assets and at least 25 percent of either income or revenues, is conclusively deemed to be a significant continuing business activity. In this calculation, activities and assets of subsidiaries whose financial statements are consolidated with the parent are deemed to belong to the parent corporation.

The 1999 amendments to MBCA (1984) authorize mergers of corporations with limited partnerships, limited liability companies or other types of entities. As indicated in the preceding text, several states currently authorize this type of transaction which permits a business to change its legal form without dissolving and reconstituting the business.

The 1999 amendments to the Model Act broadens the short form merger procedure to cover downstream as well as upstream mergers and the combination of one subsidiary with another subsidiary of the parent. In the case of an upstream merger a vote of neither the board of directors of the subsidiary nor the shareholders of the parent is required. However, if a downstream merger is involved, the shareholders of the parent corporation must approve the transaction.

Major changes are also made to the appraisal remedy. The commentary suggests that the appraisal remedy should be available only when two circumstances simultaneously exist:

(1) the action makes a fundamental change in the affected shares; and (2) uncertainty exists concerning the fair value of the affected shares that may cause reasonable persons to differ about the fairness of the corporate action.

Following this policy, the appraisal remedy is eliminated for all amendments to articles of incorporation (except for amendments involving reverse stock splits that reduce some shareholders to a fraction of a share that must be paid in cash). A "market exception" is reintroduced that differs from the earlier provision that was eliminated from the Model Act in 1978. The new market exception is applicable only where the market is "liquid" and the transaction does not involve a conflict of interest transaction. The phrase "liquid markets" is expressly defined. Another amendment eliminates access of shareholders to the appraisal remedy for shares that are entitled to vote on the transaction if the shares are not being changed or altered by the corporate action. However, minority shareholders of a subsidiary corporation that is being merged with the parent in a "short form" merger are entitled to appraisal rights.

[For unfamiliar terms see the Glossary]

*

GLOSSARY

ADOPTION is a contract principle by which a person agrees to assume a contract previously made for his or her benefit. An adoption speaks only from the time such person agrees, in contrast to a "ratification" which relates back to the time the original contract was made. In corporation law, the concept is applied when a newly formed corporation accepts a preincorporation contract made for its benefit by a promoter.

ADVANCES FOR EXPENSES refers to the payment of litigation expenses of a director or officer prior to the determination whether the director or officer has violated a duty to the corporation. See **INDEMNIFICATION**.

AFFILIATE is a corporation that is related to another corporation by shareholdings or other means of control. It includes not only a parent and its subsidiaries but also corporations that are under common control.

AGGRESSOR CORPORATION is a corporation that attempts to obtain control of a publicly held corporation, often by a direct cash tender or public exchange offer to shareholders, but also possibly by way of a merger or other transaction that requires agreement or assent of the target's management.

ALL HOLDERS' RULE is a rule adopted by SEC that prohibits a public offer by the issuer of shares that excludes designated shareholders.

ALTER EGO means "other self" and is a phrase widely used in piercing the corporate veil cases.

637

AMORTIZATION is an accounting procedure that gradually reduces the cost or value of a limited life or intangible asset through periodic charges against income. For fixed assets amortization is called "depreciation," and for wasting assets (natural resources) it is called "depletion." The periodic charges are usually treated as current expenses for purposes of determining income.

AMOTION is the common law procedure by which a director may be removed for cause by the shareholders.

ANTI–DILUTION PROVISIONS in convertible securities guarantee that a conversion privilege will not be adversely affected by share reclassifications, share splits, share dividends, or similar transactions that increase the number of outstanding shares.

APPRAISAL in corporation law is a limited statutory right granted to minority shareholders who formally dissent from specified fundamental transactions, e.g. mergers. In an appraisal proceeding a court determines the value of the dissenters' shares and the corporation must pay that value to the dissenting shareholders in cash. The Model Business Corporation Act (1984) uses the term "dissenters' rights to obtain payment for their shares" to describe this right.

ARBITRAGEURS are market investors who take off-setting positions in the same or similar securities in order to profit from small price variations. An arbitrageur, for example, may buy shares **on** the Pacific Coast Exchange and simultaneously sell the same shares on the New York Stock Exchange if any price discrepancy occurs between the quotations in the two markets. By taking advantage of momentary disparities in prices between markets, arbitrageurs perform the economic function of making those markets more efficient.

ARBS is a slang term for arbitrageurs.

ARTICLES OF INCORPORATION is the document that is filed in order to form a corporation under the Model Business Corporation Act. Under various state statutes, this document may be called a "certificate of incorporation," "charter," "articles of association," or other similar name.

ASE is an acronym for the American Stock Exchange.

AUTHORIZED SHARES are the shares described in the articles of incorporation that a corporation may issue. Modern corporate practice recommends authorization of more shares than the corporation currently planned to issue.

BENEFICIAL HOLDERS of securities are persons who own shares but who have not registered the shares in their names on the records of the corporation. See also: **RECORD OWNER**.

BLOCKAGE is a price phenomenon: A large block of shares may be more difficult to market than a smaller block in a thin market. The discount at which a large block sells below the price of a smaller block is blockage. Blockage is generally a phenomenon of shares that do not represent the controlling interest in a corporation. Compare: **CONTROL PREMIUM**.

BLUE SKY LAWS are state statutes that regulate the sale of securities to the public within the state. Most blue sky laws require the registration of new issues of securities with a state agency that reviews selling documents for accuracy and completeness. Blue sky laws also may regulate securities brokers and salesmen. A federal statute enacted in 1995, the National Securities Markets Improvement Act, preempts a significant portion of traditional blue sky law regulation.

BONDS are long term debt instruments secured by liens on corporate property. Historically, a bond was payable to bearer and interest coupons representing annual or semi-annual payments of interest were attached (to be "clipped" periodically and submitted for payment). Today, most bonds are issued in registered or book entry form, and interest is paid to the registered owner by check. The word bond is sometimes used more broadly to refer also to unsecured debt instruments, i.e., debentures.

BONUS SHARES are par value shares issued without consideration, usually in connection with the issuance of senior securities or debt instruments. Bonus shares with par values are considered a species of watered shares and may impose a liability on the recipient equal to the amount of par value.

BOOK ENTRY describes the method of reflecting ownership of publicly traded securities in which customers of brokerage firms receive confirmations of transactions but not certificates. Brokerage firms also may reflect their customers' ownership of securities by book entry in the records of a central clearing corporation, principally Depository Trust Company (DTC). DTC reflects transactions between brokerage firms primarily by book entry in its records rather than by the physical movement of securities. Shares held by DTC are recorded in the name of its nominee, Cede and Company.

BOOK VALUE is the value of shares determined on the basis of the books of the corporation. Using the corporation's latest balance sheet, liabilities are subtracted from assets, an appropriate amount is deducted to reflect the interest of senior securities, and what remains is divided by the number of outstanding common shares to obtain the book value per share.

BROKER in a securities transaction is a person who acts as an agent for a buyer or seller, or an intermediary between a buyer and seller, usually charging a commission. A broker who specializes in shares, bonds, commodities, or options must be registered with the exchange where the specific securities are traded. A broker differs from a dealer who (unlike a broker) buys or sells for his own account. Securities firms typically act both as dealers and as brokers, depending on the transaction involved.

BUYOUT is the purchase of a controlling percentage of a company's shares. A buyout often involves all of the company's outstanding shares. A buyout can be accomplished through a negotiated purchase, through a tender offer, or through a merger.

BYLAWS are the formal rules of internal governance adopted by a corporation. State corporation statutes contemplate that every corporation will adopt bylaws, though special close corporation statutes may make bylaws optional for eligible corporations.

CALL FOR REDEMPTION. See: **REDEMPTIONS**.

CALLS are options to buy securities at a stated price for a stated period. Calls are written on a variety of common shares, indexes, foreign currencies, and other securities. The person who commits himself to sell the security upon the request of the purchaser of the call is called the "writer" of the call. The act of making the purchase of the securities pursuant to the option is referred to as the "exercise" of the option. The price at which the call is exercisable is the "strike price." A call in which the market price is above the strike price is referred to as being "in the money." See also: **PUTS**.

CAPITAL STOCK is another phrase for common shares, often used when the corporation has only one class of shares outstanding.

CAPITAL SURPLUS, in the old Model Business Corporation Act nomenclature, is an equity or capital account that reflects the capital contributed for shares not allocated to stated capital. Capital surplus is traditionally the excess of issuance price over the par value of issued shares or the portion of consideration paid for no par shares that is not allocated to stated capital.

CAPITALIZATION is an imprecise term that usually refers to the funds received by a corporation for the issuance of its common and preferred shares. However, it may also refer to the proceeds of loans to a corporation made by its shareholders (which may be in lieu of capital contributions) or even to debt capital raised by the issuance of long term bonds to third persons. Depending on the context, it may also refer to accumulated earnings not withdrawn from the corporation.

CASH FLOW refers to an analysis of the movement of cash through a business as contrasted with the earnings of the business. For example, a mandatory debt repayment is taken into account in a cash flow analysis even though such a repayment does not reduce earnings. See: **NEGATIVE CASH FLOW**.

CASH MERGER is a merger transaction in which specified shareholders or interests in a corporation are required to accept cash for their shares.

CASH TENDER OFFER is a technique by which an aggressor seeks to acquire shares of a target corporation by making a public offer to purchase a specified fraction (usually a majority) of the target corporation's shares at an attractive price from persons who voluntarily tender their shares.

C CORPORATION is any corporation that has not elected S corporation tax status. The taxable income of a C corporation is subject to tax at the corporate level and dividends actually declared are taxed at the shareholder level. See **S CORPORATION.**

CEDE & COMPANY is the nominee for Depository Trust Company, the principal central clearing corporation.

CEO stands for "chief executive officer."

CERTIFICATE OF INCORPORATION in most states is the document prepared by the Secretary of State that evidences the acceptance of articles of incorporation and the commencement of the corporate existence. In Delaware the certificate of incorporation is the name given to the document originally filed with the Secretary of State to create the corporation. Many states have eliminated certificates of incorporation, substituting either a receipt for the filing fee or a notation on the filed articles of incorporation that they have been accepted by the Secretary of State.

CFO stands for "chief financial officer."

CHARTER may mean (i) the document filed with the Secretary of State, to create a corporation, or (ii) the grant by the state of the privilege of conducting business in corporate firm. "Charter" may also be used in a colloquial sense to refer to the basic constitutive documents of the corporation.

CLASS A SHARES. See **PARTICIPATING PREFERRED SHARES**.

CLASS ACTION is a suit brought by a plaintiff on behalf of all members of a class of plaintiffs suffering from a claimed common wrong.

CLASS VOTING. See: **VOTING GROUP**.

CLASSIFIED BOARD OF DIRECTORS may refer either (1) to a board of directors in which the individual members are elected by different classes of shares or (2) to a board of directors in which one-third or one-half of the directors are elected each year. See **STAGGERED BOARD**.

CLO stands for "chief legal officer."

CLOSE CORPORATION or **CLOSELY HELD CORPO-RATION** is a corporation with relatively few shareholders and no public market for its shares. Close corporations usually have never made a public offering of shares and the shares themselves are often made subject to restrictions on transfer. "Close" and "closely held" are synonymous.

COMMON SHAREHOLDERS are the ultimate owners of the residual interest in a corporation. Common shareholders typically have the right to select directors to manage the enterprise and to receive dividends out of the earnings of the enterprise when and as declared by the directors. They are also entitled to a per share distribution of the assets that remain upon dissolution after satisfying or making provisions for creditors and holders of senior securities

COMMON SHARES represent the residual ownership interests in the corporation.

CONSOLIDATION is an amalgamation of two corporations pursuant to statutory provision in which both of the corporations disappear and a new corporation is formed. The Model Business Corporation Act (1984) eliminates the consolidation as a distinct type of corporate amalgamation. See **MERGERS.**

CONTROL OF A CORPORATION by a person normally means that that person has power to vote a majority of the outstanding voting shares. However, control may effectively exist in a minority shareholder because of personal relationships with other shareholders or because the remaining shares are scattered in small, disorganized holdings.

CONTROL PERSON in securities law is a person who is in a control relationship with the issuer. Sales of securities by control persons are subject to many of the requirements applicable to the sale of securities directly by the issuer itself. In addition, controlling persons have a duty under ITSFEA to prevent insider trading by persons under their control.

CONTROL PREMIUM describes the pricing phenomenon by which shares that carry the power of control over a corporation are more valuable per share than the shares that do not carry a power of control. The control premium is often computed not on a per share basis but on the aggregate increase in value of the "control block" over the going market or other price of the remaining shares.

CONVERSION SECURITIES are the securities into which convertible securities may be converted.

CONVERTIBLE SECURITIES are securities that include the right of exchanging the convertible securities at the option of their holder for a designated number of shares of another class, called the conversion securities. The ratio between the convertible and conversion securities is fixed at the time the convertible securities are issued, and may be protected against dilution.

COO stands for "chief operations officer."

CO–PROMOTERS. See: **PROMOTERS**.

CORPORATE OPPORTUNITY is a fiduciary concept that limits the power of officers, directors, and employees to take personal advantage of opportunities that belong to the corporation.

CORPORATION BY ESTOPPEL is a doctrine that prevents a third person from holding an "officer," "director," or "shareholder" of a nonexistent corporation personally liable on an obligation entered into in the name of the nonexistent corporation. The theory is that the third person relied on the existence of the corporation and is now "estopped" from denying that the corporation existed.

CUMULATIVE DIVIDENDS on preferred shares carry over from one year to the next if a cumulative dividend is omitted. All omitted cumulative dividends must be made up in a later year before any dividend may be paid on the common shares in that year. Cumulative dividends are not debts of the corporation but merely a right to priority in future distributions.

CUMULATIVE TO THE EXTENT EARNED DIVIDENDS on preferred shares are dividends that are cumulative in any one year only to the extent of available earnings of the corporation for that year.

CUMULATIVE VOTING is a method of voting that allows substantial minority shareholders to obtain representation on the board of directors. When voting cumulatively, a shareholder may multiply the number of shares he owns by the number of director positions to be filled at that election, and cast that number of votes for any one candidate or spread that number among two or more candidates.

D & O INSURANCE means directors' and officers' liability insurance. Such insurance insures officers and directors against claims based on negligence, failure to disclose, and to a limited extent, other defalcations. D & O insurance also provides coverage against expenses and to a limited extent against fines, judgments, and amounts paid in settlement by insured persons.

DEADLOCK in a closely held corporation arises when a control structure permits one or more factions of shareholders to block corporate action if they disagree with some aspect of corporate policy. A deadlock usually arises with respect to the election of directors by an equal division of shares between two factions. A deadlock may also arise at the level of the board of directors if there are an even number of directors and no since faction of shareholders has power to elect a majority of the board.

DEBENTURES are long term unsecured debt instruments. See: **BONDS**.

DEEP ROCK DOCTRINE is a principle of bankruptcy law by which unfair or inequitable claims presented by controlling shareholders of bankrupt corporations may be subordinated to claims of general or trade creditors. The doctrine received its name from the corporate name of the subsidiary involved in the leading case articulating the doctrine.

DE FACTO CORPORATION at common law is a partially formed corporation that provides a shield against personal liability of shareholders for corporate obligations. Such a corporation may be attacked only by the state.

DE FACTO MERGER is a transaction that has the economic effect of a statutory merger but is cast in the form of an acquisition of assets or voting stock and is treated by a court as a statutory merger. Modern jurisprudence generally rejects the principle of de facto merger.

DE JURE CORPORATION at common law is a corporation that is sufficiently formed that it is recognized as a corporation for all purposes. A de jure corporation may exist even though some minor statutory requirements have not been fully complied with. See **DIRECTORY REQUIREMENTS.**

DELECTUS PERSONAE is a Latin phrase used in partnership law to describe the power each partner possesses to accept or reject proposed new members of the firm.

DEPOSITORY TRUST CORPORATION (DTC) is the principal central clearing agency for securities trades. See: **BOOK ENTRY**.

DEREGISTRATION of an issuer occurs when the assets and number of securities holders of an issuer registered under section 12 of the Securities Exchange Act of 1934 declines to the point where registration is no longer required. See: **REGISTERED CORPORATION**.

DERIVATIVE SUIT is a suit brought by a shareholder in the name of a corporation to correct a wrong done to the corporation.

DILUTION of outstanding shares may result from the issuance of additional shares. The dilution may be of voting power (if shares are not issued proportionately to the holdings of existing shareholders) or of financial interests (if shares are issued disproportionately and the price at which the new shares are issued is less than the value of the outstanding shares).

DIRECTORY REQUIREMENTS are minor statutory requirements. At common law, a de jure corporation is created despite the failure to comply with directory requirements relating to its formation.

DISCOUNT SHARES are par value shares issued for cash less than par value. Discount shares are a species of watered stock.

DISSENSION in a closely held corporation refers to personal quarrels or disputes among shareholders that may make business relations unpleasant and interfere with the successful operation of the business. Dissension may occur without constituting oppression or causing a deadlock or adversely affecting the corporation's business.

DISSENTERS' RIGHT. See: **APPRAISAL**.

DISTRIBUTION is a payment to shareholders by a corporation. If out of present or past earnings it is a dividend. The word distribution is sometimes accompanied by a word describing the source or purpose of the payment, e.g., Distribution of Capital Surplus, or Liquidating Distribution.

DIVIDEND is a distribution to shareholders from or out of current or past earnings.

DOT.COM COMPANIES are corporations formed during the 1990s to take advantage of the new computer and internet technologies.

DOUBLE TAXATION refers to the structure of taxation under the Internal Revenue Code of 1954 that subjects income earned by a C corporation to a tax at the corporate level and a second tax at the shareholder level if dividends are paid.

DOWN STREAM MERGER is the merger of a parent corporation into its subsidiary.

EARNINGS PER SHARE equals a firm's net income after distributions to senior securities divided by the number of outstanding common shares.

EQUITY or **EQUITY INTEREST** in general refers to the extent of an ownership interest in a venture. In this context, ownership interest refers to the economic concept that an owner's "equity" in a business is equal to that business's assets minus its liabilities and amounts allocable to senior securities.

EQUITY FINANCING is raising money by the sale of common or preferred shares.

EQUITY INSOLVENCY. See **INSOLVENCY.**

EQUITY SECURITY is a security that represents an ownership interest in the business, typically common or preferred shares.

EX DIVIDEND refers to the date on which a purchaser of publicly traded shares is not entitled to receive a dividend that has been previously declared. On and after the ex-dividend date the seller of shares is entitled to retain the dividend. The ex dividend date is a matter of agreement or convention established by the securities exchange. For publicly traded securities the current ex-dividend date is three days before the record date. See **RECORD DATE, PAYABLE DATE.**

EX RIGHTS refers to the date on which a purchaser of publicly traded shares is not entitled to receive rights that have been declared on the shares.

FACE VALUE is the stated value of a bond, note, mortgage, or other security on the maturity date of the security. Face value may also refer to the par value or nominal value of any instrument.

FORCED CONVERSION refers to a conversion of a convertible security following a call for redemption at a time when the value of the conversion security is greater than the amount that will be received if the holder permits the security to be redeemed.

FORWARD LOOKING STATEMENT is a public statement by a corporation that makes projections of financial data, estimates of future sales or profitability, discussion of management objectives and goals, or discussion of economic trends affecting the business.

FREEZE–OUT refers to any process by which minority shareholders are prevented from receiving financial return from the corporation in an effort to persuade them to liquidate their investment in the corporation on terms favorable to the controlling shareholders.

FREEZE–OUT MERGER. See **CASH MERGER**.

GENERAL PARTNERS are all partners in a general partnership and the managing partners in a limited partnership. General partners have power to participate in management of the business and are liable for the obligations of the business if the partnership has not elected to be a limited liability partnership.

GOING PRIVATE refers to a transaction in which smaller shareholders of a corporation are compelled to accept cash for their shares while larger shareholders retain their shares. A going private transaction may involve a merger of a publicly held corporation into its subsidiary in a cash merger.

GOLDEN PARACHUTE is a lucrative contract given to an executive of a corporation that provides additional economic benefits in case control of the corporation changes hands and the executive leaves, either voluntarily or involuntarily. A golden parachute may include severance pay, stock options, or a bonus payable when the executive's employment at the corporation ends.

GREENMAIL is a slang term that refers to a payment by the target to an aggressor to purchase shares acquired by the aggressor at a premium over the price paid by the aggressor. The aggressor in exchange agrees to discontinue its takeover effort.

HOLDING COMPANY is a corporation that owns a majority of the shares of one or more other corporations. A holding company is not engaged in any business other than the ownership of shares. See: **INVESTMENT COMPANIES**.

HYBRID SECURITIES are securities that have some of the attributes of both debt securities and equity securities.

INCORPORATORS are the person or persons who execute the articles of incorporation to form a corporation.

INDEMNIFICATION is a repayment by a corporation of expenses incurred by officers or directors who have been named as defendants in litigation relating to corporate affairs. In some instances, indemnification of amounts paid to satisfy judgments or settlement agreements also may be proper.

INDENTURE is the contract that defines the rights of holders of bonds or debentures as against the corporation. Typically, the contract is entered into between the corporation and an indenture trustee whose responsibility is to protect the bondholders.

INDEPENDENT DIRECTOR is a director of a publicly held corporation who has never been an employee of the corporation or any of its subsidiaries, is not a relative of any employee of the company, provides no services to the company, is not employed by any firm providing major services to the company, and receives no compensation from the company other than director fees. See **INSIDE DIRECTOR, OUTSIDE DIRECTOR.**

INITIAL PUBLIC OFFERING (IPO) is the first sale of equity securities to the general public by a startup business.

IN PARI DELICTO is a common law principle also known as the "unclean hands" doctrine. It prohibits a person engaging in wrongful conduct from suing another wrongdoer when things do not work out as expected.

INSIDE DIRECTOR is a director of a publicly held corporation who holds executive positions with management. See **INDEPENDENT DIRECTOR, OUTSIDE DIRECTOR.**

INSIDER is a term of uncertain scope that refers to persons having a relationship with a corporation, its directors, officers, or senior employees.

INSIDER TRADING refers to unlawful transactions in shares of publicly held corporations by persons with inside or advance information on which the trading is based. Usually but not always the trader himself is an insider.

INSOLVENCY may be either "equity insolvency" or "insolvency in the bankruptcy sense." Equity insolvency means the business is unable to pay its debts as they mature while bankruptcy insolvency means the aggregate liabilities of the business exceeds its assets. It is not uncommon for a business to be unable to meet its debts as they mature and yet have assets that exceed in value its liabilities, or be able to meet its debts as they mature and yet have liabilities that exceed in value its assets.

INSTITUTIONAL INVESTORS are investors who largely invest other people's money, e.g. mutual funds, pension funds, and life insurance companies.

INTERLOCKING DIRECTORS are persons who serve simultaneously on the boards of directors of two or more corporations that have dealings with each other.

INVESTMENT BANKERS are commercial organizations chiefly involved in the business of handling the distribution of new issues of securities.

INVESTMENT COMPANIES are corporations involved in the business of investing in securities of other businesses. The most common kind of investment company is the mutual fund. An investment company differs from a holding company in that the latter seeks control of the ventures in which it invests while an investment company seeks investments for their own sake and normally diversifies against risks.

ISSUED SHARES are shares a corporation has actually issued and outstanding.

ITSA is the acronym for the Insider Trading Sanctions Act of 1984.

ITSFEA is the acronym for the Insider Trading and Securities Fraud Enforcement Act of 1988.

JOINT VENTURE is a limited purpose partnership largely governed by the rules applicable to partnerships. In an earlier day, many states permitted corporations to participate in joint ventures but not in general partnerships.

JUNIOR SECURITIES are securities that are subordinate to other issued securities in terms of dividends, interest, principal, security, or payments upon dissolution.

LBO means leveraged buyout.

LEVERAGE refers to advantages that may accrue to a business through the use of debt obtained from third persons instead of additional contributed capital. Third party debt improves the earnings allocable to contributed capital if the business earns more on each dollar invested than the interest cost of the additional funds.

LEVERAGED BUYOUT (LBO) is a transaction in which an outside entity purchases all the shares of a public corporation primarily with borrowed funds. Ultimately the debt incurred to finance the takeover is assumed by the acquired business. If incumbent management has a significant financial and participatory interest in the outside entity, the transaction may be referred to as a management buyout (MBO).

LIMITED LIABILITY COMPANY (LLC) is an unincorporated business form that provides limited liability for its owners and may be taxed as a partnership. A certificate must be filed with a state official to create an LLC.

LIMITED LIABILITY PARTNERSHIP (LLP) is a general partnership that has elected to register under state statutes that provide protection against liability for actions of co-partners. To create an LLP, a certificate that is renewable annually must be filed with a state official. Limited liability partnerships may provide "partial shields" or "full shields" against liability, depending on state law.

LIMITED LIABILITY LIMITED PARTNERSHIP (LLLP) is a limited partnership that has elected to register under state statutes that provide protection for general partners against liability for actions of other general partners. To create an LLLP a certificate that is renewable annually must be filed with a state official.

LIMITED PARTNERSHIP (LP) is a partnership consisting of one or more limited partners (whose liability for partnership debts is limited to the amount invested) and one or more general partners who have unlimited liability. A limited partner who participates in the management of the partnership business may inadvertently assume the liability of a general partner. A certificate must be filed with a state official to create a limited partnership.

LIQUIDATING DISTRIBUTION or **LIQUIDATING DIVIDEND** is a distribution of assets to shareholders by a corporation that is reducing capital or going out of business. Such a payment may be made if management decides to sell off certain company assets and distribute the proceeds to shareholders.

LIQUIDITY refers to the market characteristic of a security or commodity that has enough units outstanding and publicly traded that purchases and sales occur routinely and usually without a substantial variation in price.

LOCKUP is a slang term that refers to a transaction designed to defeat a party in a contested takeover. A lockup usually involves the setting aside of securities for purchase by friendly interests in order to defeat or make more difficult the competitive takeover.

MANAGEMENT BUYOUT (MBO). See **LEVERAGED BUYOUT.**

MANAGEMENT'S DISCUSSION AND ANALYSIS OF FINANCIAL CONDITION AND RESULTS OF OPERATIONS is an important portion of the annual report that must be distributed to shareholders by corporations registered under the Securities Exchange Act of 1934.

MANDATORY REQUIREMENTS are statutory requirements that must be substantially complied with if a de jure corporation is to be formed.

MATURITY DATE is the date on which the principal amount of a note, draft, acceptance, bond, or other debt instrument becomes due and payable.

MD & A is an abbreviation for "Management's Discussion and Analysis of Financial Condition and Results of Operations."

MERGER is an amalgamation of two corporations pursuant to statutory provision in which one of the corporations survives and the other disappears. Compare **CONSOLIDATION.**

MUTUAL FUND is a publicly held open end investment company. An "open end" investment company stands ready at all times to redeem its shares at net asset value. A mutual fund thus provides the advantages of liquidity, diversification of investment, and skilled investment advice for the small investor.

NASD is the acronym for the National Association of Securities Dealers.

NASDAQ is an acronym for "National Association of Securities Dealers Automated Quotations" and is the principal source of information about transactions on the over-the-counter market.

NEGATIVE CASH FLOW means the cash needs of a business exceed its cash intake. Short periods of negative cash flow create no problem for most businesses; longer periods of negative cash flow may require additional capital investment if the business is to avoid insolvency.

NET WORTH is the amount by which assets exceed liabilities.

NEW ISSUE is a security being offered to the public for the first time. New issues may be initial public offerings by private companies or additional classes or types of securities offered by public companies.

NIMBLE DIVIDENDS are dividends paid out of current earnings at a time when there is a deficit in earned surplus. Some state statutes do not permit nimble dividends. The concept of nimble dividends has application only under traditional legal capital statutes.

NOMINEE REGISTRATION is a form of securities registration widely used by institutional investors and fiduciaries to avoid onerous registration or disclosure requirements. Nominee registration usually is in the form of "and Company," e.g. "Smith and Company."

NON–CALLABLE preferred shares or bonds are securities that cannot be redeemed at the option of the issuer.

NON-CUMULATIVE VOTING or **STRAIGHT VOTING** limits the number of votes a shareholder may cast for a single candidate to the number of shares he owns.

NONVOTING COMMON SHARES are a class of shares that do not have the right to vote for directors and on other issues generally coming before the shareholders. Nonvoting shares may be entitled to vote as a separate voting group on certain proposed changes that adversely affect that class.

NO PAR SHARES are shares issued under a traditional par value statute that are stated to have no par value. Such shares may be issued for any consideration designated by the board of directors. In other respects no par shares do not differ significantly from par value shares. In states that have abolished par value, the concept of no par shares is obsolete.

NOVATION is a contract principle by which a third person takes over the rights and duties of a party to a contract and that party is released from the contract. A novation requires the consent of the other party to the contract, but that consent may be implied from the circumstances.

NSMIA is an acronym for the National Securities Market Improvement Act (1996). NSMIA preempts significant portions of traditional state blue sky laws.

NYSE is an acronym for the New York Stock Exchange

OPPRESSION in a close corporation involves conduct by controlling shareholders that deprive a minority shareholder of legitimate expectations concerning roles in the corporation, including participation in management and earnings.

ORGANIZATIONAL EXPENSES are the costs of organizing a corporation, including filing fees, attorneys' fees, and related expenses. Organizational expenses may also include the cost of raising the initial capital through the distribution of securities.

OUTSIDE DIRECTOR is a director of a publicly held corporation who does not hold an executive position with management. Outside directors, however, may include investment bankers, attorneys, or others who provide advice or services to incumbent management and therefore are not independent directors. See **INDEPENDENT DIRECTOR, INSIDE DIRECTOR.**

OVER–THE–COUNTER refers to the NASDAQ securities market. In this market, brokers and dealers purchase or sell securities by computer hook-up or telephone rather than through the facilities of a securities exchange.

PAR VALUE or **STATED VALUE** of shares is a nominal value assigned to each share. At one time par value represented the selling or issuance price of shares, but in modern corporate practice, par value has little or no significance. The Model Business Corporation Act (1984) and the statutes of many states have eliminated the concept of par value.

PARTICIPATING PREFERRED SHARES are preferred shares that, in addition to paying a stipulated dividend, give the holder the right to participate with common shareholders in additional distributions of earnings under specified conditions. Participatory preferred shares may be called class A common or given a similar designation to reflect their open-ended rights.

PAYABLE DATE is the date on which a dividend or distribution is actually paid to a shareholder.

PENDENT JURISDICTION is a principle applied in federal courts that allows state-created causes of action arising out of the same transaction to be joined with a federal cause of action even if diversity of citizenship is not present.

POISON PILL is an issue of shares by a corporation designed to protect the corporation against an unwanted takeover. A poison pill creates rights in existing shareholders to acquire debt or stock of the target (or of the aggressor upon a subsequent merger) at bargain prices upon the occurrence of specified events, such as the announcement of a cash tender offer or the acquisition by an outsider of a specified percentage of the shares of the target. A poison pill is effective because it dilutes the interest being sought by the aggressor to a point where acquisition of control becomes impractical. The effect of a poison pill usually is to compel the aggressor to negotiate with the target in order to persuade it to withdraw the pill.

POOLING AGREEMENT is a contractual arrangement among shareholders relating to the voting of shares.

PREEMPTIVE RIGHTS give an existing shareholder the opportunity to purchase or subscribe for a proportionate part of a new issue of shares before it is offered to other persons. A preemptive right protects shareholders from dilution of value and control when new shares are issued. In modern practice, preemptive rights are often limited or denied by provisions in the governing corporate documents.

PREFERRED SHARES are shares that have preferential rights to dividends or to amounts distributable on liquidation, or to both, ahead of common shareholders.

PREFERRED SHAREHOLDERS' CONTRACT refers to the provisions of the articles of incorporation, bylaws, or resolutions of the board of directors that define the rights of holders of the preferred shares in question. Preferred share-holders have only limited statutory or common law rights outside of the preferred shareholders' contract. The terms of the preferred shareholders= contract may usually be amended without the consent of individual holders of preferred shares if the amendments are approved by the holders of a specified percentage of the class of preferred shares.

PREINCORPORATION SUBSCRIPTION. See **SUBSCRIPTION**.

PRICE–EARNINGS RATIO is the ratio of earnings per share to current stock price.

PROMOTERS are persons who develop or take the initiative in founding or organizing a business venture. Where more than one promoter is involved in a venture, they are called co-promoters.

PROSPECTUS is a document furnished to a prospective purchaser of a security that describes the security being purchased, the issuer, and the investment or risk characteristics of that security.

PROPRIETORSHIP is an unincorporated business owned by a single person.

PROXY is a person authorized to vote someone else's shares. Depending on the context, proxy may also refer to the grant of authority itself [the **PROXY APPOINTMENT**], or the document granting the authority [the **PROXY APPOINTMENT FORM**].

PROXY SOLICITATION MACHINERY is a phrase commonly used to describe the process by which proxy appointments are solicited from shareholders. Incumbent management of a publicly held corporation may use corporate funds to communicate with shareholders and may represent its views as the views of "management."

PROXY STATEMENT is the document that must accompany a solicitation of proxy appointments under SEC regulations. The purpose of the proxy statement is to provide shareholders with relevant information.

PSLRA IS AN ACRONYM for the Private Securities Litigation Reform Act of 1995.

PUBLIC OFFERING is the sale of securities by an issuer or a person controlling the issuer to members of the public. Normally registration of a public offering under the Securities Act of 1933 is required though in some instances exemptions from registration may be available.

PUBLICLY HELD CORPORATION is a corporation that is required to register under the Securities Exchange Act of 1934.

PUTS are options to sell securities at a stated price for a stated period. If the share price declines, the value of put option increases and the put option is described as being "in the money." A holder of an "in the money" put option may sell the put option or purchase the shares at the lower market price and "put" the shares to the put writer at the contract price.

QUO WARRANTO is a common law writ designed to test whether a person exercising power is legally entitled to do so. Quo warranto may be used to test whether a corporation is validly organized or whether it has power to engage in the business in which it is involved.

RAIDER is a slang term for an aggressor (an individual or corporation) that attempts to take control of a target corporation by buying a controlling interest in its stock.

RATIFICATION. See **ADOPTION.**

RECAPITALIZATION is a restructuring of the capital of the corporation through amendment of articles of incorporation or a merger with a subsidiary or parent corporation. Recapitalizations may involve the elimination of unpaid cumulated preferred dividends, the reduction or elimination of par value, the creation of new classes of senior securities, or similar transactions. A leveraged recapitalization involves the substitution of debt for equity in the capital structure of the corporation.

RECORD DATE is the date on which the identity of shareholders entitled to vote, to receive dividends, or to receive notice is ascertained.

RECORD OWNER of shares is the person in whose name shares are registered on the records of the corporation. A record owner is treated as the owner of the shares by the corporation whether or not that person is the beneficial owner of the shares.

REDEMPTION means the reacquisition of a security by the issuer pursuant to a provision in the security that specifies the terms on which the reacquisition may take place. Typically, a holder of a security that has been called for redemption has a limited period thereafter to decide whether or not to exercise a conversion right, if one exists.

REDUCTION SURPLUS is a term used in a few states with par value statutes to refer to surplus created by a reduction of stated capital. Many states treat that surplus as capital surplus.

REGISTERED CORPORATION is a corporation that has registered a publicly held class of securities under the Securities Exchange Act of 1934. Registration under the 1934 Act should be contrasted with the registration of a public distribution of shares under the Securities Act of 1933.

REGISTRATION of an issue of securities under the Securities Act of 1933 permits the public sale of those securities in interstate commerce or through the mails. Registration under the 1933 Act should be distinguished from the registration of classes of publicly held securities under the Securities Exchange Act of 1934.

REGISTRATION STATEMENT is the document that must be filed to permit registration of an issue of securities under the Securities Act of 1933. A major component of the registration statement is the prospectus supplied to purchasers of the securities.

REORGANIZATION is a general term for corporate amalgamations or readjustments. The Internal Revenue Code sets forth the following types of reorganizations: A Class A reorganization is a merger or consolidation pursuant to the statutes of a specific state. A Class B reorganization is a transaction by which one corporation exchanges its voting shares for the voting shares of another corporation. A Class C reorganization is a transaction in which one corporation exchanges its voting shares for the property and assets of another corporation. A Class D reorganization is a "spin off" of assets by one corporation to a new corporation. A Class E reorganization is a recapitalization. A Class F reorganization is a "mere change of identity, form, or place of organization, however effected." A Class G reorganization is a "transfer by a corporation of all or part of its assets to another corporation" in specified situations. See **RECAPITALIZATION.**

RESCISSORY DAMAGES are damages calculated on the basis of what an interest in a business would have been worth today if an invalid or voidable transaction that affected the value of that interest had not occurred.

RETAINED EARNINGS are net profits accumulated by a corporation. Retained earnings are also called "undistributed profits" or "earned surplus."

REVERSE STOCK SPLIT is an amendment to the articles of incorporation that permits a corporation to reduce the number of its shares outstanding. Reverse stock splits may create fractional shares that must be redeemed for cash. Thus a reverse stock split may be used as a device to go private by reducing the number of shares to the point that no public shareholder owns a full share of stock, and providing that all fractional shares must be redeemed for cash.

REVERSE TRIANGULAR MERGER. See **TRIANGULAR MERGER**.

RIGHTS are short term options to purchase shares from a corporation at a fixed price. Rights may be issued as a substitute for a dividend or as a "sweetener" in connection with the issuance of senior or debt securities. Rights may be publicly traded.

ROUND LOT is the standard trading unit of securities. For most securities a round lot is 100 shares.

S CORPORATION is a corporation that has elected to be taxed under Subchapter S. The taxable income of an S corporation is not subject to tax at the corporate level. Rather, it is allocated for tax purposes to the shareholders to be taxed as though all earnings were distributed. S corporation taxation is similar to but not identical with partnership taxation.

SCRIP is issued in lieu of fractional shares in connection with a stock dividend. Scrip represents the right to receive a portion of a share; it is transferable so that investors may acquire scrip from several sources and assemble the right to obtain a full additional share.

SATURDAY NIGHT SPECIAL is a surprise tender offer that expires in one week. Designed to capitalize on panic and haste, the offer may be made Friday afternoon to take advantage of the fact that markets and most offices are closed on Saturday and Sunday. "Saturday night specials" are prohibited by the Williams Act.

SECONDARY MARKET means the securities exchanges and over-the-counter markets where securities are bought and sold following their initial distribution. Secondary market transactions are between investors and do involve directly the corporation that originally issued the securities.

SECURITIES is a general term that includes not only traditional securities such as shares of stock, bonds, and debentures, but also a variety of interests that involve an investment with the return primarily or exclusively dependent on the efforts of a person other than the investor.

SECURITIES EXCHANGES are markets for the purchase and sale of traditional securities. The New York Stock Exchange is the best known and largest securities exchange.

SECURITY–FOR–EXPENSES statutes enacted in some states require certain plaintiffs in derivative litigation to post a bond with sureties from which the corporation and the other defendants may be reimbursed for their expenses if the defendants prevail. The Model Business Corporation Act (1984) does not impose a security-for-expenses requirement.

SENIOR SECURITIES are debt securities or preferred shares that have a claim on a corporation's assets and earnings that is prior to those of common shares.

SERIES OF PREFERRED SHARES are subclasses of preferred shares with differing dividend rates, redemption prices, rights on dissolution, conversion rights, or the like.

The terms of a series of preferred shares may be established by the directors so that a corporation periodically engaged in preferred shares financing may shape its offerings of preferred shares from time to time to market conditions.

SHARE DIVIDEND is a proportional distribution of additional shares to existing shareholders. A share dividend is often viewed as a substitute for a cash dividend, and shareholders may sell share dividends without realizing that they thereby dilute their ownership interest in the corporation.

SHARE SPLIT is a proportional change in the number of outstanding shares. In a 2–for–1 share split, for example, each shareholder receives one additional share for each share currently owned, thereby doubling the number of outstanding shares. A share split differs from a share dividend primarily in degree; there are, however, technical differences. For example, in a stock dividend no adjustment is typically made in the regular dividend rate per share while an adjustment in the dividend rate is usually made in a stock split. There are other technical differences in the handling of stock splits and stock dividends under the statutes of some states.

SHAREHOLDERS or **STOCKHOLDERS** are the persons who own shares of common or preferred stock. The Model Business Corporation Act (1984) and modern usage generally prefers "shareholder" to "stockholder" but the latter word is deeply ingrained in common usage.

SHORT FORM MERGER is a merger of a largely or wholly owned subsidiary into a parent through a stream-lined procedure permitted under the Model Business Corporation Act (1984) and statutes of many states.

SINKING FUND refers to an obligation sometimes imposed pursuant to the issuance of debt securities or preferred shares under which the issuer is required each year to retire or repurchase a specific fraction of the issue. A sinking fund obligation may be met each year either by redeeming a portion of the outstanding securities or by purchasing them on the open market and retiring them.

SLUSA is an acronym for the Securities Litigation Uniform Standards Act (1998). SLUSA preempts a significant portion of state securities fraud class action law.

SQUEEZE–OUTS are techniques to eliminate or reduce minority interests in a corporation. Squeeze-outs may occur in a variety of contexts. For example, in a "going private" transaction minority shareholders may be compelled to accept cash for their shares, while controlling shareholders retain their shares. New shares may be offered for purchase to existing shareholders under terms that require minority shareholders either to accept a significant reduction in their proportional interest in the corporation or invest additional capital for which they will receive little or no return. Many squeeze-outs involve the use of cash mergers.

STAGGERED BOARD is a board of directors in which a fraction of the board is elected each year. In staggered boards, members serve two or three years, depending on whether the board is classified into two or three groups.

START–UP is a newly formed business. The phrase is often used in connection with "dot.com" companies hoping to go public in the near future.

STATED CAPITAL in the old Model Business Corporation Act nomenclature represents the permanent capital of the corporation. Technically, it consists of the sum of the par values of all issued shares plus the consideration for no par shares to the extent not transferred to capital surplus plus other amounts that may be transferred from other accounts into the stated capital account.

STATED VALUE. See: **PAR VALUE**.

STOCKHOLDERS. See: **SHAREHOLDERS**.

STRAIGHT VOTING. See: **NON–CUMULATIVE VOT-ING**.

STREET NAME originally referred to the practice of regis-tering publicly traded securities in the names of Wall Street brokerage firms to facilitate the closing of securities trans-actions occurring on various stock exchanges. This practice largely disappeared in the early 1960s with the creation of the modern central clearing corporation and book entry registration of securities ownership. Today, shares regis-tered in book entry form are commonly referred to as "street name" shares.

STRIKE SUITS is a slang term for litigation instituted for its nuisance value or to improve changes of obtaining a favorable settlement.

SUBCHAPTER S refers to the subchapter of the Internal Revenue Code of 1954 that regulates the S corporation. See **S CORPORATION**.

SUBSCRIBERS are persons who agree to invest in the corporation by purchasing shares of stock. Subscribers today usually commit themselves to invest by entering into con-tracts defining the extent and terms of their commitment; at an earlier time subscribers usually executed "subscrip-tions" or "subscription agreements."

SUBSCRIPTION is an offer to buy a specified number of theretofore unissued shares from a corporation. If the corpo-ration is not yet in existence, a subscription is known as a "preincorporation subscription," that is enforceable by the corporation after it has been formed and is irrevocable despite the absence of consideration or the usual elements of a contract.

SUBSIDIARY is a corporation that is majority or wholly owned by another corporation.

SURPLUS is a general term in corporate practice that usually refers to the excess of assets over liabilities of a corporation. Surplus has a more definite meaning when combined with a descriptive adjective such as earned surplus, capital surplus, or reduction surplus.

TAINTED SHARES are shares owned by a person who is disqualified for some reason from serving as a plaintiff in a derivative action. The shares are "tainted" since for policy reasons a good faith transferee of such shares is also disqualified from serving as a plaintiff.

TAKEOVER ATTEMPT or **TAKEOVER BID** are generic terms to describe an attempt by an outside corporation or group to wrest control away from incumbent management. A takeover attempt may involve a purchase of shares, a tender offer, a sale of assets, or a proposal that the target merge voluntarily into the aggressor.

TARGET CORPORATION is a corporation the control of which is sought by an aggressor corporation.

TENDER OFFER is a public invitation to shareholders of a corporation to tender their shares for purchase by the offeror at a stated price.

THIN CORPORATION is a corporation with an excessive amount of debt in its capitalization.

TIP is information not available to the general public passed by one person (the "tipper") to another (the "tippee") as a basis for a decision to buy or sell a security. Trading by tippees in many circumstances violates federal securities law.

TRANSFER AGENT is an organization (often a bank) that handles transfers of shares for a publicly held corporation. Generally, a transfer agent assures that certificates submitted for transfer are properly endorsed and that there is appropriate documentation of the right to transfer. A transfer agent also issues new certificates and oversees the cancellation of old ones. Transfer agents also may maintain the record of shareholders for the corporation and arrange for the distribution of dividends to shareholders who hold shares in book entry form.

TREASURY SHARES are shares that were once issued but have been reacquired by the corporation. Treasury shares are economically indistinguishable from authorized but unissued shares but historically have been treated as having an intermediate status. For example, treasury shares may usually be issued without regard to the par value rules applicable to the issuance of authorized shares. The Model Business Corporation Act (1984) and statutes of several states eliminate the concept of treasury shares and treat reacquired shares as authorized but unissued shares.

TRIANGULAR MERGER is a method of amalgamation of two corporations in which the disappearing corporation is merged into a subsidiary of the parent corporation. Shareholders of the disappearing corporation receive shares of the parent corporation. In a reverse triangular merger the subsidiary is merged into the disappearing corporation so that the corporation being acquired becomes a wholly owned subsidiary of the parent corporation.

ULTRA VIRES is the common law doctrine relating to the effect of corporate acts that exceed the powers or stated purposes of a corporation.

UNDERWRITERS are persons who buy shares with a view toward their further distribution. Used almost exclusively in connection with the public distribution of securities, an underwriter may be either a commercial enterprise engaged in the distribution of securities (an investment banker), or a person who simply buys securities without an investment intent and with a "view" toward further distribution.

UP STREAM MERGER is a merger of a subsidiary corporation into its parent.

VENTURE CAPITAL FIRMS provide financing for startups hoping to go public in exchange for a substantial fraction of the corporation's equity.

VOTING GROUP is a term defined in the Model Business Corporation Act (1984) to describe rights of shares of different classes or series to vote separately on fundamental corporate changes that adversely affect the rights or privileges of that class or series. Older state statutes use the terms "class voting" or "voting by class" to refer to essentially the same concept.

VOTING TRUST is a formal arrangement to separate share voting from share ownership. In a voting trust, record title to shares is transferred to trustees who are entitled to vote the shares. Usually, all other incidents of ownership, such as the right to receive dividends, are retained by the beneficial owners of the shares.

VOTING TRUST CERTIFICATES are certificates issued by voting trustees to beneficial holders of shares held by the voting trust. Such certificates may be freely transferable and carry with them all the incidents of ownership of the underlying shares except the power to vote.

WARRANTS are options to purchase shares from a corporation. Warrants are typically long term options and are freely transferable. Warrants may be publicly traded.

WATERED SHARES are par value shares issued for property that has been overvalued and is not worth the aggregate par value of the issued shares. The phrases "watered shares" or "watered stock" are often used as generic terms to describe discount or bonus shares as well as watered shares. See **BONUS SHARES, DISCOUNT SHARES.**

WHITE KNIGHT is a friendly suitor who attempt to rescues a target corporation from an unfriendly takeover bid. The white knight typically makes it own bid in competition with the unfriendly aggressor.

*

INDEX

References are to Pages

ACQUISITION OF CORPORATION
Asset purchase, 616
Stock purchase, 616

ADOPTION
Defined in Glossary
Preincorporation contracts, 114

ADVANCES FOR EXPENSES
Defined in Glossary
Generally, 530–532

AFFILIATE
Defined in Glossary

AGREEMENT
To form corporation, 114

AGGRESSOR CORPORATION
Defined in Glossary

AIDING AND ABETTING
Securities Fraud Litigation, 571

AGENCY COST THEORY
Discussed, 412–416

AGENCY PRINCIPLES
Discussed, 324

ALL HOLDERS RULE
Defined in Glossary

"ALL OR SUBSTANTIALLY ALL"
Discussed, 626, 634

AMORTIZATION
Defined in Glossary

AMOTION
Defined in Glossary
Discussed, 235

ANNUAL REPORTS
Requirement of, 412, 608

ANTIDILUTION PROVISIONS
Defined in Glossary
See Dilution

APPOINTMENT FORM
For Proxy, 273–275

APPRAISAL
Defined in Glossary
Discussed, 627–631
Market exception, 631, 637

ARBITRAGEURS
Defined in Glossary
Discussed, 434

ARBITRATION
In voting agreement, 279

ARBS
Defined in Glossary
Arms Length Negotiation
Discussed, 349–350

ARIZONA STOCK EXCHANGE
Discussed, 382

ARTICLES OF INCORPORATION
Defined in Glossary
Amendments, 610–611
Clauses
Described, 82–95, 391–392, 490
Filing, 43–45
Vested rights, 611–613

ARTIFICIAL ENTITY
Discussed, 46–50

ASSET PURCHASE
Acquisition of corporation, 616

ASSUMED NAME
Use by Corporation, 86–87

AUDIT COMMITTEE
Discussed, 318–321

AUDITOR DISCLOSURE
Securities fraud litigation, 571–572

AUTHORITY OF OFFICERS
In general, 324–333
Apparent, 325–326
Express, 326–330
Implied, 331
Inherent, 330–333

AUTHORIZED SHARES
Defined in Glossary
Discussed, 165–166

BALANCE SHEET
Described, 171–176

BANKRUPTCY
Corporate claims, 159–161

BENEFICIAL HOLDERS OF SECURITIES
Defined in Glossary
Discussed, 258–260
Inspection of records, 605

BERLE & MEANS
Modern Corporations and Private Property, 397

BESPEAKS CAUTION
Securities fraud litigation, 563–565

BLOCKAGE
Defined in Glossary

BLUE SKY LAWS
Defined in Glossary
Discussed, 203–204

BOARD OF DIRECTORS
See Directors
Action without meeting by, 316
Classification of, 270–272
Committees of, 318–321

BOARD OF DIRECTORS—Cont'd
Compensation of, 310–311
Elimination of, 238–239, 358–362
Meetings generally, 306–310
Modification of powers, 352–353
Reduction of, 272
Telephonic meetings, 315
Vacancies, 311–313

BONDS
Defined in Glossary
Discussed, 223–227

BONUS SHARES
Defined in Glossary
Discussed, 182

BOOK ENTRY
Securities Registration, 399–402
Share ownership, 399–402

BOOK VALUE
Defined in Glossary
Discussed, 298–300

BOOKS
Inspection of, 599–608

BROKER
Defined in Glossary

BROKERAGE FIRMS
Discussed, 380–382

BUSINESS COMBINATION ACTS
Described, 441

BUSINESS FORMS
Classification of, 33–36
Conversions of, 615–616
Future Developments 45
Generally, 5–6, 26–28
Law School Curriculum 4–5
Startups, 43–44
Selection Of, 27–28

BUSINESS COMBINATION STATUTES
Discussed, 441

BUSINESS JUDGMENT RULE
Discussed, 453–467

BUSINESS JUDGMENT RULE—Cont'd
Fairness test, 484–489

BUY-SELL AGREEMENTS
Discussed, 295–301

BUYOUT
Defined in Glossary

BYLAWS
Defined in Glossary
Amendments, 243–244
Discussed, 105–106

C CORPORATION
Defined in Glossary
Discussed, 28–29

CALL FOR REDEMPTION
See Redemption

CALLS
Defined in Glossary

CAPITAL STOCK
Defined in Glossary

CAPITAL SURPLUS
Defined in Glossary
Discussed, 171–173

CAPITALIZATION
Defined in Glossary
Accounts, 171–176
Discussed, 165–171
Inadequate, 142–145
Initial, 88–89
Services as, 178–182

CARE
Duty of, 447–453

CASH CONCENTRATION SYSTEMS
Publicly held corporations, 390

CASH FLOW
Defined in Glossary

CASH MERGER
Defined in Glossary
Described, 621–624

CASH TENDER OFFER
    Defined in Glossary
Discussed, 433–437

CEDE AND COMPANY
    Defined in Glossary
Discussed, 400

CENTRALIZED MANAGEMENT
Corporation attribute, 48

CEO
Defined in Glossary

CERCLA CASES
Piercing the corporate veil in, 155–156

CERTIFICATE OF INCORPORATION
Defined in Glossary

CFO
Defined in Glossary

CHARITABLE CONTRIBUTION
Corporate power, 99–100

CHARTER
    Defined in Glossary
As contract, 51–52

CHAT ROOMS
Discussed, 381

"CHECK–THE–BOX"
Taxation, 34–36

"CHICAGO SCHOOL" OF LAW AND ECONOMICS
See Law and Economics
Described, 412–416

CHOICE OF BUSINESS FORM
Discussed, 26–44

CLASS A SHARES
Defined in Glossary

CLASS ACTIONS
    Defined in Glossary
See also Private Securities Litigation Reform Act
Abuses of, 556, 559–562
Described, 556
Preemption of state cases, 572–574

CLASS VOTING
See Voting Group
Discussed, 613–615

CLASSES OF SHARES
Discussed, 176–177, 204–210, 286–288, 353–356

CLASSIFIED BOARD OF DIRECTORS
Described in Glossary
Effect of, 270–272

CLO
Defined in Glossary

CLOSE CORPORATION
Defined in Glossary
Classes of shares, 353–356
Control devices, 352–356
Deadlocks, 362–363
Discussed, 2–4, 343–344
Dissension in, 346–348
Economic importance of, 344–346
Exit from, 288–289, 346, 347
Fiduciary duties of controlling shareholders, 373–375
Freezeouts, 365–366
Increases in quorum, 356–357
Involuntary dissolution, 369–371
Management through contract, 360–362
Oppression in, 347–348
Planning, 348–352
Share transfer restrictions, 366–369
Special statutes, 357–360
Statutory scheme, 228–231
Value of minority shares, 366–369

CLOSELY HELD
See Close Corporation

COMMITTEE ON CORPORATE LAWS
Discussed, 75, 180–182, 195–196, 292–294

COMMON SHAREHOLDERS
Defined in Glossary

COMMON SHARES
Defined in Glossary
Authorized, 165–166
Classes, 189–192
Defined, 164–165
No Par, 176–177

COMMON SHARES—Cont'd
Nonvoting, 188–189
Par value, 168–176
Price for, 168–176
Property, issued for, 178–186
Services, issued for, 178–186
Treasury, 192–194, 581–583, 581–583
Tracking, 192
Watered, 182–186

COMPACT
Corporation as, 51–52

COMPENSATION
Committee, 318–321
Directors, 310–311, 474–475
Effect of tax rules, 475–478
Fiduciary duty, 467–474
Officers, 392–394, 474–478
Waste, 477–478

COMPREHENSIVE ENVIRONMENTAL RESPONSE, COMPENSATION AND LIABILITY ACT
Piercing the corporate veil under, 155–156

CONCESSION
Corporation as, 50

CONFLICT OF INTEREST
See Self–Dealing

CONSENT
Substitute for meetings, 107–109, 257–258, 316

CONSOLIDATION
Defined in Glossary
Discussed, 615–619

CONTEMPORARY OWNERSHIP
In derivative suit, 543–544

CONTINUITY OF LIFE
Corporation attribute, 47

CONTRACT
Corporation as, 51–55

CONTROL OF A CORPORATION BY A PERSON
Defined in Glossary

CONTROL PERSON
Defined in Glossary

CONTROL PREMIUM
Defined in Glossary
Discussed, 517–523

CONTROLLING SHAREHOLDERS
Fiduciary duties, 373–375, 445–446

CONVERSION SECURITIES
Defined in Glossary
See Convertible Securities

CONVERSIONS OF BUSINESS FORMS
Taxation of, 35–36
Discussed, 615–616
Mergers of different forms, 634

CONVERTIBLE SECURITIES
Defined in Glossary
Discussed, 207–209, 226

COO
Defined in Glossary

CO-PROMOTERS
See Promoters

CORPORATE OPPORTUNITY
Defined in Glossary
Discussed, 598

CORPORATE VEIL
Discussed, 134–162

CORPORATION BY ESTOPPEL
Defined in Glossary
Discussed, 131–133

CORPORATIONS
Closely held, 2–4
Joint venture, 385
Franchise taxes 40
Publicly held, 2–4

COVERED CLASS ACTIONS
SLUSA, 573

COVERED SECURITIES
SLUSA, 573

CREDITORS
Director liability to, 497–498

CROSSING NETWORK
Discussed, 382

CUMULATIVE DIVIDENDS
Defined in Glossary
Discussed, 205–206

CUMULATIVE TO THE EXTENT EARNED DIVIDENDS
Defined in Glossary
Discussed, 206

CUMULATIVE VOTING
Defined in Glossary
Classification, effect of, 270–272
Discussed, 263–270
Minimization, 272

DAMAGES
In securities fraud litigation, 570–571

D & O INSURANCE
Defined in Glossary
Discussed, 532–534

DEAD HAND
Poison pills, 438–439

DEADLOCK
Defined in Glossary
Discussed, 362–363
Solutions,
    Arbitration, 363–365
    Buyouts, 302–303, 371–373
    Dissolution, 369–371

DEBENTURES
Defined in Glossary
Discussed, 223–227

DEBT FINANCING
Equity financing compared, 210–215
Excessive, 219–223
In bankruptcy, 221–223
In taxation, 215–223
Leverage, 216–219

DEBT SECURITIES
Discussed, 223–227

DEEP ROCK DOCTRINE
Defined in Glossary

DEEP ROCK DOCTRINE—Cont'd
Discussed, 160–161, 221–223

DE FACTO CORPORATION
Defined in Glossary
Discussed, 127–129

DE FACTO MERGER
Defined in Glossary
Discussed, 617–619

DEFENSIVE TACTICS
Takeover bids, 437–440

DE JURE CORPORATION
Defined in Glossary
Discussed, 128–129

DELAWARE
Disclosure rules, 498–499
In re Caremark, 448–449
Malone v. Brincat, 498–499
Popularity of, 66–69

DELECTUS PERSONAE
Defined in Glossary
Described, 9

DELEGATION OF AUTHORITY
Validity, 252–253

DEMAND
In derivative litigation, 544–546, 550–552

DEPOSITORY TRUST COMPANY
Defined in Glossary

DEPOSITORY TRUST CORPORATION (DTC)
Discussed, 400

DEREGISTRATION
Defined in Glossary

DERIVATIVE LITIGATION
Defined in Glossary
Abuses of, 542–543
Business judgment rule in, 463–467
Contemporary ownership, 543–544
Defenses, 552–554
Demand in, 544–546, 550–552
Described, 535–536
Distinguished from direct, 536–538

DERIVATIVE LITIGATION—Cont'd
Litigation committee, 463–467, 548–552
Plaintiffs, expenses, 539–542
Prerequisites, 544–546
Private settlement, 554
Res judicata effect, 555
Security for expenses, 546–548
Verification of complaint, 548

DILUTION
Defined in Glossary

DIRECTORS
Action without meeting, 316
Advances for expenses, 530–531
Business judgment rule, 453–457
Bylaw amendments, 243–244
Classification, 270–272
Committees, 318–321
Compensation, 310–311, 474–478
Corporate opportunities, 481–483
Decision-making role, 448
Delegation of duties, 244–253
Demand on, 544–546
Dissent from actions, 316–318
Duty of care, 447–467
Selection of, 263–270
Exoneration, 490
Fiduciary duties, 444–445, 484–489
Financially distressed corporations, 497–498
"Gatekeeping" functions, 234–235, 241–243, 610
Hold over, 313
Indemnification, 524–530
Independent, 405–406
Individuals only, 306
Informal action by, 314–315
Initial, 90–91
Inside, 405–406
Inspection of books, 599–600
Interference with, 244–251
Interlocking, 473–474
Liabilities of,
    Generally, 447–523
    Distributions, 490–493
    Limitations on, 91–92
    Loans, 102–104
    Minimum capital, 142–145
    Trading in shares, 499–517

DIRECTORS—Cont'd
Limitation of liability, 91–92, 459–460
Loans to, 102–104
Loyalty, 467–473
Meetings, 313–315
Number, 305–306
Oversight role, 448
Proxy voting by, 314
Qualifications, 304–306
    Ratification, 489–490
    Removal,
        In general, 235–237
        Effect of cumulative voting, 272–273
Roles, 232–235, 402–412
Self dealing, 467–473
Shared responsibilities, 240–244
Vacancies, 311–312
Written dissent, 316–318

DIRECTORY REQUIREMENTS
Defined in Glossary

DISCOUNT SHARES
    Defined in Glossary
Described, 182

DISCOVERY
In securities fraud litigation, 565

DISPOSITION OF ASSETS
Shareholder approval, 625–627

DISSENSION
    Defined in Glossary
Discussed, 346–348

DISSENT AND APPRAISAL
See Appraisal

DISSENTERS' RIGHTS
See Appraisal

DISSOCIATION
Of partnership, 13–14

DISSOLUTION
In general, 631–632
Involuntary, 369–371
Partnership, 13–14

DISTRIBUTIONS
   Defined in Glossary
Defined, 575–577
Of capital, 586–590
Share repurchases as, 581–583, 594–597

DIVIDENDS
   Defined in Glossary
Contractual restrictions, 590–591
Cumulative, 205–206
Discussed, 575–577
Ex-dividend defined, 583–585
Illegal, 490, 592
Mandatory, 592–594
Preferential 204–210
Property, 575–577
Refusal to declare, 592–594
Restrictions on, 490–493, 585–589
Right to compel, 592–594
Share, 577–580
Share repurchase as, 594–597
Shareholder's right to, 503–505, 589–590
Statutory restrictions on, 585

DIVISION OF CORPORATION
Compared with a subsidiary, 387

DOT.COM COMPANIES
Discussed, 346, 377–380

DOUBLE TAXATION
   Defined in Glossary
Discussed, 28–29

DOWN STREAM MERGER
Defined in Glossary

EARNINGS PER SHARE
Defined in Glossary

ECONOMICS
Chicago School, 52–61, 412–416

EMPLOYMENT CONTRACTS
Officers, 339–342

ENTERPRISE ENTITY
Defined, 151–152

ENTITY
Corporation as, 46–50

ENTITY—Cont'd
Partnership as, 11–12

EQUITY FINANCING
Defined in Glossary

EQUITY OR EQUITY INTEREST
Defined in Glossary

EQUITY SECURITY
Defined in Glossary
Debt financing compared, 210–215
Discussed, 164–165

ESTOPPEL
Corporation by, 131–133

EX DIVIDEND
Defined in Glossary
Discussed, 583–585

EX RIGHTS
Defined in Glossary

EXECUTIVE COMMITTEE
Discussed, 318–321

FACE VALUE
Defined in Glossary

FEDERAL CORPORATION LAW
Discussed, 203–204, 499–517, 566–574

FEDERAL INCOME TAXATION
Discussed, 28–39

FEE SHIFTING
In securities fraud litigation, 568

FICTITIOUS ENTITY
Corporation as, 46–50

FIDUCIARY DUTIES
Generally, 10–11, 444–447
Care, 447–467
Close Corporations, 373–375
Common directors, 473–474
Compensation, 310–311, 474–478
Competition with corporation, 483–484
Corporate opportunities, 478–483
Defenses,
    Business judgment rule, 453–467, 484–489

FIDUCIARY DUTIES—Cont'd
Defenses—Cont'd
  Exoneratory provisions, 490
  Indemnification, 524–530
  Insurance, 532–534
  Ratification, 489–490
Directors, 444–445, 484–489
Insider trading, 499–514
Improper issuance of shares, 201–203
Mergers, 624–625
Minority interests, 484–488
Promoters, 115–127
Purchase of shares or claims, 467–473
Rule 10b–5, 499–514
Section 16(b), 514–517
Self dealing, 467–473
Shareholders, 373–375
Statutory duties, 490–492
Transfers of control, 517–523

FINANCIAL REPORTS
To shareholders, 608

FORCED CONVERSION
  Defined in Glossary
Described, 226

FORMALITIES
Failure to follow, 145–147

FORWARD LOOKING STATEMENT
  Defined in Glossary
Discussed, 557–559, 563–565

FRAUD ON THE MARKET
Discussed, 559–560

FREE TRANSFERABILITY OF INTEREST
Discussed, 48, 288–295

FREEZE–OUT
  Defined in Glossary
Discussed, 365–366

FREEZE–OUT MERGER
See Cash Merger

FUNDAMENTAL CHANGES
Directors' gatekeeping function, 234–235, 241–243, 610
Generally, 609–635

GENERAL PARTNERS
Defined in Glossary

GENERAL PARTNERSHIP
See Partnership

GOING PRIVATE
Defined in Glossary

GOLDEN PARACHUTE
Defined in Glossary

GRANT
Corporation as, 50

GREENMAIL
Defined in Glossary

GUARANTEE OF INDEBTEDNESS
Corporate power, 103

HISTORY OF CORPORATION LAW
Generally, 1, 62–76

HOLDING COMPANY
Defined in Glossary

HOME OFFICE
Of publicly held corporation, 388

HYBRID SECURITIES
Defined in Glossary

"IMPLICIT" CONTRACTS
Discussed, 56–58

IN PARI DELICTO
Defined in Glossary

INCORPORATION
Generally, 77–109

INCORPORATORS
Defined in Glossary
Discussed, 81–82

INDEMNIFICATION
Defined in Glossary
Discussed, 524–530

INDENTURE
Defined in Glossary

INITIAL PUBLIC OFFERING (IPO)
Discussed, 379–380

INSIDE DIRECTORS
Defined in Glossary

INSIDER
Defined in Glossary

INSIDER TRADING
Defined in Glossary
Discussed, 499–514
Misappropriation theory, 505–509
Possession vs. use, 510–511
Section 16(b), 514–517
"Special Facts", 493–494

INSOLVENCY
Defined in Glossary

INSPECTION OF BOOKS
Discussed, 599–600

INSTINET
Discussed, 382

INSTITUTIONAL INVESTORS
Defined in Glossary
Discussed, 397–399
Use of nominees, 399–402
"Wall Street Option", 399

INSURANCE
Directors' liability, 532–534

INTEGRATION
Federal taxation, 28–30

INTERLOCKING DIRECTORS
Defined in Glossary

INTRA VIRES
Defined in Glossary

INVESTMENT BANKERS
Defined in Glossary

INVESTMENT COMPANIES
Defined in Glossary

ISSUED SHARES
Defined in Glossary

ISSUED SHARES—Cont'd
See Common Shares

ITSA and ITSFEA
Defined in Glossary
Described, 509–510

JENSEN AND MECKLING
Theory of The Firm, 412–415

JOINT VENTURE
Defined in Glossary

JOINT VENTURE CORPORATIONS
Described, 385

JUNIOR SECURITIES
Defined in Glossary

KINTNER RULES
Taxation, 33–34

LAW AND ECONOMICS
Arms length negotiation, 349–350
Chicago School,
    Discussed, 412–416
Discussed generally, 396
Nexus of contracts, 52–61

LAW SCHOOL CURRICULUM
Future developments, 45
Recent developments, 4–5

LEAD PLAINTIFFS
In securities fraud litigation, 562–563

LEVERAGE
Defined in Glossary
Discussed, 216–219

LEVERAGED BUYOUT (LBO)
Defined in Glossary
Discussed, 435–436

LEVERAGED RECAPITALIZATION
Defined in Glossary

LIMITED LIABILITY
Discussed, 16–26, 47

LIMITED LIABILITY COMPANY (LLC)
Defined in Glossary

LIMITED LIABILITY COMPANY (LLC)—Cont'd
Discussed, 23–26
Compared with corporation, 40–42
Compared with partnership, 42–43
Franchise taxes, 40

LIMITED LIABILITY LIMITED PARTNERSHIP
Defined in Glossary
Discussed, 19–23

LIMITED LIABILITY PARTNERSHIP
Defined in Glossary
Discussed, 19–23

LIMITED PARTNERSHIP
Defined in Glossary
Corporate general partner, 18–19
Generally, 16–18
Master, 28–29

LIQUIDATING DIVIDEND
Defined in Glossary

LIQUIDITY
Defined in Glossary

LITIGATION COMMITTEES
Discussed, 463, 548–552

LOANS
To officers and directors, 102–104

LOCKUP
Defined in Glossary
Discussed, 438

LOOTING
Described, 517–523

LOYALTY
Duty of, 467–473

MALONE v. BRINCAT
Discussed, 498–499

MANAGEMENT CONTROL
Discussed, 402–412

MANDATORY REQUIREMENTS
Defined in Glossary

MARKET EXCEPTION
Appraisal remedy, 631, 637

MARKET CAP
Defined, 379

MASTER LIMITED PARTNERSHIP
Discussed, 28–29

MATURITY DATE
Defined in Glossary

MD & A
Defined in Glossary
Discussed, 558–559

MEETINGS
Directors,
    Generally, 313–315
Consent as substitute, 316
Shareholders, 254–263
Telephonic, 315

MERGER
Defined in Glossary
Business purpose, 624–625
Cash, 621–622
Directors' gatekeeping function, 241–243
Discussed, 615–625
Downstream, 622–623
Reverse triangular, 620–621
Short form, 623–624
Triangular, 619–620
Upstream, 622

MILLER–MODIGLIANI THEOREM
Discussed, 218

MINIMUM CAPITAL
Discussed, 88–89
Liability for, 142–145

MISAPPROPRIATION THEORY
Insider trading, 505–509

MODEL BUSINESS CORPORATION ACT
Discussed, 72–76
History, 74–75

MUTUAL FUND
Defined in Glossary

NAME OF CORPORATION
Discussed, 84–87

NASDAQ
Defined in Glossary

NEGATIVE CASH FLOW
Defined in Glossary

NET WORTH
Defined in Glossary

NEW ISSUE
Defined in Glossary

NEXUS OF CONTRACTS THEORY
Discussed, 52–61
See Chicago School; Law and Economics

NIMBLE DIVIDENDS
Defined in Glossary

NO PAR SHARES
Defined in Glossary
Discussed, 176–177

NOMINATING COMMITTEE
Discussed, 318–321

NOMINEE REGISTRATION
Defined in Glossary
Discussed, 399–402

NONCALLABLE
Defined in Glossary

NONCUMULATIVE DIVIDENDS
Discussed, 205–206

NONCUMULATIVE VOTING OR STRAIGHT VOTING
Defined in Glossary

NONVOTING COMMON SHARES
Defined in Glossary
Discussed, 188–189

NOTICE
Directors' meetings, 306–307
Shareholders' meetings, 254–263

NOVATION
Defined in Glossary

NSMIA
Discussed, 203

OFFICERS
See Authority of Officers
Compensation, 392–394, 477–478
Designation of, 322–323
Employment contracts, 339–341
Fiduciary duties, 334–337,
Liabilities of, 335–337
Loans to, 102–104
Ratification of acts, 331–332
Roles, 239–240, 326–328
Tenure of, 338–339
Titles of, 322–323

ONE SHARE/ONE VOTE
Discussed, 190–192

OPPRESSION
Defined in Glossary
Dissolution for, 365–366, 369–371
Issuance of shares, 201–203
Mandatory buyout, 372–373

OPTIONS ON SHARES
Discussed, 580–581

ORGANIZATION OF CORPORATION
Discussed, 78–81, 104–105

ORGANIZATIONAL EXPENSES
Defined in Glossary
Discussed, 77–80

ORGANIZATIONAL MEETING
Described, 90–91, 107–109

OUTSIDE DIRECTORS
Defined in Glossary
Discussed, 405–406

OVER–THE–COUNTER
Defined in Glossary

PAR VALUE
Defined in Glossary
Discussed, 168–171
In capital accounts, 171–176

PARENT CORPORATIONS
Circular ownership of shares, 194–195
Liability of, 109–112
Transactions with subsidiary, 486–489

PARTICIPATING BONDS
See Bonds

PARTICIPATING PREFERRED SHARES
    Defined in Glossary
See Preferred Shares

PARTNERSHIP
See Limited Liability Partnership, Limited Partnership
As separate entity, 11–12
Charging order, 9–10
Compared with LLCs, 42–43
Corporate general partner, 18–19
Discussed, 7–16
Dissociation, 13–14
Dissolution, 11–12
Expulsion of partner, 11
Financial provisions, 8–10
Management of, 10–11
Power of corporation, 101–102
Taxation of, 30, 36
Winding up, 11–12

PAYABLE DATE
Defined in Glossary

PENDENT JURISDICTION
Defined in Glossary

PENSIONS
Power of corporation, 100–101

PERIOD OF DURATION
Of corporation, 87–88

PERPETUAL EXISTENCE
Discussed, 82, 87–88

PIK SECURITIES
Discussed, 225

PIERCING THE CORPORATE VEIL
Discussed, 134–142
Factors
    Failure to follow formalities, 145–147
    Inadequate capitalization, 142–145

PIERCING THE CORPORATE VEIL—Cont'd

Factors—Cont'd
  Public policy considerations, 157–159
  Subsidiaries, 147–151
In bankruptcy, 159–161
In contract and in tort, 138–142
In taxation, 159
Law controlling
  Federal, 154–155
  Generally, 152–154
Reverse, 156–157

PINK SHEETS

Discussed, 344–377

PLEADING

In securities fraud litigation, 568–570

POISON PILLS

  Defined in Glossary
Discussed, 438–439

POLITICAL CONTRIBUTION

Corporate Power, 100

POOLING AGREEMENT

  Defined in Glossary
Discussed, 278–281

PORCUPINE PROVISIONS

Defined in Glossary

POSIT

Discussed, 382

POWERS OF CORPORATIONS

Charitable contributions, 99–100
Guarantees of indebtedness, 103
Investments in shares, 101–102
Loans to officers or directors, 102–104
Partnerships, 101
Pensions, 100–101
Political contributions, 100
Purposes distinguished, 92–95
Statutory, 94

PREEMPTIVE RIGHTS

  Defined in Glossary
Discussed, 196–201

PREFERRED SHAREHOLDERS' CONTRACT
Defined in Glossary
Discussed, 51, 210

PREFERRED SHARES
Defined in Glossary
Described, 204–210
Participating, 206

PREINCORPORATION TRANSACTIONS
Agreement to form corporation, 114–115
Corporation by estoppel, 131–133
De facto corporation, 128–130,
Discussed, 110–133
Share subscriptions, 110–113

PREINCORPORATION SUBSCRIPTIONS
See Subscriptions

PRESIDENT
Of corporation, 322–323, 327, 330–331

PRICE–EARNINGS RATIO
Defined in Glossary

PRINCIPLES OF CORPORATE GOVERNANCE
American Law Institute, 444, 454, 466, 480, 482

PRIVATE CAUSES OF ACTION
Proxy regulations, 427–429
Rule 10b–5, 502–503

PRIVATE SECURITIES LITIGATION REFORM ACT (PSLRA)
Generally, 562–572
Aiding and abetting, 571
Auditor disclosure, 571–572
Bespeaks caution rules, 563–565
Damage measures, 570–571
Discovery, 565
Fee shifting, 568
Lead plaintiffs, 562–563
Pleading rules, 568–570
Proportional liability, 566–567
Safe harbor, 563–565
Settlements, 567

PRIVILEGE
Corporation as, 50

PRODUCT LIABILITY CLAIMS
Following sale of assets, 627

PROFIT CENTERS
Publicly held corporations, 386–387

PROMOTERS
Defined in Glossary
Contracts, 117–122
Discussed, 115–117
Fiduciary duties, 124–125
Organizational expenses, 125–127

PROPER PURPOSE
Inspection of books and records, 604–605

PROPRIETORSHIP
Discussed 6–7
Use of LLC in, 25

PROSPECTUS
Defined in Glossary

PROXY
Defined in Glossary

PROXY APPOINTMENTS
Defined in Glossary
Appointment form, 418–419
Directors prohibited from voting by, 314
Discussed, 418–424
Implied appointment, 280
Irrevocable appointment,
In general, 275–277
In pooling agreement, 278–281
Purchase of, 277–278

PROXY CONTEST
Discussed, 405, 429–433

PROXY FIGHT
See Proxy contest

PROXY REGULATION
Discussed, 418–423
Purchased proxy votes, 277

PROXY SOLICITATION MACHINERY
Defined in Glossary
Discussed, 418–424

PROXY STATEMENT
Defined in Glossary
Materiality, 427

PROXY STATEMENT—Cont'd
Misrepresentations, 427–429
Requirements, 420–423

PSLRA
See Private Securities Litigation Reform Act

PUBLIC CORPORATION
See Publicly Held Corporation

PUBLIC OFFERING
Defined in Glossary

PUBLICLY HELD BUSINESSES
Corporations, 2–4
Limited partnerships, 28–29
Taxation of, 29–30

PUBLICLY HELD CORPORATIONS
Defined in Glossary
Discussed generally, 2–4, 343–344, 376–377, 382–417
Cash concentration systems, 390
Chief executive officer, 391–392
Defined, 343–344
Directors, 402–412
Dividend policy, 575–577
Dot.com Companies, 377–380
"Home office," 388–391
Institutional investors, 397–399
Profit centers, 386–388
Proxy contests, 429–433
Proxy regulation, 418–429
SEC Disclosure requirements, 557–559
Share transfer restrictions, 290–291
Shareholders in,
Generally, 383, 394–397
Share registration, 399–402
State disclosure requirements, 498–499
Structure of, 384–386
Takeovers, 429–433
Tender offers, 433–437
Voting trusts in, 284

PURCHASE OF SHARES
Liability for, 493–496, 499–517

PURPOSES OF CORPORATION
Discussed, 92–95

PUTS
Defined in Glossary

QUO WARRANTO
Defined in Glossary

QUORUM
Directors, 308–310
Shareholders,
    Close corporations, 356–357
    Discussed, 255–257
Increased, 356–357

"RACE FOR THE BOTTOM"
Discussed, 63–66

RAIDER
Defined in Glossary

RATIFICATION
Generally, 489–490
Preincorporation contracts, 117–124

RECAPITALIZATION
Defined in Glossary

RECORD DATE
    Defined in Glossary
Described, 260–262, 506–507

RECORD OWNER
Defined in Glossary
Discussed, 260–263

REDEEMABLE SHARES
Discussed, 597–598

REDEMPTION
See also Repurchase of Shares
    Defined in Glossary
Discussed, 225–228, 597–598

REDUCTION OF STATED CAPITAL
Discussed, 588–589

REDUCTION SURPLUS
Defined in Glossary

REGISTERED AGENT
Discussed, 58–59

REGISTERED CORPORATION
Defined in Glossary

REGISTERED NAME
Discussed, 87

REGISTERED OFFICE
Discussed, 89–90

REGISTRARS
Described, 259–260

REGISTRATION
Defined in Glossary
Discussed, 258–260

REGISTRATION STATEMENT
Defined in Glossary

REMOVAL OF DIRECTORS
In general, 235–237
Cumulative voting, 272–273

REORGANIZATION
Defined in Glossary
Internal Revenue Service classification of, 616–618

REPURCHASE OF SHARES
Restrictions on,
    Equitable, 594–597
    Statutory, 588–590

RESCISSORY DAMAGES
Defined in Glossary

RESERVED NAME
Described, 87

RESET BONDS
Discussed, 225

RESTRICTIONS ON SURPLUS
Discussed, 587–588

RESTRICTIONS ON TRANSFER
Shares, 288–301

RETAINED EARNINGS
Defined in Glossary

REVENUE RECONCILIATION ACT
Discussed, 393

REVERSE STOCK SPLIT
Defined in Glossary

REVERSE TRIANGULAR MERGER
See also Triangular Merger
Discussed, 619–620

REVISED UNIFORM PARTNERSHIP ACT (RUPA)
Discussed, 14–16

REVLON DUTY
Discussed, 439, 462

RIGHTS
Defined in Glossary
Discussed, 580–581

ROUND LOT
Defined in Glossary

RULE 10b–5
Discussed, 499–514

S CORPORATION
Defined in Glossary
Discussed, 28–29

SAFE HARBOR
Forward looking statements, 557–559
In securities fraud litigation, 563–565

SANITIZATION OF CONFLICTS
Discussed, 469–473

SATURDAY NIGHT SPECIAL
Defined in Glossary

SCIENTER
Discussed, 501

SCRIP
Defined in Glossary

SECONDARY MARKET
Defined in Glossary

SECRETARY
Of corporation, 322–323, 328–330

SECTION 16(b)
Discussed, 514–517

SECURITIES
Defined in Glossary

SECURITIES ACT OF 1933
Discussed, 76, 203–204, 378–379

SECURITIES EXCHANGES
Defined in Glossary

SECURITIES INVESTORS PROTECTION CORPORATION (SIPC)
Discussed, 401

SECURITIES LITIGATION UNIFORM STANDARDS ACT OF 1998 (SLUSA)
Discussed, 572–574

SECURITY–FOR–EXPENSES
Defined in Glossary
Discussed, 546–548

SELF DEALING
Discussed, 467–473

SENIOR SECURITY
Defined in Glossary

SERIES OF PREFERRED SHARES
Defined in Glossary
Discussed, 209–210

SERVICE OF PROCESS
On corporation, 89–90

SERVICES
As consideration for shares, 178–186

SETTLEMENTS
In securities fraud litigation, 567

SHARE CERTIFICATES
Notation of restriction on transfer, 294–295

SHARE DIVIDEND
Defined in Glossary
Discussed, 577–580

SHARE EXCHANGE
Discussed, 616–617, 621

SHARE SPLIT
Defined in Glossary
Discussed, 577–580

SHARE TRANSFER RESTRICTIONS
Discussed, 288–295

SHAREHOLDER LITIGATION
Abuses, 542–543
Demand on shareholders, 544–546, 550–552
Litigation committees, 463, 548–552
Verification of complaints, 548

SHAREHOLDERS
Defined in Glossary
Annual meeting of, 245–263
Appraisal right, 627–631
Approval of action by,
Bylaw amendments, 243–244
Consent, 257–258
Election of directors, 263–267
Fundamental changes, 241–243
Removal of directors, 235–237
Sale of assets, 625–627
Shared responsibilities, 240–244
Beneficial ownership, 260–263
Book entry registration, 399–402
Cumulative voting, 263–270, 272
Demand on, 544–546
Derivative suits, 535–536
Direct suits, 535–536
Duties to corporation, 373–375, 445–446
Financial reports, 608
Inspection of books, 599–608
Institutional investors, 397–399
Liability for dividends, 592
Meetings, 254–263
Multiple votes per share, 190–192
Nominees, 399–402
Pooling agreement, 278–281
Preemptive rights, 196–201
Proposals by, 424–427
Proxy regulation, 418–423
Proxy voting, 394–396
Quorum, 298–299
Ratification of transactions, 489–490
Record ownership, 260–263
Removal of directors, 235–237
Role generally, 228–229, 240–241
Special meetings, 255
Straight voting, 263–270
Street name, 399–402

SHAREHOLDERS—Cont'd
Vote buying, 272
Voting agreements, 278–281
Voting list, 262–263
Voting trust, 281–286

SHAREHOLDERS LIST
Discussed, 262–263

SHAREHOLDERS PROPOSALS
Discussed, 424–427

SHARES
Circular ownership, 194–195
Classes of, 176–177, 204–210, 286–288, 353–356
Purchase by corporation, 396–401
Purchase by directors, 493–498
Repurchase restrictions, 581–583
Subscriptions for, 110–113
Transfer restrictions, 288–301
Watered, 182

SHORT FORM MERGER
Defined in Glossary
Discussed, 623–624

SHORT SALE
Defined in Glossary

SHORT SALE AGAINST THE BOX
Defined in Glossary

SINKING FUND
Defined in Glossary
Discussed, 225–226

SLUSA
See Securities Litigation Standards Act of 1998

SOCIAL RESPONSIBILITY
Of corporations, 69–72

"SPECIAL FACTS"
Insider trading, 493–494

SQUEEZE–OUTS
Defined in Glossary
Discussed, 365–366

STAGGERED BOARD
Defined in Glossary
Discussed, 270–272

START-UPS
Discussed, 43–44, 377–380

STATED CAPITAL
Defined in Glossary
Discussed, 88–89
Reduction of, 588–589

STATED VALUE
See Par Value

STATUTORY MERGER
Discussed, 615–617

STATUTORY SCHEME
Close corporations, 228–231, 244–253
Delegation of management, 352–353
Directors, 232–235, 402–412
Discussed, 228–244
Elimination of board of directors, 238–239, 358–362
Officers, 239–240, 326–328
Shareholders, 228–229, 240–241

STOCKHOLDERS
See Shareholders

STRAIGHT VOTING
Defined in Glossary

STREET NAME
Defined in Glossary
Discussed, 399–402

STREET NAME SECURITIES REGISTRATION
Discussed, 399–402

STRIKE SUITS
Defined in Glossary
Discussed, 542–543

STRUCTURAL BIAS
Of directors, 463–464

SUBCHAPTER C
Taxation, 28–29

SUBCHAPTER K
Taxation, 36–39

SUBCHAPTER S
Taxation, 29–30

SUBORDINATED
See Junior Securities

SUBSCRIBERS
Defined in Glossary
Described, 110–113

SUBSCRIPTIONS
Defined in Glossary
Described, 110–113

SUBSIDIARY
Defined in Glossary
Circular ownership of shares, 194–195
Compared with division, 387
Parental liability for, 147–151

SURPLUS
Defined in Glossary

TAINTED SHARES
Defined in Glossary

TAKEOVER ATTEMPT OR TAKEOVER BID
Defined in Glossary
Business judgment rule, 400–463
Defensive tactics, 417–418, 460–463
Discussed, 433–434
"In play", 434

TARGET CORPORATION
Defined in Glossary

TAXATION
Check the box, 34–36
Conversions of business form, 35
Debt, 215–221
Discussed, 28–39
Importance of, 28. 32
Kintner rules, 33–34
Minimization strategies, 28–39
Subchapter C, 28–29
Subchapter K, 36–39
Subchapter S, 29–30

TELEPHONIC MEETINGS
Validity, 315

TENDER OFFER
Defined in Glossary
Described, 433–437

THEORIES OF CORPORATENESS
Discussed, 50–61

THIN CORPORATION
Defined in Glossary
Discussed, 215–223

TIP
Defined in Glossary

TIPPEES
Discussed, 506–511

TRANSFER AGENT
Defined in Glossary
Defined, 259–260

TRANSFERABILITY OF INTEREST
Corporation attribute, 48

TRANSFERS OF CONTROL
Discussed, 517–523

TREASURER
Of corporation, 322, 327

TREASURY SHARES
Defined in Glossary
Circular ownership, 194–195
Discussed, 581–583
Preemptive rights, 196–201

TRIANGULAR MERGER
Defined in Glossary
Discussed, 619–620

TRUST FUND THEORY
Discussed, 183

ULTRA VIRES
Defined in Glossary
Discussed, 95–104

UNDERWRITERS
Defined in Glossary

UNIFORM LIMITED LIABILITY COMPANY ACT (ULLCA)
Discussed, 25

UNIFORM PARTNERSHIP ACT OF 1914 (UPA)
Discussed, 7–14

UPSTREAM MERGER
Defined in Glossary
Described, 622

VALUATION OF BUSINESS
Discussed, 298–301

VENTURE CAPITAL FIRMS
Discussed, 378–379

"VESTED RIGHTS"
Discussed, 611–613

VICE PRESIDENT
Of corporation, 322

VOTING
Directors, 306–310
Shareholders,
    Buying of votes, 272
    Consent, 257–258
    Cumulative, 270–272
    Discussed, 258–270
    Proxy appointment, 273–276
    Straight, 270–272

VOTING AGREEMENT
Shareholders, 278–281

VOTING GROUP
Defined in Glossary
Discussed, 613–615

VOTING LIST
Discussed, 262–263

VOTING TRUST
Defined in Glossary
Discussed, 281–286

VOTING TRUST CERTIFICATES
Defined in Glossary

WARRANTS TO PURCHASE SHARES
Defined in Glossary
Discussed, 580–581

WATERED SHARES
Defined in Glossary
Discussed, 182–186

WHITE KNIGHT
Defined in Glossary

WILLIAMS ACT
Described, 431–436